The MIT Press Cambridge, Massachusetts, and London, England

The Employed Inventor in the United States:
R&D Policies, Law, and Practice

by Fredrik Neumeyer
with legal analysis by John C. Stedman

4

Why has this book been written? Is the employed inventor different from the independent inventor? Are employers in the United States different from employers abroad?

The United States patent system is one of the oldest of the Western world. It is derived from the Constitution and after more than 175 years in use is considered a valuable institution both by the grantor and grantee. However, in the economy of large industrial countries the origin and ownership of patent rights have drifted away from the single individual, the lonely master of new inventive ideas. The vast majority of creators of important progress in science and technology today are employees. They are regularly paid for their services, and their various tasks are designated by an employer, who may be: government, through its many-armed agencies, departments, and commissions; industry, increasingly research-minded; universities and other institutions of higher learning; or certain profit and non-profit institutions.

The paramount needs of two world wars and the increase of industrial competition in international trade in peacetime have made the creation of new products and processes a requisite to survival. The general rising standard of living has contributed to the pressure to innovate. The study of the invention and innovation process in terms of finance, manpower, and efficient administration has gradually increased, and so has the general study of man's creativity.

The remarkable fact remains that the legal and practical relations between employers and employees who produce inventions during employment (whether by express order or as a by-product of work) in the different sectors of the economy have been practically neglected as a subject of research and survey in the United States.

Since almost everyone agrees that it is important to encourage inventiveness, we should at least know how making inventions in employment is regulated in practice in the United States. The main questions in this connection are naturally the allocation or assignment of ownership of rights to inventions produced by employees (including also working results and copyrightable material) and the methods—voluntary or required by law—used by employers to reward employees for inventions made in employment.

The second chapter of this book, by John C. Stedman, an American colleague, acquaints the reader with the legal status of employee inventions, patent assignment policies, the attitude past and present of the courts, and the historical background of patent law in the United States. My own subsequent chapters attempt a cross section of relations between employer and employee in three sectors of the economy—government, industry, and the universities. One chapter also deals with patent provisions in collective bargaining agreements, which are becoming more significant as labor unions tend to include more professionals. In all these fields my investigation is carried out mainly by individual case studies. These have been thoughtfully selected to stand as examples for a large mass of other undescribed cases. For all its drawbacks, I know of no better way to study this large field in a single volume.

As I look backward, the four years that it took to prepare this book are not really long in view of the lack of collected basic material. I am deeply indebted to a long series of United States institutions, government and private, and to industrial corporations and universities as well as individuals expert in questions of policy, law, and scientific work methods. Twenty-five years ago (February 1943) President Roosevelt initiated the first basic study of government employee patent policy by a letter to Attorney General Francis Biddle. John Stedman took an active part in the investigation that followed.

To start with, I acknowledge the generosity of Princeton University, which on Professor Fritz Machlup's recommendation made it possible for me to spend one and one-half years exclusively on collecting material all over the United States, discussing relevant problems on the spot, and making first drafts of the case studies. Painstaking and untiring assistance was given me by my colleague and friend Professor John Stedman and the Law School of the University of Wisconsin, which twice offered generous hospitality at their beautiful and well-equipped campus. To help me finish the writing of the book I was given a fellowship of the foundation of the Swedish Federal Bank (Riksbankens Jubileumsfond) in Stockholm. For the long periods of research in the United States I was also granted repeated leaves of absence by my understanding employer, the Swedish State Telephone Administration in Stockholm.

Working out the twenty case studies of this book was an adventure which brought in its wake a deep insight into the gigantic machinery of the American economy and the men who make that machinery work. Besides Professors Machlup and Stedman, without whose help the book could never have been written, I was fortunate enough to meet a number of experts in government and industry as well as in the universities. Cooperation with these scholars and administrators has led to personal friendship and was invaluable in reaching this first goal of my research. I mention in this connection the former Assistant Commissioner of Patents, Gerald O'Brien; Clarence Tusca, former head of the Patent Department of Radio Corporation of America; Roger O'Meara of the National Industrial Conference Board; Professor Simon Marcson of Rutgers University; Professor James Willard Hurst of the University of Wisconsin; Dr. Frank Prager, patent attorney of Philco Corporation; and Dr. Howard Forman, patent attorney of Rohm & Haas Company. The practical and intellectual lessons the author gained from these experienced representatives of the very best in American spirit will never be forgotten. None of these persons has, however, any responsibility for the ideas expressed by me in this book.

For the rest I have appropriated, consciously and unconsciously, wisdom from many sources. I express gratitude to my wife and daughter, who sacrificed family life for the long periods I resided abroad. My guiding principle was to find and to present unbiased facts. Without these we will never arrive at a basis which can be used to advantage for discussing what is right and what is wrong in this sensitive and controversial field. In the final run the question of how to manage patent policy is the question of managing human beings who are most valuable to their country and to the world.

Fredrik Neumeyer
Stockholm, January 1969

The Employed Inventor in the United States

This book treats the legal relations and relations of management between employers and employees when the latter produce inventions and discoveries during employment.

The requisites for invention are physical facilities, funds, suitable working environment, and suitable individuals.

Facilities can range from a table with paper and pencil to an atomic accelerator worth several million dollars. As a rule, facilities are research laboratories, testing grounds, computer centers, scientific libraries, or other collective means of working support.

"Funds" in this connection means moneys available to the employer or sponsor of work for salaries to employees, consultants, and contracting parties, plus money to operate the working facilities.

The working environment is an important adjunct of inventiveness. It is the tangible and intangible atmosphere, especially as expressed by the supervisors responsible for the work and by the colleagues with whom the potential inventor spends his working hours. Tangibly, invention award systems help shape the environment. But many intangible incentive policies must also be respected, whether they take the form of recognition by supervisors, the setting of particularly challenging tasks, the satisfaction of seeing one's ideas accepted and put to use, or the opportunity to learn or to take advantage of services provided by the employer (for instance, drafting, computing, testing, or clerical help).[1]

"Suitable" individuals are the persons qualified by education, experience, and inherent creative qualities to make use of the facilities and the environment. In principle, all employees who are gifted enough and who have a chance to do so under the right working conditions, can invent, although it is true that some groups of employees, by nature of their professional qualification and their assigned tasks, can be said to make up the front line. These are the research and development (R&D) personnel—scientists, engineers, technicians, and their supervisors.

To give the reader a general feeling of the size and scope of the problems treated in this book, a certain amount of statistics is presented: funds made available by government, industries, and universities in engineering R&D and numbers and categories of employed individuals available to transform these assets into inventions and other research results.[2] Public Laws, Executive Orders, departmental

[1] See John W. Riegel, *Intangible Awards for Engineers and Scientists,* Report No. 9 (Ann Arbor: Bureau of Industrial Relations, University of Michigan, 1958).
[2] No attempt is made in this book to analyze the interrelationship between R&D funds expended and manpower employed, and the inventive results derived therefrom.

and industrial regulations and rules concerned with the organization of research and with inventions usually do not address themselves directly to the individuals who are ultimately responsible for all progress in sciences and technology. They talk only to the administrative entities (agencies) or legal units (corporations, companies, contractors) as "inventors." There is, therefore, a need to indicate briefly in absolute figures and in certain percentage relations the manpower available in the United States that actually produces this progress.

Of the total labor force of more than 75 million Americans, we consider first the employee scientists, engineers, and technicians as being a primary source of inventions and innovations. There is, of course, no distinct line separating this special type of employee from others able to make inventions under certain circumstances. There is no exclusive category of employee inventors. In order to appraise these statistics a few definitions of underlying terms must be given.

DEFINITIONS

Scientists and engineers are defined as persons engaged in scientific and engineering work at a level requiring a knowledge of sciences equivalent at least to that acquired through completion of a four-year college course. They are generally classified according to the fields of their employment and not according to the discipline in which they received their major training.[3]

Technicians are persons engaged in technical work at a level requiring knowledge acquired through a technical institute, junior college, or other type of training less extensive than four-year college training. Craftsmen and skilled workers are excluded.

National Science Foundation states, in a study of 1960, that although there is no general agreement on the occupations properly classifiable within the technician group, technicians should broadly include: "All persons engaged in work requiring knowledge of physical life, engineering, and mathematical sciences comparable to knowledge acquired through technical institute, junior college, or other formal post-high school training, or through equivalent on-the-job training or experience."[4] Implicit in this definition is the type of work performed by technicians, which according to NSF usually consists of either assisting the scientist or engineer directly or performing some of the tasks that otherwise would be done by him. In either case, engineering or scientific personnel are freed for duties requiring a higher level of training or experience.

[3] *Statistical Abstract of the United States,* 1968, p. 524. Technicians are also defined on this page.
[4] National Science Foundation, *Scientific and Technical Personnel in Industry,* 1960, p. 15.

The source of these definitions are the Bureau of the Budget (*Statistical Abstract*) and the National Science Foundation. Another important governmental source is the Bureau of Labor Statistics of the Department of Labor. BLS publishes the *Occupational Outlook Handbook,* which defines several hundred professional, administrative, and related occupations in industry and government. Additional relevant definitions are found in federal laws such as the National Labor Relations Act of 1935, sec. 2 (3); the Classification Act of 1940, sec. 1112; the Taft-Hartley Act of 1947, sec. 2 (3); and in the Workmen's Compensation Acts of the different states.

Definitions of relevant types of professional employees in industrial employment are found as part of collective bargaining agreements, in the job classifications. They are modified from time to time and are basic not only for employee wages but in many cases for eligibility for invention awards given by employers.

Many statistics of interest here talk about a more limited group of employees, "R&D scientists and engineers," and for this concept an underlying definition of R&D is needed. National Science Foundation defines research as a systematic and intensive study directed toward a fuller knowledge of the subject studied, and development as the systematic use of scientific knowledge directed toward the production of useful materials, devices, systems, methods, or processes.[5] Against this background of basic definitions we can look at some recent data.

AVAILABLE R&D FUNDS

Funds to pay for building and operating research facilities and to pay employees, consultants, and contractors are prerequisite to any corporate research results. Their size shows at least the effort put out to gain the desired results, even if there is no fixed relationship between funds spent and results produced in terms of patentable inventions.[6]

[5] These definitions are cited in *Statistical Abstract of the United States,* 1968, p. 523.
[6] S. Melman has tried to analyze relationship between salaries of scientists and technical knowledge in the form of patentable inventions made by scientists and engineers, in *The Impact of the Patent System on Research,* Study No. 11, Subcommittee on Patents, Trademarks, and Copyrights, U.S. Senate, 85th Cong., 2nd sess., Washington 1958. A report on "Patents and the Corporation" was made in 1958 by nine graduate students (F. Scherer et al.) for F. Doriot at the Harvard Business School, in which a statistical analysis of patenting trends showed the disagreement between increasing total U.S. R&D expenditures and U.S. patent appiications filed (pp. 130 ff. and chart 11, in second edition, Bedford, Mass., 1959). To what extent U.S. patent applications emanate from employees has never been analyzed. The research which comes closest to this problem was done by P. Federico in his study *Distribution of Patents Issued to Corporations 1939–1955,* Study No. 3, Subcommittee on Patents, Trademarks, and Copyrights, U.S. Senate, 84th Cong., 2nd sess., Washington 1957, figures unofficially supplemented until 1963. Federico showed that more than 70 percent of all patents were issued to U.S. and foreign corporations in 1963. Corporate

The plans for financing research by the federal government are made public in the reports and messages of the President presented to Congress at the beginning of each year. In his State of the Union Message in 1967, the President called upon the genius of private industry for the most advanced technology to help realize the Model Cities program and announced an intensive fight against polluted air and water (not giving dollar figures for research in this message of January 10, however). The Budget Message of 1967 (January 24) reported that in the defense field "the vigorous research and development programs vital to maintaining the most modern, versatile, and potent forces in the world" would continue and that "capabilities for nuclear, conventional, or countersubversive conflict" would increase. Defense outlays in 1968 were to account for $75.5 billion, or 56 percent of the total budget, including military research. To support new projects in space research and technology an increase of $82 million for NASA was requested by the President for 1968 in new obligational authority. The President requested federal funds for intensified research in the economical conversion of seawater to fresh water and called for comprehensive research in such projects as intercity high-speed ground transportation and urban mass transit, as well as the development of a civil supersonic aircraft.

The second largest increase in new obligational authority of the federal budget went to the Department of Health, Education, and Welfare, which not only pays for Medicare but is in charge of extensive medical research. Air and water pollution control will be based on large-scale cooperative research efforts of federal, state, and local government agencies.

FEDERAL GOVERNMENT R&D OBLIGATIONS

From the vast statistical material illustrating annual size and distribution of federal government funds for research and development only four charts have been chosen.

Figure 1.1 shows that almost 80 percent of the research and development of federal agencies, corresponding to about $13 billion, was undertaken by extra-mural performers (industries, universities, and Federal Contract Research Centers

---

ownership of these patents can be derived by assignment either from intramural employees or outside individuals. No analysis of these possible sources has been made, but it is well known that the vast majority of these corporate patents emanate from inventions assigned by the corporation's own employees. Important analytical work on innovation activity in industry is made by Edwin Mansfield (Carnegie Institute of Technology). See abstracts in National Science Foundation, *Reviews of Data on Research and Development*, nos. 31, 34, 38 and following.

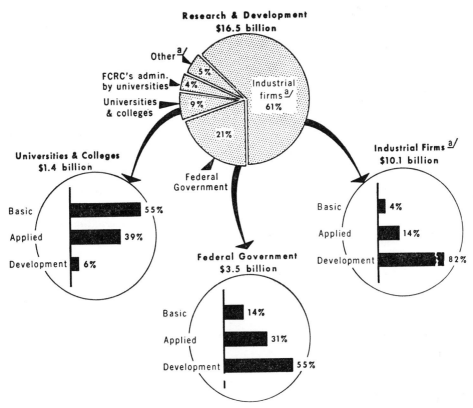

Figure 1.1 Federal R&D obligations, by performer and character of work, FY 1967 (estimated). Obligations for a fiscal year are amounts as announced in the budget, subject to later congressional action or reprogramming.

[a] Includes Federal Contract Research Centers administered by this sector.

Source: National Science Foundation

administered by them). Since all of these operate under some kind of grant or contract from government, the great importance of the contents of government research contracts— and their possible changes—for the government employee invention policy becomes obvious. That *basic research* is greatest at universities (55 percent), less in government (14 percent), and least in industry (4 percent) is no surprise; the reverse is true for *development*: universities (6 percent), government (55 percent), and industry (82 percent). Since patentable inventions are more likely to be created in applied research and in development, we can assert that these two fields, together constituting 96 percent of all research in industry, 86 percent in government, and 45 percent at universities, call for special attention regarding employer-employee relations in regard to inventions, engineering improvements, data, and other technical progress.

Figure 1.2 shows that the industrial sector has grown by far the most of all sectors in dollar value of federal R&D funds from fiscal year 1957 to fiscal year 1967, from $2.2 billion in 1957 to $10.1 billion in 1967. These figures include funds obligated for Federal Contract Research Centers administered by industrial firms. The greatest relative growth of government funds during the ten-year period occurred in the university sector (6.5 times). These figures again underline the importance of the contractual relations between government and industry and between government and universities in the research field.

Figure 1.3 illustrates that in fiscal year 1967 in government research the share of applied research was largest for the Department of Defense (44 percent) and least for the Atomic Energy Commission (3 percent), whereas government's share in the total R&D obligations of each agency is by now far largest for the Depart-

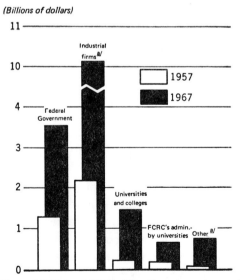

Figure 1.2 Federal R&D obligations to major performer groups, 1957–1967.
ᵃ Includes Federal Contract Research Centers administered by this sector.

Source: National Science Foundation

ment of Health, Education and Welfare (62 percent) and the Department of Agriculture (55 percent). Defense, NASA and AEC shares have decreased to 20 percent, 16 percent, and 8 percent respectively. Emphasis on inventive results should therefore be laid to the medical and agricultural fields, at least from a quantitative point of view.

Figure 1.4 shows the distribution of funds between the various sciences in the government agencies with greatest total research obligations estimated for fiscal 1967. In the overall picture for all government agencies, physical sciences dominate with 68 percent, whereas in the individual agencies, or groups of agencies, differences of research programs are marked. In the defense, space, and atomic energy group 90 percent of funds ($3.7 billion) are spent in the physical sciences, and only 7 percent in life sciences, whereas Department of Health, Education and Welfare spends 6 percent of their total funds ($1.1 billion) in the physical sciences, and 81 percent in life sciences. Obviously, the heavy involvement of the defense–space–atomic energy group with energy problems and pertaining equipment explains the extensive activity in the physical sciences. But it should not be forgotten that in recent years research programs increasingly call for a multidisciplinary approach and for interagency cooperation. This is the case in weapon construction, satellite

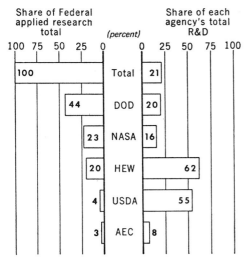

Figure 1.3 Federal obligations for applied research, by agency, 1967 estimated.
Source: National Science Foundation

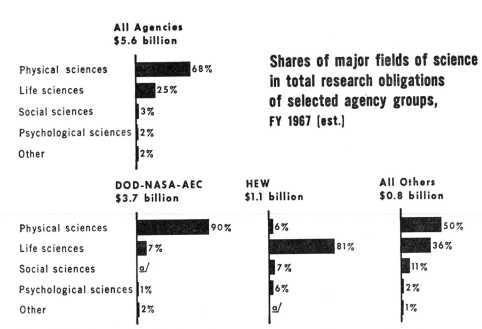

All Agencies
$5.6 billion

Physical sciences — 68%
Life sciences — 25%
Social sciences — 3%
Psychological sciences — 2%
Other — 2%

Shares of major fields of science in total research obligations of selected agency groups, FY 1967 (est.)

DOD-NASA-AEC
$3.7 billion

Physical sciences — 90%
Life sciences — 7%
Social sciences — a/
Psychological sciences — 1%
Other — 2%

HEW
$1.1 billion

Physical sciences — 6%
Life sciences — 81%
Social sciences — 7%
Psychological sciences — 6%
Other — a/

All Others
$0.8 billion

Physical sciences — 50%
Life sciences — 36%
Social sciences — 11%
Psychological sciences — 2%
Other — 1%

Figure 1.4 Total research obligations of DOD-NASA-AEC compared to HEW and all other agencies, by major field of science, 1967 estimated.
a Less than 0.5 percent.
Source: National Science Foundation

technology, and marine sciences, to mention only a few fields. This suggests that employee-invention policy in the various departments and agencies should be as uniform as possible in order to avoid illogical and unfair solutions.

INDUSTRY R&D EXPENDITURES

Statistics illustrating R&D expenditures by industry show some marked trends in regard to total increase of expenditures, use of funds for applied research, and distribution of R&D funds among leading industrial branches. Four characteristic charts and one table are selected.

Figure 1.5 shows that in ten years total industrial R&D performance (company and federally financed) had risen to $15.5 billion, about three-fourths of the total R&D performance in the nation in 1966. The number of full-time R&D employees, scientists, and engineers in industry had risen to about 380,000 including employees working in federally funded research and development centers administered by industry.

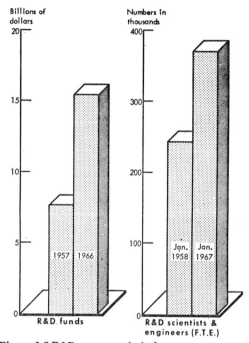

Figure 1.5 R&D resources in industry: ten-year growth of funds and of full-time R&D scientists and engineers.
Source: National Science Foundation

Figure 1.6 illustrates, not surprisingly, that in industry the dominating sector of development work is further increasing. Development involves the translation of research results into new or improved products or processes, fields which are most suitable for patentable employee inventions. The chart, therefore, demonstrates the importance of the industrial sector as a source of patent problems.

Table 1.1 shows expenditures for applied research and development in 18 industrial fields during the years 1959, 1965, and 1966. The greatest expenditures in 1966 were for communication equipment and electronic components ($2.49 billion) followed by aircraft and parts ($1.77 billion) and machinery ($1.24 billion). Regulation of employee inventions in these fields is given special consideration in this book; aircraft and space industries are treated in the chapter on collective bargaining agreements, and communications and electronics industries furnish some of the case studies in the chapter on the industrial employer invention policy.

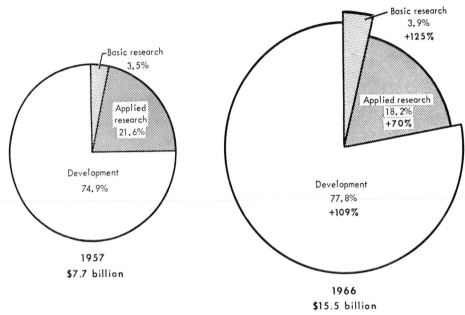

Figure 1.6 Distribution of and increase in industrial basic research, applied research, and development, 1957 and 1966.

Source: National Science Foundation

From Figures 1.7 and 1.8, we learn that five branches of industry take a lion's share of expenditures for research and development, both from government sources and company sources. Figure 1.7 tells us that compared to an overall gain of 101 percent in total industrial R&D performance, 1957–1966, federal funds for the chemicals and allied products industry rose most, 115 percent; for aircraft and missiles, 112 percent; for electrical equipment and communication, 89 percent;[7] for machinery, 26 percent; and for motor vehicles and other transportation equipment, 87 percent. Company funds for R&D performance totaled $7.3 billion in 1966. Largest percentage increases occurred in the aircraft and missiles industry (151 percent), the machinery industry (140 percent), and the electrical equipment and communications industry (130 percent). Largest percentage R&D increases

[7] These two heterogenous branches of industry are grouped together in official statistics. They can be subdivided into: "communication equipment and electronic components" and "other electrical equipment" and are broken down thus in NSF 68-5, Table 2, which provides back-up figures for Figure 7.1. Explanation of terms is found in the *Standard Industrial Classification Manual,* published by the Bureau of the Budget. Industry code number for "electrical equipment" is 36, for "communication" 48 (see NSF 64-9, pp. 95–96).

Table 1.1 Funds for Applied R&D Performance by Product Field, 1959, 1965, and 1966

Millions of dollars

Product field	SIC Code[1]	1959	1965	1966
Total	–	$9,286	$13,587	$14,931
Atomic energy devices	–	514	642	647
Ordnance, except guided missiles	19, except 192	106	103	152
Guided missiles and spacecraft	192	1,656	3,772	3,908
Food and kindred products	20	74	131	145
Textile mill products	22	–[2]	21	34
Chemicals, except drugs and medicines	28, except 283	–	1,018	1,081
Industrial inorganic and organic chemicals	281	–	–	–
Plastics materials and synthetic resins, rubber, and fibers	282	–	–	–
Agricultural chemicals	287	35	–	–
Other chemicals	284–86	196	–	–
Drugs and medicines	283	145	274	312
Petroleum refining and extraction	29, 13	147	206	205
Rubber and miscellaneous plastics products	30	–	112	127
Stone, clay and glass products	32	48	92	104
Primary metals	33	109	178	198
Primary ferrous products	331, 332, 3391, 3399	60	–	–
Primary and secondary nonferrous metals	balance of 33	49	–	–
Fabricated metal products	34	123	153	165
Machinery	35	683	1,113	1,243
Engines and turbines	351	87	–	–
Farm machinery and equipment	352	67	–	–
Construction, mining, and materials handling machinery	353	53	–	–
Metalworking machinery and equipment	354	39	–	–
Office, computing, and accounting machines	357	289	–	–
Other machinery, except electrical	balance of 35	148	–	–
Electrical equipment, except communication	36, except 365–67	326	319	371
Electric transmission and distribution equipment	361	62	–	–
Electrical industrial apparatus	362	79	–	–
Other electrical equipment and supplies	363–64 and 369	185	–	–
Communication equipment and electronic components	365–67	1,756	2,258	2,497
Motor vehicles and other transportation equipment	37, except 372	594	713	779
Motor vehicles and equipment	371	569	–	–
Other transportation equipment	373–75 and 379	25	–	–
Aircraft and parts	372	1,480	1,394	1,778
Professional and scientific instruments	38	191	372	443
Other product fields, not elsewhere classified	–	576	716	743

1 Industries and product fields are classified according to the Standard Industrial Classification Manual Codes (SIC Code).
2 Dash indicates data not separately available but included in total.

from 1957 to 1966, not visible in the figure, were recorded for textiles and apparel with 180 percent, paper and allied products 143 percent, and food and kindred products 124 percent. Lumber, wood products, and furniture industries recorded no change.

The main impression one receives from Figure 1.8 is that 58 percent of all 1966 industrial research and development was performed by two industries, aircraft and missiles and electrical equipment and communication ($5.4 billion and $3.6 billion); next were the chemical industry ($1.5 billion) and motor vehicles and machinery ($1.39 and $1.23 billion). The largest output of employee inventions and innovations is obviously to be expected from aircraft, space, and electrical industries. Employer-employee relations in these branches are of corresponding importance.

UNIVERSITY R&D EXPENDITURES

"Universities and colleges" include all organizational units owned, operated, or controlled by such institutions, except university-managed Federal Contract

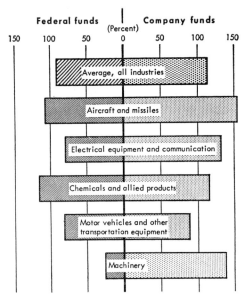

Figure 1.7 Percent change in R&D funds in the five leading industries, by source, 1957–1966.

Source: National Science Foundation

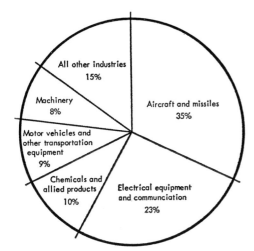

Figure 1.8 R&D funds spent by the five leading industries as percent of total R&D funds, 1966.
Source: National Science Foundation

Research Centers. Defined as parts of universities and colleges proper are graduate schools, colleges of arts and sciences, engineering schools, schools of dentistry, schools of agriculture, agricultural experiment stations, liberal arts colleges, teachers' colleges, junior colleges, and affiliated organizational units. Federal Contract Research Centers are R&D organizations exclusively or substantially financed by the federal government but managed on a contractual basis by educational or other organizations. Among the Federal Contract Research Centers so managed, the best known are the Lincoln Laboratory (Massachusetts Institute of Technology), the Jet Propulsion Laboratory (California Institute of Technology), the Los Alamos Scientific Laboratory (University of California), and the Cornell Aeronautical Laboratory (Cornell University).[8]

In the past expenditures for research and development have not always been entered as separate items in university budgets. In view of the increased role of research projects, especially federally financed research, university budgets now often carry separately budgeted research and development expenditures.

Official statistical surveys of amount and distribution of university R&D activities are, however, still relatively scarce compared with corresponding research statistics

[8] NSF, *Reviews of Data on Science Resources*, No. 9, August, 1966, p. 19.

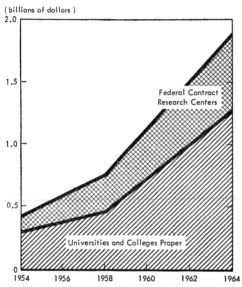

(billions of dollars)

Figure 1.9 Current expenditures for separately budgeted R&D in universities and colleges, 1954–1964, in dollars.

Source: National Science Foundation

affecting the federal government or industry. Two charts have been selected to illustrate trends in the university sector.

Figure 1.9 shows expenditures for separately budgeted R&D in universities and colleges, broken down into funds spent by universities proper and those spent by the federal government (Federal Contract Research Centers) for the years 1954–1964. One is struck by the fact that total expenditures for R&D performed in institutions of higher learning were $1.9 billion even in 1964 (the amount has strongly increased since that time). Of these expenditures the federal government financed (in 1964) virtually all performance in Federal Contract Research Centers as well as 72 percent of the separately budgeted R&D performance.[9] Coordination of government and university patent policy is obviously paramount. The research carried out by universities accounts annually for nearly one-half the basic research performed in the United States, measured in dollars.[10]

Figure 1.10 informs us that more than one-half of all R&D expenditures ($1.235

[9] NSF, *Reviews of Data on Science Resources,* No. 9, August 1966, p. 1.
[10] *Ibid.,* p. 2.

Research Expenditures - $1,235 million

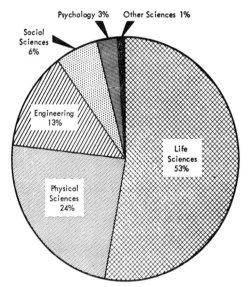

Figure 1.10 Current expenditures for separately budgeted research in universities and colleges, by field of science, 1964, in percent.
Source: National Science Foundation

billion) at universities was expended in the life sciences, comprising biological sciences, medical sciences, and agricultural sciences.[11] Nearly one-fourth of all budgeted research was carried out in the physical sciences, comprising the physical sciences proper, the mathematical sciences, and the engineering sciences.[12]

[11] Biological sciences are defined as those which, apart from the medical and agricultural sciences, deal with the origin, development, structure, function, and interaction of living things; medical sciences are those which are concerned with maintaining health and understanding disease; and agricultural sciences are directed primarily toward understanding and improving the production of animals and plants of economic and cultural importance to man. (NSF 62–37, p. 576.)
[12] The physical sciences proper are those sciences concerned primarily with understanding of the natural phenomena associated with nonliving things; mathematical sciences are those sciences that employ logical reasoning with the aid of symbols and that are concerned with the development of methods of operations employing such symbols; and engineering sciences are those sciences that are concerned with studies directed toward developing scientific principles or toward making specific scientific principles usable in engineering practice. (NSF 62–37, p. 576.)

AVAILABLE R&D EMPLOYEES (INVENTIVE MANPOWER)

"We cannot afford to squander any of our human capital, or to deny any individual an opportunity to realize his full potential." With these words ends the preface of the important report of the Committee on Utilization of Scientific and Engineering Talent published in 1964 by the National Academy of Sciences.[13] The report looks mainly to scientists and engineers for technological advances in industry-financed research and development in the civilian sector of the economy and hopes to stimulate the rate of innovation in certain areas of the economy.

What we want to know generally can be summed up in the following questions:
1. How many employees belong to this group of individuals (potential inventors)?
2. What main types of professions (occupational groups) are represented in this group of employees?
3. How are these employees distributed among three sectors of the economy (government, industry, and universities)?

It is obvious that in the gigantic total labor force of the United States—more than 75 million people—only a limited number of employees are likely to produce inventions and engineering improvements of value to an employer or to a larger entity of the economy. We often call this group by a general term, such as R&D employees or professional and technical workers. To speak of them as employees "hired to invent," a term often used in industrial circles, is unsatisfactory. Expectation of inventions is undoubtedly more justified in work assignments concerned directly and exclusively with research into new fields of technology and science or with development or improvement of products and processes, but detailed formal work assignments for employees often do not exist in practice. Where they do exist, they change frequently. Inventions are also often made by employees in fields to which they were not assigned.

R&D PERSONNEL IN ALL SECTORS OF THE ECONOMY

An important study by the National Science Foundation, *Profiles of Manpower in Science and Technology,* states that of the specialists working in science and technology some expand scientific knowledge by doing research; some apply scientific information and engineering techniques to develop new products and services, or to solve problems in health, defense, or transportation; some operate complex systems for communication or for the exploration of space; and some

---

[13] *Toward Better Utilization of Scientific and Engineering Talent: A Program for Action.* The study also called the Killian Report after the Committee chairman was approved by President Kennedy in 1961. In view of its relevance and importance, this source of information is still worth citing.

educate and train manpower.[14] Except for the last group, these persons are the subject matter of the present book.

How many persons are in the group of scientists and engineers? The Bureau of Labor Statistics showed 1,412,500 in 1966, representing about 2 percent of the total labor force. The National Science Foundation in a recent study, *Employment of Scientists and Engineers in the United States, 1950–1966*, published in 1968, found that this sector of the labor force increased from half a million in 1950, a threefold rise. In terms of percentage of total employment, the increase was—in agreement with the earlier study—from 1 percent to 2.[15]

These persons (including technicians) represent the specialists from whom inventions are most likely to arise. About one-third are actively engaged in research and development.

According to *Employment of Scientists and Engineers*, engineers in 1966 were almost 71 percent of the 1,412,500 total. Of the scientists, as distinct from the engineers, chemists in 1966 make up the largest division of personnel of the physical sciences, with more than one-fourth of all (28.7 percent). It is interesting to note that mathematicians increased much faster than the scientists as a whole, from 13,500 to 1950 to 51,800 in 1966. Their growth was second only to that of medical scientists who rose 400 percent from 9200 in 1950 to 46,200 in 1966.

Table 1.2 shows a breakdown of these manpower figures among the sectors of the economy, in 1966.

Table 1.3 shows the distribution of the special group of R&D scientists and engineers as employed by industry and federal agencies, broken down by industrial fields, in 1966. The number of R&D employees have been arranged (by the author)

Table 1.2 Distribution of Science and Engineering Manpower, 1966

	Industry[1]	Federal, State and Local Government	Universities and Colleges	Other Nonprofit Institutions[2]
Scientists	185,500	75,600	145,600	10,100
Engineers	812,200	144,100	35,100	4,600
All	997,700	219,700	180,700	14,700

1 Including all private, profit-making organizations.
2 Including foundations, independent research institutes, and self-employed.
Source: NSF 68–30, "Employment of Scientists and Engineers in the United States 1950–1966" (September 1968), Tables A-3, A-4.

14 NSF, *Profiles of Manpower in Science and Technology*, p. 3.
15 NSF, *Employment of Scientists and Engineers in the United States,* 1950–1966, p. 13f.

Table 1.3   Distribution of R&D Scientists and Engineers Employed in Industry and by Federal Agencies, by Field, in 1966

	Total	Company[1]	Federal Total	DOD	NASA	All Other Agencies
	235,900	94,300	141,600	77,600	48,200	15,800
Aircraft and missiles	95,400	17,800	77,600	43,500	30,200	3,900
Electrical equipment and communications	71,000	30,400	40,600	21,800	11,600	7,200
Machinery	21,900	1,400	7,900	4,300	3,200	400
Chemicals and allied products	17,100	13,500	3,600	1,200	NA	2,400
Other industries	16,600	9,700	6,900	4,100	1,700	1,600
Motor vehicles and other transport equipment	10,500	6,900	3,500	1,900	NA	NA
Professional and scientific instruments	3,400	2,000	1,500	900	NA	NA

[1] Covering 200 companies accounting for 93 percent of all federal funds for industry R&D performance.
Source: Statistical Abstract of the United States 1968, p. 529.

Table 1.4   Employers of Scientists, 1966

	Number	Percent
Industry and business	85,500	44.5
Educational institutions	45,600	34.9
Federal government	54,000	13.0
State and local government	21,600	5.2
Nonprofit organizations	10,100	2.4

Source: *Employment of Scientists and Engineers in the United States,* 1950–1966, NSF 68–30, Table A-4.

in seven fields in descending order. The table shows clearly the dominance of the fields of aircraft, missiles, electrical equipment and communications, both in industry and government, as the biggest sources of employment of research personnel.

The largest employers of scientists in 1966 are shown in Table 1.4.

GENERAL OBSERVATIONS

The foregoing figures may allow some preliminary generalizations of interest for this book:

1. Between 1.4 and 2 million persons are involved in the problems treated in this book. They are a small minority of the total U.S. population in absolute figures; however, they represent 2 to 3 percent of the labor force. Assuming that only half of this group produces a single invention, scientific discovery, or useful engineering improvement once a year, still a mass of working results originates continuously. To analyze and improve the effective performance of this category of employees, it is essential to explore their legal and practical relations with their employers and their own attitudes toward the prevailing situation.

More than 90,000 new patent applications for inventions are filed each year at the U.S. Patent Office.[16] The majority of these inventive ideas emanate from inventors working as employees of government, industry or universities. These employees obviously can benefit too from greater knowledge of employee attitudes.

2. Most potential groups of inventors (scientists, engineers, and technicians) as well as scientists as a single group are found in industry. Engineers are the largest single group.

3. Government agencies are the second largest employers of these groups of employees, technicians being the largest single group.

4. Among scientists, chemists are by far the largest group.

More observation can be made when looking at figures from the three sectors of the economy separately.

The Government sector

Two sets of statistics only will be presented here, to highlight the situation of government employee inventors: distribution of professional scientific and technical personnel broken down: (1) by major employing federal agency, and (2) by occupational group of personnel.

When considering the government sector, we are now (since 1964) fortunate to be able to interconnect figures concerning federal research funds and federal research personnel with figures on government patent practices, including number of invention disclosures made and submitted by various agencies' own employees and by contractors, i.e., contractors' employees. This is possible thanks to the annual reports of the Data Collection and Analysis Subcommittee of the Committee on Government Patent Policy created by the Federal Council for Science and Technology. The term invention in these statistics means an invention "which is or may be patentable under the patent laws of the United States of America or

16 There were 93,011 in 1967. See *Statistical Abstract of the United States*, 1968, p. 536.

any foreign country."[17] Comparisons between certain groups of figures will be made in connection with the individual figure or chart presented.

Figure 1.11 shows distribution of professional scientific and technical personnel in six specific federal departments compared to other departments and to all agencies together, in October 1966. Professional health personnel in four departments are also shown and compared as before. This is a breakdown from a total of 193,600 civilian scientists, engineers, and health professionals (the latter primarily medical officers, dental officers, veterinarians, and nurses). The Department of Defense (DOD) continues to be the largest employer of scientists and engineers; the total of 66,000 is almost one third of all such employees. The Veterans Administration (VA) employed 25,400 health professionals, the largest number of such personnel in any agency. Department of Agriculture was second largest employer of scientists and engineers with more than 25,000. This personnel is

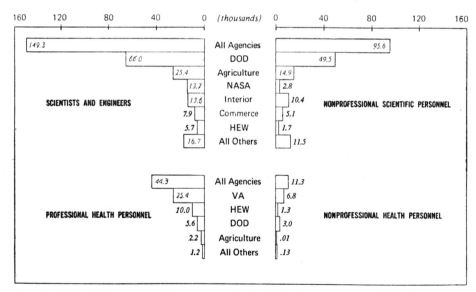

Scientific and technical personnel in the Federal Government, October 1966

Figure 1.11 Scientific and technical personnel in the federal government, 1966.
Source: National Science Foundation

[17] See definitions (sec. 4, Policy Statement), reprinted in Federal Council for Science and Technology, *Annual Report on Government Patent Policy*, June 1966, p. 16.

engaged in a wide variety of scientific work, both basic and applied. The chart does not include personnel engaged in government contract or grants or federally financed research centers. Defense, agriculture, and NASA personnel together represent more than 100,000 professional employees. It appears essential to analyze the regulation of their inventive contributions and make recommendations.

Figure 1.12 shows trends in growth of professional personnel in government by occupational group. Most occupational government employee groups increased

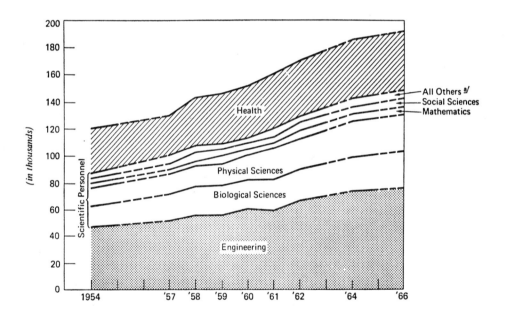

Index, 1954 = 100.0

| | Engineering | Scientific | | | | | Health |
		Biological Sciences	Physical Sciences	Mathematics	Social Sciences	All Others	
1959	122.0	131.1	124.2	132.8	143.5	99.3	113.2
1964	158.0	152.1	197.1	175.6	177.7	116.6	130.4
1966	162.1	161.5	205.4	192.9	192.5	130.6	132.4

Figure 1.12 Trends in growth of scientific and technical personnel in the federal government, by occupational group, 1954–1966.
a Includes geography, cartography, psychology, operations research and urban planning.
Source: National Science Foundation

at a similar pace. In 1966, the largest group was 76,800 engineers, followed by 72,500 scientists of all branches, and 44,300 health professionals.[18]

When trying to interconnect these figures on government personnel with inventive results produced by government agencies' own employees and employees of government contractors, we find some interesting relationships. From the statistics published by the Subcommittee of the Government Patent Policy Committee for three fiscal years (1963, 1964, 1965) covering 15 federal agencies, figures are selected comparing employee invention disclosures received from intramural employees and from contractors' employees. For the period 1963–1965, we find for some of the agencies of special interest the figures shown in Table 1.5. Preliminary generalizations of interest from Figures 1.11 and 1.12 and from the statistics in Table 1.5 from the Government Patent Policy Committee are as follows:

1. Quantitative dominance of R&D scientists and engineers in defense and space research (Figure 1.11).

2. The relatively large number of professional health employees in government employment (second after scientists and engineers) (Figures 1.11 and 1.12).

3. Quantitative dominance of employees of Department of Defense (Navy, Army, and Air Force) and employees of DOD's contractors as source of invention disclosures (Table 1.5).

Table 1.5   Invention Disclosures from Intramural and Contractors' Employees, 1964, 1965, and 1966 (three-year totals)

Intramural Employees			Contractors' Employees		
Agency	Disclosures	Rank	Agency	Disclosures	Rank
Navy	3,040	1	Air Force	6,838	1
Army	2,752	2	AEC	4,902	2
NASA	1,244	3	Navy	4,729	3
Air Force	625	4	Army	3,178	4
USDA	566	5	NASA	3,099	5
			HEW	741	6
AEC	98	9	USDA	87	9
HEW	67	10			

Source: *Annual Report on Government Patent Policy, June 1966,* Appendix D, Table II, pp. 36–37.

[18] Determination of occupations was based on standards contained in the *Handbook of Occupational Groups and Series of Classes* as published by the U.S. Civil Service Commission.

4. Relatively large amount (third in rank) of invention disclosures from NASA's own employees (Table 1.5).
5. A relatively large amount (second in rank) of invention disclosures from employees of AEC contractors (Table 1.5).
6. A small amount (tenth in rank) of invention disclosures from HEW's own employees (Table 1.5).
7. A small amount (ninth in rank) of invention disclosures from employees of USDA contractors (Table 1.5).

As a final word of caution it may be said that these observations are quantitative and do not allow qualitative conclusions with regard to special inventiveness of certain groups of government employees or employees of certain federal agencies. A single invention may be of greater value than a hundred others, but the conclusion seems to be allowable that defense personnel and NASA personnel (both in direct government service and employed by contractors) show greatest awareness regarding suggestions of new inventions. Another conclusion is that inventive activity (as expressed by number of invention disclosures) is greatest in government agencies where engineers make up the majority of professional personnel, as in DOD and NASA, in contrast to scientific personnel. Federal Aviation Agency is an exception (not shown in these charts).

Table 1.6   Employment of Scientists, Engineers, and Technicians by Major Industries, January 1, 1966 (in thousands)

Industry	Total	Scientists	Engi-neers	Techni-cians
All industries	1,627.6	178.3	776.1	673.1
Aircraft, ordnance, and missiles	196.9	15.4	127.8	53.7
Aircraft	117.7	7.0	76.3	34.4
Ordnance and missiles	79.2	8.4	51.5	19.3
Electrical machinery	245.3	9.0	135.5	100.8
Chemicals and allied products	136.0	57.1	40.6	38.3
Machinery except electrical	149.0	6.5	75.1	67.4
Engineering and architectural services	161.9	2.9	61.2	97.8
Commercial laboratories	90.4	16.1	35.4	38.9
Construction	77.4	.5	46.7	30.2
Instruments	55.8	6.0	29.6	20.2
Motor vehicles and parts	39.3	1.5	22.1	15.7
Total selected industries	1,152.2	115.0	574.0	463.0
All other industries	475.5	63.3	202.2	210.1

Source: *Monthly Labor Review,* May 1968, pp. 44, 45.

The Industrial Sector

Tables 1.6 and 1.7 illustrate the scientific and engineering manpower situation in industry as of January 1, 1966.

Table 1.6 presents a breakdown of scientists, engineers, and technicians by 10 major industries, as of January 1, 1966. It points up the leading role, quantitatively, of engineers (135,500) and technicians (100,800) in the electrical machinery industry, as well as in the aircraft, ordnance, and missiles industries (127,800 and 53,700). Scientists lead over engineers and technicians only in chemicals and allied products (57,100). Relatively many scientists work in commercial laboratories, where they represent roughly one-fifth of the total.

As a total in all industries (in 1966), engineers were the leading employee group with 776,100, followed by 673,100 technicians, and 178,300 scientists. Scientists represented not much more than 10 percent of the three-group total. The great total number of industrial professional employees illustrates the general importance of the problems treated in this book, although for the most part they are employed by only a few industries. In 1966, 10 industries, whose employment of all types of workers was only 20 percent of the total for private (nonagricultural) industries, employed about 70 percent of all scientists, engineers, and technicians.[19]

Table 1.7 is a breakdown of scientists and engineers by five primary occupational functions. It illustrates that (in 1966) about 38 percent of all scientists and engineers (361,000 of 954,600) were working with performance, management, or administration of industrial research and development, and 32.8 percent with production

Table 1.7 Scientists and Engineers Employed in Industry, by Primary Function, 1966

Function	Number (in thousands)	Percent
Total scientists and engineers	954.6	100.0
Research and development	361.0	37.8
Performance	301.2	31.5
Management and administration of research and development	59.8	6.3
Production operations	313.0	32.8
Management other than research and development	110.6	11.6
Sales and service	97.1	10.2
Other functions	72.8	7.6

Source: *Monthly Labor Review*, May 1968, pp. 44, 45.

[19] *Monthly Labor Review*, May 1968.

operations. The former group is naturally the most potentially creative, but industrial practice has shown that valuable inventions are also made by production personnel.

The University Sector

The Report of the Committee on Utilization of Scientific and Engineering Talent[20] stated that in 1964 about 175,000 scientists and engineers were employed in university educational and research activities. Since many faculty members of universities are teaching and doing research at the same time, a separation of these two functions into full-time teachers and full-time researchers may not be feasible. According to another source, all professional personnel employed at universities and colleges (including full-time employees, part-time employees, and employed graduate students) made a full-time equivalent of 192,600 individuals in 1965.[21]

Figure 1.13 attempts to present and project the number of full-time science and engineering staff in universities and colleges for three selected years, 1964–1965, 1969–1970, and 1974–1975. "Staff" includes those required for research, teaching,

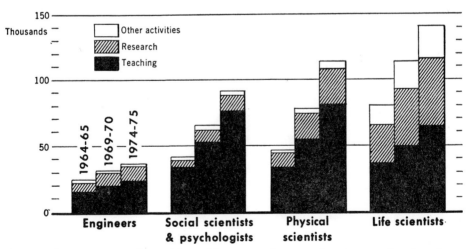

Figure 1.13 Past, present (1969–1970), and future requirements for science and engineering staff in universities and colleges. All figures in full-time equivalents.

Source: National Science Foundation

[20] "The Killian Report," National Academy of Sciences, 1964.
[21] *Statistical Abstract of the United States,* 1966, p. 547.

and "other activities," such as administration and adult education or (in medical schools) health services, diagnosis and treatment of patients in hospitals, clinics, and outpatient facilities. The figure shows that employment of scientists, excluding engineers, is expected to approximately double by 1974 as a result of expanding enrollments and research. Scientific discoveries made by this staff should increase, if not directly at least to some tangible extent.[22]

Figure 1.14 shows percentage distribution of full-time scientists and engineers employed by universities in January 1965 by field of science. It should be seen in conjunction with Figure 1.10, showing research expenditures for the different

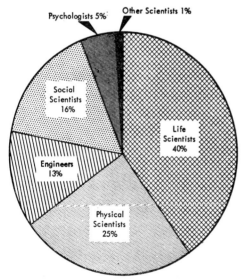

Scientists and Engineers - 250,000

Psychologists 5%   Other Scientists 1%

Social Scientists 16%

Engineers 13%

Physical Scientists 25%

Life Scientists 40%

Figure 1.14 Scientists and engineers employed in universities and colleges, by field, January 1965.

Source: National Science Foundation

[22] Many statistics on manpower in the university research field supplement figures on numbers of scientists and engineers with number of individuals awarded higher academic degrees, on the assumption that research by the federal government is mainly channeled to those academic institutions which have the most distinguished sciences and engineering faculties. See page 36 of the Report of the Committee on Utilization of Scientific and Engineering Talent, National Academy of Sciences, 1964.

sciences in universities in 1964. Life scientists dominate with 40 percent. (These include biological, medical, and agricultural scientists.) Next largest group are physical scientists with 25 percent, including scientists in mathematics and engineering sciences.

Table 1.8 presents and projects to 1974–1975 the number of research staff that will be required in four categories, in universities and colleges. From the academic year 1969–1970 to 1974–1975, the projection indicates that the total research staff in physical science in universities and colleges will increase by 9100 people, life scientists by 10,800, and engineers by 1600. Inventive research results at universities should also increase to some extent during this period. Problems regarding orderly employer-employee relations in the invention field at universities certainly will not become fewer during such expansion of professional staff.

Table 1.8   Estimated Requirements for Full-Time Equivalent Research Staff[1] in Science and Engineering in Universities and Colleges,[2] 1964–1965 to 1974–1975 (in thousands)

Academic Year	Total	Physical Scientists[3]	Engineers	Life Scientists[4]	Social Scientists and Psychologists
1964–65	54.9	11.9	7.7	29.7	5.6
1965–66	63.7	14.5	8.7	33.7	6.7
1966–67	69.9	16.5	9.3	36.6	7.5
1967–68	71.1	17.1	9.2	37.0	7.8
1968–69	74.3	18.1	9.1	38.9	8.3
1969–70	80.8	19.7	9.7	42.7	8.8
1970–71	85.4	21.3	10.0	44.7	9.5
1971–72	91.3	23.1	10.3	47.6	10.2
1972–73	95.2	25.0	10.7	48.5	11.0
1973–74	100.6	26.9	11.0	51.1	11.6
1974–75	106.1	28.8	11.3	53.5	12.4

[1] Includes full-time and part-time staff and employed graduate students.
[2] Excludes Federal Contract Research Centers administered by these institutions.
[3] Includes mathematicians.
[4] Includes medical scientists.

Employer-Employee Relations
by John C. Stedman

2

OVERVIEW

Traditionally, one thinks of the process of creating intellectual property, whether in the form of patentable inventions, patentable or unpatentable trade secrets, or "writings" in the sense that the copyright law uses the term, as being intensely and exclusively an individual process undertaken by a human being. And so it is. We have not yet reached the point where creativity is the product either of a machine or of purely pedestrian, routine acts on the part of persons or groups. On the other hand, we have witnessed a steady increase in the conduct of inventive work by employed professionals of various kinds, especially researchers, as distinguished from independent inventors working on their own. This is especially true in the areas covered by patents and trade secrets, although apparently less so in the copyright field. This development has occurred despite the fact that much of our intellectual property law—most of all our patent system—is structured in terms of the individual inventor.

This great increase in employed inventors is evidenced by the sharp expansion of both funds and manpower in the R&D area. Thus, total R&D expenditures by both industry and government increased from less than $1 billion in 1940 to $5 billion in 1953 and $22 billion in 1966.[1] Of the 1966 portion, industry performed $15.5 billion, more than half of which was financed by the federal government. Industry alone employed 371,000 scientists and engineers as of January 1967, as compared to 244,000 in January 1958.[2]

By the nature of things, we have no statistics on private, individual research and creative activity, but there is reason to suppose that the tremendous increase shown at the corporate and government level did not have its counterpart at the private level.[3] Indeed, the sharp increase in manpower employment at industry and governmental levels may have siphoned away some of the private efforts.

[1] National Science Foundation, *Reviews of Data on Science Resources*, no. 12 (January 1968), pp. 3, 4; see generally, Richard J. Barber, *Politics of Research* (Washington, D.C.: Public Affairs Press, 1966), pp. 13–31.
[2] NSF *Reviews*, pp. 1, 5; see generally Barber, *Politics of Research*, pp. 5–50. For figures on government expenditures, see Daniel S. Greenberg, *The Politics of Pure Science* (New York: American Library, 1967), p. 275.
[3] John Jewkes, David Sawers and Richard Stillerman, *The Sources of Invention* (Cambridge, Mass.: Harvard Univ. Press, 1966), pp. 108–115, discusses the reason individual invention is on the decline. See also B. F. Miessner, "Today's Inventor—A Study in Frustration," *American Engineer* (April 1963); and "Engineers and Patentry" (paper delivered before the Miami section of the Institute of Electrical and Electronic Engineers, July 23, 1963), pp. 17–18.

Further evidence of the increase in corporate activity is shown by the fact that as of 1954 approximately 60 percent of the patents issued by the Patent Office went to corporations, presumably for inventions made by employees, in contrast to roughly 35 percent in the middle 1930's.[4] Since 1954 the percentage of patents assigned to corporations has been slowly but steadily increasing.[5]

All in all, what these statistics show is that a significant amount of the creative and inventive work done in the technological area of this country today stems from the employed rather than the independent inventor.

This development suggests a number of policy problems of a social and economic nature. It is important to maintain the individuality and identity of the person responsible for the invention, including public recognition of his contribution.[6] The relationship of the employer to the employee with reference to inventions that the latter develops is a delicate and difficult one; yet a proper balancing of the interests involved in this relationship is crucially important. In terms of established national policy, we desire to encourage and promote creative and innovative activity in order to add as much as possible to the total sum of new

[4] Barker Sanders, "Some Difficulties in Measuring Inventive Activity," in *The Rate and Direction of Inventive Activity: Economic and Social Factors* (Princeton: Princeton Univ. Press, 1962) (hereafter cited as "Princeton Symposium"), Table 2, p. 62; Jacob Schmookler, *Invention and Economic Growth* (Cambridge, Mass.: Harvard Univ. Press, 1966), pp. 25–39 and Table 1; P. J. Federico, "Distribution of Patents Issued to Corporations (1939–55)" (Subcommittee on Patents, Trademarks and Copyrights, Senate Committee on the Judiciary, Study No. 3, 1957), pp. 13–15; Frank Howard, "Patents and Technical Progress," *Patent, Trademark, and Copyright Journal of Research and Education* 4 (1960 Conference number): 57, 60; Jesse Markham, "The Value of the American Patent System: An Inquiry into Possible Approaches to its Measurement," *PTC J. of Research and Education* 1 (1957): 20, 33. See also Jewkes, Sawers and Stillerman, *Sources of Inventions,* p. 104; and Miessner, "Today's Inventor." For assignment of rights, see "Rights of Employer and Employee in Patentable Inventions," *APLA Bulletin* (April-May 1966), p. 178; Federico, "Corporation Patents—Statistics of Ownership," in R. P. Calvert, ed., *The Encyclopedia of Patent Practice and Invention Management* (New York: Reinhold, 1964), pp. 178–182, Table 2.

[5] Miessner in "Today's Inventor" indicates that the early 1960's figure is about 70 percent for corporations.

[6] Jacob Rabinow, "Experiences in Electrical Invention," *J. Patent Off. Soc.* 47 (1965): 580; Miessner, "Today's Inventor" and "Engineers and Patentry," pp. 8–12; Richard Stillerman, "Resistance to Change," *J. Patent Off. Soc.* 48 (1966): 484, 498–499; U.S. Senate, Hearings before the Subcommittee on Antitrust and Monopoly of the Committee on the Judiciary, 90th Cong., 1st sess., Part 6 (1967): testimony of Richard Walton, p. 2711, and Daniel V. DeSimone, p. 2930; Jewkes, Sawers and Stillerman, *Sources of Invention,* pp. 250–260; James A. Haddad, "An Executive's View of the Employed Inventor," *J. Patent Off. Soc.* 47 (1965): 476, 478; Charles McTiernan, "Employee-Inventor Compensation Plans," *J. Patent Off. Soc.* 46 (1964): 475, 483–489; Simon Marcson, *The Scientist in American Industry* (Princeton Univ., Industrial Relations Section, 1960), pp. 73–78; Robert Calvert, "Inventor's Psychology," in *Encyclopedia of Patent Practice,* p. 494.

development and get it into use. We are also increasingly concerned to see that such creative and innovative activity goes in directions that are most useful to society, and we are no longer as sure as we have been in the past that the forces that guide the free enterprise system will necessarily take us in those directions. Finally, because R&D activity has characteristically been the special province of large corporations (and large governments) we are concerned to see that these activities do not defeat our efforts to preserve a competitive, antimonopolistic economy.[7]

The fact that most of these problems arise in an economic context should not lead us to overlook the importance of the noneconomic factors that may enter into the employer-employee relationship and play a significant role therein. These factors include the instinct of contrivance, desire for fame and prestige, intellectual inquiry and curiosity, the general level of scientific progress, and the existence of economic conditions and attitudes favorable to innovation.[8] By their nature, such factors rarely give rise to direct legal problems, although legal problems may arise incidentally from them (e.g., controversy over receiving credit for a given invention). They are nonetheless important and may well receive more attention in the future than they have in the past.

The main legal problems that arise out of the employer-employee relationship in this area are twofold:

1. The technical problems of applying for and obtaining valid patents and copyrights and of protecting trade secrets, problems that include the need for identifying the creator or inventor and defining the exact nature of his contribution.

2. The problem of determining the respective rights of the inventor and his employer in the invention he has made or at least contributed to substantially.

The rights referred to in point 2 include both the right to use the invention that has been made and the right to exclude others from using it. (A third possibility involves special compensation to the employee for inventions he makes and turns over to his employer. In the United States such compensation normally takes the form of an *ex gratia* award and rarely gives rise to a legal right.) In determining these rights one must necessarily look at the relationship between the parties, the employee's contribution as compared to the contributions of others, the under-

---

[7] Sanders "Inventive Activity," Princeton Symposium, p. 55; Barber, *Politics of Research*, pp. 71090; Schmookler, *Invention*, pp. 33–35.

[8] Floyd Vaughan, *Economics of the Patent System* (New York: Macmillan, 1925), pp. 1–10; Joseph Rossman, *Industrial Creativity: The Psychology of the Inventor* (3rd ed.) (New Hyde Park, N.Y., University Books, 1964), pp. 151–159; Marcson, *Scientist*, pp. 72–85, 147–149.

standings between the parties whether expressed or implied, the impact of public regulations and statutes, and lastly the policy considerations that may have an impact and influence on all of these.

ESTABLISHING LEGAL RIGHTS IN EMPLOYEE INVENTIONS

Whatever the employee has done in a creative sense must be translated into recognizable legal rights. These may take the form of patents, trade secrets, or copyright. In the absence of one or another of these no legal subject matter exists. Since the ultimate task is to resolve controversies involving ownership of these legal rights, it becomes necessary first to define the property being fought over.[9] One must ask two major questions:

1. What is the nature of the intellectual property that results? The "creation" may fall short of being patentable and yet be legally protectible as a trade secret or through copyright. As we shall see, the procedure for establishing the legal rights may differ depending upon whether one is dealing with a patent, a trade secret, or a copyright.

2. Just who is the "inventor" or "creator"? Defining the inventor and his contribution becomes crucial because it may have an effect upon the procedure to be used in establishing the legal rights and because it may affect the allocation procedure for establishing these rights. Also it may affect the allocation of such rights as between the employer and employee in terms of the right to use the idea or invention, the right to exclude others from using it, and the right to assign or license either of these rights to third parties.

If a given creation or invention results from the combined efforts of both the employee and others, rather than being the sole contribution of a single employee, definition of the exact nature and extent of the contribution becomes more difficult. Such multiple contributions are common at the employer-employee level. In the first place, cooperative research efforts by two or more employees in a corporate laboratory may frequently lead to joint invention. Beyond this, even though the employee may be the sole inventor or creator in the technical sense, he typically will have received assistance of an inventive or noninventive nature in the form of helpful suggestions, information and memoranda, equipment and facilities, and the like.

[9] This assumes of course, that a controversy does occur; otherwise no legal issues arise. If the employee sees fit to leave everything to the employer, retaining no rights for himself, no legal issue arises except as the employee's cooperation may be needed to establish the legal right itself. Conversely, if the employer makes no claim to the invention his employee has made, the latter simply proceeds as would an independent inventor.

Consequently, it becomes necessary to look more closely at the factors that contribute to a given creation.

Factors Contributing to Creation and Invention

One may start with the concept of "the" single creator who is solely responsible for a given creation whether in the form of an invention, a nonpatentable idea, or a piece of writing. This has been our traditional approach to this area. Indeed, the patent system is largely written in those terms, since it requires that "the" inventor be identified. Although efforts have been made to relax this requirement, it still represents the basic approach of the patent system. This is less true where trade secrets are involved. There is no legal requirement that "the" creator of a trade secret be identified. Indeed, trade secret material is more likely than not to become an amalgam of accumulated information in the files of the corporation, with no identification of the employee who was responsible for it unless the idea moved over into the patent area. As for copyright, contributions in this area are such that the writer or author is usually identifiable. This, however, is not legally required as a condition to registering a copyright. Thus, section 26 of the copyright statute identifies one who hires another to prepare a writing for him as the "author" for copyright purposes. In contrast to the circumstances that typically obtain where patenting is involved, anonymous or ghost writing occurs in magazines, newspapers, advertisements, and television and motion picture productions. In these instances the actual author remains unidentified, and such lack of identification is legally permissible insofar as the copyright law is concerned.

Irrespective of the legal requirements, actual creative contribution may reflect the cooperative efforts of a number of people. It is true that the basic idea or concrete expression of the original idea can usually be traced to a single individual or two or three persons working closely together; indeed, such person or persons are viewed as "the" inventor when it comes to the patent law. Tied to them, however, may be a substantial number of noncreative contributions. These include material aids, such as money, equipment, and laboratory facilities. They may include informational aids such as text material and other literature, or miscellaneous memoranda including confidential files. They may include various forms of assistance, such as laboratory helpers, suggestions, ideas or comments from either above or below. In this last area especially, it becomes difficult to draw the line between inventive and noninventive help to the putative inventor.[10]

[10] See *Agawam Woolen Co. v. Jordan,* 7 Wallace 583, 19 Lawyer's ed. 177 (1868); F. D. Prager, "Agawam v. Jordan, Annotated," *J. Patent Off. Soc.* (1940): 737, 771–775; Simon

Further complicating the task of identifying the contributor and his contribution is the fact that many creations reflect a continuing development rather than a single, identifiable creative step. One sees this in the accumulation of trade secret material referred to previously. One sees it even more plainly in the successive editions of a given book or treatise. It also occurs in the area of invention, although it is less apparent here because the patent law insists upon specific, isolated, identifiable inventions even though in reality these may have been simply a part of a continuing process of creation—a single frame cut from a movie strip, so to speak. Even where the creation is identified as a specific isolated phenomenon, it still may be only part of the overall development in the sense that it takes on its true and ultimate meaning and value only when it is put to actual use, and this may involve extensive and expensive experimentation, product improvement, market testing, and sales effort.[11]

With these complexities and multiple contributions in mind we turn to the problems involved in establishing the legal rights in the three major areas of inquiry, i.e., patents, trade secrets, and copyright.

Patents

Subject to minor qualifications, patent applications must be filed by "the" inventor supported by an oath signed by the inventor justifying his right to a patent. In some limited situations, application may be made by others, to wit, where (1) the inventor is dead or incapacitated, or (2) he refuses to cooperate or cannot be found to the detriment of one who has a "sufficient proprietary interest" in the patent.[12] This last provision is of especial significance in the case of the employed inventor, since it permits the employer to apply for the patent in the name of the employee.[13]

Kuznets, "Inventive Activity: Problems of Definition and Measurement," Princeton Symposium, pp. 31–35.

[11] Of the $15.5 billion spent by industry on R&D in 1966, $3.4 billion went for research and $12.1 billion for development. The recent trends (1957–1966) show that industry spends approximately three-fourths of its R&D funds for development performance. NSF *Review*, pp. 1, 8.

[12] 35 U.S. Code 117, 37 Code Fed. Register 1.42, 1.43, for the first case; 35 U.S. Code 118, 37 Code Fed. Register 1.47 for the second. See application of Louis Malakoff, 853 Off. Gazette, No. 1, p. 1 (Aug. 8, 1968).

[13] There is no express statutory authorization for the employer to sign the assignment papers that would enable the patent to issue in his own name, instead of in the name of the employee inventor, as provided in section 152, Title 35. The implications of Patent Office Rules 47 and 334, however, are that such issuance to the employer where an employee was uncooperative or could not be located would be effective just as it would be if he were dead or incapacitated. See *Manual of Patent Examining Procedure,* Sec. 409.03. There appears to be little occasion for invoking these provisions.

The requirement that "the" inventor apply has been relaxed in another respect. Sections 116 and 256 of the Statutes provide that if there has been unintentional error in naming the inventor, either as a result of naming someone who should not have been named or of neglecting to name someone who should have been named, the error can be corrected. If the misnaming is deliberate or done with deceptive intent, however, the traditional rule of the past, to wit, that error in naming the inventor renders the patent absolutely void, will continue to apply.

These relaxations in the rigorous demands of the patent statutes bring the United States law closer to the European law. The latter generally permits application by the employer if he is entitled to the patent rights.[14] Some further relaxation in this direction is currently being proposed in the United States and appears to have rather general support.

From the employee's standpoint, the strict insistence upon identifying the application with the actual employed inventor has two salutary effects. First, it provides protection against an employer claiming rights in a patent to which he is not entitled. Second, it assures the employee of proper credit for the invention he has made even though the actual patent rights may accrue to his employer.[15] On the other hand, a recalcitrant or dishonest employee can put obstacles in the path of an employer who is merely attempting to assert his legitimate rights. Such episodes, however, appear to be uncommon.

To summarize, the patent law requirements impose three primary obligations on the employed inventor.

1. He is obligated to cooperate with his employer in filing the application and prosecuting it to successful issuance. This may entail signing the application, signing the oath that he is the inventor, and filing various affidavits and statements supporting the application where this becomes necessary.

2. He is obligated to make the necessary assignments and sign appropriate papers with respect thereto, where the patent application or the issuing patent is to be assigned to the employer.

3. When controversy arises as to whether a patent application should be allowed or whether a patent, if issued, is valid, he may play a significant role in terms of

[14] Goldsmith, "Foreign Patents," in Calvert, *Encyclopedia*, p. 318.
[15] Compare *Misani* v. *Ortho Pharmaceutical Corp.*, 83 N.J. Super. 1, 198 A.2d 191, rev'd 210 A.2d 609, cert. denied, 382 U.S. Code 203 (1964). The invention by plaintiff (former employee of defendant) was patented in the name of another employee who was plaintiff's supervisor at the time of the invention. Plaintiff's action was in tort for an alleged misrepresentation depriving plaintiff of inventorship credit. The court said that while this claim may be recognized under some circumstances, it will not be recognized when the patent claim on the compound is conceded throughout the trial to be invalid as such.

filing appropriate statements and affidavits, or providing oral testimony and other evidence for the purpose of establishing the validity of the patent.[16] This cooperation may be called for at the application stage, as stated in (1), in an interference action with a competing applicant, or in an infringement suit where the validity of an issued patent is being challenged.

Finally, where the employer-employee relationship exists there is the increased likelihood of joint invention with all the difficulties and complexities that are likely to attend the issuance of patents to joint inventors.[17] In actual practice, there is some indication that corporations now and then take a somewhat cavalier attitude toward the "identification of the inventor" problem and simply assign credit for the invention, preferably to a single rather than multiple inventors, sometimes without as close attention to the actual facts as the law would seem to require.[18] Even though the Patent Office and the courts have not been disposed to hold named applicants and patentees to a rigid standard in this respect, the practice would appear to be ill-advised, however convenient.

Trade Secrets

The difficult requirements that attend the application for patents do not exist in the case of trade secrets. There is no formal law that requires that a trade secret be identified with the actual originator. Nor is there any formal law with respect to assignment by the creator to the ultimate owner. In the corporate relationship, as noted above, trade secrets tend to become a cumulative mass of knowledge possessed by employees and employers or a set of confidential documents in the corporate files. Typically, they tend to remain the property of the employer, although the employer's rights may be challenged or frustrated by indirect means. Insofar as the originating employee is concerned, his duty is simply that of disclosing the trade secret to his employer and keeping it secret to the extent that the employer is entitled to and insists upon his doing so. The difficulties that arise here center mainly upon the definition of a "trade secret," since both the obligation to

[16] At the application stage, the employed inventor may be called upon to reply to adverse Office action (Rules of Practice No. 111), to amend the application (Rules 115–127), or to respond to action by the Office (Rules 135–137). In interference actions, he may be required to make a written statement under oath (Rule 202) or file a preliminary statement (Rule 215). Although the infringement action is normally brought by the owner of the patent (employer), the employee inventor may be requested to file statements and affidavits which will rebut the infringer's defenses under sec. 282 of the Patent Laws.
[17] 35 U.S. Code secs. 116, 256, 262; Rules of Practice, nos. 45, 47, 324; Manual Patent Examining Procedure secs. 201.03, 605.04(f).
[18] Cyril A. Soans, "Who is the Inventor?" *J. Patent Off. Soc.* 28 (1946): 525.

disclose to the employer and the obligation to preserve it in secrecy will typically depend upon whether the information falls within the "trade secret" definition.[19]

Copyright

The establishment of rights in the copyright area is also simple by comparison to patents. To the extent that common law copyright (i.e., unpublished writings) are involved, these are treated by the law in the same manner as trade secrets, and the conditions for both establishing the right and transferring them from the employee to the employer are fundamentally the same.[20] Where a statutory copyright is involved, establishment of these rights becomes a matter of registering copies of the writings with the Copyright Office.[21] No need for active support in terms of identification of the author, the filing of oaths, or provision of affidavits enters into the picture. The procedure is simplified even further in the employer-employee relationship as the result of section 26 of the copyright law which defines the word "author" for purposes of obtaining a copyright as including "an employer in the case of work made for hire." Thus, in these circumstances, the employer can apply for the copyright registration without even identifying the actual author.

ALLOCATION OF RIGHTS BETWEEN EMPLOYER AND EMPLOYEE

It is necessary at the outset to define the area of "allocation." The discussion here relates both to the right to use the invention in question and the right to exclude others from using it. It also relates to the assignment of these rights to third parties. In using the term "allocation," we distinguish the apportionment of these

[19] Amédée Turner, *The Law of Trade Secrets* (Hackensack N.J.: Rothman, 1962), pp. 175–176; Roger Milgrim, *Trade Secrets* (New York: Matthew Bender, 1968), sec. 2.03, pp. 2–13.

[20] Melville B. Nimmer, *Nimmer on Copyright* (New York: Matthew Bender, 1967), pp. 183–185; Herbert A. Howell, *The Copyright Law* (Latman ed.) Washington, D.C.: Bureau of National Affairs, 1962), pp. 111–112.

[21] Nimmer, *Copyright,* pp. 301–302. Although the copyright registration process is generally a simple process, note should be taken of a current copyright problem of extraordinary complexity, difficulty, and importance—to wit, the copyrightability of computer programs. This problem and the related problem of patenting such programs are beyond the scope of the present discussion. Computer programs are currently being accepted for copyright to a limited extent. See Copyright Office, The Library of Congress, Circular 31D, April 1967; John Banzhaf, "Copyright Protection for Computer Programs," *ASCAP Copyright Law Symposium,* No. 14 (1966), p. 118.

As for patenting, a Patent Office decision denying a patent for a computer program was recently reversed by the Court of Customs and Patent Appeals. In re Prater and Wei, *U.S. Patent Quarterly* 159 (CCPA 1968): 583, reh., U.S. Patent Quarterly 162 (CCPA 1969): 541; see also David Bender, "Computer Programs: Should They Be Patentable?" *Colorado Law Rev.* 68 (1968): 241; Max W. J. Graham, Jr., "Process Patents for Computer Programs," *California Law Rev.* 56 (1968): 466; and Note (Ronald V. Thurman), "Adequate Legal Protection for Computer Programs," 1968 *Utah Law Rev.* (1968), p. 369.

intellectual property rights as between employer and employee from the payment of compensation (whether in cash or in some other form) to the employee for his contribution apart from the actual apportionment of the property rights involved. Obviously an interrelationship exists between allocation and these forms of compensation, both in terms of providing a stimulus to the employee and in terms of rewarding him for the activities he has undertaken.

The legal theories or principles upon which intellectual property rights may be allocated as between employer and employee are several. They embrace (1) common law rules for allocating such rights, including principles of equity and fairness, (2) contractual obligations, and (3) various unilateral rules, regulations and statutes covering such apportionments issued by the employer. These will be discussed in more detail later.

Important policy considerations also underlie such allocation and may affect considerably the rules that are applied and the results that follow.

1. A major policy concern is the "stimulus" effect. Both the patent and copyright statutes are consciously designed to stimulate and encourage invention and creation.[22] These statutes pose two interesting and difficult problems where the employer-employee situation is involved: First, a stimulus must be provided to *both* the employer and the employee, and this immediately poses the question whether patents and copyrights should be used to stimulate the one, the other, or both. Second, both these systems, and especially the patent system, are constructed on the theory of providing a *direct* reward to the creator when he makes an invention or creates a writing; thus, questions of operability arise in the employer-employee situation since the actual creator often sees no results accruing from his invention or writing (e.g., where it is suppressed) and receives no direct compensation from the system (e.g., where the employee is paid a salary not expressly including inventive activity, but the invention and its benefits accrue to the employer).

2. Another important policy consideration is the concern to do equity and be fair to all parties. These concepts of fairness are secondary to the "stimulus" objective, although they are stronger in the case of copyrights than of patents. They are the primary force in the case of trade secrets. In both the patent and

[22] The underlying policy considerations for both are set forth in Article I, section 8 of the United States Constitution, the relevant portion of which reads as follows: "The Congress shall have power . . . to promote the progress of science and useful arts, by securing for limited times to authors and inventors the exclusive right to their respective writings and discoveries."

trade secret areas, concepts of equity and fairness underlie the development of the common law doctrine relied upon in the allocation process.[23] Even where common law rules have been supplanted by contract, equity and fairness concepts enter into the picture to the extent that courts either refuse to enforce unconscionable agreements or require their modification as a condition of enforcement.[24]

3. Considerable emphasis is put upon the preservation of the individual identity and integrity of the actual creator. This is most apparent in the requirements of the patent law that the actual inventor be named and identified in the patent itself. It is likely to occur in the copyright field as well, although here the law does permit an employer to apply for copyright registration in his own name without identifying the actual writer. In the trade secret area, the emphasis upon identity virtually disappears. Not only is there no obligation to identify the inventor or creator as a condition to establishing legal rights, but the existence of the trade secret—and hence, necessarily, the identity of its originator—remains undisclosed to the public generally and in many instances even to the internal organization. Emphasis upon the individual is also illustrated by the law's concern to protect the individual worker's freedom to engage in his chosen line of work, to accept employment elsewhere, and to make a living.

4. A possible area of public concern, although one that has received little attention to date, is the concern to see that creations that do arise will be put to an effective and desirable usage.[25] With the current tendency to examine critically the nature

[23] As to patent "shop right" see *Cahill* v. *Regan, U.S. Patent Quarterly* 115 (N.Y. App. Div. 1957): 59, in which the court stated that the shop right is an application of equitable principles such that if the employee uses his employer's time, money, tools, and materials to produce a useful result, it is only fair and equitable that the employer should be entitled to use the product.

As to "trade secrets" see *Hoeltke* v. *Kemp Mfg. Co., U.S. Patent Quarterly* 26 (4th Cir. 1935): 114, 126. "While there was no express agreement that defendant was to hold the information so disclosed as a confidential matter . . . we think that in equity and good conscience such an agreement was implied; and having obtained the disclosure under such circumstances, defendant ought not be heard to say that there was no obligation to respect the confidence thus reposed in it."

[24] See. Roger O'Meara, *Employee Patent and Secrecy Agreements,* Studies in Personnel Policy, National Industrial Conference Board, No. 199 (New York, 1965), p. 72, which summarizes the position taken by the court in *Dalzell* v. *Dueber Watch Case Mfg. Co.,* 149 U.S. Reports (1893): 315, as follows: "If a contract is palpably unfair and inequitable and complainant is attempting to enforce an unconscionable bargain, it is not entitled either to the equitable remedy of injunction or of specific performance."

[25] NASA, more than any other governmental institution, has consciously and systematically sought to develop effective methods of maximizing desirable public usage. John A. Johnson, "Rights to Inventions Under NASA Contracts," *Fed. Bar J.* 21 (1961): 48–49; Wilson Maltby, "Need for a Federal Policy to Foster Invention Disclosures by Contractors and Employees,"

and direction of modern technology, this policy consideration may become increasingly important in the future. To the extent that it does, attention will have to be given to the important differences that may exist between government employees and private-industry employees in view of the contrasting uses to which the invention or creation might be put in the one case or the other depending upon whether the employer or employee were awarded the legal rights. This distinction has been largely ignored in the past.[26]

5. Finally, policy considerations relating to monopoly and our antitrust doctrines become important here, mainly for two reasons. First, since most research today is conducted by extremely large companies, a rule that leaves most of the rights arising out of the creation in the hands of the employer can aggravate the already existing tendency of our industrial economy to move in the direction of larger units and greater concentration, with an especially serious concentration of technology in the hands of a few entities. Second, to the extent that restrictions or limitations are placed upon the employee with respect to his own use of the ideas he develops and upon his employment by others, the more fortunate concerns may also develop an advantage, dominance, and concentration that could give them substantial control over the creative manpower upon which we depend for our technological advances.

PATENTS

Common Law Doctrine   In the absence of overriding statutes, regulations, contracts, or other specific understandings between employer and employee, a well-established body of common law doctrine determines who shall receive rights under patents resulting from inventions made by an employed inventor. Where

---

Fed. Bar J. 25 (1965): 32, 37–38; Robert Solo, "Patent Policy for Government-Sponsored Research and Development," *IDEA* 10 (1946): 143, 153, 198–199.

[26] See the reverse twist given to this difference in an ultimately deleted portion of the original opinion in *U.S.* v. *Dubilier Condenser Corp.*, 289 U.S. Reports (1933): 178; quoted in *J. Patent Off. Soc.* 15 (1933): 499. The statement reads as follows: "No Act of Congress has been called to our attention authorizing the United States to take a patent or to hold one by assignment. No statutory authority exists for the transfer of a patent to any department or officer of the Government, or for the administration of patents, or the issuance of licenses on behalf of the United States. In these circumstances no public policy requires us to deprive the inventor of his exclusive rights as respects the general public and to lodge them in a dead hand incapable of turning the patent to account for the benefit of the public." Whether the absence of patent protection will facilitate or discourage public usage depends upon a lot of interrelated circumstances that will not be discussed here. Sometimes it encourages usage, as in the case of the Babcock tester or the Salk polio vaccine, both of which went into extensive usage although their discoverers eschewed patent protection. Sometimes it discourages usage. See the rolamite invention, *Wall Street J.* 48 (June 7, 1968): 1.

the facts show that the employee was specifically hired to make inventions, the inventions that result belong to the employer and the employee is required to assign them to him. This doctrine applies, however, only to those inventions that fall within the field for which he was actually hired and not to inventions he may make in other areas.[27] At the other extreme, if the employee engages in inventive activity that is entirely independent of his job, e.g., work done at home in areas not related to his employment and not involving the use of his employer's facilities or time, the inventions that result belong entirely to the employee just as though he were unemployed. (Not in European law, where inventions made by an employee on sick leave, or when drafted, belong to the employer.) In between is the "shop right" doctrine. This doctrine is invoked when an employee, not hired to invent, nevertheless makes an invention under circumstances involving some contribution by his employer, for instance where he invents during working hours, makes use of the employer's facilities and equipment, receives assistance from coemployees or others identified with the employer, or uses information or data received from the employer. In such situations, the patent belongs to the employee but subject to a shop right in the employer. This shop right consists of a nonexclusive, nonassignable, royalty-free license to the employer to use the invention for the life of the patent.[28]

[27] For general discussion, see: Jasper Silva Costa, *Law of Inventing in Employment* (Brooklyn, N.Y.: Centeral Book Co., 1953), pp. 103–112; Arthur N. Bishop, Jr., "Employers, Employees, and Inventions," *Southern California Law Review* 31 (1957): 52–54; Note, "Rights of Employers in Inventions of Employees," *Colorado Law Review* 30 (1930): 1172, 1176–1177; Report and Recommendations of the Attorney General to the President, Investigation of Government Patent Practices and Policies 3 (1947): 136. See also: *Standard Parts* v. *Peck*, 264 U.S. Reports (1924): 52; *Martin* v. *Tennessee Copper & Chemical Corporation*, 66 Fed. Reporter 2d series (3d Cir. 1933): 187; *Hull* v. *Pitrat*, 45 Fed. Reporter (Southern Dist. Ohio 1891): 94; *Dalzell* v. *Dueber Watch Case Mfg. Co.*, 149 U.S. Reports (1940): 315; *Belanger* v. *Alton Box Board Co.*, 180 Fed. Reporter 2d series (7th Cir. 1950): 87; *Forberg* v. *Servel*, 88 Fed. Supplement (Southern Dist. N.Y.): 503; *Crown Cork & Seal Co.* v. *Fankhanel*, 49 Fed. Supplement (Md. 1943): 611; *Solomons* v. *U.S.*, 137 U.S. Reports (1890): 342.

For discussion of the doctrine that hiring must be for the express purpose of producing the object patented, see: Costa, *Law of Inventing*, pp. 103–112; *State* v. *Neal*, 152 Fla. 582 12 So.2d 590 (1943), cert. denied, 320 U.S. Reports (1942): 783; *State Board of Education* v. *Bourne*, 150 Fla. 7 So.2d 838 (1942): 323.

[28] Costa, *Law of Inventing*, pp. 9–18, 20; Note, "Rights of Employers in Inventions of Employees," p. 1173; Bishop, "Employers, Employees, and Inventions," pp. 48–49; Curt Morsell, Jr., "A Company's Right in the Invention of an Employee," *Wisconsin Bar Bulletin*, p. 11 (1968); Gloria K. Koenig, "The Shop Right—Time for Limitation," *J. Patent Off. Soc.* 49 (1967): 658, 660; John W. Leonard, "The Protected Rights of the Employee Inventor in his Invention," *J. Patent Off. Soc.* 49 (1967): 357, 360; Fredrik Neumeyer, "Employees' Rights In Their Inventions," *J. Patent Off. Soc.* 44 (1962): 674, 707.

The shop right doctrine poses two difficult questions:

1. May situations arise in which the contribution by the employer will be considered so slight as to warrant a conclusion that the invention was made independently and belongs entirely to the employee?

2. How extensive is the right of usage received by the employer under the shop right doctrine?

On the first point decisions inevitably differ, and it is virtually impossible to draw any kind of a clear line between what is too slight a contribution to recognize and what constitutes sufficient contribution to warrant granting a shop right. In general, however, the courts have been disposed to accord the employer such a right if there was any substantial contribution at all on his part.[29] The difficulty arises, of course, from the inflexible nature of the shop right and its inability to respond to variations in the extent of contributions made by the employer. In this respect it is comparable to the inflexible test of "invention" that characterizes the patent system itself, and is in contrast with the flexible "compensation" doctrine that characterizes much of the European law. As for the second point, the rules have varied. The narrowest grant to the employee takes the form of a shop right only in those areas of his business to which the invention directly relates, in some instances even being limited to specific machines produced by the employee.[30] Some cases hold more broadly that the shop right extends to use anywhere in the existing business, although some cases hold that the right does not accrue to a purchaser of the business. Even broader, some courts extend the right to all areas in which the employer is interested, including other business activities such as subsidiaries and related companies. Most broadly of all, some extend the right to include not only those businesses and interests in existence at the time the invention was made but any future activities in which the employer engages.[31]

[29] Costa, *Law of Inventing*, pp. 12–13; Bishop, "Employers, Employees, and Inventions" pp. 44–45; *Gill v. U.S.*, 160 U.S. Reports (1896): 426 (employer entitled to shop right where employee used his facilities in developing and perfecting but not in actually making the invention).

[30] Costa, *Law of Inventing*, pp. 21–35; Koenig, "The Shop Right," p. 668. In early cases the scope of the shop right often depended on whether the invention was a machine or a process or product. The shop right that was granted with respect to machines was often limited to specific machines and did not extend to additional machines. Later cases tended to extend the right to any machines used during the life of the patent. Where the patent was for a product or process the scope of the shop right was much broader. See, e.g., *City of Boston v. Allen*, 91 Fed. 248 (1st Cir. 1898), holding that if the patent is on a process or product the employer can use the invention for an unlimited term; if a machine, he can use only during the time of the inventor's employment.

[31] Costa, *Law of Inventing*, pp. 21–35; Note, Rights of Employers, p. 1174; Leonard, *The Protected Rights*, p. 360; Koenig, "The Shop Right," p. 669. Normally the shop right also

The common law doctrine is based on early concepts of what is fair and equitable as between the employer and the employee, and reflects to some extent early master-servant doctrine relating to the responsibilities and obligations of the employee to his employer.[32] In many respects, of course, it works quite satisfactorily and achieves a fair adjustment of the respective interests of the parties involved. At the two ends of the spectrum, for instance, the doctrine seems unobjectionable. The employee who engages in inventive activity entirely independent of his job surely should be entitled to lay claim to the patents that result. Likewise, an employer who hires an employee for the specific purpose of engaging in a given research activity should be entitled to claim the patents that it was expected would result therefrom. In between, however, the doctrine can result in considerable arbitrariness. A loose interpretation of the phrase "hired to invent," for instance, can result in a denial of rights to the employee that in equity should be his.[33] Even greater and more frequent inequities can result from application of the shop right doctrine, since that doctrine is applied inflexibly irrespective of whether the employer's contribution is substantial or slight, whether his use of the invention is limited or extensive, and whether the value of the invention itself is minimal or great. Consequently, the doctrine has proved somewhat unsatisfactory to both employers and employees and has to a considerable extent been supplanted by contractual arrangements.

Contract   The use of contracts has become increasingly common, especially among companies that are technologically oriented and employ research staff.[34]

---

passes with the complete sale of the business, e.g., *Lane & Bodley Co.* v. *Locke,* 150 U.S. (1893): 193, where a corporation that took over a partnership which had a shop right, succeeded to all rights of the partnership. Compare *Hapgood v. Hewitt,* 119 U.S. (1886): 226, holding that a shop right owned by a corporation is extinguished upon dissolution of the corporation. Normally, the scope of the shop right is not extended to a subsidiary corporation. *General Paint Corp.* v. *Kramer,* 68 F.2d 40 (10th Cir. 1933).

[32] Costa, *Law of Inventing,* p. 10; *U.S.* v. *Dublilier Condenser Corp.,* 289 U.S. 178 (1933); Koenig, "The Shop Right," note 43, p. 664; annotation, application and effect of "shop right rule" or license giving employer limited rights in employee's inventions and discoveries, 61 American Law Reports Annotated, 2d series (1958): 356, at p. 372.

[33] Some courts have interpreted the phrase "hired to invent" quite broadly. See, e.g., *Houghton* v. *U.S.,* 23 Fed. Reporter, 2d series 386 (4th Cir. 1928), holding that the employer's right to the invention depends, not upon the terms of the contract, but rather upon the duty which the employee owes to his employer with respect to the service in which he is engaged. Some courts have held to a stricter interpretation of the "hired to invent" phrase. See, e.g., *Hapgood v. Hewitt,* 119 U.S. Reports (1886): 226, holding that the invention belongs to the employee unless he is expressly required by his contract to exercise his inventive faculties for the benefit of his employer.

[34] See generally O'Meara, *Employee Patent and Secrecy Agreements,* pp. 22, 29–34, 93. For some sample disclosure-and-assignment provisions contained in company patent agreements see Appendix A of this chapter.

The kinds of contracts entered into follow a general pattern and structure, although they frequently vary in details and occasionally in substantive provisions. They typically include three major provisions: (1) an obligation by the employee to assign inventions he makes, (2) a duty to cooperate in disclosing inventive activities, and in providing necessary data, affidavits and testimony for purposes of patenting, and (3) an obligation to retain in confidence trade secrets and other confidential information.

While the last two items follow a fairly standard pattern, the obligation to assign inventions may vary from contract to contract. It may be limited to inventions made in the actual course of one's research employment, extend to all inventions made with help from company facilities, extend to inventions that are not in the area of the employer's interest, or extend to inventions made entirely independently of his job if they relate to the employer's business.[35] Going even further, some contracts contain trailer clauses which require the employee to assign inventions he develops after his employment has terminated. Such clauses are usually subject to certain limitations. They may apply only to inventions that relate to the employer's business. They may be limited to inventions that were started during the time of employment. They may be limited to inventions made within a certain number of years after employment ceases.[36] Some contracts attempt also to impose limitations upon an employee engaging in competition with his employer, either directly or by working for a competitor, for a given period after employment ceases.[37] These more extreme provisions, imposing con-

[35] Valid assignments may extend to (1) all discoveries relating to the machines in the employer's business, *Hildreth* v. *Duff,* 143 F. 139 (W.D. Pa. 1906); (2) all inventions related to or connected with employee's assigned work, *Paley* v. *Dupont Rayon Co.,* 71 Fed. Reporter 2d series (7th Cir. 1934): 856, and *Shook* v. *U.S.,* 238 Fed. Reporter 2d series (6th Cir. 1956): 952, which was based on USDA regulations rather than an employment contract; (3) all inventions related to any business in which the employer is engaged. *Guth* v. *Minnesota Mining & Mfg. Co.,* 72 Fed. Reporter 2d series (7th Cir. 1934): 385; or (4) "all patentable ideas and devices" affecting the employer's business, *N.J. Zinc Co.* v. *Singmaster,* 71 Fed. Reporter 2d series (2d Cir. 1934): 277. For general discussion, see Costa, *Law of Inventing,* pp. 118–120; O'Meara, *Patent and Secrecy Agreements,* pp. 27–28; Worth Wade, "Employee Inventions and Agreements" in Calvert (ed.), *Encyclopedia* 229; Fredrik Neumeyer, "The Employed Inventor—Part II, The American Situation, Lex et Scientia (1965): 2, p. 234

[36] Costa, *Law of Inventing,* pp. 116–125; O'Meara, *Patent and Secrecy Agreements,* pp. 37–39; cf. *Gas Tool Patents Corp.* v. *Mould,* 133 Fed. Reporter 2d series (7th Cir. 1943): 815, holding that employment agreements requiring the employee to assign to the employer inventions made by the former within a limited time after termination of the employment, shall be strictly construed and must be reasonable and just; *Guth* v. *Minnesota Mining & Mfg. Co.,* 72 Fed. Reporter 2d series (7th Cir. 1934): 385, holding that a contract requiring the assignment of future inventions, without a time limitation, is against public policy and therefore unenforceable.

[37] See Annotation, Validity and enforceability of restrictive covenants in contracts of

trols upon the employee after employment ceases, have been the subject of increasingly critical scrutiny on the part of the courts and more and more frequently run the risk of being held unenforceable.

As is clear from the foregoing description, many contracts of the type described are heavily weighted in the favor of the employer. They are, however, often subject to some tempering when they come before the courts. Thus, excessive contract provisions that unreasonably prevent competition or freedom of movement by the employee may be held invalid as contributing to monopoly or restraint of trade. To the extent that they deprive the employee of an opportunity to make a living or interfere with his employment mobility, they may be declared contrary to public policy. Occasionally, they may be found so inequitable and arbitrary in their terms that the court simply will not enforce them.[38] To the extent that ambiguities exist, courts are sometimes disposed, as they should be, to interpret the contracts strictly against the employer and in favor of the employee, both on the theory that the employer drew them up and on the theory that he is typically in a stronger bargaining position than the employee.

As for the remedies invoked in the event that the employee violates the contract, these tend to favor the employer. The courts, for instance, quite freely invoke the equitable remedies of injunctive relief in lieu of limiting the employer to the recovery of damages. Even when the contract terms are found to be excessive and therefore unenforceable, courts rarely declare the contract completely void; rather, they tend to throw out the provisions that are deemed unreasonable or cut them down to reasonable size and then enforce the agreement as modified.[39]

It is understandable from what has been said why an employer may prefer to require a specific employment contract rather than rely upon the vagaries and more limited sweep of the common law.

Such a contract would, of course, be subordinate to any statute with which it

---

employment, American Law Reports 9 (1920), 1467–1468; see generally R. David Lewis, "Contracts in Restraint of Trade: Employee Covenants Not to Compete," American Law Reports 21 (1967): 214; Harlan M. Blake, "Employee Agreements Not To Compete," *Harvard Law Rev.*, 73: 625–691. Normally a covenant by an employee not to compete with his employer after the termination of his employment will not be upheld or enforced in the absence of special circumstances.

[38] Bishop, "Employers, Employees, and Inventions," p. 59; O'Meara, *Patent and Secrecy Agreements,* p. 72; Morsell, "Company's Right," p. 13.

[39] For discussion of injunctive relief, see *Dinwiddie* v. *St. Louis & O'Fallon Coal Co.*, 64 Fed. Reporter 2d series 303 (4th Cir. 1933). For ways of modifying the agreement, see *Guth* v. *Minnesota Mining & Mfg. Co.*, 72 Fed. Reporter (7th Cir. 1934): 385; see also, *Fullerton Lumber Co.* v. *Torborg*, 270 Wis. 133 (1955); cf. Wis. Stat. 103.465 repudiating the Torborg doctrine.

conflicted. Such statutes are to be found in many European countries as well as Japan and Canada, but they do not exist in the United States. Recent efforts to enact statutes prohibiting employers from depriving employees of their common law rights have thus far not been effective, and there is little to indicate that they are likely to be in the near future.

Contracts may be either written or oral, express or implied. To the extent that implied contracts are involved, court determinations increasingly tend to reflect underlying policy considerations, and the line between contract and common law doctrine becomes less and less clear.[40]

The contractual approach to the employer-employee relationship has become increasingly common, especially in the case of research and development employees and companies that are oriented toward invention and innovation, and the contracts have been widely and rather uncritically accepted by the courts. Nevertheless, one may question whether they conform as well as they might to some of the prevailing premises that are important here.

In the first place, our general acceptance of contract as a desirable way of defining relationships between individuals assumes a reasonable equality of bargaining power and bargaining competence, an equality that oftentimes does not exist in the employer-employee relationship, even in a relationship involving skilled employees. In other areas of labor relations, the law has recognized this inequality and has gone to great lengths to impose substantial limitations upon the employer's freedom to lay down rules by means of contract negotiations. Such developments have not occurred except to a very limited extent in the field under discussion.

A second reservation stems from the relationship between contracts of the sort under discussion and the public policy favoring the encouragement and stimulus of inventive activity. There is some evidence, although our information in this area is relatively scant, that contracts of the sort here described fall considerably short of providing the kind of stimulus and incentive to the employee that is contemplated and sought in the public interest. To the extent that this is so, the efforts to provide such stimulus, epitomized in extensive government support of R&D and its creation of a patent system, can be frustrated through the operation of contracts of the sort described.[41]

---

[40] Note, "Rights of Employers," *Colorado Law Rev.* 30: 1175; see generally Bishop, "Employers, Employees, and Inventions," *S. California Law Rev.*, 31: 50–55. There continue to be many, including inventors themselves, who feel that free bargaining between employer and employee is still the best approach. See e.g., Rabinow, "An Inventor's View," 47 *J. Patent Off. Soc.* 469, 474–475 (1965).

[41] Miessner, "Today's Inventor"; Ephraim K. Cohen, statement, "Rights of Employer and

Unilateral Rules, Regulations, and Statutes   Somewhat akin to the contractual requirements just discussed are the unilateral rules and regulations that may be laid down by an employer as a condition of employment. Although theoretically such rules are simply imposed by the employer without consultation with the employee, in reality the process may be little different from what actually takes place in the negotiation of a contract. The only difference would be that the rules are posted on a bulletin board or published and distributed to employees for their information instead of taking the form of an actual written contract in the bilateral sense. This basic similarity is underlined by the practice prevalent in industry of simply submitting to prospective employees a standardized, printed contract which he must sign willy nilly as a condition of employment. (In actual practice, contracting procedures may be subject to more give and take than is here suggested. If the employee objects to contract conditions, the employer may make concessions if he wants that particular employee badly enough.)

Private industry relies mainly on contracts rather than unilateral regulations although, as just noted, the distinction between the two in actual practice may not be meaningful.[42] The United States government, on the other hand, makes common use of unilateral regulations.[43] So do the universities to the extent that they enter

Employee in Patentable Inventions," *American Patent Law Assoc. Bulletin,* April-May 1966, pp. 193–196; Rossman, *Industrial Creativity,* pp. 172–173; I. Louis Wolk, "An Attorney's View of the Employee Inventor," 47 *J. Patent Off. Soc.* (1965): 483, 487; Louis Lassagne, "The Legal Rights of Employed Inventors," 51 *American Bar Assn. J.* (1965): pp. 835, 838; Joseph Rossman, "Rewards and Incentives to Employee-Inventors," *Idea* 7 (1964): 431, p. 447.

[42] For a general discussion of companies that do not rely on contracts, see O'Meara, *Patent and Secrecy Agreements,* p. 13. Industry's use of unilateral regulations are discussed in this book, Chapter 3. For an early discussion of employment contracts and industry policies with respect thereto, see Joseph Rossman, "Stimulating Employees to Invent," *Industrial and Engineering Chemistry,* No. 12 (1935), p. 1512.

[43] Billy S. Holland, "Government Employee-Inventors—Invention Rights" (1964), p. 10; Marcus B. Finnegan and Richard W. Pogue, "Federal Employee Invention Rights—Time To Legislate," *Michigan Law Rev.* 55 (1957): 903, 917–924; *J. Patent Off. Soc.* 40 (1958): 252 and 322; Executive Order 10096, as amended by Executive Order 10930, Mar. 24, 1961; Report and Recommendations of the Attorney General 1 (1947): 19; *Patent Practices of Government Agencies—Preliminary Reports,* the Subcommittee on Patents, Trademarks and Copyrights of the Committee on the Judiciary, United States Senate (listed in footnote 49); Wilson Maltby, "A Government Patent Policy for Employee Inventions," *Fed. Bar. J.* 21 (1961): 127; Arthur Keeffe, *Defense Department Patent Policy—Proposed Changes in ASPR Provisions,* supplement to the Memorandum of 25 August 1960 on file in the office of General Counsel Library as Memorandum 429. For examples of enforcement of the government's unilateral regulations, see W. O. Quesenberry, "Decisions of the Commissioner of Patents on Rights Determinations" (Involving Navy Employee Inventions) (mimeo. 1964). See also Harbridge House, *Government Patent Policy Study,* prepared for the Fed. Council for Science and Technology, Committee on Government Patent Policy,

into formal arrangements with their faculty or employees at all.[44] In a few instances, uniform regulations have resulted from the collective bargaining process.[45]

The terms and conditions that regulations of these sorts lay down follow basically the same general pattern as the rather uniform contracts that were discussed in the previous section. A discussion of some of the main features of these various unilateral regulations follows.

The federal government, as just pointed out, has used such regulations extensively, sometimes as a matter of volition and sometimes as a result of statutes that require conveyance by government employees of inventions they make in the course of employment. To the extent that statutes exist, any regulations promulgated obviously must conform thereto.

Development of Federal government policy with respect to employee inventions occurred in three main stages: (1) the period prior to 1950 during which each agency was largely free to formulate its own rules; (2) the period from 1950 to 1963 during which a supposedly uniform government policy was effectuated through the promulgation of Executive Order 10096; and (3) the period from 1963 to date during which, in addition to Executive Order 10096, a Memorandum issued by President Kennedy has also been in effect. In actual operation, individual agencies tend to resist changes imposed from outside and consequently the 1950 and 1963 orders may have had less substantive impact than one might have expected although they have brought about some significant procedural changes. Even so, over the long pull there appears to have been a substantial increase in the cases in which the government has taken title; and this is presumably attributable, at least in part, to the impact of Executive Order 10096. This is especially true of the Department of Defense which prior to 1950 rarely took more than a noninclusive license under its employee inventions.

Until 1950 there existed no uniform government-wide rule directly applicable to the government-employed inventor. As a consequence, each agency was free to set its own policy. In the absence of a declared policy, the allocation of rights became a matter for common law decision. The result was considerable variation from agency

---

4 vols. (1968); and Annual Reports on Government Patent Policy, Fed. Council for Science and Technology (June 1965 to present).

[44] Archie M. Palmer, *University Research and Patent Policies, Practices and Procedures,* N.A.S.-N.R.C. Publication 999 (1962), pp. 12–16. See University chapter of this book.

[45] See O'Meara, *Patent and Secrecy Agreements,* p. 62; and Worth Wade, *Business and the Professional Unions* (Ardmore, Penna.: Advance House, 1961). See also Chapter 4 of this book. Collective bargaining agreements possess characteristics of bilateral contracts in some respects and unilateral regulations in others.

field of government work or if the government contribution is so minor as to warrant ignoring it. In situations where the government is entitled to take the
invention but waives this right upon a determination that it has "no interest"
therein, it apparently always reserves a license to itself to assure protection of its
right to use the invention in case the need for such use should come up, however
remote the likelihood may seem at the time.[49]

As a result of the various provisions allowing discretionary conduct, the generosity
of the government in leaving commercial rights to the employee inventor may vary
considerably from agency to agency.[50] The Post Office Department, for instance,
apparently takes no title to inventions from the employee even when he is
employed to invent although in at least one case the decision to leave title with the
employee was reversed upon review. It should be added that the "no interest"
proviso has been used to a considerable extent to leave foreign patent rights to the
employee, in contrast to private industry which is disposed to take whatever rights
it is entitled to whether it has an interest in using them or not.[51]

[49] This precaution is, in part, the result of a combination of circumstances that arose in
World War II, wherein the government had to pay substantial sums to one of its own
employees as a result of leaving to the latter the foreign rights in inventions made in the
course of employment. Opinion of Controller General (B-81922) of 24 Mar. 1949, regarding claim of Harry A. Knox. See Howard J. Forman, "Government Patent Policy—
Yesterday, Today and Tomorrow," *J. Patent Off. Soc.* 50 (1968): 32, 35.
[50] See Watson and Holman, "Patents From Government-Financed Research and Development," *IDEA* 8 (1964): 219–222. See generally, *Patent Practices of Government Agencies—
Preliminary Reports,* The Subcommittee on Patents, Trademarks, and Copyrights of the
Committee on the Judiciary, United States Senate. Policies of individual agencies are as
follows: Tennessee Valley Authority, favors retention of title (p. 3); National Science
Foundation, conducts no research through its own employees (p. 3); General Services
Administration, may allow employee to retain title (p. 3); Post Office Department, permits
employee to retain title and may not even require him to grant the government a license
(p. 3); Department of Health, Education, and Welfare, employees have retained title to
patents in very few cases (p. 6); Department of the Treasury, policy varies widely within
its own offices (p. 2); Government Printing Office, has allowed employees to retain title
(p. 2); Federal Aviation Agency, retains title (p. 3); Department of Defense, does not
require the taking of title from an employee unless the invention bears a direct relation
to the official duties of the employee (p. 17); Department of Agriculture, takes assignment
to all inventions made by any Department employee (p. 15); Department of Commerce,
has allowed employees to retain title (p. 6); Federal Communications Commission, retained
title in only 2 of 5 patents that were obtained by employees (p. 2); and the Department of
the Interior, has taken title in less than 50 percent of the cases (p. 5). See for details in
government chapters case studies of this book.
[51] Harrison, *An Analytical History of the Patent Policy of the Department of Health,
Education, and Welfare,* Senate Patent Study No. 27 (1960), pp. 50, 53; O'Meara, *Patent
and Secrecy Agreements,* pp. 12–13. See generally, *Patent Practices of Government Agencies—Preliminary Reports.* There appears to be little evidence to indicate that possession
of foreign patent rights in government inventions has been of any significant importance

to agency. Agencies whose primary function was to develop technology for civilia use (such as Agriculture or HEW and its predecessors) tended to require employee to assign their inventions to the government, following a policy not unlike the prevailing policies of private industry except for some disposition to waive their rights where no public interest appeared to be involved, to leave foreign rights to employees, and to refrain from imposing trailer clauses. Agencies primarily con cerned to develop technology for their own use (such as Department of Defense) usually contented themselves with a free government license and left the civilian rights with the employee.[46] In the absence of controlling regulations or agreemen it was held that established common law doctrines would apply, notwithstanding sharp differences in how the government as compared to a private concern could or would exploit patents that accrued to it as employer.[47]

Following roughly 40 years of often sporadic efforts to settle upon a uniform government policy, efforts that culminated, as we have seen, in an exhaustive Attorne General's study and report in 1947, Executive Order 10096 was finally promulgated in 1950. (See Appendix A, Chapter 5.) This Order, with some variations, follows the common law pattern described previously:

1. It provides that the government shall take title to inventions made during working hours; to inventions made with government contribution including information, employee cooperation, materials and facilities; and to inventions relating to one's official duties. A presumption of government ownership is created where the employee has been assigned to invent or engages in or supervises R&D work.

2. Title is left in the employee with a license to the government if the government contribution is so slight that it would be inequitable to take anything more than a license to use. There is a presumption of title in the government if the employe has R&D duties, but in practice the Government does not take title where the invention is not related to his actual field of activity.[48]

3. The Order permits the government to waive title, even in situations where it would be entitled to take title, if its interest in the invention is insufficient to war rant such a taking.

4. Complete title to the invention, without even a license to the government, ac to the employee in those cases where the invention is made entirely outside the

---

[46] Report and Recommendations of the Attorney General, Vo. 1 (1947), pp. 23–25.
[47] *United States* v. *Dubilier Condenser Corp.,* 289 U.S. Reports (1933): 178; *Gill* v. *Uni States,* 160 U.S. Reports (1896): 426; *Solomons* v. *United States,* 137 U.S. Reports (1890
[48] The Order appears somewhat ambiguous as to whether the Government *must* hav license in all such cases. Compare subsections (b) and (d)(2) of section 1 thereof.

The Executive Order also set up a Government Patents Board with jurisdiction to review controversies between the employing agency and the employee to the extent that disagreements resulted.[52] Even in the absence of controversy, the Board was required to review all cases in which title was left with the employee. Consequently, some protection of the public interest was afforded as against an agency that might be disposed to be unduly generous to the employee. In practical operation, however, the Government Patents Board tended overwhelmingly to uphold the determination of the agency.[53] Thus, the possibility continues that a government department may be more generous to the employee than is actually contemplated by Executive Order 10096. Such generosity has occurred in some agencies. This has sometimes been manifested, as noted previously, through the relinquishment of foreign rights, by allowing employees to retain commercial rights, and by leaving to them the rights in patents in which the government had "no interest."[54] In general, both because of the more generous provisions of Executive Order 10096 and because of the tendency in some agencies to take a fairly open-handed approach toward the employee, government treatment of employees has probably been more favorable to the employee than has been true in industry—a tendency that perhaps counteracts the greater flexibility, higher salaries, and miscellaneous fringe benefits that are likely to characterize industry as compared to government.

On October 10, 1963, a Presidential Memorandum and Statement of Government Patent Policy[55] was issued which purported to set forth "the minimum rights that government agencies should acquire with regard to inventions made under their grants and contracts." (This Memorandum and Statement are reprinted as Appendix B of Chapter 5.) The Memorandum has had no discernible effect upon

---

either to the government or to its employees. Furthermore, employees often may find it inexpedient to take advantage of the foreign rights because of the questionable value thereof, the cost of foreign patenting, and their lack of experience in administering such rights.

[52] On March 24, 1961, the Government Patents Branch was abolished and its functions assigned to the Secretary of Commerce. Executive Order 10930. He in turn delegated the functions to the Commissioner of Patents, C.F.R. Title 37.

[53] See Forman, "The Government Patents Board—Determination of Patent Rights in Inventions Made by Government Employees," *J. Patent Off. Soc.* 35 (1953): 95, 101. But see Maltby, "A Government Patent Policy for Employee Inventions," *Fed. Bar J.* 21 (1961):137.

[54] Finnegan and Pogue, "Federal Employee Invention Rights," pp. 918, 943, 947. Determinations with respect to foreign rights are made by the Government Patents Board (later relegated to the Secretary of Commerce) under Executive Order 9865, not under 10096.

[55] The "Kennedy Memorandum," 28 Fed. Register No. 200 (Oct. 12, 1963).

government policy regarding its own employees. Although the language of the Memorandum, liberally construed, would seem broad enough to cover employees as well as independent contractors, nowhere in the Memorandum are such employees specifically mentioned, and it appears quite clear that it was intended to apply only to outside contractors, not in-house employees. In any event, this is how it has been interpreted and administered.

Consequently, the Presidential Memorandum can be dismissed for purposes of the present discussion. One must be aware, however, of the possibility that it might be invoked vis à vis government employees at some future date, especially in case some quasi-employment situations arise in which persons labeled as grantees or contractors conduct themselves basically as employees or in case it becomes necessary to avoid inconsistencies between employee and grantee policies. Furthermore, as will become clear in subsequent discussion, the Memorandum may have an effect upon the policies of government grantees and contractors with respect to their own employees. In that discussion, the details and ramifications of the Memorandum will be explored more fully.

Before leaving the question of government employees, note must be taken of three federal statutes, one of which has now been repealed, that have the practical effect of creating rights in the government as against the government employee. Section 4 of Title 35 bars Patent Office employees from applying for patents. Section 266 of Title 35, now repealed, provided that a government employee might obtain a patent without the payment of the usual fee, subject to his granting a free license under the patent to the government.[56] Section 1498 of Title 28 provides that a government employee may not sue the government for use of his patented invention "where he was in a position to order, influence, or induce use of the invention by the government."[57]

Except in the cases just discussed, the United States has no general statutes applicable to the employer-employee relationship insofar as inventions are concerned. This is in sharp contrast to many other countries, notably Germany and Sweden, which have enacted comprehensive laws requiring that employees who make inven-

[56] *Squier* v. *American Telephone & Telegraph Co.,* 21 Fed. Reporter 2d series (Southern Dist. N.Y. 1924): 747, 750; affd. 7 Fed. Reporter 2d series (2d Cir. 1925): 831.
[57] An additional sentence in this section reads as follows: "This section shall not confer a right of action on any patentee or any assignee of such patentee with respect to any invention discovered or invented by a person while in the employment or service of the United States, where the invention was related to the official functions of the employee, in cases in which such functions included research and development, or in the making of which government time, materials or facilities were used."

tions be reasonably compensated therefor, primarily through cash awards based upon various criteria that we will not attempt to discuss here.[58]

There do exist in the federal statutes some limited and special statutory provisions requiring employees to assign inventions they make to the government under varied circumstances. A list of these statutes, together with a brief description of their contents insofar as they relate to employed inventors, is contained in Appendix Λ.

These statutes follow a rather uniform and sweeping pattern insofar as employee inventors are concerned, although they vary in details. Some provide generally that all research results developed in whole or in part through government expenditures shall be "freely available to the general public" (Saline Water Conversion Act, Department of Agriculture Research and Marketing Act, Helium Act, Coal Research Act, Appalachian Regional Development Act, Water Resources Research Act). The Federal Highway Administration Act contains similar provisions but is directed to grantees and outside contractors. The Solid Waste Disposal Act provides, more narrowly, that the results shall be "readily available on fair and equitable terms" to industries engaged in waste disposal or furnishing facilities therefor. It also expressly calls for adherence to the policies of the Kennedy Memorandum. Tennessee Valley Authority and National Science Foundation Acts bar employees from owning patents on their research results. Some statutes are merely enabling acts that authorize, but do not compel, the agency to make the results available to the public (Veterans Administration). Atomic Energy and Space statutes contain relatively elaborate provisions assuring public availability of research results and providing administrative devices to prevent defeat of this objective. They provide in limited circumstances for waiver of this requirement where public interest considerations warrant.[59]

[58]Fredrik Neumeyer, *The Law of Employed Inventors in Europe,* Senate Patent Study No. 30 (1963), pp. 4–66. It should be emphasized that the "reasonable" compensation provided for in these European statutes does not contemplate payment for inventive activity for which one has already been compensated. Thus, under neither German nor Swedish law does one who is hired to invent receive additional compensation for the inventions he makes in the course of such employment.

[59] The relatively limited research activities undertaken by state governments, and policies with respect to employees engaged therein, are not discussed here. See National Science Foundation, *Scientific Activities in Six State Governments,* Summary Report of a Survey, Fiscal Year 1954, NSF-58–24; National Science Foundation, *R&D Activities in State Government Agencies,* Fiscal Years 1964 and 1965, NSF 67–16. Nor have we attempted to explore the diverse policies and practices of the numerous quasi-public foundations, non-profit institutions, etc., that sometimes engage in R&D activity and employ personnel for that purpose. Nor do we find any tendency to enact state statutes covering this area.

University Relations with Employees   Within the universities, employer-employee relations have become an increasingly important matter in recent years.[60] Most university research is likely to be of a noncommercial type with the result that questions regarding rights in patents become academic. Even in the fairly recent past, most universities laid down no rules or regulations in this area, but instead left the matter entirely to the discretion of the employee or faculty member. Rules and regulations have been increasing quite rapidly, however, probably as a result of three factors:

1. The impact of the demands made by the federal government coincident to its support of university research.

2. The impact of various "success stories" that have come from selected universities, such as the University of Wisconsin (Vitamin D), Rutgers (Streptomycin) and University of California (plutonium), resulting in an increasing disposition on the part of unversities or their adjuncts to seek profit from commercially valuable research developments.[61]

3. The shift in emphasis of much university research that has resulted in considerably more research of a commercially significant type than was true in the past.

To the extent that university regulations do exist they have tended to follow four patterns[62]:

1. Regulations requiring reporting, disclosure, and such assignments as may be required to satisfy federal government conditions imposed in connection with grants.

2. The creation of university foundations, such as WARF, which offer university people an opportunity on a voluntary basis to exploit their inventions and reap a royalty return thereon. (Such foundations appear to reflect a delicate blend of profit-making and concern for the public interest.)

[60] Palmer, "University Research," 7–11, 15; Harbridge House, *Government Patent Policy Study*, p. x; Harrison, *Patent Policy of DHEW*, pp. 54–60; Clarence M. Dinkins, "Patent Practices of the Department of Health, Education, and Welfare," *Patent Practices—Preliminary Reports*, p. 10. (See for details in university chapter case studies of this book.)
[61] See Palmer, *Patents and Non-Profit Research*, Senate Patent Study No. 6 (1957), p. 43; Harrison, *Patent Policy of DHEW*; Harbridge House, *Government Patent Policy Study*, p. 1–8; and the case study of the Atomic Energy Commission, Chapter 5 of this book. One of the most strikingly successful experiments in this area, taking a somewhat different approach, is American Research and Development Corp., described later in this chapter.
[62] See Harrison, *Patent Policy of DHEW*, p. 56; Dinkins, "Patent Practices of DHEW," pp. 10–12, 41; Palmer, "Patents and Nonprofit Research," pp. 4, 31; Palmer, "University Research," pp. 9–10.

3. Adoption of a policy requiring assignment to the university of inventions made in the course of carrying out university activities.

4. Some universities adopt a negative policy of discouraging employees and faculty from seeking patents on inventions they may make. This has been characteristic of Harvard. (See university case studies of the book.)

For those universities that have no organization of their own to administer patents, there exist quasi-public organizations such as Research Corporation and Battelle Memorial Institute which undertake to administer inventions assigned to them, paying to the university inventor a share of the royalties that result.[63]

As mentioned previously, in a few instances unions or comparable organizations have negotiated agreements between employees and employers on a collective bargaining basis. The aircraft industry has been a leader in this area, although such organizations as CESO–West (a union of West coast scientific and engineering employees) and IAM, the machinists union, have shown some movement in this direction. In general, these collective bargaining arrangements have followed the common law approach or left ownership of the inventions to the employer and have emphasized instead a program of specific awards and special compensation to the employees responsible.[64]

As the foregoing discussion indicates, unilateral rules and regulations (in the strict sense) have been little used in the past except by the federal government. One may expect their usage to become more frequent in the future, however. This will become increasingly true if labor unions or professional associations get into the picture more than they have in the past. The net effect of such regulations can be rather mixed. Whether they will be more advantageous to the employer or the employee will depend upon the relative bargaining power. In the past, there has been little choice between these regulations and the contract provisions that have prevailed, but this could be less true in the future if the bargaining power of the employee increases (as it seems fairly likely to do). Such regulations, of course, limit still further the opportunity for an individual tailoring of employer-employee relationships on the basis of the individual and the type of work involved; rather,

---

[63] See Palmer, *Patents and Non-Profit Research*, pp. 32, 36–38; Harrison, *Patent Policy of DHEW*, p. 58. At the time of writing, roughly 200 colleges, universities, scientific institutions, and other nonprofit organizations have patent assistance arrangements with Research Corporation. See also Marcy, "The Endowment of Science by Invention," *Research Management* 9 (1966): 371, 377.

[64] See O'Meara, *Patent and Secrecy Agreements*, p. 64; also Chapter 4 of this book.

they push more in the direction of uniform treatment. This is true despite the fact that the kind of activity here involved is decidedly not of a uniform nature. With an increasing use of such regulations, however, one may expect more attention to be given the policy considerations underlying them. As a consequence, government efforts to influence and control the kinds of rules that are made, through statute or otherwise, may also increase.

Comment and Analysis   One is hard put to appraise the significance of the striking increase that has occurred in the area of employed-inventor activity. In a sense, such increase was inevitable if effective R&D was to be done, since much of today's research and inventive work is simply impossible to conduct except through large, well-organized and well-financed organizations. At the same time, the sharp dichotomy that results from this development, in which the employer receives the benefit of the inventive effort and the employee's primary reward or stimulus comes in the form of salary, poses some genuine problems. Confronted with a type of activity that is intensely personal in nature and relying, as we do, upon an institution (i.e., the patent system) that is basically keyed to providing a personal reward and stimulus to the actual inventor, it is a matter of legitimate concern whether our present practices and methods of conducting R&D and rewarding the contributors thereto are conducive to achieving the best results in terms of public policy and public objectives. If some means could be developed that would more effectively relate the reward and credit for inventive achievement to the actual contribution that is made, both the inventors and the public would be better for it.

Of course, some stimulus does occur under this arrangement. To the extent that the employee receives a "piece of the action" in the invention, he is directly stimulated. Public recognition of his contribution as a result of naming him in the patent also provides a direct stimulus. To the extent that returns accruing from the invention enable the employer to pay compensation to the employee that would not otherwise be paid, the stimulus again exists, even though once-removed. On the other hand, the employee has the extra burdens of reporting, keeping records, and preparing affidavits, and even so he may be denied the satisfaction of seeing his invention put to maximum use.

TRADE SECRETS

The area of trade secrets presents problems of allocation that are quite different from those in the patent area. Trade secret law embraces no formal or absolute legal right to exclude others from using an idea. Such rights as one possesses are entirely contingent upon one's keeping the information secret and preventing others from obtaining it.[65] Consequently, such legal rights as exist here are inextricably tied in with the obligation to keep such information confidential. Nevertheless, the net results in terms of right to use and right to exclude others may be very much the same as occur where patents are involved.

Under common law doctrine, one's legal rights with respect to a trade secret depend upon (1) how one obtains the information, (2) what conditions were imposed with respect to its disclosure, and (3) the nature of the information itself.

1. With respect to source, one should distinguish between confidential information that comes from outside sources and information that developed through one's own creative efforts. Actually, the law has not drawn as clear a distinction between these two situations as might be expected. Information or ideas that clearly enjoy the status of a trade secret are likely to be treated as confidential whether they originate with the employee or with someone else. Two rather slight distinctions are sometimes made, however. In the event that the employee develops the information himself, there is a chance that the court will treat it as part of his accumulated knowledge, skill, and general information, which he is free to use as he sees fit and take with him if he changes employment. The same information might be treated as a trade secret if it originated elsewhere.[66] Secondly, in the absence of an understanding, based either upon express agreement or upon the circumstances, that the information one originates is to be kept confidential, the court may hold that there was no such obligation.[67] Were the same information to originate from some other source, the court might be more disposed to construe the disclosure to the employee as confidential.

[65] Useful modern legal treatises on the subject of trade secrets are Turner, *The Law of Trade Secrets* (South Hackensack, N.J.: Fred B. Rothman, 1962) and Milgrim, *Trade Secrets*. See also Ridsdale Ellis, *Trade Secrets* (Mt. Kisco, N.Y.: Baker, Voorhis, 1953). For a report on corporate practice and policies, see O'Meara, *Patent and Secrecy Agreements*. Other general references include: 56 Corpus Juris Secundum, Master and Servant, sec. 72; Words and Phrases, "Trade Secrets"; and Worth Wade, *Industrial Espionage and Mis-Use of Trade Secrets* (2nd ed., Advance House, 1965). For a bibliographical collection of the treatises and articles on trade secrets, see Joseph Rossman, "Note on Trade Secrets," *PTC J. of Research and Education* 3 (1959): 211.
[66] For a general discussion in this area, see Turner, *Trade Secrets*, p. 172; O'Meara, *Patent and Secrecy Agreements*, p. 43; and *Lockerbie* v. *Fruhling*, 207 Fed. Supplement (Eastern Dist., Wis. 1962): 648; *Wexler* v. *Greenberg*, 339 Pa. 569; 160 Atlantic Reporter, 2d series (1960): 430; *Sperry Rand Corp.* v. *Rothlein*, 241 Fed. Supplement (Conn. 1964): 549, 564–565.
[67] Milgrim, *Trade Secrets*, sec. 5.02(2), pp. 5–9 to 5–13; Turner, *Trade Secrets*, p. 292;

It is interesting to compare the approach that the common law takes to trade secrets and its approach to patents. At the two extremes (i.e., the "hired to invent" and the "independent invention" situations), the law operates much the same. In other words, in the case of one "hired to invent" the trade secret is deemed the property of the employer. In the "independent invention" situation, it is deemed the property of the employee. In a shop right case, however, i.e., where the idea is developed by the employee but with some assistance from the employer, the patent and trade secret situations are treated quite differently. Patent doctrine gives the employer only the right to use the invention—a right which can be stripped of any value to the extent that the employee chooses to license others freely or not to patent at all. Under trade secret law, in contrast, the employer retains the control over the right to exclude (by insisting that the idea remain in secret) and the employee, if he receives anything at all, receives at most a right of usage on a nonpublic or confidential basis.[68] This right, in other words, is comparable to the shop right that the *employer* receives in the patent area.

2. Where a trade secret stemming from outside sources is disclosed to an employee, his obligation to keep it secret will depend upon the conditions attached to the disclosure. If it is revealed with no strings attached and nothing in the circumstances to suggest a confidential disclosure, the employee is free to use or disclose it as he sees fit. If restrictions are imposed, he is bound by those restrictions.[69] Where he himself is the creator, no question of confidential disclosure can arise and his

---

W.T. Collins, III, "Injunctions to Protect Trade Secrets: The Goodrich and Du Pont Cases," *Virginia Law Rev.* 51 (1965): 932–933; Research Institute of America, Recommendations, "How Safe Are Your Trade Secrets?" (Sept. 6, 1968), p. 6. See also generally, O'Meara, *Patent and Secrecy Agreements*, p. 10.

[68] Milgrim, *Trade Secrets*, sec. 5.02(4), pp. 5–26.2, 5–27; Collins, *Injunctions*, p. 922. Compare *Wexler* v. *Greenberg*, cited in footnote 64, in which the court discussed this issue, suggested that it would support an unlimited right in the employee to use and disclose but then held for the employee on another ground, to wit, that his discovery was part of his technical skill. Criticized in Comment, *Harvard Law Rev.* 74 (1961): 1473 and Milgrim, *Trade Secrets*, pp. 5–18 to 5–23. Cf. *Futurecraft Corp.* v. *Clary Corp.*, 205 Calif. Appellate Reports, 2d series (Calif. 2d Dist. 1962): 279, 288, wherein the court held for the ex-employee in an action brought by his former employer. The court suggested that (1) the idea in question was not a genuine trade secret, (2) even if it were, the employee was not in a confidential relationship, and (3) the employee was entitled to use the idea as part of his skill and experience. However, the court leaves unclear which of these criteria provided the basis for its decision.

[69] Milgrim, *Trade Secrets*, sec. 3.05(1), p. 3–34, sec. 5.02(2), p. 5–10, sec. 5.02(3), p. 5–24; Research Institute *Recommendations*, p. 6–7; Turner, *Trade Secrets*, pp. 266, 267. See generally O'Meara, *Patent and Secrecy Agreements*, pp. 8, 10. A recent Supreme Court decision casts serious doubts on the enforceability of such restrictions, *Lear* v. *Adkins* 39 S.U.S. 653 (1969).

obligation, as explained above, will depend upon the understanding and relationship between him and his employer.

3. As for the type of information involved, it must, of course, meet the definition of a "trade secret" to be protectible.[70] If it is so widely known as to be no longer subject to effective control, or if it is of a nature such that the uniqueness of the information is virtually nil, it is unprotectible. Even when it meets the "trade secret" conditions, this status can be destroyed by subsequent public disclosure or independent discovery. On the other hand, if the information lies in a twilight zone somewhere between public information and a clearly established trade secret, the fact that the employee has agreed to keep the information confidential, or the implication from the circumstances of such an understanding, may tip the scales in favor of giving it a confidential status irrespective of whether it originated with the employee or came from some outside source.[71] On the other hand, even in the face of such an understanding, the court may permit him to use the information—and possibly, although less certainly, disclose it to others—if it views the information as coming within the area of generally acquired knowledge, skill, experience and information.[72]

Confidential material may also be controlled by contract, express or implied, between the employer and employee. A common provision in employment contracts is a requirement that the employee not disclose confidential information in his

[70] Milgrim, *Trade Secrets,* sec. 2.01, pp. 2–2 to 2–8; Research Institute *Recommendations,* p. 7; Turner, *Trade Secrets,* pp. 11–13, 160; Julian O. von Kalinowski, "Key Employees and Trade Secrets," *Virginia Law Rev.* 47 (1961): 583, 595; O'Meara, *Patent and Secrecy Agreements,* p. 10. The Restatement of Torts defines a "trade secret" as follows (sec. 757, comment b): "A trade secret may consist of any formula, pattern, device, or compilation of information which is used in one's business, and which gives him an opportunity to obtain an advantage over competitors who do not know or use it. It may be a formula for a chemical compound, a process of manufacturing, treating or preserving materials, a pattern for a machine or other device, or a list of customers." See also Milgrim, sec. 2.03, p. 2–14 and 2.07, pp. 2–43 for discussion of unprotectible conditions, also Research Institute *Recommendations,* pp. 4, 5; and Coleman and Cole, "The Effect of Shifting Employment on Trade Secrets," *Business Lawyer* 14 (1959): 320.

[71] Charles E. McTiernan, "Employees' Responsibilities as to Trade Secrets," in Calvert, *Encyclopedia,* p. 246.

[72] See specifically *Wexler* v. *Greenberg,* cited in footnote 64, and Collins, "Injunctions," pp. 919, 921–922. Note 18, p. 922 in Collins, comments as follows: "this factor [i.e., that employee developed the trade secret himself] has been found significant in cases where the facts showed that the employee was actually using his own previously acquired superior skill and knowledge to such an extent that his employer acquired no interest in any trade secrets. See *Gabriel Co.* v. *Talley Indus.,* 137 U.S.P.Q. 630 (D. Ariz. 1963); *Kaumagraph Co.* v. *Stampagraph Co.,* 235 N.Y. 1, 138 N.E. 485 (1923). See also Charles M. Carter, "Trade Secrets and the Technical Man," *IEEE Spectrum* (February 1969), p. 54.

possession, including trade secret material that he himself develops. An interesting question arises whether this obligation exists only to the extent that use or disclosure would be injurious to the employer, or whether it extends to other situations as well. Reported cases on this point are virtually nonexistent since, in the absence of injury, litigation is unlikely to occur.[73]

In contrast to the trailer clauses relating to patents that are sometimes found in employee contracts, such contracts rarely call for any control over trade secrets developed subsequent to employment, although of course obligations relating to confidential materials and information acquired during employment continue after employment ceases.

With respect to remedies, the courts are rather free-handed in granting injunctive relief and generally do not limit the employer to recovery of damages, a limitation that would fall short of giving the employer what he legitimately seeks, namely, protection against the secret getting out.[74] On the other hand, the courts are concerned not to impede the employee's freedom to seek other employment, and this has caused them to refuse to enjoin an employee from taking a job with some other company even though in doing so there is danger that the secret might be revealed to a competitor. Both the employee and the new employer, however, will be subjected to an order prohibiting use or disclosure of the trade secret in question.[75]

There appears to be little in the way of unilateral rules and regulations dealing with trade secrets. Industry seems not to have used this device. Nor, in this area, has government. In fact, government shows little concern about the disclosure of trade secrets, in contrast to private industry, since it is indisposed to assert exclusive rights in ideas or inventions developed under its auspices and sees no harm in the disclosure of such confidential information. Indeed, it tends to encourage prompt disclosure through patenting, publication or other means.[76]

[73] Collins, "Injunctions," pp. 931–932; and see von Kalinowski, "Key Employees," at p. 599: "Protection should be afforded when, and only when, the information in question has value in the sense that it affords the plaintiff [i.e., ex-employer] a competitive advantage over competitors who do not know of it [i.e., the trade secret] . . . ."
[74] Turner, *Trade Secrets*, note 107, p. 458; *Collins*, "Injunctions," note 108, p. 923–931; O'Meara, *Patents and Secrecy Agreements*, note 52, p. 10.
[75] See *B. F. Goodrich Co.* v. *Wohlgemuth*, 117 Ohio Appellate Reports 493, 192 N.E. 2d 99 (1963) and *Guth* v. *Minnesota Mining and Manufacturing Co.*, 72 Fed. Reporter 2d series (7th Cir. 1934): 385; Research Institute *Recommendations*, note 91a, p. 8; J. Brooks, "Annals of Business—One Free Bite," *New Yorker* (Jan. 11, 1964), p. 37.
[76] See Presidential Memorandum of October 10, 1963; Charles E. McTiernan, "Employees' Responsibilities as to Trade Secrets," 41 *J. Patent Off. Soc.* (1959): 821; Armed Forces

There are two important exceptions to this. First, where information possessed by the government was disclosed to it in confidence, it is concerned to respect that confidence in its handling of such data.[77] Second, the government may impose restrictions upon disclosure in the interests of national security. It has sometimes been known to carry this practice to extremes, subjecting data to secrecy orders under circumstances where no discernible threat to national security appears to exit.[78]

In fact, government policies for preservation of secrecy go beyond the employer-employee relationship where either of these two elements is present. Thus, the patent statutes contain secrecy provisions pursuant to which the issuance of patents can be held up for indefinite periods of time if it appears that publication of the invention would be "detrimental to the national security."[79] They also provide that any person who has filed a patent application in the United States shall be barred from filing in a foreign country for a period of six months unless authorized by the Commissioner of Patents to do so. The purpose of this is to enable the government to determine whether the national security would be threatened by such foreign filing.[80]

The trade secret law, taken overall, is somewhat unsettled. Constituting, as it

Procurement Regulations 9–200 to 9–203, 32 Code Fed. Reg. sec. 9–200, 30 Fed. Register Doc. (May 25, 1965): 6969.

[77] See Title 5, U.S. Code sec. 552: "(a) Each agency shall make available to the public information as follows . . . (b) This section does not apply to matters that are . . . (4) trade secrets and commercial or financial information obtained from a person and privileged or confidential." Various agencies have implemented requirements of confidentiality through their own specific regulations as well. For general discussion, see Milgrim, *Trade Secrets*, sec. 6.02, p. 6–24. Sometimes, on the other hand, the government asserts a right of disclosure with respect to confidential information submitted to it, a practice that has been the subject of some criticism. See Robert E. Beach, "A Question of Property Rights: The Government and Industrial Know-How," *American Bar Assoc. J.* 41 (1955): 1024; Report, Proprietary Rights and Data, House Rept. No. 2230 (Select Committee on Small Business, House of Representatives, 1960).

[78] Walter Gellhorn, *Security, Loyalty and Science* (Ithaca: Cornell Univ. Press, 1950), pp. 111–126.

[79] Title 35, U.S. Code, sec. 181; and see *Farrand Optical Co.* v. *United States*, 197 Fed. Supplement (Southern Dist. N.Y. 1961): 756.

[80] See Note, "Sections 184 and 185 of the Invention Secrecy Act—An Ambiguous and Unnecessary Obstruction to Foreign Patenting," *Michigan Law Rev.* 64 (1966): 496. For review of the various secrecy measures imposed by the federal government, see Ansell and Hamilton, "Security Considerations in Filing Patent Applications Abroad," *American Bar Assoc. J.* 50 (1964): 946. For general discussion, see Milgrim, note 107, sec. 1.10(1); Frank L. Bate, *Criminal Prosecution in Respect of Trade Secrets*, Practicing Law Institute, 25th Annual Summer Session, 1966; John P. Sutton, "Trade Secrets Legislation," *IDEA* 9 (1965): 587, 607.

does, common law doctrine, it can differ from state to state.[81] The very nature of the law, or rather of the subject matter to which it pertains, is such that we know rather little about what really happens in this area, since most of the activity and probably most of the controversy that arises never comes to light. Only the egregious and extreme cases are likely to reach the courts.

From the standpoint of effect upon inventive and other types of creativity, trade secret doctrine is probably more an impediment than otherwise. Its primary objective, after all (in contrast to patent and copyright law), is to discourage improper conduct and wrongdoing, not to stimulate and encourage creative activity.

On balance, trade secret law probably operates more to the benefit of the employer than to that of the employee. Thus, most trade secret material ends up as the employer's property, at least as a formal legal matter. As a practical matter, however, it may be quite difficult and sometimes impossible for an employer to prevent his employee, when he changes jobs, from taking with him information and ideas he acquired in the course of employment. Consequently, as long as an employee is free to change jobs, the employer's control over his use of trade secret material is tenuous to say the least, since the employer has no sure way of knowing what goes on in the course of the subsequent employment.[82] The upshot is that, to the extent that the employer is unable effectively to prevent use or disclosure by others, his position is comparable to that of one who has received a shop right.

[81] A number of state statutes exist that deal with the protection of confidential material, These statutes are typically criminal in nature and impose rather drastic penalties for violation. They are, however, moderately limited in their application. They tend to apply mainly to outright theft and often require the actual appropriation of tangible materials, such as papers, documents, photographs, etc. In other words, the mere misuse or improper disclosure of confidential information revealed to one orally, would not bring one within the statutes. Furthermore, they ordinarily refer to information originating from sources other than the appropriator and thus are inapplicable to one who improperly discloses or uses information that originated with himself. No case is known in which an employee has been prosecuted for misappropriation of his *own* ideas. To the extent that the statutes are applicable, however, violation can be a serious matter involving heavy fines and imprisonment. There also exists a federal Stolen Property Act that operates in the same manner as the state statutes.

[82] McTiernan, "Employees' Responsibilities as to Trade Secrets," p. 832; von Kalinowski, "Key Employees," p. 598; Collins, "Injunctions," pp. 917–949; Coleman & Cole, "Effect of Shifting Employment," p. 319; "Trade Secrets: The Technical Man In Legal Land," *Chemical & Engineering News,* January 18, 1965, p. 81; William Bowen, "Who Owns What's In Your Head?," *Fortune,* July 1964, p. 175; Brooks, "One Free Bite." *New Yorker,* Jan. 11, 1964, p. 37.

In other words, he is free to use the information himself but powerless to prevent the employee from also using it or permitting its use by others.[83]

Whatever the difficulties that attend the allocation of trade secret rights and their apportionment, it seems probable that this area will increase in importance in the future as the successful practical application of patented inventions is increasingly tied in with company-owned know-how having the character of trade secrets.

COPYRIGHT

There are two types of copyright. Common law copyright applies only so long as a given writing is kept unpublished. Statutory copyright takes effect only when there is actual publication. For all practical purposes, the law of trade secrets that is applied in the technological area would apply in the "writing" area in the form of common law copyright, although the commercial significance and scope of protection may differ.

Whether copyrighted material belongs to the employer or employee depends upon the circumstances and the nature of the writing.[84] Actually, there exists little published legal doctrine in this area. The rather complex common law doctrines that prevail in the trade secret and patent areas have no application here. Many of the problems that pose serious difficulties in these areas are of no concern where copyright is involved. For instance, there is little occasion for trying to prevent the disclosure of copyrighted material; indeed, writings must be published in order to receive a statutory copyright. There is no occasion or justification for preventing the employee from entering into the employment of others, whether competitors or not. Copyright, in contrast to patents and to a lesser extent trade secrets, rarely lends itself to restrictive usages, monopolistic practices or restraint of trade.[85] Thus, the excessive and inequitable provisions

[83] An interesting but unanswered question is whether an employees who desires to preserve the confidential status of an idea developed in the course of his employment can prevent his employer from disclosing the information to others and thus destroying its exclusive nature. In one unreported instance of this kind, an employer successfully contended that his license to use the invention "in his own activities" included the right to disclose it to an outsider with whom he was negotiating a contract to supply the product covered by the invention.

[84] Nimmer, *Copyright*, p. 240. See also Howell, *Copyright Law*, at p. 52. In the absence of an express agreement, the literary efforts of an employee if not rendered as a part of his duties to his employer remain the property of the employee. See *United States* v. *First Trust Co. of Saint Paul*, 251 Fed. Reporter 2d series (8th Cir. 1958).

[85] Nimmer, *Copyright*, p. 662. See *Peter Pan Fabrics Inc.* v. *Candy Frocks Inc.*, 187 Fed.

often found with respect to patents are not likely to appear here.

How the copyright interests in a given writing are disposed of or allocated will depend to considerable extent upon the nature of the writing and most of all upon the relationship of the employer and employee and the understanding between them.[86] Occasion for controversy with respect to allocation or division of the total bundle of rights between employer and employee is unlikely. If the employee is hired to write, his product belongs to the employer, and this result is facilitated by section 26, title 17, which provides that the employer of an "author for hire" shall be deemed the author for copyright purposes. If the employee is not hired to write or otherwise produce copyrighted material, his creations remain apart from his job and belong entirely to him. Attempts to analogize from the shop right doctrine and apportion rights between the two in circumstances where the employer has contributed something to the employee's effort do not appear to have occurred in this field. Lastly, copyright law, unlike patent law, is not attended by problems of providing materials and evidence to support the application, or problems of joint versus sole authorship.

A copyright problem arises with respect to employees of the federal government. Under existing law, the U.S. Government cannot copyright "government" writings.[87] Suppose, however, that a government employee engages in writing and seeks to copyright his product. If it has no relationship to his governmental duties there is no problem. If it does relate to these duties, however, the question arises whether it constitutes a government document. If it does, then he is no more entitled to copyright protection than his government employer would be. If it is not treated as a government document (for instance, if it consists of public addresses, or if it is included in autobiographical material describing governmental operations and experiences) present law holds that it is capable of copyright protection.[88]

Supplement (Southern Dist. N.Y. 1960): 334; and *Alfred Bell & Co.* v. *Catalda Fine Arts Inc.*, 191 Fed. Reporter 2d series (2d Cir. 1951): 99, indicating that defendant in a copyright infringement suit cannot set up antitrust violations by the copyright owners as a defense thereto. But for opposing view see *United Artists Associated, Inc.* v. *NWL Corp.*, 198 Fed. Supplement (Southern Dist. N.Y. 1961): 953, and *United States* v. *Loew's Inc.*, 371 U.S. Reports (1962): 38, which seem to suggest that the doctrine of the patent cases is fully applicable in copyright actions.

86 Nimmer, *Copyright*, p. 238. An employer and employee may and often do agree that the copyright shall remain in the employee subject to a right of the employer to be exclusively licensed to use the work in a particular medium.

87 Title 17, U.S. Code, sec. 8.

88 *Public Affairs Associates, Inc* v. *Rickover*, 177 Fed. Supplement (Dist. Court, D.C.

OTHER FORMS OF COMPENSATION

Our attention up to now has been directed to the intellectual property that results from the employee's activity and to the impact of the employer-employee relationship upon this property in terms of (1) the creation of the legal rights therein and (2) the assignment or allocation of these legal rights as between the employer and the inventor. In one sense, the "allocation" device may be viewed as a means for deciding to whom the property that has been created belongs. In another sense, it may be viewed as a means for compensating or not compensating the inventor for the contribution he has made.

"Allocation" is not the only form that stimulus or compensation may take. The stimulus may be noneconomic in nature. For example, the employee may be motivated by curiosity, accident, or desire for prestige. Often the employer can contribute such stimulus with little or no cost to himself, for example, when he gives appropriate credit and publicity to the employee's achievement, enables him to attend meetings, or assists in the publication of articles on his inventions. The employer can also contribute in terms of giving the employee the satisfaction of seeing his invention put to affirmative use (assuming this is economically feasible).

Alternative forms of compensation also exist: the familiar and commonplace devices of salary increases, promotion, or award of fringe benefits. These undoubtedly represent the device most commonly used by employers today.

Aside from these general forms of compensation, however, there exist some rather special types that do apply primarily to employed inventors or creators. To these we now turn briefly.

The most common form of special compensation is the grant of an award or bonus to one who comes up with inventions or other contributions.[89] Such award programs vary in scope. Some are limited to patentable inventions. Some extend to technological ideas generally, whether or not patentable. Some go still further

1959): 601; rev'd on other grounds, 284 Fed. Reporter (Cir. Court, D.C. 1960): 260; vacated for insufficient record, 369 U.S. Reports 111 (1962). See also Schnapper, *Constraint by Copyright* (1960), pp. 110–140.

[89] See Costa, *Inventing in Employment*, pp. 213–233; Jibrin and Corry, "Government Assistance to Invention and Research: A Legislative History," Patent Study No. 22 (1960), pp. 19–23, 24–34; McTiernan, "Employer-Inventor Compensation Plans," p. 475. For general discussion of awards, see "Proposed Government Incentives, Awards and Rewards Program with Respect to Government Employees," found in Hearings on H.R. 7316, before Subcommittee No. 2 of the House Committee on the Judiciary, 82nd Cong., 2nd sess., Ser. 16 (March 10, 1952), pp. 41–56, and Hearings on S.2157 and H.R. 2383 before the Subcommittee on Patents, Trademarks, and Copyrights of the Senate Comm. on the Judiciary, 84th Cong., 2nd sess., June 7, 1956. See case studies of this book.

and include business ideas and organizational and administrative suggestions. Awards programs are found in both private industry and government, although they appear to receive greater emphasis in terms of both magnitude and scope in the governmental area.

In private industry, some companies attempt to adjust the award to the extent and nature of the contribution, but most of them incline toward a schedule of flat rates, usually rather modest in amount. Payments may be made at various stages: when a proffered idea is accepted, when a patent is applied for, when a patent actually issues. Rarely do industry programs go beyond the area of inventive ideas. While one cannot describe private industry efforts in these directions as minuscule, they are far from impressive when one considers the totality of R&D effort that private industry undertakes in this country.

Governmental awards programs are somewhat more extensive in terms of coverage, amount of awards, and total impact. (The National Aeronautics and Space Administration program appears to be the most ambitious and successful. See the section on NASA in Chapter 5.)[90] They embrace a variety of methods of rewarding, and providing incentives to employees. These include step increases for salaried employees, efficiency awards, cash awards for suggestions, and special honors in carefully selected cases. They are covered by a variety of statutes, including a general awards statute enacted in 1954[91] and a number of special statutes relating to specific subjects or particular agencies.

Another form of special compensation consists of giving inventors a share in the royalties that may be obtained. This is nonexistent in governmental policy, except for the TVA program,[92] and even there the plan has had little significance as a practical matter. Nor is such a program feasible since the government does not collect royalties on the inventions it owns.

Compensation in the form of royalties is, however, common in two areas. Organizations such as Wisconsin Alumni Research Foundation (WARF) and Research Corporation that have been set up to administer patents obtained by university personnel take title to the patents in question, administer them in a manner designed to produce income, and then pay a share of the net income,

[90] For a detailed discussion and evaluation of NASA's patent policy, see Solo, "Patent Policy for Government-Sponsored Research and Development," *IDEA* 10: 143 (1966): 152–199.
[91] 5 U.S. Code secs. 4501-4505.
[92] 16 U.S. Code 831 d(i).

usually around 15 percent, to the inventor,[93] with the remainder typically going into further research or other educational activity. There also exist a few private enterprise organizations set up for the purpose of exploiting the patents of individual inventors (primarily independents rather than employed inventors). These also typically pay a percentage to the inventor. An organization that is somewhat unique in university circles is American Research and Development Corporation, headed by Gen. Georges F. Doriot. ARDC attempts to develop faculty-originated inventions through the actual creation of new companies in which the inventor actively participates.[94]

Programs for sharing royalties with employees are comparable to the practice in parts of Europe wherein certain countries have enacted statutes that require compensation to the employed inventor, a compensation that is greatly influenced by the royalty income or other benefits that accrue from the patents in question. Nor is this European practice, found primarily in West Germany and Sweden, the only one in which compensation is determined on the basis of the value of the creation. At least seven countries have provisions for reasonable compensation to inventors as part of their patent acts. Russia and most of the other socialistic countries such as Poland, Hungary, East Germany, and Czechoslovakia, follow a practice of rewarding the inventor in this way through the issuance of an "author's certificate" which entitles him to a compensation determined on the basis of the invention's usefulness.[95] Much of the United States government program for awards is also keyed to an evaluation of what the invention contributes. Finally, there exist a few instances in private industry in which compensation is given the inventor on such a basis. (See Chapter 3.)

Most of the forms of special compensation described in the preceding discussion can be used in connection with trade secrets as well, and to some extent this is

[93] Palmer, *Patents and Non-Profit Research,* pp. 33–38, see also Chapter 6, University of Wisconsin.

[94] U.S. Senate Hearings, before the Subcommittee on Antitrust and Monopoly of the Committee on the Judiciary, 90th Cong., 1st sess. (1967), pp. 2715–2725.

[95] Neumeyer, *Law of Employed Investors in Europe,* pp. 139–140. See also Ernst H. Ruf, "U.S. Patent Concepts v. USSR Patent Concepts and Inventors' Certificates—A Comparison of Public Policies and Social Objectives," *J. Patent Off. Soc.* 49 (1967): 15, 30–31; Herschel F. Clesner, "Innovator's Payment Determination in the U.S.S.R.," *IDEA* 6 (1962): 225, 227–228; Robert C. Watson, "Soviet Law on Inventions and Patents," *J. Patent Off. Soc.* 43 (1961): 5, 35–39. At least seven countries also provide in their patent acts for "reasonable compensation" to inventors. Fredrik Neumeyer, "Employees Rights in Their Inventions," *Intl. Labour Rev.* (Jan. 1961): 35.

done. Thus, many of the awards programs that exist in government, and some of those in industry, make no distinction between patented and unpatented ideas. Such programs are, however, more difficult to administer where trade secrets are involved than where patents are involved. For one thing, the exact contribution is often uncertain and ill-defined. So, at times, is the identity of the contributor. In contrast, patented inventions must necessarily be sharply defined in both respects in order to meet the requirements of the patent law. Secondly, the pervading secrecy that exists with respect to trade secrets precludes some of the forms of reward that we have referred to, such as giving credit and publicity to the creator and otherwise adding to his prestige. Furthermore, the fact of secrecy leaves the matter largely in the discretion of the employer or those close to him since neither the public nor one's fellow workers are likely to be aware of the exact contribution that one has made, the identity of the contributor, or the comparative size of one's contribution in relation to other contributions.

Special forms of compensation based upon rewards offered by the employer seem to have played little role in the copyright field, at least in ways that are likely to lead to legal controversy. Employer-employee relationships do, of course, exist in areas involving copyright, but the basis for compensation is likely to depend upon arrangements relating to salary or commission. The tendency to limit rewards to these traditional methods is probably strengthened by the fact that contributions in the copyright area, unlike those in the patent and trade secret areas, usually do not lend themselves any too well to the use of special forms of compensation or apportionment between employer and employee. An employee usually is either simply doing his job in creating the copyrightable material, in which case it belongs to his employer, or he is operating independently of his job, in which case it belongs entirely to him. The writings of university personnel traditionally belong to them rather than to their employers.

Nevertheless, occasional instances of special compensation do occur. An employee who creates a "writing" over and above his regular employment commitments may be able to dispose of it to the employer. In such case, compensation will depend upon individual negotiations.

The foregoing examination of alternative forms of compensation to an employee for his creative contributions underlines the fact that salary adjustments, special awards, appropriate credit and publicity, and the like are in most instances considerably more flexible and administrable devices for acknowledging creative contributions than are attempts to apportion or allocate the intellectual property itself. Apportionment, as we have seen when discussing the establishment of legal rights, can become a rather inflexible and awkward device for compensating the employee because of the competing and conflicting (albeit legitimate) claims of the employer and employee. On the other hand, the kinds of compensation or reward discussed in this section offer the employer and the employee alternatives that are not only more numerous but more adaptable to delicate apportionment keyed to the various contributions of different entities. Often, also, they may be more in tune with the employee's interests and desires, since he may prefer a money award rather than to try to exploit patent or trade secret rights. These alternative forms of compensation are less subject to arbitrary or unequal treatment. All in all, both are easier to administer and more susceptible to equitable administration.

Granted all this, it is still true that both the public and individuals lose something to the extent that the allocation of rights in patents and copyright, and for that matter in trade secrets, is abandoned as a form of reward and stimulus to the employee. These systems, after all, were originally designed to stimulate and reward the individual, and they probably work best when they are so used. The interposition of the employer between the inventor and the reward that comes from the invention inevitably reduces the significance of these systems and the contributions they can make.

With creative activity being carried on more and more by employed inventors rather than by independents, we are increasingly faced with a problem that has not yet been solved adequately. The problem is this: Accepting the fact that creative contribution, whether in the field of technology or in the arts, continues to be essentially a personal and individual act, what stimuli and rewards can we provide that will induce creative employees to put forth their best efforts, will direct these efforts into the most useful channels, and will reduce the "lead time" (between conception and substantial usage) to the minimum?

It may well be that the existing system wherein the employer reaps most of the rewards that flow from the invention and then compensates the employee on a salary basis is the best way to achieve these results. On the basis of such information as we now possess, however, one is hard put to argue that this is conclusively so. A clearer understanding than we now have of what the practices in fact are, what their effects are, and how both employees and employers respond to various incentives, is needed before one can arrive at firm conclusions.

CONTRACT RESEARCH

The discussion of employee rights in inventions and other creations would not be complete without some discussion of "contract research." In a sense practically all employees "hired to invent" are engaged in "contract research." However, as used here, this term is limited to independent contractor or agency arrangements in which the individual undertaking the actual inventive activity is an employee of that contractor or agent, not of the concern that lets out the contract.

Although contract research has undoubtedly existed from early days, it has greatly increased in magnitude and importance in the last twenty-five years, mainly as a result of the vast increase in government-supported R&D and government policy of farming out the bulk of its research in lieu of doing it in its own laboratories with its own personnel.

Government contracts for R&D are entered into predominantly with private industrial concerns. Universities and other educational institutions are also substantial recipients of such contracts. To a lesser extent, so are professional research laboratories, both profit and nonprofit. Private corporations may also farm out R&D on a contract basis, most frequently to professional laboratories, and occasionally to other industrial concerns. They may also enter into research arrangements with educational institutions or faculty and other personnel connected with the latter.

The property rights resulting from these arrangements may be allocated in various ways between the organization supporting the research and the organization that conducts it. Assertion of rights by the financial supporter who lets out the contract for R&D may range all the way from claiming all rights in any patents or trade secrets that result to claiming no rights therein except the right to be informed of the results and a free license to use. The former is typical of certain types of government contracts and of contracts under which R&D is conducted by private concerns for other private concerns. The latter is typical of other types of government contracts and of research conducted by universities.

The problems and controversies that arise in this area with respect to allocation between the contracting parties are many and varied, especially where private industry has contracted to undertake R&D for the federal government. However, we are concerned with these contract provisions only to the extent that they affect the rights and duties that attach to employees of the contractor doing the research. Such arrangements are unlikely to have any significant direct impact upon the employee except in two situations:

1. Where, as a result of the contract, the terms of his own employment are modified; for instance, where the employer is obligated to turn over rights accruing from the invention that he would otherwise have left with the employee.

2. Where the conditions of the contract cause the employer to change his policies vis-à-vis the employee even though he is not legally bound to do so; for instance, where limitations upon the employer's opportunity to profit from the research cause him to be more niggardly in his bonus or awards program.

Little need be said about R&D contracts let out by private concerns, whether to other corporations, individuals, or educational institutions. Such contracts become a matter of private negotiation and are controlled by the general principles of contract law. Since parties are free to contract or not as they see fit, it is unlikely that contracts will be negotiated that conflict with the contractor's underlying policies or with his obligations to others, including employees.[96] It is, of course, conceivable that a given negotiated R&D contract could be so sweeping and demanding in its terms and so burdensome in the conditions imposed upon the contracting employer, and consequently upon his employee, as to subject the latter to burdensome employment conditions and seriously reduce his incentive to engage in effective inventive activity. Frequent occurrence of such practices would give rise to the same public policy concerns that have been expressed herein with respect to employment contracts. No such episodes have come to our attention, however; nor are we aware of any public expressions of concern in this respect insofar as the contracts of private contractors for R&D are concerned.

Contracts to engage in R&D for the federal government are another story. Such contracts have been the subject of vigorous attack by those who believe the government is too demanding with respect to the patent and other rights that it takes under such contracts. Prior to 1963, except for a few instances in which policies were set by statute, each government agency exercised its own discretion in formulating its policies with respect to such contracts.[97] Policies ranged from

[96] Such contracts may run afoul of public policy, for instance, if a university obligates itself to keep research results confidential or if a private concern agrees to conditions that restrain trade. Problems relating to such practices lie outside the scope of the present study.

[97] See Chapter 5. The following is a list of government agencies whose policy is set by statute: NSF, 42 U.S. Code 1871(a); disposition of rights should be made in a manner that will protect the public interest. USDA, 7 U.S. Code 427 i(a); results of contracts shall be made available to the public through assignment to the government, dedication to the public, or other means which secretary may determine. AEC, 42 U.S. Code 2182; all patents shall be vested in and be the property of AEC. NASA, 42 U.S. code 2457; normally the inventions shall be the property of the U.S. unless there is a waiver based upon public

insistence that all patents and other rights be assigned to the government to the other extreme of leaving all such rights with the contractor subject only to a free license in the government.[98]

In October 1963, the "Kennedy Memorandum" was issued, applicable to all agencies of the federal government. It prescribes criteria for determining the respective rights of government and contractor in patents resulting from R&D contracts entered into between them. The Memorandum provides as follows:

SECTION 1. The following basic policy is established for all government agencies with respect to inventions or discoveries made in the course of or under any contract of any government agency, subject to specific statutes governing the disposition of patent rights of certain government agencies.

(a) Where
(1) a principal purpose of the contract is to create, develop or improve products, processes, or methods which are intended for commercial use (or which are otherwise intended to be made available for use) by the general public at home or abroad, or which will be required for such use by governmental regulations; or
(2) a principal purpose of the contract is for exploration into fields which directly concern the public health or public welfare; or
(3) the contract is in a field of science or technology in which there has been little significant experience outside of work funded by the government, or where the government has been the principal developer of the field, and the acquisition of exclusive rights at the time of contracting might confer on the contractor a preferred or dominant position; or
(4) the services of the contractor are
    (i) for the operation of a government-owned research or production facility; or
    (ii) for coordinating and directing the work of others,

---

interest considerations. HEW, 45 Code Fed. Reg. 8.6; patent rights are determined in accordance with the policy set forth in 45 Code Fed. Reg. 8.2. DOD, Armed Services Procurement Regulations (ASPR) Section 9–107; adheres to a policy which promotes an incentive to invent and disclose. Additional statutes which provide expressly that patent rights resulting from government research contracts shall be made available to the public, are: "Saline Water Act," Sept. 22, 1961, 42 U.S. Code 1954(b); "Helium Act," Amendments of 1960, Sept. 13, 1960, 50 U.S. Code 167(b); "Armed Control and Disarmament Act," Sept. 26, 1961, Pub. L. 87-297, 75 Stat. 631, sec. 32; "Coal Research Act," July 7, 1960, 30 U.S. Code 666.

See also *Annual Report on Government Patent Policy,* Federal Council for Science and Technology, June 1967, Appendix F, pp. 58–64; Statement of Russell Long, Hearings, "Government Patent Policy," Senate Judiciary Subcommittee On Patents, Trademarks, and Copyrights, 89th Cong., 1st sess., 1965, Part 1, p. 329 (June 3, 1965); Anderson, "If There is an Invention Under a Government Contract—Who Should Get It?," 21 *Fed. Bar. J.* 64 (1961): 64–66.

[98] In at least one instance the license reserved by the government extends only to government activities that do not compete with those of the contractor or his licensees. See *Patent Practices of the Post Office Department: Preliminary Report,* p. 4. Apparently, no occasion to apply this limitation has occurred. In general, see Robert A. Solo, "Patent Policy for Government-Sponsored Research and Development," *IDEA* 10: 143–152 (1966).

the government shall normally acquire or reserve the right to acquire the principal or exclusive rights throughout the world in and to any inventions made in the course of or under the contract. In exceptional circumstances the contractor may acquire greater rights than a non-exclusive license at the time of contracting, where the head of the department or agency certifies that such action will best serve the public interest. Greater rights may also be acquired by the contractor after the invention has been identified, where the invention when made in the course of or under the contract is not a primary object of the contract, provided the acquisition of such greater rights is consistent with the intent of this Section 1(a) and is a necessary incentive to call forth private risk capital and expense to bring the invention to the point of practical application.

(b) In other situations, where the purpose of the contract is to build upon existing knowledge or technology to develop information, products, processes, or methods for use by the government, and the work called for by the contract is in a field of technology in which the contractor has acquired technical competence (demonstrated by factors such as know-how, experience, and patent position) directly related to an area in which the contractor has an established nongovernmental commercial position, the contractor shall normally acquire the principal or exclusive rights throughout the world in and to any resulting inventions, subject to the government acquiring at least an irrevocable non-exclusive royalty free license throughout the world for governmental purposes.

(c) Where the commercial interests of the contractor are not sufficiently established to be covered by the criteria specified in Section 1(b), above, the determination of rights shall be made by the agency after the invention has been identified, in a manner deemed most likely to serve the public interest as expressed in this policy statement, taking particularly into account the intentions of the contractor to bring the invention to the point of commercial application and the guidelines of Section 1(a) hereof, provided that the agency may prescribe by regulation special situations where the public interest in the availability of the inventions would best be served by permitting the contractor to acquire at the time of contracting greater rights than a non-exclusive license. In any case the government shall acquire at least a non-exclusive royalty free license throughout the world for governmental purposes.

(d) In the situation specified in Sections 1(b) and 1(c), when two or more potential contractors are judged to have presented proposals of equivalent merit, willingness to grant the government principal or exclusive rights in resulting inventions will be an additional factor in the evaluation of the proposals.

(e) Where the principal or exclusive (except as against the government) rights in an invention remain in the contractor, he should agree to provide written reports at reasonable intervals, when requested by the government, on the commercial use that is being made or is intended to be made of inventions made under government contracts.

(f) Where the principal or exclusive (except as against the government) rights in an invention remain in the contractor, unless the contractor, his licensee, or his assignee has taken effective steps within three years after a patent issues on the invention to bring the invention to the point of practical application or has made the invention available for licensing royalty free or on terms that are reasonable in the circumstances, or can show cause why he should retain the principal or exclusive rights for a further period of time, the government shall have the right to require the granting of a license to an applicant on a non-exclusive royalty free basis.

(g) Where the principal or exclusive (except as against the government) rights to an invention are acquired by the contractor, the government shall have the right to require the granting of a license to an applicant royalty free or on terms that are reasonable in the circumstances to the extent that the invention is required for public use by governmental regulations or as may be necessary to fulfill health needs, or for other public purposes stipulated in the contract.

(h) Where the government may acquire the principal rights and does not elect to secure a patent in a foreign country, the contractor may file and retain the principal or exclusive foreign rights subject to retention by the government of at least a royalty free license for governmental purposes and on behalf of any foreign government pursuant to any existing or future treaty or agreement with the United States.

The Patent Advisory Panel, Progress Report to the Federal Council for Science and Technology (June 1964) describes the purpose and content of this Memorandum as follows (pp. 2–3):

The Policy Statement recognizes four basic concepts as being applicable to a government-wide patent policy: first, that although it is not feasible to have a completely uniform patent practice throughout the government in view of the differing missions and statutory responsibilities of the several departments and agencies engaged in research and development, nevertheless there is a need for greater consistency; second, that a simple across-the-board "title" or "license" policy is not the answer to this difficult problem; third, that before the public can benefit from inventions derived from government-sponsored research and development, the inventions must be developed, exploited and placed before the public and used; and fourth, that the determinations as to the disposition of rights be made as early as practicable, preferably at the time of contract. The Policy Statement then sets forth guidelines for use by the agencies in determining the disposition of rights to inventions which take into consideration the need to stimulate inventors, the needs of the government, the equities of government contractors, and the interest of the general public.

The Policy Statement recognizes that there are situations where the interest of the public to have freely accessible the inventive results of government-financed research so overshadows all other considerations that the principal or exclusive rights should normally be taken by the government. Characteristic of these situations is where agencies contract for the development of products specifically intended for use by the public (as the development of material handling equipment for particular agricultural industries under Department of Agriculture contract), or where the use of the product will be required by governmental regulation (as an FAA requirement of an aircraft safety device). Other examples are where the contracts are for the development of products or processes directly related to the public health (as the development of a drug or prosthetic device under an NIH contract) or where the contract is in a field of science or technology in which there has been little significant experience outside of government funded research (as in the development of large launch vehicles for space exploration or atomic weapons). In such cases the acquisition of exclusive rights might place the contractor in a dominant position within the field.

In other situations, however, where a government contractor is expected to build upon existing knowledge in a field of technology directly related to an area in which the contractor has an established technical competence and a nongovernmental commercial position, the Policy Statement stipulates that the principal or exclusive rights to resulting inventions should normally remain in the contractor, subject to an irrevocable, nonexclusive, royalty-free license to the government throughout the world for all governmental purposes. This approach is intended to best serve the public interest by encouraging the contractor to direct his best personnel, know-how and experience towards solving the government's research problems, by recognizing the contractor's equities in the technical field, and by leaving the invention in the control of an organization qualified to further develop the invention into a commercially usable product in the shortest possible time. This situation is perhaps best illustrated by the typical Department of Defense contract which is intended to build upon a contractor's established technical competence in such fields as communications, fluid or aerodynamics, electronics, or transportation.

Where the principal or exclusive rights to an invention have been left with the contractor, and the contractor has failed to bring the invention to the point of practical application or has failed to make the invention available for licensing within three years after patenting, the Policy Statement stipulates that the government shall have the right to require the contractor to grant nonexclusive royalty-free licenses. The Policy Statement also recognizes the need for (1) flexibility to accommodate special situations, (2) deferring the determination on disposition of rights in some cases until the invention has been identified instead of at the time of contract, (3) compulsory licensing where the public necessity requires it, and (4) consideration of the foreign rights and foreign relations interests in connection with government-financed inventions.

This Memorandum lays down a policy that steers a middle course between the "title" and "license" policies theretofore followed by various government agencies. It also gives to the agencies considerable discretion to depart from the rules laid down and to waive rights the government might claim. Notwithstanding this discretionary power, the effect of the Memorandum has apparently been to temper the extremes at both ends of the spectrum, resulting in somewhat greater consistency than has heretofore been the case.

Critics of governmental "title" policy have sometimes emphasized its deleterious effect upon the employees of research contractors. No doubt, adverse effects could result under certain circumstances. To date, however, little evidence to support this criticism has appeared.[99] To the extent that the research contractor insists upon employees assigning rights to him (and, as we have seen, research-oriented concerns of the type likely to get government R&D contracts tend to require this), the employee must surrender his inventions in any event, irrespective of whether the government requires assignment from the employer. While the employer might be less generous in granting awards or bonuses as a result of being denied beneficial rights in the invention, there is little evidence that this has actually occurred.[100] One possibility of employee benefit that exists in private arrangements, namely, that the employer may waive his right to patents and leave them to the employee, still remains available as the result of a ruling that the Memorandum permits such waiver where neither the government nor the employer wishes to claim the patent rights and the public interest will not be hurt by leaving them with the employee.[101]

In contrast to government R&D contracts entered into with private industry, contracts with universities do typically deprive the research personnel of rights they would normally receive. As pointed out previously, most universities leave patents and other legal rights with the inventor. To the extent that the government contract requires that such rights be assigned to the government, this is no longer possible. Even so, there is no evidence that this deprivation has adversely affected individual initiative and activity.[102] The possible dangers here may be lessened by three factors: (1) In some instances, government has permitted these institutions to retain the rights and follow their traditional practices and policies of licensing

[99] See also statement of Russell Long, cited in footnote 95, at p. 365: "It is said that we must encourage the inventive genius of the United States, and that if we do not allow Government contractors to charge monopoly prices on the results of publicly financed research, inventors will be muffled and the scientific and technological level of our country will fall. That statement has been made by many hypocrites who themselves contract with scientists and engineers day after day and prohibit them from having the benefit of their discoveries, and yet they expect those scientists to produce good work for them. It is no wonder that this is a confidential agreement, for it shows that corporate scientists are tied hand and foot. Even their souls are shackled to corporate interests. Their very thoughts become part of the corporation's property . . . ." See also Long, "Federal Contract Patent Policy and the Public Interest," 21 *Fed. Bar J.* (1961): 7, 13–14; wherein Senator Long states that it is inconceivable that it would make any difference to the inventor, who actually does the inventing, whether this invention becomes the property of his employer or of the government. But see, William Eaton, "Patent problem: Who owns the rights?" 45 Harv. Bus. Rev. No. 4 (1967): 10.

[100] See special policy of RCA in this respect in RCA case study of this book.

[101] *Annual Report on Government Patent Policy,* June 1966, pp. 10–11, and Appendix F.

[102] See Harbridge House, Inc., *Government Patent Policy,* Vol. 1, which comments as follows (pp. 1–43): "With respect to educational and nonprofit institutions, refusal to participate for patent reasons is not normally a problem." The report does, however, refer to instances in which complications arose where joint support of research was involved.

and exploitation. (2) In many, probably most, instances university research is not commercially oriented or motivated by profit; nor are the individual researchers. (3) It is probable that the collateral financial and other advantages that accrue to the universities and university personnel from government research contracts considerably outweigh the possible disadvantages that result from being denied patent rights.

A few additional matters should be mentioned briefly in connection with government contracts. All of these can, in some circumstances, adversely affect employees of contractors but, because of the relatively slight impact, no attempt will be made here to explore them in detail or discuss their possible ramifications insofar as employees are concerned.

1. Trade secret problems arise here in a somewhat different context than they do in purely private arrangements. In general, government agencies favor publication wherever possible and, unlike private industry, usually do not concern themselves with possible commercial advantages that might flow from keeping information secret. Educational institutions are similarly publication-oriented. On the other hand, national security and defense considerations may make it necessary to maintain R&D results in secrecy. Such secrecy measures would, as previously noted, also apply to purely private research results if patents were involved.

2. At least a limited publication or disclosure of confidential data pursuant to government-private procurement contracts is reflected in occasional governmental insistence that proprietary data, submitted in confidence by a contractor, be available to second sources of supply so the government will not have to depend upon a sole source.[103]

3. Government agencies sometimes not only require that contractors assign rights in the research results as such but also require them to furnish background rights, i.e., the right to operate under patents that have previously issued and the right to operate under related patents that issue in the future.[104]

4. Government agencies, unlike private concerns, do not need the protection of trailer clauses, although two requirements that they often impose may be viewed as constituting a modified form of such a clause. One is the insistence upon the foreground rights referred to in the preceding paragraph. The other is the definition of rights arising out of the contract as including inventions "conceived"

[103] But see Milgrim, *Trade Secrets*, sec. 6.02(4), pp. 6–24, 6–25; Report, Proprietary Rights and Data, House Report No. 2230 (Select Committee on Small Business, House of Representatives, 1960), pp. 4–5.
[104] Compare Comsat patent policy.

in the course of the contract, even though not actually reduced to practice during that time.[105]

CONCLUSIONS

The basic law involving the employer-employee relationship in this area developed from the traditions and attitude of an early day. It has not progressed far. In other words, today's legal attitudes toward the employee-inventor relationship are rather similar to what one would have found in much of the nineteenth century. Much of our common law doctrine is based upon something akin to the relational or "master-servant" approach of an early day. There is extensive reliance upon "freedom of contract" concepts as an appropriate device for working out the rules.

In contrast, significant employer-employee developments have occurred over the decades in most other fields of employment. Public concern for the underprivileged and defenseless (women, children, minority groups, the unemployed) has steadily increased. So has public concern for health, safety, job security, and proper treatment of employees. Unions have played a more and more significant role, constituting both a cause and a result of the foregoing.

Few of these forces have operated with respect to inventors and other creators. This is understandable. Typically, they have not been economically downtrodden. As a class, they have been too small for the unions to become seriously concerned about. By nature, the members of the group tend to be individualistic, independent, competitive with each other. Often, they identify more with management than with the working force, an attitude that management encourages. Indeed, many do gravitate to higher management levels.

As a result, there has been little development in the areas of legislation or public policy control. We have relied upon a somewhat outmoded common law approach, the use of contract to regulate the relationship and, to some extent, a mild form of paternalism in the sense of accepting the employer's insistence that he will do right by the employee, knows what is best for him, and that government will simply be doing a disservice if it interferes. In view of the extensive changes that have occurred, one may question whether these basic approaches are as viable today as they may have been fifty years ago.

[105] Davis and Davidson, "Government Patent Policy—Another Look at an Old Problem," *Fed. Bar J.* 21 (1961): 77, note 2; Patent Practices of Government Agencies—Preliminary Reports.

We have seen a striking shift, especially in the technological fields, from the characteristically individual or small-scale effort of an earlier day to massive programs of cooperative, collective, creative activity undertaken largely in corporate, government, or university laboratories. Both the acts of invention and the developments that follow have become complex, expensive, and interrelated with other factors and other devices. The indications are that this tendency will continue. We have moved into an era in which such creative developments, especially in the technological field, are more and more becoming matters of conscious national policy and the subject of steadily increasing government support and subsidy.

In the light of these factors it seems inevitable that government will show more and more concern about the policies and practices that are adopted in these areas and use its efforts and resources to bring these policies and practices into line with the public interest, however that may be defined.

In the light of these forces at work, one may reasonably anticipate that we will see the following:

1. Increasing public insistence that employees engaged in inventive activity, whether hired for that purpose or not, be treated equitably.

2. Emphasis upon policies that will stimulate both invention and innovation and direct them into channels that appear socially important, such as areas of pollution, transportation, and conservation of natural resources.

3. Efforts to maximize the public usage of new developments to the extent that such usage appears desirable, even though this may involve to some extent taking the decisions out of private hands.

4. Possibly continued efforts to prevent developing technology from being used to strengthen monopoly or anticompetitive positions. (Past experience in this respect provides no strong basis for optimism on this score.)

In the promotion of these policies one may expect that government, primarily the federal government, will inject itself more and more into the field in an effort to influence the policies that exist (once it decides what these policies should be). This may be reflected in the formulation of policies for its own employees and government laboratories, in acts of Congress, and in other direct governmental measures. It may also take the form of rules imposed upon employers in other areas (especially private industry) and the incorporation of policy-oriented conditions in government R&D contracts. It may manifest itself in programs for making awards and providing stimuli directly to employees of other organizations, such as private industry, even to the extent of by-passing the employer and offering incentives directly to the employee.

Government programs of the sort described here would inevitably have an influence upon the policies and practices undertaken by other employers as well, even if the latter were not forced by statute to subscribe to them.

Finally, with all of these developments one would expect to see an increasingly active interest in exploring the subject and gathering more information (an activity that is sadly lacking today) on the part of public and quasi-public organization such as the government, universities and, for that matter, private industry and privately-oriented organizations as well. Indeed, there already exists within the Department of Commerce alone, a number of offices that give considerable attention to this subject, such as the Institute of Applied Technology and its subordinate organizations the Office of Invention and Innovation and the National Inventors Council. Similar interest is manifested, at least at times, by the Office of Science and Technology, the Small Business Administration, and various congressional committees, among them the Atomic Energy Committee, the Small Business Committees, the Antitrust Committees of the House and Senate, and the Aeronautics and Space Committee. Ultimately, one may hope, we will end with greater understanding than we now have of this important and complex subject, and with legal rules and guidelines more appropriately keyed to our needs than is the case at the present time.

I. Statutes asserting public rights in employee inventions.

A number of federal statutes provide expressly that inventions originating with government employees under varying, but generally broad, conditions shall be "freely and fully available to the general public." Typical provisions to this effect are exemplified by the following:

1. Saline Water Conversion Act of September 22, 1961, 42 U.S. Code sec. 1954:

"(b) All research within the United States contracted for, sponsored, cosponsored, or authorized under authority of sections 1951–1958 of this title, shall be provided for in such manner that all information, uses, products, processes, patents, and other developments resulting from such research developed by Government expenditure will (with such exceptions and limitations, if any, as the Secretary may find to be necessary in the interest of national defense) be available to the general public. This subsection shall not be so construed as to deprive the owner of any background patent relating thereto of such rights as he may have thereunder.

Similar provisions with slight modifications, are contained in the Helium Act Amendments of September 13, 1960, 50 U.S. Code sec. 167b; Coal Research Act of July 7, 1960, 30 U.S. Code sec. 666.

2. Appalachian Regional Development Act of March 9, 1965, 40 App. U.S. Code sec. 302:

(e) No part of any appropriated funds may be expended pursuant to authorization given by this Act involving any scientific or technological research or development activity unless such expenditure is conditioned upon provisions effective to insure that all information, copyrights, uses, processes, patents, and other developments resulting from that activity will be made freely available to the general public. Nothing contained in this subsection shall deprive the owner of any background patent relating to any such activity, without his consent, of any right which that owner may have under that patent. Whenever any information, copyright, use, process, patent or development resulting from any such research or development activity conducted in whole or in part with appropriated funds expended under authorization of this Act is withheld or disposed of by any person, organization, or agency in contravention of the provisions of this subsection, the Attorney General shall institute, upon his own motion or upon request made by any person having knowledge of pertinent facts, an action for the enforcement of the provisions of this subsection in the district court of the United States for any judicial district in which any defendant resides, is found, or has a place of business.

Similar provisions with slight modifications, are contained in the Water Resources Research Act of July 17, 1964, 42 U.S. Code 1961 c-3.

3. Solid Waste Disposal Act of October 20, 1965, 42 U.S. Code sec. 3253:

(c) Any grant, agreement, or contract made or entered into under this section shall contain provisions effective to insure that all information, uses, processes, patents and other developments resulting from any activity undertaken pursuant to such grant, agreement, or contract will be made readily available on fair and equitable terms to industries utilizing methods of solid-waste disposal and industries engaging in furnishing devices, facilities, equipment, and supplies to be used in connection with solid-waste disposal. In carrying out the provisions of this section, the Secretary and each department, agency, and officer of the Federal Government having functions or duties under this chapter shall make use of and adhere to the Statement of Government Patent Policy which was promulgated by the President in his memorandum of October 10, 1963. (3 CFR, 1963 Supp., p. 238.)

4. Tennessee Valley Authority Act of 1933, 16 U.S. Code sec. 8312:

"(i) . . . any invention or discovery made by virtue of and incidental to such service by an employee of the Government of the United States serving under this section, or by any employee of the Corporation, together with any patents which may be granted thereon, shall be the sole and exclusive property of the Corporation, which is authorized to grant such licenses thereunder as shall be authorized by the board: *Provided further,* That the board may pay to such inventor such sum from the income from sale of licenses as it may deem proper.

5. National Science Foundation Act of 1950, 42 U.S. Code sec. 1871:

(b) No officer or employee of the Foundation shall acquire, retain, or transfer any rights, under the patent laws of the United States or otherwise, in any invention which he may make or produce in connection with performing his assigned activities and which is directly related to the subject matter thereof.

II. Statutes asserting rights in grantee inventions.

Some statutes contain comparable provisions but directed, apparently, to grantees and other contractors rather than employees. For example, see Federal Highway Administration Act of September 9, 1966, Public Law 89–563, sec. 106, which contains the following provision:

(c) Whenever the Federal contribution for any research or development activity authorized by this Act encouraging motor vehicle safety is more than minimal, the Secretary shall include in any contract, grant, or other arrangement for such research or development activity, provisions effective to insure that all information, uses, processes, patents, and other developments resulting from that activity will be made freely and fully available to the general public.

III. Statutes requiring agencies to make R&D results publicly available.

Some statutes impose a general obligation upon agencies entering into R&D arrangements, to make the results thereof available for public use.

1. Research and Marketing Act of 1946, 7 U.S. Code sec. 1624:

The Secretary of Agriculture shall have authority to enter into contracts and agreements under the terms of regulations promulgated by him with States and agencies of States, private firms, institutions, and individuals for the purpose of conducting research and service work. . . . Any contract made pursuant to this section shall contain requirements making the result of such research and investigations available to the public by such means as the Secretary of Agriculture shall determine.

2. Veterans Administration, 38 U.S. Code sec. 216:

(a) (1) The Administrator shall conduct research in the field of prosthesis, prosthetic appliances, orthopedic appliances, and sensory devices.
(2) In order that the unique investigative materials and research data in the possession of the Government may result in improved prosthetic appliances for all disabled persons, the Administrator may make available to any person the results of his research.

IV. Atomic Energy and NASA Statutes.

These two statutes are somewhat unique, both because of the role played by the federal government in the R&D that occurs in these areas, and because of detailed provisions contained therein with respect to the allocation of rights in the R&D that results.

1. Atomic Energy Act of 1954, 42 U.S. Code sec. 2182.

Any invention or discovery, useful in the production or utilization of special nuclear material or atomic energy, made or conceived in the course of or under any contract, subcontract, or arrangement entered into with or for the benefit of the Commission, regardless of whether the contract, subcontract, or arrangement involved the expenditure of funds by the Commission, shall be vested in, and be the property of, the Commission, except that the Commission may waive its claim to any such invention or discovery under such circumstances as the Commission may deem appropriate, consistent with the policy of this section. No patent for any invention or discovery, useful in the production or utilization of special nuclear material or atomic energy, shall be issued unless the applicant files with the application, or within thirty days after request therefor by the Commissioner of Patents (unless the Commission advises the Commissioner of Patents that its rights have been determined and that accordingly no statement is necessary) a statement under oath setting forth the full facts surrounding the making or conception of the invention or discovery described in the application and whether the invention or discovery was made or conceived in the course of or under any contract, subcontract, or arrangement entered into with or for the benefit of the Commission, regardless of whether the contract, subcontract, or arrangement involved the expenditure of funds by the Commission. The Commissioner of Patents shall as soon as the application is otherwise in condition for allowance forward copies of the application and the statement to the Commission.

2. National Aeronautics and Space Act of 1958, 42 U.S. Code sec. 2457:

(a) Whenever any invention is made in the performance of any work under any contract of the Administration, and the Administrator determines that—
(1) the person who made the invention was employed or assigned to perform research, development, or exploration work and the invention is related to the work he was employed or assigned to perform, or that it was within the scope of his employment duties, whether or not it was made during working hours, or

with a contribution by the Government of the use of Government facilities, equipment, materials, allocated funds, information proprietary to the Government, or services of Government employees during working hours . . . such invention shall be the exclusive property of the United States, and if such invention is patentable a patent therefor shall be issued to the United States upon application made by the Administrator, unless the Administrator waives all or any part of the rights of the United States to such invention in conformity with the provisions of subsection (f) of this section.

(b) Each contract entered into by the Administrator with any part for the performance of any work shall contain effective provisions under which such party shall furnish promptly to the Administrator a written report containing full and complete technical information concerning any invention, discovery, improvement, or innovation which may be made in the performance of any such work.

(c) No patent may be issued to any applicant other than the Administrator for any invention which appears to the Commissioner of Patents to have significant utility in the conduct of aeronautical and space activities unless the applicant files with the Commissioner, with the application or within thirty days after request therefor by the Commissioner, a written statement executed under oath setting forth the full facts concerning the circumstances under which such invention was made and stating the relationship (if any) of such invention to the performance of any work under any contract of the Administration. Copies of each such statement and the application to which it relates shall be transmitted forthwith by the Commissioner to the Administrator.

(d) Upon any application as to which any such statement has been transmitted to the Administrator, the Commissioner may, if the invention is patentable, issue a patent to the applicant unless the Administrator, within ninety days after receipt of such application and statement, requests that such patent be issued to him on behalf of the United States.

3

OVERVIEW

This chapter presents nine case studies describing employee-invention policy as practiced by the management of eight manufacturing corporations with highly developed research and development activities and one incorporated organization dedicated exclusively to research without any industrial development or manufacturing obligations (Bell Telephone Laboratories).

Table 3.1 relates size of the corporation and its sales and net income to the number of patents issued annually to these corporations. Table 3.2 summarizes the employee-invention assignment policy of these corporations, and Table 3.3 the employee-invention award policy.

Although most companies today show wide diversification of manufacture and research, there are one or two "centers of gravity" in each case. The companies selected for this study were chosen from a spectrum of seven major industrial categories, as follows. (One company, TRW, represents two different categories.)
Electrical and electronic equipment, machinery and systems (IBM, Westinghouse, RCA, TRW)
Petrochemical products (Gulf Oil)
Steel products (tonnage items), oil and coal mining, transportation (U.S. Steel)
Optical and photographic materials and apparatus (Polaroid)
Cars, motors, power plants (including fuels, materials, components, manufacturing processes) (General Motors)
Systems and components for communication by sound, light, electrical signals with wire and wireless (Bell Telephone Laboratories)
Motors, engine components (TRW)

The size of the corporations can be described in different terms: number of employees, net sales, net income, and other criteria. In Table 3.1 they are ranked by number of employees. Other figures of importance for size would be corporation expenditures for research and development. Such figures, as a rule, are not available for individual firms, and the boundary between "research" and its transition into product development is not defined as in government-supported research (carried out by contract). This unfortunately limits the ability to draw far-reaching conclusions and comparisons regarding inventive working results of employees as based on R&D. Further studies should be made on this basis.

Table 3.1 includes five firms with more than 100,000 employees. These represent "big industry," and their appearance in a table of high-ranking patent holders is

Table 3.1   Selected Industrial Corporations Ranked by Number of Employees, 1967

	Number of Employees	Sales (1967)	Net Income (1967)	Patents[1] 1966	1967	Average Patent Rank (1966–1967)
General Motors	728,000	$20,026,252	$1,627,276	677	706	1
IBM	221,866	5,345,290	651,499	623	497	2
United States Steel	197,643	4,067,200	172,500	165	135	6
Westinghouse Electric	132,000	2,900,698	122,940	553	565	3
RCA	128,000	3,027,216	147,509	315	330	5
TRW	61,000	1,300,000[2]	64,400[2]	150	80	9
Gulf Oil	58,300	5,109,597	578,000	123	119	8
Bell Tel. Labs.[3]	15,200	—	—	436	406	4
Polaroid	6,788	374,354	57,377	136	114	7

[1] From communications to author from individual companies, October 1968.
[2] Reconstructed.
[3] Bell Laboratories is jointly owned by American Telephone & Telegraph and Western Electric Companies.

Source: Annual reports and personal communications from corporation representatives.

not accidental. Economic possibilities of carrying out large-scale research are, as a rule, more open to firms with access to large funds and great manpower. Purposeful and single-minded pursuit of specific research is, however, in no way reserved to the largest industrial corporations. The case study of Polaroid Corporation (whose 7000 employees are less than 1 percent of General Motors staff) and TRW Inc. (which began as a small metal-welding firm) illustrate this point.

A question of central interest is whether there is any correlation between an active employee-invention policy (as expressed either by a specific invention-assignment policy or by specific invention-award policy) and the working results of employees in the form of patents granted by the U.S. Patent Office. Basing this comparison on the number of patents issued in the attempt to answer whether and to what extent tangible and intangible incentives to employee inventors may yield any "interest" in terms of working results is a makeshift. The grant of a certain number of patents in a certain year depends on a series of variables such as the specific engineering field to which an invention belongs, the working speed of the U.S. Patent Office, the general patent policy of a corporation, the economic, scientific, commercial, or military situation of the country. With these

Table 3.2 Employee Invention Assignment Policy

	Assignee	Type of Agreement	For All Employees	For Specific Groups of Employees	Field of Agreement
General Motors	GM as entity including all divisions	Part of employment contract	No	Engineers and R&D personnel	Any matter relating to manufacture and business
International Business Machines	Employer and subsidiaries	Invention assignment agreement	Yes (relevant groups specified in contract)	——	Anything related to actual or anticipated business or R&D
United States Steel	Employer and consolidated subsidiaries	?	No	Group A: Title assignment Group B: Nonexclusive license	Any invention relating or applicable to any business in which company may be engaged
Westinghouse Electric	Employer, groups, divisions, subsidiaries	Invention assignment agreement	No	All technical, professional, and management employees	Within existing or contemplated scope of corporation's business
Radio Corporation of America	Employer, plants, divisions, subsidiaries	Invention assignment agreement	No	Those in touch with problems to solve (list of covered occupations	Relating to business or interests of corporation, business in which RCA has an interest or result of tasks assigned
TRW	Employer and companies he owns and controls, and their successors in business	Invention assignment agreement	No	All technically associated employees	Within existing or contemplated scope of employer's business or relating to subject matter with which employer is or may be concerned
Gulf Oil	Patent company and all affiliates (especially Gulf Research and Development Company)	Part of employment contract	No	All employees in technical and scientific work	Relating to actual or projected activities or business, opportunities afforded or knowledge gained from employment
Bell Telephone Laboratories	Employer and successors and assigns	Standard form	Yes	——	Relating to any subject matter with which the corporation is or may be concerned
Polaroid	Employer, successors, assigns, or subsidiaries	Employment contract	No	All research, engineering employees, other employees informed on Polaroid inventions	Manufacture and sale of company products and business of research in various specified general fields of science

Table 3.3   Employee Invention Award Policy

	Formal Award Plan	Cash Payments Standard	Individual	Honorary Measures	Special Suggestion Award System	Award System Modified
General Motors	No	No	No	Publicity in house organ	Yes	
United States Steel	Partly	Group A: $600 Group B: $400	No	None	Yes	Yes
International Business Machines	Yes	Yes	Yes: from $1000 to $5000 or more	Certificates, presents, honorary dinners, IBM Fellow title	Yes	Yes
Westinghouse Electric	Yes	Filed disclosure, $200; patent granted, $500	Yes	Certificates, plaques, citation programs, publicity in house organs	Yes	Yes
Radio Corporation of America	Yes	Filed application, $150; approved for publication, $75	Yes	Certificates, "Fellow" title, publicity in house organs	No	Yes
TRW	Partly	$200 on assignment to company	No	None	Yes	
Gulf Oil	Partly	Filed application, $100; patent granted, $100	No	Specific internal professional titles	No	
Polaroid	Partly	No	Yes: additional shares, salary increase based on annual business profit and base salary	Opportunity to attend scientific meetings, devote more time to publishing	No, except as covered in invention award plan	
Bell Telephone Laboratories	No	No	No	Publicity in house organ	No	

reservations in mind we compare the content of the three tables presented here. Some interesting observations may be made from Tables 3.2 and 3.3. Regarding Table 3.2 we note the following points:

1. Most employers select specific groups of employees, especially professional personnel, to sign invention-assignment agreements as a condition of employment. The scope of invention assignment for employees is rather uniform in the various corporations; the assignee includes usually not only the direct contractual employer but all his plants, divisions, groups, and subsidiaries, both domestic and foreign.[1] The assertion that invention-assignment agreements are more or less uniformly asked for from personnel with professional education and experience, as a condition of employment, is based on the author's (Neumeyer) collection of such agreements from several hundred industrial corporations belonging to various branches of manufacturing and research. This is in general agreement with the survey carried out by J. R. O'Meara for the National Industrial Conference Board, according to which 83 of 86 cooperating companies require some or all of their employees to execute patent-assignment agreements as a condition of employment.[2] Two typical assignment agreements are reproduced as Appendix A to this chapter.

2. The technical and commercial field of invention assignment appears to be extremely broad. It refers often to the existing and contemplated (or projected) business, the interests, activities, manufacture, research, and investigations of the employer without defining these broad terms. The concept of business an employer may contemplate or project in the future blurs all borderlines of the field reserved to the employee. Solution of uncertainties of interpretation of these terms or conflicts about them is in the hands of the employer. In addition, the assignment agreement often refers to inventions made "along the lines," "useful in," or "related to" the business of an employer which easily covers anything an employee can conceive in any technical field. Other agreements add all discoveries, improvements, and inventions "growing out of the contact of the employee with said art or business."

[1] Foreign subsidiaries, however, can be subject to national laws, as is the case in Germany, Denmark, Sweden, also most East European countries.
[2] See J. Roger O'Meara, "Employee Patent and Secrecy Agreements," Studies in Personnel Policy (New York: National Industrial Conference Board, No. 199, 1965), a valuable survey covering 86 "research-minded" companies.

AWARD POLICY

Table 3.3 shows that standard cash payments of fixed amounts are relatively common (even in many firms not described here).[3] Usually, one standard cash amount is paid by the employer when a submitted idea is assigned and filed as a U.S. patent application and another standard amount when a U.S. patent is granted by the Patent Office. The dollar amount paid on these two occasions varies considerably but rarely surmounts the token award of some hundred dollars, irrespective of the actual value of the assigned invention.[4] Monetary incentives in the form of shares of stock in the company are used by General Electric and Du Pont de Nemours, Inc. (not described in case studies of this book). Polaroid pays to inventive employees an additional share of between 10 and 70 percent of the salary, based on annual business profit and base salaries. Leading aircraft corporations (McDonnell-Douglas, Lockheed) pay their inventors a royalty share of income from the licensing or sale of their assigned patents.

Cash awards paid to inventors can be increased (but not created) by the practice of a number of corporations which assume all the income tax on an award or all applicable local, state, and federal withholding taxes.

An elaborate system exploiting the provisions of the current U.S. Internal Revenue Tax Act of 1954 in favor of employed inventors has been suggested by a leading patent expert, W. R. Woodward. The system is based on the following reasoning and legal facts. Section 1235 of the 1954 Internal Revenue Code makes a distinction between taxes for income from labor and income from sale or exchange of a capital asset. Whether transfer of property consisting of all rights to a patent is considered to be such a sale or exchange of a capital asset (that is,

---

[3] *Ibid.*, p. 54. Three-fifths (52) of the companies studied by O'Meara offered special cash awards for patents.

[4] Other studies on award policy have been made, especially by the National Industrial Conference Board (NICB) in New York, and by The Patent, Trademark, and Copyright Foundation of the George Washington University in Washington, D.C. (PTCF). The main studies of the NICB are found in their publication *Management Record:* August 1952 (R. O'Connor, "Patent Policies for Employees"); October 1953 (R. O'Connor, "Incentives for Inventors"); June 1956 (James J. Bambrick and Albert A. Blum, "Patent Agreements in Union Contracts"); December 1957 (J. Roger O'Meara, "Safeguarding Confidential Information"). Still more studies are in NICB's *The Conference Board Record:* June 1964 (J. R. O'Meara, "Company Patent Practices Challenged") and NICB *Studies in Business Policy:* No. 112, 1964 (Carl G. Baumes, "Patent Counsel in Industry"); No. 199, 1965 (J. R. O'Meara, "Employee Patent and Secrecy Agreements"). The PTCF studies started in 1962 and are published in installments in *IDEA, The Patent, Trademark, and Copyright Journal of Research and Education* (Washington, D.C.: Winter 1963–1964) Joseph Rossman, "Rewards and Incentives to Employee-Inventors."

an asset held for more than six months) is a question of interpretation, but the tax courts have in recent years held that payments received by employed inventors were not compensation for services rendered as an employee but for transfer of inventions, and thus taxable as capital gain.[5] Since the capital assets tax is lower than the income tax on wages, the take-home pay of employed inventors would be increased and invention encouraged by such a tax incentive.[6] The system of tax liberalization for certain inventors, including employed inventors, is now described in detail in the report of an advisory committee to the Secretary of Commerce, "Technological Innovation: Its Environment and Management," January 1967.

In addition, Congress has in recent years passed a number of special bills relieving certain individual inventors receiving large cash awards (usually between $25,000 and $100,000) from taxes, over the objections of the Treasury Department. In one case concerning secret nonpatented inventions in cryptology which were transferred to government, the inventor was given the right to treat the reward as long-term capital gain with a maximum tax of 25 percent.[7]

E. I. Du Pont de Nemours & Company has an elaborate system of bonus awards in the form of common-stock, dividend units or dividend units accompanied by an option to purchase stock of the employing company. This corporation offers its employees three bonus plans (A, B, and C). The purposes of these plans are (a) to provide greater incentive for employees to continually exert their best efforts on behalf of the company by compensation that varies with the success of the business;

(b) to attract to and retain in the employ of the company persons of outstanding competence; and

[5] Chilton v. Commissioner of Internal Revenue, Tax Court of the U.S. No. 91332, June 21, 1963, in U.S. Patent Quarterly 138: 336.
[6] To realize this idea employment contracts should not compensate an employee with a single amount both for his services and for his agreement to assign patents, but compensation for services should be distinctly and reasonably allocated, and another definite part of the compensation should be paid by the employer to purchase his inventions. The sale of his patents by a "patents purchase agreement" should entitle the employee to the benefits laid in sec. 1235 of the Internal Revenue Code. Research employees could form a joint venture among themselves and assign their interests in these inventions to the employer, all inventors becoming "holders" of the inventions. This plan is described in detail by W.R. Woodward in "Tax Aspects of Patents, Copyrights and Trademarks" in Current Problems in Federal Taxation, Practising Law Institute (New York: 1960) p. 25, giving also references to many relevant tax court decisions.
[7] F.B. Rowlett was the inventor. This and other cases are described in The New York Times, November 22, 1964, in an article by Stacy V. Jones.

(c) to further the identity of interests of such employees with those of the company's stockholders generally.

Bonus awards under "Plan A" of the Du Pont award system may be granted for conspicuous service of any nature whether or not it increases company's earnings. Earlier, eligibility for bonus awards under plan A comprised inventions and improvements resulting in a profit, saving, or important benefit, or in a reduction of risk of personal injury or damage to the company's property, or an unusually ingenious solution of a business or technical problem. Awards under "Plan A" were granted in 1969, for the year 1968, to only 162 employees, none of whom were directors or officers. The awards consisted of $290,328 in cash and 3,100 shares of Common Stock, awarded at $161.27 a share. (Proxy Statement, March 1969.) Since Du Pont at the end of 1968 employed 114,100 men and women, including its consolidated subsidiaries in the United States and overseas (excluding 6,000 employees at Government-owned plants), awards for important employee inventions—if any—played a very subordinate role (about 1.5 pro mille of all employees of the company received awards for 1968).

Awards under "Plan B" may be granted to employees, including officers of the company, who have contributed most in a general way to the company's success by their ability, efficiency, and loyalty. The three qualities of meritorious behavior cited here rest on different human grounds: "ability" being a quality of personal intelligence, "efficiency and loyalty" describing conscientious performance.

Awards under "Plan B" were granted in 1969, for the year 1968, to 13 directors and officers and 12,319 other employees in the respective amounts of $1,166,000 and $45,029,000, totaling $46,195,000. Of the total amount, $23,537,134 was awarded in cash and the balance in 147,129 shares of new common stock of the company. The awards are deliverable in four equal annual installments.

Awards under "Plan C" may be granted to employees in important managerial or other responsible positions who concurrently are, or otherwise would be, recommended for awards under Plan B. In 1969, such awards were granted, for 1968, to 11 directors and officers and 40 other employees. The awards consisted of 6,561 dividend units without stock options, and 24,711 dividend units with stock options to purchase 32,948 shares of the company's common stock at $162.25 per share.[8]

General Electric Company similarly seeks in its award policy to identify interests

8 Proxy Statement, March 1969.

of top employees with those of the company's stockholders in saying that the
substitution of a share of stock rather than a cash payment to the employee is in
line with the policy of the company to encourage stock ownership as widely as
possible among its employees.[9] This type of reward may also be cheapest for large-
stock corporations. Shares of stock as awards are made fixed payments by the
Board of Directors by the assignment of a value corresponding to the market
price of the stock at the date of delivery or option grant. At Du Pont de Nemours,
the employee is not restricted from selling or assigning his stock after it has been
delivered to him.[10]

There exists also a large variety of other awards offered to employees in return
for useful inventions (or other contributions) made for the benefit of the employer.
These have a money value corresponding to a cash award. In this group, we find
gifts such as vacation trips or rebates for goods manufactured or services rendered
by the employer.

To the group of awards having some money value, even if this value cannot be
assessed in advance, belong the cases in which the employer releases or waives all
rights to submitted inventions and patent applications to the inventor or in
which the employer retains only a nonexclusive license to use the invention within
the domestic company (a shop right) and leaves all other commercial rights—the
remaining license rights in the United States as well as all possible patentable
rights abroad—to the employed inventor. The commercial reward retained in
these cases is in accord with the initiative and commercial ability of the inventors,
which may vary considerably.

In some cases, United States employers even offer to try to exploit these unused
parts of inventive rights on behalf of the inventor, with or without provisions
to share the profits that may accrue in the form of royalty payments. This award
system is usually administered by the employer. The system carries with it some
closer financial cooperation between the inventor and his employer, the latter
functioning as exploiter and financial manager. The system, used especially by a
number of aircraft and aerospace corporations, carries with it considerable extra
accounting, disliked by most employers. A typical reaction seems to be represented
by Westinghouse when it points to the expense of accounting for royalty income
as well as the economic impossibility of increasing the selling costs of certain

[9] Cited by R. O'Connor in "Patent Policies for Employees," *Management Record,* August
1952, p. 387.
[10] Special rules apply in case of dismissal, retirement, or death of bonus beneficiary.

industrial products with very close profit margins (such as television receivers) by 1 or 2 percent for each of a number of inventions possibly involved in a more complex engineering product. It is also questioned whether a royalty system would damage the team effort in projects carried out by corporate research facilities and engineering departments.[11] On the other hand, it is asserted in circles of employees in the aircraft industry that the awards received in this way in practice amount only to a token gift.[12]

Some employers are even willing to sell patents issued to their employed inventors and share the income of this sale with the inventor. It is not clear whether in these cases the employer retains a nonexclusive license or a shop right for his own use. In the case of royalty-sharing systems, as a rule, a descending scale of shared returns is set up, from a maximum percentage of 40 percent or 30 percent for a first income between $1000 and $10,000, down to 10 percent or 5 percent for all sums collected after 3 to 5 years licensing.[13]

Honorary incentives in terms of special certificates, medals, and publicity in general press or house organs are practiced by seven of the nine corporations studied here (exceptions: U.S. Steel and TRW). Special honorary titles ("Fellows") are given by IBM and RCA. Another company practicing a similar incentive is Minnesota Mining and Manufacturing Company which has instituted a "status society" named after a former company president who did much to encourage major technical contributions. To be elected to this society, said to bring prestige and publicity, an employee must have firmly established a reputation as successful contributor to the scientific and technical growth of the company. The society is not intended to replace but rather to supplement financial rewards. Some companies have an "Inventors Club" open to any employee who has filed for or been issued a patent. Club membership brings the employee some recognition through newspaper publicity.[14]

[11] See Ted K. Bowes, in *IDEA, The Patent, Trademark, and Copyright Journal of Research and Education,* 5 (1967): 64.
[12] In the aircraft industry there is a large organized patent pool, the Manufacturers Aircraft Association, for all U.S. patents of use to the industry. It collects all patents of member industries and licenses the administered patents to all members in accordance with a royalty system geared to the number of patents assigned by members. Association committee members deciding on licensing of and payment for Association-owned patents are in many cases identical with the employers of inventing aircraft industry employees.
[13] Examples are given in the following chapter on collective bargaining agreements. See also Joseph Rossman, "Rewards and Incentives to Employee-Inventors" in *IDEA, The Patent, Trademark, and Copyright Journal of Research and Education* 7 (1964): 436 ff.
[14] J.R. O'Meara, "Employee Patent and Secrecy Agreements," p. 61.

An important question remaining is: Can any correlation be traced between incentive policy for creative employees and their output of patentable inventions made during employment?

The patent figures of Table 3.1 show

1. In absolute figures for number of patents issued the following ranking:

GM	1	U.S. Steel	6
IBM	2	Polaroid	7
Westinghouse Electric	3	Gulf Oil	8
Bell Telephone Laboratories	4	TRW	9
RCA	5		

2. Patents (average of 1966 and 1967) issued to employees as a percentage of all company employees:

Bell Telephone Laboratories	3.0%	1	TRW	0.2%	6
Polaroid	2.0	2	GM	0.09	7
Westinghouse	0.4	3	U.S. Steel	0.07	8
RCA	0.3	4	Gulf Oil	0.02	9
IBM	0.3	5			

One cannot draw far-reaching conclusions from these figures, since the statistical material is much too narrow in terms of corporations and time periods counted, but certain trends may be observed. Absolute patent figures may indicate that very large manufacturing corporations can always put out a large amount of employee patent rights irrespective of employee incentive programs. However, IBM and Westinghouse, ranking respectively second and third, are corporations with a long-standing and extensive invention-award policy.

More important are figures for employee patents as a percentage of the number of all corporate employees. Economic size is not decisive for ranking here; Bell Telephone Laboratories, the only pure R&D organization in the list, leads in spite of ranking eighth in terms of number of employees. Corporations which primarily exploit and handle raw materials have less R&D personnel and therefore minor output of inventions (Gulf Oil, U.S. Steel). The General Motors ranking appears to be low in this connection. Regarding correlation between active employee-invention award policy and output of patentable inventions, companies without any formal award policy rank (1) Bell Telephone Laboratories and (7) General Motors; companies with an active award policy rank (2) Polaroid, (3) Westinghouse, and tieing for (4) and (5) RCA and IBM.

Creative products of employees other than patents are, for instance, scientific publications. Their tangible value however, often seems entirely incompatible with their quantity. Einstein's relativity theory was set forth mainly in equations occupying a few printed lines, and the disclosure of the transistor principle was contained in a 15-line "Letter to the Editor" (of *Physical Review*). Obviously the number of publications is not a suitable measure of creative output of employed personnel. In spite of this fact, a great (formerly employed) inventor, William W. Shockley, has made an effort to judge creative results on the basis of quantity of scientific publications.[15]

Employers usually do not include any awards for publications in employee-award systems, probably because they are so hard to judge. An interesting exception is Radio Corporation of America, which gives special awards for approved publication (*RCA Technical Notes*). Since employee publications practically always communicate the company (or institute) affiliation of the author this means improved "image" and good will in the scientific community and among existing and prospective customers, which may be worth an award to the employed author. On the other hand, it is well known that scientific and engineering publications by employees are a weighty part of merits for advancement in research-minded corporations. This is the case, for instance, in Bell Telephone Laboratories, RCA, IBM, and Polaroid.

To keep a record of employee inventions and their relation to incentive awards over a long period of time is of considerable interest. This has been practiced by some large manufacturing companies. Figure 3.1 illustrates such activity over a period of 42 years in a large corporation. The corporation applied first (1935–1956) an invention-award system based on the evaluation of disclosed inventions by a corporate committee, and payment was made of a small cash award for all inventions judged to be meritorious (about 50 percent of all disclosures received). From each 50 disclosures submitted the most meritorious were awarded a cash award of about a hundred dollars. Since 1951 standard cash awards have

[15] See William Shockley, "On the Statistics of Individual Variations of Productivity in Research Laboratories," in *Proceedings of the IRE*, March 1957, pp. 279 ff., in which he tries to introduce a quantitative study of the number of scientific publications (or rather the logarithm of the rate of publication) as a measure of productivity of workers in scientific research laboratories. He believes he has found close correlation between quantity of scientific production and the achievement of eminence as a contributor to scientific journals. Shockley also studied cumulative distribution for publications and patents produced by individuals in one division of the National Bureau of Standards and in industrial laboratories. He introduced a "merit index" as a tool to study objectively the problem of quality losses of personnel in civil service laboratories ("Scientific Thinking and Problems of Growth," talk at University of California, 1963).

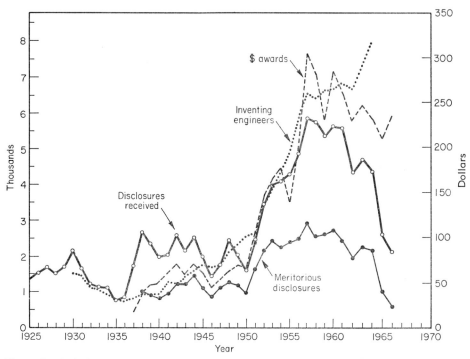

Figure 3.1 Relation between employee inventions and incentive awards, 1925–1966.

also been paid for all disclosures prepared as patent applications (implying that
their technical contents were considered useful by the employer) as well as special
cash awards for contributions of exceptional value to the employer. This system
led to a decade of heavy invention-disclosure activity by the employees. A closer
analysis revealed that this policy placed considerable emphasis on maximizing the
number of disclosures irrespective of quality. The theory behind this policy was
that if disclosures were accepted on everything, the good inventions could not be
missed. The total, however, embraced considerable worthless material, and the
efficiency factor of the system was considered poor. At the beginning of 1965
the system was radically modified. General disclosure awards as well as "most
meritorious" disclosure awards were abolished. Emphasis was now concentrated
on rewarding only the invention disclosures leading to patent applications,
"authorization to file" award being $200 per disclosure. To further increase
incentive and to award inventors in proportion to the relative values of their

contributions, a patent award was added of $100 at the issuance of each patent. It is felt that this system is adequate to encourage disclosure of all worthwhile inventions. At the same time engineering managers of the corporations are adjured to see that important inventions are disclosed by the employees.

After this general overview nine case studies follow to illustrate individual employer invention policy.

GENERAL MOTORS CORPORATION

General Survey

General Motors is the largest company of the United States and of the world.[16] Any policy, change of policy, or lack of policy in any field of labor relations of this giant employer must have a far-reaching impact upon its employees, and certainly policy toward employee inventors can be included in this statement. Yet no collected information is available, and relevant facts are widely scattered. General Motors may never have felt it necessary to report any uniform invention-assignment or invention-award policy encompassing all employees, and they may not have one.

A number of circumstances make this negative fact somewhat understandable. One is that the engineering activities of General Motors cover many different fields; in one field patentable inventions are never made or have little commercial or competitive value, whereas in others they may have great practical value. Another reason is that most branches of management of the corporation are not centralized, decentralization being one of the earliest and deepest-rooted traditions of General Motors management.[17] However, patent work is centralized, an exception to the general plan of organization. With a large central patent department in Detroit and continuous attention to employee inventions in its *GM Engineering Journal*, a conscious employee-invention policy should exist in some form.

A third reason is probably that General Motors is manufacturing and carrying on research in so many countries where legislation and management practice are at variance with the domestic situation in the United States that a unified policy on a world-wide basis would be meaningless.[18]

[16] "The Fortune Directory," June 15, 1968.
[17] See Alfred P. Sloan, Jr., *My Years with General Motors,* J. McDonald with C. Steven, eds. (New York: Macfadden, 1965), Chapter 7: "Co-ordination by Committee."
[18] A number of large U.S. corporations with their own research in many parts of the world, such as IBM, or with an international exchange of research-produced inventions by agreement, such as the Bell System (through Western Electric Company) do have a clear-cut unified policy with regard to inventions made by their own employees, contractors' employees, or employees of companies bound by license agreements.

Despite these obstacles, it is possible to describe roughly and in principle how General Motors acquires inventions made by employees and how they compensate or otherwise stimulate inventions.

General Motors' general consciousness of the importance of inventions and patents produced by their own staff goes far back in the history of the corporation. In 1920 it purchased Dayton Engineering Laboratories, and its head, Charles Kettering, became General Motors Research Corporation's first president. Kettering, whom Alfred Sloan characterized as "an engineer and a world-famous inventor, a social philosopher, and a super-salesman,"[19] the man who had invented the first practical electrical self-starter for cars, headed all General Motors' general research until 1947. Kettering was not only a prolific inventor himself but encouraged his employees to make inventions. He is supposed to have said that a patent is an order of merit granted by the government to men with imagination and an eye to the future.

Today General Motors Technical Center, completed in 1956 with an investment of more than $125 million, speaks for itself. In more than 27 buildings it houses some 5000 scientists, engineers, designers, and other specialists, of whom probably the majority is "hired to invent." The research organization of General Motors contributes to all the products of the manufacturing division. Automobiles, diesel engines, household appliances, locomotives, and jet engines depend on continuous new research. The staff is said to deal solely with fundamental long-range research in all branches of natural sciences. The basic categories of research are energy (fuel, lubricants, and power plant, also atomic energy as a possible source of automotion) and materials (metallurgical study of ferrous and nonferrous metals, glass, plastics). A new branch investigates radioisotopes as tools in manufacturing, engineering, and research.

Employee inventing, of course, is not restricted to the organized research brain trust just described. More than 20 domestic assembly plants for cars, plants producing the main automotive parts, and other operating divisions and subsidiaries invite employees of all qualifications and ages to make patentable inventions and to suggest improvements in planning, drafting, producing, measuring, and checking corporate products and processes. Yet no real invention incentive program seems to exist for either group of employees.

Historically, World War II brought about a positive postwar patent policy.

[19] Sloan, *My Years with General Motors,* p. 249.

Suggestion plans in wartime were badly needed to improve technological efficiency of weapons. An extensive and sophisticated mechanism, mainly for blue collar workers, was created to foster and reward successful suggestions for developing new products and processes. In one year, 1944, the 400,000 employees of General Motors made more than 115,000 written suggestions for improvements, of which about one quarter were usable.[20] Figures on financial rewards to employed inventors were not published.

About 90 percent of GM's commercial sales are derived from automotive products.[21] Net sales including services and rental revenues and consolidated subsidiaries were more than $20.2 billion in 1967.[22]

The weekly output of all General Motors cars oscillates in recent years between 80,000 and 110,000 assemblies a week. Relatively new products in this category are gas turbine engines, gasoline combustion rotating engines, and fuel cells. Engineering is divided between assembly and manufacture of individual parts.

As to GM's general approach to the patent system, its practice of seeking patent protection for new inventions made by the many employed engineers and scientists and its use of patents attest its positive attitude. The Corporation defrays the expenses of a patent organization with about 70 patent attorneys, five of whom serve in London. Many publications by members of the GM Patent Section, by the head of the Research Laboratories, and by top management bear witness that patentable inventions (including design patents) produced by employees are considered a stimulus to the originator and an asset to the Corporation.

In June 1967 Lawrence R. Hafstad, the Vice President in charge of the Research Laboratories of General Motors Corporation, gave the Kettering Award Address at the Eleventh Annual Public Conference of the Patent, Trademark, and Copyright Research Institute in Washington.[23] In this talk Hafstad touches on some employed-inventor problems, both in general and within his own corporation. Some of his remarks on general reward policy for employed inventors (pp. 169–170) are given here:

In addition to the controversy as to whether inventions are made by individuals or by a team, there is the question of how to reward inventors who choose to work as part of a team. It is true that this was not visualized in the early days when

20 Peter Drucker, *The Concept of the Corporation* (New York: New American Library, 1964), pp. 159–160.
21 Standard & Poor's *Industry Surveys,* Basic and Current Analysis (New York: May 28, 1964, sec. 2, and December 10, 1964, sec. 1).
22 "The Fortune Directory," *Fortune,* June 17, 1968.
23 "Lay Comments on the Proposed Patent Law," *IDEA* 11 (1967): 161–173.

the patent system was devised, and the patent system is certainly supposed to give incentive to the potentially creative individual to go ahead and create.

Does our present patent system provide adequate incentive for an inventor to invent when he is part of a large team?

I cannot presume to answer this very fundamental question, but can only give my impressions. First, let me say that I have been signing papers giving patent rights to some employee or other since 1940 when I left work in pure science. I have never felt "forced" to sign these papers, as current liberal writings never miss an opportunity to imply. Neither threats nor torture were used that I can remember, and to the best of my knowledge I wasn't drugged. Then why did I sign?

I believe the answer is that, for me as for most engineers, I like to consider myself a professional problem solver. The problems may or may not involve the need for inventions, but if they should, I feel as competent to invent as the next man. So many technical problems exist which do not involve inventions that as a "pro" I personally have preferred to work as a problem solver on a salary, with invention being incidental, rather than as a free lancer seeking riches from a single invention. . . .

If the overall group is successful, each member is or should be rewarded—by money, if the operation is commercial, by personal satisfaction in addition if it is in the national interest. . . .

This is the way it is—but this is not the way American folklore has it. From what I read, the employed inventor "alienates his stake in possible patents, et cetera, et cetera. . . ." The implication is that his rights are usurped by management and that the incentive to invent intended by the patent system for the individual is no longer effective. However, so long as the patent system provides the incentive for management to encourage its employees to invent, what has been lost? . . .

Profit is the index or measure of the effectiveness with which management does its job. Management has, therefore, every incentive for so arranging the working conditions of its technical employees as to encourage invention. In fact, the competition between industrial laboratories is specifically that of maximizing the output of useful technology and therefore of profitable inventions per dollar expended for research.

I am sure these remarks were not meant as a final analysis, but they may represent the attitude of large-scale research laboratory management.

An interesting detail on inventor patent policy at General Motors is mentioned in the same talk (p. 171):

On numerous occasions when inventions are made which the corporation chooses not to exploit, the patent rights are transferred or licensed to the inventor, who then (often with associates) resigns from the corporation as a "spin-off" and starts a small business of his own. In the GM laboratories this has occurred mainly in connection with instruments which were developed for specific uses in the business, but which for commercial reasons the corporation did not wish to manufacture.

The General Motors Engineering Journal (now discontinued) for many years reported several hundred new employee patents per year. Although the number appears small in comparison with the hundreds of thousands of employees, statistics published by the General Motors Patent Department indicate that U.S. patent applications filed for GM employees are increasing in spite of a national trend in the opposite direction. U.S. patents issued and applications filed between 1950 and 1966 are shown in Figure 3.2. The total number of U.S. patents granted in the name of General Motors Corporation per year from 1950 to 1965 shows a high level of activity with an average, up to 1962, of about 800 patent applications filed per year and between 600 and 800 granted. (Because of the lag in U.S. Patent Office processing, there may be more patents granted in a year than there are applications.)

The lists of inventions patented in the names of GM employees, as reported in the old *Journal,* gave an interesting insight into the inventiveness of members of various divisions. Not only the inventor's name but also his professional title,

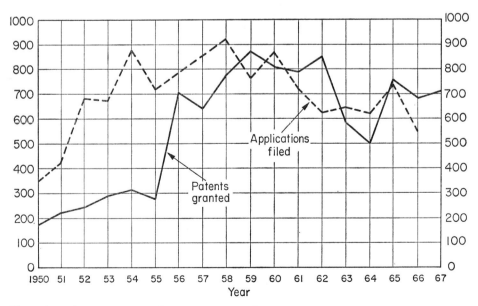

Figure 3.2 U.S. patents granted and applications filed at General Motors, 1950–1967.
Source: *General Motors Engineering Journal* and updated by GM patent department.

job title, and technical object of the patent were reported. A glance at these lists showed that the majority of patent holders had university degrees or degrees from the General Motors Institute and that many of them were senior engineers.

Assignment Policy

General Motors uses a printed standard agreement for assignment of inventions to be executed by persons seeking employment. The signing of such an agreement is asked of any employee who works with engineering or research and development. Selection of the right group of persons is left to local management and has to be exercised with some discretion, since there are no standard job descriptions and titles for employees in all General Motors corporations to serve as guideline. (That is, the job titles do not depend on education or experience, data that would be easy to obtain.) Reimbursement for the assignment of inventions and improvements (and patent applications filed or patents granted thereon) is the compensation paid for being employed by General Motors Corporation. Included in the assignment are any inventions or improvements that the signer may conceive, make, invent, or suggest. Patentability is obviously no prerequisite of assignment.

More specifically, the terms of the assignment are phrased as "relating to any matter or thing, including processes and methods of manufacture which may be connected in any way with the work (of the signer) or related in any way to the business of General Motors Corporation." The term "business" of the Corporation is extended to business "existing or anticipated."[24] The time period for which the assignment obligation is valid is any time during employment, but assignment can be requested by the Corporation at any time during or after employment. The usual condition not to reveal any information concerning these inventions, improvements, or other confidential matters is included in the assignment form. No trailer clause prohibiting an employee from entering the service of a competing company within a certain time limit occurs in the form.

It is obviously of great concern when assessing the scope of the assignment contract to define "General Motors Corporation" as employer and assignee. The Patent Section of the Corporation in "Patent Information for General Motors Employees," 1960, states in remarks on contracts involving inventions (p. 15) that "*G.M. is legally one entity*" and "*an agreement entered into for the benefit of one division will ordinarily bind the entire Corporation*" [author's italics]. This means most

---

[24] On request, information was given to the author that this may be interpreted as business "existing or anticipated" at the time when an invention was made. I do not know whether all employees are informed of this qualification, which is not contained in the contract. F.N.

likely that any invention assigned by an employee, say of the Buick Division, automatically is wholly owned by all automotive and other divisions of GM as well as by all subsidiaries in all fields, free of cost. Now, a specific invention, say improving refrigerators and assigned to Frigidaire, will have a "normal scope" within the business of this division. The picture will be different if an assigned employee invention is applicable to all passenger cars or if it is still more basic, relevant to new materials usable say in all metalworking for bodies and engines or in general metal manufacturing processes. Such inventions certainly belong to the "business" of General Motors. The interpretation does not seem unreasonable. The possible wide scope of assigned inventions of a corporation the size of GM, therefore, raises the question of special compensation or reward. Let us analyze the invention award policy of General Motors Corporation.

Award Policy

Since General Motors management strongly emphasizes decentralized operations in most of its activities, it is almost impossible to find any unified invention-award policy without access to individual management practice at a large number of plants, factories, laboratories, drafting and research departments and divisions of the Corporation. This is especially true since awards made for assigned successful inventions by employees are not based on any legal claim but have an entirely discretionary character. The employee has "contracted away" all title or other personal rights in his assignment contract. In its regular publications or press releases, General Motors reports inventions made and patents granted, but not financial or other awards given to the inventors.[25] Neither do General Motors divisions make standard payments to employees of an order of $100–300 (as is usual in some industries) for filing assigned employee patent applications and/or for patents granted. The payment of $1.00, still practiced by some GM divisions, has nothing to do with awards but satisfies the outdated formal requirement of "consideration" in patent contracts. Naturally, the ordinary incentives for good employees in industry, salary increases and promotions, are frequently used. A number of successful automotive and other inventors have later become GM directors and managers.

   A special in-house study was made by the GM Patent Section in 1963 (supplemented in 1966 on request of the author) selecting a group of 11 GM employees productive in terms of inventions and showing their experience, occupation at GM, and their

[25] Compare this procedure with that of IBM, Westinghouse Electric, RCA, and Polaroid Corp.

Table 3.4   Employment Record of Selected General Motors Employees

Starting Position at GM and Age	Final Position at GM and Age	Type of GM plant	Number of U.S. Patents Granted
1. Assistant Chief Engineer (57)	Assistant Chief Engineer (65)	Car division	1[1]
2. Metallurgist (27)	Manager, Research Staff Activities (64)	Research division	48
3. Draftsman (25)	Engineer in charge of Power Division (55)	Car division	100
4. Draftsman (23)	Executive Assistant to Vice President in charge of Engineering (55)	Car division	113
5. Development Engineer[2] (23)	Engineering Development (62)	Car division	62
6. Kiln Helper[2] (22)	Director of Research (59)	Accessory division	51
7. Toolmaker apprentice[2] (16)	Vice President and General Manager of car division (59)	Electric motor division	64
8. Designer (22)	Head, Special Problems, Research Laboratories (64)	Research laboratories	34
9. Chief Experimental Engineer[2] (28)	Staff Engineer (71)	Accessory division	87
10. Engineer (35)	Chief Engineer (63)	Accessory division	113
11. Designer (37)	Assistant Chief Engineer (57)	Research division	51

[1] Employee had 45 patents prior to employment by GM.
[2] Still employed in 1966.

advancement in the Corporation. The story is told in Table 3.4 and at more length in Appendix B.

The Corporation believes that these case histories support the point that inventive contributions of creative employees are reflected in their advancement in the Corporation. However, the examples were chosen in conjunction with awards the Michigan Patent Law Association planned to make, to recognize Michigan inventors. The aim was to choose people whose inventive contributions extended over some years; thus the list represents only long-term employees (average employment more than 33 years) who started early in almost all cases. A further limitation was that each listed employee had to be a resident of Michigan.

There exist, at least theoretically, further means of financial reward under the General Motors Bonus Plan for inventions made by employees. Such a bonus plan has been in existence since 1918, intended to provide incentive and reward to employees "who contribute to the success of the enterprise by their invention, ability, industry, loyalty or exceptional service, through making them participants in that success." Since 1957 there has also been a Stock Option Plan granting certain executive employees options to purchase General Motors common stock. These rewards, however, are not open to all employees but are restricted exclusively to a small group of high-level personnel. The minimum eligible salary rate for bonus consideration for GM employees in the United States has been $800 per month (1961), $900 per month (1963), $975 per month (1966), and $1125 per month in 1968. Stock options went in 1967 to 33 executives. Rates are fixed annually by a Bonus and Salary Committee constituted pursuant to the by-laws of the Corporation.[26] Decisions of this Committee are final and binding upon all parties but shall rely on and be bound by net earnings of the Corporation for each year (as reported in the annual statement of income), the amount of net capital, the maximum amount which may be credited to the reserve and some further figures as reported by the public accountants of the Corporation. Provisions for Bonus Plan and Stock Option Plan (before federal income tax) are shown in Table 3.5.

In 1967, 15,334 employees qualified for the Bonus Plan. They were awarded a total of $99 million. The bonus awards are partly in cash and partly in common stock, the objective being to enable the recipient to pay the income tax on his total bonus with the cash portion and retain the stock portion. The bonuses are obviously a privilege of about 2 percent of the personnel of the Corporation.[27]

Corporations in which General Motors owns substantially all the common stock and which are incorporated abroad or do most of their business abroad may have a

Table 3.5   General Motors Bonus and Stock Option Plan Expenditures 1957–1967

Year	Rounded $(millions)	Year	Rounded $(millions)
1957	80	1962	105
1958	52	1963	112
1959	84	1964	116
1960	93	1965	130
1961	81	1966	114
		1967	107

Source: *General Motors Annual Report* 1965, p. 34, and communication from Corporation, July 1968.

[26] In special cases the Committee has discretion to award bonuses to employees receiving salaries below the eligible rate.

[27] Sloan, in *My Years with General Motors,* p. 418, comes to a different figure, saying that "in 1962 some 9 percent of all salaried employees received a bonus award, compared with only 5 percent in 1922."

separate bonus plan. Separate bonus plans are actually now in effect at four
overseas manufacturing subsidiaries of the Corporation for employees not having
"home office status." Two of these subsidiaries are in England, one in Australia,
and one in Germany. Awards are payable in local currency in annual installments.

General Motors considers that substantial stock ownership by its management
is an important factor in the success of any enterprise and that this has played
an important role in bringing the Corporation to its position of industrial leadership. Further, as Alfred Sloan interprets it, this policy places executives in the
same relative position as if they were conducting a business on their own account;
each earns a reward commensurate with his own performance.[28] The incentive
is considered not solely financial but also an intangible evaluation of personal
contribution to the success of the business.

Alfred Sloan points further to the fact that the Bonus Plan provides more flexibility
in rewarding an employee than is possible under a salary system. He writes:

It may be difficult to reward a man for superior performance by raising his salary,
since the increase may upset the whole salary stratification. A salary increase,
moreover, commits the company indefinitely, whereas the bonus makes it possible
to tailor the reward to the period in which performance was unusual. And so the
Bonus Plan makes it possible for the exceptional individual to break out of the
over-all salary schedule without at the same time upsetting the schedule.[29]

These are wise words by an experienced man. They also explain why an employed
inventor "if his inventions are a superior performance" should enjoy the same
privilege. Eligibility should not be limited to a certain minimum salary per
month or year. According to statistics important inventions are, as a rule, made
by young people. Salary then is low. An incentive program should offer creative
employed inventors of all ages and degrees of education a chance "to break out of
the overall salary schedule without at the same time upsetting the schedule."
General Motors and the whole United States would derive benefit from such a plan,
especially in view of the fact that any employee by assignment in good faith turns
over all future inventions (made during employment) without special compensation.

UNITED STATES STEEL CORPORATION

General Survey

In 1967 this Corporation was the tenth largest industrial company of the United
States in terms of net sales.[30] Among the large number of companies constituting

28 *Ibid.*, p. 409.
29 *Ibid.*, p. 427.
30 "The Fortune Directory," *Fortune,* June 17, 1968.

the American steel industry the bulk of production is centered in a few. U.S. Steel Corporation belongs to the fully integrated steelmakers having blast furnaces and coke ovens to back up their steelmaking furnaces and finishing facilities. They also have their own iron ore and other mines.[31] U.S. Steel is the largest producer of most finished steel products constituting the tonnage items (flat rolled products, rails, tubular products, wire, structural steels, and heavy plate). Sales and shipments (products and services sold) amounted in 1967 to $4067.2 billion.[32] A total of 45 million net tons of ores and 19 million net tons of coal were mined; 24.3 million net tons of iron and 30.9 million net tons of raw steel. The number of employees in 1967 was 197,643. The Corporation has seven divisions: American Bridge, Oilwell, U.S. Steel Homes, U.S. Steel Products, U.S. Steel Supply, Universal Atlas Cement, and the Pittsburgh Chemical Company. It has 16 principal subsidiaries, of which 5 are foreign (3 in the Bahamas, 1 in Venezuela, 1 in Canada). The American subsidiaries include large organizations in rail and sea transportation as well as in natural gas. Equal interests (with National Distillers and Chemical Corp.) were acquired in Reactive Metals, Inc., for production of titanium and other metals and fabrication of finished mill products. The Board of Directors consists of 18 directors. There are officially 7 Executive Vice Presidents, 15 Administrative Vice Presidents, 51 Vice-Presidents, 1 General Solicitor, 3 Assistant General Solicitors, and 1 Economist.

In the steel industry, especially for fully integrated companies like U.S. Steel Corporation, wages are the principal costs in producing and transporting raw materials. The proportion of labor and employment costs per ton of steel are high. Total employment costs in the steel industry average about 40 percent of gross sales. In 1967 U.S. Steel had a total payroll of about $1.62 billion. Employee benefits for pensions, social security, taxes, insurance, unemployment, vacation, saving funds, industry welfare, and retirement funds totaled about $250 million.

Virtually all hourly employees and a sizable portion of salaried personnel in steel-producing operations are members of the United Steelworkers of America (AFL-CIO); others belong to the United Mine Workers of America.

Domestic and foreign competition for many products manufactured by U.S. Steel divisions is keen. The Corporation has suffered material "profit erosion," reflecting loss of market participation and sharply depressed results from nonsteelmaking

[31] There are approximately 22 U.S. integrated steelmakers, 60 semi-integrated companies (depending on purchase of pig iron and scrap) and 150 nonintegrated producers.
[32] Statistics in this paragraph from U.S. Steel Corp. *Annual Report*, 1967.

activities.[33] In view of relatively low profits, high labor costs, and increased competitive challenges from new technology, the Corporation is emphasizing cost reduction through more efficient steelmaking as well as elimination of unnecessary manpower. The same pressure is on innovation by research activities of other types. During the ten-year period 1957–1966 the Corporation has tripled its expenditures for research. In 1966 over 1800 scientists, technicians, and others were employed at the Research Center at Monroeville, Pennsylvania, and associated laboratories.

How does such a company approach the disposition of inventions made by its many employees? It must be stated at the outset that U.S. Steel often reports innovations and research in its annual reports and in its main house organ *U.S. Steel News*. For example, under the title "Research Pays Off"[34] the company presents three major technological developments:

A vapor-coating process, that is, an efficient, high-speed means of coating steel with other metals, for instance aluminum. The new material competes with conventional packaging materials.

A cryogenic process treating raw coke oven gas to produce a usable metallurgical fuel gas, recovering hydrogen for direct production of anhydrous ammonia.

A vacuum-deoxidized carbon steel used for heavy forgings, armor plates, heavy gauge alloy plates, and wherever ultraclean steels are needed.

In addition, a variety of new steels have been developed for specific purposes, and new column joint design and bracing systems have been devised to take hurricane loads for (to name one example) the Vehicle Assembly Building at Cape Kennedy. Roughly 1500 research projects are under study annually.

What strikes the reader when studying available publications of the company is that no attempt is made to relate these engineering achievements to the employees or groups of employees who planned the projects and translated them into reality. Neither is reference made to patents granted to company employees in connection with new products and processes. A comparison with the policy of other large companies like International Business Machines, Radio Corporation of America, and Westinghouse Electric shows the difference in approach. U.S. Steel Corporation obtained 135 patents in 1967 on employee inventions, a large majority of which are assigned to the Corporation.

Assignment Policy

U.S. Steel Corporation makes a distinction between two main groups of employees,

[33] Standard & Poor's *Industry Surveys*, 1964.
[34] *U.S. Steel News*, January 1965, p. 15.

both as to obligation in assignment of inventions, and as to types of awards given.

Group A employees are in management positions and include all salaried employees not by law, contract, or custom entitled to payment for overtime services.[35] This group of employees, by contract, assigns full title of all inventions made during employment and relating or applicable to any business in which the Corporation may be engaged.

Group B employees include all workers paid by the hour and, in short, all employees not in Group A. This group grants the Corporation a nonexclusive license to all inventions made during employment, relating or applicable to any business in which the Corporation may be engaged, and also grants an option to acquire the remaining rights on as favorable term as the employee can secure from outside parties. The reason given by U.S. Steel for the distinction of the two groups of employees is that special opportunities are open to employees in Group A to become familiar with the processes, equipment, and products of the Corporation and to conceive inventions or improvements.[36]

Neither the employees nor the business of subsidiary utility companies and subsidiary common carriers are included in the general patent policy of the Corporation as just stated. However, the assignment of title includes also all inventions and improvements relating or applicable to any business of the (consolidated) subsidiaries of the employer. The parent corporation, since it is often geographically distant from the company immediately involved, must delegate the power to manage employee patent policy to management at the spot. This policy is further supported by the fact that many operating and manufacturing divisions and plants account for their own business profits and losses. In important cases involving great sums of money central management is asked to advise and decide.

Award Policy

The monetary award system at U.S. Steel pays standard amounts geared to the two groups. Group A employees receive upon issue of each U.S. patent assigned by them to the Corporation $600, without regard to whether the invention patented is used by the Corporation. Group B employees receive $400 upon issue of each licensed U.S. patent, for which a shop right accrues to the Corporation. This payment is conditional, however; it is paid only if the invention is used by the

[35] The term "overtime" is defined in agreement with the Fair Labor Standards Act of 1938.
[36] Letter to the author, August 1966.

Corporation. The Corporation comprises in this connection all divisions and non-steel making companies as an entity.

U.S. Steel management does not believe in payment of periodical monetary awards to employee inventors. They cite the difficulty of paying awards to the proper individuals and the risk of mistakes arising from the fact that "the squeaking wheel gets the grease." Furthermore, the accounting is difficult for the employer when paying frequent awards of different size, especially when based on royalty payments.

Lump-sum awards are, however, paid to both Group A and Group B employees for inventions that in the judgment of the Corporation result in significant benefits. Such awards are not paid periodically.[37]

Like most large industrial corporations, U.S. Steel has a Stock Option Incentive Plan reserved for key management employees. One plan approved by stockholders in 1964 authorized the option and sale of up to 1,500,000 shares of common stock. The number of employees privileged by these extra payments is about 0.1 percent of the total corporate staff. None of the directors, except the three management directors, are eligible to participate in this Plan. They may have made contributions to management as inventors, but receipt of shares is not based on inventive activity.

Since U.S. Steel does not publicize or even identify employed inventors, there is no way to give typical examples or statistics. Upon inquiry information was given that even merit awards will not be mentioned "too much" in the press, house organs, or the like. Local newspapers may occasionally mention events in this field. The policy practiced by U.S. Steel deviates in this point noticeably from the practice of International Business Machines, Radio Corporation of America, and Westinghouse Electric.

INTERNATIONAL BUSINESS MACHINES CORPORATION

General Survey

IBM is the largest manufacturer of electronic data-processing systems and relevant parts and accessories such as input equipment, arithmetical units, memory units, control units, and output equipment. During 1968, sales, service, and rentals of data-processing machines and systems accounted for approximately 81 percent of the gross income; other regular products and services accounted for 15 percent.[38] The gross income from sales, services and rentals of equipment in 1968 was $6.88

[37] Communication from Corporation to the author, August 1966.
[38] IBM *Annual Report,* 1968, p. 39.

billion. The company's income is primarily derived from the rental of its own data-processing machines, but outright sale of equipment previously leased is increasing. Characteristic of IBM's activities is its extensive foreign business in sales, rentals, and research administered by a separate company, IBM World Trade Corporation. In 1967 about 30 percent of IBM's total gross revenues came from foreign operations.[39] In 1964 IBM began fully to consolidate foreign operations (subsidiaries) and domestic ones on a world-wide basis. Its participation in national space and defense programs is considerable, and it receives a continuous stream of federal government contracts. IBM furnished, in addition to data-processing equipment, advanced systems for information-handling and control for NASA's Gemini and Apollo missions.

IBM has eleven divisions in the United States and three wholly owned subsidiaries. Some of the divisions are these:

Advanced Systems Development, to explore new products and business areas.

Data Processing, to market information-handling systems and equipment in the United States.

Federal Systems, for government space and defense agencies.

Field Engineering, to service IBM systems.

Office Products, to manufacture and market electric typewriters and dictation equipment.

Systems Development and Systems Manufacturing, comprising the major development and manufacturing portion of IBM.

A research division develops advanced techniques and computer application; in addition, an Information Records division develops, manufactures, and markets punch cards, magnetic tape, paper forms and other accessories for data-processing machines and microimage equipment. The three American subsidiaries are IBM Trade Corporation which conducts all business outside the United States, Science Research Associates Inc. which develops and publishes new types of instructional materials, and the Service Bureau Corporation, offering data-processing services. IBM owns seven research laboratories in Europe, in Austria, France, Germany, Holland, Sweden, and Switzerland, and one in the United Kingdom. Advanced data-processing services are given to about 100 countries outside the United States. In Japan IBM World Trade Corp. owns a subsidiary, IBM Japan, Ltd., holding about 41 percent of the computer market. Customers are trained in IBM machine uses at more than 80 World Trade centers in all parts of the world.

Among important new products and systems are the following: IBM System 360,

[39] IBM *Annual Report,* 1968.

a comprehensive computer system; to which according to the 1964 *Annual Report,* scientific facilities in Great Britain, France, Germany, and Sweden contributed; IBM system 1050 enabling up to 40 different individuals to use the same large-scale IBM (7040) computer through a data-communication system linked to the central computer by telephone; graphic data-processing system electronically scanning, storing, and displaying graphic information; an IBM (1285) optical reader with new teleprocessing devices and units; a low-price computer with stored program; an automatic-tape typewriter for repetitive work. IBM is also extending its field of production into copying machines using electrophotography, by patent cooperation with companies in this field.

In 1968 the number of employees of the Corporation was over 241,000.[40] IBM World Trade Corporation had more than 87,000 employees of its own.[41] It opened data centers in five additional countries, bringing the count to 232 data centers in 70 countries. In a general survey of IBM's activities, one must keep in mind the impact of U.S. patent laws and antitrust laws on IBM's business. Thomas J. Watson, Jr., former president of IBM, said when talking about competitive enterprise environment as the most powerful stimulant for innovation: "Our patent laws, protecting for a specified time any individual achievements, are valuable elements of this environment. So are the antitrust laws, which help maintain both competitive stimulus to innovation and the competitive mechanism for sharing the fruits of technological change with the consumer."[42]

In January 25, 1956, the Corporation had to accommodate its actions in the patent field to a final antitrust judgment of the District Court for the Southern District of New York, which directed IBM to grant to each person nonexclusive license to make, have made, use, and vend tabulating cards, tabulating card machinery, tabulating machines or systems, or electronic data-processing machines and systems under any or all IBM existing and future patents (Section XIa). IBM was also restrained (until January 1966) from retaining the services of any individual inventor or engineer for work on the design and development of cards, machinery, and systems in these defined fields. Exempt from this ruling were employees having regular hours of employment or retired IBM employees as well as people working under contracts for research, development, or engineering services which commit the inventor or engineer to provide personal services for periods of not more than

[40] IBM *Annual Report,* 1968, p. 6.
[41] IBM *Annual Report,* 1968, p. 27.
[42] *Think Magazine,* December 1960, p. 18.

one year (Section XIIIc). The antitrust decision of the Southern District Court
will probably create a general attitude of caution on the side of the Corporation
when operating in the field of patent policy. This may have an indirect impact on
the interest of IBM to further employee inventions, at least in the United States.
In December 1968, January and June 1969, all together four civil antitrust actions
were brought against IBM (one by the Department of Justice, one by a computer
manufacturer, one by a computer-leasing company, one by a software firm). The
actions are still pending, but IBM has already decided to "unbundle" sale of
hardware and software (programs) in the United States by separate pricing
systems.[43] The independent software market will probably undergo further
upswing, and inventions in the field—if patentable—will have increased
competitive value which may to some extent accrue to programming inventors.

Assignment Policy

All employees of IBM Corporation and IBM subsidiaries in the United States on the
first day of employment must sign an "Employee Confidential Information and
Invention Agreement." The field of activities of the employing corporation in
which full title and interest must be assigned by the new employee is defined as
everything "which relates in any manner to the actual or anticipated business of
IBM or its subsidiaries, or relates to its actual or anticipated research and development; or is suggested by or results from any task to (the signee) or work performed
by (the signee) for or on behalf of IBM."

 The type of inventive work to be assigned is characterized as "any invention or
idea, patentable or not." The assignees of the contract cover IBM and its subsidiaries.
In the light of the corporate structure described in the general survey the subsidiaries at present are four United States companies. Agreements of employees
in foreign subsidiaries, in European countries and IBM Japan, Ltd., and allocation
of acquired property are regulated by agreement with the parent company. The
invention agreement enables the employer, for instance, to secure patents "in the
United States and in foreign countries." The employer limits the obligations
only to the time "while working in IBM." The consideration on which the contract
is based is the fact of employment by IBM. No provisions bind the employee after
he has left employment. Finally the assignment agreement covers any confidential
information or material relating to the business of IBM or its subsidiaries either
during or after IBM employment (except with written permission). A provision

[43] See *Datamation*, June 1969, pp. 85, 121, 276, and other computer journals.

is added that the employee will not disclose to IBM, or induce IBM to use, any confidential information or material belonging to others.

All employees have to sign an agreement of the type described, but the agreement specifies in the text that it only concerns persons "while working in IBM in an executive, managerial, planning, technical, research or engineering capacity (including development, manufacturing, systems, applied science, sales and customer engineering)." These jobs and activities seem to embrace all conceivable inventors.

In view of the fact that important inventions for IBM also stem from inventors employed in foreign subsidiaries, the invention assignment policy of IBM in other countries, especially in Germany, England, Sweden, and Japan, is of considerable interest. In general, employee-invention agreements in foreign IBM subsidiaries are patterned after the United States invention agreement to the extent permitted under local law in each country. An exception is Germany.[44] The German law concerning inventions made by employees is said to cover the relationship in such detail that IBM did not feel it necessary to adopt a specific invention agreement for its employees there. Otherwise, all employees of IBM subsidiaries sign agreements similar to the domestic one, with the respective subsidiary which employs them. Inventions become the property of the subsidiary. The eventual ownership rights in these inventions are determind by IBM intercompany agreements.[45]

Award Policy

IBM must be characterized as a corporation with a positive attitude toward incentives of different kinds for creative and inventive employees, in addition to salaries commensurate with an employee's education, skill, and performance. It is IBM's policy to reward and recognize all contributions of employees, whether domestic or foreign, and to provide the motivation and incentive for continued "excellence in performance." To fulfill this objective, when the company feels regular forms of compensation (such as salary increase and promotion) are either insufficient or inappropriate, there are several employee award plans. One of these is IBM's Invention Award Plan, which is intended to meet this objective and helps emphasize the importance of being first to conceive and develop new ideas.

All IBM employees are eligible to receive the various invention awards under

[44] See Fredrik Neumeyer, *The Law of Employed Inventors in Europe*, U.S. Senate, Subcommittee on Patents, 87th Cong., 2d sess., 1963, Study No. 30, Chapter 4.
[45] Communication to the author from IBM Vice President and Chief Scientist E. R. Piore, July 27, 1965.

the current award plan, inaugurated in 1961. The plan is in three parts. The first
part rewards employees for invention productivity prior to 1961; a total of 225
employees received awards ranging from $1000 to $3000 as provided in the Invention Achievement Award Schedule. The second part of the plan provides individual
inventor awards under the same schedule on a continuing basis. The third part
provides awards for individual inventions "of outstanding value." Each invention for which a patent application is filed is carefully evaluated to determine
both its total potential value to IBM and its possible licensing value to others. After
operating divisions and subsidiaries have made this initial determination, an
Outstanding Invention Award in the amount of $1000 is made to the inventor or
to each of several coinventors. In addition, a Corporate Headquarters' review is
made of all Outstanding Invention Awards presented during the year to determine
possible additional awards. These Corporate Awards have been $5000 or more.[46]

In addition to the awards described, inventors receive certificates confirming
their awards, and when each individual earns his first award he receives a set
of gold jewelry which identifies him within IBM as an Invention Award winner.
Each Invention Award winner is also invited to attend a dinner at the end of the
year as guest of top IBM executives, at which those inventions selected for additional corporate awards are announced.

IBM further instituted an honorary incentive system by appointing employees
"IBM Fellows"; the elected persons are scientists and engineers who have outstanding records of sustained innovation and creativity. They are free to pursue any
research project they desire in their chosen fields for a limited period of time.
They also act as consultants to other IBM scientists and executives and can in this
capacity become potential inventors and coinventors of patentable inventions.

Examples of IBM *Awards*

In May 1968 four IBM Fellows were appointed by the chairman of the board,
Thomas Watson, Jr. These appointments have a tenure of five years, renewable
at the discretion of management. One Fellow had made innovations in high-
speed circuits; another had made various contributions to laser technology. Of
the other two, one was rewarded for his work on electric typewriters and the other
for improvement of magnetic tape drives and magnetic ink character recognition
machines.

At the same time 33 IBM scientist employees received Corporate awards totaling

[46] Rules are somewhat modified where patent applications for employee inventions are
filed only in countries outside the United States.

$350,000. The largest, for $50,000, went to two employees in the Poughkeepsie plant who had analyzed a composite memory design that increases the speed and capacity of a computer. This was to be used in System 360. An award of $45,000 went to two men who had invented an automatic interrupt feature for computers; a $40,000 award was given to four people, one of them a woman, for development of algorithms to increase the efficiency of compiled computer programs. Three men received $25,000 for a print hammer actuator, and two English employees in the Hursley Laboratory received $20,000 for a functional memory concept that simplifies computer operations.

It may be interesting to note that foreign IBM employees have contributed substantially to computer developments and have been recipients of sizable awards. In 1964 four English employees shared a $40,000 award for a technique for storing machine-control information in a read-only memory for the 360 Model 40. Another $40,000 award went to eight employees, one in France the others in the United States, for the conception and design of FORTRAN, the widely accepted (but unpatented) computer language. Another French engineer, working in the French laboratory of the IBM World Trade Corporation, received $10,000 for contributions to the field of high-speed printers and data cartridges.

IBM has found that inventor reaction to the award program has been "conspicuously favorable." There is said to be much greater awareness of and interest in inventions and patents and "obvious pride in display of the certificates and jewelry, as well as satisfaction with monetary awards." The only dissatisfaction with the plan was the apparent discrimination against those employees whose work offers limited possibility for invention. This was met by introducing a complementary Outstanding Contribution Award Plan for employee achievements other than inventions.[47] The company stated that it was too early to tell if there will be a long-term improvement in invention quality, but definite increase in number and completeness of disclosures was observed, an improvement that in itself justified the cost of the program.[48]

WESTINGHOUSE ELECTRIC CORPORATION

General Survey

In contrast to IBM, General Motors, and Polaroid, Westinghouse Electric Corporation is one of the most diversified industrial corporations of the United States

[47] "Invention Award Program at International Business Machines," in Carl Baumes, *Patent Counsel in Industry* (New York: NICB Business Policy Study No. 112, 1964), p. 39.
[48] Westinghouse Electric Company had other results. See the following study.

in terms of products. The company manufactures some 300,000 variations of 8000 basic products in the electrical field at nearly 100 plants throughout the United States. The products fall into six principal groups: electric utility, industrial, construction, consumer, electronic components and specialty products, and a group of atomic, defense, and space products. Electric utility and industrial groups supply varieties of equipment for generating, transmitting, and distributing electrical energy: from steam and gas turbines, generators, and transformers to motors, marine propulsion, and welding equipment. The construction group serves the building industries with such products as lamps, elevators, and equipment for lighting and air conditioning. The electronic components group ranges from electronic tubes and semiconductor devices to ceramics and laminates. Some of the most significant defense and space systems of the United States are developed by Westinghouse's atomic, defense and space group: reactors for atomic submarines, surface ships, and atomic power plants. The consumer group concentrates on lines of products for the home and apartment builder, including such products as electric appliances, television and radio receivers, and vending machines.

This industrial empire is kept going by 132,000 employees (1967). Annual sales in that year amounted to $2.9 billion.[49] Research has been "the life-blood of Westinghouse" ever since its founder George Westinghouse started production of a new transformer in 1886. Strong tradition since that time in pioneering engineering accomplishments and patent ownership has made Westinghouse Electric "invention- and patent-minded." During his lifetime (1846–1914) George Westinghouse was credited with 316 patents, receiving his first patent at the age of 19. The company advertised in *The New York Times*, November 11, 1956:

The company recognizes this debt to its creative men, and every effort is made not only to free the engineer for his best creative efforts but to reward him for his contributions. In addition to liberal invention and patent awards, the inventor receives professional recognition for his contributions and consideration by management for advancement in his field.

Today, the Westinghouse Research Laboratories are located on a 100-acre site outside Pittsburgh; they employ some 1500 research scientists, engineers, and supporting personnel. Additional research and development is under way at a number of the company's nearly 100 plants such as the Astronuclear Laboratory and the High Power Laboratory. Pioneering work goes on in molecular electronics for outer space equipment and development of superconducting magnets as well

[49] "The Fortune Directory," *Fortune,* June 15, 1968.

as in the area of direct energy conversion by fuel cells, thermoelectricity, thermionic conversion, and magnetohydrodynamics. The company's total cost of research and engineering, including the services of about 8000 scientists and engineers, amounted in the 1960's to more than $200 million annually (more than 10 cents for every dollar of sales). The creative engineering activities of Westinghouse involve cooperation with a large number of other outside enterprises. The company engages 25,000 suppliers, and under its contract with the Atomic Energy Commission to build the nuclear reactor for the first atomic submarine (*Nautilus*) it was assisted by more than 3000 subcontractors. To distribute their products overseas the Westinghouse Electric International Company employs, besides their own company representatives, over 350 independent distributors in 166 countries and territories. Ideas for engineering development emanate also from these sources.

It is not surprising, looking at this simplified summary and at the historical origin of Westinghouse Electric Corporation, that this Corporation values new inventions and discoveries applicable to engineering. The positive view on the value of patent protection is probably a heritage from its founder, George Westinghouse, and his coworkers.

In a recent survey of the value of patents in industrial corporations, the General Patent Counsel of Westinghouse, T. L. Bowes, lists the advantages patents can offer.[50] "Patents help commercially through increased volume of sales at better profit margins," he states as a first advantage, and adds, "Patents also make it possible to realize, through lower product costs or higher sales prices, better profits than are possible when a product is just like that of a competitor."[51] In conclusion he says:

Recognition resulting from the obtaining of patents is important to engineers and is probably a factor in stimulating their creativity. Since corporate leadership requires continuous creativity, and market position benefits from invention activity, inducements to spur creativity and invention activity are worth while. Patents and the recognition they bring are one form of inducement.

There are more than 60 separate engineering activity units at Westinghouse (in the United States only) exclusive of service, repair, sales, and warehouse operations, and these are grouped under six vice presidents. The management believes that for fostering inventiveness in such a dispersed and diversified organization a

[50] T. L. Bowes, "Patents and the Corporation" in *IDEA* 10 (1966): 75 ff.
[51] In the author's opinion, this is another clear testimonial to the general value of an active employee-invention policy as part of the management of a progressive corporation.

system for stimulating employees to come forward with their new ideas is necessary as well as a means for evaluation and reward of the disclosures. Employee suggestion systems at Westinghouse go as far back as 1910 and the invention award plan (Meritorious Disclosure Award) to 1937.

In 1966, 553 U.S. Patents were granted to Westinghouse and 565 in 1967.[52] How the employee-invention policy of Westinghouse has developed is briefly described here.

Patent Assignment Policy

It is the policy of the Corporation to enter into patent agreements with all employees it believes are in a position, because of the nature of the work to which they are assigned or may be assigned, to conceive or make inventions, discoveries, or improvements within the existing or contemplated scope of the Corporation's business, or the business of companies that it owns or controls. The employee who signs the patent agreement agrees to assign all such inventions, discoveries, or improvements (whether or not patentable), together with such U.S. and foreign patents that may be obtained thereon, to the Corporation.

The agreement to assign applies to those inventions conceived or made while in the employ of the Corporation; there is no trailer clause that requires the assignment of any invention conceived or made after termination of employment. Westinghouse, like many other large corporations, does not believe that a restrictive provision of this kind is necessary or proper.[53]

The Westinghouse Patent Agreement also contains a provision to prohibit the employee, without the written approval of the Corporation, to use, publish, disclose, or authorize anyone else to use, publish, or disclose any information that is confidential or proprietary in nature (including processes and formulas) and that is acquired in the course of his employment. This provision is effective during the term of employment and subsequent thereto.

While the Division Managers of the Corporation, who are responsible for profits, have some discretion in selecting the employees who shall execute the patent agreement, it is the general policy of the Corporation that it be executed by all technical, professional, and management employees. These employees must be in

[52] Communication to the author, October 1968.
[53] There are a number of reasons for this attitude. Such clauses may be vulnerable for legal attack if too broad; there may be no practical need for them, or they may be inefficient in practice in a labor market as big as the American one. A weighty reason is that such clauses "work both ways," i.e., they impede the mobility of professional employees, which is not in the corporation's interest.

a position, because of the nature of their work assignment, degree of access to technical information and data, and working relationship with engineers and scientists to make inventions, discoveries, and improvements. Among the occupations that normally require a patent agreement are the design, research, and other engineers, scientists, draftsmen, laboratory technicians and assistants, patent attorneys, and technical writers. In technological fields that are developing fast it is felt the Corporation has to go "farther down" on the scale of employees who should sign the assignment agreement.

Even though the technical and professional employees of the Corporation are required to execute the patent agreement, the Corporation has a rather liberal invention release policy that enables the employee-inventor to personally exploit his invention. A release will usually be granted when requested on any invention covered by a disclosure on which a Disclosure Committee has decided against the filing of a patent application, provided that: (1) government rights are not involved or will not be involved, (2) the invention disclosed is not considered to be a trade secret, and (3) the release would not be adverse to the corporate interest. The release, when granted, reserves to the Corporation a royalty-free, nonexclusive license to make, use, and sell the invention, and such additional rights as are necessary to meet its commitments to others.

Award Policy

Westinghouse Electric has a long-standing tradition of incentive systems for creative employees. There are two such systems, the Suggestion System, and the Invention Disclosure System, administered separately. All employees on the active roll are eligible to submit ideas under either system. The majority of "suggestions" are submitted by nontechnical people and most awards are paid to them. (Suggestions may be of a nontechnical type or otherwise nonpatentable.) Those in executive or managerial positions are not eligible for such awards. Suggestion awards may range from $5 to a maximum of $15,000. Suggestions dealing with calculable savings are awarded 10 percent of the gross savings or 20 percent of the net savings during the first year of use of the suggestion. Some 12,000 to 14,000 suggestions are received per year from 8000 to 10,000 participants. Total annual awards paid are approximately $270,000.

The Disclosure System, as it has existed since 1937, is for the purpose of rewarding employees for meritorious disclosures of inventions and to stimulate the submission of such disclosures. The system is not rigid and has gone through different stages of evolution, a recent one being a modification in 1964, effective January 1, 1965.

This change was intended to emphasize quality rather than quantity and will be discussed after describing the basic Four-Point Invention Award Plan as it stood up to 1965.

Part 1, the Meritorious Disclosure Award   Fifty dollars was paid for each invention disclosure judged meritorious by a Disclosure Committee (about 50 percent of the disclosures submitted).

Part 2, the Most Meritorious Disclosure Award, provided for the selection of the most meritorious disclosure from each 50 submitted and evaluated. The award was $200 to a sole inventor and $300 to be divided equally among two or more inventors. This award was not limited to "cream of the crop" inventors; it could be earned by young people not yet in a position to make outstanding inventions but who were to be thus encouraged for more important disclosures in the future.

Part 3, the Award for Patent Applications   Fifty dollars was paid to each inventor on each application assigned to Westinghouse when the application was filed in the U.S. Patent Office. This award was also paid whenever the Corporation assigned the application to the government or a government agency or where the government filed a disclosure reported to it by the corporation.

Part 4, the Special Patent Award for contributions of outstanding commercial importance to the corporation. Disclosure committees made nominations to be approved by the Division Manager and forwarded for approval to a Patent Award Committee consisting of certain top executives. Two conditions had to be satisfied: the U.S. patent must have been issued (or important claims allowed), and the invention must have proved to be of exceptional value to the company in its commercial operations. The award ranged from $1000 to $5000 per inventor. If the patented invention should prove to be of continuing exceptional value to the company, a subsequent award could be made.

In addition to the substantial monetary awards each inventor received a certificate stating that "This invention is considered to be of outstanding importance by reason of its substantial contribution to advanced products for our Company, to improved service to our customers, and to the creation of employment for his fellow man."

The Westinghouse management feels that promotion by financial rewards should be supplemented by publicity for the individual and for groups receiving awards. For example, in 1964 a patent citation program was initiated by the Patent Department to give extra recognition to Westinghouse inventors. Certificates and plaques are officially given to employees on the basis of the number of U.S. patents granted and assigned to Westinghouse. Wide publication is given these events in the *Westinghouse News* and its many local editions.

Behind the intensive and widespread invention-disclosure system of Westinghouse, as described, stood a doctrine developed by the employer, that in a large multi-unit, widely dispersed company with a wide variety of personalities in management and supervision, it would be proper to establish a standard for invention submissions common to all units.[54] A minimum number of disclosures seemed to be required to cover "the design and development effort of the Corporation as a whole." A central administration operated a Disclosure Bogey System. The bogey was a numerical standard of performance, set up as a mark to be attained, as in a contest. A "bogey engineer," then, is an engineer whose job assignments are such as to make reasonably possible an opportunity to invent, encompassing all research, development, and design engineering. At least one disclosure of invention per year was expected from each bogey engineer or scientist.[55] In establishing annual "disclosure bogeys" the Patent Department considered further the possibility for inventive contributions and the past record of disclosure submissions, as well as the diversity of product. (A division producing a multiplicity of small domestic appliances has more disclosures per "bogey engineer" than one producing, say, large turbine generators.) Engineering managers reported each year the number of "bogey engineers" and their activity toward establishing a disclosure bogey set by the central Patent Department. The number of disclosures was not necessarily directly related to the development effort in dollars.

Effective January 1, 1965, the Invention Award Plan was revised primarily to place greater emphasis on quality. The "meritorious" and "most meritorious" awards were eliminated and replaced by a standard invention award of $200 to a sole inventor or $300 to be divided equally between joint inventors for each disclosure on which the filing of a patent application is authorized by a Disclosure Committee.

A new award known as the Patent Award provided for the payment of $500 to each inventor upon the issuance of each five U.S. patents after January 1, 1965. This award is payable on patents obtained by and assigned to the government

[54] Compare this to the decentralized approach by General Motors and United States Steel Corporation.
[55] Other engineers whose duties are related to less technological matter are not treated as if consistent inventive output is expected, although they also may make inventions.

based upon disclosures reported under R&D contracts as well as on patents obtained by and assigned to Westinghouse.

The Special Patent Award was retained and modified to eliminate the upper limit of $5000 so that it is now $1000 and up without limit. In this way the award can be more in line with the value of the invention to the Corporation. As under the old system, subsequent awards may be made where the patented invention is of continuing value to the Corporation, and all of these are kept confidential until the time of the presentation.

The certificate and plaque awards were also retained in the revised plan on the same basis as before. As of January 1, 1966, 16 inventors had received the bronze plaques for 50 or more patents, and 580 inventors had received certificates for 5, 10, and 25 or more patents.

Experience with the bogey system over a number of years ended with its discontinuance under the new plan, primarily because it placed greater emphasis upon quantity of disclosures than upon quality of the invention disclosed. The abandonment of the system has indeed resulted in a reduction in the number of disclosures submitted, but there is no indication so far that the number of worthwhile disclosures has been reduced. In spite of the reduction in number of disclosures submitted there has been no reduction in the number of disclosures authorized for filing by the various disclosure committees. With the elimination of the bogey these committees find the task of evaluating disclosures much less burdensome.

Under the new plan, management of each Division assumes the responsibility for (1) obtaining the submission of disclosures covering inventions resulting from its own commercial activities as well as government R&D contract activities, (2) assignment of a Division disclosure, (3) acknowledgment to inventors of receipt of disclosure, (4) evaluation of the disclosure and authorization for filing, and (5) notification to inventors of the action taken on their disclosures by use of a Notification to Inventor form.

It is obvious that the Westinghouse monetary award systems are all based on payments of lump sums. In an interesting correspondence with the Patent, Trademark, and Copyright Foundation (now the Patent, Trademark, and Copyright Research Institute of The George Washington University) in Washington in 1961, Westinghouse's Patent Counsel T.L. Bowes discusses the Corporation's objection to royalty payments.[56] Bowes points to the fact that a fair price for the

use of an employee's invention might vary from practically zero in one case
to six or seven percent or even more in other cases. An average royalty would be
too high for some inventions and not enough for others. Addition of this form
of cost to sales price is said, in certain cases, to price a product out of the market
in fields in which the profit margins are close, especially if the product embodies
a number of different patents. Television receivers are cited as an example. Bowes
further raises the question of the appropriate basis on which the royalty should
be paid. As an example he cites an invention related to the hardening of a turbine
blade: it would not be fair to give a percentage of the selling price of a complete
turbine, yet it might be difficult and costly to determine the proportionate selling
price represented by a blade itself. Design improvements of a nonpatentable
nature are hard to recompense adequately, and commercially successful products
may owe their success to a long chain of preceding improvements made by others.
Expensive bookkeeping related to payment of royalties is also mentioned.[57]

RADIO CORPORATION OF AMERICA

General Survey

RCA has been for many years a leading manufacturer and developer in all phases
of electronic engineering, television, and radio broadcasting in the United States.
During recent years its participation in electronic data-processing and computer-
building has increased. A ten-year patent-licensing accord with Siemens
A.G. of West Germany, covering the mutual granting of patent licenses for
manufacture and sale of data-processing equipment and exchange of technical
information has reinforced this position.

RCA uses patents to protect the results of its own research activities in the United
States and abroad. Up to 1956 patents were often licensed on a packaged basis,
especially in the field of radio. The consent judgment on the basis of the Sherman
antitrust law brought this part of the patent policy to an end in the United States.
RCA now licenses each patent individually in this field, and each bears its own

[57] I do not deny some of the disadvantages and costs involved in royalty award payments,
especially in large industrial corporations and in connection with complex products
consisting of many parts, but I believe that, once carefully calculated, a royalty award
in some fields gives a fair and convenient solution to the award problem. An employee
who has a managerial influence on the production, change, and sale of the product
improved by his inventions should *not* get any royalty award. In certain countries, such as
Germany, royalty payment as compensation for employee inventions is prohibited for
employees in Civil Service lest conflict of interest be involved. Even U.S. law bars or limits
some government employees from patenting activities (Patent Office employees) or from
suing the government (under certain circumstances) for compensation for use of patented
inventions.

royalty rate. The number of U.S. patents issued annually to RCA and its subsidiaries usually runs between 300 and 400.

Operation profits for the year 1967, after taxes, were $147.509 million; government sales contributed less than 10 percent after taxes.[58]

Color television has achieved the status of a billion-dollar industry in the U.S., and in this field RCA leads as top manufacturer of tubes, sets, studio equipment, service, and broadcasting. RCA has made considerable contributions to space technology in the form of new television senders, communications satellites (Relay 2), and weather satellites (Tiros series). It shares work in a lunar mobile laboratory (MOLAB), a lunar Rover vehicle and the Apollo lunar space program. In 1967 RCA was awarded a Navy contract to build 12 navigational satellites under the technical direction of the Applied Physics Laboratory at Johns Hopkins University. Electronic projects within the company include the development of devices to generate electric power directly from heat, large superconductive magnets, semiconductor improvements, integrated circuitry, lasers, and ferrite memories.

In 1967, RCA had in the United States and abroad 128,000 employees. The technical staff at the largest research center, David Sarnoff Research Center in Princeton, N.J., comprised in 1966 slightly more than 450 physicists, chemists, mathematicians, metallurgists, and electrical engineers. In addition, approximately 850 persons are employed in various administrative and service operations supporting the research program. In 1967 an experimental integrated electronic circuit was built, which will provide the basis for a new high-speed auxiliary computer memory.

RCA owns also two small basic research laboratories abroad, one in Switzerland and one in Japan. Foreign subsidiaries are located in Argentina, Brazil, Canada, Chile, Mexico, Venezuela, Puerto Rico, India, Australia, England, Italy, Spain, and Taiwan.

Assignment Policy

Anyone who is employed or is about to be employed in certain capacities by any RCA division has to sign an employee-invention agreement, the wording of which has been subject to certain changes in 1955, 1962, and 1964.

In this document the field of activities of the employer covered by the assignment are inventions that "relate to the business or interests of the Corporation or any business in which the Corporation has an interest, or (which) result from tasks assigned to the person signing by the Corporation." The concepts of "business"

[58] Data on RCA from "The Fortune Directory" and from RCA *Annual Report,* 1967.

and "interests" are supposed to be interpreted as those existing at the time of making the invention.

The types of creative work covered are "contributions and inventions," "contributions" referring mainly to unpatentable suggestions or discoveries.

The contracting party is called "the Corporation," and this includes foreign companies owned by RCA as well as all domestic plants, divisions, and subsidiaries. The agreement covers the right to obtain and protect rights for RCA "in any or all countries."

The assignment is valid during the period of employment only. If the employee is transferred by written order of the Corporation to an occupation in which his responsibilities do not include the making of technical or other contributions or inventions, the obligation to assign shall not extend to any such results made or conceived during such transfer. This provision should be interpreted to mean that an employee transferred to nonengineering work in the Corporation is not compelled to assign an invention to RCA even if the invention is in RCA's field of activity. Inventive results originating in the performance of a government contract or relating to subject matter of such a contract to be awarded in the future are excepted from this regulation. There are no provisions binding the employee in regard to his inventions after he has left the service of the corporation. RCA has intentionally abstained from the "trailer clause" which by many employers is considered detrimental to the mobility of engineering and research experts and often obstructs the hiring of valuable employees, especially R&D personnel.

The consideration necessary for a valid assignment contract is expressed as "in consideration of the salary paid," formerly as "in the consideration" of the employment of the assignor.[59]

Finally the agreement covers another group of intangible assets other than inventions, namely confidential information, including trade secrets, relating to the business of the corporation which the employee may acquire during or as a result of his employment. Such material may not be disclosed by the employee either during the term of his employment or at any time thereafter without prior written authorization from the corporation. Reference to other types of information which an employee may acquire and which he can disclose or use without detriment to the corporation was excluded from the agreement form of 1964.

[59] Salary or wages paid an employee is an adequate consideration for agreement to assign inventions made by the employee during the period of employment. See Ridsdale Ellis, *Patent Assignments*, third ed. (New York: Baker Voorhis, 1955), paragraph 164 (with citation of relevant court decisions).

The 1964 contract form modifies the groups of employees asked to sign the agreement. These groups are characterized as "those who in the natural course of events may be brought in touch with the problems which are from time to time presented to the Corporation for solution, and with the efforts which are being made by various engineers attached to the Corporation to solve these problems." This definition seems to include R&D employees. The selection of employees asked to sign assignment agreements is administered in a decentralized way by the employment managers at each company location, who have lists of covered occupations expressed in local terminology. A general listing of 13 occupations subject to assignment contract includes 11 types of engineers concerned with the following: design, development, research, machine design, tool design, manufacturing development, process, time study, installation or maintenance, sales, commercial, test equipment design, and students and trainees. To this listing belong further technicians assigned to work directly with engineering personnel, engineering supervisors, and managers who directly or indirectly supervise any listed occupation. Members of the patent staff are also included in the selected groups of employees who must sign an invention-assignment agreement. The lists are reviewed from time to time for conformity with general policy. The Corporation expects that, in the classified jobs, performance may result in patentable inventions or other contributions to the best operation of the firm. It is difficult to classify repairmen who later pass over to contract work, changing the character of their activity. Jobs are often classified differently by different branches within the firm, for instance by divisions concerned with manufacture, as distinct from those concerned with research or service. In government work, jobs usually have their own titles and definitions. In the case of RCA this is of importance in the field of government contract work, especially in atomic energy and space research. Job classification and their changes are a matter for constant surveillance by unions and professional employee organizations. As a rule, unions in their negotiations with employers object to extending the groups of union members in "covered occupations," which means occupations in which men are hired to invent or are expected to make inventions during employment. There is, on the other hand, a desire on the employer's side to avoid signing up all employees. This is said to be both impractical and expensive.[60]

Award Policy

The vice president then in charge of the Patent Department of the Radio Corporation of America wrote in 1939:

[60] For a different attitude, see the case study of Westinghouse Electric.

RCA has no system for making special awards for inventions but endeavors to compensate its inventors in proportion to the general value of their services, the same as other employees. Most inventions are made by research workers and engineers who, directly or indirectly, are assigned problems that come to the attention of RCA, and who are employed primarily or partly to solve them on its behalf.[61]

He adds that in the evolution of an article into commercial form inventions are made, and valuable but unpatentable ideas become incorporated. Under these circumstances, it is impractical in most instances to single out for special recognition the contributions of any one person without causing injustice to others. The most equitable method for compensating the participating employees is said to be by salaries commensurate with the overall value of their services.[62] However, RCA has practiced for some time a system of differential awards for employees, especially for engineers and scientists. In addition, RCA encourages employees by providing "reward satisfactions," increased rank in the organization and more autonomy in their work. The effectiveness of such rewards can be assessed only by extensive case studies.[63]

The Corporation selects annually a small number of employees in engineering and science from different parts of the organization to receive special awards. These are called The David Sarnoff Outstanding Achievement Awards. Examples (1968) of the contributions recognized are as follows:

The Individual Award in Science
"For conception and application of the solution regrowth technique for making semiconducting devices."

The Team Award in Science
"For team performance in conceiving cryoelectric memories and developing necessary theoretical understanding and technologies for their realization."

The Individual Award in Engineering
"For the conception of electronic techniques to determine accurately the response of the total television system, including lenses and photographic films."

The Team Award in Engineering
"For design, development, and installation of a computer-controlled fully automatic production test system for the on-line electrical test of color kinescopes."

[61] Otto S. Schairer, *Patent Policies of Radio Corporation of America* (New York: RCA Institutes Technical Press, 1939), p. 12.
[62] *Ibid.*, p. 13.
[63] An important study analyzing the organizational environment of an industrial research laboratory is presented by Simon Marcson in *The Scientist in American Industry* (New York: Harper & Row, 1960).

The number of employees selected for these awards is small in view of the total number of professional employees, however.

An award not immediately related to the Company but also bearing the name of David Sarnoff (a former President, now Chairman of the Board) is the Institute of Electrical and Electronic Engineers annual award of $1000, a gold medal, and a certificate to an individual or group chosen by an IEEE committee. RCA contributes the money for this award, but it may go to any persons, within or without RCA.

In addition, outstanding contributions made by members of RCA laboratories are announced annually in a special edition of RCA *News.* Between 20 and 30 achievement awards are published each year. One part of the award is given to individual employees for such attributes as ingenuity in devising new procedures, research leading to new techniques, or key contributions to a development. The other part, roughly half, is given to teams of two to five employees. Here again development is mentioned, "conceiving and developing" scientific programs, "synthesis and investigation" of new products, and others. Each recipient is presented with a gold medal, a citation referring to his contribution, and a cash award. The amount of the cash award is not disclosed.

Besides this special award policy, the Corporation also bestows a standard cash honorarium on employees who make inventions, under two conditions: The inventions must either form the basis for each original United States or complete foreign patent application assigned to RCA, or they must be approved for publication by the Corporation (as an "RCA Technical Note"). This applies also to patent applications that at RCA's request are assigned to the U.S. Government with a license or other rights reserved to RCA. These cash honoraria are used by the Corporation to recognize inventing employees engaged in government contract work (where title to inventions passes to government), in the same way as inventors who have assigned their rights to the Company. The Company feels that government-contract inventors should not be in a less favored position regarding rewards than the other employed inventors.[64] In 1967 honoraria were given for 326 patent applications and 40 "Technical Notes," of which 15 were government-filed applications.

The standard payments are $200 to each employee of RCA, including an employee of any domestic or foreign subsidiary who is named as the sole inventor of an assigned filed patent application, or a total of $250 divided equally among

[64] The government applies through the U.S. Civil Service Commission an official government reward policy for inventors from which industrial employees, including RCA employees, in many cases benefit considerably. Compare government chapter of this book.

employees named as joint inventors. The honorarium provided by this policy has also often been paid to an inventor no longer in the employ of the Corporation or a subsidiary. A honorarium of $75 is paid to each employee (or a total of $100 divided equally among joint inventors) for an invention disclosed to RCA and approved for publication as a "Technical Note." Honoraria paid to inventors are considered additional compensation and are subject to withholding and other payroll taxes.

RCA has various other ways of giving professional recognition to its employees. It bestows the title of "Fellow" on scientists of the RCA Laboratories if they have done outstanding work. This title carries no tangible reward but seems to be appreciated by the recipients, who may be allowed more freedom to pursue personal research projects. RCA also nominates (by way of its chief engineers and research directors) candidates for the degree of Fellow in the national professional societies such as IEEE and SMPT.

In addition to the award systems that have been described, RCA has a more general Incentive Plan, primarily for key employees, which must be approved annually by shareholders and which provides incentive awards "in recognition of employee's contributions to success of the Corporation's operations." These payments cover different kinds of meritorious activities of employees which may include new inventions but are not limited to them. The awards may be cash or part cash and part RCA common stock, the stock shares being valued in accordance with provisions made by the Plan. Stock payments are made in installments, with dividends, over a number of years. For instance, in 1966 the employees who received these awards had $4.214 million as first installments, with $9.723 million payable as deferred installments over the following four years. In 1964 the Incentive Plan was extended for five years by vote of the stockholders.

TRW, INCORPORATED

General Survey

Although the original corporation was active in the metal-welding field more than 60 years ago, TRW (Thompson Ramo Wooldridge) today is a firm with extensive diversification of research, manufacture, service, and sales of sophisticated engineering products in various fields, both in the United States and abroad. The principal plant and executive corporate headquarters are at Euclid, Ohio, but other plants, owned and operated by the Company and its subsidiaries are in many other states, Colorado, Connecticut, California, Florida, Illinois, Indiana, Michigan, Missouri, Montana, Nebraska, New York, New Jersey, Ohio, Pennsylvania, Tennessee, Texas, Virginia.[65]

[65] TRW *1967 Annual Report.*

TRW is organized in five groups:

Automotive group

Manufactures marine and aircraft engines and parts such as engine valves and valve train parts, pistons and piston rings, turbochargers, hydrostatic steering systems, hydraulic motors.

Equipment group

Designs and manufactures jet engine components, fuel pumps, pneumatic and mechanical actuating units for aircraft, static inverters, total energy control systems. Conducts extensive research in materials such as protective coatings for high-temperature high-strength metals.

Electronics group

Manufactures color television convergence yokes, auto radio tuners, variable capacitors, mica compression trimmer capacitors, zener diodes, specialized semiconductor subassemblies and microminiature devices.

Systems group

Designs and builds satellites for defense, space exploration, commercial and military communications. Develops systems engineering and integration of missile systems, spacecraft propulsion and related electronics systems. Conducts research in biosciences, materials, lasers and holography, and chemical processes.

Industrial operations

Provides analytical, research, and development services, electro-optical instruments, ultra high-speed cameras and spectrographic equipment, and services such as supervisory control systems.[66]

TRW owns voting control of subsidiaries in Argentina, Australia, Brazil, Canada, England, France, Japan, Mexico, Switzerland, and West Germany. It has joint international ventures and technical agreements with France, United States, United Kingdom, Sweden, and Germany.

Total net sales of TRW in 1967 passed the $1 billion mark. There were over 60,000 employees.

Invention Assignment Policy

TRW asks all technically associated employees to sign an invention and confidential information agreement. In consideration of his employment and the compensation paid for working for the employer the signing employee assigns title to TRW Inc. for certain types of defined inventions. Assignee is the Company, any other company

[66] Technical assistance in space technology is also given to member companies of the European Space Research Organization (ESRO).

it owns or controls and for whom the employee may work, or their successors in business (this may be an American or foreign corporation). TRW's domestic assignment policy has not been extended to the foreign subsidiaries.[67]

The inventions to be assigned to TRW cover all inventions made or conceived, solely or jointly with others, during the period of employment, whether patentable or not, provided they meet the following conditions:

The invention must be made or conceived "within the existing or contemplated scope of the employer's business" or relating to any subject matter with which the work of the employee for the employer is or may be concerned.

The invention must be made or conceived "with the use of the employer's time, material or facilities."

The invention must "relate to machines, processes, devices, compositions of matter, or ornamental designs for articles of manufacture, now made, used or sold by the employer, or which the employer may hereafter, during the period of employment, make, use or sell."

The invention must have been incorporated or utilized, or may hereafter "be incorporated or utilized, by the employer, in the manufacture, use or sale of machines, devices, compositions of matter, processes, or ornamental designs for articles of manufacture."

The signee must transfer all rights to unpatented inventions which the signee owns when signing the agreement (except those expressly reserved).

The invention agreement further contains a clause saying that any invention disclosed to anyone or for which a patent application is filed by the signee within six months after the termination of the employment shall be presumed to have been made during employment. Inventions conceived and made by the employee after termination of employment belong to the employee, but he expressly assumes the responsibility of proving these facts.

Regarding confidential information the agreement stipulates that the signee will not disclose nor use without the employer's written consent "any information, knowledge or data" which relate to "formulas, methods, machines, compositions, inventions, developments, improvements or otherwise which is or is treated by employer or third party as a private trade secret, or proprietary." The signee also has to comply with contract provisions between government agencies (or their

[67] Communication from TRW to the author, May 1967. One reason may be legal restrictions in other countries.

contractors) and the employer regarding invention rights and defense information. Finally, the employer reserves the right to notify anyone employing the signee after leaving TRW of the existence and provisions of the agreement.

Invention Award Policy

According to the Invention Award Plan started by TRW January 1, 1961, the company and its wholly owned subsidiaries (in the United States) paid an award of three shares of TRW common stock, plus the monetary equivalent of two shares to each employee who is applicant for a U.S. patent covering an invention that is the property of the company (or the subsidiary). This award program has been changed as of 1968; the award winner now receives a flat payment of $200, subject to deductions. The money is paid upon assignment of the disclosure to the company.[68]

Employees have to submit any invention believed to be useful to a Patent Evaluation Committee for consideration. Such a committee exists for each of TRW's divisions. The committees consist of three to five members, one of whom must be from the Corporate Staff, and others include the Chief Engineer and a member of the Patent Department responsible for the division's work. The division committee has final authority in approving the filing of a patent application and the payment of patent awards. A decision not to approve filing of a patent application does not constitute a waiver of the right of ownership by the Company. Final eligibility for an award occurs as of the date the patent application and its assignment are signed by the inventor.

The TRW Invention Award Plan does not apply to all inventions disclosed by employees but depends on selection by a company committee approving or refusing patent application and payment of award from case to case. All employees except officers, patent counsel, and members of patent departments are eligible for the invention award.

The total number of unexpired U.S. employee patents owned by TRW was 1233 in May 1967.

Employee Suggestion System

Any TRW employee can use the TRW Employee Suggestion System for submitting ideas which are beyond his job classification or work assignment. However, research and development personnel are not eligible, nor are engineers of any type, designers, supervisory employees, cost analysts, trouble shooters, department mechanics,

[68] Communication from TRW to the author, November 1968.

advertising personnel, or production planners. Why these potentially inventive employees are excluded is not known. It may be that they are in a position to influence selection of projects, or they may be rewarded in other ways. Perhaps the reasoning is that they are hired expressly to invent and improve. Other ineligible personnel includes officers of the company and its subsidiaries who are engaged in the administration of suggestion plans.

Cash awards above scheduled wages are paid to eligible employees for original suggestions adopted and put in use by TRW divisions or subsidiaries. There are two types of awards: "tangible" and "intangible." The tangible award is paid when the new idea can be calculated by a local committee and converted into dollars saved. Awards are figured on 15 percent of the net annual saving. The intangible suggestion award is paid when in the opinion of the local committee benefits cannot be calculated in terms of dollars (for instance, ideas increasing plant security, lighting, safety, housekeeping). No initial award exceeds $500, but a balance can be paid after the suggestion has been in operation for one year. Any employee can ask for reconsideration of the committee's decision.

GULF OIL

General Survey

Gulf Oil Corporation is the ninth largest industrial corporation of the United States (as of 1967), with sales amounting to $5,109,597 billion.[69] Its refining capacity is 652,000 barrels per day in the United States. Gulf owns or has an interest in 30 refineries and markets 200,000 barrels of gas liquids per day in 17 countries. Manufacture of petrochemicals offers wide diversification of products.[70] Gulf Oil is the largest merchant producer of ethylene, a major raw material for other petrochemical products. Its total ethylene capacity is 825 million pounds; its consumption is 11,000 million pounds. Other important products have resulted from engineering advances in the cracking of crude oil and its components as well as in the development of complementary processes for the synthetic production of motor and aviation fuel. Flexibility of production for refined products, larger yields, lower costs, and higher quality have been achieved by catalytic cracking methods, but constant modernization and change take place in refinery technology.

[69] Figures in this section from a communication to the author from Gulf Oil Corp., July 1968.
[70] About 5000 chemical compounds can be derived from oil and gas as raw materials. Petroleum is the source for about 65 percent of the value of all basic and intermediate chemicals and polymers produced in the United States (Standard & Poor' *Industry Surveys*, Basic Analysis).

Gulf General Atomic Inc. manufactures high-temperature gas-cooled reactors. Strong national and international competition and shift in the pattern of demand force Gulf Oil to pursue extensive and continuous research.

Gulf Oil has relatively low labor costs as compared, for instance, with the steel industry. Direct labor costs, including fringe benefits for employees run about 11 percent of revenues. The total number of employees in 1967 was 58,300. Gulf was granted 119 patents in that year, 123 in 1966.

Assignment Policy

Gulf Oil requires, as part of the contract, assignment of "all inventions and improvements, whether patentable or unpatentable, conceived or made" during employment, with the effect that they become "the sole and exclusive property of the Company." The consideration for the contract is the employment as well as undertakings of the Corporation set forth in the same contract referring to certain standard monetary awards.[71]

The assignee of the inventions is the employer company within the family of Gulf companies. Primarily these are Gulf Oil Corp., Gulf Research & Development Co., Gulf General Atomic Inc., and Warren Petroleum Corp.

The assignment covers all inventions and improvements "which the Company considers to relate to the actual or projected activities or business of the Company or its affiliates, or which the Company considers are conceived or made wholly or partly by reason of opportunities afforded or knowledge gained by Employee from his employment by the Company." The wording "which the Company considers" obviously excludes any discussion between the parties about which inventions fall within the scope of the contract.

The employment contract of Gulf Oil has an extensive trailer clause in which sales employees agree for a period of one year following termination of employment not in any manner, in competition with the Company, to solicit or accept any business from (1) customers served directly or indirectly by the employee during the three years prior to termination of employment, and (2) customers located within ten miles of any customers served directly or indirectly by the employee within three years immediately prior to the employee's termination of employment.

These stipulations are intended to protect the employer from losing commercial

[71] The express reference in the contract to invention awards is unusual in American industry and makes these awards part of the condition of employment. They cannot, therefore, be changed or abolished without giving formal notice to the employee and making a new contract.

customers (buyers of oil, gas, or chemicals) to former employees. (Salesmen and delivery men are particularly likely to build up their own clientele.) A second part of the clause binds employees "in technical or scientific work," i.e., engineers, scientists, or researchers. They agree at no time during employment to perform for others directly or indirectly the same type of work or activity that they perform for the Company and for one year after employment not to engage in the same type of work for a competitor within the same geographical area or territory. This second part of the clause covers practically all employees who are expected to be able to make patentable inventions and improvements. The phrase "within the same geographical area or territory" is aimed at a kind of employee especially important in the oil industry, namely, the prospecting geologist. No mention is made of paying a part or the whole salary to employees obliged to abstain from such professional work after termination of employment.

Award Policy

As mentioned when discussing the assignment policy, Gulf Oil Corporation formally binds itself in the employment contract as a part of the consideration of the contract to pay certain standard monetary awards for U.S. patent applications filed and assigned to the Company, and for all U.S. patents issued to the Company as assignee of the employee. The standard amount is $100 to any sole or joint inventor for each original or divisional U.S. patent application filed and assigned to the Company and another $100 for each patent issued on such applications. No other monetary award system is now in use at Gulf Oil.

Up to 1953, employed inventors working in production plants of the company could receive a share of royalty for patented inventions used by Gulf Oil, preferably by licensing these inventions to others. This practice was abolished for a number of reasons, two of which were difficulty of accounting and difficulty of identifying the right individual employee or employees. The difficulty of accounting arises from the fact that Gulf Oil does considerable business by "package licensing" many of its patents to third parties; thus it can be hard to account for the income from individual patents in such a "package," which can refer to patents protecting whole plant equipment and machinery of all kind. Yet from the point of view of sound overall management, it is felt wise by the company to allow the patent department to compensate for some of its expenses, including standard monetary awards, by licensing company patents to third parties.

The other important difficulty experienced was that awards for inventions made by a number of joint inventors became disproportionate and did not work

uniformly. Research management thought that sometimes too much was paid
for one patentable invention that led to a number of "continuations in part"
and other unexpected ramifications.

A nonmonetary incentive system affecting employed inventors at Gulf Research
& Development Company was started July 1, 1961. In order to provide additional
opportunities for advancement for scientists and engineers and for public recognition of outstanding scientific or engineering achievement, the parent company,
Gulf Oil, instituted a system called "Parallel Paths of Advancement." The system
provides equivalent opportunities for advancement, financially and professionally,
in accordance with each individual's competence and performance. These
qualities can be "ability in scientific research, administration, engineering applications or any combination of these," including presumably performance of all
professional employees as inventors. There are three parallel paths or scales for
scientific, supervisory, and technical personnel, leading to final titles "Senior
Scientist," "Division Director," and "Technical Consultant" respectively.[72]

BELL TELEPHONE LABORATORIES

General Survey

Bell Telephone Laboratories, founded in 1925, is one of the largest industrial
research laboratories of the United States and the Western world. The research
and development unit of the Bell System, Bell Laboratories is jointly owned by the
American Telephone and Telegraph Company (AT&T) and the Western Electric
Company, manufacturing and supply unit of the Bell System. AT&T owns the
Western Electric Co. There are 24 operating telephone companies in the communications network developed and currently improved by Bell Laboratories.
The cost of research and fundamental development carried on for AT&T in 1967
was $87 million.

In 1968 Bell Laboratories employed 15,300 people. More than 2364 of its technical
staff hold master's degrees in science or engineering and 1200 hold doctor's degrees,
the largest number of people with advanced degrees in any private business in the
world. Of the 15,300 employees, nearly half are engineers and scientists on the
technical staff, specializing in the fields of physics, chemistry, metallurgy, mathematics, computers, electronics, electrical and mechanical engineering, and patent

[72] The observation that additional scales of advancement for employees in the scientific
and engineering field of work within an industrial corporation should be created side by
side with opportunities for supervisory and management personnel was made by a number
of large corporations. Compare, for instance, the sophisticated system used by Bell
Telephone Laboratories.

law. Another quarter are members of the assistant technical staff, a large percentage of whom are graduates of technical institutes. And more than a quarter serve on the nontechnical staff, including administrative, plant, and clerical staff, of whom many are professionals in various aspects of business and management. For a staff of this kind salary levels and expectations of productive working results are high from the beginning.

The basic goal of Bell Laboratories is to develop and extend the science and technology of communications and to apply the results to the design of new systems and equipment. In addition to its responsibilities to the Bell System, Bell Laboratories devotes part of its effort to military projects. Typical of Bell Laboratories' military projects have been the Nike family of antiaircraft and antimissile defense systems. The staff works at 17 locations in 10 states and the Kwajalein Atoll, with four major locations at Murray Hill, Whippany, and Holmdel, New Jersey, and Naperville, Illinois. These locations include 10 smaller laboratories at manufacturing locations of the Western Electric Co. It is at these laboratories that the closely coordinated transition takes place between development and design by Bell Laboratories and production, exclusively carried out by Western Electric. The linkage between laboratory work, manufacturing activities, and operating telephone companies in the Bell System produces an uninterrupted flow of new ideas and concepts and permits their swift realization as practical engineering products.

A study titled "The Innovation Process," by Jack A. Morton, Vice President in charge of Electronic Components Development at Bell Telephone Laboratories, tries to find a systematic analytical approach to the process of converting science into new technology.[73] Since all parts of the innovation process must stem from the individually creative yet cooperative actions of people, Morton says it is most important to provide challenge and reward for the individual as the creator of the new science and technology. Innovation is said to depend vitally upon communications among people of diversified skills, knowledge, and motivation. Morton illustrates the role of systems engineering in the Laboratories in a flow sheet, as shown in Figure 3.3.

[73] *Bell Telephone Magazine,* Autumn 1966, p. 2 ff. The study avoids examples and practical cases how challenge and rewards are provided, and, therefore, offers limited value to outside research in this field. Compare also important papers of the same author: "From Research to Technology," in *International Science and Technology,* May 1964; "A Systems Approach to the Innovation Process," in *Business Horizons,* Summer 1967 (Graduate School of Business, Indiana University); additional papers and addresses about the same subjects by presidents of BTL, Mervin J. Kelley and James B. Fisk.

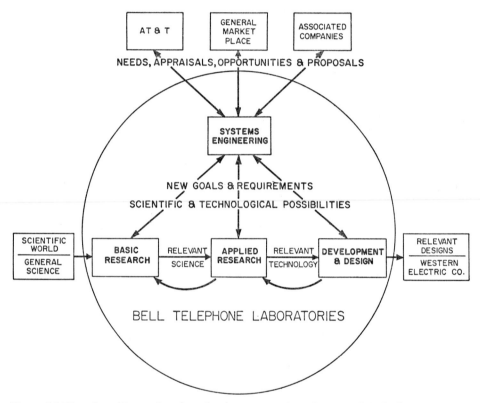

Figure 3.3 Flow sheet illustrating the role of systems engineering at Bell Telephone Laboratories.

Source: Bell Telephone Magazine, 1966.

Bell Laboratories works in three areas:

1. Short- and long-term basic research in fields of science that hold promise of yielding discoveries of value to the communications industry.

2. Development and design for manufacture; the translation of new science into functioning models of components and systems.

3. Systems engineering; the overall planning of development projects for new communications systems.

4. Military projects in communications and electronics such as antiaircraft and antimissile defense systems and satellite guidance systems.

Many major engineering achievements and inventions can be attributed to employees of the Bell Laboratories. They range from spectacular inventions such as the transistor, the solar battery, and the principles of the laser to two-way radiotelephony, microwave transmission, direct distance dialing by telephone and electronic telephone switching. A great number of basic engineering technologies were also developed at Bell Laboratories, including high fidelity sound recording, radio astronomy, digital computing, zone refining of metals, superconductivity, and solid state circuits. The carefully organized interchange and linkage between laboratory work, manufacturing activities, and operating organizations produces an uninterrupted flow of new ideas and concepts, and, in many cases, their realization as engineering products.

In such a sophisticated structure of the modern engineering world, the production of patentable inventions is almost a logical necessity. It is no surprise that the output of such inventions in the Bell Laboratories organization is both large in quantity and of a high degree of novelty and commercial usefulness. Between 1939 and 1955, 5600 U.S. patents were issued to Bell Telephone Laboratories.[74] Approximately 2000 new U.S. patents were granted to the Bell Laboratories between 1961 and 1965, and an annual rate of about 400 patents has remained fairly stable in the years that followed.

The Bell Telephone Laboratories and the other companies belonging to the Bell System are fully aware of the practical and commercial value of the patents produced by their own scientists and engineers. Two reasons are given by the Bell System companies for seeking patent protection: one, to be able to make free use, unhampered by others, of inventions made by their own employees (so-called defensive patenting) and two, to trade patent rights with others, either in exchange for licenses to use their patented inventions or for cash where the value of rights received by others is less than the value of rights granted.[75]

Broad cross-licensing agreements between the Bell System companies and U.S. corporations as well as foreign corporations play an important role and are a source of considerable royalty income. Patents are filed in foreign countries, particularly in Canada, the United Kingdom, Japan, and the nations of Western Europe, for the primary purpose of being able to use these patents for trading with

[74] In the same time period Western Electric Co. had received 2087 patents and Teletype Corp. 451. The total issued to the parent company, American Telephone & Telegraph Co., and all its subsidiaries was 8539. See P. Federico, *Distribution of Patents Issued to Corporations (1939–1955)*, U.S. Senate, Subcommittee on Patents, 84th Cong., 2d sess., 1957, p. 19.
[75] E. T. Lockwood, "Bell System Patents: Why Do We Have Them? How Are They Used?" in *Bell Telephone Magazine*, Winter 1959–1960, pp. 16–23.

other firms. There exist agreements of this kind with corporations and telephone administrations in more than 20 countries.[76]

The commercial value of inventions produced by Bell employees is therefore considerable, both in connection with the sale of Bell products and services in the United States and in the world market for communication systems.

Assignment Policy

All patent rights for inventions made by employees of Bell Laboratories staff engaged in work likely to produce inventions must be assigned to the company by general advance agreement. The field of activities of the employer, for which the general assignment is valid, is spelled out in the standard form used for this purpose as everything "relating to any subject matter with which said Corporation is or may be concerned." It is not possible to deduce any tangible field of science or engineering from this wording, or any limitation to inventions in the employee's specific field of endeavor. The creative work covered by the agreement are all "inventions" made or conceived in the course of employment or with the use of Corporation time, material, or facilities. This seems to exclude all other inventions, even if related to Bell System work. The contracting employer in the assignment agreement is Bell Telephone Laboratories, Incorporated, and "its successors or assigns." No definition or limitation is given of who the assigns can be. The scope of the contract covers inventions "in any and all countries" during the period of employment. No obligation to submit postemployment inventions is embodied in the agreement. The employee receives no extra consideration for signing the agreement. The Bell Telephone Laboratories agreement does not prescribe any express obligations to the employee regarding the keeping of trade secrets and confidential information put at his disposal. Such obligations do exist in practice, though they are not spelled out here.

Workmen employed by the Laboratories are bound by a collective bargaining agreement that does not contain any patent clause. It is felt that they are not hired to invent.[77] Inventions by workers are treated in the same manner as inventions by members of the technical staff.

Award Policy

The Bell Telephone Laboratories does not practice any special invention award

[76] The licensing of Bell patents in certain fields in the United States is mandatory on the basis of the terms of a final antitrust judgment of January 24, 1956.

[77] Inventions per year by workmen improving equipment are estimated to number 12 to 15.

policy; it considers such a system undesirable and does not intend to introduce it in the future as a part of its employee relations.[78]

Responsible leaders of the Bell System have twice (in 1954 and 1959) officially described the patent policy of the companies belonging to the system.[79] The statements they made still represent the official patent policy of the Bell system. Ralph Bown, former vice president in charge of research and patents, writes as follows:

One subject related to patents on which different companies have widely differing policies is the reward for invention. In some companies special rewards or prizes are offered for inventions which are appraised to have special value or merit. In other companies any and every application for or issuance of a patent is given a monetary recognition. In Bell Laboratories we do none of these things. We have come to our present ideas on this matter through long experience. Perhaps the best way to state our practice is to say that we class the production of inventions as a meritorious performance to be thrown into the scale along with all other merits in appraising the present and potential value of the individual to the organization, and thereby in awarding to him his fair share of our salary budget.

Bown further states that all inventing is a competitive race among individuals all over the world, and that "it is this competitive element which leads to the danger in special awards or rewards to inventors when taken outside the framework of their total contribution as compared with the total contributions of their co-workers." In other contexts, it is generally considered that competition between the employees is a salutary stimulus to greater effort.

Bell Telephone Laboratories has put a great amount of work and independent systematic planning into the general salary administration of their scientific and engineering personnel. The company is fully conscious of the fact that adequate salaries are basic in attracting and in retaining professional employees, in stimulating them to their greatest effort and in affording satisfaction in their work.[80] Bell Telephone Laboratories does not use "job categories" for its employees, but a broad category "Member of Technical Staff" includes all employees engaged in professional technical work. The administration tries for internal equity among

[78] American Telephone & Telegraph Co. had an award system about 25 years ago but abandoned it for several reasons, among which was the difficulty of identifying the right individual inventor.

[79] Ralph Bown, "Inventing and Patenting at Bell Laboratories," in *Bell Laboratories Record,* January 1954, pp. 5–10; and Edward T. Lockwood, "Bell System Patents" as cited in footnote 74.

[80] Frank D. Leamer, "Salary Administration of Scientific and Engineering Personnel at Bell Telephone Laboratories," in *Research Management* 7, No. 2 (1964), pp. 91–106.

these employees by rewarding them in accordance with the relative value of their performance to the company. Performance ratings and salary reviews are made annually. Specific contributions that include production of inventions and scientific papers are reviewed in this connection, "so that salaries will properly reflect achievement and job importance."[81]

Reservation is made by Leamer that "administration of salaries is not an exact science" and that human judgment is involved in large measure. More important is the remark that an important feature of Bell's plan is the extent to which objectives, practices, and procedures are explained to each person affected by it. This seems, indeed, to be basic in large organizations, if employee cooperation is expected.

There is no formal publicity policy relative to inventions and discoveries made by the laboratory staff. Both the periodicals published by the Bell System and the outside press often present stories and professional reports about employee inventions. The *Bell Laboratories Record* regularly publishes names, numbers, and titles of U.S. patents recently granted to Bell Laboratories employees as well as names of authors of papers published by the staff. Press conferences are held in connection with scientific discoveries, letters of congratulations are sent to inventors getting their first patent, and patent documents are displayed in Laboratory exhibits. The description of some of the Bell Laboratories inventions in *The New York Times* is considered by Bell management to have "a multiple effect," i.e., on the inventor, on the corporation, and on the patent system as such.

POLAROID CORPORATION

General Survey

Polaroid Corporation is young, founded in 1937, and small as compared with the industries described in most of the other case studies. Sales in 1967 were $374,354 million, the number of employees roughly 7000.[82]

Polaroid has manufacturing subsidiaries in the Netherlands and England (for cameras and photographic film), and sales subsidiaries in Australia, Canada, France, Germany, Great Britain, Japan, the Netherlands, Italy, and Switzerland. The character of this company and the development of its products is tightly connected with a single creative individual, Edwin H. Land, who as a freshman at Harvard in the 1920's made an important invention, a plastic material that would polarize

---

[81] *Ibid.*, p. 105.
[82] "The Fortune Directory," *Fortune,* June 15, 1968.

light rays, a synthetic light polarizer in sheetlike form.[83] His first aim was to eliminate automobile headlight glare. This synthetic polarizer was sold in the form of sheets containing submicroscopic crystals of herapathite, a quinine salt. First sales were to laboratories and manufacturers of optical instruments. By 1935 Land had obtained some ten U.S. patents covering the crystal suspension type of light polarizer, processes for its manufacture, and improved materials for use in connection with its manufacture. At about the same time he had secured license agreements with Eastman Kodak Company and American Optical Company to supply them with light-polarizing materials for photographic filters and sunglasses. World War II forced Land to abandon quinine as the base for the polarizing crystals in his polarizer; instead he invented a new highly efficient noncrystalline polarizer. The war effort directed Polaroid's production into the making of light-polarizing and other optical devices for the Armed Forces and into large-scale research for guided missiles, electronic signaling, and radiac detection devices.

At the end of the war, Polaroid found itself with a greatly expanded research division and little civilian business. Land, still the initiator and inventor of the main products of the Corporation, introduced new devices such as the phantom signal suppressor, which eliminates false signals caused by the reflection of the sun from a traffic light or railroad signal. Starting in 1944, Land devised a new type of camera and new process producing dry photographic positives from pictures taken only a few seconds earlier. He invented six or seven alternate methods of accomplishing the desired result and set up specifications for the general type of camera to be used, its weight, the size of the prints, and the maximum time for development of a negative and formation of a positive. The process and the camera were publicly demonstrated for the first time in February 1947 and were commercially introduced in November 1948. About 300 United States patents were obtained in this field before 1960, about 120 of which were issued to Land personally. This strong personal contribution of one single person as pioneer inventor necessarily had an impact on the approach to a general patent policy for the Company as a whole as well as on its labor relations with employed inventors. (As a majority shareholder, Land can hardly be considered an "employed inventor" himself.) The concept and realization of a basically new camera resulted in an

[83] The full story of the Polaroid Corporation up to the 1960's is told by its late vice president and head of Patent Department Donald L. Brown in the *Journal of the Patent Office Society* 1960, pp. 439 ff.: "Protection Through Patents: The Polaroid Story."

entirely new technology, especially in chemistry of photographic films and high-speed emulsions. Developing the new camera for both black-and-white and color film and designing a wide range of new camera accessories (all to be usable by the amateur photographer) and at the same time systematically extending the commercial and military applications of polarized light gave Polaroid a large line of quality productions.

In addition to the "instant" Land Camera, Polaroid developed apparatus and systems using linear and circular polarization of light and made these optical principles commercially significant, for instance in sunglasses, photographic lighting, and visual inspection systems. Polaroid has offered in this field devices to control glare for use with cathode-ray tube displays, for better viewing of television in brightly lighted areas, radar and sonar instruments, photoelasticity inspection systems for stress or strain of materials, and instruments measuring high-speed events in solids, liquids, and gases.

The Vectograph print, another ingenious invention, is a continuous-tone print composed of two separate images, each of which is seen by one eye. By means of polarizing analyzers the two eyes together see the picture in three dimensions. Vectograph prints are used in aerial mapping, advertising displays, electron micrographs, medical photography, radiology, and photogrammetry. It may be possible in the future to see television, radar, and X-ray pictures in "3-D" with the help of light polarizers.

Some of the new camera components offered by Polaroid include a transistorized electronic shutter, sensitive electric eye, automatic time exposures, and double-image range- and view-finder. New photographic films are offered as roll film, pack film, transparencies for projection, and X-ray film.

Since almost every product Polaroid sells (except some camera accessories) falls within the scope of claims of the Corporation's own patents, an extensive patent activity has been provided for, administered by 16 patent attorneys (in 1968). Of the total patent portfolio of roughly 700 U.S. patents, about three-fourths relate to one-step photography. Polaroid holds about 1400 patents in some 25 countries and is extending its foreign patent coverage. Obviously trademarks are also important assets to Polaroid. Relying heavily on its patent structure as distinct from contractual agreements, it can be said that the Corporation believes in the following principal uses of the patent system:

As protection against competition for the existing processes and structures developed by Polaroid internally, according to designs resulting from its own research and development.

As protection against competitive products in fields related to the main activities of the corporation including alternative processes and structures for national defense.

For exchange of patent rights with other patent owners by cross-licensing (especially with established photographic industries) in order to be able to use competitive patents and eliminate legal conflicts.

To protect new research results as assets in joint ventures or as a source of royalties when licensed to others.

As a convenient means of delegating certain branches of engineering activities to other firms by licensing one's own patents. Camera manufacture is licensed to some established firms in the field, whereas film production is retained.

Polaroid has found, in the words of its Patent Counsel, "an ability and willingness to rely upon our patents in negotiations with larger competitors has placed us upon equal footing. A recognition of the validity and strength of our patent picture seems to be a full compensation for relative commercial weakness. . . . We like that system. It has worked well for us and we shall cling to it until something better is suggested."[84]

In addition to these points of view Polaroid is underlining the importance of nonpatentable know-how material accumulated in the field of new photographic film processes, film chemicals and film products. Finally, Polaroid advises its employees that company profits depend largely upon suggestions regarding cost saving, efficient manufacture, new products and processes. In one recent year 70–80 suggestions were submitted, of which 10 were adopted, 13 were rejected, and the rest considered by a committee.

Assignment Policy

Polaroid Corporation uses an employment contract with strict and elaborate rules regarding assignment of "all inventions, discoveries, improvements or developments, whether of process, product, apparatus, or design, of whatever kind." There is no statement in the contract whether this applies only to inventions in Polaroid's field or those made as part of the job, on company time, or other detail. Another group of working results (to be returned and delivered at termination of employment) declared to be the property of Polaroid at all times are "all

[84] *Ibid.*, pp. 452, 455.

memoranda, notes, records, schedules, plans or other documents made or compiled
by or delivered to, the employee or possessed by him, concerning any product,
apparatus or process manufactured, used, developed or investigated by Polaroid."

A contract containing such assignment and property provisions (or minor
modifications thereof) has to be signed by every new employee engaged in research
or in engineering and by some of the other key employees of the company. All
inventions "which relate directly or indirectly to any of the present or future
business of Polaroid and which he (the employee) may make or aquire, either
solely or jointly with others" are expressly to be the property of Polaroid.

The fields of activities of the contracting employer are characterized as "the
manufacture and/or sale of optical materials, products, apparatus and instruments,
and in connection therewith . . . the business of research and development and of
making various inventions, discoveries, improvements and developments in various
scientific fields, and more specifically in the fields of applied physics, chemistry,
optics, sound and electricity, and in the exploitation and development of processes,
designs, apparatus and devices for use in said fields." "The manufacture and sale
of other and different products or commodities" are also mentioned, and other
possible activities are covered by saying that many of the employees of Polaroid,
whether or not directly engaged in such manufacture, sale, or research, are "by
reason of the nature of their duties informed with respect to such Polaroid
inventions and are from time to time able to contribute new inventions or
improvements on those already existing." This is said to be possible "in connection
with the study of the problems relating to such manufacture, sale and research,
and the discovery, improvement and perfection of inventions for Polaroid." The
provisions of the contract are valid for all inventions made or acquired during
employment and for one year after termination of employment (whether made
during regular hours of work or otherwise) and even though perfected or completed after the termination of employment by Polaroid.

Decision on whether any invention, discovery, improvement, or development of
an employee falls within or outside the scope of the business of Polaroid is made
by the Corporation. The decision is final and binding upon the employee.

The assignment agreement shall inure to the benefit of Polaroid, its successors,
and assigns. From other parts of the agreement it appears that this covers all
subsidiaries of Polaroid. The agreement is also equipped with a trailer clause
valid for two years after the termination of employment, stating in effect the
following points: The employee will not, anywhere in the United States or

Canada, directly or indirectly, for his own account or as an officer, stockholder, member or employee, advisor, or in any capacity whatsoever, serve, be employed by, or contribute his knowledge to, or advise any corporation, partnership, person or persons engaged in competition with Polaroid. This prohibition refers to information acquired from Polaroid respecting its formulas, processes, and methods, inasmuch as they have a substantial value and are protected against unauthorized exploitation. The employee is further prohibited from assisting in the manufacture of any product or products which he helped manufacture for Polaroid or concerning the manufacture of which he acquired knowledge or information while in the employ of Polaroid, through instructions from others, his own observations, or his original research.[85] The Corporation comments on this part of the provisions as follows:

We found in practice that there was little or no need for the provision restricting the employee from working with a competitor for a period of two years. Whenever a request for modification of this provision was made the request was granted. The provision has been used essentially only as assurance that the new employer was advised of the existence of the contract and the requirement that there be no communication of trade secrets or confidential information.[86]

Although the need to enforce the provision may not often arise, Polaroid, like other companies, exercises appropriate precautions to protect their confidential information when an employee leaves. They ask where he is going[87] and give him a release. A company employing a former Polaroid employee will not take him unless he has been released. Rather than release an employee to a competitor (where he will be doing the same kind of work) Polaroid in some cases may even pay two years of salary after termination of employment. The rigid form of agreement, according to Polaroid was essential "in connection with highly classified government research."[88] Polaroid is rather critical of present government patent policy with regard to acquiring full title for inventions arising out of government research and development contracts.

It must be stated here that the invention assignment policy of a corporation often cannot be identified, judged, or correctly interpreted without regarding a number

[85] These two provisions seem to overlap in coverage. However, they apparently do exclude ideas and improvements developed by the employee only.
[86] In a letter to Professor Fritz Machlup, Princeton University, December 1964.
[87] The leaving employee probably is not legally bound to reveal the name of his new employer. For an interesting assessment of ex-employee competition, see Harlan M. Blake, "Employee Agreements Not To Compete," *Harvard Law Rev.*, February 1960, pp. 625–691.
[88] If this explanation is adequate the agreement could be limited to "security" cases. Comment from government agencies so alluded to was not available.

of other relevant factors such as the origin, growth, and tradition of the firm, the technical fields of its activities, and its invention award policy. In the Polaroid case the role of the inventions produced by the founder of the firm, Edwin Land, is essential to the whole invention assignment policy.

Award Policy

One of Land's closest collaborators characterizes his views in the field of management-employee relations as of an advanced and liberal nature. Land is said to believe "strongly that it is a principal obligation of management in the business economy of today to see to it that employees share not only in the profits made by industry but also to a large degree in the management and direction of the company's business."[89]

How has Polaroid implemented these far-reaching ideas? The many forms of award systems with which the company has experimented will help answer this question.[90]

The Profit-Sharing System (also called Employee Incentive Plan)   Prior to 1959 Polaroid had an Executive Incentive Compensation Plan limited to company officers and salaried employees having a job rate in excess of $560 per month. After that date a new system was started letting all full-time employees take part fully in a profit-sharing plan after three years service in the company. The share paid depends in part upon the employee's base salary. A certain "goal point" in sales of the company is fixed annually, calculated from the net profit for the year. An amount is deducted equal to 20 percent of the company's net worth which, in turn, is calculated as the surplus of the company plus the par value of its outstanding capital stock. A fixed percentage of the sum so calculated is set aside for the Profit-Sharing Plan. The formula used in fixing the goal point is published and is known by all employees. The share received varies from 15 percent of the annual salary (in the group paid by the hour) to a higher figure that may reach in top management as much as 60 or 70 percent of annual salary, if the goal point has been reached. The system was adopted in the hope that it would result in a sense of participation in corporate profit throughout the employee group, and it is said to have had this effect. For example, it resulted in a considerable increase in the number of suggestions made by employees for improvement in all sorts of production and servicing activities. Suggestions of nonprofessional employees in one recent year saved the Company about three-quarters of a million dollars.

[89] Donald L. Brown, "Protection Through Patents," p. 453.
[90] Information given the author by the company in December 1964 and February 1965.

Salary Increases and Promotions   It goes without saying that these conventional means of rewarding meritorious employees are used. Salary increases of employees in the "inventive group" (who have made important or many inventions) give this group not only an increase in annual pay beyond the usual raises but also place them in a higher percentage so far as the Profit-Sharing Plan is concerned, making their returns greater not only for one year but during the whole period of employment. An inventive employee can in this way reach salary levels comparable to those which he might have attained as a Supervisor or Assistant Department Head. Concerning promotions Polaroid has experienced, as have many other corporations, that many of the best employed inventors are not qualified to act in supervisory or administrative capacities, and therefore promotions to such posts would be unsatisfactory for both the inventor and the employer. This does not, however, preclude salary returns based upon inventive contributions. This is like the "parallel paths" approach practiced by Gulf Oil, Bell Telephone Laboratories, and a number of other companies.

Stock Option Plan   A committee of the Company's Board of Directors awards stock options each year to selected employees. Although these employees are usually in the managerial group at the officer level, they may also be rewarded in this way for their inventive contributions. The stock options give the employee the right to subscribe to a specific number (for instance 100 to 200) of corporate shares at any time within 6 years from the grant of the option. The price of the shares is the market price at the date the option is granted. Since Polaroid is a "growth company," these options have proved of considerable financial value. However, considerably less than 1 percent of employees have been rewarded in this manner because of their inventive contributions.[91] Of the key inventors in different fields who have received the largest stock options and greatest salary increases, one man (in the color field) had received 37 U.S. patents over a period of 15 years, another (in the Vectograph or 3-D motion picture field) had 27 U.S. patents. The Vice President for Engineering had received 38 U.S. patents on all sorts of chemical devices, and on cameras, clutches, accessories, and X-ray devices. Of course, the number of patents granted is in itself no measure of the importance of the achievement; awards are also given for nonpatentable ideas and suggestions or for combinations of both types of contributions. The award is adapted to the commercial value of the inventions, and in some cases salary increases are given to the inventor without stock option.

[91] Information to the author in February 1965.

Nonmonetary Awards   Employees, especially in research, who are considered to have contributed substantially to the Company's business and who wish to do so are given full opportunity to attend scientific meetings on company time. Another "moral award" consists in giving an employee time to devote to writing and publishing scientific articles. The company's policy of wide patenting permits prompt publication on an equally wide basis.[92] A happier climate for research is said to be created by such a policy, since technical personnel and scientists usually want to publish their results.

Finally it must be mentioned that Polaroid earlier had tried a cash award system for employee inventions but abolished it as unsatisfactory from a management point of view. Again the reasons were given that it is difficult to ascertain the value of the contribution or invention and that jealousy may arise concerning who would be entitled to the award. It was also found that some employees tend to withhold information with respect to new inventions until they had completed the concept. Polaroid had also tried competitions, i.e., prizes or cash awards for the best inventions submitted within a certain period in a certain field. These methods were also discarded as unsatisfactory.

EVALUATION OF INDUSTRY-EMPLOYER INVENTION POLICY

The case studies of this chapter show that when industrial corporations have a conscious employee-invention policy, regulations regarding advance assignment of all future inventions an employee can make, as a condition of employment, are universally used and are in principle alike. Advance assignment provisions in contracts with employees seem to be legally permissible.[93] The scope of such assignment provisions, however, can vary substantially, for instance in defining the engineering field or field of science for which inventions are required to be assigned, the group of assignees to whom the invention rights are granted, or the time period for which assignment will be in force. A negative feature is that extra compensation or other special benefits above the salary in return for inventions are rarely promised in these contract provisions, even if invention-award systems exist.[94] Token awards in the form of standard cash amounts of some one hundred dollars each are not considered by the author to be extra compensation in this connection; neither are ordinary bonus plans to reward the merits of a small

92 Polaroid refuses permission to publish before the patent application is filed (if it is to be filed at all) to prevent automatic bar to foreign patent rights.
93 Compare the common law situation as analyzed in Chapter 2.
94 There are a few exceptions, for instance in the aeroplane and aerospace industry, and Gulf Oil Corp.

exclusive group of top employees and managers.[95] Nonmonetary (honorary) inventor awards are practiced in a great number of different ways in special award plans not a part of the employment contract. Many of these have the character of a patriarchal, eighteenth-century attitude toward the employee, a pat on the shoulder by the patron, who knows best.

Company-wide, state-wide, and nationwide publicity for successful employed inventors does occur and is sometimes encouraged by industrial employers.[96] Inventor awards expressed in salary raises, company promotion, or special work assignments are for obvious reasons difficult to assess statistically, but they naturally play an important role in research-minded industries working under hard domestic and international business competition.

The selection of groups of employees eligible for invention awards depends usually on whether the employee is required to sign an invention assignment agreement as a condition of employment. J.H. O'Meara, for instance, has found that among a group of 83 companies the types of employees required to sign assignment agreements were distributed as in Table 3.6.

To make more general statements about the employee selection policy practiced in industry, more extensive statistics would be needed, but the author's research shows a trend similar to the one related by O'Meara. The emphasis on requiring

Table 3.6 Employees Required To Sign Invention-Assignment Agreements in 83 selected companies.

Type of Employee	Number of Companies	Percentage of Total Companies
All	25	36
R&D and engineering	58	70
All management	29	35
Some management	26	31
All salesmen	20	24
Some salesmen	22	26
All production	2	2.4
Some production	37	45

Source: J. H. O'Meara, "Employee Patent and Secrecy Agreements," NICB, *Studies in Personnel Policy*, No. 199, New York, 1965, p. 15.

[95] Some exceptions: Polaroid Corporation, General Electric Co., Du Pont de Nemours extend bonus payments or shares of stock expressly to employees who are outstanding as inventors.
[96] Examples: IBM, RCA, Westinghouse Electric.

invention assignment by R&D personnel (hired to invent and to develop) is natural, but in practical industrial life there are many equivocal categories. "Occasional inventors" not hired specifically to create new technology have often produced valuable inventions during employment.

I will evaluate the material presented in this chapter by concentrating on some points only. Among suggestions that can be made for an improved industrial employee-inventor policy some are negative, aimed at abolishing certain practices, and some positive, proposing new or improved measures. My suggestions are as follows:

Abstain in invention-assignment contracts from

1. Blanket provisions covering assignment of all inventions made by an employee "in the field of business" or in the business of the employer, "present and prospective."

2. Invention assignment in favor of those other than the direct employer with whom employment contract is executed. Domestic and foreign subsidiaries, associated companies, and the like, to be excluded as assignees except with special compensation.

3. Clauses compelling employee to assign inventions made after conclusion of employment.

Express clearly in invention assignment contracts that

1. The invention assignment is limited to inventions conceived and made during employment.

2. Assignment is limited to the field in which the employee is actually intended to work at the time of employment and in which he may have special experience and education.[97]

3. All disclosures of inventions offered by an employee will be examined by the employer within a definite period and the result will be communicated to the employee, giving the reasons for the decision in writing.

4. Inventions made during employment and having substantial commercial value to the employer will result in reasonable extra compensation in cash, above salary, and some honorary measures.

5. Any productive employed inventor is eligible for bonus plan payments irrespective of his current level of salary.

6. Domestic (U.S.) rights will be treated differently from foreign rights, the latter

---

[97] If working tasks are substantially changed during employment, definition of fields of invention should be changed by modification of contract.

to be left to the inventor unless special interests of the employer require world-wide rights in his favor.

7. Inventions assigned by an employee, which after a certain period of time are not used by the employer, will be released to the inventor free of cost.

Make these provisions

1. That cash awards to inventors be constructed in such a way as to relieve the inventor partly or wholly from income tax or other tax claims.

2. That in important cases above a certain commercial level, where an invention award is given or refused to an employee, the employee has the right to appeal the company decision to a central mixed governmental-industrial arbitration board, or a special federal court (to be created).

3. That in corporate engineering and research fields in close financial cooperation with government agencies and departments invention-award provisions for employees be shaped in cooperation with the affected government offices.

Experiences from a more open, more widespread and positive industrial employee invention policy will improve the usefulness of such policy and lead to more employee inventions to choose from, expansion of industrial production and higher innovation pace, which in turn will increase employment opportunities.

Example 1:
THIS AGREEMENT made this . . . . day of . . . ., 19. . . .,
by and between . . . .
of . . . ., (hereinafter called the
"Employee") and . . . ., a corporation organized
and existing under the laws of the State of . . . . (hereinafter
called "the Corporation").
WITNESSETH:
ONE. Employee hereby covenants and agrees that for a term of three (3) months,
beginning with the date hereof and thereafter until his employment hereunder
is terminated by either party giving to the other at least thirty days notice in
writing of intention to terminate said employment, he will devote his time exclusively to the Corporation and shall faithfully and to the best of his skill and
ability perform such duties as may from time to time be assigned to him, and shall
at all times diligently and loyally serve and endeavor to further the interests of the
Corporation.
TWO. Employee hereby covenants and agrees to promptly disclose to his immediate superior or to the Patent Department of the Corporation all inventions
and improvements which he may conceive or make solely or jointly with others
during his employment hereunder, whether during or out of the usual hours of
work, which inventions and improvements shall be and remain the sole and
exclusive property of the Corporation, and that he will assign, and does hereby
assign and transfer to the Corporation, all of his entire right, title and interest in
and to such inventions and improvements and will execute and deliver all documents as the Corporation shall deem necessary or desirable to obtain Letters
Patent of the United States and foreign countries for said inventions and improvements as the Corporation may elect and to vest title thereto in the Corporation, its
successors, assigns or nominees.
THREE. Employee hereby covenants and agrees that he will promptly disclose to
the Corporation all inventions and improvements which he may conceive or
make, either solely or jointly with others, within a period after termination of his
employment equal to the duration of his employment hereunder, but not exceeding
one year after the termination of his employment, provided that said inventions
and improvements relate to the business of the Corporation or its affiliates and
arise out of his contact with said business; and that upon request of the Corporation he will, upon mutually acceptable terms, assign all of his entire right, title and
interest in and to said inventions and improvements and will execute and deliver
to the Corporation all documents as the Corporation shall deem necessary or
desirable to obtain Letters Patent of the United States and foreign countries and
to vest title thereto in the Corporation, its successors, assigns or nominees; it is
further understood that the aforesaid obligations contained in this Article THREE
shall not apply to any patent right for any inventions or improvements made by
said Employee in the course of work performed by him under a government
contract.
FOUR. Employee hereby covenants and agrees that he will not, except as expressly
authorized in writing by the Corporation, in any way disclose or authorize anyone

else to disclose orally, in writing or by publication, during his employment or thereafter, any confidential information relating to the business of the Corporation which he may in any way acquire during said employment.

FIVE. This Agreement shall not embrace nor include any inventions, improvements, applications for and/or Letters Patent owned or controlled by said Employee prior to the commencement of his employment by the Corporation, all of which, if any, are fully identified on the reverse side hereof.

SIX. Employee covenants that he is under no disability and has no undisclosed obligation, by reason of prior employment or otherwise, which might in any way affect his ability to carry out the provisions of this Agreement.

SEVEN. Employee hereby agrees that the obligation to execute and deliver documents as provided in Articles Two and THREE hereof shall survive any termination of employment hereunder and shall be binding upon his assigns, executors, administrators, or other legal representatives.

IN WITNESS WHEREOF, the parties hereto have signed and sealed this Agreement in duplicate on the day and year first above written.

. . . .

Example 2:

Memorandum of agreement made and entered into this . . . . day of . . . ., 19. . . ., by and between . . . . a corporation, hereinafter called . . . . and . . . . a resident of . . . . hereinafter called "EMPLOYEE."

1. Employee agrees to, and does hereby assign, transfer and convey to . . . ., its successors and assigns, his entire right, title and interest in and to any and all inventions and/or copyrightable material which have been or may be conceived or made by him, either solely or jointly with others, during his employment by . . . ., or any of its subsidiary or controlled companies, and which relate to automotive vehicles, engines, refrigerating devices and equipment, heating devices and equipment, air conditioning devices and equipment, and parts and accessories for any of the preceding items together with all machines, tools, methods and processes of manufacture and materials useful in the construction thereof, and other inventions and/or copyrightable material which may be useful to . . . . in the carrying on of the various phases of its business as it is now being or may hereafter be conducted, as well as his entire right, title and interest in and to any and all United States and foreign letters patent and/or copyrights covering any and all of said inventions and copyrightable material. Employee further agrees to promptly and fully disclose any such inventions to . . . . and to perform all acts and to execute and deliver upon request, without further consideration but without expense to him, any and all papers and documents including applications for patents and copyrights and assignments of the same as may be deemed necessary or as desired by . . . ., its successors and assigns, to enable it to secure and enjoy the full benefits hereof. The foregoing agreement is in consideration of the salary and/or wages paid to Employee and is not in consideration of Article 3 hereof, which is voluntarily assumed by . . . . as a token of good will.

2. It is specifically agreed that . . . . shall have the full and free right, for

itself and its subsidiary and controlled companies, to do or not to do whatever it desires with respect to the inventions, patent applications, patents, copyrights and copyrightable material referred to under the provisions of the foregoing Article 1, including, but without limitation, the right to utilize or not to utilize the same and the right to license or sell the same or to not license or sell the same, upon such terms as it may desire, with or without compensation therefor. If . . . . should decide to sell or license any of the same in connection with the acquisition or sale of other property, Employee shall have no right to participate in . . . . receipts therefrom but if . . . . shall make sales or licenses of any of them for an actual money consideration (as distinguished from other benefits) specified to be paid for them and collected by . . . . the said money consideration so specified and collected shall be shared with Employee as set forth in Article 3 hereof.

3. Subject to all the provisions of Article 2 hereof, ... hereby agrees to receive the invention disclosed to it by Employee and where said inventions, in the sole opinion of . . . ., warrant such action, to cause patent applications covering the same to be filed through its attorneys, but without assuming any responsibility for the prosecution or defense of such patent applications, or the election of one inventor over another inventor, or the election to prosecute one application in preference to another application; and to give unto Employee, in any cases where it decides to sell any of Employee's patents and/or patent applications for an actual money consideration, or to grant licenses to others to manufacture, use and sell under any such patents and/or patent applications, for an actual money consideration, a percentage of any actual money (as distinguished from other benefits), specified to be paid and which it may collect from the aggregate of all such sales and/or licenses, after deducting expenses to which . . . . may be put in connection with such licenses or sales and taxes which it may have to pay on such collections, upon the following scale:

Of the first $1,000.00 or part thereof actually collected in any one calendar year— 40%

Of the next $2,000.00 or part thereof actually collected in any one calendar year— 30%

Of the next $2,000.00 or part thereof actually collected in any one calendar year— 20%

Of the next $5,000.00 or part thereof actually collected in any one calendar year— 15%

Of all further sums actually collected in any one calendar year—10%

It is understood and agreed, however, that in cases where . . . . shall grant licenses under or shall make sales of Employee's said patents and/or patent applications and patents and/or patent applications of others, the foregoing set forth percentages of the net amount of actual money collected therefrom (as distinguished from other benefits), after deducting expenses and taxes, shall be placed in a fund from which the above percentages will be paid and Employee shall receive only a portion of said percentages. . . . . shall have the sole right and authority to fix the relative importance of the various patent applications and/or patents included in the licenses or sales and will pay to Employee such proportion of the said fund as, in the sole opinion of . . . . represents the relative importance of Employee's patents and/or patent applications with respect to the entire group of patents and/or patent applications included in such licenses or sales.

4. It is also understood and agreed that . . . . shall continue to pay any monies payable under Article 3 hereof even though Employee's employment by . . . . shall terminate, such payments to be made to Employee, or in the event of his decease, to his duly qualified executors or administrators.

5. All previous agreements of . . . . to pay said Employee in connection with inventions made by him are hereby acknowledged by Employee to have been fully paid up and satisfied to date and any such agreements are hereby cancelled, it being understood that any monies actually collected in the future by . . . . from the sale or licensing of patent applications and/or patents assigned to . . . . by Employee under such agreement shall be divided in accordance with Article 3 of this agreement.

This agreement shall be binding upon and inure to the benefit of . . . . its successors in business and Employee, his heirs, executors and administrators, but neither this agreement nor any of its benefits are assignable by Employee to any other party.

Appendix B.
Case Histories of Eleven
Selected General Motors Employees
(To be read together with case study
on General Motors, pp. 98–107.)

1. Hired in 1956 (age 57) by a car division of GM as Assistant Chief Engineer after 34 years of experience in the field of automotive engineering and 45 patents in his name. His field of education was mechanical and automotive engineering, and his inventions were primarily in this field. Patents issued to him at GM: 1.

2. Hired in 1920 (age 27) by a research staff of GM as a metallurgist after several years of experience in the field. His position on retirement was Manager, Research Staff Activities. He had held positions as head of the metallurgical research activities and as Assistant to the Vice President in charge of research activities. His field of education was mechanical engineering. His inventive contributions were primarily in metallurgy. Patents issued to him at GM: 48.

3. Hired in 1927 (age 25) by a car division of GM as a draftsman after 5 years teaching experience in aerodynamics. His position on leaving was Engineer in charge of Power Development, but he has served in various engineering capacities in the original car division including that of Assistant Chief Engineer. He also served as a special consultant and did considerable work in automatic engine controls. His field education was electrical and mechanical engineering. His inventions were primarily in the field of engine design and control systems. Patents issued to him at GM: 100.

4. Hired in 1927 (age 23) by a car division of GM as a draftsman after study in mechanical and automotive engineering. His position at the time of the survey was Executive Assistant to the Vice President in charge of Engineering. He had been in charge of transmission development for more than 18 years and had also served as Chief Engineer for one of the car divisions and as a technical director of development and engineering in several different divisions. He is recognized as one of the leaders in automatic transmission development, his inventive contributions being primarily in this field. Patents issued to him at GM: 113.

5. Hired in 1923 (age 23) by the predecessor company of the truck division of GM, this employee joined a car division of the Corporation in 1927 and then transferred to the truck division. After more than 30 years in various engineering development capacities with this division, he retired in 1964. His field of education was mechanical engineering, and his inventive contributions were in various areas of automotive engineering. Patents issued to him at GM: 62.

6. Hired in 1929 (age 22) by an accessory division of GM as a kiln helper, this employee studied ceramics and became a ceramic engineer. He was Director of Research in this division at the time of reporting and has received numerous awards for his inventive contributions in this and related fields. Patents issued to him at GM: 51.

7. This employee was hired in 1923 (age 16) by an electrical motor division of GM as a toolmaker apprentice. He continued his studies and received a degree in

electrical engineering in 1930. His responsibilities with the division increased from engineer and designer through Chief Engineer and Manufacturing Manager. He has been successively General Manager of an accessory division and a truck division and was at the time of reporting a Vice President and General Manager of a car division. His inventive contributions range over a wide area of electrical motor devices and controls and manufacturing. Patents issued to him at GM: 64.

8. This employee came to GM in 1919 (age 22) when the corporation acquired the company with which he was employed as a designer in their experimental department. He worked in the Corporation research laboratories and devoted much effort to the design and development of balancing machines, this being the principal field of his inventive contributions. His principal field of education was science and engineering, but practical experience was the significant factor in his development. His position on retirement was head of the special problems department in the Corporation research laboratories. Patents issued to him at GM: 34.

9. This engineer was hired in 1923 (age 28) as a Chief Experimental Engineer by an accessory division of General Motors. His position on retirement was Staff Engineer. Prior to joining the Corporation, he had six years experience in Europe in design and production (not for GM). His field of education was mechanical engineering, and his inventive contributions are primarily in the fields of speedometers and fuel injection. Patents issued to him at GM: 87.

10. This employee was hired in 1916 (age 35) by an accessory division of General Motors as an engineer. His position on retirement was Chief Engineer having to do mostly with spark plugs, the design and development of which accounted for his inventions. For 14 years prior to joining General Motors he was engaged in Italy and South America in research, development, and production on submarine engines, ball bearings, automobile engines, and special machinery for high production. Patents issued to him at GM: 113.

11. Hired in 1918 (age 37) as a designer in the electrical section at the research division of General Motors, this employee was responsible for some of the basic work on which the dynamic balancing machine equipment was developed. In 1926 he moved to a car division as a development engineer. In 1931 he was made Assistant Chief Engineer, and held this post until retirement. His inventive contributions were primarily in the fields of automotive engines and engine accessories as well as balancing machines. Patents issued to him at GM: 51.

4

OVERVIEW

The preceding chapter illustrated some of the practices of United States industry toward its employees, especially scientists and engineers who are expected to make inventions during employment and who sign individual agreements regarding invention assignment when entering employment. These constitute a final contractual settlement of all claims once and for all. This chapter, in contrast, is concerned with regulation of employee-invention policy by collective bargaining agreements.

A first attempt will be made here to point out the main factors at work in this field of bargaining. Is this type of agreement worth improving or should it be discarded in the future? Before reaching a decision, it would be useful to present, as a guide to the layman in labor law, the history of collective bargaining and its implications in the United States. Space is not available for this here, but basic reading can be recommended.[1]

Some reflections about the legal sources and practice of collective (wage) bargaining of employees is in order. Two flanks, employee wage bargaining and employee-invention policy, meet here on common ground—not a "battleground," one hopes. Generally speaking, policy problems emanate from the fact that there are two different groups of employees, professionals and manual workers. One basic background problem concerns legal definition and legal rights of the group of employees called *professional;* other problems are whether and to what extent this group of employees is collectively organized (unionized) in order to be able to bargain collectively, and what obstacles this group has met in the federal labor boards.

With all regard for the creativity and skill of manual workers, it seems to be a matter of experience that the improvements they contribute, as a rule, fall within the field of suggestions as distinguished from patentable inventions. The blue-collar worker, both because of his daily working situation and his lack of higher

[1] On the general history of U.S. labor law, see: James M. Landis, *Cases on Labor Law,* 2d ed. (Chicago: Foundation Press, 1942); *Documentary History of American Industrial Society,* ed. John R. Commons (Cleveland: Arthur H. Clark, 1910), Vol. 1; John R. Commons, *History of Labour in the United States* (1918–1935), Vols. 1–4 (New York: Macmillan, 1936); Neil W. Chamberlain and J. W. Kuhn, *Collective Bargaining* (New York: McGraw-Hill, 1965), chapters 1 and 2; Foster Rhea Dulles, *Labor in America,* 2d ed. (New York: Crowell, 1960); Philip Taft, *Organized Labor in American History* (New York: Harper & Row, 1964); Arthur S. Goldberg, AFL-CIO, *Labor United* (New York: McGraw-Hill, 1964); *Growth of Labor Law in the United States* (Washington, D.C.: U.S. Bureau of Standards, U.S. Dept. of Labor, 1967).

engineering education, in most cases fails to make more advanced inventions. An advantageous regulation for insuring recognition and compensation of inventions made during employment is, therefore, a matter of greater concern to the employed scientist, engineer, and trained technician. Collective bargaining, however, legally presupposes that there exist clear-cut bargaining units on the employee side, and thus in the regulation of invention rights the bargaining employee unit must have solved the question of representing two disparate groups of industrial employees, either in common or separately.[2] The logical consequence seems to be either that the employee side in such agreements must consist of a single labor union that represents both groups as an inseparable unit in relation to the employer, or that more than one bargaining agreement with one employer be made—say one agreement covering the manual labor union and one covering the professional union.[3]

In terms of numbers of employees and corporations affected, collective bargaining agreements with patent provisions are negligible in an economy the size of that of the United States. In reviewing the field the author found no more than about 11 such agreements in force, involving some 30,000 or 40,000 employees, both blue collar and professional, in a labor market of more than 70 million. Nor are there many additional agreements of this type under negotiation at the time of writing. In spite of these limitations, the facts and expectations underlying these provisions might express important principles not reasoned out by the parties to the agreements. There are many reasons for the prevailing situation: lack of time to study the problems on both sides, the small number of employed individuals concerned with making inventions (compared with the total number of employees), the failure to recognize that inventions have been founders of new industries rather than "killers of jobs," the traditional bad reputation of patents in Congress and in the federal courts, and the expected rivalry among inventors about origin of and

[2] The Labor Management Relations Act (Taft-Hartley Act), section 9(a) provides that representatives designated or selected for the purposes of collective bargaining by the majority of the employees in a unit shall be exclusive representatives of all the employees for the purpose of collective bargaining in respect to rates of pay, wages, hours of employment, *or other conditions of employment* [my italics]. Individual employees, however, keep the right at any time to present grievances to their employer and have them adjusted without the intervention of the bargaining representative as long as the adjustment is not inconsistent with the collective bargaining contract in effect and as long as the representative has been given the opportunity to be present at the adjustment.

[3] In practice the author has also found cases in which additional groups of employees (as selected by the employer) are bound by individual invention-assignment contracts side by side with the collective bargaining agreements.

profits stemming from inventions. Other reasons are these: a tendency of many researchers and inventors to identify more with management, the fact that research results are heterogeneous as compared with most labor products, the spirit of the inventor to strive to excel individually (whereas the typical union approach is to decry individual effort), and finally difference of opinion as to the strike as an effective and legitimate weapon in bargaining.

The Professional Employee

The current Labor Management Relations Act (Taft-Hartley Act) of 1947 refers expressly to the group of professional employees which I would like to call the inventive group of employees. Section 2(12) of the Act defines the "professional employee" as a person whose work is one of five types:

1. Predominantly intellectual and varied in character as opposed to routine mental, manual, mechanical, or physical work.

2. Involving the consistent exercise of discretion and judgment in performance.

3. Of such a character that the output produced or the result accomplished cannot be standardized in relation to a given period of time.

4. Requiring knowledge of an advanced type in a field of science or learning customarily acquired by a prolonged course of specialized intellectual instruction and study in an institution of higher learning or a hospital, as distinguished from a general academic education or from an apprenticeship, or from training in the performance of routine mental, manual, or physical processes.

5. Related work performed under the supervision of a professional to qualify the employee for professional work as defined in Points (1) to (4).

Some of the cited features of this definition could be used to almost exactly define an employed inventor, especially when talking about a person doing work "predominantly intellectual and varied in character," involving exercise of "discretion and judgment" and still more, work "of such a character that the output produced or the result accomplished cannot be standardized in relation to a given period of time." Such a professional employee has certain special legal rights in selecting representatives for bargaining units. According to section 9(b) of the Act the National Labor Relations Board (NLRB) decides in each case whether a unit is "appropriate for the purposes of collective bargainning." The NLRB, however, shall not decide that a unit is appropriate if it "includes both professional employees and employees who are not professional employees, unless a majority of such professional employees vote for inclusion in such unit."[4]

---

[4] This clear-cut statutory right of professional employees to sponsor separate bargaining

After the enactment of the Taft-Hartley Act in 1947, a continuous stream of decisions was rendered and is still rendered by the NLRB, regarding petitions under section 9(c) of the Act and answering what kind of employees can constitute members of a unit appropriate for the purposes of collective bargaining within the meaning of that section. These decisions reflect vividly the change and expansion of industrial technology in many fields of production and how the blue collar of many employees becomes whiter and whiter; that is, there is a trend toward making work more intellectual, involving discretion and judgment or requiring knowledge of an advanced type, fitting the Taft-Hartly Act description of "professional employee." It is also notable that many of the defendants in such cases are precisely the corporations most active in research and development (Western Electric, Radio Corporation of America, Westinghouse Electric, Boeing, Otis Elevator, Sperry Gyroscope, and Minneapolis-Honeywell).

The Role of the Federal Courts

It is not only the National Labor Relations Board that by decision interprets certain parts of the Taft-Hartley Act. Resort can also be taken to the federal courts. In 1963 a U.S. court of appeals (5th Circuit) held that collective bargaining agreements are federal contracts, to which federal jurisdiction attaches automatically.[5] Federal courts may set aside an order of the NLRB for judicial review on the usual grounds, for instance, if the findings of fact made by it are not supported by substantial evidence on the record, if the Board has made errors of law, or if the order is defective in other ways. Important questions of general interpretation of the Taft-Hartley Act have been decided by federal courts of appeal and by the Supreme Court of the United States. Here reference will be made only to some decisions clarifying two important questions: (1) the collective bargaining rights of professional employees as distinguished from nonprofessional employees, and (2) the right in principle of employees to bargain about patent and invention provisions in collective agreements.

The reason why these two areas of possible labor dispute are essential to consider in connection with collective bargaining about employee inventions is, in the

---

units, in line with their specific qualifications and working functions, is aptly described in James J. Bambrick Jr., Albert A. Blum, and Hermine Zagat, *Unionization Among American Engineers* (New York: NICB Studies in Personnel Policy, No. 155).

[5] The decision was made in connection with an airline personnel bargaining agreement, a type of contract which since 1936 has fallen under contracts pursuant to sec. 204 Railway Labor Act: *International Association of Machinists* (IAM) v. *Central Airlines,* 372 U.S. Reports 682, 692.

first case, that the "professional employees" of the Taft-Hartley Act are the group potentially able to make inventions during employment, and in the second case (whether and how inventions can be subject to collective bargaining) that this may be an important trend in future development of bargaining agreements.

On the question of representation of professional scientists and engineers as an appropriate bargaining unit pursuant to section 9(b) of the Taft-Hartley Act, the Supreme Court decision of 1958 in the case *Leedom* v. *Kyne* is relevant.[6] It concerned a petition for certification by the Westinghouse Engineers Association, Engineers and Scientists of America (Buffalo Section) a voluntary unincorporated labor organization to promote the economic and professional status of the non-supervisory professional employees at a Westinghouse Electric plant in Cheektowaga, N.Y. The Westinghouse Engineers Association received a majority of the valid votes cast in an election ordered by the Board and was certified by the Board as the collective bargaining agent for the unit. Respondent (the president of the Association) brought suit in the District Court against the Board, asserting that the Board had exceeded its statutory power in including the professional employees without their consent in a unit with nonprofessional employees, in violation of section 9(b)(1) which commands that the Board shall not do so. The trial court found that the Board had disobeyed the express comand of section 9(b)(1) and had acted in excess of its powers to the injury of the professional employees. The plaintiff's motion was granted. The Board's determination of the bargaining unit, the election, and the Board's certification of the unit were set aside.[7] The Court of Appeals affirmed the judgment that the attempted exercise of power by the Board deprived the professional employees of a right assured to them by Congress, and the Supreme Court affirmed the judgment of the Court of Appeals. The case demonstrates the strong rights professional employees have been granted by section 9(b) of the Taft-Hartley Act to bargain independently and select representation of their own choice.

The second question raised, whether a bargaining unit of employees can bargain with the employer about patent and invention provisions in collective agreements, must rest on the interpretation of section 9(a) of the Taft-Hartley Act allowing as the subjects of collective bargaining "rates of pay, wages, hours of employment, *or other conditions of employment.*" A relevant precedent for a correct interpreta-

[6] 358 U.S. Reports 184, 79 Supreme Court Reporter 180, 3 Lawyers ed., 2d series 210, reprinted in Archibald Cox and Derek Curtis Bok, eds., *Cases and Materials on Labor Law* (Brooklyn, N.Y.: Foundation Press, 1965), pp. 370 ff.
[7] 148 Fed. Supplement, 597.

tion of the term "other conditions of employment" of the Act we find in the case *Inland Steel Co.* v. *National Labor Relations Board,* decided by the Court of Appeals in 1948.[8] The facts were that the Company introduced a compulsory retirement and pension plan for its employees. The Union, United Steelworkers of America, filed a grievance protesting the action of the Company. The Company refused to discuss this or to bargain collectively about these plans with locals of United Steelworkers, even though this Union has exclusive bargaining representation of all production, maintenance, and transportation workers in the plants. The Union referred the question to the NLRB, which stated in its decision that a retirement and pension plan is included in "conditions of employment" and is a matter for collective bargaining. The Court of Appeals found itself in agreement with the Board's conclusion and was convinced that the language employed by Congress so clearly includes such plans as to leave little, if any, room for construction. The Court also stated clearly: "We do not believe that it was contemplated that the language of Sec. 9(a) was to remain static. Congress in the original as well as in the amended Act used general language, evidently designed to meet the increasing problems arising from the employer-employee relationship."

The Emergence of Collective Bargaining Agreements with Patent Provisions
National War Labor Board   The oldest documented union contracts with patent provisions stem from September 1942 and involve the aircraft industry (Vultee Aircraft Inc. and the International Association of Machinists).[9] The year 1942 seems to be significant. At the beginning of this year, January 12, President Roosevelt issued an Executive Order (E.O. No. 9017) establishing the National War Labor Board. It was agreed therein that for the duration of the war there should be no resort to strikes or lockouts and that all labor disputes should be settled by peaceful means by the new Board. The National War Labor Board (NWLB) was the first and only government tribunal in the United States to be authorized specifically to bring about final settlement of labor disputes. It interpreted and exercised its powers to include those of compulsory arbitration. The Board had a tripartite composition with twelve full members (four, including the chairman, representing the public, four, the employees, and four, the employers). The E.O. 9017 stated that the existing labor laws should be effective in any action by the new Board. (This referred mainly to the Railway Labor Act of 1926, the

[8] 170 Fed. Reporter, 2d series 247.
[9] The early contract dates are taken from J.S. Costa, *The Law of Inventing in Employment* (New York: Central Book Co., 1953), pp. 151–152, footnotes 114 to 123.

National Labor Relations Act of 1935, and the Fair Labor Standards Act of 1938.)

It was on the platform of this powerful federal emergency board that two local lodges of the International Association of Machinists were twice involved in a basic struggle about principles of employee inventions, once against Douglas Aircraft Co. (decided on November 7, 1944) and once against Lockheed Aircraft Corp. (decided on September 20, 1945).[10]

The two disputes brought out a number of ideas and statements regarding employee-invention policy on both sides of the dispute never before or after accessible in as clear a form. For this reason we will study these two cases in detail.[11]

The First NWLB *Case (November 1944)*   In the shadow of the Allied invasion of France and Germany, the National War Labor Board made a majority decision (Directive Order) in the first case on November 7, 1944, pursuant to the powers vested in it by Executive Order 9017. It adopted recommendations of the National Airframe Panel on eight certified issues remaining in dispute after one year's negotiations between the International Association of Machinists (IAM) and Douglas Aircraft Co. The IAM was certified as collective bargaining unit for all production and maintenance employees, about 10,000 of the company's approximately 15,000 employees.

The unsolved issues before the Board concerned such matters as union security, wages, hours of work and premium pay, joint wage review, and "patents and plant suggestions." The order of the Board stated that the following items and conditions of employment shall govern the relations between the parties as to this point:

In accordance with the statements of the company as to the present practice and intention, the employees subject to this agreement shall not be required as a condition of employment to transfer or agree to transfer any right to inventions which they have made or may make during their employment, except to the extent necessary to discharge, under any contract now in force or hereafter entered into between the company and the United States or any of its departments or agencies, the Company's obligations to grant to the United States a nonexclusive, irrevocable license to practice such inventions free of royalty. The company shall have the right to practice such inventions free of royalty. The company shall have

[10] 21 War Labor Reports, 760, Washington 1945, In re Douglas Aircraft Company, Inc., El Segundo, Calif., and International Association of Machinists, Lodge 720 (AFL), case No. 111–7099–D, Nov. 7, 1944; and 27 War Labor Reports, 432, Washington 1946 (In re Lockheed Aircraft Corp., Burbank, Calif.) and International Association of Machinists, Lodge 727 (AFL) case No. 111–16460–D, Sept. 20, 1945.

[11] Besides the Executive Order 9017, of January 12, 1942, establishing the National War Labor Board, relevant laws were the Act of October 2, 1942, and the War Labor Disputes Act of June 25, 1943.

the right to practice all inventions voluntarily submitted as plant suggestions. Except as indicated above, the company or the employee does not hereby waive any right to ownership of, or license to practice, or any other rights to such inventions, which accrue to them by operation of law in the absence of this article.

In this issue of the majority decision three public members (Feinsinger, Gill, and Keezer) and three labor members (Watt, Brownlow, Brant) concurred, but three employer members (Ahearn, Skinner, Adair) dissented on five points, including the patent issue.

The decision of the Board on patent provisions says clearly that "the employees . . . shall not be required as a condition of employment to transfer or agree to transfer any right to inventions which they have made or may make during their employment . . . ." However they were required "to grant to the United States . . . a nonexclusive, irrevocable license to practice such inventions free of royalty" and the company retained the right to practice such inventions free of royalty, as well as suggestions voluntarily submitted. Inventions of employees of the type "hired to invent" were not mentioned in the decision.

How did the majority of the Board arrive at this decision in the face of heavy and intense opposition of the industry members? Douglas Aircraft, the employer, had objected to negotiating the union's proposal because the language of the War Labor Disputes Act[12] expressly empowers the Board to "provide by order the wages and hours and all other terms and conditions (customarily included in collective bargaining agreements) governing the relations between the parties." The language, it was argued by the employer, prohibited the Board from assuming jurisdiction over this issue because a patent clause "is not customarily included in such contracts." The employer also alleged that according to a Department of Labor Bulletin (No. 686, 1942) only a few collective bargaining agreements contain clauses dealing with inventions and improvements made by an employee.[13] The National Airframe Panel answered that, aside from the fact that this citation was obsolete and inconclusive, two West Coast airframe companies had provisions in their collective bargaining agreements dealing with this subject. This reference concerned a contract between Boeing Aircraft and IAM and another contract between Vultee Field Division of Consolidated Vultee Aircraft Corp. and the UAW. The Boeing provision permitted employees to retain ownership of inventions made during the course of employment provided the company had a shop right,

---

[12] 50 U.S. Code Annotated, sec. 1507, par. 2.
[13] 21 War Labor Reports (WLR), 774. These reports are quoted several times on the pages that follow, and page references will be given in the text.

and the Vultee agreement established that the company not require as a condition of employment or as a part of its contract of employment that any invention made by an employee shall belong to the company except as provided in its patent compensation plan. It is probably safe to assume that the two companies had not considered that their agreements would become precedents for the War Board.

As to the jurisdiction of the Board over patent provisions the majority of the Board observed that (War Labor Reports, p. 774)

... the War Labor Disputes Act should not be construed to deprive the Board of jurisdiction over any *bona fida* dispute between management and labor simply because the disputed issue is infrequently covered in collective bargaining agreements. The Board has already had occasion to consider many novel union demands, some of which cannot be found in any collective bargaining agreements. It is important to distinguish in such cases between assumption of jurisdiction and the denial of the demands on the merits.

In their concurring opinion (WLR, p. 744) the labor members of the Board remarked that in their opinion the patent clauses would protect the employee from having to relinquish his rights to inventions as a condition of employment but would neither prevent him from entering into any plan the company might have or establish for mutual participation on a voluntary basis nor take away any shop rights the company might have (WLR, p. 791).

It must be of great interest to any student of these problems to analyze the opposing standpoint of the representatives of industrial employers of the Board and of the employer (Douglas) as revealed by this case. To start with, the industry members of the National Airframe Panel expressed their belief "that the present issue (regarding patents and plant suggestions) is one of the most important questions referred to the Board for settlement in this or any case" (WLR, p. 788). The statement is surprising and may be somewhat overstated. After making this remark the industry members developed their "dissenting opinion" on the basis of three headings: (1) diminution of common law rights, (2) effect on industrial advancement, and (3) recession of inventive development. Before starting their argument these members attacked the rest of the sitting board personally for their lack of competence by saying (WLR, pp. 789-790):

By their own admission (p. 17, Par. 2, of the panel report), the public and labor members do not profess to have expert knowledge or even familiarity with the intricacies of patent law, and it is difficult to understand how they are then willing to assume the responsibility of making recommendations on a question which has unlimited significance.[14]

[14] The regulation of rights and obligations of employed inventors certainly are *not* mere

The arguments submitted by the industry members against the majority Board order on the basis of the three headings cited above, are summarized here.

Speaking to the first point, industry members held that the ruling would deprive the company of its common law right to patents and that it was definitely contrary to the spirit and practice of established law (WRL, p. 789). As support three court precedents were cited: *U.S.* v. *Dubilier Condenser Corp.,*[15] *L. A. Young Spring and Wire Corp.* v. *Falls,*[16] and *Smoley* v. *New Jersey Zinc Co.*[17]

As to the second point (effect on industrial advancement) the industry members emphasized again that "the importance of the question transcends the mere existence of relative rights between employers and employees" (WLR, p. 789). They asserted that the provision would, if adopted, "nullify the efforts of industry in its interchange of information on important improvements." This refers to specific wartime conditions, under which the aircraft industry not only cross-licensed its various patents "to the advantage of both the country and industry" but interchanged engineering and production information of an entirely unpatentable nature. According to the industry members, the patent provision in question would restrict and hinder "the breadth and scope" of the said operations, since no company can contribute more than its employees volunteer to disclose, and mere retention of shop rights could not be given or assigned to third parties.

As a second basis for their argument under the second heading the industry members expressed a promise and a menace. They say first that "it would seem foolish to expect" that compensation and award policies would be terminated at the time government contracts end, and on the other hand "it is doubted whether industry would continue such special award plans if obligated by union contract to waive rights which are currently its own" (WLR, p. 790).

The third contention (recession of inventive development) is supported by the

---

questions of patent law, in my opinion. They involve law of contracts, constitutional law, and in the absence of law, basic high-level management decisions. (F.N.)

[15] 289 U.S. Reports 178. The *Dubilier* case classifies employees in two groups: employees hired specifically to develop existing products or methods and employees hired for general purposes. For inventions conceived by the first group the employer was held to be entitled to complete rights, and for inventions by the second group he was entitled to shop rights.

[16] Michigan Supreme Court; *U.S. Patent Quarterly* 59: 235. In the *Young Spring* case the employer was entitled to recover royalties obtained by employees for employee inventions as a result of breaches of duty and conspiracy to defraud the employer.

[17] District Court of N.J.; *U.S. Patent Quarterly* 38: 315 (Appeal *U.S. Patent Quarterly* 42: 401). In the *New Jersey Zinc* case it was held that an employee invention assignment agreement is legally mandatory. This includes also ideas perfected after employment but the conception of which occurred during employment.

following reasoning. It is asserted that American ingenuity is raised to its present capacity "almost entirely as the result of corporate and industrial enterprise in instituting research development and patent action in furtherance of the general 'ideas' usually submitted by its employees." Few inventions are held to become instruments of progress except as promoted by the vision and resources that business can lend, and they have to be improved or altered before use. If the employee is not obligated to assign his invention a loss in inventions would be noticeable. Such precedent also would be brought to bear on other industries "by labor groups more concerned with collective bargaining than with the overall advance of American industry" (WLR, p. 790).

The reasons given here induced the industry members of the panel to request the denial of the patent provision submitted by the majority of the Board. The request had no success, and the majority decision of the Board adopted its recommendations on November 7, 1944.

The Second NWLB *Case (September 1945)*   In the second case the International Association of Machinists negotiated with Lockheed Aircraft Corp. as the exclusive collective bargaining representative of the Company's employees, including about 34,000 of approximately 40,000 workers at the Company's Burbank plant. (Certain designated groups were excepted.) The parties were unable to agree on 10 issues including items such as severance notice, union security, employee representation, downgrading, employee suggestions (issue No. 2), and inventions (issue No. 3). On September 20, 1945, the National Board made the directive order on issues No. 2 and 3: "The union's request is denied" (WLR, p. 433). The decision read as follows:

Grievances; Subject matter of grievance machinery; Employee suggestions (issue No. 2).

Union is not entitled to clause providing that complaints concerning company's disposition of or reward for employee suggestions be made subject to grievance and arbitration machinery since (1) employees are not required to submit suggestions as condition of employment, (2) employees making suggestions are offering ideas for sale on company's terms, and (3) company has served notice that it will accept offers made on its own terms or not at all.

Company's attitude on this issue does not differ from that of any other company which utilizes employee suggestion plans and union has shown no evidence that its proposal is embodied in any collective bargaining agreement,

and on issue No. 3 (WLR, p. 432):

Working conditions; Assignment of inventions.

Union's request that non-research workers should be exempt from having to sign invention assignment contract is denied since company's long-standing practice of requiring execution of agreement whereby employee assigns to company inventions relating to company's work which are developed during period of employment is valid under law and constitutes reasonable device for protection of its interests. Contract provides that employees be paid for inventions patented, used or sold by company.

In the majority decision of the Board on these two issues two public members (Gill, Witte) and two employer members (Cannon, Hennessy) concurred, and two labor members (Chipman, Stewart) dissented.

Thus, in this second case, the majority of the Board followed the opinion of the industry members and denied the requests of the Union in the field of employee suggestions and employee inventions. It was held that this case was clearly distinguishable from the preceding case on its facts (WLR, p. 445), but the question of the jurisdiction of the Board was settled in the affirmative in the earlier case of Douglas Aircraft. As to the legality of Company practice to require execution of invention assignment agreements as a condition of employment, it was stated in the discussion "that by all prevailing standards this agreement is valid in law." (According to the third contention such agreement is, however, limited to the field of manufacture or operation of the company and to inventions made during employment.) Continuation of the obligation to assign inventions six months after term of employment was said not in itself to make the agreement invalid.[18] Neither did the scope of the agreement with Lockheed invalidate it, although it was said to "appear to be so broad as to render the agreement unenforceable."[19] It is added, then, that an agreement that is limited in scope and in time will not generally be considered either an unlawful restraint of trade or an unconscionable "mortgage on a man's brain."[20]

The panel finally upheld its denial of the Union's request by saying that the Company's long-standing policy of requiring an invention assignment as a condition of employment is valid under the law and "constitutes a reasonable

[18] WLR, p. 443. Five court cases were cited, of which four were Court of Claims and Appeals cases.
[19] The report adds to this statement (on page 443) in a footnote (6): "The statement above presupposes a relatively strict construction of the phrases" "business of the company" and "field of aviation." "Contract provisions of this kind are customarily limited to a particular field of endeavor," whereafter reference is made to *Guth* v. *Minnesota Mining & Mfg. Co.*, 72 Fed. Reporter, 2d series, 388 (Circuit Court of Appeals, 7th Dist. 1934).
[20] The Board referred to *Aspinwall Mfg. Co.* v. *Gill*, 32 Fed. Reporter, 697; Circuit Court, N.J. 1887.

device for the protection of its interests." It continues: "The wisdom of the law may be debatable, but that is not for this panel to say. The adequacy of the consideration given by the company in return for the promises obtained from its employees has not been called into question and is not an issue in this case."[21]

The opinions and statements made by the Board and the parties as abbreviated here present a somewhat vague picture of the legal situation as well as of the practical situation on the labor market with regard to rights and obligations of employees and employers when the former make inventions during employment, all within the framework of collective bargaining agreements. The Board tried to reconcile the issues, but they were close and might have been decided differently, as evidenced by the dissents. But after all, the decisions of the National War Labor Board had to be made in the stream of hectic world events decisive for the future of the whole country. From the point of view of the labor unions, the WLB policies served in many cases to improve the status of the country's wage earners (although the right to strike was banned for the duration of the war). Many long-term gains for all wage earners were reached, and union membership had increased to over 14 million at the close of war hostilities. On the other hand, widespread fears had been awakened that the labor unions after the end of the war would use their increased power without due regard to public welfare and industrial progress.

This chapter disregards the main subject of collective bargaining, the increase of wages, and focuses on something which in labor law and practice falls under "fringe benefits" or "supplementary benefits." Patent provisions, so far as they concern award payments or release of patent rights to employees, should be included in such benefits. The other benefits most frequently improved or established by collective bargaining are health and welfare plans, pensions, paid vacations, paid holidays, job security, paid leaves for sickness or funerals, and "premium pay."[22] What hides behind the official term "premium pay" is not known but might well cover invention-award premiums.

Concerning our specific question we find that in the period of the war years and shortly after, some fifteen collective bargaining agreements containing patent provisions were executed, about one-third of which involved the aircraft industry

[21] WLR, p. 445. The Board panel aptly indicates here that the law (common law) at that time (1945) may not yet have offered any final solution of all basic problems involved in the employee-invention field.

[22] See L. M. David, "Major Collective Bargaining Settlements," *Monthly Labor Review* 89, No. 4 (Washington, D.C.: April 1966), pp. 372 ff., especially Table 3.

(Vultee, Boeing, Douglas, Lockheed). Four of the agreements have survived, i.e., have been extended into the 1960's with Boeing, McDonnell-Douglas, Lockheed, American Potash, and one which has been shifted within different divisions of RCA. Of the labor union bargaining units nine were affiliated with CIO and six with AFL (these two federations did not unite until 1955).

Before discussing specific collective bargaining agreements of today in the latter part of this chapter some statistics are in order to enable the reader to appreciate the number of employees (mainly workers) covered by this special type of labor agreement.

Employees Covered by Collective Bargaining Agreements

In 1966, 141 unions reported to the Bureau of Labor Statistics' biennial questionnaire survey, and the Bureau estimated for another 19 unions, to total of 18.4 million workers covered by collective bargaining contracts, compared with 17.8 million union members. (The 18.4 million figure is arrived at by assuming that agreement coverage does not exceed union membership by more than 5 percent. It can be used with fair accuracy, in the Bureau's opinion, to compute collective bargaining coverage in the U.S. as of 1966.[23]) The number of workers covered by major agreements (agreements each of which covers more than 1000 workers) is 8.3 million.[24] Service trades, finance, and government bargaining agreements are omitted from this accounting.

The Bureau of Labor Statistics has also made surveys of the distribution of production workers covered by collective bargaining agreements among major industry groups.[25] All types of unions are included in these data—those affiliated with AFL-CIO, nonaffiliated unions, subordinate bodies of national unions, or unions confined to single establishments. In some cases, more than one union is entrenched in a single establishment. The transportation industry, including aircraft industries, now has the greatest number of collective bargaining agreements, with more than 80 percent of production (factory) workers in companies where the majority of all workers are covered by such agreements. Another branch of industry of special interest for this book, since four corporations in this segment were analyzed in Chapter 3, is "electrical equipment." Here close to 70 percent of production

[23] *Directory of National and International Labor Unions in the United States, 1967.* Bureau of Labor Statistics Bulletin No. 1596, pp. 68–69.
[24] The Bureau of Labor Statistics (BLS) as of 1968 had about 2000 such agreements in its files. (Communication to author, November 1968.)
[25] The BLS's data come from a sample of about 6500 establishments selected by industry, location, and size.

workers are in plants where a majority of workers are covered. "Production workers" embraced by these statistics include, in addition to manual workers, foremen and all nonsupervisory workers engaged in nonoffice functions. These figures illustrate roughly the impact any change of collective bargaining agreements has on the American labor force.

It may be interesting to see how the national and international unions are distributed by number of collective bargaining agreements with employers. Table 4.1 shows these data for 148 unions reporting, plus estimates for 36 additional ones. The number of agreements in public service—federal, state, and municipal—was estimated at about 1500. Six unions with a combined membership of 3.1 million failed to furnish data; therefore the total number of agreements in existence in 1966 is not accounted for in the table. The Bureau considers its previous estimate of 140,000 to be still valid. (This figure includes about 2500 contracts for single-plant and single-locality unions.)

The concentration of agreements among a small number of unions is marked. Thirteen AFL-CIO affiliates and one nonaffiliated union each negotiated 2000 or more agreements, and were a party to two of every three agreements signed. In contrast, about one-half the total unions, national and international, held less than 2500 contracts among them.[26]

CASE STUDIES OF ELEVEN CORPORATIONS

In this section an attempt will be made to take stock of the (accessible) collective bargaining agreements that include patent provisions, in force as of 1966. The agreements are ranked in terms of dollar sales of the employing company, which in many cases gives the same rank in terms or number of employees.

The 11 corporations in Table 4.2 totally executed more than 20 separate collective bargaining agreements containing patent provisions. Among these corporations, General Dynamics Corporation administers seven different agreements of this kind, representing three different manufacturing divisions (Convair, San Diego; Convair, Pomona, and Forth Worth). On the employee side we have professional unions (Engineers and Architects Association and its branches), one large AFL-CIO labor union (International Association of Machinists, IAM) and one independent labor union (Federated Independent Texas Unions).

To execute two different bargaining agreements (with patent provisions), one with a labor union unit and one with a professional union unit seems to be relatively common. This type of "double agreement" of two unions with the

[26] BLS Bulletin No. 1596, pp. 68–69.

Table 4.1 Distribution of National and International Unions by Number of Basic Collective Bargaining Agreements with Employers, 1966

Number	All Unions		Collective Bargaining Agreements		Union Affiliation			
					AFL-CIO		Unaffiliated	
	Number	Percent	Number	Percent	Unions	Collective Bargaining Agreements	Unions	Collective Bargaining Agreements
All unions[1]	184	100.0	115,654	100.0	124	108,026	60	7,628
No agreements[2]	3	1.6			1		2	2
Less than 25 agreements	54	29.3	373	0.3	17	108	37	265
25 and under 100 agreements	36	19.6	2,050	1.8	24	1,473	12	577
100 and under 200 agreements	19	10.3	2,620	2.3	17	2,362	2	258
200 and under 300 agreements	15	8.2	3,617	3.1	13	3,126	2	491
300 and under 500 agreements	10	5.4	3,672	3.2	8	3,065	2	607
500 and under 1,000 agreements	14	7.6	8,814	7.6	14	8,814		
1,000 and under 2,000 agreements	18	9.8	22,454	19.4	16	19,904	2	2,550
2,000 and under 3,000 agreements	6	3.3	14,461	12.5	5	11,581	1	2,880
3,000 and under 5,000 agreements	2	1.1	6,400	5.5	2	6,400		
5,000 agreements and over	7	3.8	51,193	44.3	7	51,193		

1 One hundred forty-eight unions plus 36 for which the Bureau of Labor Statistics made estimates.
2 Includes 2 unions composed of government workers.
Source: Directory of National and International Labor Unions in the U.S., 1967 BLS Bulletin No. 1596.

Table 4.2 Companies Holding Collective Bargaining Agreements with Patent Provisions

Employer	Employee Bargaining Unit	Term of Agreement
Boeing Co. Seattle, Wash.	(1) International Assoc. of Machinists (IAM) (2) (Individual invention assignment contracts are used in addition.)	October 1965–September 1968
Radio Corp. of America Camden Division	Assoc. of Scientists and Engineering Personnel	July 1964–July 1967[1]
Radio Corp. of America Moorestown Division	American Fed. of Techncial Engineers	June 1967–June 1971
General Dynamics Corp. Convair Division San Diego, Calif.	(1) Engineers and Architects Assoc., Professional division	August 1964–August 1966[1]
" "	(2) Engineers and Architects Assoc., Technical and office employees	August 1963–December 1965[1]
" "	(3) IAM	October 1965–October 1970
" "	(4) Engineers and Architects Assoc.	November 1965–December 1970
Convair Division Pomona, Calif.	(5) Engineers and Architects Assoc.	November 1965–December 1970
	(6) IAM	October 1965–October 1970
Fort Worth Division	(7) Federated Independent Texas Unions Aircraft Local 900	January 1966–January 1971
Lockheed Aircraft Corp. Lockheed Calif. Division Burbank, Calif.	(1) Engineers and Scientists Guild, Lockheed Section (2) (Individual assignment contracts are used.)	October 1965–October 1968
McDonnell-Douglas Aircraft Co.	(1) Southern Calif. Professional Engineering Assoc.	August 1965–October 1968
Missile and Space Systems Division	(2) IAM	August 1965–July 1968
Otis Elevator Co. Jersey City, N.J.	United Autoworkers (UAW) Local 980 (Individual assignment contracts are used.)	June 1961–August 1964[1]
Sperry Rand Corp. Sperry Gyroscope Co. Division Great Neck, New York	(1) International Union of Electrical Workers (IUE) (2) Engineers Assoc.	June 1967–June 1970 June 1967–June 1970
Sperry Rand Corp. Ford Instrument Division Long Island, N.Y.	(1) IUE (2) (Individual assignment contracts are used.)	June 1964–June 1967
American Bosch Arma Co. Garden City, N.Y.	(1) IUE (1) Engineers Assoc. of Arma (later IUE Engineers Unit)	October 1966–March 1969
Southern California Gas Co. Los Angeles, Calif.	Southern California Professional Engineering Assoc.	May 1967–May 1968
American Potash and Chemical Corp. Los Angeles, Calif.	United Mine Workers (UMW)	March 1962–March 1966[1]
American Oil Co. Whiting, Ind.	Research and Engineering Professional Employees Assoc.	December 1965–February 1967[1]

[1] Later agreement is not on file at the Bureau of Labor Statistics, as of November 1968.

same employer is in force at American Bosch Arma, McDonnell-Douglas Aircraft, General Dynamics, RCA, and Sperry Gyroscope. Some corporations have invention agreements with one type of bargaining unit only, either with a labor union unit (Boeing Aircraft, Otis Elevator, American Potash) or with a professional union unit (Lockheed Aircraft, Southern California Gas, American Oil). Some of the listed corporations make use of the individual invention assignment contract for additional selected groups of employees.[27]

A glance at the employee bargaining units involved shows that the blue-collar labor unions representing employees in such agreements are some of the big AFL-CIO unions. These are the International Association of Machinists (IAM), the International Union of Electrical Workers (IUE), and the American Federation of Technical Engineers, the United Mine Workers, and an engineering unit of IUE. The bargaining units for professional engineers are mostly local organizations created at the division but in some cases are company-wide. The Southern California Professional Engineering Association covers professional engineering members from a number of corporations in the West Coast area.

Of the eleven corporations, four represent large aircraft and areospace corporations (Boeing, Convair, Lockheed, McDonnell-Douglas), four electronics (American Bosch Arma, Otis Elevator, RCA, Sperry Gyroscope), one petroleum products (American Oil), one basic chemicals (American Potash), and one utility, (Southern California Gas).

Seven of the eleven corporations which executed such agreements in 1967 belonged to the group of the 500 largest U.S. industrial corporations according to the "Fortune Directory" (*Fortune*, June 15, 1968), both in terms of net dollar sales and total number of employees. The seven are presented in Table 4.3, with four additional corporations listed in Dun & Bradstreet *Million Dollar Directory*, 1968.

Even if the collective bargaining agreements of the biggest corporations have been executed only with limited groups of organized employees and only at certain of their local plants, it may be significant that very large industrial organizations seem to have some preference for handling invention problems collectively. Administration may thus be simplified and disputes in the field may be avoided or reduced. Another circumstance may be still more crucial for collective bargaining

---

[27] However, an employee can never be bound by two types of patent agreements at the same time. The collective patent arrangement excludes the individual patent assignment arrangement.

Table 4.3 Eleven Corporations Ranked by Sales

Corporation	Rank in Fortune Directory 1968[1]	Sales $	Number of Employees
Radio Corp. of America	15	3,014,074	128,000
McDonnell-Douglas Corp.	16	2,933,753	140,050
Boeing Co.	19	2,879,686	142,700
Lockheed Corp.	30	2,335,456	92,267
General Dynamics Corp.	32	2,253,336	103,196
Sperry Rand Corp.[2]	46	1,487,120	101,603
American Oil Co.[3]	–	1,800,000	24,000
Otis Elevator Co.	189	457,236	41,000
Southern California Gas Co.[3]	–	320,000	5,208
American Bosch Arma Corp.[3]	–	91,000	5,000
American Potash & Chemical Corp.[3]	–	65,000	2,165

1 "The Fortune Directory," *Fortune*, June 15, 1968.
2 Sperry Gyroscope, discussed in the text, is a division of Sperry Rand, which is primarily an operating company.
3 Dun & Bradstreet *Million Dollar Directory*, 1968.

about employee inventions. All the large corporations listed are deeply involved in government-sponsored research and manufacture. Boeing negotiates contracts with NASA for Saturn V first stages with a value of over $165 million, and RCA's Camden and Moorestown plants manufacture defense electronic products and military apparatus. Lockheed designs and produces advanced defense systems and is a prime research and production contractor for the Navy, for instance for Polaris missiles. General Dynamics' Convair division produces military cargo jets and space vehicles for the NASA Apollo project. McDonnell-Douglas (Douglas merged with McDonnell in 1967) carries out government contracts for the Atomic Energy Commission to operate AEC's $350 million atomic reactor and fuel fabrication complex at Hanford, Washington. Also Otis Elevator, as the leading producer of elevator systems, moving stairways, hoists, and accessories, belongs to the big government contractors. The company designs and manufactures Minuteman missiles, is involved in NASA's Lunar Orbiter project and Saturn V boosters, builds jet transports and weapon system fire trainers. Sperry Rand, including Sperry Gyroscope Co. as a division, designs and produces instrumentation and controls for business machines, systems and equipment, including electronic data-processing and tabulating equipment. Government business accounts for 49 percent of total sales.[28] American Bosch Arma produces electronic devices for the armed forces such as automatic fire control equipment for the Air Force, jet bombers, all-inertial navigation systems, as well as telemetering and data-handling components. American Potash's production of titanium dioxide as high-energy fuel might involve government-sponsored work. American Oil, a subsidiary of Standard Oil of Indiana, manufactures, transports, and sells a full line of petroleum products in 45 states. Southern California Gas is a large public utility in Los Angeles with appliance, chemical, and mechanical laboratories. It is involved in food, building, and air conditioning fields.

These examples may be sufficient to illustrate that the large extent of military government contracts under which most of the listed corporations work (especially the aircraft and aerospace companies) may have contributed to their mechanisms for bargaining collectively about employee inventions. Inventions made in connection with government contract work are subject to definite requirements prescribed by government agencies. However, these requirements depend on which agency has ordered the contract (all Armed Forces departments have the same procurement rules).[29]

What Do the Patent Provisions of the Collective Agreements Contain?
When looking at the contents of the patents provisions of the listed agreements we find a checkered pattern. The essential features to be looked at in all agreements concern
1. Ownership of patent and invention rights, and the field of agreement.
2. Extra compensation for assignment and/or use of invention rights.
3. The categories of employees affected by the provision.
4. The percentage of employees covered.
5. The arrangements for settling disputes.
Aircraft companies will be discussed first as each point is taken in turn.
1. *Ownership of Invention Rights and Field of Agreement*
The Boeing Company permits employees to retain ownership of inventions conceived or developed by them during employment provided that the company shall have shop rights to all such inventions. The shop right is defined to comprise the nonexclusive, royalty-free rights to use such inventions, to make, have made,

[28] Moody's *Industrial Manual 1964*, p. 1587.
[29] See Chapter 5 of this book, especially the case study on NASA. Government procurement rules are changed from time to time. General trend is now in strengthening the title policy giving government full ownership of contractor's (employee) inventions in all fields of government-sponsored R&D.

and sell products, parts, or tools incorporating such inventions. This license extends to others making use of the inventions, to the extent that they are doing work for or selling to the Company. All inventions which are not related to Boeing's business or to the employee's work are excluded from assignment. Excluded are also inventions conceived prior to employment or after termination.

General Dynamics has a series of collective bargaining agreements at Convair Division (San Diego and Pomona) and at Fort Worth Division, with provisions that the Company does not waive shop rights. On the other hand, the Company does not require as a condition of employment that any invention shall belong to it (except as required by federal statute, Executive Order, or governmental regulations).[30] In other words, the Company adopts the common law rule except as federal requirements call for greater rights.

Lockheed Aircraft. Inventions and improvements by employees "of company interest" as defined by assignment agreement are usually not "releasable," that is, they are company property. However, the Company may, in its sole discretion, release to employee inventors those inventions, even though technically within the scope of Company interest, which are clearly not directly related to Company products (in being or planned), shop methods or processes, and which will not be developed at company expense and are not subject to patent applications. The assignable inventions are those relating to the various products or manufacturing methods, processes, apparatus, machines, or operations or other business of the Company which are believed to be new and useful. In case of release the Company retains a nonexclusive, royalty-free license not entitling the inventor to special invention award.

McDonnel-Douglas provides in its patent contract that the entire title to all inventions, improvements, or developments made, invented, or suggested by certain groups of employees in defined fields become the sole and absolute property of the Company. Execution of patent contract is a condition of employment. If the Patent Board of the Company decides that a submitted disclosure does not justify the expense of a patent application the subject matter of the disclosure may be released to an employee on written request. This decision is entirely within the discretion of the Company. The field of the patent contract comprises all inventions that relate to (1) the current products of the Company, (2) any process, apparatus, or article currently incorporated in or useful in the development, manufacture, or

---

[30] This reservation is essential in view of the extensive number of NASA and AEC contracts under which the aircraft and aerospace companies work.

operation of such products, or (3) any work or investigation then being undertaken by the Company.

The collective bargaining agreements of the four large aircraft manufacturers in the case studies have one important special feature in common, not existing in agreements of other corporations. In the aircraft invention field aircraft manufacturers have contractual arrangements as members of the Manufacturers Aircraft Association (MAA). This association was originally founded in 1917 to make the aircraft patents of the Wright and Curtiss companies accessible to other aircraft manufacturers under reasonable royalty conditions.

As of December 31, 1963 the rate of payment by members of the Association for the administration of the patent pool was 20 percent of 1/8 of 1 percent of the cost of each aircraft, in addition to "arbitrated royalties" for certain patents. (This cost refers to payments to be made by the members of MAA in return for permission to use certain patents in their activities licensed to the Association, the amount of royalty being fixed by an arbitration board within the Association. On December 31, 1963, there were over 6000 aircraft patents under cross-license by MAA, of which only about 300 had been awarded special compensation by the Association.[31] The primary purpose of MAA is to administer cross-license agreements and license contracts for aeronautical patents and to serve as a collecting and disbursing agency for all payments in accordance with such agreements. All unnecessary patent litigation between aircraft patent owners shall be avoided, and the use of such patents shall be made available to all U.S. aircraft manufacturers (and to the government as potential buyer and user) at the lowest cost possible. Royalty income of large significance can hardly accrue to U.S. patent owners in this field. The Association through its Arbitration Board has to see to it that royalty costs will be kept as low as possible. Directors of MAA are taken from many different aircraft companies. In 1964, for instance, they came from 14 corporations including Martin Marietta Corp., North American Aviation, Douglas Aircraft, McDonnell Aircraft, Republic Aviation, United Aircraft, the Boeing Co., and Lockheed Aircraft. Many of the companies represented on the Board of MAA offer employed inventors in their own company patent plans a share of income from employee inventions licensed or sold to "third parties."

A legally untrained employee will undoubtedly be unable to evaluate the obligations or rights he is assuming when signing his patent agreement with his employer.

[31] H. T. Dykman, "Patent Licensing Within the Manufacturer's Aircraft Association (MAA)," *J. Patent Off. Soc.* 46 (September 1964): 646 ff, at 651.

The advantage to the inventing employee is not self-evident. Employees so involved have characterized the practical result of the promised payments as token payments. Lockheed management, however, reports a substantial record of royalty payments executed to its employee inventors. During 1964 Lockheed paid under the royalty patent plan $97,810 for 15,000 detailed ideas presented by employees during that time. It is said that ideas and individual initiative have brought more than $1 million in royalty payments to employee inventors at Lockheed, but there is no information on what time period is covered. Many of these inventions over the years have proved of great value in fields outside the aerospace industry. An outstanding example is Lockfoam plastic, originally intended as a structural stiffener in aircraft, now having more than 100 different applications. It is not known how inventors of such devices have been compensated by Lockheed.

The *Radio Corporation of America* collective bargaining agreement comprises full assignment of inventions. In the *Otis Elevator* agreement all inventions conceived, discovered, or made "along the lines of the company's work and investigations" are to be assigned to the company. In the *Sperry Gyroscope* agreement all inventions made during employment are assigned to the company. In case the employer has not filed a patent application within two years from date of receiving the disclosure, the inventor may make a written request that he do so. Within six months of the written request from the inventor, the employer must either file such a patent application or agree to grant a release of the invention provided the inventor files an application within one year from the date of such release agreement. In all release cases the employer has the right to retain a royalty-free, nonexclusive license under any patent issued to the inventor.

In the *Ford Instrument Division* of Sperry Rand agreement all inventions conceived and/or made during employment and within six months after termination of employment which are in whole or in part the result of the work with the company become the property of the company whether or not patent applications are filed thereon. Release of invention to employee is granted

... with respect to inventions, the concept, creation or development of which is outside the reasonable contemplation of his employment and which are not derived from or the result in whole or in part, of his work with the Company and are not related in any way or to any degree to any project or field of work in which the Company was employed or was actively considering during the period of employment.[32]

[32] The company could have constructed the agreement the other way round, providing that employees need not assign any inventions except for certain cases specified.

Further conditions are attached as to filing of patent applications for such inventions. If the company does not release the invention in accordance with these provisions reasonable compensation shall be made (in the discretion of the company).

The *American Bosch Arma* agreement classifies employee inventions in two groups: "in-line" inventions and "not-in-line" inventions, and treats them differently in regard to ownership and compensation. "In-line" inventions are all inventions "directly applicable to the Employer's business" and are the property of the employer, to be assigned by the inventor. "Not-in-line" inventions are all other inventions. If a patent is applied for, standard payment is made to the inventor; however, if the patent attorney for the employer considers the invention not patentable the invention shall revert to the inventor, and a full release is granted on request, subject to a nonexclusive, irrevocable license to the employer.[33] "Not-in-line" inventions remain the property of the inventor, except that the employer has a two-months option from the date of complete disclosure of the invention to file a patent application. If he does this he receives a nonexclusive, irrevocable license for such patent, but the patent may not be assigned outside the American Bosch Arma Corp., its divisions, or subsidiaries.

The *Southern California Gas* agreement prescribes for the employer the following three different courses of action regarding ownership of employee inventions.

1. A written release covering all rights in the inventions or improvements.

2. The same as (1) but subject to retention of shop rights by the Company.

3. The Company files a patent application and pays prosecution costs, but the employee may take over prosecution at his own expense, in which case the Company retains royalty-free, paid up, nonexclusive license, and employee is free to exploit the invention subject to such license.

The *American Potash and Chemical* agreement does not require as a condition of employment that any invention or improvement made by an employee shall belong to the company.[34]

The *American Oil Company* agreement, finally, provides that an employee (at the request of the Company) make specific assignment to the Company of an invention or discovery, for which he receives a fixed standard payment. Such payment must

[33] This regulation disregards the field of trade secrets and inventions patentable despite the judgment of the employer.
[34] Employee inventions that are the result of R&D for which an employee is expressly hired are not mentioned in this agreement.

obviously be based on some Company criteria regarding the nature of the invention and the circumstances under which it is made.

2. *Extra Compensation for Assignment and/or Use of Invention Rights*   When studying the compensation question we find that all four aircraft corporations offer their employees a share of the income they may collect from royalties that may be paid to the corporations by the Manufacturers Aircraft Association. All four corporations are members of the patent pool of MAA and are under obligation to offer for cross-licensing all aircraft inventions made by their employees. The licensing of employee aircraft patents to Association members is for the most part carried out free of cost. Thus no payment is made to the member company supplying its employee patents, and no royalty income arises which could be shared with the inventor.[35] "On paper" all four companies present an income-sharing scheme for employee aircraft inventions for which a patent application has been filed and revenue or royalty has been received by the employing company from MAA.

General Dynamics (Convair Division) offers employee inventors a percentage of any royalties the company may collect from licenses to others, including those from MAA. A sliding scale is applied for the use of such inventions: 30 percent of first $1000 or part thereof, 25 percent of next $1000 or part thereof, and 20 percent of any further sums in excess of $2000. These royalties are paid during the life of any patent, subject to the company invention agreement and notwithstanding possible termination of employment with General Dynamics. The company pays $50 upon execution of any U.S. patent application and $50 when a patent is granted to the company.

McDonnell-Douglas offers the inventor from the net amount of any "money consideration" received and retained from licensee: 30 percent of the first $10,000, 20 percent of the next $10,000, and 10 percent of all above $20,000. The "net amount" is defined as the total amount of any actual money specified to be paid, and actually received and retained from the licensee (or purchaser), less cost of exploiting and protecting the invention, other than cost of filing and prosecuting the patent application. The company pays standard cash awards, $25 when a U.S. patent application is assigned and $75 when a "mechanical" patent is granted.

Lockheed Aircraft has the following schedule in its Patent Plan (1966) governing income participation for inventor-employees: 20 percent on the first $100,000

[35] At the end of 1963 a special compensation (royalty) was awarded for about 5 percent of MAA-administered aircraft patents.

received, 10 percent on the next $400,000, and 5 percent on any further sums in excess of $500,000.

Any special invention award granted to the inventor by the company shall be balanced against royalty revenue that may accrue for the same invention from outside licensing of such invention. As standard cash award Lockheed pays $100 whether the invention is assigned or title transferred under government contract, and $500 as final award, if a patent is allowed.

The *Boeing Company* pays the inventor 20 percent of any royalty received from outside sources for patented employee inventions. As standard award, $50 is paid for any filed U.S. patent application and an additional $50 when a patent is granted to the company.

In the schedules presented by McDonnell-Douglas and Lockheed a percentage is offered inventors for the first $10,000 (McDonnell-Douglas) and the first $100,000 (Lockheed), to be applied also to royalties within these amounts. This is the case for General Dynamics, too, which talks about the first $1000 and the next $1000, "or part thereof."

Radio Corporation of America provides a standard cash award in its two collective-bargaining agreements, upon filing of each patent application assigned to the Corporation by employees. The amount of the award is, however, different in the two agreements. The employees covered by RCA's agreement with the Association of Scientists and Engineering Personnel as bargaining unit receive $150 for each assigned application, and the employees covered by the American Federation of Technical Engineers as bargaining unit with RCA receive $100 for each assigned application.

American Bosch Arma pays the inventors of any "in-line" invention (directly applicable to the company's business), idea, or suggestion for which the company shall apply for patents the sum of $100 per inventor (to a maximum of $300 per invention). For "not-in-line" invention the employer, if he elects to bear the costs of a patent application, has a nonexclusive, irrevocable license. The license is nonassignable outside the company, its divisions, or subsidiaries, provided the company pay the inventor a royalty at no lesser rate than that paid by any other licensee under the same patent. The expense of the employer in procuring such patent shall be offset against any royalty so earned by the inventor.

According to the *American Oil* agreement each employee represented by the professional association as bargaining unit receives for each specific assignment to the company of an invention or discovery a sum of $50,

Sperry Gyroscope pursues two different ways. In the agreement with the Engineers Association it pays $25 upon the assignment of an application for a patent; in the agreement with the International Union of Electrical Workers (IUE) no additional payment is made for disclosed inventions.

No extra compensation for any invention is provided by *Otis Elevator* and by *Southern California Gas,* but the latter company pays costs of filing and prosecuting U.S. patent applications relating to inventions for any phase of the company's work or investigations, and it retains a royalty-free, paid up, nonexclusive license.

Neither does *Ford Instrument Co.* Division of Sperry Rand Corporation make any additional payment for inventions patented and assigned by an employee, which are in whole or in part the result of his work with the company. The Company, however, has a general policy, described before, to release to the employee inventions not derived from his work with the Company and not related to any project or field of work the Company was actively considering during the period of his employment. In case such inventions are not released by the Company, it offers a "reasonable compensation."

3. *Categories of Employees Affected*   As we have seen earlier, it is the duty of the National Labor Relations Board pursuant to sec. 9(b) of the Taft-Hartley Act to determine what group of employees constitutes a unit appropriate for bargaining with their employer. This discretion of the Board is limited by the same section when it states that professional employees may not be included in a unit of nonprofessional employees unless a majority of the professional employees vote to be included. (The definition of professional employee is given in sec. 2(12) (a) of the Taft-Hartley Act.) These provisions of the law are highly relevant for the present study, since the two different bargaining units, professional and non-professional, most likely have different attitudes toward the importance of invention provisions in a collective bargaining agreement. Professional employees are obviously more likely to make inventions, discoveries, and improvements during employment. There is, however, no definite borderline between different employees in their capacity as inventive individuals. The collective bargaining agreements analyzed in this chapter demonstrate this fact rather well. We find that the six bargaining agreements of the four aircraft corporations in regard to "appropriate bargaining units" show three different types of employee representation:

1. One collective bargaining agreement is executed with only a blue-collar labor union as bargaining unit (Boeing and International Association of Machinists, IAM).

2. Two collective bargaining agreements are executed with only white-collar professional independent associations as bargaining units (Lockheed Aircraft and Engineers and Scientists Guild, Lockheed Section; and General Dynamics, Forth Worth Division, and Federated Independent Texas Unions, Aircraft Local No. 900).[36]

3. Three collective bargaining agreements are executed with two separate bargaining units coetaneously, one a blue-collar labor union and one a white-collar professional association.

The agreements can be charted as follows:

General Dynamics Convair Division, San Diego, Calif.	Engineers and Architects Association International Association of Machinists (IAM)
General Dynamics Convair Division, Pomona, Calif.	Engineers and Architects Association International Association of Machinists (IAM)
McDonnell-Douglas Missiles and Space Systems Divisions	Southern California Professional Engineering Association International Association of Machinists (IAM)

These relationships are important but do not furnish particulars on how many and what kind of workers, technicians, and engineers are covered by the collective bargaining agreements and their patent provisions. Taking the General Dynamics Convair Division (both San Diego and Pomona) bargaining agreements as examples, we find that the agreements between Convair Division and the Engineers and Architects Association, San Diego Chapter, recognize this Association as exclusive representative of all employees located there (and at a number of other plants and test facilities), and job classifications are listed as part of the agreement. The bargaining agreements between Convair Division in San Diego (and six other plants, test facilities, and five offsite bases in California, Florida, and New Mexico) and the International Association of Machinists at these plants recognize IAM as exclusive representative of all employees as listed in extensive job classifications set forth as appendices of the agreement. Expressly excluded are professional, management, confidential and security employees, and all classifications of employees excluded by law. Also excluded are those employed in about 26 different

---

36 FITU is very small, covering only about 200 employees. The union is defined by the National Labor Relations Board in Case No. 16–RC–1153, on February 24, 1953. The case seems not to be officially reported, either in NLRB cases or in LRRM.

functions, sections, or departments of the Company such as the offices of the president, base managers, technical directors, contracts, financial control, audit and factory method sections. About 6400 employees are covered by the IAM as exclusive bargaining representative in this local bargaining agreement.

The agreement between Convair Division in Pomona and the IAM at this plant recognizes the union as the exclusive representative of the production and maintenance employees in the job classifications set forth in one appendix of the agreement covering about 225 factory job classifications (from all kinds of mechanics, assemblers, and machine operators to utility workers and groups of factory inspectors) and in another appendix covering 23 technical and office job classifications (from chauffeur to data-processing librarian). The actual number of workers covered by this local agreement is about 1850.

From these examples it can be seen that job classifications are usually a part of larger collective bargaining agreements and thus are of importance to the scope of patent provisions in these agreements.[37] Large mixed groups of workers, technicians, and engineers are in this way automatically and collectively bound to the total agreement. Depending on how many types of classified jobs are covered by the agreements, groups of potential inventors may or may not be included. Professional employees of higher education and long experience probably will not like this kind of collective bargaining-invention tie-up. But from the viewpoint of the employer this arrangement must mean a simplification compared with individual invention contracts. Whether such invention arrangements stimulate inventive work has not yet been analyzed. Employers and employees should be interviewed about attitude and practical results.

A similar pattern as to categories of employees involved in collective bargaining agreements we find at McDonnell-Douglas. The agreements of this corporation with the Southern California Professional Engineering Association as exclusive bargaining agent define the types of employees covered in job classification lists attached to the agreements. In one case 21 classes of jobs are listed (covering altogether 5300 employees) and in the other case 23 classes of jobs (covering 1100

[37] Job classifications were originally introduced by management in connection with setting of wage rates. The evaluation of categories in this system is made on the basis of a number of factors such as the amount of training or experience necessary to learn a job, the hazards involved, responsibility entailed in the work, and the "pleasantness" of working conditions. The factors are scored in a point system, and labor grades are introduced as basis of basic wage rates. Modification and introduction of new grades are often subject to negotiation between unions and management. (See Neil W. Chamberlain, and J.W. Kuhn, *Collective Bargaining*, pp. 327 ff.)

employees). Among the engineers represented in this way we find "engineer/scientists," engineering research assistants, flight test engineers and analysts, production designers, service publication writers, and many other professional engineers. The corresponding agreements between McDonnell-Douglas and the IAM coordinate 58 job classifications with such for which employees are obliged to execute the patent contract (with obligation to assign inventions as a condition of employment). The jobs described there cover electronic technicians, milling operators, precision mechanics, toolmakers and diemakers, engineering planners, materials analysts, and many others. About 10,500 employees are covered by these agreements with the IAM. The IAM is obviously the labor union primarily active in this type of special collective bargaining agreement.[38]

The other bargaining agreements outside the aircraft and aerospace field cover minor groups of workers and professional employees: in the two RCA agreements they cover totally about 1500 employees for the Association of Scientists and Professional Engineering Personnel in the one agreement, and 1050 employees for the AFL-CIO-affiliated American Federation of Technical Engineers in the other agreement. In the Ford Instrument agreement (Sperry Rand) about 450 employees for the International Union of Electrical Workers (IUE) are covered, and in the American Oil agreement about 350 employees for the Research and Engineering Professional Employees Association.

4. *Percentage of Employees Covered*   The total labor force of the four aircraft corporations in 1967 was, in rounded numbers:
Boeing, 142,00 employees
McDonnell-Douglas, 140,000
General Dynamics, 103,000
Lockheed, 92,000.

The number of employees covered by collective bargaining agreements with patent provisions, compared to these totals, is indeed limited, not more than about 10 to 15 percent. This observation does not imply that the agreements are of negligible interest, however, in the author's opinion. Inventive employees are a highly valuable asset for any progressive industrial corporation. Except in pure research

[38] The IAM is probably the most diversified union in the U.S. labor movement. It has over 8000 agreements with approximately 15,000 firms, ranging from one-man auto repair shops to the giants of the nation's aerospace complex. These agreements are in nearly 250 different industries. The union has substantial membership in the airlines, electronics, shipbuilding, and railroad and trucking industries. (Communication from IAM to the author, June 1966.)

organizations such as Bell Telephone Laboratories, they will always constitute a minority in terms of totals. The task of working out contractual provisions which result in an increase of quantity and quality of disclosed inventions and improvements by competent employees should be one of high priority. Labor unions and professional unions which are alert to chances for improved income and advancement of their members should carefully consider the undeveloped possibilities of this field of bargaining, even if it has no direct impact on all members. Since in many industrial jobs the blue collar is gradually replaced by a white collar and since more and more jobs call for higher working training, the chances and need for making contributions in terms of inventions reach more employees than ever before. The conventional disinterested outlook of labor unions in this field is bound to change some day. The union attitude in this field is elaborated later in this chapter.

5. *Arrangements for Settling Disputes*   In theory there is no need for any mechanism to settle disputes arising from collective bargaining agreements in U.S. industry, since both parties to the agreement put their signature voluntarily under the contract. In practice many of the provisions in these agreements, however, are the result of last minute decisions and of changes or addition of wording, especially in parts other than the traditional ones. Patent provisions in such agreements belong to these newer, less common subjects. It seems therefore to be of considerable importance to find out how interpretation and application of such invention clauses are regulated within the total framework of a collective bargaining agreement.[39] As a first step, employers listed in the preceding section might be asked.

The essence of a grievance procedure as part of collective bargaining agreements is to provide a means by which an employee without jeopardizing his job can express a complaint about his work or working conditions and obtain a fair hearing through progressively higher levels of management. Since bargaining agreements for large companies usually are more complicated, need more rules and formalities, and have more "layers of authority" on both sides, formal

[39] European laws, for instance in Great Britain, Germany, and Sweden, have created permanent government boards to settle conflicts in this field, either independent ones (Great Britain, Sweden) or in the Patent Office (Germany). In the United States machinery is provided by the Government Patents Branch at the Patent Office. This is, however, restricted to the settlement of specific differences of opinion between government employees and their employers (government departments and agencies). It does not include disputes about compensations or awards for inventions, nor does it treat any nongovernment employees.

grievance and arbitration procedures have rapidly developed in this connection. They are held to be one of the major accomplishments of postwar collective bargaining.[40]

It has been said that in the long run any substantial accumulation of grievances not covered by the contract and not admissible into the grievance procedure will very likely work itself out, either in open conflict or in a revision of the contract to accommodate the issue or the type of grievance. This may be true, but how much friction, lost production, or other negative factors of work can occur before a boil bursts of itself? Employee benefit plans that can to some extent be considered analogous to patent provisions are in some agreements specifically excluded from the grievance process; other agreements specifically include such issues.

We now turn to the various corporations and their grievance mechanisms. General Dynamics, Convair Division, in its collective bargaining agreement with the professional division of Engineers and Architects Association, appoints a Committee which meets at least once every month to discuss any problem the Company or the Union may have. Suggestions made by both parties for the improvement of efficiency and morale will be considered. Matters passed by unanimous vote of the Committee are considered final and binding on the Company and the Union. The Company reserves to its sole discretion the determination of additional payments to employees for sales of patents, or royalty income collected from licenses for employee patents to others (including those from Manufacturers Aircraft Association). The Company also reserves the same right if it elects to grant royalty-free licenses for the use of such employee inventions or to waive future royalties for a definite or indefinite period of time on any license issued (Invention Agreements, sec. 2(d) and 4).

The other aircraft corporations have taken different paths to arrange settlements. McDonnell-Douglas provides in its collective bargaining agreements, both with the labor union (IBM) and the professional union (Southern California Professional Engineering Association), that grievances and disputes of employees concerning the Patent Plan (containing award provisions) and Patent Contract may be adjusted under the grievance procedures of the agreement but shall not be subject to arbitration under the agreement.

It is not known whether these grievance procedures have actually been used to

40 R. T. Selby and M. C. Cunningham, "Grievance Procedures in Major Contracts," in *Monthly Labor Review*, October 1964, p. 1125.

settle invention disputes of employees, since there is no access to settlements that have not been arbitrated.

Lockheed in their agreement with the Engineers and Scientists Guild provides general grievance and arbitration procedures for employee relations, departmental relations, and Lockheed-Guild relations. Interpretation or application of the Company's Patent Plan is expressly excluded from these procedures, however.

In the collective bargaining agreements of nonaircraft corporations, only in the American Bosch Arma agreements can provisions regarding settlement of disputes in the patent field be found.

The arrangements to settle invention disputes as sketched here do not seem to present an ideal solution. "Sanctity of contracts" is an acknowledged principle of law. Strict construction and interpretation of a contract is also desirable. Any unsuitable provisions should be amended and renegotiated upon expiration of the agreement. On the other hand, the partial or complete exclusion of grievance procedure in the patent and invention field (as practiced by some large corporations) takes this whole field out of reach of general study and analysis. In spite of the fact that grievance and arbitration decisions cannot set any precedents to be followed by other parties, these decisions are most likely carefully watched and studied by other corporations and union organizations having access to them. Well-reasoned individual solutions will be influential with the labor market. There should be no fear of giving unbiased students of the field a chance to follow the practical solutions found acceptable to management and inventive employees. They would give most valuable insight into the institutional problems that arise in the employee-invention field. As in other fields of law, cooperation of the parties and finally peace in the labor market could be fostered by practicing a more open and unified procedure to settle disputes about employee inventions. The experience with official arbitration boards in this field in some European countries, whose decisions are published, have been rather good. They have not started any employee-inventor's dictatorship or other misuse of the impartial and informal forum opened to the parties. The European boards short-circuit formal court procedures and work faster and at less cost than courts. Their decisions are often by agreement declared finally binding on the parties. As the American practice stands, the McDonnell-Douglas way of handling disputes seems to be reasonable. It opens one safety valve (i.e., by allowing grievance prcedures) even though it forbids arbitration procedures.

The lack of general access to settlements (regarding inventions) between corporation and bargaining unit, or between corporation and individual employee, is a disadvantage. A leading labor union expresses this in a typical way:

We at headquarters have little if any information regarding the benefits gained by our membership through the existence of these clauses. Since patents are excluded from the grievance and arbitration provisions, contracts regarding this item are usually between the individual and management with the union unaware of them.[41]

Attitude of Unions and Management to these Agreements

The approach of the parties to a collective bargaining agreement regarding such specific questions as inventions and patent rights is composed of a number of more general attitudes. The opinion which the parties might have—if they have any—is a result of how they feel : about the patent system as such, about engineering progress (especially automation) in their branch, about the collective bargaining system, and how they appraise the value of the inventive contributions.

Attitude of Labor Unions

The usual attitude of labor unions toward professional unions is still a wary one. It must be remembered that the economic situation of blue-collar and white-collar employees in the labor market is very different. The educated and skilled scientists and engineers are in constant high demand, and they have not known unemployment since before World War II. Blue-collar workers without higher education and long job experience are subject to unemployment and fear it. Labor expresses doubts as to the usefulness (toward the end of eliminating unemployment) of certain kinds of engineering progress and inventions, namely those resulting in "labor saving." There is no doubt that a considerable number of inventions made by skilled workers, technicians, engineers, and scientists on the job can affect directly the quantity, quality, and speed of the laborer's work or even abolish his job entirely. New machinery, new methods of production, or other installations may indeed result in a lower requirement of employees. All new labor-saving or new shortcut devices have a direct and important impact on the income of the pieceworker who is paid on a basic hourly rate as a minimum, plus an incentive bonus for production over and above the norm fixed by management. There is a risk that such improvements may speed up the inventor's own work or that of his colleagues beyond the pieceworker's capacity and that the pieceworker will not be compensated commensurately with the actual increase in production. Such a contingency predisposes this group of employees against suggestions and inventions

[41] Communication from International Association of Machinists to the author, June 1966.

systems. The labor union is bound to have a keen ear for this kind of experience and for the resulting attitude of members. The following statement shows where the shoe really pinches:

Like salaries, patents are a matter for collective bargaining where unions are concerned. But unlike salaries, patents affect only a relatively few employees. They are, in other words, hardly a striking issue. Progress will be slow even where a more militant union spirit exists. I must leave for our engineering unions the job of defining a policy on patent rights for these employees.[42]

In the protracted controversy about ownership of patent rights developed under government research funds, unions support the doctrine of Senator Russell Long that government shall have full title to all inventions originating in any way in connection with contracts financed by it, irrespective of what the role of these funds is in individual cases or to what extent government funds are used in such contracts. The political slogan Long coined in this respect is that the American taxpayer should not pay twice, first for the research financed by government, then additionally as consumer because of patent monopoly granted to private government contractors. This reasoning was willingly accepted by the spokesman of labor unions, Oscar Jager, in an investigation of labor attitudes toward the patent system conducted by the American Patent Law Association in 1962.[43]

In rebuttal to this point of view, A. J. Hayes, former International President of IAM, pleads for the rights of employed inventors as follows[44] " . . . and corporations do not invent. People invent. Some authorities much closer to this field than I point out that corporate expropriation of patents is not only inequitable but contravenes the constitutional purpose in that it actually discourages rather than promotes the progress of science and the useful arts."

The individual, the only source of inventions, has somehow become the victim of either Big Government or Big Business. Ownership of his inventions and reward for them seem to be going to either of the two powers but rarely to him. Naturally I do *not* advocate that employed inventors should be exclusive owners of inventions made with substantial support, economic or other, of the employer (whether government, industry, a university, or anybody else). But complete ownership by government or by contracting corporations without other reward than wages to the

[42] "Labor, Inventions, and Patents," *American Patent Law Assoc., Bulletin,* June 1962, pp. 211 ff. The statement quoted here was made by Oscar Jager, then Director of Publications and Public Relations of the Industrial Union Department of AFL-CIO.
[43] *Ibid.,* p. 237.
[44] "The Independent Inventor's Interest," a talk reprinted in *J. Patent Off. Soc.* 47 (April 1965): 298 ff.

employed inventor is not a satisfactory solution in all situations.[45] The indiscriminate wholesale decision governing employee inventions as suggested (and practiced) seems to be unfair to many inventors and not be in agreement with the spirit of Article I of the Constitution. As John Stedman said:

It is clear that the common law, as applied to employed inventors, is something less than a perfect instrument for dealing with the infinitely varied and delicate relationships that may exist between an employer and his inventive employees. As has been said in other contexts, the case calls for a surgeon's scalpel, not a butcher's cleaver.[46]

The absence of carefully developed provisions that are fair to both parties of the collective bargaining agreement and that satisfy the public interest merely indicates, as was aptly stated by Vernon Jirikowic, Director of Research of the International Association of Machinists, "the degree of both employer resistance and employee indifference."[47]

Attitude of Professional Unions

Whereas labor unions are recognized as such and their existence and function is the basis of collective bargaining, this is by no means the case with professional engineering unions as bargaining organizations. Their *raison d'être* in the United States labor market is still controversial. Neither management nor the labor unions believe that they are needed and—the real weakness—engineers and scientists themselves have serious doubts. The first successful period of development of professional unions as independent organizations throughout the country came during World War II.[48] A number of circumstances made employed engineers

[45] The government's objective of administering patents for the public interest justifies full ownership in specific cases.

[46] "The Law of the Employed Inventor in the United States," a talk February 20, 1965 at the Conference on the Employed Inventor, Lake Arrowhead, Calif. (Univ. of California).

[47] Communication to the writer in June 1966.

[48] Unionism among engineers and scientists has in recent years become subject to some careful research. Among valuable studies should be especially mentioned: James J. Bambrick, A. A. Blum, and H. Zagat, *Unionization Among American Engineers* (New York: NICB Studies in Personnel Policy, No. 155); Eldon J. Dvorak, in Symposium: Will Engineers Unionize? *Industrial Relations* 2, No. 3 (May 1963), p. 45; Bernard Goldstein, "Some Aspects of the Nature of Unionism among Salaried Professionals in Industry," in *American Sociological Review* 20 (April 1955): 199; Bernard P. Indik and Bernard Goldstein, "Professional Engineers Look at Unions," *Proceedings of the 16th Annual Meeting of Industrial Relations Research Association* (Boston: December 1963); John W. Riegel, *Collective Bargaining as Viewed by Unorganized Engineers and Scientists* (Ann Arbor: Bureau of Industrial Relations, 1959); James W. Kuhn, "Success and Failure in Organizing Professional Engineers," *Proceedings 16th Annual Meeting, Industrial Relations Research Association* (Madison Wis.: 1964), p. 194; Joel Seidman and Glen G. Cain, "Unionized Engineers and Chemists: A Case Study of a Professional Union," *Journal of Business of the University of Chicago* 37, No. 3 (July 1964), p. 238;

and scientists amenable to the idea of organizing as independent unions to bargain for their own working conditions. One reason was that in large-scale defense manufacturing, especially in aircraft, electronic, instrument, and machine industries, technical qualified personnel was employed on a mass employment basis in working conditions similar to those of manual workers. The imposition by big defense manufacturing corporations of strict control of working hours (time clock) and working results, together with the general uncertainty of employment for the postwar years, were among the reasons for union organization of their own group. Two more factors added to the favorable climate for union action at the time: the increasing specialization of work and the threat that professional engineers might be "submerged" by the shop union representing exclusively the blue-collar worker (encouraged by decisions of the NLRB on the basis of the Wagner Act of 1937).

The motives for union organization for professional engineers mentioned here were recognized by the six largest occupational societies in the engineering field active at that time (still the dominating ones today)[49] but were not strongly supported by them.[50] As George Strauss points out, a major problem faced by these organizations is that they are dominated by people already well up in the management hierarchy who may conceivably speak up for the interests of the profession as a whole but are less likely to represent the economic interests of individual professionals, particularly those in lower ranks.[51]

George Strauss, "Professional or Employee-Oriented: Dilemma for Engineering Unions," *Industrial and Labor Relations Review* 17 (July 1964): 519; Richard E. Walton, *The Impact of the Professional Engineering Union* (Boston: Harvard Business School, 1961); Everett M. Kassalow, "Prospects for White Collar Union Growth," *Industrial Relations* 5, No. 1 (October 1965), p. 37.

[49] American Society of Civil Engineers, American Institute of Mining and Metallurgical Engineers, American Society of Mechanical Engineers, American Institute of Electrical Engineers, American Institute of Chemical Engineers, National Society of Professional Engineers.

[50] Professional unions (general white-collar unions and engineering unions) in many European countries are almost generations ahead of the American ones. For basic information see, for instance, Everett M. Kassalow, "The Development of Western Labor Movements: Some Comparative Considerations," in Richard A. Lester, ed., *Labor: Readings on Major Issues* (New York: Random House, 1965), pp. 71–88; "White Collar Unionism in Western Europe," in *Monthly Labor Review*, July 1963, p. 765, and August 1963, p. 889; Adolf Sturmthal, ed., *White-Collar Trade Unions, Contemporary Developments in Industrialized Societies* (Urbana: Univ. of Illinois Press, 1966).

[51] George Strauss, "Professional or Employee-Oriented," p. 524. Similar observations were made by Joel Seidman and Glen G. Cain, "Unionized Engineers and Chemists," p. 256 ff. (Both references are cited in footnote 48.)

Some of the more important professional engineering unions with bargaining rights were developed at Western Electric, RCA Victor, Minneapolis-Honeywell, and Westinghouse Electric. Several of the local unions started to form independent engineering federations on a nationwide basis, but they all experienced a short lifetime. Among them were the Federation of Architects, Engineers, Chemists, and Technicians (FAECT), which existed from 1934 to 1946, the Engineers and Scientists of America (ESA) from 1953 to 1961, and the Engineers and Scientists Guild, from 1957 to the 1960's. The remaining independent engineering unions hold bargaining rights, especially in West Coast aircraft companies, but the loss of bargaining rights for engineering unions through decertification by the NLRB under sec. 9(c)(1) of the Taft-Hartley Act has weakened the general strength of these organizations.[52]

Returning to the question of collective bargaining for invention rights by the engineering unions, it seems obvious that without numerically large and economically strong organizations there is no efficient basis for development of collective bargaining provisions. Since the scientists, engineers, and technicians represent the main source of inventions, discoveries, and improvements in industry, their attitudes and methods of action in the bargaining process are important to know. If bargaining in this field is taken over by the existing large blue-collar unions, this would hardly strengthen the bargaining position of the qualified inventor employees. These employees often recognize both the commercial value of patents and their value as proof of personal meritorious performance. They are not deterred from disclosing inventive ideas for fear of unemployment, as is often the case in worker's circles.

It is true that scientists, in many cases, give preference to publication over patenting. Some reasons for this attitude are these: standing tradition in a specific field of work; unfamiliarity with the fact that publication and patenting do not exclude each other; regulations in certain nonprofit institutions, universities, and government departments; the fact that in some fields of basic science (for instance, medicine or mathematics) patents cannot be obtained. In addition, there may be a desire for rapid dissemination of new knowledge and for bringing ideas to maximum usage (otherwise limited by the patent system); a feeling that

[52] A decertification is an official statement by the NLRB that a particular recognized or certified union is not the chosen bargaining representative of a majority of the employees in a certain unit. It is given when a union loses a decertification election, or in the event of a tie vote. The NLRB has not indicated for how long a period a decertification will remain valid, but sec. 9(c)(3) prohibits more than one valid election per year in any bargaining unit. The Board may amend or revoke a decertification.

the patenting process is awkward, expensive, and haphazard in operation and that the advantages resulting from patents accrue to others; a feeling that it is difficult to exploit patents and dispose them freely and that awards by the employer are not in proportion to inventive performance. Unfortunately, there is no neutral institution or forum in the United States to decide such questions.

An opinion on the invention problem from organized professional engineering quarters is that of Eph Cohen, the spokesman for the Council of Engineers and Scientists Organizations-West (CESO-W). The Council is made up of five bargaining organizations representing 14,000 engineers, scientists, and allied technicians in Southern California, all of which are party to the collective bargaining agreements with patent provisions treated in this chapter, at McDonnell-Douglas, General Dynamics (Convair Divisions), Lockheed, Southern California Gas (and, in addition, the City of Los Angeles). Cohen writes as follows:

Every engineer, and scientist, and technician, feels a sting of resentment the moment he is told he must sign his first agreement giving away the rights in all his inventions to his employer. It shatters an American dream of a pot at the end of the rainbow containing fame and fortune which will reward the maker of a great and useful invention, and that this pot of gold is somehow guarded, somehow assured, by the patent right.

We make a big mistake when we give no credence at all to this dream—when we simply write it off as folklore and tell the engineer that he is being well taken care of even without his patent, and to get back to his drafting board, or computer, and not worry about it. Because in spite of all our reservations, invention and patentable invention in particular, is a very important thing. It is important to the country. It is important to business, and, in order to flourish, it *must* be important to the inventor.[53]

A major problem for all professional engineers and scientists and their organizations should be to find out the legal and practical implications of invention assignment policy as practiced by industrial employers.[54] Patent provisions in collective bargaining agreements are still the exception; practically all scientists and engineers sign individual invention assignment contracts as a condition of employment. In both types of agreement employees "contract away" their future property rights once and for all, and there is no legal action left for them in case of serious disagreement with the employer other than court action or leaving

[53] *American Patent Law Assoc., Bulletin,* April-May 1966, pp. 194–195.
[54] The invention assignment (title) policy of U.S. Government as employer is today based on the interpretation of the so-called Kennedy Memorandum on Government Patent Policy of October 1963, which was meant to bring about greater unification regarding patent ownership in all fields of government-financed research. See Chapter 5.

employment.[55] The major drawbacks to legal action by an employee are the slight chance of winning in view of costs, the sweeping definitions of fields of activity, and the legal doctrine imposed upon them.

Attitude of Management

It will be safe to say that management of most industrial corporations with their own research activities and working in competitive business branches consider ownership and use of patents a valuable asset. The purpose of patents can be restricted to protecting the inventive results of one's own development work and to keeping a temporary monopoly for products and methods created in that way. Patents can also be used as a source of income by licensing others, or to get access to technology developed by others through cross-licensing of patent rights. Combinations of two or more of these uses of patents is common.[56]

Chemical, pharmaceutical, electrical, electronic, aircraft, and mechanical industries are most conscious of the value of patent ownership. To acquire these rights from their employees is of basic importance to such corporations. As we have seen before, the way to acquire inventions from potential inventors is in most cases by individual assignment acquired by standard procedure at the moment an individual enters employment. Acquisition of ownership by way of collective bargaining agreements as described in this chapter is less frequent. The conditions of acquisition, free of cost and without any obligations on the side of the employer (other than payment of a salary), are practically the same in individual assignment agreements and in collective bargaining agreements.

The attitude of management to engineering progress, especially automation, is obviously positive, since it means in most cases an increase of income and profits, as well as an increase in competitive power and expansion of production. In many fields it also means an increase of quality of products or services.

The attitude of management to collective bargaining by different groups of employees is a field of complex development and gradual change. Today there is a

[55] In the cited literature (footnote 48) these problems have found little attention. Goldstein (p. 204) has, however, observed that this aspect of professional work (i.e., patent rights) "creates special collective bargaining issues." Dvorak (p. 47) says that most engineers as employees of business firms experience considerable restriction of research activities to conform to the firm's objectives. Results often were kept secret and patent rights were retained. Walton (p. 90) states that "patent payments were an important objective for the engineers' unions during their early history when most of the provisions covering patent payments were negotiated."

[56] There are of course, other uses of patents as a device for excessive monopolizing through assertion of questionable or invalid patents, litigious harassment, various forms of cartelization, and agreements restricting competition.

conspicuous difference of attitude of management toward collective bargaining by labor unions and by professional unions; the first are widely accepted as bargaining units but the latter are not. The resentment management felt toward labor unions in the nineteenth century is the resentment management now feels toward professional unions.

The relatively strong activities of engineering unions during the first two decades after World War II led to intense and sometimes violent discussions between the employee groups interested in such collective organization and management. The hardest fights, which most likely took place "behind the scene," are not reported in print, and it can be assumed that no detailed history of what was said and what actions were taken now survives. Representatives of industrial management have, however, stated their general viewpoint to collective bargaining efforts by engineers and scientists, and still do. As Richard Walton rightly stated with regard to the need for cooperative arrangements among research workers:

The effectiveness and efficiency of any industrial organization depend largely on the collaborative relationships that exist among its members. This is decidedly true in engineering and research organizations in which the nature of the work often requires team effort—teamwork on the idea level. The cooperative, integrative arrangements within and among such groups are delicately balanced mechanisms; they can easily go haywire.[57]

One good illustration of management attitude of recent years toward these problems comes from a talk by Gerry E. Morse, vice president in charge of industrial relations at Minneapolis-Honeywell Regulator Company.[58] The doctrine he presents is that the engineer in modern industry works in areas that are close to the very core of management decision and that he is responsible for the technical development of the products, processes, and customer applications on which the success of the business depends. His ability creates, tests, controls, and improves the product, and the soundness and practicality of his professional judgments are important elements in determining the fortunes of the organization. Because the engineer is entrusted with work that others in the organization cannot do and often cannot even check, it is essential that he be clearly aware of the ethical requirements of his profession.

Membership in a collective bargaining organization by itself alone, says Morse, does not constitute a breach of ethics for the individual engineer. Those who were

[57] Richard E. Walton, *The Impact of the Professional Engineering Union* (Boston: Harvard Business School, 1961), p. 328.
[58] Gerry E. Morse, "Engineering Ethics From the Viewpoint of Industry," in *J. Engineering Education,* November 1954, p. 214.

instrumental in creating and developing collective bargaining organizations of professional employees are said to have "made the fundamental error of assuming that a collective bargaining relationship between a group of professional employees and management could be very cordial and dignified and that problems would be solved forthrightly without resort to the exercise of power or the strategical and tactical maneuvering of the typical collective bargaining situation." Morse is convinced that there is "a fundamental conflict between the practices inherent in collective bargaining and the kind of unregimented atmosphere that must prevail in an engineering organization if it is to function professionally and accomplish the results for which it is employed." He continues, "Engineers are not conditioned by temperament or training to feel comfortable in the pulling and hauling of the collective bargaining process." Morse also refuses to accept the idea that the technical societies should try to meet the problem of unionization and considers it fatal for them to become collective bargaining agencies: "They would inevitably then find themselves moving in the direction of the typical labor union behavior and practices."[59]

In February 1966, Milton F. Lunch, the general counsel and director of the National Society of Professional Engineers, gave a talk on "The Engineers in a Changing Society"[60] in Ottawa, where proposed Canadian laws to permit collective bargaining for engineers were under discussion. Lunch presents the problem of unionism for engineers in the United States substantially as a matter of past history. For existing unions he says it is "not a serious or important factor in present discussions how to improve employment relations for engineers." From personal opinion and analysis he made the following points:

Trade unions are based on the concept that the worker has found his niche—he is a steelworker and will remain a steelworker. His only effective means of improving his economic status, therefore, is through collective approach to secure higher wages and fringe benefits. The employed engineer, on the other hand, starts his employment career with the concept that he is on the first rung and that he will climb the ladder to successively higher and better paying positions. He may not go as far as he anticipated in his youth, but he is not resigned to a niche in the company structure.

[59] Morse's talk contains additional arguments on the basic problems of the management-employee relation. In this context, see also H. Metz, "Management and the Professional Employee," *Addresses on Industrial Relations*, 1954 Series, Bull. No. 22 (Ann Arbor: Bureau of Industrial Relations, 1954), relating RCA's experience with its unionized design and development engineers.
[60] Remarks to Ontario Association of Professional Engineers (February 1966), reprinted in BNA White Collar Report No. 470, March 10, 1966, C-1.

... Engineering unions have been notoriously ineffective. When the subway workers strike the subways stop, when the steelworkers walk out steel production stops, when the bricklayer puts down his trowel the construction ceases. But when the engineers strike, as did happen a few times, nothing much else happens. Production continues, management men with engineering background step into the breach to the extent necessary and the engineers find that they really do not have effective economic leverage. In short, they cannot hurt the company very much.

Statements of this type appear to be rather paternalistic. They express however, the feelings of some representative management groups. What is needed is that corporations conscious of the unsolved questions in this field look for more analysis and guidance in the interest of both parties.[61]

The former Secretary of Labor, Willard Wirtz, observed that "the established institution of free collective bargaining faces a challenge which arises in significant part from the advances of science, the new discoveries of the technologists. Why is it that there is such an obvious, in some ways ominous predominance today of scientific over institutional invention?"[62] The questions treated in his book concern a new type of bargaining regulation in regard to inventions in the engineering sense of the word. Bargaining should be protected by an "institutional invention," as Secretary Wirtz calls it, that is, by equitable and fair contractual provisions to be reached in open discussion. By "open discussion" is meant discussion not under the pressure of time and of tactical moves, as is the rule in actual collective bargaining negotiations. The present analysis hopes to contribute to this discussion.

SUMMARY

1. The number of collective bargaining agreements with patent provisions is still small in comparison with the total number of such agreements.

2. Of the eleven industrial corporations studied in this chapter which have executed such agreements, four represent large aircraft and aerospace corporations and four electronic companies. The others were one for petroleum products, one for heavy chemicals, and one for natural gas.

3. Seven of the eleven corporations belonged (in 1967) to the group of the 500 largest U.S. industrial corporations.

4. Double agreements (one with a labor union unit and one with a professional

[61] The best analysis is Richard Walton's *Impact of the Professional Engineering Union*, 1961, cited in footnote 47.

[62] W. Willard Wirtz, *Labor and the Public Interest* (New York: Harper & Row, 1964) "Constructive Bargaining" talk, Feb. 1, 1963, to the National Academy of Arbitrators, Chicago, p. 54.

union unit) were executed by five corporations, a single agreement with a labor union unit only were concluded by three corporations, and a single agreement with a professional unit only, by three corporations.

5. Bargaining units for professional engineers are mostly local organizations created at the level of a company division. Bargaining units for blue-collar labor unions are some of the big nationwide AFL-CIO unions such as IAM and IUE.

6. Invention provisions in collective bargaining agreements are in principle similar to individual assignment contract provisions, with the exception of provisions in the aircraft industry agreements. All four aircraft and aerospace corporations offer their agreement partners a percental share of the income from inventions licensed to the Manufacturers Aircraft Association (MAA).

5

OVERVIEW

A survey of the activities of United States Government as initiator of engineering research and as employer of inventors reflects important features of the general history of the country.[1] The two oldest fields of inventive activity in the United States are agriculture, man's mother trade, and the production of tools of warfare and military defense. These two fields were well established by the second half of the nineteenth century. With the geographical expansion of the country, radio communication, electricity as a source of power and light, agricultural machinery,

[1] This section deals with the recommendations of national committees and of commissions especially over the years 1938 to 1947. However, the literature in the field of general government patent policy is scattered through decades of official discussion and attempts at independent analysis in and out of Congress. Of independent legal papers and articles, some of the most relevant work has been presented by Lawrence Caruso, Howard I. Forman, M. B. Finnegan and R. W. Pogue, Mary A. Holman, Wilson R. Maltby, and Gerald D. O'Brien. See, for instance, L. R. Caruso, "Inventions in Orbit: The Patent Waiver Regulations of the National Aeronautics and Space Administration Revisited," *Howard Law J.* 12 (Winter 1966): 35; H. I. Forman, *Patents, Their Ownership and Administration by the United States Government* (Brooklyn: Central Book Co., 1957); Statement in Testimony Hearings House Subcommittee No. 3, Committee on the Judiciary, March 3, 1958, Series 15, Washington, D.C., 1958, pp. 2–9; "Wanted: A Definite Government Patent Policy," in *IDEA: The Patent Trademark and Copyright J. of Research and Education* 3 (Winter 1959): 399; "Forgive My Enemies For They Know Not What They Do," *J. Patent Off. Soc.* 44 (1962): 274; "Impact of Government's Patent Policies on the Economy and the American Patent System," in "Patent Procurement and Exploitation," *Inst. on Patent Law*, 1963, p. 181; "President's Statement of Government Patent Policy: A Springboard for Legislative Action," in *Fed. Bar. J.* 25, No. 1 (Winter 1965): 4–23; M. B. Finnegan and R. W. Pogue, "Federal Employee Invention Rights—Time To Legislate," in *Michigan Law Rev.* 55, No. 7 (1957), or *J. Patent Off. Soc.* 40 (1958): 322; Mary A. Holman, "The Utilization of Government-Owned Inventions," *IDEA* 7 (1963): 109; M. A. Holman and D. S. Watson, "Patents from Government-Financed Research and Development," *IDEA* 8 (1964): 199; "Government Research and Development Inventions: A New Resource?" *Land Economics,* August 1965; Wilson R. Maltby, "A Government Patent Policy for Employee Inventions," in *Fed. Bar. J.* 21 (Winter 1961): 127; "Need for a Federal Policy to Foster Invention Disclosures by Contractors and Employees," in *Fed. Bar. J.* 25 (Winter 1965): 32; Gerald D. O'Brien, "Federal Patent Policy," speech of May 20, 1965, North Carolina Inventors Congress, Raleigh, N.C.; with Gayle Parker, "Property Rights in Inventions Under the National Aeronautics and Space Acts of 1958," in *Fed. Bar. J.* 19 (July 1959): 255. See also Jacob Schmookler, *Invention and Economic Growth* (Cambridge, Mass.: Harvard Univ. Press, 1966).

Of government reports the most important is: *Investigation of Government Patent Practices and Policies,* Report and Recommendations of the Attorney General to the President (U.S. Dept. of Justice), Vols. I–III, Washington 1947. See also "Patents and Technical Data," Government Contracts Monograph No. 10, Government Contracts Program, George Washington University, Washington, D.C., 1967, pp. 1 ff. ("Patent Rights"), pp. 106 ff. ("Technical Data"), pp. 156 ff. ("Trade Secrets"). And see Harbridge House, Inc., *Government Patent Policy Study, Final Report,* 4 Vols. (Washington, D.C.: Government Printing Office, 1968). This is the report sponsored by the Committee on Government Patent Policy or the Federal Council for Science and Technology.

and airplane traffic, large fields of research were opened. The systematic fight against diseases of men and animals gave rise to another large area of research. In all of these the federal government had a stake. The two world wars were powerful primers to advance almost all fields of inventions either directly or indirectly. It is not surprising, therefore, that the Department of Defense contracts for more scientific research than all other agencies combined.[2] At the end of World War II atomic energy emerged as a gigantic field of military and civil research, which since 1946 has been administered by an independent government agency, the Atomic Energy Commission. The major portion of AEC's research is conducted in about ten government-owned laboratories supplemented by far-reaching expensive work performed by universities as well as industrial and other privately owned organizations. In 1958, spurred by achievements made by Soviet government science, another independent government agency, the National Aeronautics and Space Administration (NASA), was created by Federal Act to conduct fundamental nonmilitary research and development in aeronautics and space flight.[3] The military activities in this latter branch of research remain with the Department of Defense. NASA has been the most heavily endowed government research organization in the United States and probably in the Western world. It is expressly authorized to enter into R&D contracts, which are granted to industry, universities, and nonprofit organizations. For the fiscal year 1966 funds for such contracts amounted to $6.9 billion for all kinds of space projects. The chances of producing new inventions, discoveries, and improvements in the course of these extensive aerospace pograms are high, and the need for an efficient and unified invention policy is obvious.

The path from the oldest documented law cases of government employee inventions of the 1870's to the streamlined central organization of employee invention administration by NASA in 1968 demonstrates convincingly how the U.S. Government's role as employer of inventors has developed from the incidental into a major field of federal law and administration. The case studies that follow in the latter part of this chapter deal with the Department of Agriculture, Department of Health, Education and Welfare, the Atomic Energy Commission, and the National Aeronautics and Space Administration. These four are chosen to illustrate

[2] "Report of the Committee on the Judiciary, U.S. Senate Subcommittee on Patents" (Report together with individual views), 87th Cong., 1st sess., Report No. 143, 1961, p. 13.
[3] *U.S. Government Organization Manual* 1960–1961, p. 452.

government agencies as employers of inventors and as owners of invention rights of contractors.

The prolific literature in this field exists mainly in the form of special government reports, Congressional committee studies and hearings (both in the House of Representatives and in the Senate) and articles in law reviews and engineering journals. The author has found no overall review of this policy in a single source.

The deep disagreement on policy as to the right of ownership of inventions between different government agencies on the one hand, and between the agencies and Congress as legislator and supervisor of governmental activities on the other hand, can be studied in the literature under the general heading of "government patent policy." At the same time one realizes the fight over the right use to be made of inventions produced by government employees or employees of government contractors.[4] The main issue, however, is always whether government or the contractor shall own patents, with the implication that if government-owned, the technology will be publicly available.

The difficulty of reaching a unified policy in the field of inventions made by employees of government and its contractors is surprising in view of the fact that U.S. Government in many other complex fields of activities, say in defense, commerce, or health policy, for purposes of international negotiations, has reached unified policy rules and decisions. One of the reasons why such results are not as easy to achieve in the field of inventions may be that the inherent needs of different government departments and agencies are basically different and may be best served by individual solutions. Undoubtedly the research within the armed forces departments, for instance, has little regard for commercial consideration, whereas federal research in agriculture or health is almost entirely consumer-oriented.

Another reason for not reaching agreement on federal policy may be a political one. The gulf between two schools of thinking in Congress, both citing as their basic belief the free private enterprise economy, is deep. The one school asks for uncompromising and total government ownership of all inventions made under publicly financed research without even regarding the varying share of government funds used (which sometimes is much less than 50 percent). This position, taking all property rights from the creators of the inventions, has for a number of years

---

[4] A list of important general publications is given in footnote 1. Literature relevant to specific agencies is given in footnotes in connection with the individual agencies and departments described.

been represented by Senator Russell B. Long.[5] The other school of thought is that the United States already leans too much on government management and that the products of scientific research should be reserved to the individuals or the research teams that have originated the inventions. According to this latter policy, the initiative and inventive talent that give rise to the innovation should be protected and encouraged by government patent policy.[6]

Patent Policy: Some Bills and Public Laws

The continuing dispute about the patent policy of government as originator of research contracts and as source of funds has primarily concerned the questions of ownership and use of the results of research in form of inventions. At the Congressional level the fight has been carried on mainly in two different contexts: in connection with discussion of bills involving improvement of technology and in connection with the annual authorization of funds for new research programs of federal agencies.

As an example of bills in the field of government patent policy, the following are the more important. They were introduced or reintroduced during the 89th and 90th Congresses. Those of the 89th Congress are as follows:

H.R. 5918, March 8, 1965, by George Brown, Jr.
"A Bill to amend the Labor Management Relations Act, 1947 . . . ." Purpose: to make it unlawful for any employer to require any employee to agree to assign

[5] The standpoint of Senator Long (D., Louisiana) has been expressed in Congress and in the literature. For some of his basic statements see *Congressional Record,* Jan. 28, 1965, pp. 1495–1503, and May 4, 1965, pp. 9023–9034. See also the following brochures of the Senate Subcommittee on Monopoly of the Select Committee on Small Business: "Patent Policies of Government Departments and Agencies, 1960" (Conference on Federal Patent Policies) April 8, 1960; "Space Satellite Communications, Review of the Report of the Ad Hoc Carrier Committee," Nov. 8 and 9, 1961; "Government Patent Policies in Meteorology and Weather Modification, 1962," March 26, 27, and 28, 1962; "Economic and Legal Problems of Government Patent Policies," June 15, 1963; "Economic Aspects of Government Patent Policies," March 7, 8, 13, and 14, 1963; See also "National Patent Policy," Hearing, Senate Subcommittee on Patents of the Committee on the Judiciary, June 2, 1961.

Several articles are also relevant: "Federal Contract Patent Policy and the Public Interest," *Fed. Bar. J.* 21 (Winter 1961): 7–25; and "A Government Patent Policy To Serve the Public Interest," *Am. Bar Assoc. J.* 47 (July 1961): 675–681; and B. Gordon (Staff Economist of Senate Select Committee on Small Business), "Government Patent Policy and the New Mercantilism," *Fed. Bar. J.* 25 (Winter 1965): 24–31.

[6] This viewpoint is represented in Congress by Congressman Emilio Q. Daddario, as evidenced in a number of Congressional Documents such as in U.S. House of Representatives, 88th Cong., 1st sess., Committee on Science and Astronautics, Subcommittee on Science, Research, and Development: Hearings October–November 1963 ("Government and Science"), Washington 1964; and Reports of the same subcommittee, No. 1 ("A Statement of Purpose"), 1963, and No. 2 ("Fiscal Trends in Federal Research and Development"), 1964. See also "A Patent Policy for a Free Economy" in *Amer. Bar Assoc. J.* 47 (July 1961): 671 ff.

patents to him as a condition of employment. This Bill was assigned to the Committee on Education and Labor of the House of Representatives for consideration and went on to the Committee on Science and Astronautics in 1965, but there is no record of any action by these Committees. No such bill was reintroduced in the 90th or 91st Congress.

S. 789, January 27, 1965, by Leverett Saltonstall.
"A Bill to prescribe a national policy with respect to the detrmination and disposition of property rights to inventions ... conducted under contracts ... with the U.S. Government ... to provide incentives to invention by rewarding inventors ..." (National Inventions Act). Purpose: to liberalize invention title policy in favor of invention license policy and to introduce cash award compensation for government-employed inventors.

S. 2756, August 1, 1969 (and several earlier versions of the same bill) by John McClellan.
"A Bill to establish a uniform national policy concerning proprietary rights in inventions made through the expenditure of public funds, and for other purposes" (Federal Inventions Act). Purpose: to instrument the Kennedy Memorandum and procedure regarding determination of ownership of rights.[7]

S. 1899, by Russell Long.
"A Bill to prescribe a national policy with respect to the acquisition, disposition, and use of proprietary rights in inventions made, and in scientific and technical information obtained, through the expenditure of public funds, and for other purposes" (Federal Inventions Act). Purpose: to create a unified government administration taking title of inventions made by all government employees, with amendents of ten other federal acts in this direction.

S. 2326, July 23, 1965, by Everett Dirksen.
"A Bill to establish a uniform national policy concerning proprietary rights in inventions made through the expenditure of public funds, and for other purposes" (Federal Inventions Act).

S. 2715, October 22, 1965, by Philip Hart and Quentin Burdick.
"A Bill to establish a uniform national policy concerning property rights in inventions made through the expenditure of public funds, and for other purposes" (Federal Inventions Act).

In the 90th Congress were filed:

H.R. 458, January 10, 1967, by Emilio Daddario, identical to H.R. 17167 of 89th Cong.
A Bill to establish "a uniform national policy concerning rights in inventions resulting from expenditure of public funds." The Bill defines the shop right of the contractor and the rights of government (right to prompt disclosure, shop right with free nonexclusive world-wide license, right to compel the contractor to license others in certain circumstances); then specifices other situations in which government or the contractor shall receive rights in the invention.

[7] Hearings before the Subcommittee on Patents, Trademarks and Copyrights of the Committee on the Judiciary, U.S. Senate, 89th Cong., 1st sess., June 1, 2, 3, 1965. See also the important Senate Report No. 1461, of August 16, 1966, to accompany S. 1809.

H.R. 3095, January 19, 1967, by Abraham Multer, identical to H.R. 857 (1965) and S. 1432:
"A Bill to establish a Federal Invention Administration to administer all government-owned patents."

Surprisingly, no bill later than H.R. 3095 was introduced in the 90th Congress. Senate Bill 1809 of Senator McClellan is still the most discussed bill in the field. It was once favorably reported by the Committee on the Judiciary and was carefully supplemented by individual views of Senators Burdick, Hart, Tydings, and Edward Kennedy. The Brown Bill H.R. 5918 (Representative George E. Brown, Jr.) represents a legal experiment of considerable interest. It tried to attack the problem of invention assignments as a condition of employment by suggesting changes in the Labor Management Act of 1947, but the Bill was not acted upon by the committees to which it was referred.

A number of public laws have been promulgated (up to January 1968) in which government patent policy is expressly defined in some provisions. This is the case in the following Public Laws or amendments to Public Laws.

1. Helium Gas Act of 1925, as amended 1960, sec. 4.
2. Tennessee Valley Authority Act of 1933, as amended 1959, sec. 831r.
3. Agricultural Research Act of 1946, sec. 10(a).
4. Veterans Administration Prosthetic Appliances Research Act of 1948, P.L. 80–729, sec. 2.
5. Housing Research Act of 1948, as amended 1949, sec. 301(a).
6. National Science Foundation Act of 1950, sec. 12.
7. Atomic Energy Commission Act of 1954 and 1958, sec. 151–153.
8. National Aeronautics and Space Administration Act of 1958, sec. 305(a-j), 306(a).
9. Coal Research and Development Act of 1960, P.L. 86–599, sec. 6.
10. Saline Water Act of 1961 and 1964, P.L. 87–295 (1961) and P.L. 88–379 (1964), sec. 4(a, b).
11. Desalination Act of 1961, P.L. 87–295, sec. 4(b).
12. Water Resources Research Act of 1964, P.L. 88–379, sec. 303.
13. Appalachian Regional Development Act of 1965, P.L. 89–4; sec. 302(d).
14. Solid Waste Disposal Act (Clean Air Act Amendment) of 1965, P.L. 89–272, sec. 204(c).
15. National Traffic and Motor Vehicle Safety Act of 1966, P.L. 89–563, sec. 106(c).

Thirteen of these 15 public laws have riders consisting of a provision concerning government patent policy incorporated in the wording of the respective act. They were all sponsored and carried through by Senator Russell Long. With some deviations these patent provisions stipulate in the acts that no part of any appropriated funds may be expended for any scientific or technological research or development activity unless "all information, uses, products, processes, patents, and other developments" resulting from such research will be made freely and fully available to the general public. This means in relation to patented inventions that their title belongs to the government for its unlimited use or licensing to others, free of cost. The actual inventors of these patented ideas, whether in government service or in the service of government contractors, go with empty hands.

The lists of enacted Public Laws and pending law bills show that considerable effort is made—although by a limited number of members of Congress—to confer on government in its capacity as a direct employer as well as an indirect employer through contractors, a definite role as owner of all created rights. The authors of almost all bills belong to the Democratic Party.

Before the role of the government as employer is described more in detail, it must be stated that in relation to employee inventors the U.S. Government is neither an entity nor a single employer. Theoretically all ten executive departments,[8] all autonomous federal agencies, commissions, and boards as well as two quasi-official agencies[9] are independent (government) employers entitled in principle to accept assignment of and take title to inventions made by their employees. On the other hand, as a rule, patent rights acquired belong to "government" and may be used by all government entities.

Over almost a hundred years several dozen different statutes have provided this right of title to government in one or another form.[10] The United States or one of its agencies may also constitutionally acquire property deemed necessary or desirable for governmental purposes.[11] As early as 1881 the Supreme Court treated the acquisition by the government of inventions made by a federal employee.[12] Also the rulings by the Comptroller General (and his predecessor, the Comptroller of the Treasury) and the Attorney General of the United States recognize either expressly or inferentially the right of government to receive assignment of employee patents.[13] As to the purchase of patent rights by government, statutory authority is requisite since an appropriation must be available, but the power to acquire such

[8] State, Treasury, Defense, Justice, Post Office, Interior, Agriculture, Commerce, Labor, and Health, Education, and Welfare.

[9] National Academy of Sciences and American Red Cross.

[10] *Investigation of Government Practices and Policies, Report and Recommendations of the Attorney General to the President*, 3 Vols. (Washington, D.C.: U.S. Department of Justice, 1947). Vol. 3, 127 ff.: "Monograph on the Principles of Law Applicable to the Interest of the United States in Inventions made by its Employees and Contractors." This volume will be referred to hereafter as "Law Monograph" or (LM).

[11] LM 129.

[12] *James* v. *Campbell*, 104 U.S. Reports, 356 (1881): 358.

[13] Early cases cited by Forman, *Patents,* p. 28 (footnotes 60, 61).

rights by donation, by agreement, or as a result of the employee-employer relationship under common law principles needs no express statutory sanction.[14]

Government-Employed Inventors: Early History

The earliest cases concerning government personnel as employed inventors to be discussed by a federal department and submitted to court occurred in the Navy Department and in the Department of Agriculture. The Navy case concerned the use of an employee invention made by a lieutenant assigned to ordnance duty (John Dahlgren, later Chief of the Bureau of Ordnance). Lieutenant Dahlgren in 1850 started experiments on improved guns at the Washington Navy Yard, and these guns were patented in 1861. After his death his widow filed a petition with Congress in 1874 asking compensation for the use of Dahlgren's inventions by the United States. This led to a Special Act in 1878 vesting the Court of Claims to hear and determine Mrs. Dahlgren's claim. The Court decided that Congress, rather than rewarding Dahlgren for the success of a suggestion made in the line of his ordinary duty should award him the maximum compensation allowed by statute for the *use* of the patented property ($65,000).[15]

The case of the Department of Agriculture concerned the question of ownership of patents made by a government agent, Magnus Swenson, who was employed in 1886 to superintend experiments at the plant of an industrial government contractor regarding manufacture of sugar from sorghum and sugarcane. Swenson filed a patent application for improvement in the manufacture of sugar and received a patent in 1887. The Senate passed two resolutions in the same year inquiring, first, whether any departmental employee had obtained a patent on an invention connected with experiments conducted under the auspices of the government and, second, requesting the Attorney General to take appropriate court action against Swenson. In 1888 suit was instituted, and in 1891 Swenson by court injunction was permanently restrained from asserting any right or claim under the patent.[16]

These early cases exemplify the two legal problems that are still basic today, two generations later, exactly as they were in 1878 and 1888: the right to use, and the right to own inventions made by government employees.

Since the legal and practical situation of the employed inventor in government service or contractor's service is a part of the broad general field of government

---

[14] LM 131.
[15] Attorney General's Report, Vol. 2, pp. 246–250.
[16] Attorney General's Report, Vol. 2, pp. 4 ff.

patent policy, it is appropriate to mention government statements, orders, and rules
that treat this subject along with related questions such as the proper use of patents
owned by government or general change and improvement of the patent laws.

Looking backward about 30 years, the development of government policy toward
employed inventors can be tied to the promulgation of more than a dozen Public
Laws or Executive Orders and the institution (or change) of a number of federal
boards or panels. The impact of common law on government policy in this field
is discussed in Chapter 2.

When President Roosevelt on April 29, 1938, sent his message to Congress
"transmitting recommendations relative to the strengthening and enforcement of
antitrust laws," he started the greatest political and intellectual effort ever made
in the United States to appraise the general economic state of the country.[17] The
times were grim. The Second World War was in preparation and the disorganized
economy in the United States was unable to handle an army of ten to eleven
million unemployed. In a message of unusual length, sketching basic principles
of democratic government against the background of "unhappy events abroad,"
the President outlined a program for "a thorough study of the concentration of
economic power in American industry and the effect of that concentration upon
the decline of competition." The President stated expressly that "the study
should not be confined to the traditional antitrust field. The effects of tax, patent,
and other government policies cannot be ignored." When the twelve-man committee, established by Congress in June 1938, presented its final report in March
1941 against the background of more than 20,000 pages of direct testimony,
interrogation of 552 leading American industrialists, 3300 technical exhibits, and
43 independent scientific monographs,[18] it suggested only 5 legislative changes in
the antitrust laws. One group of changes concerned procedure and substance of
the existing patent laws.[19] None of these suggested changes concerned relations
between employers and employed inventors except possibly the one recommending
that any sale, license, assignment, or other disposition of any patent be evidenced
by an instrument in writing, to be filed and recorded with the Federal Trade
Commission. However, this recommendation was not directed toward the assign-

[17] The message is reprinted in Hearings Before the Temporary National Economic Committee (TNEC), "Investigation of Concentration of Economic Power," 75th Cong., 3rd sess.,
December 1938, Part 1, Economic Prologue, Washington, D.C.: 1939, Exhibit No. 1, pp. 185–
191.
[18] *Final Report and Recommendations of the* TNEC, March 1941, p. 20.
[19] TNEC *Final Report*, pp. 36–37.

ment of inventions as a condition of employment. An analysis of the TNEC (Temporary National Economic Committee) hearings in the light of the problems of this book, therefore, is unproductive, but the same cannot be said about the extensive dialogues which took place in the Senate between December 1938 and January 1939.

In these Senate hearings, the chairman of the TNEC, Senator Joseph O'Mahoney, and his colleagues in Congress as well as some of the high officials of government departments, members of the Committee, heard witnesses who presented evidence or suggestions on a large scale. They were frequently involved in discussions about the basic value and meaning of the U.S. patent system as such. Without giving a complete analysis of everything that was said during the lengthy days of testimony, it can be stated that it was especially the executive secretary of the committee, Leon Henderson, Commissioner of Patents Conway P. Coe, and some leading industrialists such as George Baekeland (vice president of the Bakelite Corp.), Vannevar Bush (president of the Carnegie Institute), and Frank Jewett (president of the Bell Telephone Laboratories) who gave views of what they thought was the value and the operation of the patent system. Although no honest witness could deny the basic role of the inventor as the source of inventions made in any field, the witnesses' presentation of the inventor's position in the patent system was unclear and sometimes illogical. Of course, the statements made by the witnesses were oral, not always prepared in advance, and often the result of answers given to sudden questions thrown out by Committee members. It seems obvious that the TNEC did not consciously consider the situation of employed inventors to be of any importance. Characteristic is the wording in which Richard Patterson, Assistant Secretary of Commerce, described the purpose of the hearings: to hear witnesses "typical of successful, independent inventors who have controlled the manufacture of their products, independent inventors who have turned over the results of their invention to other enterprises for exploitation, and inventors who function in research groups attached to large corporations."[20] The last group of inventors was obviously meant to represent the employed inventors. A similar statement was made by the executive secretary, Henderson, talking about the basic assumptions of the United States' competitive capitalistic system. He said:

> In the first place, the American system has emphasized the dignity of the individual, his resourcefulness, and has had essential reliance on the ability of individuals, in free association, to design affirmatively the main forms and directions of life. Its basic legal institutions have included private property and

[20] TNEC Hearings, Part 3, January 1939, p. 837.

freedom of contract, with the collateral assumption of approximate equality of bargaining power.[21]

In his presentation of the American patent system, Coe, the Commissioner of Patents, stated:

It is not the principal purpose of the patent laws of our own country or of any nation to reward an individual. The purpose is much deeper and the effect much wider than individual gain. It is the promotion of science and the advancement of the arts looking to the general welfare of the Nation that the patent laws hope to accomplish. The individual reward is only the lure to bring about this much broader objective. . . . An inventor will not be rewarded and society will not be benefited until the invention passes into commercial channels.[22]

This attitude was in agreement with that of other witnesses such as Jewett from Bell Telephone Laboratories, who said, ". . . we don't want to give too much consideration to inventors, it is the public that should interest us."[23] In his interpretation of the first British patent system he also said:

They weren't thinking particularly of the individual himself, but they could only do it through the individual, and what they did was to offer what was in effect a bribe to the individual by being willing to agree in advance and to pledge the faith of the nation to inventors unknown, even unborn, that if they would do certain things, the nation pledged itself to do certain other things.[24]

Vannevar Bush was more optimistic and recognized the impact of the inventor as an individual:

While a great research laboratory is a very important factor in this country in advancing science and producing new industrial combinations, it cannot by any means fulfill the entire need. The independent, the small group, the individual who grasps a situation, by reason of his detachment is oftentimes an exceedingly important factor in bringing to a head things that might otherwise not appear for a long time.[25]

The chairman of the Committee, Senator O'Mahoney, thought that ". . . the big problem is to find how that system [the patent system] can be made to serve the better interests of the individual" and added that he was thinking of the question of employment of individuals and that it was important to know whether or not collective research ". . . redounds to the benefit and liberation of the individual or of a collective group."[26] Only one member of the Committee, Representative Carroll Reece, asked the Commissioner of Patents directly about "the custom of the assign-

[21] TNEC Hearings, Part 1, p. 167.
[22] *Ibid.,* Part 3, p. 857.
[23] *Ibid.,* p. 977.
[24] *Ibid.,* p. 950.
[25] *Ibid.,* p. 872.
[26] *Ibid.,* pp. 873–874.

ment of patents to corporations," referring to a diagram on the distribution of issued patents, exhibit No. 186, produced by Coe. (This exhibit was produced once more, as No. 187. It showed the percentage distribution of patents between large corporations, small corporations, foreign corporations, and individuals, and showed that, in 1938, 57.1 percent of patents were issued to corporations.)[27] However, all discussions and statements made about the inventors and their position in the patent system in the TNEC hearings or publications were obviously of a more casual nature and not in any way central in assessing whether the U.S. patent system was working satisfactorily in this special field.

The National Patent Planning Commission

Only nine months after the TNEC had submitted its final report to Congress President Roosevelt came back to the patent question. On December 12, 1941, he issued an Executive Order (No. 8977) obviously thinking ahead toward the full utilization of the nation's war-expanded industrial capacity with return of peace. He established the National Patent Planning Commission and ordered a comprehensive survey and study of the U.S. patent system to consider "whether the system now provides the maximum service in stimulating the inventive genius of our people in evolving inventions and in furthering their prompt utilization for the public good" and "to what extent the government should go in stimulating inventive effort in normal times."[28]

After a first basic report on the general operation of the patent laws in 1943, the Commission took up in its Second Report of January 1945 the questions of law and administration of government-owned patents and inventions of government employees and contractors. Existing practices in various government agencies were investigated, and legislative proposals, congressional hearings, reports, and general literature were studied. The Commission stated that the government at that time owned approximately 500 unexpired patents, that nearly the same number had been dedicated to the public, and that the government had a royalty-free license under about 3000 unexpired patents. It was further found that it was general practice of the several departments to grant to anyone a nonexclusive license free of cost. The Commission went on to say that ownership of a patent by government is "somewhat anomalous," that commercial and industrial interests require an exclusive right for which government has no need. Specific statutory

[27] *Ibid.,* p. 865.
[28] Fed. Register Doc. 41-9471, filed December 16, 1941. From Fed. Register, December 17, 1941; Vol. 6, No. 244.

power authorizes government from 1910 to use any patented invention without license from its owner.[29]

After general codification of the patent law in 1952, the new section now provides that government, or somebody acting in its behalf (e.g., a contractor), may use a patented invention without permission of the owner of the patent. The section further provides that the *sole* remedy of the patent owner shall be an action in the Court of Claims against the government for reasonable compensation for the unauthorized use of the invention. In this way contractors performing services for the government were insured against the possibility of having to defend an infringement suit.

The Commission recommended that two principles established by court decisions, which operate in the absence of a contract to the contrary, should be made uniformly applicable throughout the government service:

1. Inventions made within the specifically designated duties of the employee shall be assigned to the employer, because the employee has produced only that which he was employed to invent.

2. Inventions made by an employee on his own time, without the use of his employer's facilities, and in a field unrelated to his employment, shall be the exclusive property of the employee, who shall be entitled to all patent rights.[30]

In the area not covered by these two cases it did not seem practicable, in the opinion of the Commission, to devise a uniform law or order. Policies and regulations adopted by any agency should be submitted to a central body for approval, and this body should also serve as an appellate tribunal with power of final decision on appeals that employee inventors may desire to take from agency decisions.

The proposal that employee inventors be granted special awards "for unusually meritorious services" was regarded with favor by the Commission. Any agency should negotiate for funds "in the regular manner," consulting with the Bureau of Budget and then justifying the proposal before the appropriate Congressional committees. Qualified agencies should be authorized independently to make individual awards up to a specified amount. Award above this amount, up to a maximum, were to be approved by the central control body.[31] The question of

[29] Act of June 25, 1910, 35 U.S. Code, title 35, sec. 68; now 28 U.S. Code, 1498.
[30] *Ibid.,* p. 11.
[31] Compare similar suggestions dealing with inventions by government employees in England in the 1920's, in F. Neumeyer, *The Law of Employed Inventors in Europe,* Study No. 30 of the Senate Subcommittee on Patents of the Committee on the Judiciary, 87th Cong., 2nd sess., 1963, pp. 69 ff.

extra compensation for inventions was not specifically brought up but was probably considered to be covered by awards for "unusually meritorious services."

As to government-sponsored research, the Commission found that in connection with inventions made under such contracts the practice has been that the government either retained blanket power to determine disposition of rights, took complete ownership, or left ownership with the contractor. In the latter case government received a royalty-free license with or without power to require the licensing of others.

As to a single uniform practice in this field, the Commission found this to be "unfeasible and undesirable" and that ownership of inventions could not be fairly determined in advance by an arbitrary or fixed rule. It was further found that the establishment of the central body vested with authority to review and approve important agency proposals becomes "almost essential." This body should be placed under the Executive Office of the President, preferably within the Bureau of the Budget. The body should have power to promulgate general policies, to supervise, and approve departmental policies regarding employee inventions, and determine disputed cases. It should further supervise and approve the manner of disposing patent rights (including the power to grant exclusive licenses and sell government-owned patents), instruct and advise departments, collect information, conduct investigations, and make recommendations.

These recommendations, made more than 25 years ago in the middle of World War II, are remarkable for their well-balanced judgment, clear-cut suggestions, and their concentration on essential terms, avoiding piecemeal suggestions of minor importance.

Regarding rights in employee inventions the policy recommended was that there should not be any rigid rules prescribed in advance for all departments and all cases. As to the two extreme practical cases: (1) when an employee "is hired to invent" and (2) when an employee "makes an unrelated invention by use of his own time and facilities," the rule of the general law should be followed. The ownership of inventions resulting from research contracts (from government) could not be determined in advance by an arbitrary or fixed rule but should be decided in each instance in accordance with the facts involved.[32]

In September 1945 the National Patent Planning Commission submitted a short third report to President Truman, which in regard to problems relating to the stimulation of discovery and invention recommended (point 8, subpoint 12(c)):

[32] This and the preceding recommendations of the Committee are discussed *ibid.*, pp. 13–15.

"study of employee-suggestion systems and rewards for distinguished service."[33]

Two years earlier, on February 5, 1943, President Roosevelt had started a new action in the same field by sending the Attorney General (Francis Biddle) a letter asking for an investigation of the patent policies of government agencies. The President stated: "There appears to be need for a uniform government-wide policy with respect to the ownership, use or control of inventions made by employees of the Federal Government, or by employees of government contractors in the course of performing contracts financed by the United States."[34]

The Attorney General's Investigation

This letter resulted in 1947 in the most comprehensive study of United States government patent policy ever made before or after, published in three volumes by the Department of Justice under the title *Investigation of Government Patent Practices and Policies, Report and Recommendations of the Attorney General to the President*. The publication covers the patent practices of 15 government departments and agencies (508 pages), of more than 50 nongovernmental educational and industrial organizations (75 pages), a legal study of the principles of law applicable in this field (34 pages), a survey of prior studies and legislative proposals (151 pages), a final report with findings, conclusions, and recommendations (Volume 1, 146 pages) and a bibliography (13 pages). The final report proper (Volume 1) presents all essential problems connected with inventions made by government employees and employees of government contractors as these problems appeared shortly after World War II. The central problems taken up there are the same today: primarily the question of ownership of employee inventions, the use of these inventions, and the question of special rewards to employees. Since no study of similar comprehensiveness has been published since that time and since the recommendations made by the Attorney General had some impact on the succeeding development, the main results regarding employed government inventors will be reported here.

The findings and conclusions of the Attorney General are collected under seven titles which concern law as well as government practice:

1. Ownership of inventions made by the government employees.
2. Special rewards to employees.
3. Inventions made by government contractors.
4. Administration of government-owned inventions.

[33] H.R. 283, 79th Cong. 1st sess., 1945.
[34] Letter reprinted in the Attorney General's Report, Vol. 1, p. 9.

5. Foreign (patent) rights to inventions made by federal employees.

6. Secrecy rules for government employees and contractors.

7. Uniform patent policy and procedure.

Ownership of Inventions   The findings presented leave no doubt what the Department of Justice felt about these different problems; many basic statements are quite blunt. Regarding ownership of inventions made by government employees the summary states:

Inventions financed with public funds should inure to the benefit of the public, and should not become a purely private monopoly under which the public may be charged for, or even denied, the use of technology which it has financed. The weight of informed opinion and the evidence of experience establish that the ownership of patent rights is not a necessary form of incentive to the great majority of Government scientists and technicians. Such opinion and experience further establish that patent rights are in fact an undesirable form of incentive because they may induce lack of cooperation and secretiveness among research workers; may unduly emphasize the patentable phases of their work; would provide an unequal form of reward for performance of comparable merit and usefulness.[35]

In spite of the statement that patent rights (presumably meaning the private ownership of patent rights) are considered an undesirable form of incentive to the employee, the Attorney General continues in his findings to divide employee inventions into three categories not unlike the categories used in a number of European laws in this field.[36]

In the first category government should obtain all rights, if the inventions (1) are made during working hours, or (2) are made with a substantial contribution by the government in the form of facilities, equipment, materials, funds, information, paid time, or services of other government personnel, or (3) bear a direct relation to the employee's official functions.[37]

As a second category, the Attorney General cites cases where there is some contribution by the government or some relationship between the invention and the employee's official functions, but where these are clearly insufficient to warrant the assignment to the government of all rights in the invention. On the decision of the government agency concerned, with the approval of the Patents Administrator (a post to be established on recommendation of this Report) ownership of

[35] *Ibid.,* Vol. 1, p. 2.
[36] Compare Neumeyer, *The Law of Employed Inventors in Europe,* Chapters 2 (on Sweden) and 4 (on Germany).
[37] This specification comes very close to the one used in the Swedish special law of 1949 regarding the right to inventions of employees, see Neumeyer *ibid.,* p. 6.

the invention should then be left to the employee, subject to a nonexclusive, irrevocable, royalty-free license to the government to make, have made, use, and dispose of the invention. In this case the employee or his assignee is also subject to the obligation to exploit the invention diligently or to grant nonexclusive licenses thereunder at a reasonable royalty to all applicants. In other words, he is made subject to a provision of compulsory licensing (not to be found in the Federal Patent Act).

In the third category—"in all other cases"—the federal employee should retain all rights to his invention, subject to existing provisions of law.

Substantiating the Attorney General's opinion that ownership of patent rights by employees "is not necessary as incentive, is unsound and undesirable as such," the Report gives a detailed list of reasons. In essence the following points are made:
1. If rights are left to the employee, inventions may be suppressed or a "private toll" may be levied for the use of an invention financed with public funds and resulting from functions of government undertaken in the public interest.
2. The employee may keep his scientific papers and accomplishments secret from his fellow workers and avoid cooperating with them.
3. Private ownership may create conflicts of interest which disable the employee from acting in the very fields in which he is most qualified.
4. The research employee may become patent-conscious, that is, dissatisfied with assignments to tasks not likely to lead to commercially valuable results, and he may be prone to neglect such work for research more likely to result in pecuniary profit.
5. Individual ownership is inequitable to federal employees as a whole, since it singles out for special treatment one of many federal functions and gives no comparable reward to nonresearch workers who may render equally meritorious service to the government.
6. The public would be subjected to a 17-year monopoly by the employee. It may be argued that this compensates for the alleged inadequacy in his salary, but higher salary or cash reward would serve the public interest better. For one thing, the burden would be distributed more fairly in the form of taxation.[38]

This catalogue of disadvantages and possible misuses has never been officially analyzed or refuted. Some experienced writers, however, such as M.B. Finnegan and R.W. Pogue, both formerly with the Office of the Judge Advocate General

[38] Attorney General's Report, Vol. 1, pp. 46–54.

(Department of the Army), have aptly pointed out some of the doubtful arguments in this official argumentation.[39] It seems worth repeating here that the grave criticism of private ownership, whether by government employees or by government contractors, assumes a lack of loyalty of federal employees and seems to criticize the structure and soundness of the U.S. patent system. The findings also pass over in silence possible legal remedies that may be available outside of the patent laws in the more extreme cases of misuse, to deal with theft of ideas, breach of duty, misappropriation of inventions, and other obvious punishable crimes. Further valuable points in a critical review of these findings have been given by Wilson R. Maltby, an expert in this field, formerly Navy Staff Patent Attorney and General Counsel to the Government Patents Board.[40]

Special Awards   The next important subject matter of the Report of the Attorney General treats the question of special rewards to employees. "Any system of special financial rewards, promotions or salary increases to employees on account of their making a patentable invention or discovery is undesirable." The argument is that a premium to the employee inventor may induce secrecy and lack of cooperation, may mean administrative difficulties in selecting the right person in cases of group endeavor, and may create dissatisfaction among unrewarded members of a research group or among personnel assigned to functions unlikely to produce inventions.[41] These reasons are obviously similar to those for not granting ownership of inventions to employees. The Attorney General recommends, however, a general system of cash bonuses, promotions, and salary increases for meritorious suggestions or ideas, *regardless of whether they are patentable.* [My italics.] The system should not be limited to or emphasize patentable inventions but should cover all types of scientific or technological contributions, and it should provide for reward of entire research groups or teams producing valuable scientific advances. These rewards should be initially determined by each federal agency. Another variety of this award system providing "for public, official and professional recognition of meritorious scientific contributions and advances" was proposed, to be under the direction of the Government Patents Administrator. This officer should correlate the experiences of the agencies and inform, advise, and make recommendations regarding the system. Recognition could also be made through issuance of certificates of merit (by the President or the head of the agency),

---

[39] Finnigan and Pogue, "Federal Employee Invention Rights," cited in footnote 1.
[40] Maltby, "A Government Patent Policy," cited in footnote 1.
[41] Attorney General's Report, Vol. 1, p. 3.

announcements to the press, or articles in scientific periodicals.[42] The rewards may take several forms such as retention of some or all of the commercial patent rights by the employee, financial awards such as cash bonus or participation in royalties,[43] and promotion to a higher salary grade. The Attorney General's Report states: "Scientific advances and improvements should be taken into account in rating the employee or in determining his eligibility for promotion or salary increase."[44] The discussion of salary promotion raised the question of whether government salary scales for scientific and technical employees were adequate.

The Attorney General thought (probably correctly) that a system of public recognition meant increased prestige and professional standing for the individual and was likely to lead to improved position in public or private life.[45]

Inventions Made by Government Contractors   In this field the Report recommended that as a basic policy all contracts for research and development financed with federal funds should specify that all rights to inventions produced in the performance of the contract belong to government.[46] Cooperative research projects are also subject to this policy.[47] Exceptions can be made in an "emergency situation" in a particular case in respect to inventions "to which the contractor has made a substantial independent contribution prior to the award of the contract." Every exception is subject to a number of conditions such as:

1. That the agency in question must show it had made a reasonable effort to enter into a contract on the basis of the basic patent policy (i.e., taking all rights) but has been unsuccessful.

2. That the United States has been granted a nonexclusive, irrevocable, royalty-free license to make, have made, use and dispose of any inventions awarded to the contractor under the contract.

[42] Attorney General's Report, Vol. 1, pp. 3–4.
[43] At the time of the Report of the Attoney General the chief proponents of cash awards to inventive employees were the Department of Interior (which suggested legislation) and War and Navy Departments.
[44] Attorney General's Report, Vol. 1, p. 73.
[45] *Ibid.*, p. 74.
[46] *Ibid.*, p. 76. At this point the surprising fact must be stated that the official government discussion practically never mentions the inventor or the employee making inventions when discussing contractor relations. The rights of contractors' employees are therefore entirely neglected, and their impact on government patent policy and public interest is not considered.
[47] By cooperative research project is meant the situation in which a certain agency (for instance, Department of Agriculture) and outside institutions or contractors contribute facilities, personnel, or funds in varying degrees. Inventions resulting from such projects

3. That the contractor agrees to place the invention in adequate commercial use within a designated period.[48]

By "emergency situation" the Attorney General had in mind situations in which a federal agency finds itself obliged to award a contract to a corporation having the best background or facilities in the field. However, this specific considered contractor may, when working on his own, prefer to do further investigations in a direction less likely to achieve the results desired by government, or he may prefer to complete the work at a date later than the government would find desirable. In order to direct the research into the desired channels or to expedite its completion an agency may make use of the "emergency clause" (with certain minimum safeguards described earlier in the Report).[49] The title of government to inventions made by contractor's employees and the belief that the public interest will be served best thereby is extensively defended in the final report of the Attorney General.[50]

General Recommendations   Of the further findings and recommendations made by the Attorney General in 1947 the final ones concerning a uniform policy and procedure are relevant for the general history of the U.S. Government as employer of inventors and sponsor of invention-producing contracts. The Attorney General stated in this respect that a uniform government policy is desirable in order to avoid competition among agencies, to strengthen the government's bargaining power, and to spread "the benefits of sound patent principles" throughout the government. To implement such a policy an Executive Order of the President is recommended.[51] On the other hand, each agency in the Executive Branch has the authority to prescribe rules and regulations for the conduct of its affairs, including policy regarding disposition of patent rights, and to enter into agreements with employees in respect to such measures. Such agreements may take the form either of an employment contract or a regulation applicable to all employees. The President may direct and correlate the exercise of the powers of each agency similar to the case of a corporation. No new statute is considered to be necessary, but it is recommended that the clear expression of government policy should be supplemented by centralized administrative control with regard to application and

---

should either be dedicated to the public, assigned to government, or made available at reasonable royalty rates.

[48] Attorney General's Report, Vol. 1, p. 76.

[49] *Ibid.*, p. 103.

[50] *Ibid.*, pp. 88–109.

[51] *Ibid.*, pp. 143–144. The President can issue Executive Orders by virtue of his general control over the Executive Branch of government.

interpretation of such policy. Leaving the respective rights to the common law "has resulted in controversies, litigation, and other difficulties." The proposed administration should consist of a Government Patents Administration headed by a Patents Administrator, assisted and advised by an Advisory Patents Board. This Board should have seventeen members: one each for industry, labor, academic institutions, and the general consuming public, and thirteen for certain government agencies (for instance, Agriculture, Commerce, Interior, Justice, Navy, War). The Administration should apply, construct, and supervise the uniform policy established by the President. Among its duties is "the determination of any controversies or disputes between the government and its employees or contractors, concerning the ownership, use or disposition of inventions and patent rights."[52] This would entail the creation of an administrative "quasi-judicial" federal institution to decide all ownership disputes in the employer-employee relation between government and employed inventor.

The voluminous Report of almost 1000 pages was presented to President Truman (President Roosevelt, the originator of the order, had died in April 1945), and the drafting of an Executive Order was begun in the Attorney General's office, starting December 1947.[53] The majority of agencies were in favor of the uniform patent policy suggested by the Attorney General, leaving the entire right and title in all inventions made by government employees to the government. The National Military Establishment and the Federal Works Agency, however, had a contrary view; the former took the stand that commercial patent rights are a necessary incentive to employees engaged in research and development and that elimination of that incentive would require the payment of higher salaries.[54] The War Department expressed a similar view, pointing out the value of encouraging ingenuity on the part of employees. The hope of financial reward, it was felt, offers the strongest incentive to invent. A system of cash bonuses or promotions and salary increases was suggested.[55] Also the Navy dissented strongly from the recommendations of the Attorney General.

[52] *Ibid.,* p. 145.
[53] The history of the first Executive Order in this field (No. 10096 of January 1950) is most carefully analyzed and presented by Forman in Chapter 6 of *Patents,* pp. 81–108. See footnote 1.
[54] Director of the Bureau of the Budget (James E. Webb) to the President in a Memorandum of January 28, 1948, reprinted, Forman *ibid.,* p. 86.
[55] Under Secretary of War (Robert P. Patterson) to the President, January 27, 1948, reprinted, *ibid.,* pp. 88–90.

Executive Order 10096
Numerous revisions of the Executive Order relating to patent policy were made
over a period of two years, but the amendments which would have resulted in a
policy more liberal to employees (as desired by the branches of the Defense Department) were not adopted, with a few exceptions. A last attempt to find a compromise
between the employee policy envisaged by the defense agencies and that desired
by the majority of other agencies was prepared January 21, 1950. A letter reached
the Secretary of Defense on January 23 for signature, but President Truman signed
an Executive Order on the same day, and the correspondence was returned to the
Defense Department without having been considered.[56] The previous history of
this Executive Order (No. 10096) is given here somewhat extensively because it
illustrates that important branches of government believed (and still believe) in
more actively encouraging employees who create patentable inventions during
their work. (The Order is reprinted as Appendix A of this Chapter.) The Assistant
Secretary of Defense in a memo to the Secretary of Defense of January 21, 1950,
mentioned that employees of this department filed 82 percent of the total government-wide employee patent applications, and he felt that for that reason alone
their opinion should be respected.[57]

By signing Executive Order 10096 with the title "Providing for a uniform patent
policy for the government with respect to inventions made by government employees and for the administration of such policy,"[58] President Truman established
a board of a character entirely unknown before in government administration.
The preamble of the Order stated that inventive advances in scientific and technological fields frequently result from governmental activities carried on by
government employees and that these advances constitute a vast natural resource.
The inventive product of functions of the government by its employees should be
available to the government, and the rights of these employees in their inventions
should be recognized in appropriate instances.

The Executive Order created for the first time federal administrative law in two
essentially different directions. It stated (1) a clear-cut basic policy for all government agencies with respect to inventions made by any government employee, and
(2) it established the administrative forum to handle legal problems involved
herein (except for compensation).

Invention Categories   The first part of the patent policy (Executive Order 10096)

[56] *Ibid.,* pp. 92–97.
[57] *Ibid.,* p. 94.
[58] Fed. Register, No. 16, Jan. 25, 1950, pp. 389, 391.

defines with exactness three categories of employee inventions. The first category concerns "all inventions made by any government employee (1) during working hours; or (2) with a contribution by the government of facilities, equipment, materials, funds, or information, or of time or services of other government employees on official duty; or (3) which bear a direct relation to or are made in consequence of the official duties of the inventor." In this first category of inventions the government shall obtain the entire right, title and interest.

The second category is: "in any case where the contribution of the government, as measured by any one or more of the criteria set forth in paragraph (a) last above [the first category] to the invention is insufficient equitably to justify a requirement of assignment to the government of the entire right, title and interest to such invention, or in any case where the government has insufficient interest in an invention to obtain entire right, title and interest therein" (even though it could obtain some right under the first category).

In this second category the agency shall, subject to approval of the Chairman of the Government Patents Board, leave title in the employee, and reserve a nonexclusive, irrevocable, royalty-free license with power to grant licenses for all governmental purposes in any patent, domestic or foreign, which may issue on such invention.

The third category is expressed as follows: in any case wherein the government neither pursuant to the first category obtains entire right nor pursuant to the second category reserves a nonexclusive license of the described scope, the government shall leave the entire right, title, and interest in and to the invention in the government employee (subject to law).

The third part of the first category in the Executive Order (in which government owns title) is qualified by supplementary criteria regarding the kind of government employees to whom it applies and their "official duties." Any invention falls within this category if it is made by an employee who is employed or assigned

To invent or improve or perfect any art, machine, manufacture, or composition of matter.

To conduct or perform research or development, or both.

To supervise, direct, coordinate, or review government-financed or government-conducted research, development work, or both.

To act in a liason capacity among governmental or nongovernmental agencies or individuals engaged in such work.

In addition, inventions are included if they are made by employees who fall within any other category of employees specified by regulations issued pursuant to sec. 4(b) (a section authorizing the Chairman of the Board to formulate rules).

The Government Patents Board   The second main part of the policy introduced by Executive Order 10096 instituted a "Government Patents Board," an independent government institution with a chairman appointed by the President and one representative from each of the following ten departments or agencies: Agriculture, Commerce, Interior, Justice, State, Defense, as well as Civil Service Commission, Federal Security Agency, National Advisory Committee for Aeronautics, and the General Services Administration. The Atomic Energy Commission is expressly excluded from the jurisdiction of the Board (sec. 7(a)). The Board shall advise and confer with the chairman concerning the operation of the Order. The functions of the chairman are to consult and advise with government agencies concerning application and operation of the policy, to formulate rules and regulations, and to submit annual reports to the President.

However, the most important duty vested in the chairman is "to determine with finality any controversies or disputes between any government agency and its employees, to the extent submitted by any party to the dispute, concerning the ownership of inventions made by such employees or rights therein" (sec. 4(d)).

One other important function was given the chairman by transferring to him some of the functions and duties of the Secretary of Commerce under an earlier Executive Order (No. 9865) of June 14, 1947. This Order provided for the protection abroad of inventions resulting from research financed by the government.[59] For these inventions the agencies shall acquire the right to file foreign patent applications, and they shall inform the chairman of such applications together with recommendations as to which inventions should be protected abroad. As to the scope of the Executive Order, it shall be added here that the concept "invention" as used therein comprises only such inventions as are or may be patentable under the patent laws of the United States (sec. 7(c)) and that the term "government employee" includes any officer or employee, civilian or military, of any government agency, except such part-time consultants or employees as may be excluded by certain special agency regulations (sec. 7(b)).

Before describing the procedure and the judicial activities of the Patents Board during its lifetime from 1950 through 1961 (when its functions were delegated to the Secretary of Commerce by President Kennedy), it should be remembered that

[59] Executive Order reprinted in "Patent Practices of the Government Patents Board," Preliminary Report of the Senate Subcommittee on Patents of the Committee on the Judiciary, Washington, D.C., 1959, Appendix B, p. 21.

this Board was vested with the power finally to determine the "apportionment"
or allocation of all invention rights by all government employees. At the time of its
creation this meant considerably more than 100,000 highly qualified military and
civilian scientists and engineers, disregarding the vast amount of "casual employed
inventors" whose results often were of considerable importance to the advancement
of the research and improved operation of government agencies. Remembering
further that the chairman of the Board through the years handed down more than
3500 decisions regarding the so-called "Rights Determinations" under sec. 4(d)
of the Executive Order, it must be stated that here a body of judicial precedents
was developed which must be valuable as guidelines for any future policy in this
field.[60]

For proper perspective of this activity of the United States Government in the
field of employee inventions we should remember the international situation at
this time (1950). Executive Order 10096 was substantially based on the Report and
Recommendations of the Attorney General submitted to President Truman in
1947. The collection of data for this report was concluded in 1946. In spite of the
laudable intent of the authors of this Report that "a study of the patent practices
of the United States Government, made with a view toward the framing of a
sound uniform policy, may properly embrace, for purposes of comparison, a study
of the practices of other governments with respect to the inventions of their employees and contractors, particularly in countries whose patent systems and
industrial development are comparable to ours,"[61] the report "missed the boat"
for several reasons. One was, of course, that the material for the ten foreign countries described was collected during the war years, which made it impossible to
obtain a complete and unbiased presentation of the Nazi legislation.[62] A second
reason was that the important special law of Sweden, for example, was enacted in
the very interval between the Final Report of the Attorney General in 1947 and

[60] The mass of material incorporated and analyzed in 11 years of the Board's arbitration
activities shows not only relevant solutions in cases of government employee inventions in
all fields of military and civilian technology but represents at the same time object lessons
in the general field of employee inventions. These decisions up to the present time have
not been printed, in spite of attempts by the first Chairman of the Board in this direction,
and they are treated as administratively confidential. An exception is the valuable analysis
of early *ex parte* decisions of the Board between 1950 and 1957 presented by Forman in
1957 in Appendices C and D of his book *Patents,* pp. 296–334.
[61] Attorney General's Report, Vol. 3, p. 79.
[62] Discussing Germany, the Report says that "the drastic economic and political changes
which characterized the Nazi regime render the experience between 1933 and 1945 an
inadmissible precedent" (Vol. 3, p. 111).

the promulgation of Executive Order 10096 in January 1950. The remarkable fact remains, however, that the classification of categories of employee inventions and the establishment of a central quasi-judicial body in the government adminis- tration as presented by Executive Order 10096 are closely related to (and defined in a similar way) as in some of the laws promulgated in this field in Europe.[63]

Returning to the year 1950, the newly established Government Patents Board started its activity in July of that year and created a small staff of seven persons including the chairman. The nature of the work of the Board was fixed by its chairman in rules issued by him on April 20, 1951, and approved by President Truman the same day.[64]

The operation of the Patents Board is described roughly in the following pages. Whether the results of research, development, or other activity within an agency constitute invention in the meaning of the Executive Order is determined by each government agency itself (sec. 300.5). Originality, priority, or patentability as well as when and by whom an invention was made are decided by the employing agency of the inventor.[65] In case of disagreement the employee may appeal to the Board, the chairman of which may approve, reverse, or modify the agency deter- mination with administrative finality (sec. 300.7). Another function of the Board is, according to the Executive Order (sec. 2(a)), to decide in cases in which govern- ment is entitled to full ownership of an invention and the invention is disclosed to the chairman, whether a patent application should be filed or publication effected. When government is not entitled to assignment of all rights and the employee files a patent application on his own, the chairman must give approval. All rights determinations by agencies must be reported to the Board chairman as well all inventions in which the employee retains the rights. All cases of disagree- ment between employee and his agency are decided by the chairman, whose decisions must be consistent with pertinent court decisions.[66] Finally in any case in which the chairman has decided that government is entitled to a greater right than that

[63] Compare with material on Sweden, Germany, Great Britain, Holland as well as Austria and Italy, Neumeyer, *The Law of Employed Inventors in Europe,* chapters 2, 4, 5, 6, and 8(A).

[64] Administrative Order No. 5, April 26, 1951, title 37, Chapter III, Part 300, sec. 300.1– 300.11.

[65] The operation of the Government Patents Board is described by Forman, *Patents* (1957), pp. 125 ff.; "Preliminary Report of the Senate Subcommittee on Patents" (1959), pp. 3–12; Wilson R. Maltby, "A Government Patent Policy for Employee Inventions," pp. 131–141. Maltby's article gives the most detailed presentation of the procedure.

[66] In spite of the fact that these decisions are administratively final, they can be reviewed by the courts. No such review has occurred as of this writing. See Maltby (1961), p. 135.

determined by an agency, the employee may petition for reconsideration (sec. 300.6(c)). In this case the chairman must reopen and reconsider the case.

The chairman obviously had a heavy workload. It was his responsibility to survey noncontested agency decisions and to review decisions on appeal or on request for reconsideration. At the same time he must clarify and interpret Executive Order 10096, under which he worked. He was especially concerned with interpretation of three concepts in the Executive Order: (1) when an invention is "made" in regard to the Patent Act, (2) what is meant by "part-time consultants and part-time employees" (exempted from the definition of government employee in sec. 7(b) of the Executive Order), and (3) what is meant by the provision that in certain cases the entire right, title, and interest to an invention shall be left in the inventor, "subject to law" (sec. 1(d)). It was found in connection with this latter term that various statutes such as the so-called Non-Fee Act of 1883, the Atomic Energy Act, and the Tennessee Valley Authority Act, and statutes relating to incentives and awards can give government certain property rights. The rights could also be acquired by contract, agreement, purchase, voluntary grant or gift.[67]

In the field of *foreign* patent protection of government-owned employee inventions, sec. 5 of the Executive Order had transferred these activities to the chairman of the Government Patents Board. On September 6, 1950, however, he redelegated this responsibility to the Secretary of Commerce who in turn assigned this function to the Office of Technical Services. In spite of repeated interdepartmental discussions nothing of a substantial nature had been accomplished to implement the order in this area. Neither Congress nor industry provided necessary funds for such activities.[68] The Executive Order that took up this matter for the first time was Executive Order 9865 of June 14, 1947, which ordered all departments and agencies to inform the relevant authority (now the chairman) which inventions should be protected abroad and where. The employing agency had to indicate "the immediate or future industrial, commercial or other value of the invention concerned, including its value to public health."[69] The agencies found the kind of analysis and motivations asked for here somewhat outside their ordinary competence and experience.

How did the Government Patents Board work in practice? Some statistics are to be found in scattered places, for different time periods, dealing with the number

[67] The interpretations are reported in Forman, *Patents*, Appendix B III, pp. 274–278.
[68] "Preliminary Report of Senate Subcommittee on Patents" (1959), p. 12.
[69] Executive Order 9865, Point 2, last sentence.

and character of the decisions made by the chairman and the agency sources from which the cases were submitted.

One source[70] reports that the chairman rendered 2357 decisions during calendar years 1950–1958. Of these 2333—in other words practically all—arose from automatic reviews of individual agency determinations, 24 decisions arose from the appeals to the chairman by employees protesting the determinations made by an agency. Petitions to the chairman for reconsideration of an agency reversal were received from employees in 7 cases. Of the total number of agency determinations, the chairman approved 2241 and reversed totally 116 (5 percent). By far the greatest number of decisions for review came from the Navy (1087); the Army was second with 424, and the Air Force third with 272. At the time the Government Patents Board started operations in 1950 there were 5844 inventions fully owned by government and 16,556 inventions licensed to government.[71]

Maltby, on the other hand, reports that from 1950 to 1961 the number of decisions made by the chairman exceeded 3500, of which about 80 were on appeal from employees, on determination whether to publish a government-owned invention or to patent it, or on reconsideration of prior decisions.[72]

Forman,[73] investigating the type of decision made by the chairman when determining the question of ownership of employee inventions, analyzed 1163 decisions rendered from the beginning of 1950 through December 31, 1954. He found that in 8 cases title was taken by government, in 668 cases title was entirely left with employees, in 467 cases title was left with employees subject to license to government, and in 20 cases publication or dedication of rights was ordered.

Forman's analysis indicates that the Government Patents Board under its first chairman in the vast majority of reviews between 1950 and 1954 made determinations of invention ownership in favor of the employed inventors. Since only those decisions came before the Board in which employees appealed from the agency's prior decision, it cannot be assessed in how many cases the agencies took full title from the beginning *without* a final review of these cases by the Board. There are strong indications, however, that the first chairman of the Board did not interpret the rules of Executive Order 10096 narrowly, regarding the employee's right of ownership. During this same time period (1950–1954) the percentage of full patent assignments to government by employees increased from 20.12 to 40.74 percent,

[70] "Preliminary Report of Senate Subcommittee on Patents" (1959), pp. 4–5.
[71] *Ibid.*, p. 6.
[72] Wilson R. Maltby, "A Government Patent Policy," p. 137.
[73] Forman, *Patents*, p. 141.

and the percentage of free patent licenses acquired by government decreased correspondingly from 79.88 to 59.26 percent. Since the chairman of the Board had determined title of inventions accruing to government in only 9 cases of 1163 (less than 1 percent), the increase of cases in which title was *de facto* assigned to government must be attributed to primary agency decisions (according to Forman). The Chairman of the Board also made public (in a talk of May 27, 1953) that he was "going to change" the wording "the Government shall obtain the entire right" into "the Government may be entitled to obtain the entire right." During this period the criteria of Executive Order 10096 were obviously applied rather loosely in cases of review by the Board, resulting, as noted previously, in the fact that the majority of cases were decided in favor of employees. Government patent experts consider Executive Order 10096 to be a restatement of the common law, not to be interpreted literally.

Employee Awards   Concerning the concept of award systems with extra compensation or other means of personal encouragement for inventive government employees, the first draft of Executive Order 10096, prepared in December 1947 provided for "a system of cash bonuses, promotions and salary increases." The succeeding drafts and the final Executive Order 10096, however, omitted any reference to this subject.[74] In his report to President Eisenhower, the chairman of the Government Patents Board stated in 1953:

Because of general interest in the subject and because of the desirability of giving appropriate recognition to government employees who make meritorious creative contributions useful in the performance of governmental functions and operations, consideration has been given to the development of a comprehensive Government incentives, awards, and rewards program.[75]

The chairman also had appointed an interagency working committee that recommended enactment of legislation with a comprehensive program to reward government employees making all types of meritorious contributions, including inventions and discoveries of basic scientific principles, and to find the most effective application of existing statutory provisions in this field.[76] At the same time the chairman urged all departments and agencies to do the following:

1. See that existing awards programs be made applicable to meritorious inventive contributions.

[74] *Ibid.*, p. 102.
[75] "Report of the Chairman, Government Patents Board, through June 30, 1953, to the President of the United States," Washington, D.C., 1953, p. 7.
[76] "A Proposed Government Incentives, Awards and Rewards Program with Respect to Government Employees," Office of the Chairman, Government Patents Board, March 1952.

2. See that such programs be reviewed for the fullest possible advantage.

3. Assure application to the employee inventor.

4. Give publicity to the fact that employees making inventive contributions of merit are rewarded.

It was on this active policy of the Board Chairman that legislative proposals were worked out.

Within two years these proposals led to the Government Employees' Incentive Awards Act of 1954 (Public Law 763, 83d Congress, 2d session).[77] With this Act government-employer policy splits into two separate fields of administration, one for "rights determinations" deciding ownership of government-employee inventions, and the other for incentive-award decisions for the same group of employees.[78] The nucleus of the Incentive Act is section 304, instituting two basic types of awards:

1. Cash awards for employees "who by their suggestions, inventions, superior accomplishments, or other personal efforts contribute to the efficiency, economy, or other improvement of government operations, or who perform special acts or services in the public interest in connection with or related to their official employment." These awards are paid by heads of departments.

[77] U.S. Code 2121–23 Stat. 1112–1114. Cash awards for suggestions of employees in the federal service originated with the Act of July 17, 1912, authorizing the Secretary of War to make such awards to workers in the Army's ordnance shops. A similar program was initiated in the Navy Department in 1918 under Acting Secretary Franklin D. Roosevelt. Probably both actions grew from the increasing number of successful suggestion programs in private industry after the National Cash Register Company introduced the idea in 1894.

Suggestion programs in the federal government grew notably during World War II when leaders from private industry came to Washington with strong feelings about the value of suggestion programs. As a result, the War Production Board strongly encouraged cash award suggestion programs in all industries having government contracts, and Congress passed legislation authorizing such awards throughout the Army, Navy, and Air Force. Similar authority was given to the Department of Interior and the Maritime Commission in 1944. A few offices, such as that of the Post Office, operated employee suggestion programs on an honorary recognition basis. The War Department's "ideas for victory" program was particularly noteworthy, saving more than $100,000,000 during its two years of wartime operation. At the end of the war the chairman of the War Production Board estimated that employee suggestions in wartime industry saved more than 200 million man-hours per year, or the equivalent of 80,000 full-time workers. The legislative history of the Incentive Awards Act of 1954 is described in *Congressional and Administrative News* 1954, 83rd Cong., 2d sess., Vol. 3, p. 3825. For this summary of employee awards the author thanks the Director of the Federal Incentive Awards Program of the U.S. Civil Service Commission.

[78] In Europe both determinations, as to ownership and as to extra compensation, are as a rule governed by the same law, and in Germany and Sweden for instance, they are administered by the same administrative board. See Neumeyer, *The Law of Employed Inventors in Europe,* Germany, pp. 52–55; Sweden, p. 10; Holland, pp. 117–122.

2. Cash awards for employees "who by their suggestions, inventions, superior accomplishments, or other personal efforts contribute to the efficiency, economy, or other improvement of Government operations, or who perform exceptionally meritorious special acts or services in the public interest in connection with or related to their official employment." These are awarded by the President.

Both awards are aimed at all civilian officers and employees of the government (not military personnel) and are awarded in addition to regular compensation. The use of any idea, method, or device for which the award is made shall not form the basis for any further claim by the employee. An award of this type shall be given due weight in qualifying and selecting employees for promotion.

The law permits agencies to make awards up to $5000 on their own authority and in special cases as high as $25,000 if approved by the Civil Service Commission. It also permits an employee to receive awards from all agencies that benefit from his suggestion or invention. The Civil Service Commission is given general responsibility for administering the government-wide awards program, and in practice this is carried out by the director of the Federal Incentive Awards Program who reports to the Office of Career Development under the executive director of the Commission. This official reports directly to the chairman of the Civil Service Commission. There are no separate appropriations to the Civil Service Commission for the cash awards; they are to be paid from the appropriations already established for the agency that primarily benefits from the achievement of the employee. The regulations of the Civil Service Commission contain the guidelines which the individual agencies follow in setting up their own programs. These regulations require each agency to "establish and operate a plan which provides for the use of incentive awards as an integral part of supervision and management." The objective of this requirement is to have an incentive-awards program in each agency which assists supervisors and management in carrying out their responsibilities for encouraging high performance and proposals for improvement from their work force.

Each agency has final responsibility for making awards under plans set up in accordance with the Incentive Awards Act and Commission guides and principles. Although incentive-awards systems may vary from agency to agency, depending on size, mission, and resources, certain basic features are the same throughout the federal service. For example, the awards scale for contributions resulting in measurable benefits is the same for all agencies.

Assistance to the agencies, including personal consultation with agency officials, is extended by the Civil Service Commission through development of principles and standards for the guidance of the agencies. Results of programs in the agencies are currently summarized and reported. Regional offices of the Commission evaluate the actual operation of award plans in federal field establishments. Two types of employee contributions have to be processed by the Civil Service Commission section: those for which an award of over $5000 is proposed and those which may have an application in agencies other than the one in which they originated.

The Commission has to consider both cash and honorary awards for contributions resulting in measurable or intangible benefits. If the benefits can be measured in money value (savings in man-hours, productive time, supplies, equipment, or space) the amount of the award is determined according to the award scale contained in the Commission's regulations (minimum award $15). When benefits are intangible (giving better service to the public, achieving more effectively the mission of the organization, or reducing accident hazards) the amount of a cash award is determined by the importance of the program affected by the contribution and its impact on that program.

To be eligible for a federal incentive award, an employee's contribution must be described in writing. The contribution may be of a variety of types. For example, it may be sustained excellence in performance of assigned duties, a particular achievement of special value, or a useful idea in the form of an employee suggestion.

A contribution may be either within or outside the employee's job responsibilities, but if within it must be so superior as to warrant special recognition.

Honorary awards may be granted independent of or in addition to cash awards. The highest honorary award granted under the program is the President's Award for Distinguished Federal Civilian Service.[79]

As a result of an in-depth study conducted in 1968, the CSC has revised the current government-wide incentive awards program. The changes which grew out of the study have been incorporated in the basic Federal Personnel Manual (Chapter 451) and became effective July 1, 1969.

Main changes in the awards program were the following: The scope of agency awards for employee suggestion is now limited to proposals that "directly contribute to economy or efficiency, or directly increase effectiveness in carrying out the Government mission." Other employee ideas relating to employee services or benefits, working conditions, housekeeping, buildings and grounds, and routine

[79] The fact that an idea is not new or patentable does not necessarily mean that it may not merit an award; the test is whether it will improve operations if adopted.

safety practices should be handled through normal administrative channels. A change of the kind made will result in fewer suggestions (and fewer awards), but shall lead to prompt processing and decision by the employing agency and rapid reply to the employee. A majority of government employees have been in favor of focusing the suggestion system on economy, efficiency, and effectiveness. Another change was to raise the minimum award level and the minimum level of benefits required for award. Minimum award level is now based on ten percent of tangible benefits, up to benefits of $1,000. In addition, management is asked to initiate a positive effort toward awards where there is objective evidence of successful program achievement in order to supplement the more passive process of waiting for the first-line supervisor to initiate award recommendations. CSC also advocates that ordinary performance evaluation of employees include consideration for awards. Another detail refers to establishing express recognition of private citizens who have made useful minor contributions to an agency's mission or operations.[80]

To give the activities of the Civil Service Commission the right perspective, it must be remembered that it is in principle responsible for the reward of creative achievements arising from a base of more than 2.5 million government employees, of whom considerably more than 100,000 are professional scientists and engineers, that is, potential innovators. Approximately 100,000 employees each year receive awards for adopted suggestions, and approximately 75,000 employees receive awards for superior on-job performance or for special achievements.

The benefits received by government as an employer conscientiously encouraging voluntary contributions of improved operations and new research results can only be partly measured, but the Commission says that the measurable benefits have averaged about $100 million annually. For the fiscal year 1968 the measurable benefits from adopted suggestions were $149,761,851 and from superior achievements $99,460,059. The number of adopted suggestions for the same time period was 145,623 (5.3 per 100 employees) and the number of recognized superior achievements 97,390 (3.3 per 100 employees). Cash awards totally paid by all agencies for 1968 for suggestions were $4,799,686, i.e., about 4.8 million and 14.3 million for superior achievements. The year 1968 has set an all time record.

The award programs in government civil service cover a broad spectrum of achievements in which inventions numerically make only a small proportion of the total.[81] In this connection it has to be remembered that two of the largest

[80] U.S. Civil Service Commission ("Changes in the Incentive Awards Program"), Bulletin No. 451–1, March 4, 1969.
[81] Communication to the author, December 1964.

agencies in the natural science and engineering field, the Atomic Energy Commission and the National Aeronautics and Space Administration, apply separate award systems authorized by specific provisions of acts of Congress. These systems will be described in the latter part of this chapter concerned with the invention policies of specific agencies.

Some examples of awards approved by the Civil Service Commission are these: To Vice Admiral H. G. Rickover, 1964, the Enrico Fermi award of $25,000 (on proposal of the Atomic Energy Commission) for his outstanding engineering and administrative leadership in development of safe and reliable nuclear power and its successful application to national security and economic needs.

The Enrico Fermi award to John A. Wheeler, 1968, for "pioneering contributions to understanding nuclear fission. . . ." Wheeler had done important work on problems of reactor shielding and control and later turned to work on control of thermal fusion.

A group award to postal clerks and letter carriers of the Anchorage, Alaska post office for restoring postal service after the earthquake of 1964, shared by seven mathematicians of the National Bureau of Standards for computer work in connection with the National Fallout Shelter Survey.

In 1966 the largest award for group achievement ($5000) was shared by sixteen employees of the Navy's Bureau of Ships (Technical Library).

It is easy to understand that in the operations of U.S. Government, whether in its capacity as the largest producer and keeper of warships and aircrafts or as the largest map surveyor, book printer, or hospital administrator of the Western world, there is unlimited opportunity for improvements. An adequate picture of the ingenuity of the employee inventors should embrace "dollar stretching" accomplishments as well as sophisticated defense improvements and advances in health service, to mention only two major fields. The career professionals who create new solutions may present them in different ways; often they appear as publications or patents, but many are also secret or directly put into use. A cursory study shows that many professionally qualified civil service inventors are patent holders and expressly recognized as such.[82] Some examples are:

William N. Sullivan, USDA entomologist with some 80 scientific publications and 22 patents, who revolutionized aerosol packaging.

Joseph W. Horton, technical director of the Navy Underwater Sound Laboratory,

[82] Examples: *Civil Service Journal,* July–September 1962 and October–December 1962.

the father of modern sonar, who holds 56 patents in sonar and electrical communication.

William B. McLean, Naval Ordnance Test Station, the creator of the conception of the Sidewinder air-to-air guided missile, holding some 24 patents.

William A. Geyger, electrical engineer in the Applied Physics Department of the Naval Ordnance Laboratory, world authority on high-sensitivity low-power-drain magnetic devices, who has published 3 books, over 100 articles and holds 11 patents.

Miss Marilyn Levy, research chemist at the Applied Physics Division of the Army Signal Research Laboratory at Fort Monmouth (now the Army Electronics Command), a pioneer in developing prints without the use of chemicals, with 9 patents in the field of photographic processes and materials.

These random examples could be multiplied many times. The impact of such inventions cannot be exactly evaluated—neither for their benefit to government nor for their commercial applications outside government—but the incentive funds set up for such innovators seem to be well invested. In 1965 the head of the Federal Incentive Awards Program calculated that total cash awards to productive civil servants is roughly one tenth of one percent of the total annual payroll of the agencies.

The application of the Incentive Awards Act naturally presents a number of difficulties, among them the problem of who is eligible for awards and who is excluded when making a contribution or performance as part of his "line of duty." The Federal Personnel Manual (as of August 1967) cites as examples of the types of ideas and performances which warrant consideration for incentive awards (Chapter 451, sec. 3-2) the following:

Ideas which result in improved operations. The fact that the idea is not original does not necessarily make it ineligible for award consideration.

An invention which is, or may be, patentable under the patent laws of the United States.

Exemplary performance of assigned tasks whereby previously unattained records of production are achieved.

Sustained above-average performance that merits recognition.

Performance which has involved the overcoming of unusual difficulties.

Exemplary or courageous handling of an emergency situation in connection with or related to official employment.

Creative efforts that make important contributions to science or research.

In order to determine the "line of duty" of a government employee the Civil Service Commission has drawn up guidelines which suggest consideration of job descriptions, performance requirement statements, or supervisor's interpretations.[83] Another criterion may be whether it was necessary for the employee to obtain the approval of higher authority in order to place a suggestion into effect. In making awards for superior performance, it must be determined to what degree the performance has exceeded the normal requirements of the employee's job. In general the Civil Service Commission approach is that doubt is resolved in favor of the employee.

The policy of the Civil Service Commission is also to keep to a decentralized method of operation. The diversity and the geographic dispersion of government operations argue strongly for flexibility and local control of this kind of activity. Delay, red tape, and paperwork are avoided in this way. The key objective of these award programs to make full use of employee skill and resourcefulness has been strongly supported and endorsed by recent Presidents.

The Incentive Awards Office of the Civil Service Commission is striving to spread knowledge about the federal award systems and their winners. An "Awards Story" appears in the issues of the *Civil Service Journal,* films are produced, and banquets are given for groups of award winners. Formal ceremonies in which outstanding achievements are rewarded by the President or heads of departments find their way automatically to the press. Cases in which successful government inventions come about in cooperation with industrial corporations as contractors are also publicized by the industry involved.

The Government Patents Branch   Returning now to the fate of the Government Patents Board, on January 10, 1955, the procedural instructions for submitting agency reports regarding employee inventions were revoked and revised. In the fall of 1954 the Department of Defense had recommended to the Bureau of the Budget that the Government Patents Board should be abolished by Executive Order and a new basic policy should be administered by each federal agency.[84] By an Executive Order (10695) of January 16, 1957, the records relating to government-owned or government-controlled inventions were transferred to the Department of Commerce.

The next step in the development of government patent policy to affect employees

[83] In Swedish government practice, importance is also attached to the wording of newspaper ads and public notices of new jobs for government employees.
[84] Forman, *Patents,* p. 175.

decisively was Executive Order 10930 of March 24, 1961, issued by President Kennedy.[85] This Order abolished the Government Patents Board and transferred all its functions (except the functions of conference and consultation between the Board and the Chairman) to the Secretary of Commerce. All rules and orders not inconsistent with this Order continued in full force. On the same day the Department of Commerce authorized the Commissioner of Patents "to arrange for the performance of these designated functions."[86] Within about one year the Acting Commissioner of Patents (E. L. Reynolds) implemented this authorization by a set of rules issued on February 6, 1962[87] and approved by President Kennedy. These regulations changed Part 300 of Chapter 3 of title 37 (Patents, Trademarks, and Copyrights), giving it the new heading "Government Inventions Jurisdiction, Patent Office, Department of Commerce." The First Assistant Commissioner, E. L. Reynolds, was made responsible for this new jurisdiction, called the Government Patents Branch.

The crucial legal and factual decision to be made by the head of the Patents Branch was whether an invention is directly related to the duties of the inventor employed in the agency and could reasonably be expected to arise therefrom. In this case the title to the invention belonged to government and had to be assigned to it, if the presumption of assignability was not rebutted. The head of the Government Patents Branch in the automatic review of cases from the agencies assigned title to government in many more cases than under the first chairman of the Government Patents Board (1950–1956). One consequence of this strict title policy was said to be that some government agencies, especially the Navy Department, could sidestep the provisions of Executive Order 10096 of 1950 by not forwarding all their rights determinations for automatic review. Many prolific government inventors were said to be well rewarded, in cash and honors, by their own agency, and this policy no doubt contributed to their decisions to remain with their government jobs in spite of higher salaries offered by industry.

The Kennedy Memorandum On October 10, 1963, President Kennedy issued a "Memorandum for the Heads of Executive Departments and Agencies" followed in the same document by a three-page "Statement of Government Patent Policy."[88] (See Appendix C.) The action was an unusual one; on the one hand the Memorandum was addressed to the heads of government departments and as such aimed for

85 26 Fed. Register, 2583.
86 *Ibid.,* p. 3118.
87 27 Fed. Register, 3289.
88 28 Fed. Register, 10943–10946, October 12, 1963.

internal government operations, but on the other hand it was published in the Federal Register as a kind of notice to the public. As a matter of law, the document is no Executive Order (being short of a statute) but a new type of executive procedure. It has been suggested that a possible reason for this action by the President was that at this time congressional action in the field of government patent policy was imminent on the basis of intensive activity by Senators Estes Kefauver and Russell Long. (Senator Long's measures on behalf of government title to inventions were discussed at the beginning of this chapter.) The Statement of policy by the President was meant to block Congressional interference by premature legislation.

Legal History

In a hearing before the Select Senate Committee on Small Business on March 14, 1963, Jerome Wiesner, director of the Office of Science and Technology in the Executive Office of the President, testified about policies concerning patents resulting from federally financed research and development.[89] This office, a "staff arm" of the President, advises on the coordination of science and technology. It analyzes patent policy, "this complex and tangled situation," from a "neutral corner," assessing what in the view of this office the public interest requires.[90] Allocation of patent rights under government contracts was examined, and the rationale behind current practices and the feasibility of developing criteria to guide agency judgment were explored. The final result was the Presidential document of October 10, 1963.

Briefly, the Memorandum states that complete uniformity of patent ownership practice throughout the government is not feasible but that significant common ground exists. This common ground is that a single presumption of ownership of patents does not provide a satisfactory basis for government-wide policy on the allocation of rights to inventions and that the government has a responsibility to foster the fullest exploitation of government-owned inventions.

The Policy Statement attached to the Memorandum is divided into seven "basic considerations," and four sections are devoted to the establishment of a basic policy with respect to inventions made under contract of any government agency. Since this book is primarily concerned with the question of ownership of employee inventions and compensation for them, the statements on the best use of government patents will not be discussed here. The basic considerations in the Presidential

[89] U.S. Congress, Senate Select Committee on Small Business, Subcommittee on Monopoly, Hearings March 1963 ("Economic Aspects of Government Patent Policies"), 88th Cong., 1st sess., 1963, pp. 323–345.
[90] *Ibid.*, p. 323.

Statement only once come close to talking about the employees who make all inventions: "The use and practice of these inventions and discoveries should stimulate inventors, meet the needs of the government, recognize the equities of the contractors, and serve the public interest."

The Statement goes on to say that the public interest requires that expeditious development and civilian use be encouraged, and to that end the need for incentives to private initiative and to healthy competition in industry must be weighed. In the Statement the "Contractor" is defined as "any individual, partnership, public or private corporation, association, institution, or other entity which is a party to the contract" (sec. 4(c)). Since the employees of contractors are not a party to the contract, they are not mentioned and the treatment of the inventions originating from them are left to the discretion of the contractor employing them.[91]

Ownership of inventions or discoveries made under contracts is discussed in two sections: (1) one group of five cases in which "the principal or exclusive rights throughout the world" shall be reserved to government, in other words, government title; (2) one group of three cases in which a contractor "may acquire greater rights than a nonexclusive license," i.e., principal or exclusive rights throughout the world (subject to an irrevocable, nonexclusive royalty free of cost throughout the world "for governmental purposes").

The five cases in which government always shall own title to employee inventions (made under any contract) are as follows:

1. Where a principal purpose of the contract is to create, develop or improve products, processes, or methods which are intended for commercial use by the general public (at home or abroad).
2. Where a principal purpose of the contract is to explore fields which directly concern the public health or public welfare.
3. Where the contract is in a field of science or technology in which there has been little significant experience outside of work funded by the government, or where the government has been the principal developer of the field and acquisition of exclusive rights might confer a preferred or dominant position on the contractor.
4. Where the services of a contractor are for the operation of a government-owned research or production facility.
5. Where these services are for coordinating and directing the work of others.

Exclusive rights can be acquired by contracting parties "in exceptional circum-

[91] In practice government contractors in industry own the inventions of their employees by contractual assignment.

stances." The three cases in which such circumstances obtain are as follows:

1. When the head of a department or agency certifies that such action will best serve the public interest.

2. When the invention is not a primary object of the contract (provided its acquisition is consistent with the intent of the provision regulating title ownership of government as listed above and is a necessary incentive to bring the invention into practical application).

3. When the purpose of the contract is to build upon existing knowledge or technology to develop information, products, processes, or methods for government use and when the work called for is in a field of technology in which the contractor has acquired technical competence such as know-how, experience, and a patent position directly related to an area in which the contractor has an established nongovernmental commercial position.

These rules are surrounded by a number of safeguards, among others by an obligation to report to government the use of inventions and an obligation to bring them to practical application.

The Memorandum finally ordered the establishment of a Patent Advisory Panel under the Federal Council for Science and Technology with the function to develop common guidelines for implementation and to recommend the use of government-owned patents. This Panel was created in November 1963 and in December 1964 made an Interpretive Statement on the Kennedy Memorandum.[92]

This Statement is a complex and extensive legal commentary interpreting more than a dozen key phrases and words within the Policy Statement and practically redrafting parts of the Presidential Memorandum. Its purpose is to achieve greater consistency and guidance of the various departments and agencies. (It is said that additonal such statements may be issued in the future to implement the Kennedy Memorandum.) Eight of thirteen interpretations refer to terms in section 1(a) of the Memorandum, setting forth contracting situations where the government normally should acquire exclusive invention rights in the public interest.

The Interpretive Statement on the President's Memorandum is of considerable importance for a more uniform application of government patent policy, especially concerning relations between government sponsors of research and industrial contractors (i.e., corporations as research contract parties). Since both government and private corporation employees in the vast majority of situations are bound in

[92] The statement is reprinted on pp. 15–23 as Appendix C of the "Annual Report on Government Patent Policy," of the Federal Council for Science and Technology, Washington, D.C., June 1965.

advance to assign all inventions produced by them, this Interpretive Statement does not have direct impact on their personal situation as inventors. Nor is the character of the tangible or intangible awards affected by this Statement. In fact, the "Kennedy Memorandum and Statement" itself does not suggest any measures regarding incentives to inventing employees in the service of government or its contractors. It seems obvious, therefore, that the treatment of inventing government employees as to ownership of inventions is administratively governed by the individual agencies, subject to review by the Government Patents Branch. The quoted statement in the Memorandum saying that the use and practice of inventions resulting from work performed under government contracts "should stimulate inventors" is entirely noncommital.

The Patent Advisory Panel provided for by the Presidential Memorandum considers the field of employee invention policy (emphasizing rights and obligations of the employed inventor) as outside their primary field of interest. There is, however, one part of the activities of this Panel which turns out to be of great value in regard to these rights. At its first meeting on January 24, 1964, the Patent Advisory Panel recommended the setting up of four subcommittees to investigate and study particular areas of government patent policy. One of these committees was the Data Collection and Analysis Subcommittee whose purpose was to encourage the acquisition of data by "every federal agency and department having a research and development program of the type likely to produce patentable subject matter."[93] Data designed to reflect type and size of the agencies' patent operations are now collected annually from 15 agencies. Information ascertained in this way on a broad official basis covers for the first time important current figures basic to the exact knowledge of government employee invention policy such as number of invention disclosures made by employees and the use made by government of these disclosures (patenting, publication, or no action).[94]

The Subcommittee figures include current information on the number of U.S. and foreign patents to which the government receives either title or license rights,

[93] "Patent Advisory Panel Progress Report" to the Federal Council for Science and Technology, June 1964," Washington, D.C., 1964, p. 6.
[94] When coming down to details the Subcommittee experienced many problems due to variations in practices and different methods of maintaining statistics as well as different definitions given by the individual agencies to the information requested ("Annual Report on Government Patent Policy," June 1966, p. 7). The Subcommittee work is, however, most encouraging and meritorious giving a hope that, at least in the government sector, more exact knowledge of existing policy and trends of policy through a number of years will lead to a more uniform and equitable government policy. Such a government policy could inspire private employers to improve their policy in the same field.

the number of invention disclosures received by the agencies, the practice of publishing disclosures in lieu of patenting, and the size of the government patent portfolio.[95] In the *Annual Report* of 1966 the Subcommittee for the first time started an analysis of the statistical material that the agencies had begun to submit in 1964. Summarizing the information received, the Committee provided averages of three-year statistics for fiscal years 1963, 1964, and 1965. The Subcommittee now annually records the following data:

1. Number of invention disclosures received by government.
2. Determination of rights in intramural employee disclosures.
3. Determination of rights in contractor disclosures.
4. Number of U.S. patent applications filed by government on intramural employee disclosures.
5. Number of U.S. patent applications filed, by government and contractor, on contractor disclosures.
6. Number of contractor disclosures on which no patent protection will be obtained by government.
7. Number of U.S. patents issued to government.[96]

Data included in points (2) through (7) undoubtedly offer an opportunity to study and judge important parts of government patent policy toward its employees.

For fiscal year 1966 the figures regarding patent policy for 15 federal departments and agencies are shown in Table 5.1. They can be compared with average figures for the four fiscal years 1963–1966 in the last column.

Before drawing any conclusions from these figures it must be kept in mind that they are averages from 15 federal agencies. The final average figures, therefore, may be rather misleading when remembering that patent activities vary strongly between individual agencies.[97] The column of 1966 figures in some cases shows a significant departure from the four-year average, too.

To illustrate the background of four-year average figures, some maximum and minimum figures for agencies as four-year totals are given here. They correspond, as far as possible, to the eight points presented in the Subcommittee's *Report* of 1967.[98]

[95] "Patent Advisory Panel Report" (cited in footnote 93), p. 6.
[96] "Annual Report on Government Patent Policy," Federal Council for Science and Technology, June 1967, p. 34.
[97] There are also included one department (Treasury) and one agency (National Science Foundation) which naturally have very little patent activity.
[98] Summary and breakdown figures taken from "Annual Report on Government Patent Policy," June 1967, pp. 34–35, and Appendix E, Table I.

Table 5.1   Agency Statistics on Patent Practices 1963–1966

	1966	Average 1963–1966	
1. Number of invention disclosures received by government			
From own employees	2,931	3,000	
From contractors	9,869	8,500	
		11,500	Total
2. Determination of rights in employee disclosures			
Government has title	1,179	900[1]	
Government has license only	263	300	
No rights in government	72	70	
		1,270	Total
3. Determination of rights in contractor disclosures			
Government either acquired or had right to acquire title	7,242[2]	7,000[2]	
Government has license	1,788	1,600	
		8,600	Total
4. Number of U.S. patent applications filed by government on employee disclosures			
Government has title	1,002	1,000	
Government has license	245	300	
	1,247	1,300	Total
5. Number of U.S. patent applications filed on contractor disclosures			
Government has title—filed by government	924	850	
Contractor has title—filed by contractor	1,777	1,600	
	2,725	2,450	Total
6. Total number of U.S. patent applications filed by government and by contractor (in latter case on contractor disclosure only)			
By government on employee and contractor disclosures	2,170	2,150	
By contractor on contractor disclosures	1,777	1,600	
	3,947	3,750	Total
7. Number of disclosures on which no patent protection will be obtained			
Employee disclosures	1,440	1,445	
Contractor disclosures	6.267	5,800	
	7,707	7,245	Total
8. Number of U.S. patents issued to government			
Employee disclosures	968	650	
Contractor disclosures	609	600	
	1,577	1,250	Total

[1] Voluntary assignments from inventor to Dept. of the Army not included.
[2] Totals do not include Dept. of the Army.

Source: "Annual Report on Government Patent Policy, 1967," Federal Council for Science and Technology, pp. 40ff.

Point 1

Average invention disclosures received by government from own employees = 3000. Breakdown reveals maximum contribution from Navy (four-year total of 3961), minimum of zero from National Science Foundation. In 1966 NASA (National Aeronautics and Space Administration) and Air Force pulled ahead of Navy with 3667 and 2447 disclosures to 2259.

Average invention disclosures received by government from contractors = 8500. Breakdown reveals maximum contributions received by Air Force, 6516 contractor disclosures, minimum by Veterans Administration, Treasury, and Tennessee Valley Authority, zero.

Point 2

Average determinations of rights in employee disclosures = 1270. Breakdown reveals maximum of rights determinations over the four-year period was made by the Navy, 2183, minimum by NSF, zero.

Total number of employee inventions to which government acquired title over the four-year period was 3921. Breakdown shows maximum contribution from Navy, 1586; minimum by NSF, VA, AEC, zero.

Point 3

Average number of determinations of rights in contractor disclosures = 7950. Government had title or right to title in an average of 6350 cases, and had a license only, in 1600. Breakdown shows maximum total in the Air Force, 6516 with title and 2484 with license; minimum, zero, in VA, TVA, and Treasury.

Point 4

Number of U.S. patent applications filed on employee disclosures to which government has title = 1000 average. Breakdown shows maximum in the Navy, 1586 total; minimum in NSF and Treasury, zero. Navy also had the highest total of license-only applications, with 565, compared to the average of 300.

Point 5

Average number of U.S. patent applications filed on contractor disclosures to which government has title = 850. Breakdown shows Atomic Energy Commission slightly leading Navy, with a total of 1101 to 1092. Contractor had title in an average of 1600 cases, on applications filed by contractor. Air Force contractors led with 2484 total.

Points 6 and *8* cover, respectively, patent applications filed by both government and contractor and number of U.S. patents issued to government. They appear in Table 5.1 but are not singled out here.

Point 7

Average number of contractor disclosures on which no patent protection is obtained = 5800. Breakdown shows maximum for Air Force, 7295 total, second largest Atomic Energy Commission, 5082. Minimum Treasury, VA and TVA, zero.

It seems rather obvious that the size of patent activities of all agencies in many respects is greatest in the branches of the Department of Defense, especially the Navy and the Air Force. Contractor invention disclosures and their processing is also markedly large at the Atomic Energy Commission. The number of inventions published rather than patented is largest at DHEW. Any future change of policy, therefore, should be decided in close consultation with these departments and agencies. A functional difference between defense patent policy, on the one hand, and health and agricultural patent policy, on the other hand, will always exist.

During the years 1964 to 1967 the government appointed at least three important national commissions, the objectives of which bear on the problems treated in this book. These commissions are

1. The National Commission on Technology, Automation, and Economic Progress, established in August 1964. It furnished a report in February 1966, *Technology and the American Economy,* in three volumes.

2. The President's Commission on the Patent System, established in April, 1965. It furnished a report in November 1966, *To Promote the Progress of . . . Useful Arts in an Age of Exploding Technology.*

3. Ad hoc Panel on Invention and Innovation, established in 1964. It furnished a report in January 1967, *Technological Innovation: Its Environment and Management.*

It must be stated at once that none of these national commissions has taken up the legal and managerial problems of inventive employees as a central theme. The first commission had the mandate from Congress to identify effects and pace of technological change and its impact on production and employment, to define areas of unmet needs, and to channel new technologies into promising directions. It was to recommend action on the part of management and labor as well as legal steps by government to promote technological change, facilitate occupational adjustment, and alleviate adverse impact of change. In this context problems of labor relations (for instance, collective bargaining as a vehicle for management of change) and federal and private research policy occur at several points. Automation is the direct result of innovations and inventions produced by employees (mostly men employed to do so), but this commission had to work substantially on the problem of how to marshall technology rather than how to improve employer-employee relations.

The second commission (on the Patent System) limited its objectives to six restricted and interrelated points: (1) to raise the quality of the U.S. patent, (2) to shorten the period of pendency of patent applications, (3) to accelerate public disclosure of technological advances, (4) to reduce expenses of obtaining and litigating patents, (5) to make U.S. patent practice more compatible with that of other major countries, and (6) to prepare the patent system to cope with the exploding technology. The framing of these main objectives shows clearly that any provisions of the patent system concerned with the inventors themselves (except for new rules governing what persons shall file patent applications and be cited as inventors) fall outside of the study and its recommendations. It seems therefore logical that at the only point of direct confrontation with problems of employee-inventors in the Government Patent Policy Report (sec. XXXII) "the Commission decided not to address itself to the question of the distribution of rights in inventions resulting from research and development work financed wholly or in part by the Government." The Commission holds that "this question is being considered actively elsewhere in the Executive Branch and by Committees of the Congress."[99]

The third commission (an ad hoc panel on Invention and Innovation) limited its study to three main factors affecting invention and innovation: taxation (encouraging or discouraging innovation), finance (such as distribution of costs in innovation or technological balance of payments), and competition (interaction between innovation and competition). The commission made seventeen recommendations, of which three are directly concerned with certain tax alleviations for inventors and innovators (irrespective of their employment), one broadens and complements studies of the innovative and entrepreneurial processes including preparation of empirical data and case materials, and one calls for a White House conference on understanding and improving the environment for technical innovation followed by a series of regional innovation conferences (expressly including scientists and engineers).

It becomes clear from this overview of government patent policy that uniformity as to legal and practical treatment of government employees and employees of government contractors making inventions in the course of their work has not been looked upon by executive offices as a matter of prime concern, and it has not

[99] *Ibid.*, p. 53.

been considered in their statements. The remarkable exception is the Investigation of the Attorney General reported in 1947 and described in detail earlier in this chapter.

Any past analysis and overall judgment of the situation regarding inventions made by employees of the U.S. Government and of government contractors had to be based substantially on the policy applied by the individual government agencies as reviewed by the determinations of the Government Patents Branch (regarding ownership) and as approved by the Civil Service Commission (regarding awards larger than $5000).

A complete evaluation of government as an employer of inventors in all respects is hampered today by some federal agencies and boards involved, which claim it is traditional to keep "rights determinations" of ownership administratively secret.[100]

FOUR CASE STUDIES

Four federal departments or agencies are selected for detailed description of their general employee invention policy, including their policy toward inventors employed by government contractors. The four examples chosen are the Department of Agriculture; the Department of Health, Education, and Welfare; the Atomic Energy Commission; and the National Aeronautics and Space Administration.

It must be remembered that most federal agencies differ basically from each other in general purpose and with regard to patent policy, both from a point of view of legal authority and from a point of view of traditional practice. One group, to which the Department of Agriculture and the Department of Health, Education and Welfare belong, is heavily "population oriented." Their activities are aimed directly at the people as producers and consumers of agricultural products in one case and as persons in need of safeguards to their health and general well-being in the other. Both departments have broad statutory authority to carry out and to assist research for the benefit of the nation. On the other hand, the Atomic Energy Commission and the National Aeronautics and Space Administration belong to a group guided by statutory directives in special federal acts created in the 1950's exclusively for their operation. They have to create new technology not ordinarily used by the general public. A third group (not described here) is represented by the Department of Defense and is exclusively concerned with the procurement of the best material and equipment for its own use, i.e., for the defense of the nation. It

[100] Principles of administrative secrecy are controversial. See Walter Gellhorn, *Security, Loyalty, and Science* (Ithaca: Cornell Univ. Press, 1950), Chapters 2, 3, and 7; also Kenneth Culp Davis, *Administrative Law* (St. Paul: West Publishing Co., 1965), Section 4.16.

gives no direct public service to the population. This department has broad authority to engage in its own research and development or to assign it to others by contract.

DEPARTMENT OF AGRICULTURE

Legal Authority

When considering the legal authority of the Department of Agriculture (USDA) to pursue research and to make innovations, its unique position becomes obvious. Congress created this department more than a hundred years ago (in 1862), but 26 years earlier (in 1836) the first Commissioner of Patents, Henry Ellsworth, started to distribute plants to farmers and promote publication of agricultural statistics. An agricultural division was established within the Patent Office at an early date, and when the Department of Agriculture was started the Assistant Commissioner of Patents, Isaac Newton, became the first Commissioner of Agriculture. As early as 1849 the *Annual Report* of the Commissioner of Patents remarked:

The inventive genius of mechanics, by improving the various implements of husbandry, has done much for the tillers of the soil. Their newly invented horse-powers, their threshers and separators, their seed-sowers and grain crushers, and other valuable machines, do much to expedite the labors of the farm.[101]

Some of the oldest U.S. patents belong to agricultural machinery. Reapers were patented by Obed Hussey in 1833 and by Cyrus McCormick in 1834. The *Annual Report* for 1848 listed 33 agricultural implements patented that year. The Department of Agriculture was developing at the same time as the breakthrough in basic areas of modern engineering such as communications, electricity, transportation, and medical science. Congress declared it to be its policy to promote the efficient production and utilization of products of the soil and a sound and prosperous agricultural and rural life. Agriculture in this declaration was expressly assured a position in research equal to that of industry, with the purpose of maintaining an equitable balance between agriculture and other sections of the economy.

The research tasks officially assigned to the Department since the beginning of its activities are enormous. It is now authorized to develop and improve methods of production, marketing, distribution, processing, and utilization of plant and animal commodities at all stages from original producer to ultimate consumer; to develop production of dairy products; to introduce and breed new crops, plants, and animals; to conserve and use land, forest, and water resources; to design and

[101] Cited by D. R. Rush, "A Stout Man To Bear On," in *Power to Produce, The Yearbook of Agriculture,* Washington, D.C., 1960, p. 13.

develop farm buildings, homes, and machinery, and establish agricultural industries.

Ever since its birth date in 1862, the Department has been further required by law to acquire and diffuse among the people of the United States useful information on subjects connected with agriculture in the most comprehensive sense of the word. This obligation was later extended to cover agricultural research under foreign contracts and grants.

The intent of Congress is to let the Department carry out its vast program through existing research facilities owned by government, by state agricultural experiment stations and federal and state extension services.[102] The Department maintains regional agricultural research laboratories in each of the four major farming areas of the United States; these laboratories are authorized to cooperate with other government agencies, states, counties, municipalities, business organizations, associations, universities, scientific societies, and individuals. In addition there is the Forest Products Laboratory, the principal research organization of the Forest Service since 1910, concerned wholly with the investigation of wood and wood products and their adaption to diversified uses.

The Department may enter into contracts with organizations and individuals to carry on research, if it can be performed more efficiently or at less cost than by the Department itself. All such contracts require that the results of research and investigation be made available to the public through dedication, assignment to the government, or by other means determined by the Secretary of Agriculture. This policy is implemented through the use of research contracts and grants with patent clauses.

The Department of Agriculture holds authority to provide for research in specific fields. This list offers some examples.

Processing and transporting agricultural products.

Soil erosion.

Culture of forest trees and other forest products, utilization and preservation of wood and material for pulp and paper-making; study of diseases of trees.

Causes, cure, and prevention of animal diseases.

Use of cotton and its by-products.

102 7 U.S. Code, 427, Bankhead-Jones Research Act (1935) as amended by Research and Marketing Act, Title I, 7 U.S. Code 427(i) and 1624 (1946) and Hatch Act, 7 U.S. Code 361(a), part of Agricultural Experiment Station Act (1887), reenacted 1955.

Improvement of ginning plants and ginning machinery.
Study of foreign plants and animal husbandry suitable for introduction into the United States.

To consolidate these enormous programs within a single organization the Agricultural Research Service (ARS) was established in 1953 to conduct and supervise most of the physical, biological, chemical, and engineering activities and to enforce regulatory programs involving plant and animal diseases. The ARS, now the Consumer and Marketing Service, works in four main areas: nutrition, utilization (consumer industrial use) and farm research. It is this branch of the Department which administers the departmental patent policy.

Size of USDA *Activities Working Funds*

What funds for research and development are appropriated to the Department of Agriculture and how are they used? Statistics collected by the Federal Council for Science and Technology illustrate the distribution of federal funds for R&D for fiscal years 1963–1966. These are shown in Table 5.2.

The figures show that the greater part of the funds for USDA are spent for research by its own institutions and laboratories, and that among outside contractors educational institutions predominate.[103]

Working Facilities

The Agricultural Research Service (ARS), the most important research arm of the Department, works through five large laboratories in Pennsylvania, Louisiana, Illinois, California, and Maryland:
Eastern Utilization Research and Development Division Wyndmoor, Philadelphia
Southern Utilization Research and Development Division New Orleans
Northern Utilization Research and Development Division Peoria, Illinois
Western Utilization Research and Development Division Albany, California
The Agricultural Research Center Beltsville, Maryland

An example of a Department of Agriculture branch with considerable inventive activity is the Forest Products Laboratory in Madison, Wisconsin. The Laboratory is part of the Forest Service and is concerned with the more efficient and diversified utilization of forest materials. Research is directed to chemistry of wood, its growth and structures, and to physical and mechanical properties of wood from American tree species. The Laboratory has five research divisions: wood quality, solid wood products, wood engineering, wood fiber products, and wood chemistry. Cooperation

---

[103] Compare the contrasting situation at Atomic Energy Commission where almost all research is carried out extramurally.

Table 5.2 Funds Obligated for R&D, USDA (in millions)

Total Funds Obligated	1963	168.0
	1964	189.2
	1965	227.4
	1966	243.7[1]
For intramural use	1963	117.7
	1964	130.2
	1965	155.7
	1966	171.4
For domestic extramural use	1963	42.5
	1964	51.3
	1965	61.7
	1966	62.1
1. Profit organizations	1963	.9
	1964	1.1
	1965	2.2
	1966	1.1
2. Educational organizations	1963	40.6
	1964	48.6
	1965	57.2
	1966	60.1
3. Other nonprofit organizations	1963	1.0
	1964	1.6
	1965	2.3
	1966	.9
For foreign use	1963	7.8
	1964	7.7
	1965	10.0
	1966	10.3

1 For 1968 National Science Foundation estimated $267.2 million, in *Federal Funds for Research, Development, and Other Scientific Activities*, NSF 67–19, p. 122.

Source: Federal Council for Science and Technology, "Annual Report on Government Patent Policy," June 1967, pp. 52–54.

with the University of Wisconsin assures collaboration in scientific matters and interchange of research facilities for staff and graduate students. The Laboratory serves governmental agencies, industry, and the general public. Nine Forest Experiment Stations complement the work of the Madison Laboratory. The personnel of the Madison Laboratory is only about 450, of which about one-third are technical staff.

The Rural Electrification Administration (REA) is an agency of USDA which acts under its own federal statute.[104] Its main function is to make loans for financing

104 Public Law 600, August 2, 1946, 50 U.S. Code, 55a.

rural electric and telephone systems without owning or operating such facilities. It is also responsible for adequate design of the property it finances. Testing and some research and development work therefore became necessary. Existing industry system designs and equipment were found not to be entirely satisfactory for certain coverage of rural telephone service, and standardization and R&D outside of the Bell System were negligible. REA was authorized in the 1952 appropriation bill to use funds to finance its own R&D program on a contract basis. Patent clauses in these contracts after 1952 were similar to the patent clauses in departmental research contracts.[105]

USDA *Manpower*   As Figure 1.11 shows (Chapter 1), the USDA in 1966 had about 40,000 scientific personnel, of whom 25,400 were scientists and engineers and 2200 professional health personnel. (The balance was made up largely 15,000 of nonprofessional scientific personnel.) In other words, professional scientists and engineers, including professionals in health fields, constituted almost one-quarter of the total USDA labor force of 117,000. The Department ranked second only to Department of Defense in its employment of scientists.[106]

A further breakdown of scientific fields represented in USDA is shown in Table 5.3.

Implementation of Legal Authority

Since all research conducted by the Department of Agriculture, as directed by statute, must benefit either the farmer or the consumer, there was from the beginning strong emphasis on its public service character. However, there were no regulations within the department relating to inventions made by employees and patents resulting from research. Early attempts by employee patentees to commercialize their own inventions led to adverse criticism by Congress. An important law suit regarding ownership of patents made by departmental employees in the 1880's (Magnus Swenson) led in 1891 to a permanent injunction whereby the employed inventor could not assert any right under his patent.[107]

In 1900 a controversy arose between the Weather Bureau (at that time part of the Department of Agriculture) and a scientific contractor (Reginald Fessenden) as to disposition of patent rights resulting from a contract to make improvements in the field of wireless telegraphy. According to the contract, inventions developed belonged to the contractor subject to a free license for the use of the Weather

[105] H. F. Clesner, "Patent Practices of the Department of Agriculture," Preliminary Report of the Senate Subcommittee on Patents, 87th Cong., 1st sess., Washington, D.C., 1961, pp. 18, 19, and Appendix J.
[106] "Scientific and Technical Personnel in the Federal Government, 1966," NSF 68–16, April 1968, p. 1.
[107] This case is described earlier in this chapter, on page 214.

Table 5.3   Technical and Scientific Personnel in USDA, by Occupational Group, October 1966

Total USDA employees	117,1841
Total professional employees	27,625
Physical sciences	1,530
Mathematics	601
Biological sciences	19,119
Biology (general)	93
Microbiology	163
Agricultural sciences	10,373
Animal sciences	630
Plant sciences	1,543
Forestry	5,434
Fishery and wildlife	94
Other biological sciences	789
Social sciences	997
Geography and cartography	95
Engineering	3,090
Health professionals	2,187

1 *World Almanac 1967*, p. 124, listing as of June 30, 1966.

Source: "Scientific and Technical Personnel in the Federal Government, 1966," NSF 68–16, April 1968, pp. 14–17.

Bureau only. As a result of public criticism of this and similar cases, the Secretary of Agriculture promulgated in 1905 the first departmental patent regulations for employed inventors,[108] in which employees were directed to apply for patents through the department for all such inventions as were connected with the work of the department through government expenditure or time. Any citizen of the United States was allowed to use the patented article or process without payment of royalty, and under the regulation any invention of this kind was, in effect, to be dedicated to the public—even if, as in this case, the inventor was no regular employee but a contractor or consultant. Between 1905 and about 1931 all patents of the department were dedicated to the public.

The decision of the Supreme Court in the Dubilier case in 1933[109] and employee antagonism caused some shift in departmental invention practice. In November 1936 a new regulation provided that if the employee's invention by determination of the Secretary of Agriculture was found to be within his specifically assigned duties, he was required to dedicate it to the public. When an invention "does not come within the scope of employment of the inventor employee and where the subject matter is of interest to the government" a patent application was to be

108 Clesner, "Patent Practices," p. 11.
109 See Chapter 2, footnote 26.

filed through the department under which it would retain a shop right. All other commercial rights were to remain in the inventor. This regulation remained in force for about ten years, and many inventors are said to have retained commercial rights to their inventions during that period. The regulation was amended several times, both in view of criticism by an employees' union and later in view of Executive Order 10096 of 1950 creating the Government Patents Board. In 1937 a memorandum in the department set forth that the employee inventor might dedicate the invention to the public or assign it to the Secretary of Agriculture, or retain commercial rights subject to a shop right in the government under applicable law. Unless the bureau chief or the employee requested reconsideration within 30 days the Department solicitor's opinion on these alternatives was decisive. This regulation was intended to reflect the principles of the Dubilier case, but in practice it only led to a broad construction of "assigned duties."[110]

In the 1960's the Department of Agriculture's policy has been to require assignment of submitted employee inventions and file patent applications. The Department believes that securing of patents serves to protect the public; when the patents are assigned to the Department, it can make use of these property rights in various ways to foster the public interest. For example, it can institute quality control over products manufactured for the Department under assigned patents, by obtaining information through license requirements or by granting royalty-free or royalty-bearing licenses to others. The Department feels that a patent license relationship also stimulates the creation of further independent invention by licensees. Finally, it is better to patent an invention than to publish information concerning it; the published patent presents a more accurate description and delineation of scope, and contributes more to existing technical knowledge than publication.[111] The employee invention rules were further developed on the basis of an outside report made for the Department of Agriculture (Newton Report) which appraised the USDA's research on utilization, including the handling of domestic and foreign patents.

The main source of patentable employee inventions (about 90 percent) is the Agricultural Research Service (ARS); others emanate from the Forest Products Laboratory, the Soil Conservation Service, and the Consumer and Marketing Service (formerly Agricultural Marketing Service). According to department regulations (sec. 7.918) all administrative functions relating to the acquisition and

[110] For details and further references, see Attorney General's Report, Vol. 2, p. 13.
[111] Clesner, "Patent Practices," pp. 13–14.

administration of patents involving the Department of Agriculture are delegated
to the Agricultural Research Service on behalf of the Department.

Inventor Rights of USDA *Employees*

Questions regarding employee inventions are governed by Title I, Chapter 15, of
the Administrative Regulations of the Department of Agriculture.[112] These regulations are an express condition of employment for all employees of the Department,
embracing full-time employees, part-time employees, and part-time consultants—
the two latter groups insofar as they make inventions during periods of official
duty. (Exemptions are subject to approval of the Government Patents Branch.)

Ownership of the domestic patent rights of Department of Agriculture employees
will be determined in accordance with Executive Order 10096 implemented by
Title 3, Part 300, Code of Federal Regulations, as amended Feb. 6, 1962. (The
seven criteria which settle the question whether government shall obtain the entire
title to domestic rights were described on page 229).

In any case where the government neither obtains this right nor reserves a
nonexclusive, irrevocable, royalty-free license in the invention, it shall leave the
entire right to the invention in the government employee, "subject to law."[113] If a
U.S. patent application is filed subject to ownership by the government, the
domestic right shall either be dedicated to the public, or "in the event it is desirable
to retain control of the invention in the department" it shall be assigned to the
government as represented by the Department of Agriculture (sec. 2.881). The
Office of the General Counsel in charge of handling patent applications has to
determine impartially whether or not the inventor is entitled to retain commercial
rights.[114] The determination is subject to approval of the Commissioner of Patents.
If the domestic patent rights are assignable to the government but the Department
decides not to file a patent application, the General Counsel must be informed
as to the manner in which it is intended that the invention will be placed in the
public domain, or as to any other disposition to be made of it (sec. 2.884). The
foreign patent rights of employees are determinable in accordance with Executive
Order 9865 and Administrative Order No. 6, but no employee of the Department
shall file patent applications in any foreign country (sec. 3.892) except as will be
described a little later. Plants bred by employees shall not be patented by them

[112] Reprinted (as of 1961) in Clesner, "Patent Practices," Appendix F, pp. 150–156.
[113] This phrase means that the pertinent common law as defined in court decisions must
be considered.
[114] "Commercial rights" include according to the regulations of the Department of Agriculture (sec. 2.879) the patent rights subject to the license rights of the government arising
pursuant to these regulations, or subject to law.

in this country (sec. 4.900); neither shall employees assist others in preparing or prosecuting plant patents (sec. 4.901).

The Department, however, acquires options to the foreign rights in all inventions in which a U.S. application is filed and in which the domestic rights are assigned or dedicated. If at the end of six months the government has not exercised its option, the employee obtains all rights to foreign patents. In these employee patent rights the Department, however, has a "world-wide license," i.e., a nonexclusive, irrevocable, royalty-free license "for all purposes of the U.S. Government," including the power to grant sublicenses. For most government agencies, the power to grant sublicenses extends only to licensing others to practice the invention for or in behalf of the government. However, in the case of the Department of Agriculture, any American firm or individual who obtains a license under the government-owned United States patent may also obtain a royalty-free, nonexclusive license under any foreign patents which may be granted to the employee. The employee, on the other hand, is under no requirement to report the use he is making of his rights abroad.[115]

Invention Rights of Contractors' Employees

Other sources of inventions for the Department of Agriculture are its contractors. These may be domestic corporations or institutions with which the Department has cooperative agreements or state experiment stations to which it makes direct grants (about 30 percent of the funds appropriated for R&D). USDA also makes foreign agricultural research grants or contracts. All these research contracts authorized by law must provide in principle that the patentable results of the work shall be made available to the public through dedication, assignment to the government, publication, or such "other means" as may be determined by the contracting officer of the Department. By "results" is, in addition, meant all nonpatentable information or data developed under the terms of the contract, during or subsequent to the period of contract.

Standard patent clauses with provisions of this type are used in practically all USDA contracts with profit or nonprofit organizations as well as with individuals. Under such a clause contractors as a rule have obligations to submit progress reports and to receive Department scientists as visitors. The Department determines whether data will be made public by it or by the contractor, and whether this will be done through patenting or a combination of publication and patenting.

[115] Foreign rights to some employee inventions of the Department have been successfully sold by the employed inventor. Examples are Moyer's vat fermentation process for production of penicillin and Cording and Willard's dehydrated potato flakes process.

In contracts with public organizations such as state universities, the standard patent clause is modified but has the same effect as the one described. Universities have a right to publish information concerning nonpatentable innovations resulting from such contracts.

Another standard patent clause in these cooperative agreements says that inventions made jointly by employees of the Department of Agriculture and employees of the "cooperator" shall be fully disclosed, either by publication or by patenting in the United States, and that such patent shall either be dedicated to the free use of United States citizens or shall be assigned to the United States at the discretion of the Department. The Department shall also have an option to acquire the foreign patent rights for any particular foreign country within six months after the filing of a U.S. patent application. Any invention made independently by departmental employee or contractor's employee shall be disposed of in accordance with the respective policy.[116]

This strict policy has been modified in certain branches of the Department. For example, the Forest Products Laboratory investigated at the request of a private firm (Southern Extract Co.) the possible use of chestnut chips in the manufacture of pulp and paper, major research costs being paid by the private company. The experiments did not lead to the expected results, but Forest Products employees developed instead a process and machinery for making chestnut board from the chips. Resulting U.S. patent rights were assigned by the Department in trust to a trust company which in turn licensed Southern Extract exclusively for 5 years. The company agreed to put a plant in full operation to manufacture the new products within 28 months. After the 5-year period the patents were reassigned outright to the government.[117]

About one-third of the R&D funds of the Department are given to state experiment stations as direct research grants. These funds are expended under their own statutory supervision.[118] In this connection the agricultural experiment stations are allowed by the Department to set their own guidelines for the disposition of inventions developed under such federal grants. One of the reasons why the Department allows this is that the Hatch Act of 1887,[119] as amended in 1955, does not have provisions governing patent rights for agricultural experiment stations, and federal patent policies do not apply to funds provided to these stations. The

[116] Administrative Regulations of USDA, title 7, sec. 185d, 1(a) and 1(b).
[117] Clesner, "Patent Practices," p. 19.
[118] 7 U.S. Code, 361.
[119] 7 U.S. Code, 361(a)-361(i), "Agricultural Experiment Stations."

Comptroller General has further ruled that federal grant funds allotted to a state become institutional funds.[120] As a result, state agricultural experiment stations have established rules within the framework of their state laws. On the other hand, since these stations are public institutions and tax-supported, most of them do not allow individual researchers to obtain title for patentable inventions resulting from such work. Legal conflicts about invention ownership have arisen between some state agricultural experiment stations and their employee inventors, as in the state of Florida.[121]

Another legal conflict concerned Harry Steenbock, a staff employee of the Agricultural Experiment Station at Wisconsin (and member of the Chemistry Department of the University), and his patents on a process to produce vitamin D. The inventions had resulted from research using funds both from state and federal governments and were assigned by the inventor to a patent-exploiting organization (Wisconsin Alumni Research Foundation, WARF).[122] A lawsuit instituted by the Department of Justice against this foundation for violation of the Sherman Act ended in January 1946 with a consent judgment cancelling the patent agreements for the vitamin D patents and the right to collect royalties under them and dedicating the patents to the public.

In 1956, the U.S. Court of Appeals (Sixth Circuit) held that a research chemist at the Northern Regional Research Laboratory of the Department of Agriculture at Peoria, Illinois, was hired to devote his efforts to a particular problem and to conduct experiments for a specifically assigned purpose. He made an invention that evolved as the direct and natural result of the execution of his assigned duties in the laboratory and therefore belonged to the employer (i.e., the United States as represented by the Department of Agriculture).[123]

In its general provisions applicable to grants (Public Law 85–934) the Agricultural Research Service provides regarding "Patent Provisions and Publication of Results" (paragraph 15) that with respect to patentable results the grantee agrees to cooperate in the preparation and prosecution of domestic and foreign patent

[120] 28 Comptroller General, 54.
[121] The Florida court cases involved questions of ownership of new varieties of sugarcane and a process to use dried citrus waste as dairy feed, both developed by Florida State Experiment Station employees. See the case study of the University of Florida.
[122] The foundation is a membership corporation of Wisconsin. See the case study of the University of Wisconsin.
[123] *C. R. Shook* v. *The United States of America*, U.S. Court of Appeals, Sixth Circuit, Nov. 8, 1956, rehearing denied, Dec. 21, 1956, 238 Fed. Reporter 2d Series 952; certiorari den. 353 U.S. 924, 11 Supreme Court, 684.

applications, to execute all papers requisite, and to secure the cooperation of any employee of the grantee. With respect to nonpatentable results of research and investigations the grantee agrees that in grants with public organizations such results may be made known to the public only in such a manner and with such credit or recognition as the parties hereto may agree upon. In all other grants such results may be made known to the public only at the discretion of the Contracting Officer. In case of publication by the grantee, reprints shall be supplied at no cost to the Department, and support is to be acknowledged in the publication.

Finally, in contracts and grants of the Department of Agriculture with *foreign* agricultural research stations (under Public Law 480) the departmental policy is that the American public shall be granted all benefits and information of any patentable results of such research conducted abroad, through dedication, assignment, publication, or other means determined by the Office of the General Counsel. In foreign countries the U.S. Government shall have an irrevocable, nontransferable and royalty-free license to use such inventions.[124] If no U.S. patent application is filed, the research results shall be made known through publication. If publication is made in a country other than the United States, this shall be done in accordance with the policy of the grantee. An important part of the agreement gives U.S. government representatives the right to inspect and make observations of the status of a foreign research project and to have access to all data, information, records, reports, and accounts relating to such project. In many private international research and patent agreements today emphasis is given to the same type of arrangement, giving one partner access to essential know-how and technical information developed by the other partner. The Department of Agriculture has no official record regarding foreign patents obtained by contractors, cooperators, and grantees.[125] Cooperation in agricultural research is world-wide. It includes countries such as Finland, France, India, Italy, Israel, Poland, Spain, Turkey, and the United Kingdom.

Invention Award Policy

Lacking specific statutory orders in this respect the invention award policy and the policy to award other contributions of employees of the Department of Agricul-

[124] The term used in connection herewith, "throughout the world," is unclear, since the right of use for the U.S. government cannot be broader than its legal basis. Since patent rights are strictly national rights based on national laws, no license right can be received in other parts of the world than that in which a foreign receiver of a contract or grant has a patent. In most cases, this means his own country only.

[125] Clesner, "Patent Practices," p. 22.

ture is based on the provisions of the Government Employees Incentive Awards Act of 1954. The relevant rules are implemented in the Department's Administrative Regulations, Chapter 451 (Incentive Awards), Subchapter 3 (Awards).

Four types of employees are eligible according to departmental rules: current employees, former employees, "nonemployees," and "other persons." Current employees of the Department are eligible when their contributions have received administrative approval. Suggestion contributions must be adopted within two years of initial proposal. Any employee may request reconsideration of his suggestion. Former employees are eligible for a period of two years from their last day on the rolls of the Department. "Nonemployees" refers to employees of a county Agricultural Stabilization Committee, a Cooperative Extension Service, or a State Agricultural Agency. If their achievements constitute a notable contribution to agriculture and to the public service, they may be considered for the Department's Distinguished or Superior Service Awards, but they are not eligible for cash awards. "Other persons" can be recognized by certificate or letter of appreciation if they have participated in an achievement for which a group Distinguished Service or Superior Service award is made by the Department.

In accordance with the federal Incentive Awards Act the Department makes a distinction between two types of cash awards: those based upon suggestions, including inventions, and those for high performance. Suggestions are eligible for cash awards only if not covered by normal job responsibility or if exceptionally outstanding or meritorious.

In addition, honor awards are given for "distinguished" and "superior" service.

The departmental regulations give four examples of ideas, special acts or services, and performance which would "warrant consideration."

1. An idea which results in marked improvement or savings in excess of $50 or its intangible equivalent in operations.

2. The suggestion or development of a usable invention which does not infringe on existing patents or copyrights, whether or not it is patentable.

3. Major scientific and technical contributions may, at the discretion of the Secretary of Agriculture, Director of Personnel, or agency head be considered for award. These contributions are classifiable as "Special Acts or Services" and are eligible for awards fixed under a Tangible and Intangible Awards Table.

4. Contributions to solution of difficult management problems.

From these regulations it can be seen that the activities for which either cash awards or honorary awards are given to employees are divided into two broad categories: those not related to the employee's official duties and those that are related but represent outstanding accomplishments.

The first category includes, for example, awards to a nonprofessional employee for simplifying the distribution of correspondence or the keeping of records, for improving the means for storing and retrieving information, and the like. Another example could be an improvement by a laboratory technician or research scientist in any technique or apparatus, the recovery of waste materials, or the salvaging of dirty or broken equipment. In both these examples the improvements or inventions are essentially extracurricular in the sense that the employee was not hired to make them. The amount of the award in this instance generally depends on the tangible savings in carrying out any particular program or service to the public. The primary object is to induce employees to develop a personal identification with their jobs and to wish to contribute beyond the routine performance of duty.

The second category, where accomplishments are directly related to assigned duties, generally requires different criteria for evaluation. Ordinarily, when a scientist officially engaged in some field of applied research makes a discovery or invention in his field of work, it is considered that he was merely doing what was expected of him. The reward is primarily the recognition given him by fellow scientists, which can lead to promotion to a position of greater responsibility and independence from supervision. Occasionally, a scientist or group of scientists will either solve a particularly difficult problem or obtain results which materially affect a specific industry, field of technology, or the public interest in general. In such instances, the Incentive Awards Act provides for special individual or group recognition in the form of cash or honorary awards.

Probably the Department of Agriculture does not single out employees with patentable inventions for special treatment. When overall work is evaluated for a promotion, one of the items considered is the number of papers the employee has written or delivered at scientific meetings. His patents are treated in the same way, being added to the number of papers. Such a practice is customary in most departments with civilian activities.

Invention Statistics

In 1966 the Department reported that between 80 and 100 patent applications are filed each year for employee inventions. In about five of these commercial rights

are claimed, and during the last 10 years departmental determination to grant
these rights has been upheld in all but three instances. They were reversed in two
cases when employees appealed adverse determinations.

Clesner in Appendix A of "Patent Practices of the Department of Agriculture"
reported that from more than 70 research projects the Department (in 1961) had
obtained more than 180 patents, constituting slightly less than 10 percent of
patents held by the Department. The great majority of these were employee
inventions.

The Patent Advisory Panel of the Federal Council for Science and Technology
was created in 1964 on the basis of the October 1963 Statement of Government
Patent Policy (the "Kennedy Memorandum") and through its Data Collection and
Analysis Subcommittee has collected extensive data concerning patent practices
and policies, reflecting the type and size of the various agencies' patent operations.
Thanks to the work of this Subcommittee, we have exact figures for fiscal years
1963 through 1966, with a breakdown of invention disclosures (the basis of all
patentable inventions) for USDA.

These are shown in Table 5.4.

The majority of invention disclosures offered to USDA are first submitted to a
screening process performed by patent advisors connected with each of the four
Agricultural Research Service regional offices and with the Forest Products
Laboratory. The ARS regional laboratories, whose function is primarily utilization
research, account for about 90 percent of the invention disclosures submitted by
employees to the Department's Office of the General Counsel. After screening,
the Department filed in Fiscal Year 1967 97 U.S. patent applications (one from
a contractor), and in 1968 108 applications (eight from contractors).

Before screening, 286 employee disclosures were received in Fiscal Year 1967,
and 216 contractor disclosures. In 1968 there were 268 employee disclosures and
62 from contractors. Here it should be observed that the term "invention disclosure" is interpreted in varying ways. Some use it narrowly to mean material
expressly submitted for possible patenting; others include progress and other
work reports, both from employees and contractors.[126] Reporting of invention
disclosures by contractors is low, because the number of USDA contractors
is low. The cases in which the Department determined to publish the reported
disclosure instead of patenting it are surprisingly few.

[126] Communication from Patent Counsel, USDA, Research & Operation Division, November
1968.

The Forest Products Laboratory in Madison makes a special attempt to inform its personnel about the patent situation and reports the number and nature of U.S. patents granted its employees. Employee inventions cover wide engineering fields from manufacture of paper pulp to refinement of wood alcohol, from moisture-indicating instruments to prefabricated buildings.

Patent Licensing

To what extent does the Department of Agriculture license its patents to others? As of the end of fiscal year 1967, 1244 unexpired patents were available for licensing, of which 670 had been licensed at one time or another. At the end of fiscal year 1968 these figures stood at 1315 and 671. In 1967, 28 of the available unexpired patents were licensed, and in 1968, 29 were licensed.

Some departmental employee inventions have found wide commercial application and represent great potential money value if they were to be licensed on a commercial royalty basis. For the employee patents listed in Table 5.5 more than 10 licenses each have been granted to commercial firms by the Department.

Invention Award Statistics

The following Table 5.5 gives an idea of the commercial importance of some of the Department of Agriculture employee inventions. The question arises: Do inventors in USDA receive any special award from their department or from other government sources? Did they receive cash awards as provided for by the Government Employee Incentive Awards Act of 1954, or other honorary incentives?

The Civil Service Commission, which administers the Government Employee Incentives Act, shows in its review of incentive awards for fiscal year 1966 that the Department of Agriculture adopted in its "Improvements Through Suggestions" 3.3 suggestions per 100 employees and awarded an average cash amount of $49. In the program called "Top Results Through Superior Performance" it gave 2809 awards for an average value of $218. The rate per 100 employees was 3.1.

These results and the intra-Department breakdown are shown in Tables 5.6 and 5.7. Table 5.6 shows only the top ten agencies in terms of rate of suggestions adopted per number of employees and average cash award granted.

Table 5.7 shows a breakdown of five USDA divisions contributing most in terms of absolute numbers of suggestions adopted and performance awards granted. Table 5.7 does not attempt to rank divisions within USDA by rate per 100 employees because a rather misleading picture would result, from divisions having less than 100 employees, for example. In terms of first-year dollar benefits, Forest Service was greatly in the lead with $3,230,527, followed by Consumer and Marketing

Table 5.4   Invention Disclosures in USDA Compared to Total of 15 Agencies

	Fiscal Year	USDA	Agencies (including USDA)
Total Invention Disclosures			
	1963	153	10,439
	1964	182	10,939
	1965	318	11,759
	1966	174	12,800
From government employees	1963	144	2,832
	1964	135	3,069
	1965	277	3,172
	1966	160	2,931
From contractors	1963	9	7,607
	1964	37	7,870
	1965	41	8,587
	1966	14	9,869
Employee Invention Disclosures			
For which government has title	1963	157	803
	1964	144	955
	1965	126	984
	1966	130	1,179
For which government has license only	1963	0	304
	1964	1	316
	1965	6	278
	1966	1	263
For which government has no rights	1963	1	64
	1964	0	69
	1965	1	74
	1966	3	72
Total U.S. patent applications filed by agency	1963	145	1,245
	1964	146	1,444
	1965	129	1,315
	1966	131	1,246
U.S. patents issued to agency (government has title)	1963	87	539
	1964	55	550
	1965	81	711
	1966	70	737
U.S. patents issued to employee (government has license)	1963	2	241
	1964	4	250
	1965	1	312
	1966	4	231
Disclosures for which no patent applications are filed	1963	17	1,237
	1964	17	1,537
	1965	144	1,566
	1966	43	1,440

(table continued)

Table 5.4. (continued)

	Fiscal Year	USDA	Agencies (including USDA)
Agency decision to publish instead of patenting	1963	10	28
	1964	11	25
	1965	28	89
	1966	38	64
Contractor Invention Disclosures Determined to Be under Government Ownership	1963	8	5,509
	1964	25	6,475
	1965	41	6,175[2]
	1966	12	7,242[2]
Government leaves contractor with exclusive license	1963	0	60[3]
	1964	0	80
	1965	0	40
	1966	0	29
Disclosures for which contractor has option to acquire title but elected not to do so	1963	–	–
	1964	–	–
	1965	–	–
	1966	0	2,961[4]
Patent applications filed by agency (government has title)	1963	1	731
	1964	5	834
	1965	3	980
	1966	4	924
Patent applications filed by contractor (government has license)	1963	0	1,742
	1964	0	1,527
	1965	0	1,315
	1966	3	1,777
No U.S. patent application filed	1963	2	5,345
	1964	18	5,945
	1965	37	5,639
	1966	6	6,267
Determination to publish instead of patenting	1963	2	177
	1964	3	293
	1965	6	239
	1966	5	222

[1] Voluntary assignments from inventor to Department of the Army not included.
[2] Totals not including Dept. of the Army in this group of four figures.
[3] This group of four figures refer to AEC; the situation occurred in no other agency.
[4] Almost entirely from Dept. of Defense.

Source: *Annual Report on Government Patent Policy, June 1967,* Federal Council on Science and Technology. The other 14 agencies are CIA, HEW, NSF, VA, Commerce, Treasury, TVA, FAA, Interior, AEC, NASA, Army, Navy, Air Force.

Table 5.5   Some Examples of USDA Employee Inventions Licensed to Others

		Number of Licenses
Lyle Goodhue William Sullivan	Aerosol bomb	107
Chester Thompson	Contributions to preservation of forage crops	43
Jacob Schaffer	Pullorum disease test	37
August Miller Roger Brown Ralph Rusca	Cotton-carding apparatus	22
James Cording, Jr. Miles Willard, Jr.	Drum drying of cooked potatoes	15
James Cording, Jr. Miles Willard, Jr.	Method for control of texture of dehydrated potatoes	15
James Cording, Jr. Miles Willard, Jr.	Dehydration of cooked potatoes	15
Edison Lowe William Rockwell	Continuous belt-trough drier	13
Daniel Swern Thomas Findley	Epoxidized oils	12
Ray Young Ralph Rusca	Cotton opener	12
Clarence Asbill, Jr. Ray Young	Cotton-working machine	12
Edison Lowe William Rockwell	Apparatus for treating particulate material with gaseous media	11

Source: Incentive Awards Program F.Y. 1966, USDA

Service despite the fact that the number of suggestions adopted and suggestion awards made (100 and 91) were not enough to place it in the top-ranking five of the table. Highest cash awards for performance went to Soil Conservation Service ($150,529) and highest awards for suggestions were paid to Forest Service ($25,065).

Examples of Inventions by USDA *Employees*

Pamphlets published annually by the Department of Agriculture report the results of the Incentive Awards Program and give both statistics and short stories of individual and group achievements.

For fiscal year 1965, for instance, we learn that B. M. Meeks, Assistant to the Poultry Division Director of CMS, made annual administrative savings of about one-quarter million dollars and received a Presidential Citation. Two program specialists, H. H. Walker and R. A. Bell of the Ohio ASCS State Office, developed a plan for reproducing aerial photographs and using them to determine acreage of food crops. The photographs were used to assess crops in 38 counties in 10 states,

Table 5.6   Improvements Through Suggestions, F.Y. 1966, by Agency

	Number of Suggestions Adopted	Rate per 100 Employees	Value of Measurable Benefits	Average Cash Award
Air Force	23,327	7.9	$ 57,390,465	$ 49
Post Office	42,736	7.7	8,268,645	25
Navy	24,889	7.4	20,788,932	48
Railroad Retirement Board	113	6.7	32,516	32
Army	23,064	6.1	25,021,498	51
Veterans Administration	8,179	5.4	663,995	22
Treasury	4,696	5.2	1,455,024	38
Agriculture	3,021	3.3	1,324,845	49
GSA (General Services Administration)	1,191	3.3	474,561	35
NASA	844	2.5	2,449,034	159
Total 40 agencies	140,779	5.7	123,395,573	42

Table 5.7   Suggestions and Performance Awards Within USDA, F.Y. 1967

	Suggestions Adopted	Number of Cash Awards for Suggestions	Performance Awards Approved	Number of Performance Awards Granted
Forest Service	592	380	455	292
Agricultural Stabilization and Conservation Service	298	268	412	90
Soil Conservation Service	374	266	946	610
Agricultural Research Service[1]	196	181	572	133
Farmers Home Administration	166	141	135	110
USDA Total[2]	1,841	1,433	3,251	1,590

1 Includes Research Program Development and Evaluation Staff.
2 Includes 30 divisions.
Source: USDA Incentive Awards Program, F.Y. 1967, based on Annual Report, SF–69.

saving over $1 million for the fiscal year. The two men shared a cash award of $2080 for "superior accomplishments."

For another "superior accomplishment" K. Messenger, Chief Staff Officer of the Methods Improvement Staff of ARS, received a cash award of $1723. He had developed low-volume aerial spraying for insect pest control under a cooperative program in two states (Texas and Indiana). As a result over $600,000 was saved.

Eight employees of the ARS Energy Metabolism Laboratory of the Animal Husbandry Division were credited for a "cost avoidance," i.e., annual saving of about one-half million dollars in a method for completing metabolism trials on lactating cows. A total cash award of $1480 was shared by these employees.

For "sustained superior performance" of an administrative nature 7 employees of the Livestock Section of the Economic and Statistical Analysis Division (Economic Research Service) earned a cash award of $1150 each and a Certificate of Merit. They made an economic analysis affecting livestock and meat, thus aiding "high-level policy formulation."

DEPARTMENT OF HEALTH, EDUCATION, AND WELFARE

Legal Authority[127]

The Department of Health, Education, and Welfare (DHEW) was created by President Truman in 1953 under a Reorganization Plan No. 1[128] essentially as successor to the Federal Security Agency established in 1939 by President Roosevelt. The Plan was designed to bring those agencies whose major purposes are to promote social and economic security, educational opportunity, and the health of the people under one Department head.[129] The Federal Security agency had been an assembly for various minor government agencies and government functions derived from several departments of the most varying traditions and goals. The "public welfare oriented" agencies were thus united in one structure, an executive department reporting directly to the President. The Department comprises today six main operating agencies: the Office of Education, the Social and Rehabilitation Service, the Social Security Administration, the Consumer Protection and Environmental Health Service, the Health Services and Mental Health Administration, and the National Institutes of Health. The three last agencies are of special

[127] Main sources for the earlier periods of this study are listed here: *United States Government Organization Manual 1964–1965,* pp. 338 ff.; Subcommittee Patents, Trademarks, and Copyrights of the Committee on the Judiciary, U.S. Senate, 86th Cong., 1st sess., Preliminary Report by C. M. Dinkins, "Patent Practices of the Department of Health, Education, and Welfare," Washington, 1960; G. Harrison, *An Analytical History of the Patent Policy of the Department of Health, Education, and Welfare,* Study No. 27, Washington, 1961; P. M. Banta and M. B. Hiller, "Patent Policies of the Department of Health, Education, and Welfare," *Fed. Bar J.* 21, No. 1 (Winter, 1961): pp. 88–98. The discussion of current activities is based on personal interviews with officials of the Department and internal documents of the Department.
[128] 67 Stat., 631 (1953), 5 U.S. Code, 133z–15n.
[129] President Roosevelt's message upon sending Reorganization Plan No. 1 (sec. 201, 53 Stat. 1424 (1939), 5 U.S. Code, 933t) to Congress.

interest for the present study, since they belong to the Public Health Service, and have far-rearching tasks in the field of scientific research and in the support of research and dissemination of its results to professional groups and to the people.

Size of DHEW *Activities*

Expenditures and Appropriations   Medical research is at the center of DHEW research, and appropriations increased rapidly after World War II. Federal medical research expenditures totaled more than $1 billion annually through the 1960's, and not surprisingly DHEW has had the lion's share, with $1.16 billion of a total of $1.6 billion in 1968. Table 5.8 shows the totals spent for medical research nationally during the five years 1964–1968, with breakdown.

Table 5.8   Medical Research in the United States, Distribution by Sources of Funds (in millions)

Source	1964	1965	1966	1967	1968
Total	$1,652	$1,841	$2,057	$2,280	$2,490
Industry	400	450	511	580	640
Private	153	162	169	177	180
State and local government	50	55	61	65	69
Federal	1,049	1,174	1,316	1,458	1,601
DHEW	not available	826	925	1,070	1,166

Source: National Institutes of Health, Department of Health, Education, and Welfare. Communication from DHEW, February 1969.

These figures can be seen in a context of total national expenditures for such research which have increased from $161 million in 1950 to $2.49 billion in 1968, at a rate of 12 percent per year. Federal expenditures accounted for two-thirds of this increase, but other sources of investment have risen too—from less than $100 million in 1950 to about $900 million in 1968.[130]

The National Institutes of Health accounts for the major share of federal expenditures for medical research. In 1968, NIH research expenditures constituted 54 percent of federal medical research funds ($873 million of $1,601 million) and a little more than 30 percent of total national expenditures for medical research.

The spectacular expansion (since 1950) of NIH programs supporting extramural research has meant significant increases both in the number of institutions receiving financial support and in the amounts received. In 1950, NIH research grants

[130] Resources Analysis Branch, Office of Program Planning and Evaluation, NIH, 1968.

were awarded to 241 institutions. The average amount received per institution was $60,000.[131] In 1968, 849 institutions of all kinds were receiving grants from NIH, of which 347 were institutions of higher education. The average amount per institution (general) was $884,000, including construction grants, and the average for institutions of higher education was $1,642,000.[132] In addition to money for construction, these grants go for support of health research in general and for training of personnel.

As an example of the great expectations that Congress places on research of scientists, engineers, and other health-related personnel assigned to carry out the various DHEW programs, appropriations to the National Cancer Institute (NCI) might be mentioned specifically. In 1956 the funds for chemotherapy research amounted to $900,000. In 1967 NCI had $30,732,000 for such research alone, in a total picture of $160,418,000 for general research in the Institute.[133]

Table 5.9 shows how DHEW's support of medical and health-related research fits into the total picture of federal support for such research. In the year 1968 the overall increase in federal support was to be less than 10 percent, the smallest since 1952–1953, when the Korean war imposed budgetary restraints. However, the increase was not uniform throughout the agencies; NASA's aerospace medicine program was up by 30 percent, and PHS's program for study of air pollution and environmental control was up by 25 percent.

The Food and Drug Administration (FDA) consists of five bureaus: the Bureau of Medicine, the Bureau of Scientific Standards and Evaluation, the Bureau of Scientific Research, the Bureau of Regulatory Compliance, and the Bureau of Education and Voluntary Compliance.

Working Facilities

The Food and Drug Administration (FDA) administers a number of special federal acts, such as the Federal Food, Drug, and Cosmetic Act, the Tea Importation Act, the Import Milk Act, the Caustic Poison Act, the Hazardous Substances Labeling Act, and the Filled Milk Act.[134] The activities of FDA are directed mainly toward promoting purity, standard potency, and truthful and informative labeling of consumer products. FDA has five bureaus that specialize in the following: scientific standards and evaluation, medicine, scientific research, regulatory compliance, and education and voluntary compliance. It has headquarters in 18 district territories,

[131] DHEW *Program and Management Progress,* A Report to the President, March 1965.
[132] Communication to author from Office of the Secretary, DHEW, November 1968.
[133] *Ibid.* Figure for 1956 from Harrison, *Patent Policy of the* DHEW, p. 19.
[134] *U.S. Government Organization Manual,* p. 362.

Table 5.9   Federal Support for Medical and Health-Related Research, 1968 Estimated
(in thousands of dollars)

Agency	$
Total	1,600,689
Atomic Energy Commission	96,938
National Aeronautics and Space Administration	108,185
National Science Foundation	13,055
Tennessee Valley Authority	2,107
Veterans Administration	46,461
Dept. of Agriculture	45,734
Dept. of Commerce	1,038
Dept. of Defense	113,347
Dept. of Health, Education, and Welfare	1,166,374
Public Health Service	(1,110,110)
National Institutes of Health	(873,230)
National Institutes of Mental Health[1]	(114,244)
Other PHS	(122,636)
Other DHEW	(56,264)
Dept. of Interior	1,970
Dept. of Transportation[2]	3,080

[1] A separate bureau of the Public Health Service since January 1, 1967.
[2] Represents programs of the Federal Aviation Administration.
Source: Resources Analysis Branch, Office of Program Planning and Evaluation, NIH, 1968.

each manned by chemists and inspectors and fully equipped with testing laboratories. The Washington laboratories conduct fundamental research to determine
characteristics of consumer products and production techniques, and they establish
standards and tolerances for consumer protection. They evaluate the safety and
efficacy of medicines; the toxicity of ingredients used in the manufacture of foods,
drugs, and cosmetics; the effect of pesticidal and radioactive residues on food
crops; the normal composition of all products covered by the federal acts administered; the potency of drugs and vitamins; and methods of processing, packaging,
preserving, and storing products under adequate controls. In addition, applications for distribution of new drugs are evaluated and must be approved before
they are placed on the market. Safety and efficacy of antibiotics, food coloring
agents, and household chemicals are tested and checked.

The Public Health Service (PHS) is the most important research arm of DHEW.
It is administered by the Surgeon General, in whom is vested broad statutory
authority of various kinds. Section 301 of the Public Health Service Act of 1944[135]
sets forth his duties, as follows:

[135] 58 Stat. 691 (1944) U.S. Code, 241.

... to conduct (in the Service) and encourage, cooperate with, and render assistance to other appropriate public authorities, scientific institutions, and scientists in the conduct of, and promote the coordination of, research, investigations, experiments, demonstrations, and studies relating to the causes, diagnosis, treatment, control and prevention of physical and mental diseases and impairments of man, including water purification, sewage treatment, and pollution of lakes and streams.

Medical research is, of course, the central field of research of PHS. Its share of total federal expenditures for such research through DHEW rose from 52 percent in 1953 to an estimated 89 percent in 1967.[136] The Surgeon General is further charged "to assist the states and other governments in the application of new knowledge for the prevention and control of disease, the maintenance of a healthful environment, and the development of community health services"[137] as well as to "collect and make available through publications and other appropriate means, information as to, and the practical application of such research and other activities."[138] Thus DHEW is seen as a source and a clearing house of research results. The Public Health Service Act has by repeated amendments through the years brought fields of research under its administration which must be solved with the cooperation of private industrial engineering, for instance, air pollution.[139] Conflicts relating to inventions may arise between industrial contractors in these areas and the Department.[140]

The Public Health Service carries out its research programs primarily through the National Institutes of Health (NIH). For fundamental laboratory and clinical research in causes, prevention, and methods of diagnosis and treatment of diseases this organization has the assistance of ten medical institutes: the National Cancer Institute, National Heart Institute, National Institute of Allergy and Infectious Diseases, National Institute of Arthritis and Metabolic Diseases, National Institute of Dental Research, National Institute of Neurological Diseases and Stroke, National Eye Institute, National Institute of General Medical Sciences, the National Institute of Environmental Health Sciences, and the National Institute

[136] *Federal Funds for Research, Development, and Other Scientific Activities,* F.Y. 1966, 1967, and 1968. National Science Foundation 67–19, 1967, p. 36.
[137] *U.S. Government Organization Manual,* p. 343.
[138] 58 Stat. 691 (1944), 42 U.S. Code, 241.
[139] The Air Pollution Control Act (69 Stat. 322, 1955, 42 U.S. Code 1857–1957 ff.) is administered by the Surgeon General.
[140] Less reason to expect conflict of interest as to industrial property rights may be found in other fields of research now under the administration of HEW, concerned with purely medical purposes such as the statutory authority to do research or contract for research in the field of cancer (42 U.S. Code 282), heart diseases (42 U.S. Code 287), dental diseases (42 U.S. Code 288), or hospital development and utilization (42 U.S. Code 291 n).

of Child Health and Human Development.[141] The Division of Biologics Standards is particularly active in research and development. It was here the rubella vaccine was developed.

An additional statutory authority of great importance, granted to the Surgeon General, is to make grants-in-aid to universities, hospitals, laboratories, and other public or private institutions, by the National Advisory Health Councils, appointed by the Surgeon General to oversee operation of the Institutes. The Councils in general follow the recommendations of many (more than 50) study sections. Four special councils for the medical fields of cancer, mental health, heart diseases, and dental diseases also receive grants.

The Saint Elizabeth's Hospital plans, develops, and carries out coordinated research programs and projects in the field of mental illness. As of January 1, 1967, the National Institutes of Mental Health became a separate bureau in the Public Health Service; prior to that time it had been one of the National Institutes of Health.

Manpower   As of March 1967, HEW had a total of nearly 101,000 employees, of whom about 5 percent were life scientists and 1 percent engineers. Public Health Service in the same year had 38,322 employees, NIH 10,659, and FDA 4500.[142]

NIH awards from 15,000 to 25,000 research grants each year. In addition, NIH support for training has had a significant impact on the nation's research manpower resources in medical and health-related fields. In 1968 $136,806,000 was spent by NIH for approximately 2500 training grants. About 25,000 principal investigators and collaborators were at work on them.

After "general medical," heart diseases and arthritis received most grant funds. NIH staff in 1967 was engaged in direct research, collaborative studies, and other functions, as follows:[143]

Direct research	3,432
Collaborative studies	515
Extramural research	1,255
Central services	4,269
Program direction (OD-NIH)	181
Other program staff	1,007
Total	10,659.

[141] *Basic Data Relating to the National Institutes of Health*, NIH, March 1968.
[142] *Basic Data Relating to the National Institutes of Health*, 1968, p. 44.
[143] *Ibid.*, p. 48. The total figure includes full-time civil service employees, commissioned officers, staff fellows, and visiting scientists at Bethesda, Maryland, and in the field.

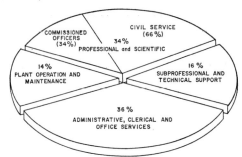

10,659 FULL TIME SCIENTISTS AND SUPPORTIVE WORKERS

COMMISSIONED OFFICERS (34%)

CIVIL SERVICE (66%)

34% PROFESSIONAL and SCIENTIFIC

14% PLANT OPERATION AND MAINTENANCE

16% SUBPROFESSIONAL AND TECHNICAL SUPPORT

36% ADMINISTRATIVE, CLERICAL AND OFFICE SERVICES

Figure 5.1 Distribution of staff at National Institutes of Health, 1967.
Source: NIH *Basic Data*

Figure 5.1 shows the percentage distribution of NIH scientists and supporting staff in 1967.

Industrial and University Contractors   The liberally supported anticancer program of the Department calls for cooperation with industry, especially chemical and pharmaceutical firms. As early as February 1, 1959, industrial research contracts with 10 large pharmaceutical manufacturers were in effect in connection with the cancer chemotherapy program. By 1967 the list had grown to almost 100.

The character of the research work of the Department makes it practically mandatory to delegate important parts to universities and other nonprofit educational and scientific institutions, especially for medical research projects. The research work of the Department takes the form of two distinct types: contract research and research grants. In 1967, 78 universities and medical schools were research contractors.

On the other hand, there were in the same year 347 institutions of higher education in every state and region in the United States receiving grants from NIH. All told, NIH accounted for about one-fifth of the total support by federal agencies to institutions of higher education, almost $700 million of $3300 million. The greatest number of institutions were receiving support for research projects and resources, averaging $1.6 million per institution.[144]

Institutions of higher education receiving the most considerable support from NIH in fiscal year 1967 are listed in the fellowship Table 5.10.

[144] Office of the Secretary, DHEW, February 1969.

Table 5.10   Universities Receiving Most NIH Support, FY 1967

1 Harvard University	$21,598,000
2 Johns Hopkins University	20,061,000
3 University of Wisconsin	19,228,000
4 University of California, L.A.	18,031,000
6 Columbia University	17,379,000
6 Columbia University	17,379,000
7 University of Michigan	16,658,000
8 University of Washington	16,506,000
9 Washington University	14,957,000
10 University of Minnesota	14,880,000
11 Stanford University	13,942,000
12 University of California, S.F.	13,706,000
13 Duke University	13,617,000
14 University of Chicago	13,434,000
15 Yale University	13,073,000
16 Cornell University	12,894,000
17 New York University	12,877,000
18 Yeshiva University	12,687,000
19 University of California, Berkeley	10,945,000
20 University of North Carolina, Chapel Hill	10,547,000

Source: Office of the Secretary, DHEW.

In many invention cases the Department came in contact with Research Corporation (New York), a nonprofit patent administrator and licensing agent for inventions produced at more than 100 universities. PHS has approved the licensing and handling of inventions arising in research contracts with university institutions in those situations where the university has been permitted to retain title under the Department's institutional patent agreement program. In such cases the universities can use an approved nonprofit patent management agent such as Research Corporation.

How university patent policy toward faculty and staff members has developed under the impact of government research contracts, including DHEW contracts with universities, is illustrated in the case studies of universities, Chapter 6. In general, their reactions to contract requirements regarding inventions range from satisfaction to distrust and concern about their relations with the Department.

Patent Policy Regulations

No statutory directive with respect to patent matters has been provided for the Department by Congress in the Public Health Service Act, in contrast to the detailed provisions drafted and accepted by Congress in promulgating the Atomic Energy Act (in 1954) and the National Aeronautics and Space Act (in 1958).

However, agencies of the Department had experience in the administration of
inventions resulting from their work through the overall federal agency patent
policy as set forth in Executive Order 10096. The Public Health Service has also
had a traditional policy, similar to that of E.O. 10096, of complete dedication
to the public of inventions resulting from its research.[145] This policy had been
expressly approved by a court decision in the late 1920's that inventions made in
the course of PHS studies and experiments must not be monopolized for private
gain nor tribute levied upon the public which has paid for its production.[146]

With the great increase of research conducted or financed by the Department, the
need for a more definite patent policy grew. The policy as it now stands had its
roots in an early Report of Federal Security Agency Committee on Patent Policy
(1950), the General Administration Manual and General Administration Manual
Guide HEW No. 1 (Patents and Inventions), October 1956, and an Explanatory
Statement, 1958, clarifying an important distinction between contract research
and research grants.[147]

Research Grants   The regulations, as set forth in the General Administration
Manual, Part 6, after stating the general policy of safeguarding the public interest,
encouraging individual or cooperative achievement, and after assigning general
responsibility to the Assistant Secretary for Health and Scientific Affairs, go on to
specify conditions to be included in research grants (sec. 8.1). Here two categories
can be immediately identified: (a) in which ownership and manner of disposition
of rights shall be subject to determination by the Assistant Secretary; and (b) in
which ownership and disposition of rights shall be left for determination to the
grantee institution. In the latter case the grantee institution's own procedures are
acceptable to the Department, being "such as to insure that the invention will be
made available without unreasonable restrictions or excessive royalties." The
condition is also made that the government shall receive a royalty-free license with
right to sublicense and that it shall have an option to file foreign patent applications.

Rights to inventions arising from research grants, to be determined according to
8.1(a), by the Assistant Secretary, may fall into four classes listed in 8.2 as follows:
1. Rights may be left to the grantee if he satisfies the Assistant Secretary that the
invention will either be effectively dedicated to the public or that any patent obtained will be available for royalty-free, nonexclusive licensing.

[145] P.M. Banta and M.B. Hiller, "Patent Policies of DHEW," p. 92.
[146] *Houghton* v. *United States*, 23 F. 2d 386, 391 (4th Cir., 1928), cert. den. 277 U.S. 592.
[147] All three documents are reprinted in Harrison, *An Analytical History of the Patent Policy of DHEW*, pp. 66–87.

2. The invention may be assigned to a "competent organization" for development and administration if the Secretary finds that the invention will thereby be more adequately and quickly developed.

3. Rights to the invention may be left to another contributing government agency if its interest in the invention is paramount to that of DHEW or when this is legally required or in the public interest. In such a case the invention will be developed according to the policy of the other agency.

4. In all other cases domestic rights in the invention shall go to the government. Exceptions are made for an invention of such "doubtful importance" that protective measures are not needed[148] and for inventions in which the government's equity is minor.

HEW fellowships, handled by the Office of Education, contain no patent clause. However, the Assistant Secretary may provide for the reporting of any invention arising during the term of a fellowship and for its disposition. Disposition may be made by the Assistant Secretary in accord with 8.1(a) or, if the institution where the research was performed meets the requirements of 8.1(b), disposition may be left to it. Fellows in some agencies with HEW may not be required to report at all.

Research Contracts   Right to inventions arising under contracts are disposed in a manner analogous to that of grants, namely, by the Assistant Secretary in the case of institutions other than nonprofit institutions, or by the institution itself if it is nonprofit and meets the requirements of 8.1(b)—a policy of its own which is acceptable to HEW.

An important exception is made for industrial research contracts having to do with research on cancer chemotherapy. Here the contractors are permitted to retain title to inventions and to acquire a license for government. Limitations and alternatives are left to the discretion of the Assistant Secretary. This exception was made in order to obtain the cooperation of pharmaceutical firms in the screening of compounds.

Patent Licensing   In agreement with the general principle that "the inventive product of research aided under research programs of the Agency are made freely available to the Government, to science, to industry, and to the general public" (as stated in the basic FSA report of 1950), the Department in the patent regulations of its General Administration Manual (sec. 6.3) states that

... licenses granted under government-owned patents will be royalty-free, revocable, and nonexclusive. Except for unusual cases when, on recommendation of the head of the constituent organization (for instance, NIH) that unconditional licensing would be contrary to the public interest, licenses are issued to all applicants and

148 As of 1969, HEW had never refused rights for this reason.

contain no limitations or standards relating to the quality of the products to be manufactured, sold, or distributed. To reduce the need for individual license applications, patents held for unconditional licensing shall be dedicated to the public as may be feasible.

In connection with agreements for research grants, fellowship awards, and contracts for research, the head of the constituent organization within DHEW may determine to assign an invention to a competent organization for development and administration for the term of the patent or for such lesser period as may be deemed necessary. This policy was stated in 8.2 of the Regulations, reprinted in the preceding discussion of research grants. The paragraph also states that for such assignment the Assistant Secretary must find that there are satisfactory safeguards against unreasonable royalties and repressive practices.[149]

FSA in its basic report of 1950 felt that there might occasionally be situations in which the effective development of an invention of potentially great significance might be prevented or delayed unless exclusive control of the invention can be permitted, at least temporarily for development and exploitation. Such a case existed in connection with the Department-developed drug Cortisone. On the other hand, the FSA report recognized dangers inherent in giving preference to any private interest for inventions financed even in part by government.

Invention Assignment Policy

Inventions of HEW *Employees*   The basic patent policy set forth in E.O. 10096 is that all inventions made by agency employees which are directly related to their official functions, or to which the federal government has made a substantial contribution, should be owned and controlled by the government for the public benefit. This is in accord with the recommendations of the basic Report of the Attorney General of 1947. The FSA, precursor to DHEW, had stated an equivalent policy in 1950 in a Report, and further underlined that, for employees engaged in scientific research or in the supervision of research, the nature of the work itself and the cooperative effort of research staffs warrant the requirement that the product should belong to the government. Further, the Report stated that in the field of health all doubts as to whether the government contribution was sufficient to warrant the requirement of assignment (of inventions) should be resolved in favor of assuring the availability of the invention to the public. This statement also referred to "many physicians and scientists" having the same opinion as a matter of professional ethics.

[149] The difference between unconditional (exclusive) licensing and assignment of a patent is substantially only that with any type of a license, final ownership remains with the (licensing) patent owner, who can revoke such license, whereas assignment transfers ownership to the assigned party.

This recommendation regarding employee-invention policy was well in hand when a draft of the forthcoming Executive Order 10096 came to FSA for comment. The basic requirements of the Executive Order regarding inventions made by a government employee with contribution of government time or facilities, or which bear a direct relation to his work, were considered to be in line with FSA's own recommendations in this respect, as were the other provisions of the Order. HEW, for example, took over the rules governing determination of ownership of employee inventions together with all criteria and distinctions as established in E.O. 10096. Even the four classes of employees to which full assignment of inventions applies, as specified in detail in E.O. 10096, are repeated in the rules of HEW. Regarding assignment of foreign rights, HEW complies with the principles expressed in Executive Order 9865 reserving to government the option to require assignment of rights in all or any specified foreign countries. This is the Order governing rights in foreign countries for all government agencies.

Inventions Under Research Grants, Fellowships, and Research Contracts   In spite of its strict adherence to E.O. 10096 in its policy toward its own employees (which is the policy of all government agencies), DHEW has developed a flexible ownership policy in regard to inventions arising from research grants, fellowship awards, and contracts for research. The Department in its Explanatory Statement of January 1958, with respect to contract research and research grants, points to the distinction between "contracts for research," a procurement or a purchase, and "grants for research," assistance or support. Under the research contract, research for which the government is to pay is undertaken by an institution pursuant to contractual obligations and in accordance with specifications prescribed by the government. In contrast, a research grant is made in support of some research activities or projects proposed by an applicant institution. Patent policy of DHEW has been framed in the light of these distinctions, as was shown in the summary of the regulations.

In research grants (as defined in the Explanatory Statement) the ownership and disposition of all domestic rights may be waived by DHEW and left for determination to the grantee institution in accordance with the grantee's established policies and procedures. In 1968, 21 universities and their research foundations had their institutional agreements with DHEW according to Table 5.11 below. The standard agreement, offered to all qualified grantee institutions, is reproduced in Appendix D.

How have these institutional patent agreements worked in practice? Many universities depend on federal grants and are willing to accept DHEW's conditions

Table 5.11   Institutions Having Standard Institutional Patent Agreements with DHEW

California Institute of Technology
Cornell University
Florida State University
Iowa State University
Kansas, University of, and University of Kansas Medical Center
Massachusetts Institute of Technology
Michigan State University
Minnesota, University of
Mount Sinai Hospital, and Mount Sinai School of Medicine of the City University of New York
New Hampshire, University of
New York, State University of, and The Research Foundation of State University of New York
Ohio State University, and the Ohio State University Research Foundation
Pennsylvania, University of
Princeton University
Purdue University, and Purdue Research Foundation
Stanford Research Institute
Utah,   University of
Washington, University of
Washington State University
Wisconsin, Regents of the University of
Wistar Institute

in the patent field. If a university has once formalized its patent policy in accordance with the "outline" of DHEW it will hardly change again on short notice. In this way leading universities that have entered patent policy agreements with DHEW have become pacemakers for a rather definite type of patent policy in the health research field. Institutions about to enter negotiations with DHEW, especially when they are inexperienced in the field or hesitating what course to take, are influenced by these agreements, in many of which the equities of the Department, the contractor, the faculty, and laboratory or staff members producing the research results are well safeguarded. However, the position of the Department as sponsor may make it relatively easy to win over a negotiating applicant to its concept of a reasonable patent policy. Many universities support research with their own funds or those of industrial sponsors, and in these cases DHEW patent policy must be modified.

Harbridge House, in their recent four-volume *Government Patent Policy Study* prepared for the Federal Council of Science and Technology, found in their interviews with pharmaceutical firm representatives that 19 firms refused to participate in NIH projects because of the restrictive features of HEW patent policy.[150] The par-

[150] Harbridge House, Inc., *Government Patent Policy Study,* Boston, 1968. See especially

ticularly objectionable clauses were those naming conditions under which the contractor could not obtain patent rights, especially in the situation in which the grantee (working with the contractor) participated in conception or reduction to practice of an invention. (Two other conditions under which no rights for contractor were obtainable were eliminated in 1966: where the patent would impede intended use of the invention, and where the new use of the invention was in the field of the research supported by an NIH grant.) The contractors were also alienated by the likelihood, as they saw it, that the Assistant Secretary, acting for HEW, might claim products or methods paralleling NIH's research. They referred to this as "contamination," meaning that their own research staff would be exposed to ideas or results coming from NIH-sponsored research. If the new ideas, new compounds, or new testing methods were found to be useful in an area in which the contractors were already conducting research, and if they then developed a salable product, HEW might be in position to press its claims to the product.

The years in which noncooperation of pharmaceutical firms was a serious impediment to general public welfare were from 1962, when the new requirements were instigated, to late 1966, when two restrictive clauses were removed by HEW, and several less objectionable features were eased. Testing of compounds possibly useful in cancer was never subject to as strict controls as compounds in the general medicinal chemistry program.

University Contractors and Grantees

Universities and other nonprofit organizations with medical schools, hospitals, and scientific laboratories are important contractors of DHEW in point of research. As stated in the summary of the Regulations, the Department applies, mainly through PHS and NIH, a definite patent policy toward academic contractors, to be administered either through the Assistant Secretary or through the institution itself if its procedures are acceptable to DHEW. The features of the policy are like those governing grants and are summarized on pages 282–283 of this chapter.

In its basic report of 1950, FSA, the predecessor of DHEW, touched on the principles of a patent policy applicable to institutions engaged in research for noncommercial purposes. This report cited the patent policy of some universities (as of 1950) and said

---

Vol. 1, Part 5, pp. 42–47, "Effect of Patent Policy on Industry Participation in Government R&D Programs." The NIH research programs and a closer view of the withdrawal of the pharmaceutical industry from participation in screening programs for NIH is treated in Vol. 2, pp. 1–29.

Some of these (for example, Chicago University, Yale University) have adopted the general policy that neither university nor members of its faculty shall in any way profit from inventions made in connection with work connected with the institution. Others (such as Columbia and Wisconsin) leave individual faculty members free to assign or not to assign rights to the institution but encourage assignment of rights to a research body set up by the university to secure patents in appropriate cases and to administer such rights on a licensing and revenue-producing basis. Obviously, the vital question in the case of cooperative projects is not so much whether rights are required to be assigned to the Government or to any other body but whether rights to the invention, however assigned, will be so administered that the invention will be readily available to the public, to science, to the Government, and to industry.

This basic principle was stated even earlier in a letter to Armour Laboratories, by James Conant, former president of Harvard, on July 2, 1947.

The research conducted by the department of physical chemistry is financed in large part by funds given for the advancement of science for the benefit of the public and it would be most embarrassing for the university if inventions which are directly or indirectly the outgrowth of that research, particularly inventions in human therapeutic or public health fields, are made the subject of privately owned patents administered for profit and not for the benefit of the public.[151]

Not all universities have this approach regarding ownership and commercial exploitation of university-employee inventions. The varying policies are discussed in Chapter 6.

Two early cases of university contractor agreements illustrate how employee inventions may be handled. One concerned a specific invention produced by an employee of the University of California and the other an invention by an employee of Johns Hopkins University. Both cases involved the problem of employee inventions resulting from research supported by contributions from several sources. In the California case, there was an institutional patent agreement with DHEW; in the Johns Hopkins case there was no such agreement.[152]

The University of California invention concerned a synthetic antigen for use in detection of cancer, and necessary research was continued with contributions and assistance of qualified technicians of a private drug firm. The Surgeon General in 1953 approved an arrangement whereby the private firm received a five-year exclusive license with a limit of 5 percent of net sales on any royalty charge. In 1958 the government received a license under the pending patent application. In 1959 the university abandoned all of its rights on condition that the inventor fulfill his obligations to the government.

The Johns Hopkins invention involved amplification of X-ray fluoroscopic

[151] Letter cited in Harrison, p. 64, footnote 117.
[152] Dinkins, "Patent Practices of the DHEW," pp. 15–16.

screens. Research contributions to the university-employed inventor were paid up to 1955, one-third from the university and two-thirds from PHS. Further technical development of the invention was undertaken by a private firm holding patents with exclusive right of use until 1965 with approval of the Surgeon General. At the end of this period the patent owner had to grant nonexclusive licenses with royalties limited to 6 percent, with a nonexclusive, irrevocable license free of cost for government.

Harrison[153] reports another case from New York University Postgraduate Medical School. Here the invention arose from research to which several organizations had contributed. None of the contract parties was interested in patent rights, and the university inventor had no desire to patent either, except to safeguard the interests of the government and the general public.

One university agreement considered to be typical of those executed by DHEW with grantee institutions was executed by the Surgeon General with the University of Washington in Seattle. The Department left the ownership and disposition of all domestic rights in inventions arising under PHS grants and awards for administration by the university. DHEW considered, in this case, that the arrangements between the university and Research Corporation were adequate safeguards of the public interest. Their procedure included patent licensing on a royalty basis in conformance with "normal trade practices," the university being opposed to the grant of any exclusive licenses. PHS in this agreement further required that the university report each invention which appeared patentable, that a nonexclusive, irrevocable, and royalty-free license be reserved in any patent application for such invention, and that an option be reserved to government to file foreign patent applications for six months from the date of U.S. patent filing.[154]

There have been other cases, of course, in which universities have asked for patent protection, giving as reason the need to assure economic development, the need to protect the public interest, or the usefulness of royalties in financing other research.

DHEW is aware of such arguments in favor of patent protection and states in its *General Administration Manual* (Part 8, sec. 8.0(c)) that "in some cases it may be advisable to permit a utilization of the patent process in order to foster an

[153] Harrison collected a series of university invention cases, trying to give a cross section of the views expressed by inventors and grantee institutions and the disposition made by the Surgeon General. Twenty-seven cases are discussed, from July 1956 to July 1959.
[154] Agreement (in form of a letter) reproduced in Dinkins, "Patent Practices of the DHEW," pp. 12–13.

adequate commercial development to make a new invention widely available."

Senator Russell Long presented to the Senate in May 1965 a case that was debated there a month later. It may illustrate some of the problems arising for DHEW when supporting a medical university grantee.[155]

Robert Guthrie, a Ph.D. and M.D. of the University of New York at Buffalo between 1959 and 1964 worked under formal research grants of the Public Health Service and the Children's Bureau, both part of the Department of Health, Education, and Welfare. Total DHEW support was almost $750,000 and the total support for his project by other sources about $100,000. In the total from DHEW was included a grant-in-aid by the Children's Bureau for his special project at the university at Buffalo, including costs for staff, supporting services, test kit materials and equipment, and the costs for field tests made by 30 states in many hospitals across the country.[156] One of the inventions Guthrie made in the course of his research (in 1962) was a new type of blood test and a test kit making it possible to detect phenylketonuria within three days after birth. This condition leads to mental retardation for life if not detected during the first month of a baby's life. Since the University of New York at Buffalo did not have an institutional agreement with DHEW, Guthrie was bound to forward invention reports to PHS as soon as any invention was conceived by him. PHS (which in some way must have been informed about the invention without a report from the inventor) requested in January 1962 a formal invention report but did not receive any such report from Guthrie until December 1962. In the meantime, Guthrie both filed a U.S. patent application in his name (in April 1962) and entered shortly thereafter into an exclusive patent license agreement for the life of the patent with Ames Company, a subsidiary of Miles Laboratories, Inc., a pharmaceutical manufacturer. This action was approved by two voluntary health associations involved in the research but not by PHS. Further, Guthrie and Children's Hospital of Buffalo petitioned PHS to leave exclusive rights to the licensed manufacturer.[157] Hospitals in Massachusetts and in other states were producing a test kit of their own according to Guthrie's invention for $6, including all costs. The selling price charged by the industrial patent licensee would have been $262, over 40 times as much. According to Senator Long, a

---

[155] Congressional documents: *Congressional Record,* Senate, A, May 17, 1965, pp. 10343–10347, and B, June 3, 1965, pp. 12083–12087.

[156] The exact breakdown of the support budget for Guthrie's research project is in dispute, but the author of this book has no means of checking the correctness of the figures presented in the Senate debate. A different figure, however, would not change the basic situation of conflict of interest.

[157] *Congressional Record,* Senate, A, p. 10347.

number of states contemplating setting up the Guthrie test on a routine basis could not afford a state-wide program if they had to purchase the kits from Ames Co. (the licensee) or if they had to pay royalties on the materials in the kit (in the event they were manufacturing it themselves).[158]

Upon disclosure of the price the industrial patent licensee intended to charge for the kit, the inventor helped try to destroy his existing agreement. After studying the situation, PHS through the Deputy Surgeon General determined that ownership belonged to the United States, and an assignment of the patent application was executed accordingly. A suggestion by the patent advisor of NIH to reimburse the industrial licensee for certain costs and expenses incurred in the meantime was refused by PHS.

It appears from a letter from the DHEW Patents Officer to the PHS Inventions Coordinator, of March 25, 1965,[159] that in research projects cosponsored by PHS and by other DHEW agencies, the latter did not use a patent clause in their research grants, whereas PHS did. The Department Patents Officer continues in this letter as follows:

This is difficult to explain to the institution and the grantee investigator when they ask why. This also makes it difficult to require reporting of such inventions. . . . Under all the circumstances it appears that the Public Health Service and other Department of Health, Education, and Welfare policies and practices ought to be as consistent as possible with one another and that cooperation should exist in order to carry out DHEW responsibilities.

Senator Long expressed his criticism on this and similar cases in various ways. He wished to call a halt to "this immoral and evil practice"—the desire to make monopoly profits at the public's expense even when it adversely affects the health of children.[160] He said that allowing private patents on government-financed research will inevitably result in delaying disclosure of new knowledge, inventions, and discoveries, at least for as long as it takes to prepare patent applications and file them. Senator Long also expressed the opinion that allowing universities, hospitals, and nonprofit institutions to control and administer patents resulting from publicly financed research is contrary to the public interest, that educational institutions should not be in patent licensing, should "stay out of business." He accused the inventor of holding up "the formal invention report . . . for almost a whole year so that a patent could be filed" and fulminated against the exorbitant price to be charged by the licensee.

[158] *Ibid.*, p. 10344.
[159] *Ibid.*, p. 10347.
[160] *Ibid.*, p. 10344. This statement is not correct. (F.N.)

The charge of exorbitant pricing seems not to be so easily justified either. Senator Bayh in his answer to Senator Long on the Senate floor on June 3, 1965[161] gave an account of the situation as seen by the licensed manufacturer, which had been involved in phenylketonuria research for nearly 10 years before becoming Guthrie's licensee. Ames Company spent considerable time in refining the Guthrie PKU test to meet essential standards of quality and uniformity of ingredients. It appears plausible that, as Senator Bayh reported, additional effort, investment, and expense had been incurred by the licensed manufacturer. Total unrecovered costs were claimed to be somewhat more than $131,000, and official auditors attested that this amount represented fairly the data shown in the company's statement.

A short evaluation of the Guthrie case illustrates how difficult it may be for a research-supporting agency to receive invention reports from a research grantee, not only to receive them early but to receive them at all. Another problem is obviously to "reduce to practice" (as patent law says) inventions submitted to DHEW in the health field, such as new medical test methods, new or improved drugs, and medical appliances or instruments. To develop a marketable product of high and even quality, safe for human use and saleable at a reasonable price requires cooperation between the inventor and experienced industrial manufacturers. Additional costs of development are, as a rule, difficult to avoid. The supporting agency, naturally, has the right and obligation to rule whether additional industrial development costs are reasonable, but in many cases it can hardly refuse them. They should be considered as part of the total research grant. Discovery of new means of medical treatment (like other improvements) has little value to the country if they remain at an experimental stage without nationwide use.

An additional problem demonstrated by the Guthrie case has to do with DHEW departmental patent policy. It seems that this Department despite its heterogeneous structure will sooner or later be compelled to accept a consistent patent policy as asked for by the Department Patent Counsel in the letter of March 25, 1965, quoted previously. A research grantee need not be acting in bad faith if he fails to follow exactly the provisions of his research contract or contracts in regard to his various obligations. The reporting of inventions, right of ownership, the question of patenting or publishing his results, and similar legal questions are not part of his ordinary competence as a scientist. Lack of uniformity of policy and unclear language can further complicate correct action by a grantee-inventor or a grantee-institution.

[161] *Congressional Record*, Senate, B, June 3, 1965, pp. 12083–12087.

One other group of sources of academic inventive research results is important in view of the worldwide supporting functions of DHEW. Several foreign universities and scientific institutions are among its grantees. PHS grants submitted to foreign applicants include a standard patent clause, reserving to the Surgeon General the right to determine ownership of inventions and questions of patenting or publishing all research results under a grant. Serious doubts have arisen on the side of the foreign party to DHEW research contracts, such as the University of Manchester, the University of Leyden, or the University of Stockholm (School of Engineering).[162] The standard patent clause applied by PHS or NIH covering industrial property rights abroad can be in conflict with national laws. Modifications of the standard patent clause is also needed when research support comes from several sources at the same time, United States and foreign. Often foreign governments, institutions, and industries are involved as partial supporters.

According to the DHEW Patent Regulations (Part 8, sec. 8.0(c))

... it is recognized that inventions frequently arise in the course of research activities which also receive substantial support from other sources, as well as from the Federal grant. ... It would not be consistent with the cooperative nature of such activities to attribute a particular invention primarily to support received from any one source. In all these cases the Department has a responsibility to see that the public use of the fruits of the research will not be unduly restricted or denied.

Disposition of such inventions is governed by the individual situations. According to the Department *Manual* (Part 8) the Assistant Secretary for Health and Scientific Affairs may determine, if the facts so warrant, that the government's equity in an invention is minor, and its rights may be waived subject to a royalty-free license for governmental purposes (sec. 8.2(d)).

Invention Award Policy

Like the other agencies, DHEW acts on the authority of the Federal Government Employees Incentive Awards Act to pay cash awards and incur expenses for the honorary recognition of employees who by their suggestions, inventions, superior accomplishments, or other personal efforts contribute to the efficiency, economy, or other improvements of the operations of the Department.

Aside from this general policy, the Department has no specific patent award system or procedure, probably because it has no specific statutory directive with respect to patent matters. The character of a public service activity has been strongly

[162] Harrison, p. 55, footnote 110, regarding the two first cases. The latter case is personally known to the writer.

emphasized in all work of the Department, and health and welfare personnel, especially, are urged to remember the public service character of their work.[163]

The widespread fields of research within the framework of DHEW, from testing of food to cancer cures, do not make for any unified approach to the problem of an employee invention incentive policy. The main discussion in this field is aimed at the question whether to patent or to publish research results. The reward and incentive effect of these measures *upon the employee* as the creator of improved service, new medicines, or new testing and manufacturing processes has been entirely in the background. Harrison reports in her study some casual early cases on invention awards to employees of the Food and Drug Administration, the Communicable Disease Center, the Robert E. Taft Sanitary Engineering Center, and the National Institutes of Health (as research center of the Public Health Service).[164] As in all federal agencies, under E.O. 9865 foreign rights can be retained by the inventing employee, in some cases giving the inventor "substantial consideration." It has, however, been a strict policy of the Food and Drug Administration that none of its employees who has any part in making policies or in enforcement operations should have any financial interest or receive income, including royalty income, from any firm whose business or whose sale of commodities is subject to laws enforced by the Administration.[165] (Exception is made for the employee whose invention is outside government title. No "conflict of interest" rules are contained in E.O. 10096.) Harrison refers to some cases in point, as follow.

Henry A. Welch, former director of the Division of Antibiotics, had made inventions developing some important therapeutic compounds. Later he was asked by his Administration to dedicate his remaining foreign rights to the public, in keeping with the policy just cited. Another case, in the same Division, concerned two bacteriologists in the Sterility Testing Branch who had invented a new method for the production of penicillinase, used to inactivate pencillin in laboratory testing. They received cash awards of $200 each under the employee award system, and the method was prepared for publication. They received no other income from the invention. Harrison also discusses 13 invention reports from the Communicable Disease Center and its affiliated stations during the period 1949–1959

---

[163] The Surgeon General now administers, however, a number of new research fields which may involve cooperation with private industrial firms having earlier research experience.

[164] Harrison, *An Analytical History of the Patent Policy of* DHEW, pp. 25–35.

[165] Cited in Harrison, *An Analytical History of the Patent Policy of* DHEW, p. 28. A similar policy is expressed in a number of countries, both by court decisions and by law. The German law of 1957 regarding employee inventions refers to this problem.

covering inventions that were the direct outgrowth of work in the laboratories of the Center. "In no case was there a claim of personal interest."[166]

Another reported invention case refers to three employees of the Technical Development Laboratories of the Communicable Disease Center who invented DDVP, "beta-substituted alpha ketophosphates," a compound with outstanding insecticidal properties useful in the fields of both public health and agriculture. Domestic patent rights were assigned to the government, and technical publication was supplemented by mimeographed announcements. Foreign rights were left to the inventors and assigned to a corporation for a fixed amount plus a share in receipts from foreign patents (if realized).[167]

Another employee of a field station of CDC, the venereal disease experimental laboratory in North Carolina, patented a process for preparing a serologically active fraction of virulent *Treponema pallidum* in 1955. The invention had potential value for programs of syphilis control by controlling the potency of a diagnostic reagent. In 1959 the inventor received the Distinguished Service Award from the Department "for outstanding contributions to venereal disease control."

At the Occupational Health Field Headquarters technical assistance is provided to state and local health departments and industrial hygiene agencies. Tests of the diagnostic and analytical methods of such agencies and improvement of instruments purchased from outside sources are some of the tasks of this office. Technical descriptions written by the employed scientists are published, and no patents have been developed. An award presented to the members of this office by an outside organization, the American Medical Association, as a certificate of merit for sustained activity in contributions to public health is said to be particularly prized.

Administrative machinery for patent matters, including awards, in connection with grants and employee inventions is operated by the National Institutes of Health, with seven main medical institutes in Bethesda, its Clinical Center, and its divisions of General Medical Services, Biological Standards, and Research Grants. PHS uses an information form for employees listing a number of points on which

---

[166] *Ibid.*, pp. 28–29. "Personal interest" probably means the right to patent, publish, or receive monetary award.

[167] *Ibid.*, p. 30. The inventors commented on their case by expressing their belief that when assigning patent rights to government "this recognition as a patentee may be the only public acknowledgment of the inventor's work" and that the right to seek foreign patents for themselves "serves as a stimulus not only to gain recognition but to obtain unexpected remuneration." This would have the effect of attracting better personnel to the government in all fields.

answers are sought, of which one asks whether he personally desires a patent on the discovery. Information regarding general patent policy is available in the Regulations as set forth in the Department Manual.

Regarding award questions, two cases of appeal by employees from final determinations of the Department were particularly interesting. One involved the question of monetary reward through ownership of patent rights, the other the question of honorary recognition through patenting.[168] In both cases NIH employees expressed dissatisfaction with the declared policy.

The first case may be significant in the light of the invention-award policy current in most departments. A physicist in the Ophthalmology Branch of the National Institute of Neurological Diseases and Blindness had invented a tangent screen for visual fields, for which government claimed full title, to be met by publication of the device, whereas the inventor wished patent protection. The inventor relied in his appeal action largely on the concept of separation between his work on physical optics, in which he admittedly was employed to exercise originality and inventive faculties, and his work in clinical optics (from which the invention had developed).[169] The Department presented its view of an "integrated research effort" of the NIH in May 1955 to the Government Patents Board, stating that

... these combined Institutes [i.e., NIH] constitute one of the largest centers in the world devoted primarily to research, both laboratory and clinical, in the field of health. The Clinical Center, within the Institutes, is devoted entirely to research. Its scientific and professional personnel are in effect a team brought together solely for the purpose of seeking in the public interest better methods of preventing, diagnosing, and treating the diseases of man. It is to be expected that important inventive advances, many of them patentable, will arise as a natural product of such an institution, and as a matter of policy, that the full product of the public investment in the institution will be preserved for the public benefit.[170]

The Chairman of the Government Patents Board upheld in his decision the determination of the Department.[171] He found that the facts did not support the separation of official duties claimed by the inventor. He noted that the Clinical Center is "a medical research center staffed by selected personnel of the type of the inventor and combines both laboratory research and related clinical functions."

[168] *Ibid.*, p. 33.
[169] The problem raised here is exactly the same one as in connection with the classification of employee inventions provided in the special laws of Sweden, Denmark, and Germany, making a difference between inventions made by an employee in the field of his employment and those in other fields. See Neumeyer, *The Law of Employed Inventors in Europe,* Senate Subcommittee on Patents, Study No. 30, Washington 1963, Chapters II, III and IV.
[170] Department Memorandum, May 18, 1955, to the Chairman of the Government Patents Board, cited by Harrison, p. 34.
[171] Government Patents Board determination 6–48, not published.

The second case, which arose in 1958, involved the Chief of the Laboratory of Biophysics (at NIH), a scientist of standing who had invented a bridge circuit for temperature measurement with semiconductors. He wished patenting (under restricted licenses), but the Department determined that it was entitled to the entire right and that the publication of the invention would protect the public interest. The inventor was dissatisfied with this result. The period for taking an appeal to the Government Patents Board had lapsed; however, the chairman of the Board had agreed with the Department's determination that the public interest did not require patenting and would be met by publication. A special review of the case before the Department Patents Board was allowed. The inventor commented on the determination in his memorandum to the Board as follows.

I understand that under certain circumstances the results of medical research should be protected by means of scientific publication, but I am concerned when inventions of the type that would actually be recognized by patent protection in a university or industrial environment, that the Government does not find a way to patent such inventions. The issuance of a patent is in my opinion a nonremunerative recognition of the work of scientists who choose Government as a career; furthermore, I am of the opinion that a policy favoring publication as a means of protecting Government interests discourages the exercise of creative imagination and initiative of those individuals with "inventive" minds who hold Government jobs.[172]

The decision of the Department in this case is not known. However, the bridge circuit was published by the Department in *The Review of Scientific Instruments*.

Another division of NIH doing extensive engineering development work is the Instrument Section Laboratory serving all the Institutes. In the course of a year this Laboratory "fashions" several thousand instruments which are not available in the general market and which are required by scientists belonging to NIH. Some 60 percent of these instruments are said to be new, and many represent new discoveries. The practice of the Laboratory has been that in any case of extensive outside need technical publication of the device is made. About a hundred such publications have been made during the 22-year life of the section up to 1961. Inventions that are novel and have potential commercial utility are patented (as of 1967), and the remaining are published. The inventions generated by the Laboratory are processed in the same manner as all other inventions made in any Department program.[173]

When duplicating instruments for use by a nonprofit institution, drawings and designs are furnished by the Laboratory upon execution of an "acknowledgment

[172] Reprinted in Harrison, p. 35.
[173] Communication by DHEW to the author, July 1967.

form" by the receiver. For commercial firms another form of acknowledgment (with publication references listed) is used.[174] No monetary awards or other recognition for the draftsmen of these instruments are mentioned in accessible reports or publications describing HEW patent policy.

Parke Banta, former general counsel of HEW, and Manuel Hiller, assistant general counsel, have a negative outlook regarding employee patent policy in government health research. They say that there is no support for such patent policy "in the contention that it would increase employee incentive, by no means a certain result," and further:

Employee incentive is extraneous to this problem. The basic consideration here is the Department's fulfillment of the research missions entrusted to it by Congress. It is, of course, helpful to this mission that employees be provided with incentive, but not at the sacrifice of the ultimate goals of research programs. The solution to the employee incentive problem must be found through other means which are consistent with the basic purpose of Government research such as granting significant incentive awards and promotions for achievements.[175]

Harrison, however, points to a positive effect of invention awards, valid at all times, when she says

Inventive talent is not limited to the research worker or to those in shops and laboratories whose function is to fashion instruments and devices needed by the scientists to conduct their work most effectively. It is latent in many a worker whose official duties are far removed from scientific pursuits and who is stimulated to activity simply by needs observed in the course of the performance of routine tasks. . . . It is not a part of the basic bargain of the Government with such an employee that he should exercise inventive ingenuity or push back the horizons of science or improve the mechanics of humble devices. Whether or not the employee develops the concept of an improvement which occurs to him in the course of his work may very well depend upon the stimulus of a possible monetary or other award.[176]

European law is intimately familiar with such a line of thought. Both administrative and court decisions in a number of countries have been based on the differentiation between groups of employed inventors.[177]

In her study Harrison gives five early illustrative examples of inventions or improvements made by (substantially manual) workers employed by DHEW (in PHS, Food and Drug Administration, Social Security Administration, Clinical Center, and at a PHS hospital), in which cases the Department made different

---

[174] Harrison, Appendix I.
[175] Banta and Hiller, *Patent Policies of HEW*, p. 98.
[176] Harrison, p. 38.
[177] See Neumeyer, *The Law of Employed Inventors in Europe*, 1963.

determinations regarding ownership of rights (full title, license, or no assignment at all).[178]

In spite of the subordinate role played by awards to staff employees in DHEW's official personnel policy, inventions of DHEW employees are honored and widely published in the publications of the Incentive Award Office of the Civil Service Commission. On the basis of the Government Employees Incentive Awards Act of 1954 all civilian officers and employees of the government service are entitled to receive departmental or presidential awards (in cash) under certain conditions defined in this federal act (P.L. 763, 83rd Congress, 2d sess., sec. 304). Employees of DHEW and of DHEW contractors are included in this award system. The story of creative NIH employees is related from time to time in federal pamphlets and professional journals. For instance, an NIH instrument maker, Carl Mencken, invented an automatic serum test machine,[179] and a team composed of a PHS chemist and a retired pharmacologist, Everette May and Nathan Eddy, discovered a potent and completely synthetic pain-killer called phenazocine, which does not addict the user.[180] The annual statistical surveys presented by the Civil Service Commission include award figures for employees of all departments. Those for DHEW are reported later in this chapter.

Other Features of Invention Policy

Invention Reporting An efficient mechanism for reporting inventions from all employees, grantees, and contractors is basic for any centralized patent administration. According to the DHEW *General Administration Manual* (Part 7, sec. 7.1, and the *U.S. Government Organization Manual Guide*, sec. 5) any Department employee is required to report promptly to the constituent organization (for instance, PHS or NIH) in which he is employed any invention made by him that bears any relation to his official duties or that he has made, in whole or in part, during working hours, or with any contributions of government facilities, equipment, material, funds, or information, or with the time or services of other government employees on official duty.[181] Reports of inventions shall be forwarded through appropriate channels to the head of the office or organizations having administrative jurisdiction over the inventor at the time the invention was made

---

[178] Harrison, footnote 85.
[179] Publication under the title "Increased Effectiveness Through Employee's Ideas for Improvement, Superior Accomplishments" (Incentive Awards Program), 1962.
[180] "Civil Service Inventors," in *Civil Service Journal,* Washington, July–September, and October–December 1962, p. 3.
[181] This definition is very close to the "service invention" definition of Executive Order 10096 of 1950.

and thereafter shall be forwarded with recommendations and determinations to the Department Patent Officer. All employees of the Department, including commissioned and other officers, part-time employees and consultants, are subject to the reporting requirements.

All DHEW contractors are bound by the provisions of section 8.6 in the Regulations to report inventions to the Assistant Secretary either at the conception or at the first actual constructive practice, or when evidence of utility of a "subject invention" has developed in a health field or other field. Usually the contractor cannot file a patent application himself, but there are exceptions, as when he is participating in the cancer therapy program or when he is covered by an institutional policy offering this alternative. If under such conditions he does not intend to file a patent application, he must promptly inform the contracting officer of any known or contemplated publication of such invention. A contractor is further required to submit periodic "certifications" every year stating what inventions reasonably believed to be patentable were conceived or reduced to practice during this period. Reporting is also required from subcontractors and their employees as well as from federal employees making inventions jointly with others.

In practice, the Inventions Office of DHEW receives individual invention reports from employees of the Institutes and from grantees and contractors, the groups together constituting over 90 percent of the source of invention reports in the Department as a whole. Invention-reporting obligations of essentially the same type are included in the special Cancer Chemotherapy Industrial Research contracts.[182]

Patent or Publication   Before discussing DHEW regulations regarding decisions whether to seek patent protection for employee inventions or publish them, it should be stated generally that in many cases there is no choice. Most research results in DHEW's fields of activities have their origin in investigations, experiments, and diagnosis of diseases; in other words, they concern purely medical research, often of a basic scientific character. Such results, as a rule, cannot be protected by patents since they do not comply with section 101 of the U.S. Patents Act regarding patentability.[183]

In other cases both publishing and patenting are permissible. If the work falls

[182] See Harrison, Appendix B (6–10–20), point B1, p. 76.
[183] 35 U.S. Code (Patents) section 101 says that whoever invents or discovers any new and useful process, machine, manufacture, or composition of matter, or any new and useful improvement thereof, may obtain a patent therefor, subject to the conditions and requirements of this title.

within the definitions of section 101, the inventor may file a U.S. patent application on his invention, provided he does so within one year of the date of publication.[184]

In its *General Administration Manual* (Part 6, sec. 6.2), regarding publication or patenting of inventions DHEW makes the following statement:

It is the general policy of the Department that the results of Department research should be made widely, promptly and freely available to other research workers and to the public. This availability can generally be adequately preserved by the dedication of a Government-owned invention to the public through publication. Determination to file a domestic patent application on inventions in which the Department has an interest will be made only if the circumstances indicate that this is desirable in the public interest, and if it is practicable to do so. Department determinations not to apply for a domestic patent on employee inventions are subject to review and approval by the chairman of the Government Patents Board [now the Government Patents Branch]. Except where deemed necessary for protecting the patent claim, the fact that a patent application has been or may be filed will not require any departure from normal policy regarding the dissemination of the results of Department research.

With the approval of the Department Patents Board the HEW *General Administration Manual* provides criteria supplementary to those reported here (Part 6, sec. 6.2 of the Manual) for the use of management personnel of the Department charged to make recommendations in this question.[185] In these instructions the Department states

The Department's interest in inventions is almost the reverse of that which generally prompts a private patent application. Its concern is not to withhold the invention from the public or to charge royalties for its use but to assure the availability of the invention to all (45 Code Federal Register 6.2). This assurance with respect to an invention may be lost if an individual claiming priority of invention files a patent application [6–30–10A].

In the next point these supplemental criteria regarding patenting or publications of inventions refer to an obligation under Executive Order 10096 "to take appropriate defensive action to protest the interest of the Government and the public against potential adverse claims."[186] Such defensive action may take the form of a patent application or may be made through publication. Recommendation concerning patenting should be made in any case, identifying originality of concepts and elements of novelty and usefulness. Reports on these points by

184 In the Scandinavian countries and in Germany entirely new patent acts issued in 1968 modify this problem, since *all* patent applications filed after January 1, 1968, at the Patent Office automatically become open to the public after 18 months.
185 HEW *General Administration Manual*, Chapter 6–30.
186 "Government interest" is explained (6–30–30C) as its right to use its inventions in its own operations, to purchase products embodying its inventions, and to preserve for the public the products of its work and investment.

research workers in the particular field are considered valuable. Patenting is further recommended (HEW *General Administration Manual*, 6–30–40B) in the following circumstances:

1. In the case of an invention of high potential significance to the public health, safety, or welfare, to obtain maximum assurance against potential claims.[187]

2. For reasons of health or safety, to retain control of the invention itself, with legal authority to impose restrictive conditions on its use.[188]

3. When other federal agencies have such interest in the invention that they would be prepared to prosecute the patent application.

Patenting is further recommended "as a protective device when there is likely to be a considerable lag between conception and actual reduction to practice and the invention is in a highly competitive field, or when the invention is a basic one likely to constitute a key to subsequent advances in the art." (6–30–40C). The DHEW Manual, on the other hand, appears to disfavor patenting for other reasons. Under 6–30–40D we read, "The inventor's interest, as a matter of prestige and professional reputation, in having a patent issued in his name does not justify a recommendation for a patent application to be prosecuted at the expense of the Government."[189] As to the question, patent or publication, the Department no longer applies the former standard policy for both employee inventions and inventions arising from work supported by grants, to dedicate them by publication without recourse to the patent process.[190] The determination of the Department to protect the interest of government by publication of disclosed employee inventions is subject to review by the Government Patents Board.[191] To the knowledge of the DHEW patent staff, this Board had never (as of 1968) reversed a Department determination to publish or patent an invention when brought to their attention.[192] Harrison believed (in 1961) that the policy of DHEW "represents a middle ground between undesirable

[187] Probably in interference procedure before the U.S. Patent Office.

[188] DHEW has had cases of inventions in the field of narcotics which require restrictions because of health risks.

[189] This statement is not in agreement with general experience on how prestige and professional reputation are acquired in the scientific community. Further, no patent "is issued" according to the U.S. Patent Act on any grounds other than the ones stated in the Act. "The inventor's interest" in having a patent issued does not affect the objective grounds on the basis of which a patent is granted by the Patent Office.

[190] Communication to the author from DHEW, September 1969.

[191] Copyright rules for research contracts regarding scientific and technical data are found in the Atomic Energy Commission Procurement Regulations (9–9.5100 and following). See the case study of the Atomic Energy Commission on page 354.

[192] Communication to the author, December 1968.

alternatives, i.e., the amassing of Government-owned patents devoid of normal patent significance, or a general abandonment to private and potentially monopolistic interests of the funds of publicly financed research."[193] The fact that DHEW gives preference to publication of research over patenting is in line with the statutory functions of this Department. In most areas of medical research publication is the simplest way to disseminate results.

One argument for patenting, recommended by inventors and supervisors of DHEW, is that it serves to control the quality of a product. The idea is to compel licensees of a DHEW patent to follow standards of quality control prescribed in connection with license agreements, potentially enforceable against lawful and unlawful (not licensed) users. The question of "quality control licensing" under DHEW-owned patents was considered in connection with some important drugs developed at DHEW agencies. Some examples follow.

1. The drug Primaquine was invented under a PHS grant at Columbia University. The drug, which was patented, has highly effective antimalarial properties and is toxic. Great care is required in its manufacture to prevent harmful effects. Quality standards for the manufacture of Primaquine were furnished by one of the inventors to the patent licensees, but in the end the only "quality condition" used was one making the manufacture and sale subject to compliance with the Federal Food, Drug, and Cosmetic Act (which was applicable in any event).

2. A patent was asked for and obtained on the Surgeon General's recommendation, for a serologically active fraction of virulent *Treponema pallidum*, useful in the detection of syphilis. Quality control was considered to be a primary factor, both by DHEW and the Department of Defense. FDA administration, however, indicated that the reagent would constitute a drug under federal food and drug legislation and thus would fall within FDA's control.

[193] Harrison, p. 19. Many objections can be made against this appraisal of DHEW policy. Whether government-owned patents are "devoid of normal patent significance" depends on how they are administered. If government is satisfied with full license rights under the patents there is no need to "amass" patents with full ownership. If patents were owned by their creators (government employees, contracting institutions, or industries) no "general abandonment" exists, since a government license is reserved as a minimum right in most cases. A misuse of patents by "potentially monopolistic interest" is illegal under the antitrust laws, as more than 60 years of basic court decisions attests. Therefore, no "undesirable alternatives exist" (between which DHEW must choose "a middle ground"). The policy of government ownership or private ownership of the fruits of publicly financed research, or a negotiated compromise between both types, is in many fields of such government research a satisfactory solution.

3. A patent was obtained by PHS (before becoming a part of FSA and DHEW in 1953) on Metopon, a morphine derivate, i.e., a narcotic. Quantity and quality control in this area is provided by the Harrison Narcotics Act. Licenses to manufacturers and distributors were issued following recommendations of the former Bureau of Narcotics. In 1951 the Committee on Drug Addiction and Narcotics found these licenses to be retarding the medical use of the drugs and recommended that they be revoked and that the patent be dedicated to the public. The patent was finally made available for unrestricted licensing, but it was not revoked.

Foreign Patent Rights   The patent policy of DHEW regarding patenting or publishing research results in the United States does not tell the entire story. In the field of general human welfare, particularly in the health field, there is a strong trend in recent years toward freer sharing of information and techniques on an international basis, for instance, through the World Health Organization. On the other hand, there is strong international competition in the manufacture and sale of pharmaceutics, drugs, and medical instruments, between United States companies and foreign ones, especially European.

The legal framework for government policy in this field is given by Executive Order 9865 of June 14, 1947, establishing a government foreign patent program. The Order, antedating Executive Order 10096 of 1950 by three years, requires all government agencies (when practicable) to acquire foreign rights in inventions resulting from research financed by government. It also provides machinery for prosecution of foreign patent rights and delegates their administration to the respective agencies. DHEW, however, expressed the view that it had no funds and no general authority to administer foreign patent controls.[194] Despite the fact that Executive Order 10096 regulating government patent policy (since 1950) does not make any distinction between domestic and foreign rights (talking only about "the entire rights, title, and interest"), the Department conforms "to the established pattern" and draws distinctions in its treatment of foreign rights. Since neither means nor mandate for foreign patenting of government inventions exist, DHEW

[194] Harrison, p. 49. A working committee of the former Government Patents Board in 1955 could not reach unanimous recommendations as to disposition of ownership and administration of foreign patent rights by government agencies. In 1959 the implementing administrative orders 6 and 7 to E.O. 9865 issued by the Government Patents Board in 1954 regarding reporting foreign patent protection were declared to be "suspended" and "temporarily inoperative" by the chairman of the Board. The program contained in E.O. 9865 failed to receive support from industry; neither were necessary appropriations granted by Congress. No executive action seems to have been taken since that time, and under these circumstances each agency seems to follow its own course with regard to foreign rights.

believes that it is better to leave the foreign rights to the employee with a license reserved to government.[195]

In the case of the narcotic drug Phenazocine, option for foreign rights was exercised by DHEW under Executive Order 9865. The Department offered acquisition and administration of foreign rights to the World Health Organization. WHO declined the offer in 1959 on considerations "parallel to a striking degree" with the ones which have shaped the thinking of the Department on patent matters. The WHO reasoned roughly in the following way:

1. Administration of patent rights would involve the organization in a quasi-commercial field, conceivably outside its legal competence.

2. Impartiality might be prejudiced by its administration of rights in a particular drug, involving, for instance, determinations as to which country should be permitted to manufacture a narcotic drug.

3. The patent laws of many countries present "formidable difficulties" in securing and maintaining patents, particularly on medicaments, and the alternative of publication would furnish reasonably adequate protection against exclusive appropriation by others.[196]

There were also two cases in which a foreign institution, the Medical Research Council of Great Britain, requested patent agreements with PHS, which were reached in 1957 and in 1960.[197] In both instances inventions had been made by an employee of PHS in collaboration with employees of the British Government. In the first agreement rights to the invention in the United States were assigned to the United States and the foreign rights to the Medical Research Council of Great Britain. Terms regarding foreign patent rights in the second agreement are not known. DHEW has information regarding foreign rights sought and obtained by its employees, since they have to provide the department with royalty-free license on such rights.

An early case (in the period 1947–1949) illustrates the uncertainty of policy in the health field regarding foreign patent rights. The Director of the Division of Antibiotics in FDA, Henry A. Welch, had received six patents, on which domestic rights were assigned to the United States and foreign rights left to him. The government would have been entitled to the entire rights under the Executive Order, but prosecuting and policing of foreign rights was considered too expensive and onerous. On the other hand, purchase of foreign rights from the inventor by

[195] *Ibid.*, p. 50.
[196] *Ibid.*, p. 52.
[197] Dinkins, "Patent Practices of the DHEW," p. 14.

certain companies gave rise to fears that the impartiality of the Food and Drug Administration, the employer of the inventor, might be impaired in its certification services (the inventions included important therapeutic compounds). The inventor, then, was asked to make, and did make a dedication of foreign rights to the public, insofar as he still retained such rights.[198]

Independently of how individual cases of foreign patent disposition and administration were decided by DHEW and its predecessors in the past, it seems correct to summarize that for DHEW generally publication will suffice to protect government-owned inventions against claims of prior invention abroad. Patent applications in foreign countries are rarely filed by the Department.

In 1965 the Patent Advisor of NIH, Norman Latker, and the Contract Operations Officer, R. J. Wylie, in a public address reexamined the general problems of utilization of HEW-owned inventions. They found that under departmental policy (based on the Presidential Memorandum of October 10, 1963[199] and a 1924 Attorney General's decision)[200] no guarantee of exclusive patent licensing could be given by DHEW. (One of the four categories of the contracts outlined in sec. 1a of the Presidential Memorandum of 1963 deals expressly with the contracts for exploitation in fields which directly concern the public health or public welfare. According to Latker and Wylie, all contracts or grants entered into by DHEW can be construed as falling within this category, ibid., 873.) The authors stated, however, that the emphasis of DHEW on basic research, the need of great effort and expenditures for the development of new drugs and medical instrumentation, and the urgent needs for bringing all products to a point of utilization make it necessary to investigate mechanisms offering inducements for such development. Exclusive licensing of patents was believed to be one such mechanism. Such licensing is now practiced on a limited scale.

---

[198] An interview with the inventor about the patent policy indicated, according to Harrison p. 28), that there was no incentive to patent, since unless an employee could get some return from foreign rights, he could not afford to go to all the effort involved in working up the details of a patent application, an elaborate and exhausting process. Welch is said at the same time to have approved the alternative of publication as a matter of government policy, avoiding the complexities of the pursuit of patent rights. Welch is also reported to have said that the inventive talents of the research worker in government are not at all dependent upon the patent incentive. Contradiction seems to exist here in the opinion of this author.

[199] "Utilization of Government-owned Health and Welfare Inventions," *J. Patent Off. Soc.* (November 1965): 868.

[200] 34 *Opinions of the Attorney General*, 320, 328 (1924).

Cancer Chemotherapy Industrial Contractors
In fiscal year 1956 Congress appropriated for the first time $900,000 for a major research attack to explore exhaustively and rapidly the potentialities of certain chemical compounds in the control of cancer. The idea of the program was to mobilize the resources of pharmaceutical and chemical firms with a minimum of delay, to "coax from the shelves of the large chemical and drug companies, for testing purposes, a vast number of compounds and chemicals whose utility was as yet unestablished, and the formula for whose manufacture was as yet undisclosed."[201] For this purpose the Surgeon General received power to enter into industrial research contracts free of some of the controls normally attendant on government contracts. The Cancer Chemotherapy Program was carried out for the Department by PHS, the importance of the program being emphasized by the fact that Congress increased special appropriations from $900,000 for fiscal year 1956 to $21,142,000 for fiscal year 1960. The 1960 Appropriation Act extended the contract authority of the Department to all research (and training) projects of the Public Health Service without limitation to nonprofit organizations. The patent policy applicable to anticancer research contracts by industry was spelled out in the Department's *Administration Manual* (Patents and Inventions, 6–10–20). The criteria in the patent field were first approved in 1957 and modified in 1958.[202]

The main tool of control of research results by the Department is an extensive patent clause included in the research contracts. From the beginning there was a "standard patent clause," reserving generally to the Surgeon General the right to determine the disposition of inventions arising from the performance of contract. A modification arose in the form of "standard alternative clauses," leaving the right to patent and exploit such inventions to the contractor, subject to certain limitations deemed necessary to protect the public's interest in the result of the contracted research. In negotiating and operating the "alternative clauses" the Department applied the policy that these clauses be made available to all contracting companies without discrimination and that the operation of these clauses be closely reviewed to maintain the following basic objectives:

1. Availability of information about results of research and right to make disclosures, without undue delay, to the extent essential to serve the research need.
2. Availability of inventions for development and health purposes (irrespective of

[201] Harrison, p. 19.
[202] DHEW *General Administration Manual*, Part 6, Appendix B, "Patent Policy Applicable to Cancer Chemotherapy Industrial Contracts," reprinted in Harrison, *ibid.*, p. 75.

whether actual development and production is to be made by the contractor or by others).

3. Concentration of all resources on the anticancer objective. Close consultations between the parties are observed to impose extensive and specific limitations on products of the inventions, to protect the public interest as to their supply, price, and quality.

Seven main limitations are cited in the policy declaration of the Department in connection with the grant of alternative patent clauses in favor of contractors, as follows:

1. *Reporting.* Any invention must be promptly reported to the Surgeon General, as well as the filing of domestic or foreign patent applications (or election not to file such applications). Invention report is required after conception or first actual reduction to practice of each invention that reasonably appears to be patentable and, in any event, as soon as evidence of utility in a health field or other field has developed.

2. *Disclosure.* Right to make a disclosure of the invention is reserved to the Surgeon General, allowing the contractor reasonable opportunity to protect his rights (perhaps specifying a respite of not less than six months from the time the Surgeon General determines the invention was or should have been reported).

3. *License to government.* Reservation to the government of an irrevocable, nonexclusive, royalty-free license to practice or cause to be practiced, by or for the government throughout the world, each subject invention (whether patented or unpatented) in the manufacture, use, or disposition according to law, of any article or material, or in the use of any method or process.

4. *Failure to meet health needs.* Right of the Surgeon General to "make the invention available" for health purposes to others than the contractor and his licensees, if he has ground to believe that such invention is at such stage of development that if it were more generally available, it would meet a health need, and if the public interest (with respect to supply, quality, or price) requires. Appropriate steps include issuance of licenses to additional manufacturers of the contractor's own selection. A 90 days' respite and hearing opportunity for the contractor are provided. The measures open to the Surgeon General in a case of failure of the contractor to meet the requirements are the right to dedicate all rights in the invention to the public, or to issue nonexclusive, royalty-free licenses on a nondiscriminatory basis to all qualified applicants to use, manufacture and sell embodiments of the invention for any health purpose.

5. *Failure to patent.* The right of the Surgeon General to require the assignment to the government of all domestic rights except for a nonexclusive, royalty-free license to the contractor, in the event the contractor elects not to file a domestic patent application on the invention, or when filing an application fails to diligently prosecute such application.

6. *Foreign rights.* The same type of right for the Surgeon General in regard to foreign patent applications.

7. *Renegotiation on new leads.* The right of the Surgeon General (no mandatory provision) to renegotiate the application of the contract patent provisions to any

new lead which the contractor identifies in the course of the performance of the contract and which he wishes to develop at his own expense without utilization of facilities financed by government.[203]

In carrying out the contractor research programs, supply and animal testing of compounds for anticancer properties became important in contracts with industrial suppliers "for controlled screening and screening only." The Department applied a policy (point C in *Administration Manual*, 6–10–20) that for compounds or products not otherwise available to the Service and in which the supplying company has a proprietary interest, the contract may provide that all rights shall remain in the company. The contract may additionally provide for confidentiality of the results (of screening and testing) for a limited period not exceeding 12 months after the completion of these processes and the report of the results to the supplier.

Contracts with suppliers (as well as contracts for research and development) in which federal employees participate in any way require that inventions made by such employees, or by such employees jointly with others, be subject to applicable Executive Orders and Department regulations (point D in *Administration Manual*, 6–10–20). The Surgeon General, finally, may also negotiate for a license under existing patents (background patents) or a license involving the use of patented or unpatented compounds or processes for the effective prosecution of the cancer chemotherapy program (point E in *Administration Manual*, 6–10–20).

The patent clauses and provisions of research contracts discussed here were not issued without considerable dispute between the Department and industrial manufacturers. The Surgeon General had been unable to conclude product-development contracts under the contract terms of 1957 (with the original patent clause). Industry had urged that the power of publicity and public opinion would be sufficient to force general licensing of the research inventions, if the facts of a situation justified it. They expressed fear that the Surgeon General might be unable to resist "the pressure for general licensing," even when circumstances did not justify.[204] The negotiations resulted in the creation of the first alternative patent clause giving the contractor exclusive rights defeasible only after formal proceedings of a quasi-judicial character.[205]

[203] General Administration Manual (Patents and Inventions) 6–10–20, point B, see Appendix B, p. 76, also in Harrison.
[204] Among industry leaders pleading before the Department were former Secretary of Commerce (John T. Connor), at that time president of Merck & Co., as well as Messrs. Volwiler of Abbott Laboratories and Brown of Schering Co., representing the American Drug Manufacturers Association and the American Pharmaceutical Association, respectively.
[205] Harrison, p. 23.

The Harbridge House study of government patent policy found that the NIH medicinal chemistry program had suffered considerably through clauses naming conditions under which the contractor pharmaceutical firm could not obtain rights to inventions. In late 1966 two restrictive conditions were removed, but considerable damage had been done in the form of lost contacts between academic research workers and drug firms and inability of university laboratories or independent laboratories to screen the thousands of compounds which until 1962 had been tested free of charge by pharmaceutical firms. Compounds possibly useful in malaria or cancer did not fare as badly as those in other parts of the program, since the government operates its own screening services here and develops those that seem useful.[206]

Invention and Patent Statistics

The studies on DHEW patent policy which have been cited repeatedly in this chapter do not deal with employee invention statistics and administration. This serious gap has now been filled by the Federal Council for Science and Technology. The Data Collection and Analysis Subcommittee has collected extensive data concerning patent practices and policies of 15 agencies.

The statistics of patent and invention practices of DHEW presented here as Table 5.12 are a simplified extract from this extensive statistical report covering figures for the fiscal years 1963, 1964, 1965, and 1966. Only two columns are presented here: one showing DHEW figures for these years and one showing the total figures for all 15 agencies (including DHEW) as means of comparison. The figures are substantially based on the different types of invention disclosures submitted by department employees and department contractors (for their employees). Because of differences in methods of tabulating and reporting between the agencies, the data cannot be taken as precise measurements. Even with this substantial reservation the figures are most valuable.

Table 5.12 shows that DHEW in certain parts of its patent and invention policy makes no exceptions in treatment of invention-disclosing, whether dealing with its own employees or with contractors' employees. No employee invention disclosures exist for which government DHEW has no rights. That is to say, for all such disclosures DHEW has either title or a license. No U.S. patents have been issued to DHEW employees. No contractor has been left sole license by DHEW for his invention disclosure. Disclosures of inventions which DHEW determined to publish rather than patent are relatively low in view of the many research results in the medical field, usually suitable for publication only.

[206] Harbridge House, Inc., *Government Patent Policy Study*, 1968, Vol. 1, p. I-45.

The second column representing a total of all fifteen agencies, shows a certain parallelism with the DHEW column regarding number of disclosures received from contractors and determined to be under government ownership, or number of such disclosures for which no U.S. patent applications have been filed. The comparison between the trend of figures in the two columns has to be made with extreme caution since the total agency figure includes the three branches of the Department of Defense, AEC, and NASA—all potential invention-producing agencies with invention-producing contractors.

Invention and patent statistics would not be complete without reference to the number of research contracts and grants awarded by DHEW which contain patent clauses. Patent clauses are the legal means of regulating control and ownership of all inventions conceived by the employees of contractors and grantees. The accumulated figures for DHEW, together with the corresponding figures for other agencies[207] having such information for fiscal year 1966 are shown in Table 5.13.

At the end of 1968, DHEW had 96 unexpired patents available for licensing. On 16 of these 24 nonexclusive, royalty-free licenses had been issued.

During fiscal years 1963 through 1967, the Department issued determinations to dedicate 791 inventions to the public by publication. Unfortunately, the Department has no data regarding use of such published inventions.[208]

Invention Award Statistics

Earlier in this chapter an attempt was made to trace some types of award incentives actually granted by DHEW to its own employees and to contractors' employees for extraordinary performance in the field of inventions, discoveries, and engineering improvements. The emphasis on the ethical character of research in the health field seems to preclude monetary awards for inventive employees. It would be interesting to know the income from a series of commercial patent licenses granted by the Department to drug manufacturers under patents assigned to DHEW by its own or its contractors' employees. These licenses, like all other licenses, are, however, granted free of royalty to the licensees on a nonexclusive revocable basis. Accordingly, there is no income or royalties for employee inventors from licensure of patents they have assigned to DHEW.

Publication of research results in the name of the originator seems, however, to

[207] In a relatively large number of instances, as shown in Table 5.13, DHEW used a clause in which it acquired less than title. This results from its policy of allowing nonprofit educational institutions to retain title when their patent administration policy has been deemed by the Department to be in the public interest.
[208] Communication to author from Office of the Secretary, DHEW, November 1968.

Table 5.12 Invention Disclosures in HEW Compared to Total of 15 Agencies

	Fiscal Year	DHEW	Agencies (including HEW)
Total Invention Disclosures			
From government employees	1963	238	10,439
	1964	324	10,939
	1965	246	11,759
	1966	313	12,800
From contractors	1963	228	7,607
	1964	292	7,870
	1965	221	8,587
	1966	294	9,869
Employee Invention Disclosures			
For which government has title	1963	7	8031
	1964	8	9551
	1965	18	9841
	1966	12	1,179
For which government has license only	1963	0	304
	1964	2	316
	1965	1	278
	1966	0	263
For which government has no rights	1963	0	64
	1964	0	69
	1965	0	74
	1966	0	72
Total U.S. patent applications filed by agency	1963	1	1,245
	1964	6	1,444
	1965	9	1,315
	1966	3	1,246
U.S. patents issued to agency (government has title)	1963	3	539
	1964	2	550
	1965	0	711
	1966	2	737
U.S. patents issued to employee (government has license)	1963	0	241
	1964	0	250
	1965	0	312
	1966	0	231
Disclosures for which no patent applications are filed	1963	6	1,237
	1964	7	1,537
	1965	16	1,566
	1966	13	1,440
Agency decision to publish instead of patenting	1963	6	28
	1964	0	25
	1965	10	89
	1966	10	64

(table continued)

Table 5.12   (continued)

	Fiscal Year	DHEW	Agencies (including HEW)
Contractor Invention Disclosures	1963	49	5,509
Determined to Be under	1964	174	6,475
Government Ownership	1965	204	6,175[2]
	1966	254	7,242[2]
Government leaves contractor	1963	0	60
with exclusive license	1964	0	80
(government has title)	1965	0	40
	1966	0	29
Disclosures for which contractor	1963	—	—
had option to acquire title but	1964	—	—
elected not to do so	1965	—	—
	1966	44	2,961[3]
Patent applications filed by	1963	5	731
agency (government has title)	1964	6	834
	1965	11	980
	1966	6	924
Patent applications filed by	1963	10	1,742
contractor (government has	1964	3	1,527
license)	1965	17	1,315
	1966	14	1,777
No U.S. patent application filed	1963	74	5,354
	1964	185	5,945
	1965	189	5,639
	1966	281	6,267
Determination to publish	1963	74	177
instead of patenting	1964	185	293
	1965	163	239
	1966	189	222

[1] Voluntary assignment from inventor to Dept. of the Army not included.
[2] Totals do not include Dept. of the Army.
[3] Almost entirely from Dept. of Defense.

Source: *Annual Report on Government Patent Policy, June 1967,* Federal Council on Science and Technology. The other 14 agencies are CIA, USDA, NSF, VA, Commerce, Treasury, TVA, FAA, Interior, AEC, NASA, Army, Navy, Air Force.

dominate DHEW emloyee-award policy. Since publication is called "dedication to the public," it is obvious that the donor is not expected to draw any financial advantage from his gift to the public. Inventors and discoverers have had other types of publicity but there are no available DHEW departmental statistics on the subject.

In a survey of the "10th Anniversary Year" (fiscal year 1964) of the Federal

Table 5.13   Contracts and Grants, 1966, with Patent Clauses Designed To Implement Kennedy Memorandum of 1963.

| | Number of Prime Contracts and Grants | |
	Government Having Acquired (or Having Right To Acquire) Title	Contractors Having First Option To Acquire Title
DHEW	30,269	5,910
NASA	2,576	30
Army	892	5,509
Navy	542	5,351
AEC	239	151
Interior	522	13
USDA	209	1
NSF	27	1,329

1 Contractor has option in nonatomic areas only.

SOURCE: Federal Council For Science and Technology, *Annual Report on Government Patent Policy*, June 1967, p. 38.

Incentive Awards Program, operated by the Civil Service Commission, 11 federal agencies with 20,000 to 100,000 employees were studied. The following figures for DHEW as an "awarding agency" are shown:

Average cash award for improvements through suggestions: $37 (7th in rank).

Value of measurable benefits of these improvements to the Department: $180,278 (7th in rank).

Average cash award for top results through superior performance: $164 (7th in rank).

Value of measurable benefits of such performance to the Department: $913,201 (3d in rank).

From other federal award statistics for the same year it appears that DHEW had paid a total of $39,960 in cash awards to employees for improvements through suggestions and $251,024 for superior performance awards.[209] A three-year survey of incentive awards granted to federal agency employees on the basis of the Federal Government Employee Incentive Awards Act shows the following result for DHEW (Table 5.14).

Table 5.15 shows how awards are assorted by category of employee.

The types of employee performance rewarded in accordance with Tables 5.14 and 5.15 are based on guidelines laid down in the regulations of the Civil Service Commission for all government agencies. Figures must be furnished annually by all

[209] Civil Service Commission, 1964.

Table 5.14   DHEW Employee Awards Under Programs According to Civil Service Commission
Regulations (fiscal years 1963-1965)

	1963	1964	1965
Awards for Suggestions			
For tangible benefits	165	152	162
Cash value	$ 11,215	$ 9,025	$ 9,925
For intangible benefits	984	1,059	892
Cash value	$ 26,095	$ 30,935	$ 30,377
Awards for Superior Accomplishments			
For tangible benefits	249	272	223
Cash value	$ 45,698	$ 52,178	$ 34,828
For intangible benefits	1,133	1,262	930
Cash value	$177,902	$170,421	$141,761
Top Level Honorary Awards			
"Continued Excellence of Service"	72	73	75
Honor awards with cash	1	1	1
Honor awards without cash	71	72	74

Table 5.15   DHEW Cash Awards for Three Employee Categories[1] (fiscal year 1964)

Category of Employee	Awards for Suggestion or Invention	Awards for Sustained Superior Performance	Awards for Specific Act or Service and Singular Achievement	Average Number of Employees
GS–6 and below	605	1,010	141	37,734
GS–7 through GS–11	415	618	114	22,843
GS–12 and above	50	72	30	8,176
Total	1,070	1,700	285	68,753
Nonsupervisory	73	86	10	6,321
Supervisory	23	13	3	470
Total	96	99	13	6,791

1 The Federal Classification Act of 1949 distinguishes employee categories with 18 grades of
difficulty and responsibility of work, GS–1 through GS–18.

Source: Civil Service Commission.

agencies to the Commission, on the basis of which the Commission makes an annual
report to the President and to Congress.

A glance at Table 5.14 shows that in DHEW awards for "intangible benefits" of
employee contributions are in the majority. Table 5.15 shows that employees of
GS–6 and below and nonsupervisory personnel dominate as receivers of awards.
The highest percentages of awards are for "sustained superior performance" by the
two lower categories of employees, in each case a little less than 3 percent of the

average total number of employees listed. Awards for "suggestion or invention" (the two categories are not separated) are also highest for employee category GS–6 and below, and for category GS–7 through GS–11, about 1.5 percent of the average total number of employees. In the employee category GS–12 and above, the percentage of all employees is only about 0.6.

Evaluation of DHEW *Patent Policy*

The studies on DHEW patent policy by Dinkins, Harrison, and Banta and Hiller (cited in full in footnote 127) are divided in their appraisal of past patent policy of DHEW. The views expressed in these studies are obviously based on a close knowledge of past internal department conditions.[210] These authors' basic apprehension of the value of incentives for employees and of the patent institution varies and leads them to different conclusions and recommendations.

Dinkins reports that DHEW felt that its practice regarding patent matters was working reasonably well (as of 1959). The Department had reached no conclusion as to whether greater flexibility of authority in the administration of government-owned patents would facilitate or impede the realization of its research objectives. No recommendations for future policy were offered.

According to Banta and Hiller "to date (1961) the Department's policy has served both to protect the public interest and to avoid discouragement of the researcher, whether employee, grantee or contractor. This is not to say that the policy should not be constantly re-examined and re-appraised in the light of our expanding experience." Banta and Hiller report, however, that DHEW officials strongly oppose a general government policy leaving invention rights with inventors, subject only to a nonexclusive royalty-free license to government. They argue that such a policy would not take cognizance of the various government agencies engaged in research, would frustrate the statutory mandate to make widely available to the public the results of government-sponsored research in the health, education, and welfare fields, and would confer upon employees (grantees and contractors) greater rights than are usually possessed by employees in private industry. The policy would also discourage free interchange of information among researchers and would create inequities by conferring property rights upon one employee even if the invention is actually the result of collaborative group effort. Assignment of inventions to employees "would create an incentive in the direction of private patenting, and thus, deemphasize investigation and research in fields not likely to result in patentable inventions," and thereby "seriously affect the entire research design." The Department officials go further (according to Banta and Hiller); they seem to know that the

[210] The time of writing was for Dinkins, November 1959, for Harrison, September 1960, and for Banta and Hiller, at the end of 1961.

contention that this policy would increase employee incentive is not valid. They also believe that "employee incentive is extraneous to this problem" and that "the solution of the employee incentive problems must be found through other means which are consistent with the basic purpose of Government research such as granting significant incentive awards and promotions for achievement."

Regarding procedural requirements (valid also for DHEW), Harrison says that "the recommendations of the Attorney General's report to the President in 1947 and the requirements of Executive Order 10096 and the administrative orders of the Chairman of the Government Patents Board are excessive and unrealistic in this respect." She holds further that "the requirement in every case of an invention report, and a formal determination of rights as to the method of protecting the Government's interest (by publication or patenting) is unwieldy and wasteful. It tends to clog and render less effective the administrative channels which should be kept open for prompt and careful determination in two types of situations: (1) where there is a claim of interest adverse to the Government, and (2) where, if the invention is one to which the Government is entitled, there are factors which point to the need for patenting or other steps to protect the Government's interest."

For patenting and maintenance of patents in foreign countries Harrison suggests that the government should act through a public agency equipped by specialized experience and financed with adequate appropriations for this purpose. "The lingering controls supposedly, but not actually exercised under Executive Order 9865, are unrealistic, stale, and unprofitable."

The use of patent protection in the DHEW fields of activities is generally rejected by Harrison. "Inventions which are the outgrowth of such research should not, through patenting, be made the subject of exploitation for profit or for private ends" and "Patenting of inventions assignable to the Government as the employer as a system for regulation and control of the product is undesirable; the Government has other more direct, more modern, and more appropriate means for achieving such purposes." Harrison further opposes the prosecution at public expense of patent applications in respect of employee inventions as having "no place as an instrument of personnel policy."[211] However, she does not mind leaving to non-profit institutions the disposition of inventions arising from grants or contracts when their policies are generally compatible with the principles of assignment or license acquisitions as laid down in the rules of Executive Order 10096 of 1950.

---

211 At the same time she points to the fact that "it is perhaps unfortunate that members of the commissioned corps of the Public Health Service, which is a career system modeled closely upon the military, are not covered by the awards program" (the Federal Government Employee Incentive Awards Act).

The Atomic Energy Commission as a government employer of research personnel and sponsor of research work differs from practically all other U.S. government agencies. The dominant role which the development of weapons has played and still plays in the activities of this agency makes it necessary to consider this branch of work apart from the activities concerned with the development of peaceful and civilian applications of atomic energy. Construction and use of military weapons are governed by rules other than those for civil research and production. Economic laws operative in regard to fair competition, a free labor market, mobility of the labor force, and price formation for goods and services are to a great extent thrown out of gear in military research. The same is the case regarding many statutory federal laws, especially in connection with laws governing working relations, compensation and salaries, and other personal privileges of individuals, secrecy and publicity of documents (including patents and patent applications), and the right to claim various special compensations, damages, and rewards. Freedom to accept work may be curtailed if the work is in the area of activity of an individual's federal employment but offered by an outside employer.

The patent policy of the AEC has historically developed from an autonomous military government monopoly. Only gradually has it expanded toward peaceful and civilian uses. The conditions of employment and compensation to which inventors employed by the AEC and its many contractors are subject have been very different in times of war and peace and are still very different depending on whether the employee is, for instance, an officer of a defense agency or, say, a university faculty scientist, bound directly or indirectly by a research contract or an employment contract.

No attempt is made here to separate artificially the pattern of interaction and cooperation which exists in practice between the persons and groups of persons working for the development and advance of nuclear science and technology under the auspices of the AEC. Some primary facts and features are presented in order to make it possible to present the research policy of the Atomic Energy Commission side by side with other government departments and agencies in spite of its basic differences.

Legal Authority

Shortly after the end of World War II, in 1946, the first Atomic Energy Act was enacted in order to protect production, use, and research surrounding the first atomic bomb.[212] The first Act contained a number of basic provisions on patents and inventions, prohibiting the grant of patents useful solely for and used for military weapons or useful solely in the production of fissionable material. Others were prohibited to the extent they covered materials or processes used in the conduct of atomic energy research and development. Patents were permitted for other types of inventions in the atomic energy field. Thus even in the very beginning the basic doctrine for this specific field of science and technology was created: that patents concerning certain types of nuclear material or energy could be declared "to be affected with the public interest."[213] These industrial property rights could become subject to "public regulation" by compulsory licensing by the Atomic Energy Commission. The first Act also established a system for compensating persons whose patents were revoked or who were barred by the statute from obtaining patents. A leading court case in the Court of Claims in 1955 interpreted the provision (sec. 1498 of title 28 U.S. Code) on the right to recover reasonable compensation from the AEC for manufacture and use of inventions patented to a private party. The interpretation in effect precluded persons or firms from any such action.[214]

In 1954 the Atomic Energy Act of 1946 was modified in various ways.[215] All further discussion here is based on this second Act in force at the time of writing. This Act states in the first sentence of its first section its most difficult dilemma: "Atomic energy is capable of application for peaceful as well as military purposes." This means one of the great difficulties in a patent policy is to be fair to inventors employed by the AEC itself and inventors employed by its many contractors. The main problems connected therewith will be dealt with later in this chapter.

As the general functions of atomic energy policy of the United States the Act states:

... to make the maximum contribution to the general welfare, subject at all times to the paramount objective of making the maximum contribution to the common defense and security. (sec. 1(a)) . . . to promote world peace, improve the general welfare, increase the standard of living, and strengthen free competition in private enterprise. (sec. 1(b))

[212] P.L. 585, 79th Congress.
[213] The legal doctrine of a business "to be affected with the public interest" was first created in United States constitutional law in 1873 in connection with legislative determination of maximum rates for grain elevators and was laid down in the leading Supreme Court precedent *Munn* v. *People,* 69 Ill. 80, 93 (1873).
[214] *Consolidated Engineering Corporation* v. *United States,* Ct. Cl. 104, *U.S. Patent Quarterly* 111, January 11, 1955.
[215] P.L. 703, 83rd Cong., 2d sess., ch. 1073.

These objectives embrace broad military, political, social, and economic goals, both of a national and international character.

The Act sets up six specific programs to effect its policies (sec. 3), of which three have an essential and direct impact on the invention and patent policy of the Commission. The first three read as follows:

... a program of conducting, assisting, and fostering research and development in order to encourage maximum scientific and industrial progress. (sec. 3(a))
... a program for the dissemination of unclassifed scientific and technical information and for the control, dissemination, and declassification of Restricted Data, subject to appropriate safeguards, so as to encourage scientific and industrial progress. (sec. 3(b))
... a program to encourage widespread participation in the development and utilization of atomic energy for peaceful purposes to the maximum extent consistent with the common defense and security and with the health and safety of the public. (sec. 3(d))

These three programs give the framework for the entire R&D policy, information-dissemination policy, and policy of cooperation with industry and the scientific community. These policies are implemented by other sections of the Atomic Energy Act, by rules and regulations issued on the basis of the Act, and by decisions (determinations) made by administrative boards instituted with the authority of the Act.

Of the 21 basic definitions given in sec. 11 of the Act two groups of definitions are highly relevant for the present analysis of patent and invention policy, one group covering definitions of terms generally affecting the creative activities of employees and another explaining the fields of science and technology that fall within the activities of the AEC. Definitions affecting all creative employees working under the Atomic Energy Act are, of course, "research and development," "design" (as part of "working results"), and "restricted data."

Research and development
1. Theoretical analysis, exploration, or experimentation.
2. The extension of investigative findings and theories of a scientific or technical nature into practical application for experimental and demonstration purposes, including the experimental production and testing of models, devices, equipment, materials, and processes. (sec. 11(g))

Design
1. Specifications, plans, drawings, blueprints, and other items of like nature.
2. The information contained therein.

3. The research and development data pertinent to the information contained therein. (sec. 11(i))

Restricted data

1. All data concerning design, manufacture, or utilization of atomic weapons.

2. All data concerning the production of special nuclear material.

3. All data concerning the use of special nuclear material in the production of energy, but shall not include data declassified or removed from the Restricted Data category pursuant to section 142. (sec. 11(r))[216]

The definitions of the Atomic Energy Act determining and outlining the borderlines of its research efforts in science and technology are laid down mainly in the following five technical definitions:

Atomic energy: all forms of energy released in the course of nuclear fission or nuclear transformation. (sec. 11(c))

Atomic weapon: any device utilizing atomic energy, exclusive of the means for transporting or propelling the device (where such means is a separable and divisible part of the device), the principal purpose of which is for use as, or for development of, a weapon, a weapon prototype, or a weapon test device. (sec. 11(d))

By-product material: any radioactive material (except special nuclear material) yielded in or made radioactive by exposure to the radiation incident to the process of producing or utilizing special nuclear material. (sec. 11(e))

Special nuclear material

1. Plutonium, uranium enriched in the isotope 233, or in the isotype 235, and any other material which the Commission, pursuant to the provisions of section 51 determines to be special nuclear material, but does not include source material.[217]

2. Any material artificially enriched by any of the foregoing, but which does not include source material. (sec. 11(e))

Source material

1. Uranium, thorium, or any other material which is determined by the Commission pursuant to the provisions of section 61 to be source material.[218]

[216] Sec. 142 regulates classification and declassification of restricted data by the AEC, and AEC jointly with the Department of Defense, including determination of data which can be published without undue risk to the common defense and security.

[217] Authorizing the Commission to determine from time to time that other material is "special nuclear material" in addition to that specified in the definition of sec. 11(c).

[218] Section 61 authorizes the Commission to determine from time to time that other material is source material in addition to materials specified in the definition of sec. 11(s).

2. Ores containing one or more of the foregoing materials, in such concentrations as the Commission may by regulation determine from time to time. (sec. 11s)

The five definitions cited here contain the basic fields of work and are open to interpretation. The defined working areas may overlap each other and may also overlap activities carried out by the Department of Defense and the National Aeronautics and Space Administration. They may also become obsolete or too narrow and require change or extension in view of the fast general development of science and technology in atomic energy research. The definitions are, however, sufficient to give an idea of the enormous scope of atomic energy work.

In the research field the Atomic Energy Act gives the Commission additional explicit instructions in sec. 31(a) "to insure the continued conduct of research and development activities by private or public institutions or persons" and "to assist in the acquisition of an ever-expanding fund of theoretical and practical knowledge." To this end the Act authorizes the Commission to make "arrangements" including contracts, agreements, and loans, for R&D in specified fields. This section in the Act is obviously the legal basis for the AEC to do research with the help of contractors of all kinds, usually industrial corporations, universities and other nonprofit institutions. The power to make R&D contracts is conditional. It must relate to one of the following:

1. Nuclear processes.

2. The theory and production of atomic energy, including processes, materials and devices related to such production.

3. Utilization of special nuclear material and radioactive material for medical, biological, agricultural, health, or military purposes.

4. Utilization of special nuclear material, atomic energy, and radioactive material and processes entailed in the utilization or production of atomic energy or such material for all other purposes, including industrial uses, the generation of usable energy, and the demonstration of the practical value of utilization or production facilities for industrial or commercial purposes.

5. The protection of health and the promotion of safety during research and production activities. (sec. 31(a))

In the military field sec. 91 gives the AEC special authority to conduct experiments and to do research and development comprising the military application of atomic energy and the production of atomic weapons or parts thereof.

A further worldwide extension of activities of the AEC is created by sec. 124 of the Act authorizing the President of the United States "to enter into an international arrangement with a group of nations providing for international cooperation in the nonmilitary applications of atomic energy." This authorization is realized by agreements and cooperation with the United Kingdom and Canada (since 1956), with Euratom, the research arm of the six European Common Market countries in the atomic energy field, and with IAEA in Vienna. These international agreements affect atomic energy inventors employed by AEC and its contractors in different ways. The Atomic Energy Act regulates (in sec. 173) one special case in this area, and that is, if the AEC "communicates to any nation any Restricted Data based on any patent application not belonging to the United States." In such case the government pays the (private) owner of the patent application just compensation as determined by the AEC.

In practice most overseas cooperation of the U.S. Government is in the form of bilateral agreements. There are "research bilaterals" containing no provisions with respect to patents and "power bilaterals" involving communication of restricted data to other nations. The latter contain patent provisions to protect U.S. Government-owned patents.[219]

AEC *Statutory Patent Provisions*

Chapter 13 of the Atomic Energy Act is dedicated entirely to the field of patents and inventions and includes ten separate sections 151 to 160.

Section 151, Subsections (a) and (b) refer to military utilization of patents; subsection (c) to reporting of nonpatented inventions to AEC; subsection (d) to notifying AEC of atomic energy patent applications.

Section 152 refers to inventions conceived during commission contracts as the legal basis of patent policy toward contractors.

Section 153 refers to nonmilitary utilization of patents. Eight extensive subsections (a) to (h) contain the doctrine of declaring patents to be affected with the public interest and the compulsory license system following thereon.

Section 154 refers to injunctions against patent licensees licensed by the AEC.

Section 155 refers to prior art, a special provision extending the ban on patenting of an invention under the Patents Act when comprising prior knowledge or use existing under secrecy within the atomic energy program of the United States.

Section 156 refers to Commission patent license, establishing standard specifications for licenses to use Commission-owned patents.

Section 157 refers to compensation, awards, and royalties, with three extensive sub-

[219] Atomic Energy Law Reports (Commerce Clearing House), par. 4520.

sections (b) to (c) regulating for the first time by statute a broad field of different types of monetary compensations.

Section 158 refers to monopolistic use of patents, creating sanctions against the use of patents in the field of utilization or production of special nuclear material or atomic energy in a manner to violate any of the antitrust laws.

Section 159 refers to federally financed research, providing that "nothing in this Act shall affect the right of the Commission to require that patents granted on inventions, made or conceived during the course of federally financed research or operations, be assigned to the United States." In other words, this section asserts the general power of discretion of the Commission to decide about assignment of title to all patented inventions made by employees of the AEC and employees of AEC contractors.

Section 160 refers to a "Saving Clause" for patent applications, for which a patent was denied by the Patent Office under certain parts of sec. 11 of the original Atomic Energy Act of 1946, making possible reinstatement of the right under certain conditions.

This rough sketch of the 10 patent provisions of the Atomic Energy Act reveals the entirely heterogeneous character of this piece of patent legislation. Provisions of subordinate, specific, or formal content (such as sections 154, 155, 156, 160) are arranged among provisions dealing with absolutely basic and far-reaching government research and patent policy (such as sections 151, 152, 153, 157, 158 and 159).

This discussion of the Atomic Energy Act, for the purpose of this book, can be limited to five sections:

151 regarding treatment of atomic weapon inventions, patent applications, and patents.

152 regulating the field of contractor inventions.

153 regarding treatment of all nonweapon patents.

157 regulating various inventor compensation systems.

159 authorizing the AEC to use the patent assignment principle.

In addition to these paragraphs, another provision of the Atomic Energy Act is relevant to the patent field, and that is section 161g, giving the Commission general authority to acquire, purchase, lease, and hold real and personal property, including patents, as agent of and on behalf of the United States.

These sections will be the basis of the discussion to follow, on assignment policy and on awards.

The Size of AEC *Activities*

Working Funds and Operation Costs   In fiscal year 1968, $2,466.6 million was appropriated for AEC, $200 million more than in fiscal 1967 but $200 to $300 million less than in the years 1960–1965. Completed plant, at cost, was estimated at $8.8 billion as of June 30, 1968, and the estimated cost of plants under construction and projects authorized (but not started) at that date totaled $1.3 billion. A major portion of this authorized plant expansion is for construction of reactors and related facilities, facilities to be used in high-energy physics research, and facilities in support of the weapons program.

The acquisition costs of plants, by type of facility was as follows: for production of raw materials, $3.2 million; for production of feed materials, $217.3 million; for gaseous diffusion plants, $2.3 billion; for production reactors and separation areas, $1.7 billion; for weapons production and storage, $647.8 million—in a total of $5.3 billion acquisition costs. Acquisition of plants and equipment for research and development accounted for almost $3 billion, principally for laboratories, $1.7 billion; reactors, $628 million; and accelerators, $442 million, and $148 million for other research facilities.[220]

The summary of net operating costs of the AEC for the various programs shows a shift in emphasis over the decade 1959–1968, from procurement of raw material and production of nuclear material to research and development activities of various kinds. This is illustrated by a comparison of figures for the years 1959 and 1968, in Table 5.16.

Table 5.16   AEC Operations, 1959 and 1968
($ millions)

	1959	1968	Percentage of Total Operations, 1968
Procurement of raw materials	700	125	5
Production of nuclear materials	713	507	20
Weapons development and fabrication	492	784	31
Reactor development	356	549	22
Physical research	112	310	13
Biology and medicine	43	99 ⎰	9
Other[1]	81	133 ⎱	

1 Administrative expenses, community operations, and miscellaneous expenses and income net.

Source: U.S. Atomic Energy Commission, 1968 Financial Report, pp. 44–45.

220 U.S. Atomic Energy Commission, *1968 Financial Report,* U.S. Government Printing Office, Washington, pp. 30-31.

Net costs incurred by AEC in fiscal year 1968 in connection with the physical location of contractors and AEC offices for operation (excluding depreciation) were totally $2.507 billion. The largest costs for authorized plant and equipment were incurred in Tennessee ($1.810 billion) and South Carolina ($1.371 billion).

Cost for raw materials procurement mainly involves uranium concentrates (U_3O_8) and until 1961 referred to uranium from foreign countries (Canada, South Africa). The trend was reversed after 1961 when over half the uranium came from domestic U.S. sources. Today all procurement comes from domestic sources. A smooth transition from a government to a private market for uranium is under way.

Cost of producing nuclear materials for weapons, research, and civilian needs has decreased as a result of increased production efficiency in all processes and reductions in the use of electric power. Costs of developing, testing, and producing atomic weapons were directed to the atomic stockpile, to improving yield-to-weight ratios, and to incorporating the latest design and technological concepts to improve reliability, safety, and efficiency of stockpiled weapons. Total costs of designing, developing, fabricating, and testing nuclear weapons increased mainly as a result of costs related to the safeguards commitments in connection with the test ban treaty in Moscow, including increased underground testing, maintenance of weapons laboratories, and developing a readiness capability for the conduct of atmospheric tests. In fiscal year 1968 total cost was $784 million.

Major R&D Areas and Projects

The reactor development program is largely oriented toward acquiring and utilizing knowledge for the development, demonstration, improvement, and safe operation of nuclear reactors and nuclear systems to generate electricity, produce heat, and propel vessels. Recent years have seen a leveling off of costs in the areas of civilian, Army, and Navy programs, along with rapidly increasing costs for space propulsion and auxiliary power sources. For nuclear space propulsion a joint AEC-NASA program, the so-called Rover program has gone on since 1956, using a graphite reactor as the basis for a nuclear rocket engine for space propulsion. Systems for compact nuclear auxiliary power for use in space are already developed for navigation satellites, navigation light buoys, and unmanned weather stations. For naval reactors by the end of fiscal year 1968 Congress had authorized 106 nuclear-powered submarines. Four nuclear-powered surface ships were then in operation. The Army power reactor program has developed reactors for remote areas of the world and will largely eliminate the need for fossil fuel.

The civilian power reactor program has as its basic objective to develop a broad technology which can be used by the utilities to extend fuel resources and to achieve economic generation of electricity with nuclear power plants. Civilian power reactors are developed for power plants to compete in some areas with conventional (fossil fuel) plants. They include sodium-cooled, gas-cooled, pressurized, light water, heavy water, boiling light water, and organic-moderated reactors. More than 40 percent of all the new electricity-generating capacity from steam announced by U.S. companies during fiscal year 1968 was nuclear, and the cost of developing central station nuclear power reactors during that year was $167 million. Efforts are concentrated on developing reliable and economically attractive high-gain breeder reactors. Twenty-three domestic power reactors were in operation in 1968.

There are 15 cooperative power reactor projects in which the Atomic Energy Commission and either public or private utility corporations share the cost of development and construction. The cost of operation of such reactor projects is still shared by AEC on ten projects (two in Michigan and California, one each in Minnesota, S. Dakota, Pennsylvania, Wisconsin, Connecticut, Colorado). Costs of $28 million were incurred for the cooperative power reactor demonstration programs in F.Y. 1968. The reactor program comprises, finally, nuclear safety and general research to develop technology applicable throughout the reactor development effort, especially to develop high-gain breeder reactors. The latter program includes the area of fuels and materials, plutonium utilization, chemical separation, and reactor physics. A program called Advanced Systems Research and Development comprises experiments in molten salt and molten plutonium reactors, direct conversion of energy, beryllium oxide and ultra high temperature reactors, and test reactors.[221] Production of fresh water by utilizing nuclear energy to desalt is a national and international cooperative aim. Total general reactor research and development costs in F.Y. 1968 were over $117 million.

The Physical Research Program is concerned with seven principal areas: high-energy physics, medium-energy physics, low-energy physics, controlled thermonuclear power, metallurgy and materials, chemistry, and mathematics and computers.

The high-energy physics research is directed toward comprehensive understanding of elementary particle phenomena, using as a main tool particle accelerators with energies above one billion electron volts (BeV). In 1968 there were seven such AEC accelerators in operation: at Brookhaven, Lawrence Radiation Laboratory,

[221] Some costs are incurred as accruing to Euratom activities in Europe.

Argonne National Laboratory, Stanford, Cambridge, Princeton, and California Institute of Technology. The largest accelerator (a 33 BeV alternating gradient synchroton) is located at Brookhaven, the next biggest at Stanford (with 20 BeV). The costs for this high-energy physics program have grown from $50 million in 1960 to $137 million in 1968. Some doubt is rising in Congress and among scientists whether such a large share of the federal science budget should be used for this branch of atomic energy research.[222]

Controlled thermonuclear or fusion power research seeks to determine the possibility of obtaining energy from the joining of the nuclei of light elements. Cost for devices and experiments for this research amounted in 1964 to $22.9 million. Scientific approaches include the (Princeton) Stellarator, direct current, magnetic mirror, pinch, magnetic shock compression, rotating plasma, and relativistic electron methods.

Biological and medical research is conducted to determine the direct and indirect biological effects of radiation, both short-term and long-term, on man. Total costs for this research amounted for fiscal year 1968 to $98.6 million. Main fields of biomedical research concern somatic effects of radiation, environmental radiation, and molecular and cellular level studies, to further research on cancer and radiation genetics.

Research on ways to preserve food by radiation pasteurization is under way. It may be feasible to extend the refrigerated storage life of selected marine products and fruits in this way. To develop technology for production, separation, purification, and encapsulation of radioisotopes and uses of high level radiation, $8.37 million were spent in 1968.

Large-scale research with a view to producing fresh water at competitive prices is under way by AEC contractors. A report by the Bechtel Corporation indicated that seawater can be transformed into fresh water at low cost by using nuclear fission to produce heat for distillation. For peaceful uses, in industry and science, of nuclear explosives (program "Plowshare") costs in 1968 were totally $20 million. The program studies uses of nuclear explosions for large-scale excavation, underground engineering (to recover and utilize reserves of natural gas, oil shale, and copper), and experiments on the effects of high pressures, high temperatures, and varying electromagnetic conditions on earth's crust.

[222] The AEC proposes that studies be made for a future national accelerator in the range of 600 to 1000 BeV, which would cost roughly $1 billion and would be about 2 miles in diameter.

Working Facilities

AEC programs are conducted both intramurally and with the assistance of the research facilities already owned or especially erected for the purpose by industries and universities of the country. A major portion of the AEC research and development is conducted in laboratories owned by the Commission but operated by contractors. On June 30, 1968, the investment in research facilities totaled $2.9 billion. These facilities include the expensive research reactors and particle accelerators, as well as general laboratory buildings, equipment, and research devices. Major production facilities owned by the Commission are located at Oak Ridge, Tennessee; Richland, Washington; and at sites near Paducah, Kentucky; Aiken, South Carolina; and Portsmouth, Ohio. The ten principal AEC-owned research centers and their 1968 operating expenses are as follows:

	1968 Costs ($ millions)
Ames Research Laboratory (Ames, Iowa)	9.4
Argonne National Laboratory (Chicago)[223]	102.0
Bettis Atomic Power Laboratory (Pittsburgh)	73.6
Brookhaven National Laboratory (Long Island, N.Y.)	63.1
Pacific Northwest (formerly Hanford, at Richland, Wash.)	51.0
Knolls Atomic Power (Schenectady, N.Y.)	65.4
Lawrence Radiation Laboratory (Berkeley and Livermore, Calif.)	184.0
Los Alamos Scientific Laboratory (New Mexico)	104.6
Oak Ridge National Laboratory (Oak Ridge, Tenn.)	90.4
Savannah River Laboratory (Aiken, S.C.)	13.6

The largest laboratory in terms of acquisition of the completed plant is the Argonne National Laboratory in Chicago, and the largest laboratory in terms of operating costs is the Lawrence Radiation Laboratory in Berkeley and Livermore (including facilities in Nevada). In addition to the laboratories listed here the AEC owns Mound Laboratory in Miamisburg, Ohio; Cambridge Electron Accelerator (operated by Harvard and M.I.T.) in Cambridge, Massachusetts; Princeton-Pennsylvania Proton Accelerator and Princeton Plasms Physics Laboratory at Princeton, New Jersey; and National Accelerator Laboratory near Batavia,

223 By order of the AEC this laboratory on October 21, 1964, was turned over to a nonprofit corporation formed by the AEC, the University of Chicago, and the Midwestern Universities Research Association consisting of 15 universities of the area, as a tripartite agreement for operation and management of the laboratory (*The New York Times*, October 22, 1964). The operations figure includes the National Reactor Testing Station in Idaho.

Illinois. It also has testing stations and proving grounds for atomic energy
equipment of civil and military type.

Manpower

Who translates these programs of Atomic Energy Commission into bombs,
satellites, ships, radioactive isotopes, power, heat- and energy-producing machines?

On June 30, 1968, the Commission listed a total employment of 129,959 (not
including employees in small research contracts, principally at educational institutions). Of these only 7,665 were its own employees. AEC contractors employed at the
same time 122,294 individuals, of whom 111,846 were operating contractor employees and 10,448 construction contractor employees working for AEC.[224] The
figures reflect the heavy engagement of outside contracting organizations in industry and nonprofit institutions for the Commission. The official figures are not
broken down to give a clear picture of how many scientists and engineers employed
by industrial and university employers are engaged in Commission research and
development.

Glenn Seaborg, chairman of the AEC, has stressed that "the development of nuclear
energy, probably more than any other one factor, tended to break down the arti-
ficial wall which had for a long time separated the scientist and the engineer.[225]
Seaborg points to "engineering achievements of unparalleled magnitude" in designing and constructing the facilities and plants necessary to the production of the
first nuclear bomb. When plutonium was discovered in 1940 in Berkeley it was
soon visualized that this element could be used in a nuclear weapon. A chemical
process for separating plutonium isotopes was developed, yielding microgram
amounts visible only under a microscope. The engineers of the Manhattan Engineer District (from which the AEC took control of atomic energy in 1947), working
side by side with university chemists had to translate the discoveries of the tracer
experiments and the microscope-scale experiments into huge facilities for producing the world's most powerful explosive. In view of the war, this had to be done
without going through most of the stages of development which normally lie between basic research and industrial production. Plants of novel design had to be
constructed, which consumed materials by the ton to deliver products by the gram.
Engineers were asked to produce, and succeeded in producing, a full-sized chemical processing plant (at Hanford, Washington) from ultramicrochemical experiments. This was possible only by extrapolating by a factor of some 10^9. Urgency of

[224] U.S. Atomic Energy Commission, *1968 Financial Report.*
[225] Talk before the Swedish Engineering Academy of Science in Stockholm, September
14, 1962.

these projects meant that engineers had to draft and construct even while the scientists were continuing their unfinished basic experimental and analytical work. Immediate "make do" decisions had to be adapted with a view toward later modification. Seaborg characterizes this performance as "one of the proudest accomplishments of engineering history."

Similar contributions are produced by engineering personnel in the field of nuclear reactor technology. Paramount engineering problems have to be solved to establish nuclear power as competitive with power generated through conventional fossil fuels. For example, corrosion engineering is vital for safe operation of reactors, and all radioactive parts of a reactor must be managed by "indirect maintenance methods." Problems of heat transfer, radiation shielding and instrumentation, and many others have been posed by the use of the new source of energy.

The intensive cooperation of men in theoretical science with practical engineers, as underlined by Seaborg, makes for delicate situations in the individual treatment of employees of the AEC and of AEC contractors when it comes to weighing their contributions and merits as inventors. However, the Commission has at all times applied a carefully thought-out policy of recognizing and awarding meritorious inventors on the basis of its statutory and discretionary power.

Faculty or staff members of universities and other nonprofit research organizations find their "prize," as a rule, in undisturbed working conditions and liberal grants of research equipment and staff. Their desire is rather to have the right to publish their results in their own name. This requirement may sometimes come into conflict with government procurement regulations for copyrightable material or secrecy regulations in the military field. In these circles monetary awards are usually not expected from the employer or sponsor of work.

Invention and Copyright Policy

Policy Regarding All Inventors (and Writers)   The patterns of assignment policy usual in other government departments and agencies do not fit the atomic energy field, whose military origin has separated it entirely from the legal status of government research in other fields of engineering.

The basic patent laws of the United States as codified in the 1952 Patent Act[226] have been circumscribed by a number of provisions of the Atomic Energy Act (AEA), especially by sections 151 and 153. The exclusive right accorded by the Patent Act to make, use, assign, or sell a patented invention or to refrain from so doing has been superseded by section 151 of the AEA which provides that no patent shall

226 66 Stat. 792 (1952), 35 U.S. Code, sections 1–293.

be granted for any invention useful solely in the utilization of special nuclear material or atomic energy in an atomic weapon (sec. 151(a)). If such a patent has been granted it is revoked by the AEC, including any rights conferred by such patent. The principle of a just compensation for the patent owner for the act of revocation is stated in the same section.

Not only military but also all nonmilitary inventions "of primary importance in the production or utilization of special nuclear material or atomic energy" (sec. 153a(1)) are subject to direct interference by the Commission on ownership rights. The Commission may declare any such patent "to be affected with the public interest," giving the Commission the sole authority to grant compulsory licenses to others to use such inventions under certain conditions.

In December 1956 rules of practice were adopted by the AEC on how to declare patents to be affected with the public interest.[227] A second requisite to interfere with such nonmilitary inventor rights is that the licensing must be "of primary importance to effectuate the policies and purposes of this Act" (sec. 153a(2)). The AEC, therefore, has wide discretion and quasi-judicial power to determine ownership in broad fields of atomic energy inventions made by all kinds of employed and independent inventors as well as to determine compensation paid for such rights. The AEC, however, regards its authority to grant compulsory licenses as a "reserve power" and does not anticipate exercising it "except under compelling circumstances."[228] All decisions about patent ownership and granting of licenses and all pertaining terms of use and compensation for such use are issued by a special Patent Compensation Board which the Commission is authorized to designate according to sec. 157a, of the AEA.

From the foregoing description of the statutory "confiscating powers" of the AEC in the field of inventions and discoveries made by any type of inventor (including employed inventors), it follows that there is no general unified type of invention policy in the AEC which can be called "assignment" policy. Inventions the patents for which are revoked, declared to be "affected by the public interest," or deemed to be made by the Commission itself need not be assigned to it, since they are either non-existent or already owned wholly by the AEC. The Atomic Energy Act, however, gives the Commission (in sec. 159) express power to require that patents granted

---

[227] *Federal Register*, December 11, 1956, title 101, Atomic Energy, ch. 1, AEC, Part 2, Rules of Practice.

[228] Hearings on Development, Growth, and State of the Atomic Energy Industry, 1955 p. 192. The same position was reiterated by the Commission in the Hearings on Atomic Energy Patents, Joint Committee on Atomic Energy, 1959.

on inventions made or conceived during the course of federally financed research or operations (by any kind of employee) be assigned to the United States.

The conditions, terms, and limitations of patent licenses to third parties which the Commission may fix for the three types of licenses (of which two are defined in sec. 153a and the third in sec. 153c) are established in standard specifications issued in AEC Rules and Regulations of June 1, 1962.[229]

1. The conditions and limitations of a license granted for Commission-owned United States patents to third parties are as follows:

The license shall be nonexclusive, revocable, and royalty-free.

Neither the license (nor any right under the license) shall be assigned or otherwise transferred.

The license shall be one of two types defined in sec. 156.

The AEC makes no warranty and assumes no liability that the exercise of the license will not result in infringement of any other patent.

The licensee shall observe all rules, regulations and orders of the AEC (sec. 81.12).

2. The conditions of a license for patents by the AEC declared "to be affected with the public interest" are that

The license shall be nonexclusive and revocable.

Neither the license nor any right under the license shall be assigned or otherwise transferred.

The licensee shall pay a reasonable royalty fee. This fee may be agreed upon with the owner, or in the absence of such agreement it may be determined by the AEC pursuant to sec. 157.

The licensee shall observe all rules, regulations, and orders of the AEC (sec. 81.22).

3. The conditions of license for "other patents useful in the production or utilization of special nuclear material or atomic energy" (under secs. 53, 62, 63, 81, 103, or 104) are the same as for patents affected with the public interest, except that such license is expressly limited to the purposes for which it is issued (sec. 81.33(c)).

The principles of payment for "reasonable royalty fees" to owners of revoked patents are described in connection with invention-award policy of the AEC.

Policy Regarding AEC *Contractors and Their Employees* A definite statutory rule is found in amended section 152 of the Act for inventions or discoveries made or conceived in the course of or under any contract, subcontract, or arrangement entered into with or for the benefit of the Commission. This rule is valid regardless

[229] *Federal Register,* June 1, 1962, Part 81, "Standard Specifications for the Granting of Patent Licenses," 81.30.

of whether the contract involved the expenditure of funds by the Commission. The types of inventions concerned here are those "useful in the production or utilization of special nuclear material or atomic energy." Inventions in this field and made under the above relations to any contractor to the Commission shall, according to sec. 152, "be deemed to have been made or conceived by the Commission." According to this statutory doctrine the invention right arises and has its origin directly within the Commission itself. Naturally, no rules of assignment of inventions are necessary if the inventions automatically are owned by the Commission. This rule applies also to contractors and inventions made by their employees.

Waiver Policy The Commission has authority to waive its claim to an invention made at any laboratory described in sec. 33 (the Commission's own facilities for conducting R&D for other persons), or (sec. 152) "under such other circumstances as the Commission may deem appropriate." This general wording gives the AEC discretion by statute to work out waiver regulations adapted to the needs of different research contracts, but always in regard to inventions "useful in the production or utilization of special nuclear material or atomic energy." Since the authority to waive its claim to inventions and discoveries is also found in this section (152) of the Atomic Energy Act, headed "Inventions Conceived During Commission Contracts," it can only be applied to contractors of the Commission and their employees. Waiver of claims to inventions made by AEC's own employees is obviously not provided for in the Act, and the Commission, therefore, has no authority to favor its own inventing scientists and engineers by releasing title to submitted inventions in the same way as is possible for contractors and their employees. This seems to be a disadvantage for AEC employees. The Commission, however, has only one small laboratory staffed by its own employees. It can also be argued that employees of contractors and direct AEC employees are treated alike in that inventions arising from either group are covered by an employment agreement (to be discussed later in this chapter).

Through the issuance of the Kennedy Memorandum of 1963 regarding government patent policy, new guidelines for government waiver policy were drawn up.[230] The interpretation of this Memorandum is expected to result also in new waiver regulations of the AEC. Since 1946 the AEC has worked out invention policies

---

[230] The Memorandum indicates that an agency should acquire patent title mainly when the end aim is for general public use, when public health or welfare is involved, when the field is government-financed, and when the contract is for operation of a government-owned facility.

and practices for different contract types in detailed procurement regulations.[231] There are three types of patent provisions. Provisions securing patent rights to the government are applied to research and development contracts, operating and service contracts, architect-engineer contracts, special contracts and subcontracts, and purchase orders thereunder (9–9.5002). The insertion of patent provisions in contracts is determined primarily by the character of the work to be performed under the contract (R&D, routine development, construction, supply, or quantity production) and by the industrial and patent position of the contractor in the field of work of the contract (sec. 9–9.5002(a)).

Part of all such contract provisions is a waiver by the contractor or his employees for pecuniary awards or just compensation under the AEA. A similar provision is included in employee agreements with respect to any invention made or conceived in the course of or under the contract. The contractor has to obtain patent agreements from all persons who perform any part of the work under the contract. Excepted are only "such clerical and manual labor personnel as will not have access to technical data" (sec. 9–9.5003(c); sec. 9–9.5004(c); sec. 9–9.5005(c)). The same provision is applicable to subcontractors and their employees. If the contractor or his employees desire to publish information on scientific or technical developments made or conceived in the course of a contract, approval of release and publication shall be secured from the Commission. In certain specified fields a contractor may publish if the publication does not disclose an invention. If an invention is disclosed it shall be promptly reported to AEC and withheld from publication for four months (or less, at AEC's discretion).

The three types of patent provisions used by the AEC are as follows:

Type A, for contracts probably relating to some phase of the research or development that AEC conducts or sponsors (sec. 9–9.5003).

Type B, for contracts probably relating only incidentally to the basic research or development work that AEC conducts or sponsors but relating to a field of work in which the contractor has an established industrial and patent position (sec. 9–9.5004).

Type C, for contracts of the same type as type B but with the additional characteristic that the invention will result from routine development or production work by the contractor (sec. 9–9.5005).

231 The procurement regulations were issued during the Manhattan Engineer District period. Part 9–9, Patents and Copyrights, has been revised from time to time, in December 1964 and May 1965 (AECPR Circular No. 1, January 1966).

Under the Type A clause the Commission has the sole and final power to determine the disposition of title and whether patent applications shall be filed (no right to inventions remains with the contractor).

Under the Type B clause the Commission has the same powers as under Type A except that the contractor shall retain at least a nonexclusive, irrevocable, royalty-free license under said invention (limited to manufacture, use, and sale for purposes other than the production or utilization of special nuclear material or atomic energy).

Under the Type C clause, the Commission has the same powers as under Type A, except that the contractor shall retain at least a sole, irrevocable, royalty-free license (except as against the government or its account), with the sole right to grant sublicenses (but limited in manufacture, use, and sale as in Type B). Settlement of the questions of ownership of inventions made by contractor's employees and compensation for such inventions under Type C clause (where the contractor may keep a sole license) are matters between the employing contractor and his employees.

As is seen from these three clauses, the AEC has the right to determine whether and where a patent application shall be filed. AEC thereby is in a position to comply with E.O. 9865 of June 14, 1947, which requires all government agencies, wherever practicable, to acquire the right to file foreign patent applications on inventions resulting from research conducted by the government (through its departments and agencies) (sec. 9–9.5013).

Finally, the AEC Procurement Regulations of 1962 (like preceding regulations) cover policy and practices as to use and publication of technical data and copyrightable materials (sec. 9–7.5006–13; and sec. 9–9.5100 to sec. 9–9.5106). The Commission employs, as a rule, a provision under which all scientific and technical data, specifications, reports, papers, articles, and other memoranda shall be and remain the property of the government, and the government shall have the right to use such scientific and technical data in any manner without claim for additional compensation from the contractor or his employees. This provision is included in research and development and other contracts, including contracts for translations or for the preparation of articles, books, or other publications, under which material subject to copyright may be furnished in the form indicated previously. Certain of these materials may be government publications for which copyrights are specifically excluded in accordance with section 8, title 17, U.S. Code. In contracts not containing a copyright provision of this type, provisions are incorporated giving the government the right to determine the disposition of copyrightable material or to receive at least a royalty-free, nonexclusive, and irrevocable license to such material, if it is first produced, composed, or furnished under the contract. This type of copyright license gives the government the right to authorize others to reproduce, publish, and use the material but leaves the contractor who has created these documents free to take out a copyright in his own name if he so desires.[232]

If a contractor incorporates in governmental work material that he or others already own, the government secures a license in such material whenever appropriate. Provisions as to government rights are included in contracts, whether the material subject to copyright is the main item of the contract or is merely incidental. In case a translation or preparation of articles or books is the principal subject matter of a contract, special provisions are used.

Policy Regarding AEC *Employees*   We have seen that section 159 of the Atomic Energy Act entitles the Commission to ask generally for assignment of all patents granted on inventions made during the course of federally financed research or operations.[233] The Commission has had rules of this kind since 1947, revised in May 1954, four months before the issuance of the amended Atomic Energy Act of August 30, 1954. These rules are found in the AEC *Manual,* Appendix 4108 V. F3 and VI. E6 and Appendix 4139, II, A.9.[234] The instructions cited there give orders to the managers of AEC operations that all AEC employees, advisors, and consultants shall enter into an agreement covering discoveries, inventions, and improvements. Clerical and manual-labor personnel who will not have access to technical data are excepted. The procedure specifies that this agreement shall be executed concurrently with engagement or employment by "each AEC employee or officer employed by contract or otherwise, each member of an advisory board established by the AEC, and each AEC consultant, with or without fee, including personnel assigned to or on loan to the AEC." (AEC *Manual,* Appendix 4108 V., F3). The scope of the agreement embraces all inventions "arising from or related to work conducted or sponsored by the AEC." The inventions must be made or conceived during the engagement or employment of the signee. The consideration of the agreement is the engagement or employment by the Commission. A standard form is used for this agreement, in

232 All details regarding government rights in copyrightable material in the atomic energy field can be studied in 9–9.5100 and its subsections of the AEC Procurement Regulations, of December 6, 1962.

233 The cited section is, however, restricted to assignment of granted patents, obviously not including the other groups of unpatentable or not yet patented inventions, discoveries and improvements; neither does the section specify to what extent federal funds must have been used to be applicable.

234 This is part 0300 (Legal) in the (General Administration) Manual of the AEC.

which the employee agrees that the Commission shall have the sole power to determine the disposition of the title and the rights under such inventions and to determine whether a patent application shall be filed. The AEC may determine in each case what rights (if any) shall be retained by an AEC employee. The judgment of the Commission is accepted by the employee as final. Any claim for a pecuniary award or compensation under the Act is waived with respect to such inventions.[235]

Invention-Award Policy

Statutory Award Provisions   The Atomic Energy Act is the first federal law with detailed rules regarding pecuniary compensation to inventors in lieu of patent grants. They are laid down in section 157(b) and concern three main types of compensation:

1. "Reasonable royalty fees" for all owners of patents subject to the three types of compulsory patent licenses the Commission can issue (under secs. 153(b), 153(e), or 158).

2. "Just compensation" to owners of patents in the atomic weapon field whose patents have been revoked (under sec. 151).

3. "Award" to any person making any invention or discovery useful in the production or utilization of special nuclear material or atomic energy, who is not entitled to compensation or a royalty under (1) or (2) and who has filed a report of his invention with the Commission.

We are concerned here only with the third type of compensation, the "award" which is open to all AEC employees and employees of AEC contractors. The AEA provides for two such awards, one under sec. 157b(3), first sentence, which was just described under (3) and which is granted by the Patent Compensation Board of the Commission, and the other under sec. 157b(3), second sentence, which is granted by the Commission upon the recommendation of the AEC General Advisory Committee and must be approved by the President. This second award is reserved for "any especially meritorious contribution to the development, use, or control of atomic energy." This second award is an *ex gratia* award.

The AEC Patent Compensation Board   The determination of these awards (and the other types of compensation) is prepared by a special administrative board of the Commission, the Patent Compensation Board, established under sec. 157(a) of the Atomic Energy Act. General rules of procedure before this Board were first established in 1949 and amended under the 1954 Act.[236] The Patent Compensation

---

[235] This waiver does not prohibit the Commission from making voluntary awards under sec. 157(b)(3); neither does the waiver exclude awards under the Federal Government Incentive Awards Act of 1954.

[236] *Federal Register*, August 15, 1960, Part 80, "General Rules of Procedure on Applica-

Board is qualified to accept applications for the three main types of claims pursuant to sec. 157(b) ("just compensation for restricted data of a patent application not belonging to the United States which the Commission has communicated to any foreign nation (sec. 80.10(d)) and claims for the damage caused by an order of secrecy and/or for the use of an invention disclosed to the Commission. Each application for an award must contain a concise statement of all the essential facts upon which it is based. Nine different specific data are recommended to accompany the application (sec. 80.11). Of these the following are of special interest:
A statement of the extent to which the invention was developed through federally financed research, the degree of its utility, novelty, and importance.
The actual use of such invention to the extent known to the applicant.
The cost of developing the invention.
The amount sought as award.

The Board prepares findings and a determination with statement of the reason or basis thereof. The decision of the Board becomes final unless any party files a petition for review within 60 days to the Atomic Energy Commission.

The Atomic Energy Act lists expressly and by statutory provision (in sec. 157(c)) standards which the Commission shall take into account when determining the amount of any award. These four criteria are:

1. The advice of the Patent Compensation Board.
2. Any defense, general or special, that might be pleaded by a defendant in an action for infringement.
3. The extent, if any, to which such patent was developed through federally financed research.
4. The degree of utility, novelty, and importance of the invention or discovery, and the cost to the owner of the patent of developing such invention or discovery or acquiring such patent.[237]

The policy applied and the trends of policy in granting awards to various inventors, including employed inventors, on the basis of section 157b(3) of the AEA can be found partly by studying the decisions rendered by the AEC Patent Compensation Board.[238] Between March 1950 (when the first decision was rendered by

---

tions for the Determination of Reasonable Royalty Fee, Just Compensation or the Grant of an Award for Patents, Inventions or Discoveries." Last printing of rules in June 1962.
[237] The final decision about the novelty of an invention by the AEC takes away this statutory power from the U.S. Patent Office and the federal courts for the field of atomic energy as defined in the AEA. See, for instance, the Board decision, in re Kerner, January 31, 1958, in *U.S. Patent Quarterly* 116: 268.
[238] The decisions are usually published in the *United States Patent Quarterly* and from time to time in the *Atomic Energy Law Reports* of the Commerce Clearing House.

the Board under the original Atomic Energy Act of 1946) and May 1965, 37 cases
(docket numbers) can be identified. Of these cases about 10 percent refer twice
to the same case, as reviewed by the AEC. Some important cases have also been carried on by parallel or subsequent court actions before the U.S. Court of Claims[239] or
before the U.S. Court of Appeals, District of Columbia Circuit.[240]

A number of the earlier Board cases were started by applicants pursuant to the
provision of sections 11(a), 11(b), and 11(e) of the original Atomic Energy Act of
1946. However, the basic similarity of these provisions to section 157 of the amended
Atomic Energy Act of 1954 welds all Board decisions into a somewhat coherent and
continuous body of law. From a formal point of view applicants have asked the
Board for compensation either for complete or partial revocation of a U.S. patent
or for a discovery or invention (in the technical field of the Act) disclosed to the
Commission by certain designs, descriptions, patent applications, or granted
patents, and asserted to be useful and operative within the military or civil purposes
of the Act.

The decisions of the Board and the reasons given for these decisions in no way
offer a complete system of "law of ownership and compensation" for atomic energy
inventions and still less a complete body of valid criteria for all inventors making
such inventions. However, there have emerged a limited number of Board decisions
since 1950 which illustrate and to some extent clarify the position of inventors who
are employees of U.S. or foreign corporations or institutions and who claim an
award under the Atomic Energy Act. Of general interest in this connection are five
Board cases.

In three Board decisions [A. A. Matheson, May 11, 1957 (Docket No. 8),[241] N.V.
Philips' *Gloeilampenfabrieken,* November 14, 1961 (Docket No. 16)[242] and *Commissariat à l'Energie Atomique,* CEA, February 28, 1963 (Docket No. 18)],[243] the
claims set forth by the applicants involve some dispute about the significance of
assignment of employee inventions. In the Matheson case the applicant conceded
that the patent upon which his claim for an award was based was assigned to and at

---

[239] For example, G. M. Giannini and Co., Inc., *et al.* concerning the famous Fermi U.S.
patent, discussed at the end of this chapter.
[240] Examples: *Grossman* v. *United States Atomic Energy Commission,* 101 U.S. App. D.C.
22 (1961), 246 Federal Reporter 2d, 709; 355 U.S. 285, rehearing denied 355 U.S. 942;
N.V. Philip's Gloeilampenfabrieken et al. v. *Atomic Energy Commission et al.* U.S. App.
D.C., March 21, 1962, *U.S. Patent Quarterly* 137, 90.
[241] *Atomic Energy Law Reports* (Patents) 10,126; 10,128.
[242] *Ibid.,* 10,168; 10,173.
[243] *Ibid.,* 10,173; 10,17.

the time of application of his claim was owned by the corporation which employed him, although he asserted that the assignment "was subject to a condition which has not been performed."[244] The Board held that the applicant does not have title to the patent, so his application is "fatally defective." In argumentative statement the applicant contested the proposed findings of fact, the determination and statement of reasons of the Board by reporting that the Matheson Pneumatic Machinery, Inc. (his employer), had been reinstated under the laws of the State of Colorado and that he had the controlling interest in the corporation. The Board held that these facts did not affect its findings and determination.

In June 1968, there was a settlement between the CEA and the AEC, in which $35,000 was paid to the individual innovators, and a citation and plaque were given the Commissariat. The Patent Compensation Board then dismissed the proceedings before the Office of the General Counsel, in view of the settlement.

In the Philips case the Board held (referring to compensation for foreign patents, for expired U.S. patents, and the defense of the Statute of Limitations) that the Atomic Energy Acts of 1946 and 1954 authorize awards to corporations as well as to individual inventors.[245] In a subsequent court decision the U.S. Court of Appeals, District of Columbia Circuit, in 1963 remanded the Patent Compensation Board in this case in some respects, making statements about just compensation under constitutional power of eminent domain.[246]

In December 1968 the AEC settled the Philips claim for $50,000 with a letter of commendation. The Patent Compensation Board dismissed the proceedings upon stipulation of the parties.

In the case of the *Commissariat à l'Energie Atomique* (this agency of the French government had applied to the Board for awards), the same question of individual inventors versus corporate assignees was in dispute. In the proceedings before the Board the Office of the General Counsel of the Commission filed a motion to dismiss the applications of the *Commissariat,* stating that the Atomic Energy Acts of 1946 and 1954 authorize awards only to individual inventors and not to corporate assignees and that the *Commissariat* is not a "person" and thus may not be the recipient of an award. The Board, however, considered the grounds of the motion and reached the following conclusions in regard to this point:

It is, of course, true that the U.S. Patent Office issues patents only when the appli-

[244] *Ibid.,* 10,126.
[245] *Ibid.,* 10,168.
[246] *N.V. Philip's Gloeilampenfabrieken et al.* v. *Atomic Energy Commission et al.,* Court of Appeals, D.C., March 21, 1963, in 137 *U.S. Patents Quarterly* 90.

cations therefor have been executed by individual inventors, or groups of inventors (with the minor exceptions provided for in Patent Office Rules 42, 43 and 47), even though most patents are currently issued to corporate assignees. Neither the Patent Act of January 1, 1953, nor any act of earlier date, gave to the U.S. Patent Office the authority vested in this Board by the Atomic Energy Acts of 1946 and 1954, to consider as equals individuals, corporations, and other organizations, in carrying out the intent of the legislation.[247]

Reference is made to sec. 11(n) of the 1954 Act defining a "person" in agreement with the above statement. The contention that the Acts authorize awards only to individual inventors and not to corporate assignees was, therefore, denied by the Board, which held that language of "the atomic energy legislation . . . shows an intent to encourage groups of persons, gathered together for an organized effort, to also engage in the effort to advance the art." According to the author [F.N.], this interpretation of the Atomic Energy Act seems to be not very well chosen. The statement is somewhat misleading in its general language and seems not to have support in the relevant common law.

Two remaining relevant compensation cases before the Board touch relations with employee inventors, one regarding four university staff members and one a person employed as a consultant by a government contractor.

The first case in the form of an AEC release on June 26, 1955,[248] concerns Glenn T. Seaborg et al. (Docket No. 7). The Patent Compensation Board approved a settlement payment to the four academic atomic scientists Glenn Seaborg, Joseph Kennedy, Arthur Wahl, and Emilio Segré, at that time all associated in teaching or research with the University of California. A settlement of $400,000 was granted to these four univerity members for the acquisition of all rights, title, and interest in certain inventions in plutonium separative processes developed prior to their engaging in research work in connection with government contracts. All rights in pending classified patent applications on these early inventions were assigned to the Commission. The inventors filed an application for award before the Board in 1950 (amended in 1953). Their early work included highly important discoveries pertaining to the recovery of plutonium from solution in its lower oxidation state. Subsequently, the four university-employed scientists were engaged in work under the Office of Scientific Research and Development and the Manhattan District, where they made further valuable contributions and a considerable number of inventions which they assigned to the government (AEC) pursuant to their employment agreements.

[247] *Atomic Energy Law Reports* 10,174.
[248] *Ibid.,* 10,133–134.

A second case concerns a different type of employed inventor, James C. Hobbs (Dockets No. 22 and No. 23).[249]

Hobbs was employed as a consultant by a government contractor engaged on an R&D contract for the construction of the original gaseous diffusion plant at Oak Ridge, Tennessee. On February 18, 1963, the Board denied his combined application for just compensation for two new valve types developed by him during that time. The Board concluded that the work was within the scope of his employment in his role as consultant and "within the expected accomplishments and duties of a man of his standing and the order of his compensation." The inventions the applicant may have made were based upon knowledge of problems acquired by him only by way of disclosures made to him as a part of his employment as consultant on the Oak Ridge project. The inventions were based upon work completely financed by AEC, including the use of tools, machinery, and equipment. Thus, the Board held, the inventions were made under such circumstances and conditions as would give to the government (AEC) shop rights (the Board did not ask for full title to the inventions) and the application by Hobbs for just compensation was denied.[250]

Hobbs asked the U.S. Court of Appeals (Fifth Circuit) to review the adverse decision and the Commission's refusal to review it. The Court found that Hobbs was a mechanical engineer of excellent reputation working half time as a consultant to a government contractor, Kellex Corporation. He had made his position clear regarding assignment of inventions by refusing to assign or license any of his anticipated patent rights either to the government or to Kellex. (It was not until July 1944 that the government became aware of his refusal to execute a waiver form.) The main thrust of the Board's opinion was that the United States had obtained shop rights in Hobbs's inventions. Since government was said to have an implied nonexclusive, royalty-free license to use the inventions, the Board's theory was that AEC's use of the inventions took nothing for which compensation must be paid.

The Court held, however, that the Atomic Energy Act of 1946 totally obliterates patent rights in certain areas and provides that just compensation be paid for this obliteration. The Act had to be viewed as a whole. Section 11(a)(2) terminated the inventor's rights, which are held to derive their value not only from potential royalties from the government but from potential sale or licensing to private parties as well (reference is made to section 11(c)(2) of the Act in this regard). In other words, other valuable rights which should be the property of the inventor are terminated in this way. The inventor, therefore, was held to be entitled to compensation regardless of the government's license. The Board's statement that nothing was taken from the inventor was held to be erroneous. The Board's consideration of the

249 *Ibid.,* 10,199.
250 The applicant asserted that the government's manufacture and use of the valves invented by him constituted a "taking," within the meaning of the AEA of 1946, for which he was entitled to just compensation. The Board ruled that the property which the applicant maintained was "taken" by the government was, in fact, government property at the time that the "taking" took place. Case completely reported in 136 *U.S. Patent Quarterly,* pp. 489 ff., and *Atomic Energy Law Reports* 10,433; 10,439.

shop rights defense was held proper in itself but did not require a total denial of compensation in this case. Further, it was held that shop rights could not arise here in favor of the government since Hobbs was not directly employed by, nor was he a contractor of, the government. (Shop rights were held generally to arise only where there is a direct employer-employee relationship.)

The Court also made some interesting pronouncements in connection with section 11(e)(3) of the 1946 Act, where the Commission is directed to take into consideration, when setting just compensation, "the extent to which, if any, such patent was developed through federally financed research." The Court said that the "federal research" provision was intended to apply to persons not directly employed by the government, whether hired to invent or not, and that this clause fitted the facts of this case more closely than the shop rights doctrine. Further, the Board's opinion that Hobbs's inventions "were developed completely through federally financed work, whether it be called research or some other name" was opposed by the Court. The Court held that the statute uses the word "research" rather than "work." "Research" was said to imply more than "work." "It involves the notion of lengthy, complex technical investigation," said the Court, and it concluded that an invention developed in connection with a federal contract is not necessarily the product of "federally financed research" as the term is used in the Act.[251] Hobbs's inventions were held not to be the product of an intensive investigation but ideas coming suddenly one night in a hotel room and reduced to practice without exhaustive experimentation and at very little cost to the government. On April 7, 1967 the decision of the AEC Compensation Board was reversed by the Court of Appeals, and the case was remanded to the Patent Compensation Board "for further proceedings consistent with this opinion."[252]

Special Ex Gratia Awards   Section 157b(3) of the Atomic Energy Act gives statutory authority for a second type of award "for any especially meritorious contribution to the development, use, or control of atomic energy." The Commission established two such separate awards, one in 1956 called the Enrico Fermi Award, and the other in 1959, the Ernest O. Lawrence Memorial Award. These two awards have a broad field of application—outstanding contributions to development, use, or control in the general field of atomic energy. Yet contributions in this complex field are based on advanced and abstract theories and imply a degree of knowledge and scientific standard which is out of reach of average experienced and educated scientists.

The purpose of the Fermi Award is twofold, to give merited recognition to outstanding achievement and to stimulate creative work in the development and applications of nuclear science. The Commission specified that the award could be

[251] The same term appears in the corresponding section, 159, of the amended Act of 1954.
[252] *Atomic Energy Law Reports*, 10,439. A rehearing on the Hobbs docket was held in April 1968; the docket was still pending at time of writing.

applied to contributions "in the physical or biological sciences, including medicine" and could be made to an individual or to several individuals, for separate or cooperative achievements. It could also be made on an international basis. A gold medal was awarded and $50,000 (in 1954 reduced to $25,000).[253]

The Fermi Award is tax-free and entails no surrender of property rights (patents or the like). No age limit for a recipient is prescribed. Most recent recipients have been professors (von Neumann, Lawrence, Wigner, Seaborg, Bethe, Teller, Oppenheimer, and Wheeler). Admiral Rickover was an exception. In 1964 the Commission reviewed the Fermi Award and extended the award criteria to recognize not only scientific achievement but also contributions to engineering and technical management in the development of atomic energy.

The recipients of the Fermi Award were no "inventors" in the meaning of patent law, but many of their abstract scientific achievements sooner or later evolved into practical engineering results, like computers in the case of John von Neumann; the cyclotron, Ernest Lawrence; atomic reactors, Eugene Wigner; plutonium manufacture, Glenn Seaborg; the hydrogen bomb, Edward Teller, and the atomic submarine in the case of Hyman G. Rickover.

In 1959 the Commission established the second type of *ex gratia* award for especially meritorious contributions to atomic energy, as a recognition of Ernest O. Lawrence's work. The award consists of a medal, citation, and cash payment of $5000 for each (annual) recipient. The award is made in areas of all sciences related to atomic energy, including medicine and engineering. Recipients must be under 45 years of age. Not more than five recipients may be selected in any year, and the total award may not exceed $25,000 per year. The Commission makes the award on recommendation of the General Advisory Committee of the AEC and with the approval of the President. The first Lawrence award was granted to five scientists in 1960. Since that time the number of academic scientists receiving the Lawrence award has been about equal to AEC employees so honored. Scientist employees of the University of California have accounted for several recipients, and AEC's contractor employees have come from Oak Ridge National Laboratory, Los Alamos Scientific Laboratory, Argonne National Laboratory, and Brookhaven National Laboratory.

253 The first award under the AEA, sec. 157b(3), the precedent for later Fermi awards, was granted to Enrico Fermi in November 1954 in recognition of his "contributions to the basic neutron physics and the achievement of the controlled nuclear reaction," together with $25,000 and a medal (posthumously to Mrs. Fermi). Fermi and his coworkers had achieved the first sustained controlled nuclear chain reaction on December 2, 1942, at Stagg Field, Chicago.

Industries have been represented too; recipients have come from Babcock & Wilcox Company, General Electric Research Laboratory, the Rand Corporation, and General Dynamics Corporation.

The great mass of employees of the Commission and its many industrial and academic contractors do not reach the level of inventions and improvements eligible for these awards, of course. But all government employees are eligible under the rules of the Federal Government Employees Incentive Award Act of 1954 for awards up to $5000, which can be granted them directly by their own agency for suggestions and improvements, including new inventions.

There is yet another kind of award for inventors employed by AEC contractors. The Commission can in connection with research and development contracts "buy a company policy as it is," meaning that the costs to the contractor of an internal invention-award policy for employees is reimbursed by the Commission under certain premises. The rules for such reimbursable costs are laid down in detail in the AEC Procurement Regulations and in the ASPR (Armed Services Procurement Regulations) if applicable. Universities as government contractors do not follow this type of policy; their systems are described in Chapter 6.

University or other contractors' employees are not eligible for awards under the Federal Government Employees Incentive Award Act of 1954, since they are not government employees. At the same time the industrial employer feels in most relations of this kind that without ownership of his employees' inventions he has no commercial advantage other than payment by government, and he will not pay the inventive employee any extra reward.[254] Here it must be stated, however, that the AEC in its Procurement Regulations allows reimbursement of costs of a contracting corporation for internal invention awards under certain premises. This means that an industrial contractor to AEC would not lose money by rewarding an employed inventor working in government-supported research and making useful improvements of a patentable type. From the standpoint of the industrial employer this kind of payment to an employee is just a delivery of a government payment.

An employer may have another motive for paying invention awards to employees in that his corporation in return has received a property right which provides him, directly or indirectly, with increased income or an advantage in his competitive position on the market. A farsighted employer could reason that voluntary payment

[254] There are a few exceptions in which the industrial employer pays employees working on government contracts the same award as to employees making and assigning inventions in nongovernment fields. Radio Corporation of America is an example.

of an award or other tangible incentive by him to employees working on government contracts would be valuable for the company in the long run, since government contracts may cease some day and the creative employee might be an asset in connection with other company work.

In the cases in which AEC releases exclusive license rights to the contractor for invention disclosures under government ownership, the contractor gets back some property right of commercial value. This situation occurred in 2.3 to 4.5 percent of cases of contractor inventions disclosures over the years 1963 through 1966.[255] In this situation the industrial employer has lost little or nothing and should compensate his employee out of his own funds.

Restricted Data Policy   The origin of atomic energy research and production in the United States as a purely military weapon has led to a secret character of research data, and broad rules of restricted use and classification were established. On the other hand, it is highly compatible with the basic purpose of atomic energy policy of the United States as stated in the Atomic Energy Act that free competition shall be strengthened in private enterprise, that research and development shall be conducted and fostered in order to encourage maximum scientific and industrial progress, and that widespread participation in development and utilization of atomic energy for peaceful purposes shall be encouraged.

"Restricted data" are defined by the AEA in section 11r as follows:

... all data concerning (1) design, manufacture, or utilization of atomic weapons; (2) the production of special nuclear material; or (3) the use of special nuclear material in the production of energy, but shall not include data declassified or removed from the Restricted Data category pursuant to section 142.

Restricted data as defined here are only a part of the enormous field of technical data. Property rights in such valuable material are regulated in different ways depending on whether they are considered to be "restricted data," or data "which can be published without undue risk to the common defense and security" (sec. 142a of the AEA). Still other categories are (1) restricted data contained in patent applications not belonging to the United States (General Rules of Procedure before the AEC Patent Compensation Board, August 1960), (2) technical data in general (AEC Procurement Regulations 9–7.5006–13), and (3) "background technical data," that is, secret processes, technical information, and know-how developed or acquired by a contractor prior to the contract or prior to completion of a contract but independent of contract work (AEC Procurement Regulations 9–9.5008–7). In 1962 the Commission amended the rules for access to classified technology that can

255 *Annual Report on Government Patent Policy,* 1967, pp. 42–43.

be of benefit to private industry and removed certain criteria formerly required for such access.[256] The Commission grants waivers from the secrecy of classified data under certain conditions and when not constituting "an undue risk to the common defense and security." The government, however, at the same time secures nonexclusive, irrevocable licenses to use all U.S. patents, or patent applications on any invention "made or conceived during the term of the permit and for one year thereafter, by the permittee or the employees, or others engaged by the permittee, in the course of the permittee's work" if the work is in the gaseous diffusion field (sec. 25.23(d)(1)). In its regulations of permits for access to restricted data of August 1962, the Commission defined the restricted data available in this connection. They fall into the following main fields."[257]

1. Isotope separation by the gas centrifuge method.
2. Nuclear technology.
3. Plutonium production.
4. Nuclear reactors for ramjet propulsion.
5. Nuclear reactors for rocket propulsion.
6. Systems for nuclear auxiliary power (SNAP).
7. Advanced concepts for future applications such as reactor experiments and energy conversion devices.
8. Military compact reactors (MCR).

The Atomic Energy Act (except for restricted data of special type) does not frame expressly its policy regarding general scientific and engineering (technical) data. Guiding principles as to ownership and release of ownership (waiver) of such property are generally covered in the chapter of the Manual previously cited, covering employees' conduct. In many cases such data are represented by specifications, reports, papers, memoranda, and similar material and thus fall under the legal concept of "copyrightable material" which is regulated by part 9 of the AEC Procurement Regulations of December 1965. These regulations concern only AEC contractors. The assignment agreement for AEC employees, advisors, and consultants does not contain any provision regarding "writings."

That publication of patentable or copyrightable data by the Commission against the will of its author can be controversial is evident from a case that came to the AEC Patent Compensation Board, in which an applicant, F. P. Fulmer, claimed

[256] 27 *Fed. Register* No. 163, August 22, 1962, title 10, ch. 1. Part 25 "Permits for Access to Restricted Data."
[257] Appendix A, of the Regulation on Permits for Access to Restricted Data, of August 22, 1962.

damages for the publication of a disclosure as a press report by the Commission. Another case came to the Supreme Court, on whether the Commission may publish features of a U.S. patent application which had been formerly prohibited by a secrecy order. This prohibition prevented filing the application abroad within the so-called priority year of the Paris Convention.[258]

Industrial Contractors

Private industrial organizations under contract perform most of the AEC's production and much of its research and development. In 1968 AEC's principal prime industrial contractors accomplished work amounting to some $1.645 billion. AEC had more than 40 industrial contractors for supply, production, and R&D, with costs to the Commission of more than $5 million. The five largest contractors in 1968 were Union Carbide ($284 million), Sandia ($198 million), General Electric (103 million), du Pont de Nemours ($90 million), and Reynolds Electrical ($88 million). The costs include construction and capital equipment but exclude depreciation.

University Contractors

The highly scientific character of atomic energy research has made it necessary to engage all available and suitable institutions of higher learning. Faculties of mathematics, physics, chemistry, metallurgy, medicine, astronomy, and others are needed to reach the ambitious aims of the Commission. In 1968 the Commission had contracts with 229 colleges or universities whose work cost the Commission about $164 million, including construction and capital equipment, and excluding depreciation. (These costs are distinct from the operating costs of AEC laboratories listed earlier, several of which are operated by these universities.) By far the largest university contractor is Stanford which incurred contract costs for 1968 of $29.625 million. The list of the largest university contractors is as follows:

Stanford	$29.625(millions)
Princeton	16.612
M.I.T.	9.617
California	9.146
Harvard	6.792
Chicago	5.330

The figures for research expenditures and costs give little clue to the creative

---

258 Fulmer's case is reported in 86 *U.S. Patent Quarterly,* p. 116. For the second case, see *Spevak* v. *Strauss et al.,* 257 *Fed. Reporter* 2d 208, cert. granted U.S. Supreme Court, 358 U.S. Reports 871 (1958).

results reached. Many of the purely scientific results have a preliminary character. They must be verified and supplemented; sometimes they are contested and may even be recalled.[259] Undoubtedly, the University of California with its Lawrence Radiation Laboratory, established as long ago as 1936 as part of the University's Department of Physics, has been and still is the stronghold of basic scientific discoveries having an impact on fundamental aspects of physical science, chemistry, biology, and medicine. Of all eleven new elements (the so-called transuranium elements), nine were discovered at the University of California in Berkeley, and two by Berkeley scientists at the University of Chicago. These basic discoveries were substantially made with facilities owned by the AEC and in the course of contracts sponsored by the AEC. The results were, as a rule, presented in printed publications (except for the discoveries made before the end of World War II). Various awards and recognitions were received by these academic discoverers, from Presidential Citations to monetary compensation for patent rights (Fermi, Seaborg), from the Nobel Prize to membership in the exclusive societies and academies of the international community of science. The university scientists working on the basis of broad government research sponsorship usually do not think of themselves as "employees," but the concrete and tangible relationship with the sponsor is legally one governed by the statutory law and common law of employer-employee relations. This becomes a cold reality each time a university receives a government contract containing among many other provisions painstaking details regarding its obligation to report working results and "data" of various kinds and to assign title of all inventions, discoveries, and improvements made by faculty members and staff members in the course of contract work.

International Activities

The research efforts of the AEC go beyond the borders of the United States. Not only has the Commission invested research plants and equipment by contract to organizations in Puerto Rico, Canada, Japan, and some other countries, but an extensive program of international cooperation unites the AEC with foreign countries in the practical development of peaceful uses of atomic energy. As of June 30, 1968, the AEC had agreements with 33 foreign countries supporting and exchanging atomic energy research. In addition the European Atomic Energy Community (Euratom), administered in common by the six European Common Market countries is supported by AEC funds. Through fiscal year 1968 the Commission and Euratom had each spent over $25 million on research and development.

[259] In 1957, for instance, in Stockholm, element 102 (nobelium) was reported found by an international team of scientists, but further research failed to duplicate the Stockholm findings, since the half-life of the element is only three seconds.

AEC's research and development costs incurred in connection with these programs amounted to $2.6 million. The AEC has a further agreement with the International Atomic Energy Commission (IAEA) in Vienna which, however, has the function rather of control and sale or lease of materials. As of June 30, 1968, 19 power reactors built or designed in the United States had been sold abroad and about 352,000 kg of enriched uranium had been committed under bilateral agreements. A long-term toll-enrichment supply contract with a Swedish utility was signed in fiscal year 1967, and at the end of fiscal year 1968 similar contracts were negotiated with Euratom, Japan, and Switzerland. Most international research agreements of the AEC contain provisions regarding inventions made by employees of either contracting party (or government). These can be of practical importance to employed inventors, both in governmental and industrial service (and at universities) on both sides, but they are outside the scope of this book. The legal problems involved here are a matter of private and public international law which in recent years have had some attention.[260]

Invention and Patent Statistics

The statistics presented in Table 5.17 bring to light some interesting circumstances. The first observation is the dominating role of the industrial and university contractors of AEC as suppliers of new inventions. The second is the policy of the Commission to acquire full title, as it has done in the vast majority of these contractor invention disclosures. The third observation is that on only about 15 to 20 percent of U.S. applications are foreign patent applications filed. This may result in many foreign patent applications for the same inventions, however, since each invention may be filed in 7 or 8 countries. Of these, AEC files more than 80 percent, some are filed by contractors, and some by foreign governments.

The total portfolio of AEC-owned foreign patents at the end of 1965 numbered 2624. Foreign patents exist mainly in the United Kingdom, Canada, Belgium, Japan, France, Germany, and Sweden. Total number of foreign patents from contractors' inventions issued, to which government (AEC) has title, were 1542 (from 1963 through 1966).[261] Between 5 and 10 percent of contractor inventions disclosures are published rather than patented, but in many cases publication has been made prior to the decision to file a patent.

Invention disclosures by government employees in the atomic energy field are obviously few compared with inventions by contractor employees—only about 2

[260] See publications by Godenhielm, Helsingfors (Finland), and Troller, Lucerne (Switzerland).
[261] Statistics in this paragraph from *Major Activities in the Atomic Energy Programs,* January–December 1967, U.S. Atomic Energy Commission, January 1968, p. 236.

Table 5.17   Invention Disclosures in AEC Compared to Total of 15 Agencies F. Y. 1963 through 1966

	Fiscal Year	AEC	Agencies[1] (including AEC)
Total Invention Disclosures			
From government employees	1963	29	2,832
	1964	33	3,069
	1965	36	3,172
	1966	11	2,931
From contractors	1963	1,598	7,607
	1964	1,691	7,870
	1965	1,613	8,587
	1966	1,260	9,869
Employee Invention Disclosures			
For which government has title	1963	26	803[2]
	1964	30	955[2]
	1965	20	984[2]
	1966	0	1,179
For which government has license only	1963	3	304[3]
	1964	3	316
	1965	0	278
	1966	0	263
For which government has no rights	1963	0	64[3]
	1964	0	69
	1965	0	74
	1966	0	72
Total U.S. patent applications filed by agency	1963	1	1,245
	1964	4	1,444
	1965	4	1,315
	1966	2	1,246
U.S. patents issued to agency (government has title)	1963	1	539
	1964	1	550
	1965	6	711
	1966	2	737
U.S. patents issued to employee (government has license)	1963	0	241
	1964	0	250
	1965	0	312
	1966	0	231
Disclosures for which no patent applications are filed	1963	25	1,237
	1964	28	1,537
	1965	14	1,566
	1966	26	1,440
Agency decision to publish instead of patenting	1963	0	28
	1964	0	25
	1965	0	89
	1966	0	64

(table continued)

Table 5.17   (continued)

	Fiscal Year	AEC	Agencies[1] (including AEC)
Total Invention Disclosures			
Total foreign patent applications	1963	9	–
filed	1964	17	–
	1965	32	–
	1966	11	266
Contractor Invention Disclosures	1963	1,377	5,509
Determined to Be under	1964	1,961	6,475
Government Ownership	1965	1,508	6,175[4]
	1966	1,241	7,242[4]
Government leaves contractor	1963	60	60
with exclusive license	1964	80	80
(government has title)	1965	40	40
	1966	29	29
Disclosures for which contractor had option to acquire title but elected not to do so	1966[5]	0	2,961[3]
Patent applications filed by	1963	270	731
agency (government has title)	1964	232	834
	1965	315	980
	1966	284	924
Patent applications filed by	1963	23	1,742
contractor (government has	1964	26	1,527
license)	1965	23	1,315
	1966	21	1,777
No U.S. patent application	1963	1,082	5,354
filed	1964	1,653	5,945
	1965	1,235	5,639
	1966	1,112	6,267
Determination to publish	1963	100	177
instead of patenting[6]	1964	100	293
	1965	18	239
	1966	22	222
Total foreign patent	1963	363	385
applications filed[7]	1964	369	391
	1965	424	433
	1966	385	–

1 Other agencies included: CIA, USDA, NSF, VA, Commerce, Treasury, TVA, FAA, Interior, NASA, Army, Navy, Air Force.
2 Voluntary assignments from inventor to Department of the Army not included.
3 Almost entirely in Department of Defense (group of four figures).
4 Totals do not include figures for Department of the Army.
5 Not reported prior to 1966.
6 In many instances prior to patent recommendation a determination to publish has been made.
7 Only other applicants: NASA, Army, and Navy.

Source: *Annual Report on Government Patent Policy, June 1967,* Federal Council for Science and Technology.

percent of the latter. Government takes title to about 90 percent of the inventions of its own employees. In F.Y. 1963 through 1966 there were 109 government employee inventions at AEC, compared to 6162 from AEC contractors' employees (both prime and subcontractors).

Patent Licensing

The accumulated amount of unexpired AEC-owned U.S. patents available for licensing as of the end of the fiscal years 1963 through 1966 was large (more than 3600 by the end of 1966). The number of available foreign patents increased from about half the amount of the available U.S. patents to two-thirds of them. There are, however, about 1000 U.S. patents and patent applications already licensed in earlier years, as at the end of fiscal year 1965. Licenses directly granted by U.S. government to foreign governments or retained by contractors are not included in these figures. In January 1968, 661 nonexclusive licenses were retained by AEC contractors and 531 exclusive licenses in fields other than atomic energy. At the same time, 1350 nonexclusive licenses had been issued on some 600 government-owned unexpired patents and patent applications administered by AEC.

From the foregoing the following conclusions can be drawn in regard to employees making inventions during employment. The vast majority of inventions in the atomic energy field are made by the employees of contracting private industrial firms, universities, and other nongovernment institutions. Title of practically all inventions made in this context goes to AEC or other government agencies such as Department of Defense. The property incorporated in invention and patent rights, therefore, stays out of reach of the originating inventor.

Table 5.18 summarizes patent-licensing activity in AEC 1963–1966.

Three Board Decisions in AEC Invention Awards

Some cases of awards granted to inventors disclosing their inventions to the AEC pursuant to sec. 11a(2), (3), 11b and 11e(2c) of the first Atomic Energy Act of 1946 or sec. 157 of the amended Act of 1964 can be studied in the decisions of the AEC Patent Compensation Board. In three cases summarized here (of more than 36) the Board granted compensation for the use of inventions assigned to the AEC.

1. Cyril E. McClellan had independently designed an apparatus and a method of separation of isotopes and had disclosed these to the AEC. The separation method was the basis for a U.S. patent application. The Commission utilized apparatus incorporating the principle disclosed in research on isotope separation. In 1951 the applicant was awarded the sum of $7500 for his invention.[262]

2. In 1948 G. M. Giannini and Co., Inc., Pasadena, filed an application for just compensation and reasonable royalty for partial revocation of a U.S. patent for a process

[262] Cyril E. McClellan, Docket No. 4, November 20, 1951, 91 *U.S. Patent Quarterly*, 278.

Table 5.18   AEC Patent Licensing Activity[1]

	Fiscal Year	AEC	Total of 15 Agencies (including AEC)
1. Unexpired government-owned	1963	3,085	13,970
U.S. patents available for licensing	1964	3,299	14,670
	1965	3,524	15,979
	1966	3,681	16,539
2. Number of U.S. patents	1963	556	1,223
licensed, from row 1	1964	596	1,309
	1965	602	1,318
	1966	618	1,330
3. Unexpired foreign patents	1963	1,344	1,645
available for licensing	1964	1,703	2,057
	1965	2,086	2,475
	1966	2,324	2,808
4. Number of foreign patents	1963	2	4
licensed, from row 3	1964	5	8
	1965	5	8
	1966	15	18

[1] Excluding licenses reserved or accorded to contractors under their contracts.

Source: *Annual Report on Government Patent Policy*, June 1967, Federal Council for Science and Technology, pp. 46–49.

for the production of radioactive substances. The patent had been granted to seven atomic scientists, Enrico Fermi, Bruno Pontecorvo, Edoardo Amaldi, Oscar d'Agostino, F. Rasetti, Enrico Segré, and G.C. Trabacchi. Legal owner was G.M. Giannini and Co., Inc. The invention was based on work carried out by the seven inventors in Rome prior to 1934. The principle of the patent has been applied by the AEC in its atomic energy program. Pursuant to settlement, payment of $300,000 as a compensation for partial revocation of the U.S. patent was granted in 1953. (Giannini and Co. had in different actions claimed compensation of $1.9 million, $2.1 million, and $10 million.[263])

3. In 1955 the AEC approved a settlement of $400,000 to four atomic scientists, Glenn T. Seaborg, Joseph Kennedy, Arthur Wahl, and Emilio Segré, all formerly associated with the University of California, for the acquisition of all rights in certain inventions in plutonium separative processes developed prior to their engaging in research work in connection with government contracts. All rights in pending classified U.S. patent applications in the inventions were assigned to the Commission.[264]

The Patent Compensation Board seems not to have rendered any decisions for awards to inventors directly employed on AEC-sponsored research. The Hobbs case before the Board in 1963, reviewed by the U.S. Court of Appeals in April 1967,

[263] G. M. Giannini and Co., Inc. *et al.* Docket Nos. 2 and 11, July 31, 1953, *Atomic Energy Law Reports*, Chicago, No. 10,109.
[264] Glenn T. Seaborg *et al.* Docket No. 7, June 26, 1955, *ibid.*, p. 133.

covers compensation for an inventor employed as a consultant by the government contractor. The Court in this case made some important pronouncements regarding the scope of government rights to inventions in connection with federally financed research and on the *principia* position of an employee of a contractor, attributing to this inventor a right to just compensation. The case was remanded to the Board.

NATIONAL AERONAUTICS AND SPACE ADMINISTRATION

Legal Authority

NASA, the youngest of the agencies studied in this chapter, was triggered into existence by the launching of the first Sputniks by the Soviet Union in October and November 1957. Incited by these events, President Eisenhower and Congress agreed on the need to legislate and to organize new activities in space with greatest urgency. Proposals for broad research programs within the framework of a new civilian government agency were drafted, and a bill to create such an agency to coordinate a wide program "for research into problems of flight within and outside the earth's atmosphere, and for other purposes" was prepared at the request of the President through the Bureau of the Budget.[265] The only government organization in a related field, the National Advisory Committee for Aeronautics, assisted in the preparation, and hearings were held during the second session of the eighty-fifth Congress in 1958 before a House Select Committee on Astronautics and Space Exploration and a Senate Special Committee on Space and Astronautics (whose

[265] Reference will be made in this section only to papers treating legal aspects of NASA, especially those of inventions and patents. For basic information see: Gerald D. O'Brien and Gayle Parker, "Property Rights in Inventions under the National Aeronautics and Space Act of 1958," *Fed. Bar J.* 19, No. 3 (July 1959): 255 ff.; O. Brooks, "Ownership and Use of Space Age Ideas—A Legislative Approach," *Fed. Bar J.* 21, No. 1 (Winter 1961): 26 ff.; John A. Johnson, "Rights to Inventions under NASA Contracts," *Fed. Bar J.* 21, No. 1 (Winter 1961): 37 ff.; Wilson Maltby, "A Government Patent Policy for Employee Inventions," *Fed. Bar J.* 21, No. 1 (Winter 1961): 127 ff.; Wilson Maltby, "Need for a Federal Policy to Foster Invention Disclosures by Contractors and Employees," *Fed. Bar J.* 25 (Winter 1965): 32 ff. See also Harbridge House, *Government Patent Policy Study* (4 vols.) (Washington, D.C.: Govt. Printing Office, 1968); George Washington Univ., "Patent Policies of the National Aeronautics and Space Administration," September 1966; *A Review of NASA's Patent Program,* NASA Headquarters, March 1967; Wilson Maltby, "The National Aeronautics and Space Act of 1958 Patent Provisions," *George Washington Law Rev.* 27, No. 1 (October 1958): 49 ff.; Lawrence R. Caruso, "A Study in Decision-Making: The Patent Policies of the National Aeronautics and Space Administration," *Howard Law J.* 7, No. 2 (Spring 1961): 93 ff. In addition, various Congressional Hearings and Reports deal with NASA problems, including NASA invention policy. See especially committees on use of space as part of a general inquiry on government patent practices, committees under chairmanship of Senators Long and McClellan.

chairman was Lyndon Johnson). After repeated redrafting, a public law was enacted on July 29, 1958, to be cited as the "National Aeronautics and Space Act of 1958."[266] The law consists of 16 sections under three titles (sec. 101–103, sec. 201–206, and sec. 301–307). The statutory functions of the NASA were expressed in the Act (sec. 102c) stating that activities shall be conducted so as to contribute materially to one or more of the following objectives:

1. To expand human knowledge of phenomena in the atmosphere and space.

2. To improve the usefulness, performance, speed, safety, and efficiency of aeronautical and space vehicles.

3. To develop and operate vehicles capable of carrying instruments, equipment, supplies, and living organisms through space.

4. To establish long-range studies of the potential benefits to be gained from the opportunities for, and the problems involved in the utilization of aeronautical and space activities for peaceful and scientific purposes.

5. To preserve the role of the United States as a leader in aeronautical and space science and technology and to further application thereof to the conduct of peaceful activities within and outside the atmosphere.

6. To make available to agencies directly concerned with national defense the discoveries that have military value or significance and to help such agencies furnish appropriate information to the civilian agency established to direct and control nonmilitary aeronautical and space activities as to discoveries which have value or significance to that agency.

7. To further cooperation by the United States with other nations and groups of nations in work done pursuant to this Act and the peaceful application of the results thereof.

8. To most effectively utilize the scientific and engineering resources of the United States, with close cooperation among all interested agencies of the United States in order to avoid unnecessary duplication of effort, facilities, and equipment.

The new federal act defined the term "aeronautical and space activities" as follows:

1. Research into, and the solution of, problems of flight within and outside the earth's atmosphere.

2. The development, construction, testing, and operation for research purposes of aeronautical and space vehicles.

[266] P.L. 85–568, 85th Cong., H.R. 12575.

3. Such other activities as may be required for the exploration of space (sec. 103(1)).

The term "aeronautical and space vehicles" is defined as meaning "aircraft, missiles, satellites, and other space vehicles, manned and unmanned, together with related equipment, devices, components, and parts" (sec. 103(2)).

It is apparent from the sections of the Act cited here that it is intended to further an all-out effort to produce scientific and engineering results worthy of the new technology. James E. Webb, second head of the new agency, said in 1963 "NASA, like its predecessor NACA, is a research and development organization."[267] It is, therefore, appropriate to look for statutory provisions, in the NASA Act which regulate questions like determination of ownership and compensation for inventions made by individuals (usually scientists and engineers in the service of the agency or of its contractors). Section 305 with ten subsections regulates "Property Rights in Inventions," and section 306 with two subsections regulates "Contributions Awards" for any scientific or technical contribution to the NASA administration. These sections of the NASA Act represent an unprecedented piece of federal legislation. Their scope, interpretation, and practical administration are the main target of this study. The Atomic Energy Act of 1954 and the NASA Act are the only public laws containing specific statutory rules for rewarding inventors.

Legislative History of Patent Provisions   The unusual conditions surrounding the genesis of the NASA Act, especially the hurry of Congress to draft a law and to get it enacted, are reflected in the legislative history of its patent provisions. There seems little reason for the inclusion of the special patent provisions which became part of the Act. However, some prior federal laws and Executive Orders have a direct bearing on these new provisions. There is a relationship with sec. 831(d) of the Tennessee Valley Authority Act of 1933,[268] with sec. 1871 of the National Science Foundation Act of 1950,[269] and with sections 151–152 of the Atomic Energy Act of 1954.[270] These acts contain express provisions regarding ownership of inventions made in the conduct of assigned work or by virtue of and incidental to service as a (government) employee.

Hearings held by the House and Senate Committees working on the draft of the NASA Act in Spring 1958 touched the questions of patent rights. The clearest state-

[267] Keynote address, Feb. 11, 1963, to the Second NASA—Industry Program Plans Conference, Washington, D.C., Feb. 11–12, 1963. Reprinted in *Government Patent Policies* (Washington, D.C.: Gov't Printing Office, 1963), Appendix v, pp. 373 ff.
[268] 48 Stat. 58, 16 U.S. Code.
[269] 64 Stat. 154, 42 U.S. Code.
[270] 68 Stat. 919, 42 U.S. Code.

ment on the intent of Congress in enacting the "invention section" 305 was made by House Speaker McCormack who was the House Majority Leader and Chairman of the Select Committee of the House of Representatives considering the Space Act. In submitting to the House of Representatives the report of the conference committee which drafted section 305 on July 19, 1958, he spoke as follows:

The patent provisions of the House bill is the only part of the bill extensively revised by the conferees. . . . The review and the redrafting were wise. The select committee created a special subcommittee to study the matter, and after talking with many experts in and out of government arrived at a new version. The original [House-passed] patent provision was too closely patterned after the stringent requirements in the Atomic Energy Act which are not fully applicable to the space field. The substitute provision agreed to by the [House-Senate] conferees protects both the interests of the Government and affords enough flexibility to the Space Administrator to let him meet needs for preserving the incentives of the individuals and companies whose efforts it is public policy to encourage.[271]

Caruso[272] tries to reconstruct the impact Senator Clinton Anderson may have had on section 305 of the NASA Act. Anderson, for many years member and chairman of the Congressional Joint Committee on Atomic Energy, was known to have a critical attitude to private enterprise in government work. Similarities can be seen between the wording of the patent sections of the Atomic Energy Act and of the NASA Act.[273]

As to determination of the rights of Government in the inventions of its own employees, the criteria of Executive Order 10096 of 1950[274] are applied by NASA. Under sec. 305(a) of the NASA Act, invention disclosures by employees of NASA contractors are processed. NASA, applying the rules of the Executive Order, obtains entire title in those inventions made by government employees which "bear a direct relation to" or "are made in consequence of the official duties of the inventor." Finally, O'Brien refers to common law as providing valuable assistance in analyzing the intent of Congress. He mentions court cases dealing with the rights to inventions evolved in the performance of a research contract (with the Navy), or inventions by intramural employees, also delineation of "the positive and negative extremes" of employment.[275]

271 Cited in *A Review of* NASA's *Patent Program,* March 1967, p. 15.
272 Lawrence R. Caruso, "Study in Decision-Making," pp. 100–103, cited in footnote 265.
273 See O'Brien and Parker, "Property Rights," p. 262, cited in footnote 265.
274 15 Fed. Reporter 389.
275 O'Brien and Parker, "Property Rights," pp. 262–263. Recognized common law principles have been that a person employed to make an invention is bound to assign it to the employer, but a person having only general employment is not required to do so. On "middle ground" the so-called shop right doctrine has been developed. "In between the two

Size of NASA *Activities*

Working Funds   NASA has become the second most heavily financed government agency, surpassed only by the Department of Defense. No civilian government agency in the Western world has been allowed to spend so much money on creating a new technology (space technology) nor so much on expanding an existing one (aeronautics). NASA's research runs the gamut of the technological sciences. Since fiscal year 1959, NASA's first year, its budget has grown from a modest $339 million to $4.588 billion in fiscal year 1968, including $2.789 billion for manned space flight. In its first 10 years, NASA has spent approximately $25 billion on research. The share of funds not used for the conduct of manned space flight goes partly to basic scientific research, development and fabrication of spacecraft and instruments, and partly to other research in space technology.

NASA has some far-flung engineering projects it shares with the Atomic Energy Commission. These are classed as "advanced technology" and concern "hardware" not assigned to any specific space mission. One is SNAP (Space Nuclear Application Program). SNAP is part of a three-part program to obtain more efficient power for space flight, the other areas being chemical and solar power. The nuclear power program will rely on two types of mechanical systems for converting reactor heat into electrical power—a gas cycle turbogenerator system and an alkali-metal turbogenerator system.

Through fiscal year 1968 NASA has spent approximately $82,600,000 for the power conversion system, and AEC spent about $62,000,000 for the reactor research. Work on safety in nuclear flight is also being carried on in conjunction with AEC and Department of Defense.[276]

Two new engines, the M–1 liquid hydrogen–oxygen engine, and a 260-inch-diameter solid-propellant rocket engine, were discontinued in 1966 because of reductions in research funds. However, the F–1, H–1, RL–10, and J–2 engines are being modified and improved continuously. These are the engines that have been used in the launch vehicle programs.

The funds available for NASA research during a single fiscal year are larger than the total government budget of a country of the size of Sweden.

---

extreme limits lies the turbulent area which provokes the great mass of judicial controversy," as O'Brien aptly states.
276 1969 NASA Authorization Hearings before the Subcommittee on Science and Astro-
278 James E. Webb, Feb. 11, 1963. See footnote 267.

Working Facilities   Four major headquarters program offices are primarily responsible for planning and directing NASA's programs.[277]

The offices, with their field installations are listed here.

Office of Manned Space Flight

John F. Kennedy Space Center, Cocoa Beach, Florida.

Manned Spacecraft Center, Houston, Texas.

George C. Marshall Space Flight Center, Huntsville, Alabama.

Office of Space Science and Applications

Goddard Space Flight Center, Greenbelt, Maryland.

Jet Propulsion Laboratory, California Institute of Technology, Pasadena, California.

Wallops Station, Wallops Island, Virginia.

Office of Advanced Research and Technology

Ames Research Center, Moffett Field, California.

Flight Research Center, Edwards, California.

Langley Research Center, Hampton, Virginia.

Lewis Research Center, Cleveland, Ohio.

Electronics Research Center, Cambridge, Massachusetts.

Office of Tracking and Data Acquisition

No specific field center.

In addition to these major centers for technical programs, there are under the Office of Organization and Management an Office of Industry Affairs, an Office of Technology Utilization, and an Office of University Affairs (among others). Under the Associate Administrator is an Office of Policy and an Office of Program Plans and Analysis.

NASA's own research centers and installations are, naturally, an important source of employee inventions, discoveries, and improvements. But in the overall picture the facilities of a large part of U.S. industry and nonprofit institutions are NASA's most important source of technological progress. More than 90 percent of its work is done under contract with industry, universities, and private research organizations.[278]

More than 3000 (3246) contractor invention disclosures were reported to NASA during 1966, compared to 1526 in 1965.[279] According to NASA the increasing rate at

---

[277] *United States Government Organization Manual, 1964–1965* (Washington, D.C.: Govt. Printing Office, 1965), pp. 449 ff.

[278] James E. Webb, Feb. 11, 1963. See footnote 267.

which contractor inventions are reported is due to the fact that NASA programs have matured to the stage at which actual hardware or components are being built and tested and to the greater effort it is expending to identify new technology. Another factor may be the greater appreciation by contractors of NASA's patent program—a flexible one in which a contractor's privately financed position may be respected.[280]

Among the prime contractors of NASA in aerospace work are to be found practically all large domestic aircraft manufacturers such as Lockheed, Boeing, McDonnell-Douglas, and North American Aviation; the leading electrical and electronic manufacturers such as General Electric, Radio Corporation of America, Westinghouse Electric, Bell Telephone, Philco Corporation. The mechanical, metal, and chemical industries of the country are also represented. It would be impossible to enumerate all laboratories and research divisions which by means of contracts must be considered indirect NASA facilities, whose employees produce inventions and discoveries that pass to NASA and government ownership as soon as they are conceived and disclosed.

Manpower   When counting the employees occupied in R&D for NASA, the same dualism exists as in regard to working facilities. As of June 30, 1968, NASA had 34,641 employees, of whom 13,889 were engineers and scientists, 332 supporting professional engineers, and 4,977 supporting technicians.[281] But the great mass of employees contributing to the new space technology and science are bound in contractors' and subcontractors' research departments. In addition, a considerable number of NASA inventors are professors, assistants, graduate students, and staff members of university institutions and laboratories engaged in NASA research contracts. It is impossible to give an exact number of employees working indirectly for NASA, but Administrator James Webb in 1968 estimated 300,000. At the end of fiscal 1968, about 300 universities, engineering schools, colleges and other nonprofit institutions had NASA research contracts.[282]

Invention Rights of NASA Contractors

Section 305 of the NASA Act with its ten subsections establishes a policy which shall govern the division of rights in inventions made by employed inventors in the performance of NASA contracts. (Inventors employed directly by the agency, therefore, are not affected by this section.) This specific structure of law provisions

279 Federal Council for Science and Technology, *Annual Report on Government Patent Policy*, 1967, p. 43.
280 *A Review of NASA's Patent Program*, March 1967, p. 11.
281 Communication from Office of General Counsel, NASA, December 1968.
282 *Ibid.*

has not come about by chance. As the Administrator of NASA, James E. Webb, said in his keynote address of February 1963:[283]

In the National Aeronautics and Space Administration, basic in all of our decisions is the concept that we will encourage widespread participation in the space program by American industry to develop a broad base of competence in space technology by contracting out to industry the maximum possible amount of our work, and utilizing the competitive forces of the marketplace to obtain topnotch performance. More than 90 percent of our work is now performed under contract with industry, universities, and private research organizations. Inventions made by employees of NASA contractors are, therefore, the main source of inventions to the Agency and demand special regulations.

Section 305(a) talks about inventions made "in the performance of any work under any contract" (of NASA). Gerald O'Brien, a former Assistant General Counsel for Patent Matters of NASA, interpreted the term "work" as "work of the kind performed by research employees," not covering *all* inventions made under *every* contract entered into by NASA such as supply contracts for delivery of off-the-shelf items.[284] The NASA Act does not limit the "invention" concept technologically, but it can be interpreted to refer to all "research development or exploration work," an expression repeatedly used in section 305(a). At the time it refers to any invention having a relation to employment but in a specific type of contract.[285] The inventor must have been employed or assigned to perform this inventive work, or the work must have been within the scope of his employment duties. In this connection it does not matter whether the invention "was made during working hours, or with a contribution [by the government] of the use of Government facilities, equipment, materials, allocated funds, information proprietary to the Government, or services of Government employees during working hours."[286]

The second group of employed inventors, expressly cited by sec. 305(a) are those "*not* employed or assigned to perform research, development, or exploration work, but [where] the invention is nevertheless related to the contract, or to the work or duties he was employed or assigned to perform and was made during working hours, or with a contribution from the Government." All inventions within these two categories made by inventors employed by a NASA contractor become the exclusive property of the United States.

283 To the NASA—Industry Program Plans Conference, as cited in footnote 267.
284 O'Brien and Parker, "Property Rights," pp. 256–258.
285 The Atomic Energy Act, in contrast, requires in sec. 152 a specific type of invention under any contract with the Commission.
286 Similar criteria appear in Executive Order 10096 of 1950 for the determination of government rights in the inventions of all its own employees. See the Overview of this chapter.

The Administrator of NASA has at his discretion the right to waive "all or any part of the rights of the United States to such invention" made by any person or class of persons in the performance of any work required by any contract of NASA.

According to sec. 305(f) the Administrator may do so if he "determines that the interests of the United States will be served thereby." Each such waiver shall, however, "be subject to the reservation of an irrevocable, nonexclusive, nontransferable, royalty-free license for the practice of such invention throughout the world by or on behalf of the United States or any foreign government pursuant to any treaty or agreement with the United States."

To insure consistency of action and policy questions regarding waiver of invention rights, such proposals are referred to an Inventions and Contributions Board (ICB) established within the Administration which, after an opportunity for a hearing for each interested party, shall transmit its findings of fact and its recommendations for action to the Administrator. The Administrator, then, acts according to his discretion (presumably in accordance with recommendations made by his Board). The government agency is empowered by statute to make these quasi-judicial decisions as to (industrial) property rights independent of the courts. Another federal quasi-judicial institution created to make analogous decisions regarding *all* government employees is the Government Patents Branch.

In order to facilitate the decisions concerning acquisition of ownership to inventions made by employees of NASA contractors or release of ownership by waiver, sets of special rules and regulations have been issued by the Administrator. Special regulations have been issued three times since the establishment of NASA in 1958. The first time was on October 29, 1959, in order to implement basically the provision in sec. 305 (a)(2) and 305(f) authorizing the Administrator of NASA to waive all or any part of the invention rights belonging to NASA.[287] The second time was almost five years later on August 27, 1964,[288] and the third time on May 28, 1966, effective June 1, 1966.[289] The reason for a revision of the rules governing patent waivers was to put into effect the patent policy recommended by President Kennedy in his basic Memorandum on Government Patent Policy, of October 10, 1963.[290] The new NASA Patent Waiver Regulations of 1966 continue in their 17 sections (Part 1245, sections 100–116) to implement fully the President's patent policy and

[287] 24 Fed. Register 8788–8790, October 29, 1959, Title 14, Chapter V, Part 1201 "Patents," Part 1245 "Patents (Waivers)."
[288] 29 Fed. Register 12273–12275, August 27, 1964, Title 14, Chapter V, Part 1245 "Patents," Subpart 1 "Patent Waiver Regulations."
[289] 31 Fed. Register 7677–7679 No. 104, May 28, 1966.
[290] Discussed in the Overview of this chapter.

to improve procedures in carrying out this policy. Under the 1964 regulations waivers could be granted in three ways:

1. The NASA contracting officer applies the waiver to a contract prior to execution.
2. A petition for an advance waiver prior to invention identification is submitted to and acted upon by the ICB.
3. A petition is made to the ICB following identification of a particular, individual invention.

According to the 1966 waiver rules (sec. 104–106) all three types of waiver actions are now submitted to the ICB. Remembering the several NASA field centers with a number of contracting officers in different parts of the country, it is obvious that consistency of policy is better safeguarded in this way. In addition to these procedural changes which now involve the ICB in all waiver actions, the 1966 revision expands the so-called "march-in rights" which NASA retains whenever a waiver is granted. A new subsection (b of sec. 109) provides that waiver of title is voidable with respect to any particular invention if the patent claiming such invention "is held to have been used in violation of the antitrust laws in an unappealed or unappealable judgment or order of a court or administrative tribunal of competent jurisdiction." The provision is intended to underscore the consistency between NASA patent policy and the principles underlying the antitrust laws.

A new section (116) requires NASA to publish, at least annually, the following:
The findings and recommendations of the Board with respect to each petition for waiver.
Statistics regarding inventions made under NASA contracts and actions taken with respect thereto.
Decisions of the Board in each proceeding under section 108c.[291]

The reasoning of NASA (Office of General Counsel) concerning this new provision is as follows:

It was felt, first, that such publication would serve to alleviate any concern regarding NASA's waiver policy and its application to specific cases, and secondly, that decided cases would serve as precedent to guide future actions of the Board, and to provide contractors with guidelines useful in determining whether to petition for waiver in any given case.[292]

In connection with this statement the author feels compelled to emphasize here

[291] Section 108 refers to cases in which a contractor is given opportunity to show cause before the Board why he should not be required to grant a license as prescribed by the Administrator according to sec. 108a, subsections 1–3 in connection with the contractor's failure to bring the invention to the point of practical application or make it available for nonexclusive licensing.

[292] *Program Review Document,* Patent Program, prepared by the Office of General Counsel, April 1966, NASA, Washington, D.C., 1966, p. 37.

that finally a responsible government agency in clear-cut words expresses the
necessity and value, both to government institutions (here the NASA Invention and
Compensation Board) and to contractors, to publish findings and recommendations
of a government invention board. The purpose cited by NASA, that the provision
would serve as precedent to guide future actions of the Board and the second party
(contractors and their employees, and NASA employees) is undoubtedly in the public
interest. This new publishing policy of NASA should be followed by the Government Patents Branch (administered by the U.S. Patent Office), which works almost
in the same field on a government-wide basis. The motivation for such a policy,
as given by NASA and cited previously, applies to a still higher degree to the Government Patents Branch, on whose findings thousands of government employees
depend. The failure of this Branch to publish its determinations makes impossible
any guidance for future actions of the public and any attempts at consistency between the actions of different boards of this type.

Invention Rights of NASA *Employees*

The evaluation of section 305 of the NASA Act in the preceding section dealt with
NASA's right of ownership (title policy and title-waiver policy) of various results of
research work. However, this discussion was limited to results produced by the employees of outside contractors only. To do so was appropriate in view of the strong
emphasis laid by NASA administration on carrying out their objectives substantially
by U.S. industrial corporations and outside research institutions. There is, of
course, much parallel in-house research and development carried out by more
than 30,000 of NASA's own employees. The legal treatment of these employees of a
government agency as inventors is governed by Executive Order 10096 of 1950.
According to this Order, government (i.e., the respective agency) acquires title to
all government employee inventions made during working hours with contribution
by government and in direct relation to official duties. This Order is binding upon
NASA[293] and has been implemented through the issuance of a NASA *Management
Manual* instruction (3450.2) requiring each employee of NASA to submit disclosures
of each invention made under the three conditions cited in Executive Order 10096.
NASA patent personnel make an initial determination of rights as to ownership
and submit findings to the Government Patents Branch and the Commissioner of
Patents, whose decision is final, subject to appeal by an aggrieved employee to
the Commissioner. According to the Annual Report on Government Patent Policy,
issued by the Federal Council for Science and Technology, 1967, government acquires title in more than 90 percent of the inventions disclosed by employees.

[293] *Patent Policy, Program Review,* sec. D, May 11, 1963, NASA, Washington, D.C., D–9.

At the Office of Technology Utilization of NASA a matter of concern has been whether government employees owning their inventions themselves generally can undertake adequate promotion of their inventions, and if not, whether they may impair the transfer to industrial use of technological advances resulting from government work. NASA patent officials noticed (in 1963) that implementing Executive Order 10096 by instructions alone was inadequate for a successful program of utilization. Patent staff has been assigned at various NASA field centers—where most inventions of NASA employees are conceived—for personal monitoring.

The fact that in some circumstances NASA employees can keep personal ownership of inventions constitutes an incentive not generally available to government employees. The Federal Government Employee Incentive Awards Act of 1954 aimed to equalize treatment of government employees by setting up awards to all government employees making inventions.

NASA *Ownership of Data Policy*

The term "invention," as used in the NASA act and in the various rules and regulations connected with it, embraces more than patentable inventions. In practice many creative results in scientific research as well as engineering development have the character of technical know-how or data outside the field of patentable inventions. Such data are much broader in scope than technical data in connection with inventions, but both are of value to the employer.

What are the relations between these proprietary data and the employer-employee issue? In contrast to the field of patentable inventions there are no clear-cut legal or practical definitions that can be applied to this large and important field of working results. Executive Order 10096 governing the invention field does not expressly cover technical data and technical information produced by employees. The two main questions considered in this book in connection with inventions made by employees: allocation of patent rights and systems of reward, are to be approached quite differently when the inventions lie in the area of technical data and know-how. Some of the basic questions then are: In what ways are such proprietary data produced? By whom are they produced? Are they identifiable as the product of individual performance of an employee? These questions as a rule go unanswered.

Data are produced by an agency's own employees, by the employees of contractors (employees of industrial corporations, faculty and staff members of universities or other scientific institutions), or by individual grantees. To the author it seems that in many cases two main types of data produced by employees could be distinguished:

1. Data resulting from a single, direct, and specific order given by a supervisor or sponsor.

2. Data resulting from a step-by-step, long-time development accumulating into a total body of working material not created by single individuals but increased, enlarged, changed, or improved by many direct and indirect contributors over a long, indivisible period.

Only data of the first type can be allocated and rewarded. In the vast majority of cases all proprietary data produced by employees are the result of their employment and are therefore considered to be the full property of the employer by both parties. The reward ("consideration") for these products is the salary.

Conditions in the field of copyrightable items, such as books, manuals, films, charts, photographs, computer programs (protectable as copyrights since June 1965) are more specific. As a general principle of law, a copyright does not prevent others from using the information contained in an item protected by such right but prohibits only reproduction or copying of the specific form in which it is expressed, without permission. Moreover, under the copyright law one who hires another to write for him is deemed the copyright owner without formal assignment. Government agencies generally reserve the right to publish, reproduce, and use such items as are produced by any kind of employees, without limitations if they are first produced in the performance of a contract. For other data incorporated in a contractual performance but not first produced in connection with it, government keeps a nonexclusive royalty-free license to publish, use, and dispose in any manner, and it allows others to do the same. For authors of data who are faculty members or scientific staff employees of nonprofit institutions these regulations are of great importance.

The government through its different agencies is eager to identify these general technical data, to receive current reports about them, and to acquire title when possible. In the case of the Atomic Energy Commission and the National Aeronautics and Space Administration this right of acquisition is legally based on the AEC and NASA acts (Executive Order 10096 does not contain any provisions in regard to such data) and concerns their own employees. Acquisition of data from contractors and their employees is naturally based on specific provisions in the individual contracts.

Much effort, therefore, is put into a legal and administrative mechanism by government to "catch" the hundreds of thousands of reports, notes, diagrams, drawings, and descriptions written and drafted in the course of government-financed research. In dealing with contractors it was necessary for government agencies to introduce the "contracting officer," who is designated with the authority to enter into and administer contracts and make determinations and findings with respect thereto. This officer, or a representative (often the patent attorney or—in the case of NASA—the "new technology representative") must check continually the reporting obligations entered into by contractors' employees.

The legal rules applicable in this complex and important field are collected in procurement regulations, which are published by most government departments and agencies. By far the most important are those issued by the Department of Defense for its three branches, under the name Armed Services Procurement Regulations (ASPR), supplemented by an Army Procurement Procedure, a Navy Procurement Directive, and Air Force Procurement Instructions.

The needs for data at NASA are different from those of the Department of Defense, since NASA is concerned principally with research and development work where needs for data often are not determinable at the time of contracting. NASA, therefore, has developed its own set of procurement rgulations, issued in August 1964, and prescribing contract clauses and instructions with reference to section 305(b) of the NASA Act. Section 305(b) prescribes that each contract for performance of any work shall contain effective provisions under which the party shall furnish promptly a written report containing full and complete technical information concerning any invention, discovery, improvement, or innovation made. According to the NASA procurement regulations (referred to by paragraph here and on the following page) a "New Technology" clause obliging the contractor to report all "reportable items" must be included in every contract for one of the following purposes: Conduct of basic or applied research.

Design or development or manufacture for the first time of any machine, article of manufacture, or composition of matter to satisfy NASA specifications or special requirements.

Development of any process or technique for attaining a NASA objective not readily attainable through the practice of a previously developed process or technique.

Testing or experimenting with a machine, process, or technique to determine whether the same is suitable or could be made suitable for a NASA objective (9.101–2).

Certainly NASA administration cannot be accused of ambiguity when defining what kind of working results of its contractors should be reported. The obligation of written reports is supplemented by the requirement that contractors shall conduct frequent periodic reviews of the work performed, and, of course, extend their own obligations in this respect to any subcontractor (9.101–4 (II)).[294] NASA has, in addition, worked out a number of procurement regulations for "nonprofit institutions of higher education" and "nonprofit institutions whose primary purpose is the conduct of research" (9.101–5) and "nonprofit institutions including educational institutions" (18–9.204–51).

NASA defines data as follows (9.201):

Data means writings, sound recordings, pictorial reproductions, drawings, or other graphic representations and works of any similar nature whether or not copyrighted.[295]

Proprietary data means data providing information concerning the details of a contractor's secrets of manufacture, such as may be contained in but not limited to his manufacturing methods or processes, treatment and chemical composition of materials, plant layout, and tooling, to the extent that such information is not readily disclosed by inspection or analysis of the product itself and to the extent that the contractor has protected such information from unrestricted use by others.[296]

Other data means all data other than "proprietary data" and includes information suitable for operation, maintenance, or testing, and *descriptive data,* providing design specifications which, although not including proprietary data, may nevertheless be adequate to permit manufacture by other competent firms.

Against this background of definitions NASA has developed a so-called "data requirements clause" for its contracts to serve its special needs (9.202–1(e)). The data shall be furnished by the contractor upon written request of the Contracting Officer of NASA at any time during contract performance (or within one year after final payment). These data cover, for example, engineering drawings to enable reproduction or manufacture of any equipment or items furnished under the contract; data to help government technical personnel understand any equipment, items, or process developed under the contract and furnished to the government; including drawings and other technical data used in the development, practice, and testing of any process required under the contract, or with the development, fabrication, and testing of prototype models. The contractor shall also furnish a report of all studies made in planning the work and in developing background research

---

[294] The term "working results" does not include financial reports, cost analyses, and other information incidental to contract administration.

[295] This definition is similar to the definition of confidential information or know-how as used in industrial employment contracts or in court cases in this field.

[296] Definitions are not quoted word for word.

for the work, and a copy of design studies, parameter and tolerance studies, specifications, test results, and any other technical information.

The clause as sketched here is not used in all NASA contracts. It can be modified and even deleted by negotiation with the Contracting Officer of NASA.

NASA also reserves "rights in data" in contracts concerning products which can be of a rather nontechnical character. The administration may order the production of motion pictures, musical compositions, sound tracks, translations, adaptations, and the like, including drawings or other graphical representations. Productions of this kind are sometimes called "subject data" and shall be the sole property of the government, if first produced in the performance of a contract for such production. The contractor shall not publish or reproduce such data without the written consent of the government. For all data of a type not first produced or composed in the performance of such contract but incorporated in the work furnished, the contractor agrees to grant to the government a royalty-free, nonexclusive, and irrevocable license throughout the world to publish, translate, reproduce, deliver, perform, use and dispose of, in any manner. This license covers also the right of the government to authorize others to use these data in the described manner (9.204–2).

The "rights in data" provisions show that NASA makes use of the provisions of the copyright law, according to which one who hires somebody to write for him is copyright owner without formal assignment. It is no secret that the question of rights in data to be furnished by contractors under a contract with the government constitutes a major controversy between government and industry.[297]

Also universities are bound by special provisions in NASA contracts for basic or applied scientific research regarding inventions subject to reporting obligations of sec. 305 of the NASA Act (9.101–5). In other special research contracts (NASA Form 419S) nonprofit institutions, including educational institutions, are bound by a clause saying that the government "may publish, reproduce and use, without limitation, drawings, studies, research notes, technical information, and other scientific data resulting from this contract." The government may also inspect or otherwise evaluate the work performed by the institution (sec. 9.204–51).

Dissemination of Research Results and Working of Inventions

One other area of NASA invention and patent policy has an impact on the relations of the Administration with employed inventors. NASA has from the beginning considered itself to have a broad mission and definite obligation to collect and dis-

[297] O'Brien in *Patent Policy, Program Review*, sec. D, NASA Headquarters, May 11, 1963, D, p. 45.

seminate to industry and the public all technical innovation (not of a purely military or otherwise restricted nature). This policy is similar to that of both the Department of Agriculture and of Health, Education, and Welfare. The NASA administration has also resorted to manifold measures through the years to realize a closely related principle "that the Government has a continuing interest in making sure that inventions produced in the course of research and development work financed with public funds are actually put to practical use."[298] In the patentable invention field NASA has adopted a waiver and licensing policy which is based on the principle that any private person—whether a government or contractor patentee or an outside licensee of government-owned rights—who acquires NASA-financed inventive results be required to prove that he is trying seriously to exploit the invention within a reasonable period of time prescribed. As a sanction all NASA licenses are revocable if the licensee fails to use his continuing best efforts to put the invention to work. The time period allowed for working varies with the type of license granted by NASA but is in many cases as short as the end of the second year after the issuance of a U.S. patent.

The statutory basis for this policy is the function given to NASA administration in sec. 203a(3) of the Act to "provide for the widest practicable and appropriate dissemination of information concerning its activities and the results thereof" and sec. 305g authorizing the Administrator to promulgate regulations specifying terms and conditions upon which licenses of any invention for which the Administrator holds a patent on behalf of the United States will be granted for practice by any person. Such patent-licensing regulations were issued by the Administrator on October 26, 1962.[299] The principle of compulsory working of all NASA inventions licensed in any way runs like a red thread through the regulations. The license agreements granted by NASA contain obligations for the licensee to furnish annual reports of all activity and progress in developing the invention to the point of commercial utility and in making the developed invention available to the public (Regulations sec. 1245.207c(1)). The revocation clause included in license agreements specifies that the license will be revoked "if the licensee at any time shall fail to use his best efforts to develop at least one embodiment or process of the invention to the point of commercial utility and to offer the benefits of the development invention to the public in accordance with normal business practice" (Regulations sec. 1245.207c(3)).

[298] John A. Johnson, "Rights to Inventions Under NASA Contracts," p. 48.
[299] 27 Fed. Register, 10446–10448, Title 41, Chapter V, Part 1245, "Patents," Subpart 2, "Patent Licensing Regulations."

In addition, NASA in 1962 promoted the efficient and immediate transfer of new technology by establishing an Industrial Applications Division, now called Office of Technology Utilization, to identify and disseminate to industry new ideas and innovations arising from space research that might have commercial applications.

As of June 30, 1968 almost 13,000 invention disclosures from NASA contractors had been received. (See Table 5.21.) This new technology is made available for wide industrial use in a variety of ways, for example, by issuing hundreds of single-page technical briefs. Computer-based regional centers take care of most of the dissemination for the general economy. One of the first such centers, the Applied Research Application Center (ARAC) at the University of Indiana had 48 member companies in 1966 who pay a substantial portion of the cost to obtain ready access to NASA technology. Four regional centers of this type now serve 134 companies, which pay annual membership fees for the service. Further, almost 10,000 copies of the NASA Star (*The Scientific and Technical Aerospace Reports Abstract Journal*) are distributed to over 4000 recipients.

Considerable significance is also given by NASA administration to the channeling of important research results through its university contractors. Studies have been made to develop closer relationships between university-based scientists and engineers and those in the industrial community. NASA Administrator James E. Webb reported in 1963[300] that NASA university facilities have grants provisions that say essentially: "The university will undertake, in an energetic and organized manner, to create a broadly based multidisciplinary team to explore mechanisms whereby the progress and research results achieved in space science and technology may be fed into the industries and segments of the economy with which the university normally has close relations."

NASA tries to maximize utilization of the technology developed under its research programs irrespective of patent ownership. On the other hand, it seeks to extend commercial use of its own patents as part of the public domain.

Statutory Award Provisions

NASA management has implemented the Federal Awards Act through the issuance of NASA *Management Manual* Instruction (3450.2). The Instruction says that all employee inventions, for which the Office of General Counsel (at NASA headquarters in Washington) determines that an application for a U.S. patent should be filed, shall be considered for an award. However, authorization to seek patent protection is used more selectively than this implies. The decision to file an application for a

300 Address to the Second NASA–Industry Program Plans Conference.

patent is made only after technical evaluation by in-house NASA officials and after a search to determine patentability.

NASA has also undertaken a program through its Office of Technology Utilization to have employee inventions published. This is supposed to offer "some modicum of protection and serves to disseminate the technology."[301]

In the NASA Act the following provisions are found for awards. The Act dedicates a complete and detailed section (306) to the subject matter of "contributions awards." The only similar case in federal legislation is in the Atomic Energy Act of 1954, which in sec. 157, subsections (b) and (c), regulates eligibility for and standards to determine compensations, awards, and royalties for persons making inventions. Section 306 of the NASA Act authorizes the Administrator of NASA upon his own initiative or upon application of any person to make a monetary award, the amount and terms of which are determined by him. The subject matter of awards is "any scientific or technical contribution to the Administration which is determined by the Administrator to have significant value in the conduct or aeronautical and space activities" (sec. 306(a)).

This wording has to be interpreted and the policy applied by the NASA Inventions and Contributions Board, established in accordance with section 305(f).

This Board consists of seven members, including a chairman, a vice chairman, and an executive secretary. The Board's procedure is to make monthly reviews of all contributions produced by NASA employees and contractors' employees, to evaluate the disclosed inventions and innovations, and award compensation for such disclosures. The Board also reviews requests for waivers by contractors and makes recommendations to the NASA Administrator (but the Board plays no part in requests for title by NASA's own employees, which are heard by the Government Patents Board). The Board prepares quarterly presentations of awards amounting to $1000 or more at NASA headquarters in Washington and annual honor award ceremonies for a large number of federal and nonfederal awards. Taking into consideration the enormous amount of research going on continuously in NASA's research centers and in the divisions and laboratories of thousands of the country's largest industrial corporations and universities working for NASA, the activities of this unique government inventions board and its general experiences arouse considerable interest when studying government employee invention policy. The NASA Board has developed sets of sophisticated rules of practice.

Contributions eligible for awards under the NASA Act need not be patentable but

301 *A Review of* NASA's Patent Program, D, p. 14.

include patentable inventions. They must be determined by the Administrator to have significant value in aeronautical and space activities. The persons entitled to apply for awards include not only NASA's own employees or employees of NASA contractors, but any person, even of other nationality.

In determining awards the NASA Act prescribes that the following criteria shall be taken into account:

1. The value of the contribution to the United States.
2. The aggregate amount of any sums expended by the applicant for the development of his contribution.[302]
3. The amount of any compensation (other than salary received for services rendered as an officer or employee of the government) previously received by the applicant for or on account of the use of such contribution by the United States.[303]
4. Such other factors as the Administrator shall determine to be material (sec. 306a).

The Invention Board uses awards evaluation questionnaires to implement the general guidelines of sec. 306a of the Act and has developed about ten main areas for a fair evaluation of invention disclosures. In view of the interest in such evaluation methods, not restricted to government invention administration, the more important questions asked by the NASA Inventions and Contributions Board in its evaluation questionnaire are reproduced here (abridged by the author).

1. General identification of program, project, or area to which the invention pertains.
2. Possible use of the invention: operational, experimental, or contemplated; extensive, considerable, little, or none; as disclosed, slightly modified, or considerably changed?
3. Is the invention likely to be retained or replaced?
4. Functions of the invention: Are the assigned functions accomplished in all, many, or some respects? Is their degree of difficulty great, moderate, or small? Has their accomplishment been proved?
5. Type (category) of invention: Is it a new device or a modification of an existing device? Is it a large overall arrangement, a small overall arrangement, a subarrangement, or a component?
6. Type of personal contribution made by the employee. Was the challenge to the

---

[302] Here, obviously, industrial employees and university research employees have to report the assistance given by their employers to make the contribution possible.
[303] This covers awards received by an employed inventor from his own employer under any award system in industry and awards granted under The Federal Government Employees Incentive Awards Act, to a government-employed inventor.

inventor exceptional or routine? Did the inventor's performance exceed or equal expectations?

7. Field of technology of the invention. Is the field highly developed, moderately developed, or undeveloped? On the technological level of accomplishment, does the invention represent a basic finding, a new approach, or a modified approach?

8. Use of invention in other government applications. Can it be used as is or only when modified? Is the extent of such use large, moderate, or small? Would it serve the same purpose in other government applications? A similar purpose? A different purpose? Does the demand for such use exist? Is it likely or unlikely?

9. Use of invention in other commercial applications. Can it be used as is or only when modified? Is the extent of such use large, moderate, or small? Is the purpose of such use different, similar, or identical? Does the demand for such use exist? Is it likely or unlikely?

10. Savings from invention. What monetary savings can be expected in labor or materials?

According to Board rules, each applicant for award is afforded an opportunity for an oral hearing before the Inventions and Contributions Board of NASA. Testimony will be under oath or affirmation. Strict rules of evidence do not apply, but "reasonable grounds of materiality, relevance, and admissibility will be observed." The contributor as well as NASA may be represented by counsel, but hearings are held with a minimum of persons. Verbatim transcript of the hearing is provided by the Board. Such hearings are expensive and time-consuming; there have been no more than a half dozen or so in NASA's history.

If no hearing is requested, the Board will evaluate the contribution on the basis of the material submitted. Recommendations of the Board to the NASA Administrator reflect the views of the majority of the Board members. (Dissenting views may be transmitted with the majority opinion.[304])

According to sec. 306b of the NASA Act the Administrator shall, further, apportion any award if more than one applicant claims an interest in the same contribution. A legal condition to receive any award from NASA is that the applicant surrender all claims to compensation (other than the award) for the use of the contribution or any element of it at any time by or on behalf of any foreign government pursuant to any treaty (or agreement) with the United States (sec. 306b(1)).

Finally, the NASA Act expressly limits the right of the Administrator to make

[304] 32 Fed. Register 6273, No. 77, April 21, 1967, "Inventions and Contributions," Subpart 1, "Awards for Scientific and Technical Contributions."

monetary awards exceeding $100,000 unless he has transmitted a complete report concerning amount, terms, and basis for the proposed award to the appropriate committees of Congress, with allowance of thirty days for possible objection (sec. 306(2)).

Regarding cash awards to NASA's own employees, the NASA Act of 1958 was implemented by administrative regulations and procedures in its *Management Manual* of June 27, 1961, reprinted December 14, 1968.[305] The instruction refers only to awards for patentable inventions, made by any of its employees. Determination as to whether an invention is patentable is made by the Office of General Counsel, NASA Headquarters in Washington.[306] This Office further determines whether an application for a U.S. patent is filed; if so, it refers the invention to the Inventions and Contributions Board for award consideration. If application has not been filed, the Office returns the invention to the employee with the suggestion to submit the invention under the suggestion plan of the NASA Incentive Awards Program.

Types of Awards

Awards for patentable employee inventions are made in accordance with expected tangible savings or intangible benefits. The Board, at its own discretion, grants cash awards in amounts up to $100,000, and recommends those over that amount for the approval of the Administrator and Congress, as previously stated.

Regardless of the special individual cash awards just discussed, a minimum of $50 is paid for each invention of an employee, for which a patent application is filed by NASA. The awards usually range from $250 to $500. NASA presents each cash award with a letter setting forth the basis for the award, signed by the Chairman of the Board (if $1000 or less) or the Administrator (if more than $1000). Awards are presented in appropriate ceremonies. Field installations report awards each fiscal year to NASA Headquarters, where all reports are consolidated in an Annual Incentive Awards Program report required by the Civil Service Commission.

In addition to the above discussed cash awards "morale" awards are also given. They are usually awarded for performance merits other than inventions and may take the following forms:

Medals for exceptional scientific achievement, for outstanding leadership, excep-

---

[305] See also a Policy Directive of that date, 33 Fed. Register 18574–18575, Dec. 14, 1968; and 32 Fed. Register 11263, "Awards for Reported Technical and Scientific Contributions—NASA and Contractor Employees."

[306] This can only be a preliminary decision on patentability which is regulated by the U.S. Patents Act.

tional service, public service, length of service.

Certificates of appreciation, for engineering research performance, management, planning, community relations development.

Trophies, especially to the astronauts.

Honorary titles, such as "Outstanding Young Engineer."

Presidential Citations, "for an outstanding contribution to greater economy and improvement in Government operations" under the Federal Incentive Awards Program.

NASA awards are given to individuals or to groups of individuals. Geographically, they are widely distributed. Awards go to those in NASA's own research centers and launching and tracking stations, to employees of other government agencies and contractor firms, and to staff of universities and research institutions all over the United States.

In addition to the standard award for an invention on which patent application has been filed, NASA has a $25 minimum award for new technology, familiarly called the "Tech" award. Inventions considered for the Tech award need not be patentable, may be only a concept (not reduced to practice) and may or may not be classified. They are judged by the Technology Utilization Office.

Also, as in other federal agencies, NASA's in-house employees are eligible for awards under the Government Employees Incentive Awards Act of 1954. These may be in the order of "suggestions," carrying a $10 gift, or they may be considerably more important, with higher amounts given.

Tables 5.19 and 5.20 show that by the end of the first half of fiscal year 1969 NASA had awarded in all $465,893 to 1724 persons.

It is clear from this description of NASA awards that contributions may cover wide fields of intellectual effort. The statutory definition in sec. 306a of the NASA Act is, as mentioned before: "any scientific or technological contribution to the Administration, which is determined by the Administrator to have significant value in the conduct of aeronautical and space activities."

Individuals, groups or divisions, and research centers receive awards by NASA management for such partly noninventive contributions in the following areas, or in combinations of the areas.

Outstanding executive management of finance, personnel, legislative affairs, recruiting and research.

Flight records (of research pilots).

Outstanding publications in the aerospace field.

Space medicine results.

Various fields of technology, such as propulsion systems, sounding rockets, vehicle control, computers for data recording and reproducing.

Part of any active employee award policy, governmental or nongovernmental, is the *publicity* given. NASA has developed a current and extensive program serving as incentive to award recipients. The quarterly and annual ceremonies of award presentations at NASA Headquarters (or in the White House for a Presidential Citation) have already been mentioned. Award checks to contractors' employees are often forwarded to the contractor for a presentation ceremony, but the checks are always made out to the individuals. In connection with these events programs are printed presenting the names of employees distinguished in this way, their education, a detailed description of the invention made, the amount of award given, and perhaps even the savings realized by the invention. Award-winning inventions are often displayed, and the inventors are available for detailed explanation. To the extent that awards emanate under the Government Employees Incentive Awards Act current publicity is taken care of by the Civil Service Commission in their numerous pamphlets and illustrated reports published annually. The daily press, local and nationwide, as well as house organs of corporations and university publications all take part in the publicity for employed scientists and engineers distinguished by awards. From the point of view of public recognition, NASA-employed inventors seem to be rather favored.[307]

Award Statistics

Table 5.19 shows monetary awards recommended by the Inventions and Contributions Board and granted by the Administrator of NASA over the period 1959–1969. Awards authorized by the Space Act were made to NASA in-house employees and NASA contractor employees; in addition the incentive awards authorized by the Government Employees Incentives Awards Act are shown. Table 5.20 shows the $25 minimum Tech Awards, as authorized by an amendment of 1968, and the $50 minimum awards to NASA employees or contractors' employees submitting an invention disclosure on which a U.S. patent application is filed.

The largest award granted to date went to a husband and wife team, Francis and Gertrude Rogallo, in 1963. The Rogallo's were responsible for two inventions which arose from their hobby of kite flying and have to do with the concept of flexible, packageable wings. These led to large-scale developmental work on

[307] As are the employees of the Atomic Energy Commission and the Department of Defense.

Table 5.19   NASA Monetary Awards, 1959–1969

Fiscal Year	Space Act Authority		Incentive Awards Act Authority	
	Number	Dollar Amount	Number	Dollar Amount
1959	0	0	0	0
1960	0	0	1	200
1961	1	3,000	0	0
1962	1	5,000	26	7,560
1963	12	57,100[1]	110	33,525
1964	9	20,000	110	48,050
1965	5	7,400	80	31,650
1966	4	4,500	108	55,750
1967	11	14,600	150	55,558
1968	22	12,825	197	63,100
1969[2]	23	12,400	38	12,100
Grand Totals	88	$136,825	820	$307,493

[1] Includes Rogallo Award for $35,000 (see preceding text).
[2] First-half of F.Y. 1969.

Source: NASA Office of the General Counsel.

Table 5.20   NASA Technology Utilization and Patent Application Awards, 1968–1969

Fiscal Year	$25 Tech Awards		$50 Patent Application Awards	
	Number	: Amount	Number	Amount
1968	518	$12,850	41	$2050
1969[1]	247	6,175	10	500

[1] First half of F.Y. 69.

Source: NASA, Office of the General Counsel.

paragliders, carried out by NASA and the military services. The paragliders are expected to make possible the recovery of expensive rocket boosters, which now are lost when jettisoned because of friction damage upon reentering the atmosphere.

The Rogallo's were awarded $35,000 for their two inventions, because they had developed them on their own initiative and expense, patented them, and reduced them to practice, and indeed they had found nobody interested when they first approached government agencies in 1950.

Listed in Table 5.20 are the minimum cash awards introduced in 1968.

Compared with the total number of 34,641 employees of NASA, of which almost

14,000 are scientists and engineers, the number of award recipients seems rather modest. In this connection it must be stated that these purely quantitative considerations may not give a fair and impartial picture of the inventive effort of employees working for the NASA space programs, since one single invention may balance the importance of most of the others together. The award figures should also be compared with the figures showing invention disclosures from employees, patent applications filed, patents issued, and patent waiver petitions received and granted. An attempt will be made in the next section to give some statistics illustrating these four areas.

The minimum $50 award to each employee reporting an invention on which a patent application is filed is usual in government agencies and in private industrial corporations, but the NASA Patent Program booklet adds, "The awards granted are often many times this amount."[308] No further details are given. The report of 1967 makes another short statement regarding contractors: "Plans are currently being formulated to make the awards program more meaningful to NASA contractors, for example, by recognizing the cooperation of a contractor in the NASA Technology Utilization Program with the recognition of a Space Act Award."

General Invention Statistics

Total invention disclosures received by NASA up to June 30, 1968, were 15,809. Of these, 2878 were from NASA employees and 12,931 from NASA contractors' employees. These and other figures are reported in Table 5.21.

The patent-licensing program of NASA is "designed to encourage early use of inventions covered by NASA-owned patents and patent applications." The NASA Administrator has broad licensing authority to implement the intent of Congress "that the traditional incentives afforded by the patent system were to be utilized in making the results of NASA research activity available to benefit the entire economy, including use in commercial products."[309] The licensing policy of NASA, therefore, differs somewhat from that of other government agencies. Through fiscal year 1968, as Table 5.21 shows, 128 nonexclusive licenses were granted and 3 exclusive licenses. The former figure includes some licensing of patent applications, which does not occur, as a rule, at other agencies.

Invention Waiver Policy

NASA places strong emphasis on transfer of its newly created technology from space-related applications to nonaerospace purposes by waiving its commercial

308 *A Review of NASA's Patent Program,* March 1967, p. 8.
309 Both quotes from *A Review of NASA's Patent Program,* March 1967, p. 29.

Table 5.21   NASA Invention Disclosures, Waivers, and Licenses, as of June 30, 1968

Invention disclosures from NASA employees	2,878
Invention disclosures from contractors' employees	12,931
U.S. patent applications filed by NASA for employee inventions	959
Patent applications filed by NASA for contractor employee inventions	502
U.S. patents issued to NASA for employee inventions	412
U.S. patents issued to employee for employee inventions	82
U.S. patents issued to NASA for contractor inventions	193
Total petitions for waiver received (for individual inventions)	598
Granted	423
Denied	93
Withdrawn	49
Pending	5
(Total for blanket waiver of all inventions received)	458
Granted	199
Denied	193
Withdrawn	61
Pending	5
Nonexclusive licenses granted by NASA for patents or applications for patent	128
Exclusive licenses granted by NASA for patents	3
Total NASA-owned patents available for license	692

Source: NASA, Office of General Counsel, December 1968.

invention rights to contractors. Applicants for such waivers are all types of contractors—industrial corporations and universities and other nonprofit institutions. It may happen that the contractor does not want the commercial rights he would get under the waiver, but the contractor's employee does want them. In this case, if the employee can show that he is capable of commercializing his invention, he will get two waivers, one directly from NASA and one from the contractor.

The total number of waivers granted by NASA is modest, however. As of June 30, 1968, there had been (over the life of the agency) 598 petitions for waiver of individual inventions received, with 423 granted and 93 denied. (The others were either withdrawn or pending at the end of this fiscal year. See Table 5.21.) There had been 458 petitions for blanket waiver of all inventions received, with 199 granted and 193 denied.

When commercial rights are waived to a contractor, NASA retains "march-in" rights. Under these rights NASA can compel a contractor to grant a license to a responsible applicant, even though he has had a waiver, under the following circumstances:

1. If the contractor has failed to work the invention or make it available to the public over a period of three years from time of issuance of the patent.

2. If the invention is needed to fulfill health needs.

3. If the invention is required for public use by government regulations.

In addition the waiver may be voided if the patent is used in violation of the antitrust laws or if the contractor fails to file a patent application, to furnish copies of patent applications filed, to formally confirm the rights reserved by government, to grant licenses as NASA may require, or to submit reports on the use he is making of the invention (all within a reasonable margin of time).[310] As of June 30, 1968, NASA had used "march-in" rights in 30 cases. In almost all of these the waiver was voided because the contractor did not file or prosecute a patent application. In no case was compulsory licensing invoked.

NASA has always considered that its waiver policy is in line with the antitrust laws, because it furthers commercial use of the invention with all that this implies of competitiveness. However, during the costly period of development the contractor receiving the waiver is protected. The Patent Program booklet presents some selected cases of the waiver policy in operation, which serve also to exemplify the kind of inventions NASA contractors' employees have made.[311] Five examples are given here.

A temperature transducer was waived to Ball Brothers Research Corporation. This firm had developed an ultra-sensitive transducer to be used as a temperature probe in the Orbiting Solar Observatory B-2 satellite. With the protection of the patent, Ball proceeded to invest $25,000 in improvement and adaptation of the transducer for industrial use.

A moisture-removal system, replacing a conventional pump, was developed by Allis-Chalmers for the fuel cell system in the Saturn boosters. Water vapor is formed in the electrochemical fuel cell and must be drawn off. Allis-Chalmers used a specially treated asbestos membrane, lightweight and reliable, and is now promoting sales of the improved fuel cells in university and other research laboratories.

Magnetic memories improvements. One error that creeps into magnetic memories arises from a residual direction of magnetization that develops gradually. Univac, a division of Sperry Rand, found a means to alternately pulse a plated magnetic wire in a direction opposite the one desired for recording, prior to recording, and thus do away with this bothersome residue.

The other inventions waived to Univac under an advance waiver have to do with a storage matrix of exceptionally high bit capacity and a means for regulating the

[310] *A Review of NASA's Patent Program,* March 1967, pp. 23–24.
[311] *Ibid.,* pp. 42, 44, 39, respectively.

red current pulse in nondestructive readout. A sizable part of Univac's several million dollar engineering and development program of its 9200 and 9300 computer models was directed toward commercialization of these inventions.

Remarks on NASA *Patent Provisions*

What is the general impact of NASA's Patent Policy on the flow of discoveries and inventions, whether from intramural employees or from the employees of the thousands of industrial and institutional contractors? Criticism has been raised by members of Congress, industrial corporations, and private legal experts and is addressed both to the established invention and patent policy of the administration and to the statutory provisions on which this policy is based.[312] These studies, however, do not evaluate whether or to what extent creative personnel have been stimulated to disclose inventions.

Wilson Maltby pointed out in an early stage of development (1958) that inventive contributions to NASA programs may come in comparable number from two different government sources,[313] from NASA's own government laboratories (including research done there by NASA's predecessor, National Advisory Committee for Aeronautics, NACA) or from employees of the large laboratories of the three armed service branches within the Department of Defense. Maltby cautions that two different standards of rules must be applied in such case, one for inventors employed directly by NASA and one for inventors employed indirectly through loan or agreement with another agency, usually the Department of Defense. The DOD's patent title policy differed from NASA's, which had to rely substantially on the strict rules of E.O. 10096 of 1950. However, the former NASA Counsel for Patent Matters, *Gerald O'Brien,* writes that there is no such dual standard inasmuch as the Department of Defense and other government agencies, including NASA, are all governed by the provisions of Executive Order 10096, and the determinations of all government agencies must be approved by the Government Patents Branch.[314]

In the opinion of *James E. Webb,* former NASA administrator, there is no lack of cooperation between NASA and other agencies, even when statutory status and functions are different. In his keynote address of 1963[315] he says, "Thus, we work

[312] Two recent studies are: "An Evaluation of the Patent Policies of the National Aeronautics and Space Administration," prepared for NASA by the Dept. of Economics, George Washington Univ., *The George Washington Law Rev.* 27, October 1968; and *Government Patent Policy Study,* Harbridge House, Inc., Boston, 1968; for other studies see footnote 265.

[313] "NASA Patent Provisions," p. 53, as cited in footnote 265.

[314] O'Brien, *Patent Policy, Program Review,* pp. 54, 58.

[315] Cited in footnote 267.

in close cooperation and collaboration not only with the Department of Defense, but with many other agencies such as the Weather Bureau, the Communications Satellite Corporation and the Atomic Energy Commission in order that what we do will meet their needs." Final consistency of government employee invention policy, therefore, depends on the determinations of the Government Patents Branch as coordinator.

From Congressional quarters, Congressman *Overton Brooks,* from Louisiana, former chairman House Committee on Science and Astronautics, had a number of objections regarding government invention title policy. Although he was speaking of government policy in general, he was thinking especially of NASA, since he wrote after the first few years of experience with the NASA patent provisions:

So far as inventions are concerned the people have delegated to Congress the power to secure to inventors the exclusive right to their discoveries. The Constitutional delegation does not itself contemplate the issuance of patents to the Government, nor is it contemplated that the Government or the people should have the free use of the inventions conceived and patented under the guarantees provided. This is true whether the scientific research from which the inventions arise is financed or subsidized by the Government, by private enterprise or by the inventor himself. . . .

Yet while the Congress gave the Administrator [of NASA] the power to waive title in the public interest, it failed to give him any criteria for determining what was in the public interest. . . .

Some say that "team research" has replaced the "garret inventor." As a matter of simple logic, is it really possible for a "team" to conceive anything in the nature of a mental act or mental concept? The individual human mind is the agency through which conceptions must necessarily take place. It is true that through team effort the conception of one mind may be enlarged and improved upon by others, but, in the final analysis, the germ of an idea must originate in a single mind. It may sometimes be crossbred with other ideas arising in the minds of other individuals. The ultimate product of the mental effort of one or more individuals will usually yield a plurality of inventions.

It is the brain children of the inventors of our country which our Constitution gave to the Congress responsibility for protecting. In addition, we must stimulate the inventive mind by preserving the incentive to create. If we take away the incentive to invent, we can expect our standard of living to fall with all of the implications of such an occurrence. . . .

But I believe we tend to break faith with our inventors when we insist upon the Government taking title to their inventions. This is "Indian giving." If the Governments grants a patent, it should honor its obligations under the patent without trying to find excuses for taking back the very grant which was the inducement offered the inventor to extend his best efforts on behalf of society.[316]

[316] "Ownership and Use of Space Age Ideas—A Legislative Approach," *Fed. Bar J.* 21, No. 1 (Winter 1961): 26 ff.

Brooks makes here a passionate defense for the incentives and rights of the individual employee as inventor and interprets the Constitution as in agreement. Having in mind the opposite attitude of Senator Long which led to the enactment of more than a dozen federal laws giving government full title to all inventions of contractors' employees made with support of any government funds, the statements of Congressman Brooks, made in connection with NASA patent policy in 1961, earn attention. According to the author a reasonable solution lies between these two standpoints. To find this solution one must look at the practical situation in each case and state the contribution made in terms of money, facilities, working hours, know-how furnished on both sides as well as the experience and education of the inventor, before allocating the invention as a property right. A number of industrial nations have accepted this method of "rights determination," with satisfactory results.

In 1962 another colleague of Brooks, Congressman *Emilio Daddario,* as chairman of the Subcommittee on Patents and Scientific Inventions of the House Committee on Science and Astronautics, transmitted a report on "Ownership of Inventions Developed in the Course of Federal Space Research Contracts" containing findings and recommendations on the basis of 14 days of hearings and testimony from 37 witnesses.[317] This Subcommittee and its chairman were trying for a change of the patent provisions (sec. 305 and part of sec. 306) of the NASA Act, doing away with subsections (c), (d), and (e) of sec. 305 (the so-called flushing provisions) and substituting for the government title policy of sec. 305(a) a policy emphasizing title to prime contractors, who would then license the government. The report gives a valuable summary of arguments in favor of and against changing NASA's existing patent provisions.

The main arguments for a change of provisions are as follows:

A shift to the license policy will speed the space program.

A license policy will result in easier contracting and improved research.

Contractor ownership increases incentive and lowers costs.[318]

A NASA license policy would accord with traditional concepts.

Unless title remains in private hands the invention will not be used commercially.

Arguments against changing NASA's patent provisions are these:

Patent ownership should follow federal financing.

Government ownership promotes flow of information.

[317] 87th Cong., Second sess., April 5, 1962 (Committee Print), Washington 1962.
[318] To this point the Subcommittee says, "Common sense and an understanding of human nature, though, tell us that men respond to material rewards." *Ibid.,* p. 12.

Government title policy may allow recovery of expenditures.

Title retained by government will discourage monopoly.

The Subcommittee, further, remarks that industry has seen fit to make substantial changes in its patent relationships with employees and with subcontractors. Efforts to learn what "research industries" may be doing along these lines has shown, according to the report, "that the research industry of the United States today is markedly liberalizing its incentive plans for employees, its royalty-sharing plans for employees, and its handling of the ownership of inventions where subcontractors are concerned."[319] The Subcommittee offers no evidence for the truth of this statement. [The author has tried to come closer to hard facts in this field.]

The report finishes, following a review of all testimoney and evidence furnished to the Subcommittee since August 1959, with a bill intended to liberalize sec. 305 of the NASA Act, following the general philosophy set out in the National Science Foundation Act of 1950.[320] The bill was reintroduced by Daddario, on January 6, 1965, in the House of Representatives, and referred to the Committee on Science and Astronautics.[321]

In the Subcommitte's report the former Assistant Attorney General, Lee Loevinger, through Subcommittee member William F. Ryan (New York), announced a separate view strongly supporting invention title policy as set forth in sec. 305 of the NASA Act, especially "in view of serious anticompetitive consequences for enterprises dependent on that technology," in case of modification.

In connection with this dissenting view Loevinger made the following generalization about employed inventors:

Where an inventor has not devoted his own independent efforts and resources to the development of an invention but has used his employer's resources, it is a well-known common law doctrine that any resulting invention is the property of the employer. Similarly, when the contractor has used Government money or facilities, or both, and has been compensated by the Government for his efforts, is there a justification for giving to him also the title to the invention? In that case it is the expenditures by the public which have made the invention possible,

[319] The other half of "patent relationships with employees," the invention assignment policy, is not mentioned in the Subcommittee's Report.
[320] This Act (64 Stat. 154, 42 U.S. Code sec. 1871) contains patent provisions that each contract or other arrangement . . . which relates to scientific research shall contain provisions governing the disposition of inventions produced thereunder in a manner calculated to protect the public interest and the equities of the individual or organization with which the contract is executed, and further, that no officer or employee of the Foundation shall acquire, retain, or transfer any rights, under the patent laws of the United States, in any invention he may make in connection with performing his assigned activities and which is directly related to the subject matter thereof.
[321] H.R. 1683, 89th Cong., 1st sess.

and the public should get what it has already paid for. The patent philosophy should not apply to this type of case.[322]

Finally, criticism from industrial corporations regarding NASA patent provisions seems to be plentiful. Naturally, in many cases responsible managers of manufacturing and research corporations are unwilling to attack government policy in print. Still, they express misgivings about acquisition of exclusive title by government to all inventive results from NASA-financed contracts. Some companies also hold that employees working exclusively on government contracts lose the incentives and benefits offered by the employer to all employees who assign their invention rights to the company. They argue that where ownership of rights accrues to government, government should also be responsible for benefits. In some firms employees making inventions which go automatically to government receive monetary awards and other benefits in the same way as other inventing employees.

Employers complain also about the costs arising for such payments when they get no property right in return. To this last argument it must be stated that the Armed Services Procurement Regulation (ASPR) gives carefully designed compensation in connection with supply and research contracts referring to cost items of this kind. ASPR is generally used by NASA with the exception of the section relating to patents. Under 15–205.6, "Compensation for Personal Services" (last edition, 1 March 1963) it is expressly stated that "compensation for personal services includes all remuneration paid currently or accrued, in whatever form and whether paid immediately or deferred, for services rendered by employees to the contractor during the period of contract performance." This includes, but is not limited to, among many items: "bonuses (including stock bonuses)," "incentive awards," "employee stock options," and "management employee incentive compensation plans." In addition, under 15–205.26, "Patent Costs" (last edition, 1 April 1965) in the Contract Cost Principles and Procedures of ASPR it is stated:

Costs of preparing disclosures, reports, and other documents required by the

[322] Report of Subcommittee on Patents and Scientific Inventions, p. 26. The statement, made in this sweeping fashion, does not help us to a solution of the complex problems of employee inventions in modern industry. European law has tried to find some legally based policies which take into account the varying situations under which employee inventions are made and how they should be distinguished. Different solutions are offered in Great Britain, Germany, Italy, Sweden, and other industrial nations such as Canada or Japan, but all try to strike a fair balance between the expenditure and other help given by the research sponsor or employer, on the one hand, and the inventing employee and his identifiable efforts, on the other hand. See Study No. 30, Senate Subcommittee on Patents, Trademarks and Copyrights, Washington 1963.

contract and of searching the art to the extent necessary to make such invention disclosures, are allowable. In accordance with the clauses of the contract relating to patents, costs of preparing documents and any other patent costs, in connection with the filing of a patent application where the title is conveyed to the Government, are allowable.

These procurement rules seem to indicate that complaints about costs arising for contractors in connection with employee inventions the title of which is owned by government, are substantially unfounded.

Evaluation of Government-Employer Invention Policy

As we saw in the Overview of this chapter, serious thought on the creation of a nationwide federal invention and patent policy goes back about 30 years. Criticism of patent policy and suggestions for change are as old as the policy itself. The discussion gained intensity as government became more and more engaged as sponsor of research and development on a large scale after the end of World War II. Particular impact on the general discussion of federal patent policy was made by the Atomic Energy Act of 1954 and the National Aeronautics and Space Act of 1958, both containing extensive special provisions on inventions and patents applicable to their new fields of technology. Senator Russell Long's periodic forays injecting "title provisions" for employee or grantee inventions into more than a dozen federal laws concerned with scientific and engineering research and frequent Congressional hearings preceding such legislation "kept the pot boiling."[323] (The more important of these federal laws are listed on page 212 of this chapter.)

Consistent with the subject matter of this book, my evaluation of employee patent policy is restricted to those parts of the policy which concern the relations of *employers*—in this chapter government agencies, departments and commissions—in their capacity as employers, sponsors, and contract-ordering principals of their own employees, grantees, or contractor's employees. These relations have been evaluated in the light of the specific studies of four government departments as presented in the preceding part of this chapter. All conclusions and suggestions for future policy here presented are made with a strong feeling of caution. Some of the great obstacles to recommendations for an efficient uniform government-employer policy toward inventive employees and grantees are, of course, the heterogeneous premises with regard to the type of people representing employees, on the one hand, and with regard to the objectives of their performance (inventions, discoveries, improvements, suggestions) on the other hand.

[323] Research by Caruso, Forman, Holman, O'Brien, Rossman is mentioned in footnote 1 of this chapter.

An efficient, reasonable, and uniform policy must be guided by an acceptable compromise between the public interest, the employers' interests and the employees' (and grantees') interests. The employees range from those with a minimum of professional training, education, and experience up to research and science leaders with a lifetime's accumulation of those assets. It will be easier to establish common policy rules for assignment, release, or other allocation of inventions produced by all employees than to establish rules for reasonable awards, because the merit of reaching certain research results or other valuable performance and the usefulness of these results to the employer when expressed in dollars and cents will rarely be more than a rough guess. These difficulties, however, should not prevent us from establishing an improved employee-invention policy. Any chosen system is open to future improvement.

Some conclusions and suggestions of the author of this part of the book are the following:

1. Uniform regulations regarding disclosure and submission of all inventions made by government employees within their assigned job responsibilities and official duties should be drafted and brought to the knowledge of all employees upon starting the job. (Executive Order 10096 is not uniformly applied by all departments and agencies, neither is its text presented to all employees.)

2. Determination to patent, publish, or keep secret patentable employee inventions should lie with the employing agency, but the employee should have the express right to appeal these determinations to a special court or board.

3. Similar regulations should apply to important technical, commercial, and educational information, data, trade secrets (for industrial employees), know-how, and other nonpatentable results produced by government employees and employees of government contractors.

4. Decentralized handling by individual employing departments and their subordinate divisions and bureaus to determine allocation of employee inventions and to give awards seems appropriate.

5. Copies of all rights and awards determinations should be collected and surveyed by a central federal office, suitably the Civil Service Commission or the Department of Justice. Summaries of such determinations should be printed regularly.[324]

6. A special federal court or board should be established as a place of appeal for all determinations (regarding both allocation and awards) made on departmental

---

[324] Provisions must be made for exemptions from publication in special cases of military secrecy or substantial commercial competitive interest.

level. It must be open to both parties. Chairman of such a court should be a federal judge assisted by assistant judges or a jury with competence in law, government personnel administration, and engineering. Procedure of the court should be public, free of cost, and without compelling the parties to choose legal advisers (lawyers) to represent them.[325] The Government Patents Board at the Patent Office must be dissolved, and its rulings must be published without delay. The functions of this new special federal court have to be defined in order not to interfere with ordinary federal courts, especially in regard to contract litigation. Existing Atomic Energy Commission and National Aeronautics and Space Administration invention boards should become divisions of such a court.

7. A division within a suitable government agency (for instance, the Civil Service Commission or the Bureau of Standards) should be established to advise government employees on all legal and commercial questions regarding government inventions. This organization should be staffed by experts in patent prosecuting and in patent licensing and selling, both domestic and foreign.[326] The Division's work would be similar to that of the nonprofit invention-exploiting institutions such as Research Corporation and Battelle Memorial Corporation.[327]

8. A federal periodical should be started, reporting regularly the pending and decided law cases regarding allocation of inventions and awards for inventions of government employees. Surveys and annual statistics based on the extensive material accessible at the Award Office of the Civil Service Commission and the Federal Council for Science and Technology (Patent Advisory Panel) should be published. Invention incentive and patent plans introduced by industrial corporations and faculty and staff invention regulations at universities should be reported. Important developments in law, government and industry policy in the field of employee-invention management from other countries and international institutions are to be reported.[328] Abstracts of individual case histories of employee inventions of general interest should be presented in some way, perhaps in brochures like those of the Civil Service Commission or like NASA's annual incentive award programs.

325 The latter point makes it possible to the employee as the weaker party economically and in law competence to freely choose personal legal advice.

326 A great number of such experts have been working for many years in various government agencies, especially in the branches of the Department of Defense, AEC, NASA, and the Patent Office.

327 Foreign examples: National Research Development Corporation in London, INFOR and EFOR in Sweden, now Swedish Development Corporation.

328 These should include work prepared by the International Labor Office, the *Bureaux Internationaux pour la Protection de la Propriété Intellectuelle* (BIPPI), and the *Association Internationale pour la Protection de la Propriété Industrielle* (AIPPI).

9. Government experiment stations should be established to carry out developing and prototype work for government employee inventions not developed and used by the government and owned by the employee.[329]

10. Employees of foreign corporations or institutions supported by U.S. government funds or foreign grantees of U.S. government should normally leave title to U.S. patents to the U.S. government but should be allowed to keep rights in their own country.[330]

11. Inventive capacity of government employees (as shown by granted patents, published articles, awards and prizes) should be officially accepted by government employers as substantial merit for promotion.

12. In industrial research supported by the federal government or in cooperative government-industry research both governmental and industrial employees should receive the same invention awards and honors (not excluding "special treatment" by their direct employer irrespective of the individual award). The same should apply to state government employees, who now are sometimes bound by special provisions of state laws regarding state-supported research.

Other Evaluations of Patent Policy

The reader may be interested in the following summary of three evaluations of patent policy by other authors. I have chosen for this purpose the work of Wilson Maltby, analyzing invention award policy under the NASA act, the work of Robert A. Solo, raising objections to the general "invention procurement" system of government with special regard to NASA activities, and W. W. Eaton's experience with the basic problems of determining distribution of patent rights jointly developed by federal and private funds.

Wilson Maltby[331] is one of the few authors no longer in active government service who has taken the pains to analyze federal employee award policy as an essential part of employee patent policy. He wrote at an early stage of patent policy development, in 1961. Robert Solo's work is a more recent example (1966) of a comprehensive analysis of various aspects of government patent policy touching the practical (managerial) and legal relations between employees making inventions in government service (and those in the employ of contractors)

[329] Such a suggestion was made by former Assistant Attorney General Wendell Berge in his book *Cartels—Challenge to a Free World* (Toronto: Progress Publishing Co., 1945), but it was never adopted.
[330] In Germany and Sweden this is, in fact, a national legal obligation.
[331] Wilson R. Maltby, "A Government Patent Policy for Employee Inventions," *Fed. Bar J.* 21 (Winter 1961).

and their employers.[332] Finally, an article of William W. Eaton published in July 1967[333] deserves serious attention, in part because the author until 1966 had been Deputy Assistant Secretary of Commerce for Science and Technology and had served as Chairman of the Patent Advisory Panel of the Federal Council for Science and Technology. Eaton's criticism is mainly directed against a federal patent policy asking for total title ownership of all inventions produced under government-sponsored research regardless of the size of the government share.

Wilson Maltby directs his objections against the Government Employees Incentive Awards Act of 1954 and its effects. He considers that this Act has not become a strong force for encouragement of innovations, discoveries and inventions for these reasons: (1) The authority delegated to the Civil Service Commission is "primarily local rather than under a (central) board." (2) The vast majority of awards granted by the Commission are for trivial rather than significant contributions, and evaluation often is made by industrial relations officers rather than by scientific or patent personnel. (3) Military personnel are not included. (4) No provision is made for awards to employees of government contractors.

To the objections raised by Maltby the following can be said: (1) The emphasis of the Civil Service Commission on local rather than centralized administration of the federal award systems is intentional and in agreement with the needs of large, differentiated, and widespread government activities. Strict uniformity—which could be attained by a central board—is not considered necessary by the Commission. (2) Regarding importance and quality of rewarded contributions, the federal system is aimed at all types of improvements. The judges who evaluate contributions of a scientific character are most likely the top officials of a number of agencies; rewards for the mass of suggestions which emanate from nonprofessional personnel are made by personnel officers. (Whether there is any assurance that the contributions get to the right people for review is not known.) Since all contributions can be rewarded irrespective of patentability, patent experts are not absolutely necessary for evaluation but could undoubtedly in many cases give good advice and judgment. (3) Military personnel are excluded by law. They come under rules administered by the Department of Defense. (Military inventions made

332 Robert A. Solo, "Patent Policy for Government-Sponsored Research and Development," IDEA 10 (Summer 1966): 143–206.
333 William W. Eaton, "Patent Problem: Who Owns the Rights?" *Harvard Business Review* (July-August 1967), reprinted in *Congressional Record* (Senate), July 24, 1967, Suppl. pp. 10093–10097.

by civil government employees are included in the federal incentive system,
however.) (4) Finally, in regard to the lack of express provisions for employees of
government contractors, there is no rebuttal. This seems, indeed to be a draw-
back.[334]

When talking about award systems aimed at government employees as inventors,
it must be mentioned that "any officer, enlisted man, or employee of the government" formerly had a special privilege in the patent field. The "Non-Fee Act" of
1883 as amended in 1903, 1928, 1946, 1952, and 1965 (22 Stat. 625 c. 143) entitled
all federal employees to obtain a U.S. patent on inventions without payment
of fees and also meant that patent applications would be handled by government
patent personnel without cost for prosecution on the basis of Executive Order
10096, sec. 2(a). Two conditions were attached to this privilege: (1) that the head
of the department or agency certify that "the invention is used or likely to be used
in the public interest" and (2) that government "may manufacture and use the
patented invention for government purposes without payment of royalties."[335]
The Non-Fee Act was repealed in July 1965.

Robert Solo presents in his article the evolution of patent policy for government-
sponsored R&D with specific regard to NASA's experience and makes certain policy
recommendations for promoting outflow and transfer of technology. For purposes
of this book only the part of Solo's paper which treats promotion of inventiveness
and creativity (of employees) in contracted-for R&D is relevant.

Solo finds the (well-known) gap between the inventions actually reported by
employees and the level of inventiveness that might be expected. He states two
grave weaknesses (which he considers due to the structure of government procurement) in relation to encouraging creativity in research and development and the
disclosure of invention. One is the lack of managerial motivation to encourage
inventiveness in government-sponsored R&D beyond fulfillment of contractual
obligations. The other is "indirect reporting of invention." At NASA, Solo asserts,

[334] The fact that employees of government contractors in some cases have received awards
by their own employers does not alter this judgment. By including some obligation to
contractors to reward employees making valuable inventions or improvements in connection
with government contract work, the government reward system could be extended to private
enterprises on a limited justifiable scale. Employers are already reimbursed for payments
of this kind under cost-plus arrangements in government research contracts.
[335] The proper scope of the government license under the Non-Fee Act was subject to
litigation and was discussed at length both in the majority opinion and in the dissenting
opinion of the Dubilier case, *United States* v. *Dubilier Condenser Corp.*, 289 U.S. Reports
178, 201–203 (1933). See also 28 U.S. Code sec. 1498(a) which bars recovery from patents for
government use in a great many circumstances.

reports from inventors arrive "through intermediaries who are motivated to minimize disclosure." He suggests that a more direct relationship be cultivated between company inventors and the government office (here NASA) responsible for promoting inventiveness. Awards and commendations should be made by the agency to company employees, for instance, by engaging them for short periods as consultants to the agency ("inventor fellowships") to advise applicability of their contributions for government purposes. Such leaves of absence of course should carry job security. Solo also stresses the urgent need to understand the role of the university in producing and advancing technology. He makes a series of recommendations to improve government's policy of waiving commercial rights to inventions when the inventions are contractor-made. He wants to wake industry from its statistically proved "general, pervasive, sometimes absolute indifference" to ask for exclusive commercial rights for inventions made under government R&D contracts. Finally, he asks for integration of agency patent policy with a more general policy for facilitating the commercial application of technologies developed for government use.

In a chapter presenting problems of inventiveness and disclosure of inventions by government employees (still NASA) and contractors' employees, Solo makes a number of valuable and provocative statements. He sees three categories of personnel involved in the output and disclosure of invention: research personnel, research supervisory staff, and company (agency) management, and asks himself whether there may be significant differences affecting invention and disclosure depending on whether R&D is carried on in government centers or in private companies. For example, it has been contended that government scientists devote too much time to evaluation of proposals, project supervision, monitoring, and training of contractors. Men engaged in such tasks of course have less opportunity to invent than "bench researchers." Solo suggests that, on the other hand, government scientists may have opportunity to "contract out" routine work and perhaps reserve the more invention-provoking elements for themselves.

Research supervisors are assigned the job of seeing to it that projects are promptly and adequately carried out. Inventions per se are never prespecified as R&D contract requirements. Creative ideas of employees may even be in conflict with the objective of supervision which is to fulfill the specifics of an assignment to the letter as quickly as possible. Activities such as exploring and developing the general values of an R&D employee invention so that others can comprehend, appreciate, and apply it would require time and effort aside from current assignments. Development and reporting of inventions may be considered a diversion of the employee from the R&D task at hand. According to Solo then, supervisors, whether in-house or extramural, would seek to minimize these inventive "excursions and diversions."

Top management may either encourage or discourage inventiveness and disclosure of inventions. Solo finds that government management (NASA) is clearly motivated to encourage these activities, as evidenced by the fact that a high official is assigned to every NASA research center to encourage the flow of disclosed inventions. The administration also has an incentive system, examining inventions and rewarding inventors. On the other hand, the private company interest in inventiveness of employees working on government contracts is equivocal. The company has a defensive advantage in the disclosure of contract inventions, since publishing or patenting such inventions protects it against later infringement suits. Exclusive commercial rights to contractors may encourage disclosure, but this motivation is discounted as of small significance in practice. It is asserted that quantity or quality of the company's inventive contributions is not rewarded under existing government R&D procurement and that this circumstance militates against promotion and disclosure of employee inventions under government contracts. Disclosed inventions are said to be quickly assimilated and freely used by competitors for government business. Further, the contractor may be motivated to siphon off inventions or researchers who have proved their creativity, from government-supported programs to R&D on company account. No matter where conceived, inventions born in the research programs of the contracting firm serve to strengthen the company's position in its bargaining with government or in its relationships with its rivals. According to Solo, enlightened management might also promote invention as incident to its efforts to increase overall creativity within the company. Inventors who had established themselves as possessing "exploitable capabilities" would be rewarded. The employee would enhance his self-interest by establishing a reputation for inventiveness whether he is engaged on government contract work or company research.

Solo also considers it a grave weakness of government R&D procurement that company employees do not report directly to government, at least in the case of NASA, but to company research supervisors. From the latter, inventions are "infiltrated upward" to patent lawyers and are disclosed only at the volition of company management, where too often there is indifference or even antipathy to disclosures.

Many more facts are undoubtedly needed as a basis of unbiased overall criticism and of recommendations for improvement of the employer-employee relation in this field. Solo's attempts to point out weaknesses in the procedure of "procurement" of employee inventions is valuable and should stimulate additional studies.

In his paper of July 1967 William Eaton gives first an overall survey of the history of government patent policy similar to that in the Overview of this chapter, except that he does not take into regard the extensive basic work done by and presented to the Attorney General in 1947.

As the first chairman of the Patent Advisory Panel created as a consequence of the Presidential Policy Statement issued on October 10, 1963 (the "Kennedy Memorandum"), Eaton is deeply familiar with the objective to make government patent policy of all agencies more consistent and to develop sound principles for the allocation of patent ownership of inventions arising from federally financed research policy. Eaton reminds the reader of what he calls the chaotic situation prevailing in 1963, which led to serious inconsistencies in contract terms, such that different government agencies could present entirely different patent clauses to the same contracting company for similar types of research work in the same field. According to Eaton, "The Policy Statement (of 1963) is not an Executive Order, but it does have the force of persuasion of the White House."

Eaton continues, basing himself on the summary of the 1966 report on Government Patent Policy of the Federal Council for Science and Technology, to say that there is ample evidence that the President's Policy Statement has been effective, that it has achieved its stated objectives reasonably well, and that the practical operating experience under its principles has been satisfactory. The policy has been effective in two respects: in bringing patent practices of federal departments and agencies into closer harmony and in obtaining a greater degree of protection of the public interest through provisions for compulsory licensing. There is no evidence that the discretion given the agencies in the Policy Statement has been exercised other than consistently with its purposes. The statistics of the 1966 report also show that agencies which prior to the Policy Statement seldom made use of clauses acquiring or reserving the right to acquire title to inventions on behalf of the government are now doing so, at least in those situations recommended for such action in the Policy. Eaton is strongly in favor of having Congress legislate without delay along the lines of the Presidential Policy Statement of 1963. As the best basis for such legislation, he recommends the McClellan bill of 1966 (S. 1809) which was intended to enact into law most of the features of the Presidential Policy Statement. The Judiciary Committee reported the bill favorably on August 16, 1966, but it never reached the Senate floor and died with the 89th Congress. On January

10, 1967, Representative Emilio Q. Daddario introduced H.R. 458 which is basically identical to the McClellan bill of 1966. Final legislative action is still out of sight. Eaton directs his severest criticism against what he calls "a small, but extremely vocal and emotional minority who seem to feel that the enactment of any kind of legislation other than an ironclad across-the- board title policy will be roughly equivalent to the end of the world." He refutes this group and their suggested patent policy in detail, saying that their position is that regardless of the extent of support in any kind of research contract or grant, the government must always take all patent rights, any other procedure being a "patent give-away program."[336]

Eaton's opposition to the "absolute title" policy group seems justified. Compulsory assignment to government of *all* contractor inventions irrespective of the extent of government support cannot be in the public interest; it chokes the incentive of the grantee to invent and improve. It is also in disaccord with general principles of commerce, according to which there should be a balance between the worth of goods or services furnished and the price paid for them by the customer.

Most relevant to this book is Eaton's criticism directed against "extremist arguments" concerning employee invention policy practiced by industry as compared with government patent policy. It has often been said in support of a complete title acquisition policy by government that business enterprises insist that their own employees sign away in advance all patent rights to the employing corporation. Therefore, the analogy goes, these same companies should be equally willing to sign away to the government all rights to inventions developed under contract. Eaton holds that such a superficial view overlooks some basic differences between the two situations. First, an employee in a corporation is generally on a full-time basis, whereas the contracting corporation is essentially on only a part-time schedule, hired on government contract to do a specific job. Individuals agreeing to the assignment of rights expect full support in the way of facilities as well as some degree of permanence of employment—conditions that seldom hold for independent government contractors (and rightly not, in the American competitive system, according to Eaton). Most inventive individuals would not make such assignment of future patent rights to a corporation for temporary or part-time employment.[337] A second crucial flaw in the analogy is the contention that a

[336] Eaton does not mention the name of Senator Russell Long as the most influential representative of this policy.
[337] Government R&D contracts, however, pay more than the amounts required to pay the salaries of the R&D personnel actually assigned thereto. The comparision is rather to

corporation like an individual is a member of the free enterprise system and can, if it owns a patent, "respond to the basic incentives of the patent system for the ultimate benefit of all the employees and stockholders," as the government cannot. The argument is questionable. A main tenet of the free enterprise system is the maintenance of competition, whereas the ideological background of the patent system is a time-restricted private monopoly in exchange for the inducement to apply the patented invention for the benefit of the nation and to release its use to the public after the end of the monopoly period. Finally, Eaton refers to the fact that inventive individuals in corporations are usually given rewards commensurate with their contributions, inventions or otherwise, even when they agree to assign all patent rights. This argument by Eaton would be strong if all American industry had employee-inventor award systems, but world-famous corporations with outstanding employee inventors, for instance, Kodak or Bell Telephone Laboratories, refuse to consider any such award systems as do many other industrial corporations. In government, on the other hand, there are at least the Government Employee Incentive Awards Act of 1954 and the specific award provisions of the Atomic Energy Act and the National Aeronautics and Space Act. Eaton's arguments on reward policy, however, invite the suggestion that there should be some federal law with guidelines inducing industrial employers and other private employers to start an employee award incentive policy. The industrial case studies describing positive employee-award policies in Chapter 3 of this book should not be interpreted as characteristic for all corporations or as comprising the majority of industrial enterprises of the whole country, even if they influence the policies of other companies.

Eaton finally points out that the phrase "patent give-away program" is often used to describe any policy that involves leaving commercial rights to any patented invention with the contractor, even under the carefully described conditions of the Kennedy Memorandum. He holds that the phrase is without foundation "although it has a demagogic surface appeal." Commercial inventions are left with a contractor when there is likelihood that the public will get some additional benefits, and nothing is "given away." He further attacks a number of other arguments brought forward against a suggested "McClellan-type" bill as presenting misleading and inaccurate analogies. In short, Eaton pleads intensely for a legal solution as laid down in the Kennedy Memorandum of 1963, which he considers moderate, flexible,

---

private corporations contracting out research and the invention policy applied in this connection.

and reasonably workable in practice. He wants thoughtful businessmen to speak out firmly in favor of continuing the vital incentives and benefits of the patent system wherever possible even when government funds are involved. Otherwise, the "present drift toward what can only be described as socialized technology will surely continue."

The author of this chapter of the book believes that it may have been in the mind of President Kennedy and his science advisor at that time, Jerome Wiesner, to make the contents of the Statement of Government Patent Policy of 1963 the basis of future federal legislation. That the President chose the form of an interdepartmental memorandum seems to have been a tactical measure dictated by the state of congressional debate about this subject at that time. An interdepartmental memorandum avoids official comments (and objections) by various agencies. In case government patent policy takes the shape of a public law based on proposed legislation introduced by Senator McClellan (Congressman Daddario in the House of Representatives) it should be supplemented with provisions to make such federal law a model for the policy of private employers (in industry and research institutions). Certain basic principles as to allocation of ownership and right to special awards should be valid for employees in all fields of employment.

APPENDIX A. EXECUTIVE ORDER 10096

Draft 5, January 23, 1950

PROVIDING FOR A UNIFORM PATENT POLICY FOR THE GOVERNMENT WITH RESPECT TO INVENTIONS MADE BY GOVERNMENT EMPLOYEES AND FOR THE ADMINISTRATION OF SUCH POLICY

WHEREAS inventive advances in scientific and technological fields frequently result from governmental activities carried on by Government employees; and

WHEREAS the Government of the United States is expending large sums of money annually for the conduct of these activities; and

WHEREAS these advances constitute a vast national resource; and

WHEREAS it is fitting and proper that the inventive product of functions of the Government, carried out by Government employees, should be available to the Government; and

WHEREAS the rights of Government employees in their inventions should be recognized in appropriate instances; and

WHEREAS the carrying out of the policy of this order requires appropriate administrative arrangements:

NOW, THEREFORE, by virtue of the authority vested in me by the Constitution and statutes, and as President of the United States and Commander in Chief of the armed forces of the United States, in the interest of the establishment and operation of a uniform patent policy for the Government with respect to inventions made by Government employees, it is hereby ordered as follows:

1. The following basic policy is established for all Government agencies with respect to inventions hereafter made by any Government employee:

(a) The Government shall obtain the entire right, title and interest in and to all inventions made by any Government employee (1) during working hours, or (2) with a contribution by the Government of facilities, equipment, materials, funds, or information, or of time or services of other Government employees on official duty, or (3) which bear a direct relation to or are made in consequence of the official duties of the inventor.

(b) In any case where the contribution of the Government, as measured by any one or more of the criteria set forth in paragraph (a) last above, to the invention is insufficient equitably to justify a requirement of assignment to the Government of the entire right, title and interest to such inventon, or in any case where the Government has insufficient interest in an invention to obtain entire right, title and interest therein (although the Government could obtain same under paragraph (a), above), the Government agency concerned, subject to the approval of the Chairman of the Government Patents Board (provided for in paragraph 3 of this order and hereinafter referred to as the Chairman), shall leave title to such invention in the employee, subject, however, to the reservation to the Government of a nonexclusive, irrevocable, royalty-free license in the invention with power to grant licenses for all governmental purposes, such reservation, in the terms thereof, to appear, where practicable, in any patent, domestic or foreign, which may issue on such invention.

(c) In applying the provisions of paragraphs (a) and (b), above, to the facts and circumstances relating to the making of any particular invention, it shall be presumed that an invention made by an employee who is employed or assigned (i) to invent or improve or perfect any art, machine, manufacture, or composition of matter, (ii) to conduct or perform research, development work, or both, (iii) to supervise, direct, coordinate, or review Government financed or conducted research, development work, or both, or (iv) to act in a liaison capacity among governmental or non-governmental agencies or individuals engaged in such work, or made by an employee included within any other category of employees specified by regulations issued pursuant to section 4(b) hereof, falls within the provisions of paragraph (a), above, and it shall be presumed that any invention made by any other employee falls within the provisions of paragraph (b), above. Either presumption may be rebutted by the facts or circumstances attendant upon the conditions under which any particular invention is made and, notwithstanding the foregoing, shall not preclude a determination that the invention falls within the provisions of paragraph (d) next below.

(d) In any case wherein the Government neither (1) pursuant to the provision, of paragraph (a) above, obtains entire right, title and interest in and to an invention nor (2) pursuant to the provisions of paragraph (b) above, reserves a non-exclusive, irrevocable, royalty-free license in the invention with power to grant licenses for all governmental purposes, the Government shall leave the entire right, title and interest in and to the invention in the Government employee, subject to law.

(e) Actions taken, and rights acquired, under the foregoing provisions of this section, shall be reported to the Chairman in accordance with procedures established by him.

2. Subject to considerations of national security, or public health, safety or welfare,

the following basic policy is established for the collection, and dissemination to the public, of information concerning inventions resulting from Government research and development activities:

(a) When an invention is made under circumstances defined in paragraph 1(a) of this order giving the United States the right to title thereto, the Government agency concerned shall either prepare and file an application for patent therefor in the United States Patent Office or make a full disclosure of the invention promptly to the Chairman, who may, if he determines the Government interest so requires, cause application for patent to be filed or cause the invention to be fully disclosed by publication thereof: *Provided, however,* That, consistent with present practice of the Department of Agriculture, no application for patent shall, without the approval of the Secretary of Agriculture, be filed in respect of any variety of plant invented by any employee of that Department.

(b) Under arrangements made and policies adopted by the Chairman, all inventions or rights therein, including licenses, owned or controlled by the United States or any Government agency shall be indexed, and copies, summaries, analyses and abstracts thereof shall be maintained and made available to all Government agencies and to public libraries, universities, trade associations, scientists and scientific groups, industrial and commercial organizations, and all other interested groups of persons.

3. (a) A Government Patents Board is established consisting of a Chairman of the Government Patents Board, who shall be appointed by the President, and of one representative from each of the following:

Department of Agriculture
Department of Commerce
Department of the Interior
Department of Justice
Department of State
Department of Defense
Civil Service Commission
Federal Security Agency
National Advisory Committee for Aeronautics
General Services Administration

Each such representative, together with an alternate, shall be designated by the head of the agency concerned.

(b) The Government Patents Board shall advise and confer with the Chairman concerning the operation of those aspects of the Government's patent policy which are affected by the provisions of this order or of Executive Order No. 9865, and suggest modifications or improvements where necessary.

(c) Consonant with law, the agencies referred to in paragraph 3(a) hereof shall as may be necessary for the purpose of effectuating this order furnish assistance to the Board in accordance with section 214 of the Independent Offices Appropriation Act, 1946, 59 Stat. 134, 31 U.S.C. 691. The Department of Commerce shall provide necessary office accommodations and facilities for the use of the Board and the Chairman.

(d) The Chairman shall establish such committees and other working groups as may be required to advise or assist him in the performance of any of his functions.

(e) The Chairman of the Government Patents Board and the Chairman of the Interdepartmental Committee on Scientific Research and Development (provided for by Executive Order No. 9912 of December 24, 1947) shall establish and maintain such mutual consultation as will effect the proper coordination of affairs of common concern.

4. With a view to obtaining uniform application of the policies set out in this order and uniform operations thereunder, the Chairman is authorized and directed:

(a) To consult and advise with Government agencies concerning the application and operation of the policies outlined herein;

(b) After consultation with the Government Patents Board, to formulate and submit to the President for approval such proposed rules and regulations as may be necessary or desirable to implement and effectuate the aforesaid policies, together with the recommendations of the Government Patents Board thereon;

(c) To submit annually a report to the President concerning the operation of such policies, and from time to time such recommendations for modification thereof as may be deemed desirable;

(d) To determine with finality any controversies or disputes between any Government agency and its employees, to the extent submitted by any party to the dispute, concerning the ownership of inventions made by such employees or rights therein; and

(e) To perform such other or further functions or duties as may from time to time be prescribed by the President or by statute.

5. The functions and duties of the Secretary of Commerce and the Department of Commerce under the provisions of Executive Order No. 9865 of June 14, 1947 are hereby transferred to the Chairman and the whole or any part of such functions and duties may be delegated by him to any Government agency or officer: *Provided,* That said Executive Order No. 9865 shall not be deemed to be amended or affected by any provision of this Executive order other than this paragraph 5.

6. Each Government agency shall take all steps appropriate to effectuate this order, including the promulgation of necessary regulations which shall not be inconsistent with this order or with regulations issued pursuant to paragraph 4(b) hereof.

7. As used in this Executive order, the next stated terms, in singular and plural, are defined as follows for the purposes hereof

(a) "Government agency" includes any executive department and any independent commission, board, office, agency, authority, or other establishment of the Executive Branch of the Government of the United States (including any such independent regulatory commission or board, any such wholly-owned corporation, and the Smithsonian Institution), but excludes the Atomic Energy Commission.

(b) "Government employee" includes any officer or employee, civilian or military, of any Government agency, except such part-time consultants or employees as may be excluded by regulations promulgated pursuant to paragraph 4(b) hereof.

(c) "Invention" includes any art, machine, manufacture, design, or composition of matter, or any new and useful improvement thereof, or any variety of plant, which is or may be patentable under the patent laws of the United States.

HARRY S. TRUMAN

THE WHITE HOUSE
23 JANUARY 1950

APPENDIX B. PRESIDENTIAL MEMORANDUM AND STATEMENT OF
GOVERNMENT PATENT POLICY ISSUED OCTOBER 10, 1963
(Published Federal Register, Vol. 28 No. 200, October 12, 1963)
Memorandum for the Heads of Executive Departments and Agencies
Over the years, through Executive and Legislative actions, a variety of practices
has developed within the Executive Branch affecting the disposition of rights to
inventions made under contracts with outside organizations. It is not feasible to
have complete uniformity of practice throughout the Government in view of the
differing missions and statutory responsibilities of the several departments and
agencies engaged in research and development. Nevertheless, there is need for
greater consistency in agency practices in order to further the governmental and
public interests in promoting the utilization of federally financed inventions and
to avoid difficulties caused by different approaches by the agencies when dealing
with the same class of organizations in comparable patent situations.

From the extensive and fruitful national discussions of government patent practices, significant common ground has come into view. First, a single presumption of
ownership does not provide a satisfactory basis for government-wide policy on
the allocation of rights to inventions. Another common ground of understanding
is that the Government has a responsibility to foster the fullest exploitation
of the inventions for the public benefit.

Attached for your guidance is a statement of government patent policy, which I
have approved, identifying common objectives and criteria and setting forth the
minimum rights that government agencies should acquire with regard to inventions made under their grants and contracts. This statement of policy seeks to
protect the public interest by encouraging the Government to acquire the principal
rights to inventions in situations where the nature of the work to be undertaken or
the Government's past investment in the field of work favors full public access to
resulting inventions. On the other hand, the policy recognizes that the public
interest might also be served by according exclusive commercial rights to the
contractor in situations where the contractor has an established nongovernmental
commercial position and where there is greater likelihood that the invention
would be worked and put into civilian use than would be the case if the invention
were made more freely available.

Wherever the contractor retains more than a nonexclusive license, the policy
would guard against failure to practice the invention by requiring that the
contractor take effective steps within three years after the patent issues to bring
the invention to the point of practical application or to make it available for
licensing on reasonable terms. The Government would also have the right to insist
on the granting of a license to others to the extent that the invention is required for
public use by governmental regulations or to fulfill a health need, irrespective of
the purpose of the contract.

The attached statement of policy will be reviewed after a reasonable period of
trial in the light of the facts and experience accumulated. Accordingly, there should
be continuing efforts to monitor, record, and evaluate the practices of the agencies
pursuant to the policy guidelines.

This memorandum and the statement of policy shall be published in the Federal
Register.

John F. Kennedy

STATEMENT OF GOVERNMENT
PATENT POLICY

Basic Considerations

A. The government expends large sums for the conduct of research and development which results in a considerable number of inventions and discoveries.

B. The inventions in scientific and technological fields resulting from work performed under government contracts constitute a valuable national resource.

C. The use and practice of these inventions and discoveries should stimulate inventors, meet the needs of the government, recognize the equities of the contractor, and serve the public interest.

D. The public interest in a dynamic and efficient economy requires that efforts be made to encourage the expeditious development and civilian use of these inventions. Both the need for incentives to draw forth private initiatives to this end, and the need to promote healthy competition in industry must be weighed in the disposition of patent rights under government contracts. Where exclusive rights are acquired by the contractor, he remains subject to the provisions of the antitrust laws.

E. The public interest is also served by sharing of benefits of government-financed research and development with foreign countries to a degree consistent with our international programs and with the objectives of U.S. foreign policy.

F. There is growing importance attaching to the acquisition of foreign patent rights in furtherance of the interests of U.S. industry and the government.

G. The prudent administration of government research and development calls for a government-wide policy on the disposition of inventions made under government contracts reflecting common principles and objectives, to the extent consistent with the missions of the respective agencies. The policy must recognize the need for flexibility to accommodate special situations.

Policy

SECTION 1. The following basic policy is established for all government agencies with respect to inventions or discoveries made in the course of or under any contract of any government agency, subject to specific statutes governing the disposition of patent rights of certain government agencies.

(a) Where

(1) a principal purpose of the contract is to create, develop, or improve products, processes, or methods which are intended for commercial use (or which are otherwise intended to be made available for use) by the general public at home or abroad, or which will be required for such use by governmental regulations; or

(2) a principal purpose of the contract is for exploration into fields which directly concern the public health or public welfare; or

(3) the contract is in a field of science or technology in which there has been little significant experience outside of work funded by the government, or where the government has been the principal developer of the field, and the acquisition of exclusive rights at the time of contracting might confer on the contractor a preferred or dominant position; or

(4) the services of the contractor are

(i) for the operation of a government-owned research or production facility; or

(ii) for coordinating and directing the work of others,

the government shall normally acquire or reserve the right to acquire the principal or exclusive rights throughout the world in and to any inventions made in the course of or under the contract. In exceptional circumstances the contractor may acquire greater rights than a non-exclusive license at the time of contracting, where the head of the department or agency certifies that such action will best serve the public interest. Greater rights may also be acquired by the contractor after the invention has been identified, where the invention when made in the course of or under the contract is not a primary object of the contract, provided the acquisition of such greater rights is consistent with the intent of this Section 1(a) and is a necessary incentive to call forth private risk capital and expense to bring the invention to the point of practical application.

(b) In other situations, where the purpose of the contract is to build upon existing knowledge or technology, to develop information, products, processes, or methods for use by the government, and the work called for by the contract is in a field of technology in which the contractor has acquired technical competence (demonstrated by factors such as know-how, experience, and patent position) directly related to an area in which the contractor has an established nongovernmental commercial position, the contractor shall normally acquire the principal or exclusive rights throughout the world in and to any resulting inventions, subject to the government acquiring at least an irrevocable nonexclusive royalty-free license throughout the world for governmental purposes.

(c) Where the commercial interests of the contractor are not sufficiently established to be covered by the criteria specified in Section 1(b), above, the determination of rights shall be made by the agency after the invention has been identified, in a manner deemed most likely to serve the public interest as expressed in this policy statement, taking particularly into account the intentions of the contractor to bring the invention to the point of commercial application and the guidelines of Section 1(a) hereof, provided that the agency may prescribe by regulation special situations where the public interest in the availability of the inventions would best be served by permitting the contractor to acquire at the time of contracting greater rights than a nonexclusive license. In any case the government shall acquire at least a non-exclusive royalty-free license throughout the world for governmental purposes.

(d) In the situation specified in Sections 1(b) and 1(c), when two or more potential contractors are judged to have presented proposals of equivalent merit, willingness to grant the government principal or exclusive rights in resulting inventions will be an additional factor in the evaluation of the proposals.

(e) Where the principal or exclusive (except as against the government) rights in an invention remain in the contractor, he should agree to provide written reports at reasonable intervals, when requested by the government, on the commercial use that is being made or is intended to be made of inventions made under government contracts.

(f) Where the principal or exclusive (except as against the government) rights in an invention remain in the contractor, unless the contractor, his licensee, or his assignee has taken effective steps within three years after a patent issues on the invention to bring the invention to the point of practical application or has made the invention available for licensing royalty free or on terms that are reasonable in the circumstances, or can show cause why he should retain the principal or exclusive rights for a further period of time, the government shall have the right to require the granting of a license to an applicant on a non-exclusive royalty free basis.

(g) Where the principal or exclusive (except as against the government) rights to an invention are acquired by the contractor, the government shall have the right to require the granting of a license to an applicant royalty free or on terms that are reasonable in the circumstances to the extent that the invention is required for public use by governmental regulations or as may be necessary to fulfill health needs, or for other public purposes stipulated in the contract.

(h) Where the government may acquire the principal rights and does not elect to secure a patent in a foreign country, the contractor may file and retain the principal or exclusive foreign rights subject to retention by the government of at least a royalty free license for governmental purposes and on behalf of any foreign government pursuant to any existing or future treaty or agreement with the United States.

SECTION 2. Government-owned patents shall be made available and the technological advances covered thereby brought into being in the shortest time possible through dedication or licensing and shall be listed in official government publications or otherwise.

SECTION 3. The Federal Council for Science and Technology in consultation with the Department of Justice shall prepare at least annually a report concerning the effectiveness of this policy, including recommendations for revision or modification as necessary in light of the practices and determinations of the agencies in the disposition of patent rights under their contracts. A patent advisory panel is to be established under the Federal Council for Science and Technology to

(a) develop by mutual consultation and coordination with the agencies common guidelines for the implementation of this policy, consistent with existing statutes, and to provide overall guidance as to disposition of inventions and patents in which the government has any right or interest; and

(b) encourage the acquisition of data by government agencies on the disposition of patent rights to inventions resulting from federally-financed research and development and on the use and practice of such inventions, to serve as basis for policy review and development; and

(c) make recommendations for advancing the use and exploitation of government-owned domestic and foreign patents.

SECTION 4. Definitions: As used in this policy statement, the stated terms in singular and plural are defined as follows for the purposes hereof:

(a) *Government agency*—includes any Executive department, independent commission, board, office, agency, administration, authority, or other government establishment of the Executive Branch of the Government of the United States of America.

(b) *Invention* or *Invention or discovery*—includes any art, machine, manufacture, design, or composition of matter, or any new and useful improvement thereof, or any variety of plant, which is or may be patentable under the Patent Laws of the United States of America or any foreign country.

(c) *Contractor*—means any individual, partnership, public or private corporation, association, institution, or other entity which is a party to the contract.

(d) *Contract*—means any actual or proposed contract, agreement, grant, or other arrangement, or subcontract entered into with or for the benefit of the government where a purpose of the contract is the conduct of experimental, developmental, or research work.

(e) *Made*—when used in relation to any invention or discovery means the conception or first actual reduction to practice of such invention in the course of or under the contract.

(f) *Governmental purpose*—means the right of the Government of the United States (including any agency thereof, state, or domestic municipal government) to practice and have practiced (made or have made, used or have used, sold or have sold) throughout the world by or on behalf of the Government of the United States.

(g) *To the point of practical application*—means to manufacture in the case of a composition or product, to practice in the case of a process, or to operate in the case of a machine and under such conditions as to establish that the invention is being worked and that its benefits are reasonably accessible to the public.

APPENDIX C. STANDARD INSTITUTIONAL PATENT AGREEMENT GOVERNING GRANTS AND AWARDS FROM THE DEPARTMENT OF HEALTH, EDUCATION, AND WELFARE

This Agreement made and entered into this _____ day of _____, 19____, by and between the United States of America as represented by the Assistant Secretary (Health and Scientific Affairs) of the Department of Health, Education, and Welfare, hereinafter sometimes referred to as the Grantor, and _____ hereinafter referred to as the Grantee.

WITNESSETH:

WHEREAS, the Regulations of the Department of Health, Education, and Welfare, *covering inventions* resulting from research grants, fellowship awards, and contracts for research (45 CFR Parts 6 and 8), provide in Secs. 8.1 through 8.5 that upon approval by the Assistant Secretary (Health and Scientific Affairs), the ownership and disposition of domestic and foreign rights to inventions arising out of activities assisted by grants and awards may be left to the Grantee pursuant to its approved established patent policy, with such modifications as may be agreed upon; and

WHEREAS, the Grantee is desirous of entering into an agreement whereby it has a first option to retain principal rights in and to administer inventions made in the course of or under research supported by grants and awards from the Department of Health, Education, and Welfare, pursuant to the aforesaid Regulations; and

WHEREAS, the Assistant Secretary (Health and Scientific Affairs) has reviewed the patent policy of the Grantee as set forth in _____, dated _____, and its practices thereunder and has found them to be acceptable, subject to the provisions of this Agreement, and that said policy provides for administration by the Grantee of patents in the public interest and is consistent with the stated objectives of the President's Statement and Memorandum of Government Patent Policy, issued October 10, 1963;

NOW, THEREFORE, in consideration of the foregoing, the parties hereto agree as follows:

I. *Scope of Agreement*

This Agreement shall define the rights of the parties hereto regarding disposition of title to inventions made in the course of or under research supported by grants and awards from the Department of Health, Education, and Welfare, which are subject to the Department Patent Regulations and are issued after the date hereof.

II. *Definitions*

(a) The term "subject invention" as used in this Agreement means any process, machine, manufacture, composition of matter or design, or any new or useful improvement thereof, and any variety of plant which is or may be patentable under the Patent Laws of the United States made in the course of or under research supported by grants and awards from the Department of Health, Education, and Welfare.

(b) The term "made" when used in relation to any invention or discovery means its conception or first actual reduction to practice.

III. *Disposition of Principal Rights to Subject Inventions*

The Grantee shall have the right to elect to file patent application in the United States and in foreign countries on any subject invention and to administer such invention pursuant to the provisions of this Agreement. Grantee shall notify Grantor at the time each subject invention is reported to Grantor as required by paragraph V hereof, if it intends to file patent application(s) on and to administer the invention. If Grantee does not elect to file a U.S. patent application on and to administer a subject invention, it shall notify Grantor in sufficient time to permit Grantor to file a U.S. patent application thereon. In such event, all rights in and to such invention, except rights in any foreign patent application filed by Grantee, shall be subject to disposition by the Grantor in accordance with its Regulations then in effect.

IV. *Supplementary Patent Agreements*

(a) The Grantee shall obtain patent agreements from all persons who perform any part of the work under a grant or award from the Department of Health, Education, and Welfare, exclusive of clerical and manual labor personnel, requiring that such persons promptly report and assign all subject inventions to Grantee or its approved patent management organization.

(b) The Grantee shall include the following provision in any contract it enters into involving research and/or development for which DHEW research grant or award funds are utilized.

"The Contractor hereby agrees to report fully and promptly to _____
                                                                    (Grantee)
any invention conceived or first actually reduced to practice in performance of this contract (hereinafter referred to as "such invention(s)", and to assign all right, title and interest in and to such invention to _____ or its
                                                                    (Grantee)
designee.

"In addition, the Contractor agrees to furnish the following materials, disclosures and reports:

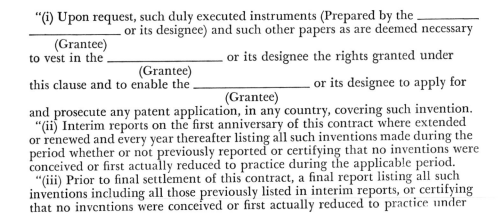

"(i) Upon request, such duly executed instruments (Prepared by the _____ _____ or its designee) and such other papers as are deemed necessary
(Grantee)
to vest in the _____ or its designee the rights granted under
(Grantee)
this clause and to enable the _____ or its designee to apply for
(Grantee)
and prosecute any patent application, in any country, covering such invention.

"(ii) Interim reports on the first anniversary of this contract where extended or renewed and every year thereafter listing all such inventions made during the period whether or not previously reported or certifying that no inventions were conceived or first actually reduced to practice during the applicable period.

"(iii) Prior to final settlement of this contract, a final report listing all such inventions including all those previously listed in interim reports, or certifying that no inventions were conceived or first actually reduced to practice under the contract."

V. *Report of Invention*

(a) The Grantee shall submit a written invention report to the Grantor of each subject invention promptly after conception or first actual reduction to practice.

(b) Such invention report shall be furnished directly to the Grantor in addition to any other requirement under any grant or award for the submission of progress or financial reports, and whether or not reference to subject invention has been made in any progress or other report furnished to the Grantor; such report shall include description of such invention, appropriately illustrated by a simple sketch or diagram, to permit the invention to be understood and evaluated, and such other information as Grantor may require.

(c) The report shall specify whether or not Grantee intends to file a U.S. patent application or any foreign patent application on the invention. Notice of an election not to file a U.S. patent application shall be given Grantor not less than ninety (90) days prior to the date a statutory bar becomes effective.

(d) If the Grantee specifies that no U.S. patent application will be filed (or having specified that it intends to file, thereafter notifies the Grantor to the contrary), the Grantee shall promptly inform the Grantor of the date and identification of any known publication of subject invention made by or known to the Grantee or, where applicable, of any contemplated publication to be made by or known to the Grantee, and also the date subject invention or any embodiment thereof was first in public use or on sale in the United States and shall furnish such other information (and have executed such documents as provided in VIII(f) as may be required to enable the Grantor to make disposition of subject invention rights).

VI. *Administration of Inventions on Which the Grantee Elects to File Patent Applications*

(a) The Grantee shall require assignment to it of all right, title and interest in and to each subject invention on which it elects to file any patent application for administration by it in accordance with and subject to the terms and conditions herein set forth. Assignments from the inventor to the Grantee under U.S. patent applications shall be promptly obtained and recorded by the Grantee in the United States Patent Office and copies of the recorded assignment shall be furnished to the Grantor.

(b) The Grantee shall grant to the Government of the United States a non-exclusive, irrevocable, royalty-free license for governmental purposes and on behalf of any foreign government, pursuant to any existing or future treaty or agreement with the United States under each U.S. or foreign patent application it elects to file on a subject invention. The form of the license to be granted shall be as set forth in Exhibit "A", attached hereto, and by this reference made a part hereof. Any license issued by Grantee shall be made expressly subject to the license to the Government of the United States.

(c) The Grantee shall administer those subject inventions to which it elects to retain title in the public interest and shall, except as provided in paragraph (d) below, make them available through licensing on a nonexclusive, royalty-free or reasonable royalty basis to qualified applicants.

(d) The Grantee may license a subject invention on an exclusive basis if it determines that nonexclusive licensing will not be effective in bringing such inventions to the commercial market in a satisfactory manner. Exclusive licenses should be issued only after reasonable efforts have been made to license on a nonexclusive basis, or where the grantee has determined that an exclusive license is necessary as an incentive for development of the invention or where market conditions are such as to require licensing on an exclusive basis. Any exclusive license issued by Grantee under a U.S. patent or patent application shall be for a limited period of time and such period shall not, unless otherwise approved by the Assistant Secretary (Health and Scientific Affairs), exceed three years from the date of the first commercial sale in the United States of America of a product or process embodying the invention, or eight years from the date of the exclusive license, whichever occurs first, provided that the licensee shall use all reasonable effort to effect introduction into the commercial market as soon as practicable, consistent with sound and reasonable business practices and judgment. Any extension of the maximum period of exclusivity shall be subject to approval of the Grantor. Upon expiration of the period of exclusivity or any extension thereof, licenses shall be offered to all qualified applicants at a reasonable royalty rate not in excess of the exclusive license royalty rate.

(e) Any license granted by the Grantee to other than the Government of the United States under any patent appplication or patent on a subject invention shall include adequate safeguards against unreasonble royalty and repressive practices. Royalties shall not, in any event, be in excess of normal trade practice. Such license shall also provide that all sales to the U.S. Government shall be royalty free.

(f) If permitted by its patent policies and the terms of the grant or award under which an invention is made, the Grantee may share royalties received with the inventor(s), provided that the Grantee shall not pay the inventor(s) more than (1) fifty percent (50%) of the first $3,000 gross royalty paid under the patent, (2) twenty-five percent (25%) of the gross royalty income between $3,000 and $13,000, and (3) fifteen percent (15%) of the gross royalty in excess of $13,000. The balance of the royalty income after payment of expenses incident to the administration of all inventions assigned to it pursuant to the provisions of this Agreement shall be utilized for the support of educational and research pursuits.

(g) All licenses issued by the Grantee to other than the Government of the United States under any patent application or patent on a subject invention shall be subject to the conditions of this Agreement and shall specifically reserve to Grantor those rights specified in paragraph XII hereof. The Grantee shall, upon request, promptly furnish copies of any license agreements entered into by it to the Department.

VII. *Patent Management Organizations*

The Grantee shall not assign any subject invention to parties other than the Grantor in circumstances as set forth in this agreement except it may assign rights in the invention to a nonprofit patent management organization, provided that the patent administration agreement between such organization and Grantee is approved by the Grantor. Any reference to a Grantee in this Agreement shall also include a patent management organization when applicable and an assignment to such an organization shall be subject to all the terms and conditions of this Agreement.

VIII. *Patent Applications*

(a) Grantee shall promptly furnish Grantor with a copy of each U.S. patent application filed in accordance with this Agreement specifying the filing date and the serial number. Grantee shall promptly notify Grantor of each foreign patent application filed, including filing date and serial number, and shall furnish a copy of each application upon request.

(b) Upon request, Grantee shall fully advise the Grantor concerning all steps and actions taken during the prosecution of any patent application covering a subject invention and shall, upon request, furnish copies of any final actions, amendments, petitions, motions, appeals, or other papers relating to the prosecution of said application.

(c) Upon request, the Grantee shall promptly furnish to the Grantor an irrevocable power of attorney granting the right to inspect and make copies of any patent application covering a subject invention or any of the final actions, amendments, petitions, motions, appeals, or other papers relating to the prosecution of said application.

(d) The Grantee shall include the following statement in the first paragraph of the specification following the abstract of any patent application filed on a subject invention:

"The invention described herein was made in the course of work under a grant or award from the Department of Health, Education, and Welfare."

(e) The Grantee shall not abandon any U.S. patent application filed on a subject invention without first offering to transfer all rights in and to such application to the Grantor not less than forty-five (45) days prior to the date a reply to the Patent Office action is due. If the Grantor does not request assignment within thirty (30) days of receipt of this offer, the Grantee may permit the application to go abandoned.

(f) If the Grantee elects to file no patent application or to abandon prosecution of a U.S. patent application on a subject invention, he shall, upon request, execute instruments or require the execution of instruments (prepared by the Grantor) and such other papers as are deemed necessary to vest in the Grantor all right, title and interest in the subject invention to enable the Grantor to apply for and prosecute patent applications in any country.

IX. *Invention Reports and Certifications*

Notwithstanding the provisions of this Agreement, the Grantee shall provide invention reports and certifications as may be required by the terms of any grant or award.

X. *Disclosure and Publication*

The Grantee shall not bar or prohibit publication of disclosures of inventions on which patent applications have been filed.

The Grantor shall have the right to publish and make disclosure of any information relating to any subject invention whenever deemed to be in the public interest, provided that upon request reasonable opportunity shall be afforded the Grantee to file U.S. and foreign patent applications.

XI. *Reports on Development and Commercial Use*

The Grantee shall provide a written annual report to the Department on or before September 30 of each year covering the preceding year, ending June 30, regarding the development and commercial use that is being made or intended to be made of all subject inventions left for administration by the Grantee. Such reports shall include information regarding development, the date of first commercial sale, gross sales by licensees, gross royalties received by the Grantee, and such other data and information as the Department may specify.

XII. *Additional Licenses*

(a) The Grantee agrees that if it, or its licensee, has not taken effective steps within three years after a United States patent issues on a subject invention left for administration to the Grantee to bring that invention to the point of practical application, and has not made such invention available for licensing royalty-free or on terms that are reasonable in the circumstances, and cannot show cause why he should retain all right, title and interest for a further period of time, the Grantor shall have the right to require (1) assignment of said patent to the United States, as represented by the Grantor; (2) cancellation of any outstanding exclusive licenses under said patent; or (3) the granting of licenses under said patent to an applicant on a nonexclusive, royalty-free basis or on terms that are reasonable in the circumstances.

(b) The Grantor reserves the right to license or to require the licensing of other persons under any U.S. patent or U.S. patent application filed by the Grantee on a subject invention on a royalty-free basis or on terms that are reasonable in the circumstances, upon a determination by the Assistant Secretary (Health and Scientific Affairs) that the invention is required for public use by governmental regulations, that the public health, safety, or welfare requires the issuance of such license(s), or that the public interest would otherwise suffer unless such license(s) were granted. The Grantee and its licensees shall be given written notice of any proposed determination pursuant to this subparagraph not less than thirty (30) days prior to the effective date of such determination, and that if requested, shall be granted a hearing before the determination is issued and otherwise made effective.

XIII. *Inventions by Federal Employees*

Notwithstanding any provision contained in this Agreement, inventions made by Federal employees, or by Federal employees jointly with others, shall be subject to disposition under provisions of Executive Orders, Governmental and Department Regulations applicable to Federal employees.

XIV. *Termination*

This Agreement may be terminated by either party for convenience upon thirty (30) days written notice. Disposition of rights in, and administration of inventions made under grants or awards entered into during and subject to this Agreement will not be affected by such a termination except that in the event the Department terminates this Agreement because of a failure or refusal by Grantee to comply with its obligations under Articles V or VI of this Agreement, the Department shall have the right to require that the Grantee's entire right, title and interest in and to the particular invention with respect to which the breach occurred be assigned to the United States of America, as represented by the Secretary of the Department of Health, Education, and Welfare.

XV. *Limitation*

It is agreed and understood that this Agreement shall not apply to any grants or awards issued under statutes containing requirements for disposition of invention rights with which the provisions of this Agreement are inconsistent. It is further agreed that any constituent agency of the Department of Health, Education, and Welfare may, with the approval of the Assistant Secretary (Health and Scientific Affairs), provide as a condition of any grant or award that this Agreement shall not apply thereto. It is also agreed that any constituent agency of the Department of Health, Education, and Welfare may provide, subject to approval by the Assistant Secretary (Health and Scientific Affairs), that this Agreement shall apply to specific research contracts.

IN WITNESS WHEREOF, each of the parties hereto has executed this Agreement as of the day and year first above written.

UNITED STATES OF AMERICA

By _____

Title _____

(Corporate Seal)

By _____

Title _____

CERTIFICATE

I, _____, certify that I am the Secretary of _____ named above; that _____ _____, who signed this Agreement on behalf of said corporation, was then _____ of said corporation; and that this Agreement was duly signed for and in behalf of said corporation by authority of its governing body and is within the scope of its corporate powers.

Witness my hand and the seal of said corporation this _____ day of _____, 19_____.

By _____

(Corporate Seal)

Rev. 8/26/68

APPENDIX C. GOVERNMENT-WIDE INCENTIVE AWARDS PROGRAM

I. Civil Service Commission Notable Employee Achievements-Awards/1968

A few examples of achievements earning awards over $1,000:

Man Hours Conserved Award: $1,175

28,000 fewer man hours per year, worth $120,000, are needed to process certain overseas mail as a result of a simplified procedure suggested by a distribution clerk in the San Francisco Post Office.

Patient Care Improved Award: $1,250

Patients confined to wheel chairs with spinal cord injuries can engage in more activities as a result of a special device designed by a manual arts therapist at the VA Hospital, Memphis, Tenn. Device enables patients to assume different positions and also prevents occurrence of body ulcers.

Paperwork Costs Cut Award: $1,175

A reduction in clerical, supply and printing costs, totaling $124,000 for one year, stemmed from an improved paperwork procedure proposed by an employee of the SBA Regional Office, Kansas City, Mo. New system eliminates a number of steps and forms.

Air Safety Advanced Award: $2,000

Greater safety for the air traveling public is expected to result from the efforts of a 4-man team of electronic engineers at FAA's National Aviation Facilities Experimental Center, DOT, Atlantic City, N.J. They demonstrated and convinced the communications and aviation industries that satellites could be used for relaying short-range, static-free communications with planes over the ocean.

Cancer Treatment Advanced Award: $1,500

Development of the Blood Separator machine, a major advance in the treatment of cancer, is due in great part to the inventiveness of a medical technician at the National Cancer Institute, HEW, Bethesda, Md. His design of a crucial part of the machine led to its successful development.

Packing Costs Cut Award: $1,315

A reduction of $260,000 in cost of packing 1 million rocket motors and warheads for overseas shipment was realized from a suggestion by an inventory management specialist at Hill Air Force Base, Utah. His idea enabled the two items to be packed in the same box, instead of separate boxes.

Mapmaking Improved Award: $2,000

Better maps and increased mapping production results from the invention of a research engineer with Geological Survey, Interior, McLean, Va. He developed the

Stereo Image Alternator, a greatly improved system of viewing aerial photographs in 3-D for depiction of map detail.

Material Costs Cut Award: $1,110

A $93,000 reduction in the cost of replacement hose for vacuum cleaners resulted from a suggestion by an equipment specialist with GSA's Region 3, Washington, D.C. His idea: replace rubber hose formerly used with plastic hose which is 25% cheaper, more durable, and lighter.

Supply Costs Cut Award: $1,150

Cost of purchasing GI laundry bags was reduced an estimated $99,000 per year as a result of an idea suggested by a sewing machine operator at Army's Fort Jackson, S.C. Her idea to make the bags with flat rather than round bottoms saves 18 cents on material and labor costs per bag.

Consumers Protected Award: $1,500

A more wholesome meat supply for the nation's consumers was insured as a result of the special efforts of 3 meat inspectors with Agriculture's Consumer and Marketing Service. Their alertness and initiative in detecting and reporting the source of a potentially serious meat contamination problem led to remedial action by the Department.

Equipment Costs Cut Award: $1,165

One-year procurement costs of tropical combat boots was cut an estimated $114,000 as a result of a suggestion by a quality control representative at DSA's Defense Contract Administration Services Region, Atlanta, Ga. His idea: eliminate the 5 cents leather heel pad since it doesn't affect the boot's serviceability.

Space Technology Advanced Award: $1,500

An improved design of future spacecraft stems from an invention of 2 aerospace engineers at NASA's Ames Research Center, Calif., which greatly simplifies the hardware required for stabilization about the pitch, roll, and yaw axes.

II. Civil Service Commission Distribution of Awards 1967

Table II.1   Federal Department Breakdown of Incentive Awards Statistics for Fiscal Year 1967

Department or Agency	For Suggestions and for Superior Performance					
	Number Received		Number Adopted			
	Total	Annual Rate per 1000 Employees	Total	Annual Rate per 1000 Employees	First Year Measurable Benefits to Government	Amount Paid in Cash Awards
Agency for International Development	93	6	12	0.8	$ 3,678	$ 455
Agriculture, Department of	4,878	52	1,753	18	3,866,127	80,461
Atomic Energy Commission	395	55	119	17	17,654	3,190
Civil Aeronautics Board	47	61	3	4	0	0
Civil Service Commission	392	83	75	16	10,211	1,581
Commerce, Department of	2,502	81	762	25	200,902	28,660
Defense, Department of	258,386	225	66,212	58	133,563,190	2,773,455
Air Force	102,339	343	20,229	68	60,097,530	748,635
Citizen only	100,905		19,997		59,943,810	742,360
Army	83,434	205	23,133	57	40,406,919	962,468
Citizen only	75,215		20,984		38,655,909	901,151
Navy	57,209	155	19,703	53	24,870,925	944,585
Defense Supply Agency	14,673	252	2,963	51	8,124,554	113,201
Other Defense Activities	731	–	184	–	63,271	4,566
District of Columbia Govt.	131	4	84	3	14,680	3,090
Federal Power Commission	46	41	6	5	2,094	155
Federal Trade Commission	11	10	7	6	2,500	310
General Accounting Office	36	9	4	1	0	105
General Services Admin.	3,649	98	1,291	35	339,791	44,730
Government Printing Office	976	139	228	33	29,692	5,870
Health, Education & Welfare	6,137	62	965	10	308,785	54,271
Housing & Urban Development, Dept. of	618	44	132	9	330,793	9,274
Interior, Dept. of	4,706	70	1,682	25	495,848	78,801

(table continued)

Table II.1   (continued)

Department or Agency	For Suggestions and for Superior Performance					
	Number Received		Number Adopted			
	Total	Annual Rate per 1000 Employees	Total	Annual Rate per 1000 Employees	First Year Measurable Benefits to Government	Amount Paid in Cash Awards
Interstate Commerce Commission	41	18	3	1	2,000	135
Justice, Dept. of	2,656	80	668	20	114,193	12,632
Labor, Dept. of	815	86	184	19	19,151	6,305
Library of Congress	17	5	2	0.6	1,830	150
National Aeronautics & Space Admin.	3,906	113	866	25	4,133,817	101,460
National Labor Relations Board	70	31	14	6	0	305
Panama Canal & Canal (Govt.) Zone	639	54	138	12	49,780	5,060
Post Office Department	209,968	357	50,467	86	8,710,762	767,541
Railroad Retirement Board	343	203	96	57	21,464	2,675
Securities & Exchange Commission	6	4	5	4	1,153	245
Selective Service System	746	107	113	16	10,450	1,345
Small Business Admin.	297	74	56	14	36,243	3,642
Smithsonian Institution[1]	153	68	35	16	21,207	1,240
State, Dept. of	669	26	136	5	72,797	6,702
Transportation, Dept. of	6,679	157	1,336	31	591,590	59,750
Treasury, Dept. of	21,790	236	4,753	51	1,814,383	181,401
U.S. Information Agency	169	14	34	3	38,048	2,480
Veterans Administration	18,542	121	9,066	59	788,393	119,274
Others	1,255	–	228	–	959,269	35,965
Totals	551,764	205	141,535	53	$156,572,489	$4,392,715

[1] Includes National Gallery of Art.

(table continued)

Table II.1   (continued)

Department or Agency	Superior Performance Awards[2]				
	Number Approved				
	Total	Annual Rate per 1000 Employees	First Year Measurable Benefits to Government	Amount Paid in Cash Awards	Honor Awards for Distinguished or Meritorious Service
Agency for International Development	135	8	$ 23,582	$ 14,536	54
Agriculture, Department of	3,251	35	66,067,334	362,080	94
Atomic Energy Commission	252	35	828,227	74,193	3
Civil Aeronautics Board	28	36	0	1,200	0
Civil Service Commission	168	36	36,450	13,976	17
Commerce, Department of	3,723	121	3,085,281	485,674	85
Defense, Department of	45,056	39	96,414,120	5,655,414	549
Air Force	11,263	38	1,387,510	1,653,920	178
Citizen only	10,700	16	1,386,160	1,608,680	
Army	23,395	57	69,683,886	2,501,151	249
Citizen only	16,207		69,660,739	2,102,677	
Navy	8,631	23	24,386,649	1,280,863	36
Defense Supply Agency	1,473	25	956,075	197,755	53
Other Defense Activities	294	–	0	21,725	33
District of Columbia Govt.	289	10	0	34,705	0
Federal Power Commission	123	108	0	250	6
Federal Trade Commission	87	78	0	3,800	91
General Accounting Office	242	60	20,060	24,275	120
General Services Admin.	1,045	28	107,896	163,632	23
Government Printing Office	293	42	155,464	65,698	7
Health, Education & Welfare	1,250	13	1,132,880	281,070	100
Housing & Urban Development, Dept. of	404	29	78,000	60,100	536
Interior, Dept. of	2,218	33	1,314,881	437,795	347

[2] Includes awards for superior performance and special acts or services.   (table continued)

Table II.1   (continued)

| Department or Agency | Superior Performance Awards[1] | | | | Honor Awards for Distinguished or Meritorious Service |
| | Number Approved | | | | |
	Total	Annual Rate per 1000 Employees	First Year Measurable Benefits to Government	Amount Paid in Cash Awards	
Interstate Commerce Commission	0	0	0	0	0
Justice, Dept. of	1,926	58	11,570	381,225	2
Labor, Dept. of	324	34	0	48,496	53
Library of Congress	10	3	0	400	5
National Aeronautics & Space Admin.	1,046	30	2,368,708	248,610	51
National Labor Relations Board	19	8	0	4,600	0
Panama Canal & Canal (Govt.) Zone	378	32	1,047,400	68,150	378
Post Office Department	9,388	16	4,472,953	1,305,253	14
Railroad Retirement Board	124	73	174,314	12,413	5
Securities & Exchange Commission	72	53	0	11,051	3
Selective Service System	437	63	3,000	31,489	3
Small Business Admin.	111	28	46,000	28,680	9
Smithsonian Institution[2]	51	23	11,760	7,820	44
State, Dept. of	581	23	315,664	33,536	254
Transportation, Dept. of	2,161	51	6,456,221	437,709	18
Treasury, Dept. of	5,309	58	1,515,038	784,638	35
U.S. Information Agency	134	11	250	3,812	86
Veterans Administration	7,232	47	474,579	617,290	0
Others	557	–	784,010	71,120	86
Totals	88,424	33	$186,945,642	$11,774,690	3,078

[1] Includes awards for superior performance and special acts or services.
[2] Includes National Gallery of Art.

Table II.2   Civil Service Commission Fact Sheet for Government-Wide Incentive Awards
Program, Fiscal Year 1967

Improvements Through Suggestions		Top Results Through Superior Performance	
Total Adopted	141,535	Total Cases Approved	88,424
Adopted per 100 employees	5.3/100	Approved per 100 Employees	3.3/100
Total Measurable Benefits	$156,572,489	Total Measurable Benefits	$186,945,642
Number of Cash Awards	104,283	Number of Cash Awards	78,179
Amount in Awards	$4,392,715	Amount in Awards	11,774,690
Average Cash Award	$42	Average Cash Award	$151
% Adopted of Total Recd.[1]	25.7%		
% Adopted of Total Processed	27.8%		
Cash Awards for Tangible (Measurable) Benefits		Cash Awards for Tangible (Measureable) Benefits	
Number with Measurable Benefits (31.7% of total)	33,052	Number of Measurable Benefits (8.1% of total)	6,322
Average Benefits per Case	$3,552	Average Benefit per Case	$17,293
Amount in Awards (57.3%)	$2,515,511	Amount in Awards (7.3%)	$857,745
Average Cash Awards	$76	Average Cash Award	$136
Cash Awards for Intangible Benefits		Cash Awards for Intangible Benefits	
Number with Intangible Benefits (68.3% of total)	71,251	Number of Intangible Benefits (91.9% of total)	71,857
Amount in Awards (42.7%)	$1,877,204	Amount in Awards (92.7%)	$10,916,945
Average Cash Award	$26	Average Cash Award	$152

[1] Total number of suggestions received—551,764
Rate received—205/1,000
1967 Total Government strength—2,692,712
Total processed—508,673

Table II.3   Civil Service Commission Improvements through Employee Suggestions, Breakdown by Agencies/1968

Agency	Number Suggestions Adopted	Number Adopted per 100 Employees	Value of Measurable Benefits	Average Cash Award
Defense	(70,325)	(5.5)	($133,387,111)	($ 56)
Army	25,705	5.9	56,263,960	61
Navy	19,614	4.9	28,724,151	57
Air Force	21,261	7.1	44,364,005	53
Defense Supply	3,500	6.0	3,927,442	46
Post Office	51,910	8.3	6,586,106	24
VA	9,220	5.9	791,049	23
HEW	1,158	1.1	427,428	51
Agriculture	1,618	1.7	3,016,189	71
Treasury	3,480	3.9	935,112	41
Interior	1,497	2.2	317,000	47
Transportation	1,350	2.4	851,916	58
GSA	1,367	3.5	388,744	36
Commerce	587	1.7	164,975	37
NASA	758	2.2	1,795,312	159
Justice	676	2.0	166,129	52
D.C. Government	38	0.1	117,878	48
State	130	0.5	110,751	51
AID	13	0.1	11,440	89
HUD	124	0.8	73,534	68
Panama Canal	155	1.2	33,358	30
USIA	17	0.1	33,887	93
Labor	188	1.9	635	32
GPO	271	3.7	57,720	30
AEC	107	1.5	20,226	32
Selective Service System	150	2.1	23,900	43
CSC	112	2.2	12,494	34
Small Business Admin.	103	2.3	141,240	56
GAO	5	0.1	1,550	115
Library of Congress	3	0.1	0	250
Smithsonian Institution	31	1.3	3,000	37
NLRB	4	0.2	0	18
ICC	4	0.2	1,511	33
RRB	85	4.9	14,908	28
SEC	0	0	0	0
FTC	4	0.3	0	38
FCC	6	0.4	0	18
FPC	12	1.1	1,042	18
CAB	3	0.5	0	25
EEOC	5	1.4	3,000	50
Government-Wide	145,623	5.3	$149,761,851	$ 44

Table II.4   Civil Service Commission Top Results through Superior Achievements[1], Breakdown by Agencies/1968

Agency	Number of Awards Approved	Number Approved per 100 Employees	Value of Measurable Benefits	Average Cash Award
Defense	(52,865)	(4.2)	($57,230,916)	($130)
Army	27,187	6.3	36,593,414	115
Navy	11,037	2.8	13,607,425	150
Air Force	12,336	4.1	2,320,155	148
Defense Supply	1,822	3.1	4,691,888	154
Post Office	12,583	2.0	14,424,571	228
VA	4,649	3.0	168,875	132
HEW	1,401	1.3	468,879	226
Agriculture	3,376	3.6	21,402,820	244
Treasury	4,093	4.6	717,650	163
Interior	2,367	3.4	892,104	253
Transportation	2,911	5.1	520,218	196
GSA	1,567	4.1	100,902	173
Commerce	4,055	11.8	1,189,219	146
NASA	546	1.6	128,400	367
Justice	1,957	5.8	35,999	236
D.C. Government	430	1.4	0	93
State	701	2.6	95,862	96
AID	213	1.2	1,352,679	309
HUD	385	2.6	3,000	208
Panama Canal	507	4.1	387,530	176
USIA	45	0.4	0	57
Labor	304	3.1	0	185
GPO	352	4.8	165,649	229
AEC	222	3.1	77,424	339
Selective Service System	397	5.6	1,500	90
CSC	164	3.2	52,756	72
Small Business Admin.	334	7.6	0	253
GAO	132	3.1	0	301
Library of Congress	7	0.2	0	167
Smithsonian Institution	28	1.2	8,656	324
NLRB	22	0.9	0	202
ICC	1	0.1	0	176
RRB	51	3.0	27,450	147
SEC	39	2.8	4,000	301
FTC	74	6.3	0	172
FCC	55	3.7	0	304
FPC	156	14.0	0	250
CAB	24	3.7	0	284
EEOC	6	1.6	0	196
Government-Wide	97,390	3.5	$99,460,059	$159

[1] Includes awards for superior performance and special acts or achievements.

6

Of the seven universities selected for case studies in this chapter, six have a formalized patent policy. They are Massachusetts Institute of Technology, Princeton, and four state universities—Florida, California, Wisconsin, and Iowa State University. The exception is Harvard, which limits itself to advising.[1]

Since academic learning is traditionally communicated by teaching, the role of research has often been considered secondary, and some of the old cavalier attitude toward such practical matters as inventions and patents no doubt remains. University administrators may often prefer to treat inventions as private, since they mean additional administrative work, and faculty members may resent formal relations with the university as employer in this respect. They may also wish to retain rights in possible inventions to use as they see fit.

On the other hand, a number of leading universities and engineering schools are highly conscious of the value of efficient administration of research; they know that its results are indispensable to the advancement of knowledge and the enrichment of teaching and are of great service to the public.

The need for formal organization has also been emphasized by experts in university research. In 1960 Henry de W. Smyth, the chairman of the Research Board of Princeton University, said:

> What concerns me more are the dangers inherent in the size, costs, and complexity of modern scientific equipment. The casualness and absence of formal organization, so important to scientific research, becomes too expensive a luxury for a department running a big accelerator. For such a machine, a pseudo-business or military operating organization is necessary. . . . There is a real problem in reconciling this necessity with the advantages of a typical university organization.[2]

The work of Research Corporation (New York)[3] demonstrates that there really

[1] A pioneer in collecting important factual material on university patent policies is Archie M. Palmer, who has published the following special studies: "University Patent Policies," in *Journal of the Patent Office Society*, February 1934; "Patents and University Research," in *Scientific Monthly*, February 1948; "Survey of University Patent Policies," Washington 1948; "University Patent Policies and Practices," Washington 1952 (and supplement 1955); "Patents and Nonprofit Research," Study No. 6, Senate Subcommittee on Patents, Trademarks, and Copyrights, 85th Congress, 1st sess., Washington, 1957; *University Research and Patent Policies, Practices and Procedures*, Washington, 1962.

[2] Proceedings of a Conference on Academic and Industrial Basic Research, Princeton University, November 1960, sponsored by National Science Foundation (NSF 61–39), *Role of the University in Basic Research*, p. 20.

[3] Research Corporation has no substantial invested endowment and relies upon earnings on royalties from patents assigned to it, the net income of which is used for grants to academic and scientific institutions. See Annual Reports of the Corporation; also C. H.

is a flow of inventions from university faculty and staff. This nonprofit organization, specializing in the administration and exploitation of inventions of university
origin, provides patent services to some 200 nonprofit organizations, mostly
universities and colleges.

The great variety of universities in size, structure, local traditions, and fields
of science emphasized in the United States makes it natural to expect no single
pattern of operation of employee inventions. Allan M. Cartter, pioneer in
analyzing universities as economic entities, describes this negative attitude thus:

Some of our academic colleagues would deny the relevance of economic rationality
to such a serious matter as education. Economics is for the world of wheat, automation, and stock markets, they would argue, while higher education is the world
of humane learning, scholarly inquiry, and freedom of the spirit.[4]

Further, in certain fields of research private ownership or even any attempt to
file patent applications (irrespective of their later use or dedication to the public)
by university employees of any kind is considered unethical, and in many institutions it is directly prohibited by university procedures. (See the discussion of
Harvard Medical School in the field of public health and therapeutics, p. 000.)

An opposite stand was taken by Karl T. Compton, former President of Massachusetts Institute of Technology, in his annual report of 1932:

Responsibility does not always end with the mere publication of a patentable
scientific discovery or invention; the public benefits derivable from the patent laws
and contemplated by the framers of those laws should not be lost through a failure
to solicit patent protection.[5]

The problems of a formalized uniform patent policy for the use of colleges and
universities arose in earnest at the end of World War II, when government agencies
started to distribute research funds on a large scale to these institutions.[6] Much
of the advanced defense research in space sciences, medicine, agriculture, and
the exploration of the atom is entrusted by government agencies to university
faculties and institutions closely associated with them.

In 1967 the estimated federal funds for industrial R&D amounted to $10.1 billion.
This figure compares to total federal government expenditures for R&D of $16.5

Schauer, "Research Corporation—Experiment in Administration of Patent Rights for
the Public Good," in *Research Management* 5, No. 4 (1962): 229.
[4] "Economics of the University," in *American Economic Review* 55, No. 2 (May 1965):
481.
[5] Annual Report M.I.T., *Technical Review,* December 1932, p. 101, cited by A.M.
Palmer, in "Patents and University Research," *Scientific Monthly* 66 (February 1948):
149.
[6] The first universities to establish a formal patent policy were Lehigh University and
University of Florida in 1924. See Palmer, *University Research,* 1962, pp. 15, 84.

billion, of which universities and colleges (not including federal contract research centers) had about $1.4 billion. Research in the universities and colleges was largely devoted to basic studies (55 percent in terms of funds), with applied research next (39 percent) and development 6 percent. As one might expect, this is in sharp contrast to the case in industry, where development gets the lion's share (82 percent), applied research 14 percent (in 1966), and basic research not quite 4 percent.[7]

Another fact is important for the survey of university patent policy in connection with federal research support. The pattern of government-supported research grants to universities shows a marked concentration in a relatively small number of institutions. In 1966 the first ten institutions ranked by size of total federal grants accounted for a total of 23 percent of all federal funds in research allocated to universities. These institutions ranked as in Table 6.1.[8]

Table 6.1 Ten Institutions Receiving Largest Amount of Federal Funds, 1966

	Dollars	% of U.S. total
Massachusetts Institute of Technology	62,762	2.89
University of Michigan	61,489	2.83
Stanford University	57,288	2.64
Columbia University	54,291	2.50
University of Illinois	52,957	2.44
University of California (Los Angeles)	47,983	2.21
Harvard University	47,183	2.17
University of California (Berkeley)	45,959	2.12
University of Chicago	39,574	1.82
University of Pennsylvania	36,736	1.69

Source: National Science Foundation 67–14.

The annual survey of university research published by *Industrial Research* showed that approximately one-third of the nation's $2.7 billion spent on academic research by the federal government in 1966 was being conducted by four institutions in the following order[9]:

[7] National Science Foundation, 67–19, p. 24. See also discussion in Chapter 1 of this book and Figure 1.1.
[8] NSF 67–14 *Federal Support to Universities and Colleges 1963–1966,* Table 16, abbreviated.
[9] *Industrial Research,* April 1967. All figures given here may be subject to some adjustment depending on ways of calculation. *Industrial Research* calls the $2.7 billion figure used here "an educated guess based on reported figures from 174 institutions that perform the bulk of academic R&D."

University of California (when adding $255 million for Lawrence Radiation Laboratory, Los Alamos Scientific Laboratory, and Naval Biological Laboratory)	$316 million
California Institute of Technology (when adding $245 million for the Jet Propulsion Laboratory operated by the Institute)	$258 million
University of Chicago (when adding $86 million for Argonne National Laboratory expenditures)	$172 million
Stanford University (when adding Stanford Resarch Institute and all affiliated R&D activities)	$152 million

The former President's Special Assistant for Science and Technology, Donald F. Hornig, confirmed this official federal policy in an address, by saying: "We have a number, perhaps something like 20 really outstanding institutions which set the tone and standard for the whole enterprise. This number will grow, but we will always look to a limited number of institutions to perform this function."[10]

It is, therefore, obvious that, as in the industrial sector, the research and invention policy of a minority of leading universities and colleges as "chosen instruments" has an impact on and will set the scene for many other institutions of the country, at least for the many universities and colleges with little or no experience of their own in this recent branch of university administration.

In his thought-provoking book *American Universities and Federal Research,* Charles V. Kidd submits as his central thesis "that large-scale federal financing of research has set in motion irreversible forces that are affecting the nature of universities, altering their capacity to teach, changing their financial status, modifying the character of parts of the federal administrative structure, establishing new political relations, and changing the way research itself is organized."[11] In this context Kidd could also have mentioned a probable change in the relations between the universities in their capacity as employers and supervisors of federal research and their employed scientists when administering their tangible research results in sponsored research.[12] This part of administrative university policy claims increased attention.

To get a better grip of the factual situation, this chapter presents seven case studies of university invention and patent policy, but no attempt is made to give a complete

[10] *Science* 150 (November 12, 1965): 850.
[11] (Cambridge, Mass.: Harvard University Press, 1960), Preface.
[12] In *University Research,* 1962, pp. 21 ff., Archie Palmer had noticed this same problem and touches on some of the recognized advantages and concomitant hazards for universities when accepting financial support of scientific and technological research from government, industry, foundations, and other external sources.

nationwide survey in this fast-changing and increasing field. A first investigation by the author shows that there is a vast variety of approaches to these problems at different universities, ranging from a strict hands-off attitude, leaving all responsibilities to determine ownership and disposition of rights entirely to the academic employee, to a formalized overall control and administration of tangible research results emanating from university research as patents, printed publications, and various forms of scientific data. The latter policy has been developed, more or less voluntarily, under the pressure of government research contracts prescribing detailed and continuous duties of reporting inventions, improvements, and scientific data, as well as transfer of ownership of these results by university contractors.[13] Some educational institutions have adopted an employee-invention policy only with regard to those results of scientific investigation that affect public or private health, others only with respect to sponsored research. Whether variety in university patent policies is desirable or undesirable depends on whether it reflects considered but differing policy positions or whether it stems from abdication or unwillingness to change and refusal to face up to the existing situation.

From a legal point of view there exist a few patent policies for all educational institutions on a state-wide basis. (State laws describe handling and allocation of all industrial property rights in state universities.) This is the case, for instance, in Arizona, Florida, Mississippi, Montana, Ohio, and Oregon.[14] University of Florida policy is described as an example of this group in a case study in this chapter. Other state university patent policies are described in the case studies on Iowa State University of Science and Technology, University of California and University of Wisconsin of this chapter.

This chapter presents seven case studies in all, describing the main features of a university's patent policy toward its various faculty and staff employees. The investigated universities are:

Harvard University
Massachusetts Institute of Technology
Princeton University
University of California
University of Florida
University of Wisconsin
Iowa State University.

Among these examples there are three leading private universities of the East

---

[13] The contractor can be a university as entity, a university faculty, or an individual faculty or staff grantee.
[14] Palmer, *University Research*, 1962, p. 14.

Coast: Harvard, M.I.T., and Princeton, and four state universities: California, Florida, Iowa, and Wisconsin. Two very large universities are included, California and Wisconsin, and three small universities, Florida, Iowa State, and Princeton.[15] In terms of R&D funds available, one university, California, had funds amounting to about $142 million in 1966–1967, excluding federal funds for three major AEC contracts. M.I.T. had $50 million for on-campus sponsored research, excluding Lincoln Laboratory and Instrumentation Laboratory, and Wisconsin had the same amount. Iowa State University's total expenditure for R&D in the same year was $23 million, $15 million of which were federal funds. Princeton spent (and committed) $29 million, almost all of which (close to $28 million) was federal. Harvard had roughly $49 million of federal research funds in contracts and another $6.5 million federal money spent indirectly. Florida had about $22.5 million in federal money.[16]

It is the hope of the author that this limited collection of cases may give a first glance at the current trends of employee-invention policy in the academic world.

HARVARD UNIVERSITY

Harvard University in Cambridge, Massachusetts, was founded as Harvard College in 1636. Harvard College is now part of the Faculty of Arts and Sciences, which in turn is only one element in a complex including the Medical School and the School of Dental Medicine, the Divinity School, the School of Business Administration, the School of Public Health, the Graduate School of Design, the School of Education, and the John F. Kennedy School of Government.

Among the thirty departments and two divisions (Engineering and Applied Physics, and Medical Sciences) of the Faculty of Arts and Sciences, inventions are most likely in architectural sciences, biology, chemistry, geological sciences, and mathematics and physics. In the Division of Engineering and Applied Physics research has to do with digital computers, electrical and electronic engineering, solid state physics, nuclear reactor theory and reactor materials, and properties of various other materials. Much research is also carried out in the Harvard Medical School and School of Dental Medicine, which cooperate with more than a dozen hospitals, infirmaries, sanatoriums, and hospital medical centers. The Harvard School of Public Health (devoted to graduate education) does extensive work on industrial hygiene. Military, naval, and air science are also taught.

[15] California in 1967–1968 had 5886 full-time academic faculty and 84,317 students enrolled in graduate and undergraduate colleges. Wisconsin had 4358 full-time academic staff and 57,052 students. On the other hand, Florida had 2100 faculty and 18,508 students, Iowa State 1025 and 17,755 students, and Princeton 551 faculty and 4707 students.
[16] From catalogues and letters to the author, October 1968. The Florida figure from NSF 67–14, Federal Support to Universities and Colleges 1963–1966.

Harvard in 1967 had a teaching staff of 5237, including part-time assistants. Overall enrollment, including all graduate schools, was 12,648 men and 2520 women (many of whom were enrolled in affiliated Radcliffe College). There were 4834 students in Harvard College.[17]

The working results of research and publications by faculty members and staff of Harvard University have had and still have great impact on science in the United States and on international science. Most research projects are concentrated in the great number of natural science laboratories operated by the University under the Faculty of Arts and Sciences. These laboratories include the biological laboratories, five chemical laboratories, seven laboratories of engineering and applied physics (of which especially the Howard Hathaway Aiken Computation Laboratory[18] and the Cruft Laboratory are world-famous), a laboratory of the department of geologial sciences, and four laboratories of the department of physics (including the Cambridge Electron Accelerator operated jointly with Massachusetts Institute of Technology).

Government research contracts and grants take a share of supported research activities which increases from year to year. In 1967 such research amounted to $55.4 million. This compares to the University's expenditures from sources other than the federal government of $94.3 million.[19]

Sponsored research increases at about 10 percent per year. Government research sponsors include National Institutes of Health, Atomic Energy Commission (which pays for the atomic energy accelerator operated by Harvard jointly with Massachusetts Institute of Technology), National Science Foundation, and Department of Defense.

General University Patent Policy

Harvard University as of 1967 had no formalized patent and copyright policy for its faculty members and staff.[20] The University has intentionally refused to be involved in questions of this kind and does not sympathize with universities that have developed an active employee policy in the inventions field. Harvard considers itself a purely educational institution, and "President and Fellows" of the University have never taken title to inventions or discoveries made by faculty or staff members.

The only definite statement of policy in this field was made more than 30 years

[17] Harvard University Catalogue, 1968.
[18] Here Professor Aiken in 1944 completed the first large-scale automatically sequenced digital calculator (i.e., computer).
[19] Communication to author from Harvard comptroller, October 1968.
[20] Among important universities without such a policy are Columbia University, University of Chicago, and Johns Hopkins University.

ago and was brought up by the Harvard Medical School. It is called "A Statement of Policy in Regard to Patents on Discoveries or Inventions Bearing on Health Therapeutics," and it is still in force. On recommendation of the Faculties of Arts and Sciences, Medicine, Public Health, and Engineering, Harvard University stated in May 1934:

No patents primarily concerned with therapeutics or public health may be taken out by any member of the University, except with the consent of the President and Fellows; nor will such patents be taken out by the University itself except for dedication to the public.[21] The President and Fellows will provide legal advice to any member of the University who desires steps to be taken to prevent the patenting by others of such discoveries or inventions.[22]

In cases where it may be deemed necessary to take out a patent and dedicate it to the public in order to prevent others from obtaining a patent for their own benefit, members of the University are asked to report to the Dean of the appropriate Faculty any such discovery or invention made by them, with a recommendation as to whether an application for patent should be filed.

The many and valuable government-sponsored research projects granted to Harvard University faculty and staff have to be signed directly by the individuals themselves. They are considered to be employed by the University to comply with all government requirements. The University itself, however, promises at the same time to exert its best efforts to make the researchers comply. Having in mind the large amount of government funds spent by Harvard faculties and laboratories and the strict regulations existing in regard to reports on research progress and inventions made in the course of most government-financed research, a more formalized patent policy for Harvard University seems likely to be necessary sooner or later.[23]

It must also be mentioned that as of 1968 there was no formal regulation of copyrights for Harvard University faculty and staff; that is, there are no written rules to be followed.

Some Harvard Inventors

Harvard has a long tradition of top-flight faculty and students with new ideas, but inventions and discoveries in the form of legally protected property rights have

[21] Obviously, it is not always easy to label an invention as *primarily* concerned with therapeutics or public health. The Office of Research Contracts refers to a "gray zone" of inventions more difficult to classify.
[22] This advice is given by a leading Boston law firm.
[23] Conversation of the author with the Director of the Office of Research Contracts of Harvard University, May 1965.

always been considered and treated as "private assets."[24] Thus the University never officially collected facts and figures regarding university employee inventions and their fate. Some faculty inventions, however, are too well known to be unknown to the University administration. They occur mainly in biology, mathematics, physics, chemistry, and medicine.

A famous Harvard faculty inventor, whose way of inventing and making use of his inventions now belongs to the past, was George Washington Pierce (1872–1956), who served the department of physics for 39 years and directed the Cruft Laboratory for electrical communications.[25] Pierce invented the crystal oscillator (1923) and the magnetostriction oscillator (1928). His basic discoveries were first disclosed in scientific papers and technological applications later protected by patents. Each contribution "produced one or more major publications and a portfolio of patents."[26] Pierce defended vigorously his priority in these inventions, but once his rights were legally recognized he granted licenses liberally. During World War II he engaged in antisubmarine research but had conflicts with the Navy about the use of his patents. The proceeds from his inventions Pierce used to extend generous financial help to needy students and assistants. Such paternalism does him honor but is a kind of benevolence that has gone forever.

World-famous are the discoveries and inventions of Howard Aiken, professor of mathematics, who during and after World War II worked on Navy research contracts concerning the basic principles of computer operations. (The patents are in the public domain.) Nicolaas Bloembergen, of the Division of Engineering and Applied Physics, invented a three-level solid state maser; Richard Goody, in atmospheric sciences, a new optical relay in connection with a National Science Foundation grant. In the chemistry department Louis Fieser pioneered in laboratory production of vitamin K (blood-clotting agent) and in antimalarial drugs. Robert Woodward is known for the first complete synthesis of quinine (1944), for the polymerization of protein analogues (1947), and for the first total synthesis of a steroid (1951).

The invention in 1929 of the iron lung by Philip and Cecil Drinker has been of great benefit. One of the brothers, Philip, was a Harvard Medical School faculty

[24] This, of course, cannot apply to inventions made by Harvard University members in the course of government-sponsored research.
[25] See *Biographical Memoirs: George Washington Pierce 1872–1956*, by Frederick A. Saunders and F. V. Hunt, Vol. 33 (New York: National Academy of Sciences, 1959), pp. 351–380.
[26] *Ibid.*, p. 360.

member. Edwin Cohen, also of the Medical School, found a way of separating blood plasma from blood cells, a procedure that simplified problems of storage and of tolerance to transfusions.

When needed, Harvard University utilizes the services of Research Corporation for patent protection and development.

MASSACHUSETTS INSTITUTE OF TECHNOLOGY

The Massachusetts Institute of Technology (M.I.T.) in Cambridge, Massachusetts, is the most important engineering school of the United States. It is a private institution organized as a corporation by charter. A chairman presides over the M.I.T. Corporation; the President and Vice President and Treasurer of the Institute also belong to it *ex officio*. In 1968 the M.I.T. Corporation had 35 life members and 10 special term members. Many of these represent large industrial corporations, banks, and insurance companies. The Commonwealth of Massachusetts is represented by its Governor, the Chief Justice of the Supreme Judicial Court, and the Commissioner of Education. The Institute is organized into five academic schools: Architecture and Planning, Engineering, Humanities and Social Sciences, Management, and Science. The School of Engineering has eight departments: aeronautics and astronautics, chemical engineering, civil engineering, electrical engineering, mechanical engineering, metallurgy and materials science, naval architecture and marine engineering, and nuclear engineering.

In 1968 there were 7730 students, half of whom were undergraduates, and 974 faculty members (professors, assistants, and associates) in a total teaching staff of 1646.[27] Compared with the engineering schools of the large State universities these numbers are rather small. The ratio of students to total teaching staff runs about 8:1.

M.I.T. is no ivory tower of teaching and research. The Institute is deeply involved in the advance of many essential engineering sciences, cooperating with civil and military branches of government, industries, and foundations fostering natural sciences. As the vice president for the research administration of M.I.T. expressed it in 1963: "The explosion in university research that has occurred in the last two decades—particularly in that research supported by such outside sponsors as government agencies, foundations and industrial concerns—has been a healthy development."[28] The positive attitude of M.I.T. management to sponsored research, however, dates farther back than two decades. During World War II M.I.T. played

[27] Massachusetts Institute of Technology Bulletin, The General Catalogue Issue, 1968–1969.
[28] Carl F. Floe, "Massachusetts Institute of Technology," *Industrial Research*, April 1963, pp. 45 ff.

a basic role in military weapon and defense research. The contribution of members of the M.I.T. staff to the gigantic National Defense Research Committee is well known; they have advised the Office of Scientific Research and Development as to what research contracts should be written, for what purpose, in what amount, and with whom, in all defense research fields (except medical research). Of the nineteen divisions of NDRC, M.I.T. staff participated actively in eleven, including fire control, subsurface warfare, rockets, bombs, incendiary warfare, guided missiles, optical problems, and metallurgy.[29]

The powerful achievements of M.I.T. in research are based especially on its famous research laboratories. The Cambridge Electron Accelerator, operated jointly with Harvard, is one; others are the Center for Space Research, the Laboratory for Nuclear Science, the Instrumentation Laboratory, and the National Magnet Laboratory. The Lincoln Laboratory, in suburban Lexington, is sponsored by the federal government and derives its support largely from the Department of Defense. It is staffed and operated by M.I.T., and its facilities in many areas are available for research by M.I.T. faculty members and advanced graduate students.[30]

Lincoln Laboratory was established in 1951 at the joint request of the Army, Navy, and Air Force to advance the design of modern air defense systems. It is operated under Air Force Department contract, with support from the three armed services and from the Advanced Research Projects Agency (of the Department of Defense). The research covers advanced electronics as well as fundamental research in solid state, information processing, communications, control systems, radar, radio physics and astronomy, and space surveillance techniques. The largest single subject area in applied research was detection and discrimination of ballistic missiles, reentry systems, and integrated tracking communication systems for NASA. Lincoln's personnel numbers approximately 1800 persons.

The Instrumentation Laboratory has applied a major portion of its efforts in recent years to NASA's Project Apollo, designing guidance and navigation systems for the mooncraft. Participating contractors are General Motors, Raytheon, Kollsman Instruments, and Sperry Gyroscope. Guidance systems used in Thor, Titan, and Polaris missiles also grew out of Instrumentation Laboratory design. It employs about 1900 people. Of these, 325 were directly involved in Apollo in 1967, and twice that number were indirectly at work on it through support and service groups.

Other M.I.T. research activities are carried on by interdisciplinary centers such as

[29] John Burchard, *M.I.T. in World War II*, Q.E.D., New York, 1948.
[30] M.I.T. Bulletin, General Catalogue Issue, July 1968, p. 13.

the Research Laboratory of Electronics which works for 11 different academic departments in general physics and engineering, plasma physics and dynamics, and communication sciences, or the M.I.T. Laboratory for Nuclear Science and the National Magnet Laboratory. New centers for Earth Sciences, Materials Science and Engineering, and for Space Research are all supported by federal government funds.[31]

The dollar investment in research at M.I.T. is on a high level. In fiscal 1967 the total expenditure on sponsored research was $165,628 million, of which on-campus research took $50.6 million, Lincoln Laboratory $66.6, and Instrumentation Laboratory $48.3 million. Federal funds supported an overwhelming majority of this sponsored research, 89.4 percent of the on-campus, all of Lincoln Laboratory's, and 99.6 percent of Instrumentation Laboratory's.[32]

M.I.T.'s on-campus "current operating" budget for 1967 was just over $85 million. On-campus sponsored research accounted for 59.5 percent of it.

General Institute Patent Policy

The Executive Committee of the Corporation adopted, in April 1932, with the approval of the Faculty Council a formal statement of policy regarding inventions.[33] The policy has in general remained unchanged, but it has been modified in certain particulars several times. The revised document of 1964 "Patents and Patenting Procedures" is part of "Policies and Procedures," a printed general statement for the guideance of M.I.T. staff. It gives interesting information on M.I.T.'s relations with government, industry, and foundations.

The patent policy document starts with a preamble saying that the basic aim of this policy is to promote the progress of science and the useful arts by utilizing the benefits of the established patent system in accordance with Article I, section 8 of the Constitution. The Institute patent policy was established to insure four principles:

1. To utilize inventions in a manner consistent with the public interest.

2. To direct attention to effective individual accomplishment in science and engineering.

3. To make inventions resulting from Institute research available to industry and the public on a reasonable and effective basis.

[31] Carl F. Floe, "Massachusetts Institute of Technology." See note 28.
[32] The reader should note that the figures in this paragraph and the next refer to research administered by the Division of Sponsored Research. Considerable research is carried on by professors on department-controlled funds; this probably amounts to 10 percent or more of the on-campus figure. [Communication to the author, October 1968, from the Division of Sponsored Research.]
[33] Archie M. Palmer, *University Research*, 1962, p. 130.

4. To provide adequate recognition to inventors.[34] The relations of M.I.T. with staff and students in the patent field are regulated in eleven sections of that Patent Policy document. The Institute reserves the sole right to determine the disposition of inventions by staff and students resulting from a program of research supported wholly or in part by funds administered by the Institute. (This covers outside sources.) Disposition of rights shall be in the best interest of the Institute, the public, and the inventors.[35] In cases not specifically controlled by contract the Institute will seek advice from the Committee on Inventions and Copyrights.

Inventions not related to any Institute program of research and to which the Institute contributes no special funds, space, or facilities shall be the exclusive property of the producing individuals. The Institute will not construe the payment of salary nor the provision of normal academic environment as constituting grounds for equity in such invention. Students receiving no financial aid from funds administered by the Institute and not connected with Institute research programs shall have full rights in any inventions they may make. Scholarship or fellowship awards normally do not alter these rights, since they are gifts to the recipient.

If government and industrial sponsors require formal agreements between the Institute and those connected with sponsored projects, the Institute may in such cases require formal agreement to assign inventions to the Institute.[36] All staff members connected with sponsored research programs and also those engaged "in consulting work or in business" are warned to make sure that patent clauses in their agreement are not in conflict with the patent policy of the Institute. The Institute reserves ultimate right to resolve conflicts of interest arising from outside activities.

Special cases not covered by the foregoing regulations may be submitted to the Committee on Inventions and Copyrights for resolution. The Institute recognizes the traditional academic freedom of its staff and students in matters of publication and copyright.[37] Where a research sponsor requires the Institute to determine conditions of publication and disposition of copyrights, the Institute reserves the right to apply a policy similar to that set forth for inventions.

[34] The term "recognition" is not further explained here, but a communication to the author states that it comprises both economic and honorary recognition, including recognition resulting from publications.
[35] These interests are often in conflict with each other. F.N.
[36] This may be interpreted as meaning that the Institute does not ask for assignment of inventions in other cases.
[37] Publication and copyright belong in practice to the author, and this is true of publications connected with Institute-sponsored research too. However, the right to dispose of these rights is reserved to the Institute.

The Institute will endeavor to negotiate contracts on sponsored projects regarding patent and copyright commitments on such terms as will further the Institute's basic aims in patent and copyright matters.

When the Institute has an opportunity to acquire patent rights, they will be exercised only when its basic aims would be furthered, otherwise the rights may be waived to the inventor, the government, or other sponsoring agency. In making these determinations the Institute will give full consideration to reward of inventors and will judge whether commercial exploitation will be best served by waiving the invention to the inventor.

Where a research contract is made with an industrial sponsor with provisions for payment of all expenses (direct and indirect) the sponsor may be granted "full patent rights" (exclusive rights). The sponsor may in such case file and prosecute applications at his expense and in his own name. Donors of funds for grants-in-aid (or donors under the Industrial Liaison Program of the Institute) are entitled to a license under any patents the Institute may acquire as a result of work to which the funds are eligible to be applied. Such rights may not be granted in cases of inventions made by students who have been awarded fellowship or scholarship funds from grants-in-aid.

The part of the patent policy document just described regarding relations of M.I.T. with staff and students, is followed by a section on "Patent Organization and Procedure" where the Institute's Committee on Inventions and Copyrights is discussed. The Committee is appointed by the President of M.I.T. It advises the Institute on patent problems (of staff and students) such as inventorship, equities between coinventors or between inventors and the Institute, inventor participation in financial returns, and the disposition of patent. This Committee also gives advice on copyrights and publication matters. *Ad hoc* committees to treat equity questions can be appointed at any time.

The Vice President for Research Administration of M.I.T. serves as chairman of the Committee.He is responsible for administrative matters relating to inventions, patents, and copyrights. Procurement of Institute patents is handled either through patent counsel or through contractual arrangements with an appropriate outside organization. This work is carried out by a Patent Section belonging to the Division of Sponsored Research, which has the immediate responsibility for all business administration aspects of all contract research projects sponsored either by government, industry, or foundations (including patent problems). Government-sponsored research of the Institute is carried out under D.S.R. contracts. In case of industry- or foundation-sponsored research, a decision must be made as to whether a given project is handled as a D.S.R. contract, a grant-in-aid, or as a fellowship. A D.S.R. contract is in order if there is a proprietary interest in the research results on the part of the sponsor, restrictions on expenditures or publications, or special patent rights.[38] If the project is to be a grant-in-aid, the research must be of direct benefit to the educational program of the Institute and must not carry any restrictions on disclosure of results, publication, or patent rights.[39] Such agreements often omit all reference to patents but may specify that any patents arising out of the work supported by the grant-in-aid will be handled in accordance with the Institute's established patent policy. If a student receives financial aid from a grant for thesis expenses or utilizes laboratories and equipment that are partly or wholly financed by special funds, he must relinquish his rights (particularly with respect to inventions and publication) to the extent that the Institute is obligated to those who give financial aid to its educational and research programs.[40]

These invention-policy rules for staff members at M.I.T. are implemented by three types of invention and copyright agreements drafted by the Division of Sponsored Research.

1. A standard patent agreement, "card form agreement," to be signed by nonstaff employees engaged to work on sponsored research projects says that the signee is aware that M.I.T. has research contracts that include patent obligations and that he "may work on projects under such a contract." He agrees, in consideration of his employment by M.I.T., that inventions made while employed and relating to such projects shall belong to M.I.T. The signee also agrees to report all such inventions to his superior and to help in obtaining patents if requested to do so by M.I.T.

2. A second standard invention and copyright agreement is prepared for M.I.T. academic staff and full-time students engaged on sponsored research or using special facilities. This type of personnel agrees—either in consideration of their employment by the Institute on a sponsored project, or having available the opportunities or facilities maintained through funds derived from sponsors—to communicate all discoveries or inventions made in the field of any sponsored project on which they are employed or whose facilities are made available to them. Further, they agree to assign all such rights to M.I.T. or its designate. The same applies to all copyrights and reproduction rights to any material written or prepared by this personnel in connection with work on the project. Where merely reproduction

[38] M.I.T. "Policies and Procedures," revised August 1961, p. 22.
[39] *Ibid.*, p. 26.
[40] *Ibid.*, p. 28.

rights are required to be granted to the sponsor, the signer may publish and copyright such material himself.

3. A third type of invention and copyright agreement, the D.S.R. patent agreement, for all staff members employed full time on sponsored work (D.S.R. staff). This agreement says expressly that the signer recognizes that the making of inventions (and transferring them to M.I.T.) is an important part of the work for which he is employed. In other words, he is an employee "hired to invent." He is obliged to communicate and to assign all inventions to M.I.T.

D.S.R. employees further agree to assign to M.I.T. any and all copyrights and reproduction rights to any material prepared in connection with their work. For example, all employees of Lincoln Laboratory and the Instrumentation Laboratory sign this type of patent agreement. Academic staff members not employed on sponsored research projects do not sign any patent agreement.

The M.I.T. Patent Policy in Practice

After discussing the acquisition of employee-invention rights, our interest is directed to the invention and patent policy for Institute employees in practice. The actual assignment of inventions made by M.I.T. inventors occurs only when a patent application is filed by M.I.T. or the U.S. Government. The number of assigned inventions for which such applications have been filed runs approximately 30 per year. Most of these are filed by M.I.T. and about one-third by the government. There have been years that differ substantially from these averages; for instance, at the end of World War II the government filed a large number of inventions on work done by M.I.T.'s Radiation Laboratory. Unlike the present practice, those inventions were assigned directly to the government with no licensing rights retained by M.I.T.

The number of patent applications held by M.I.T. in April 1967 was 130, the number of patents held for licensing approximately 150. The number of patent applications filed abroad is negligible, possibly not averaging as much as one application per year.

M.I.T.'s general policy is to issue nonexclusive licenses, although in special circumstances an exclusive license for an initial limited term may be issued. Such a special case might exist in connection with a new product requiring substantial development or research expenditure.[41]

Full patent rights are given to a sponsor by M.I.T. only in projects where the sponsor

---

[41] Information in this section from a letter from M.I.T. Patent Administration to the author, April 1967.

pays all overhead costs. On the other hand, waivers of invention rights are requested from time to time by M.I.T. from certain government agencies such as NASA in cases where inventions fall within M.I.T.'s licensing activities. This is the case, for instance, in the field of computers, and computer memories in particular. M.I.T. has not requested waivers on behalf of individual inventors for government-assigned inventions.[42]

Until 1964 when it began administering its own patent program, the Institute had referred practically all assigned inventions, both for purposes of patenting as well as for commercial exploitations, to Research Corporation in New York. This nonprofit organization utilizes the proceeds derived from applied research for the further advancement of science and technology. The Institute was Research Corporation's first client. The two parties had an arrangement by which the Institute could request Research Corporation to accept an invention for management, even after it had been rejected by them, and they would do so. If M.I.T. made this specific request that Research Corporation accept the invention, M.I.T. paid for patent prosecution and any litigation, and the income was divided 80 percent to M.I.T. and 20 percent to Research Corporation. The more normal basis was a 50–50 share of net income with Research Corporation paying prosecution costs. From the beginning, a percentage of gross income was assigned to the inventor, in accord with the principle acknowledged by M.I.T. that the inventor should participate financially in any proceeds from his invention even though it arises from an Institute-administered program of research. This percentage has been raised over the years to 12 percent of gross royalties (but not more than the Institute's net share). When, in 1964, M.I.T. formed its office of Patent Administration, Research Corporation assigned all of the M.I.T.-originated patents which were unexpired as well as outstanding licenses. From that time, the Institute has handled all exploitation of its own patents through the Patent Administration Office, the Patent Prosecution Office (D.S.R. Patent Office), and the Institute's outside patent counsel in close cooperation.

Several of M.I.T.'s inventions have been of significance as far as both income and furtherance of technology is concerned. Among them are the Van de Graaf Generator; the Milas synthesis of Vitamins A and D and organic perioxides; the well-known work of Charles Stark Draper and his Instrumentation Laboratory in gyroscopic controls, navigation, and space flight instrumentation. Perhaps the best known from the standpoint of patent licensing and management is the invention

42 Princeton's policy differs in this detail. See the case study.

by Jay W. Forrester of the core memory now in use in most digital computers. This invention was conceived during a government contract for the United States Navy (Project Whirlwind) at M.I.T. M.I.T. retained title and licensing rights to the invention after issuing a royalty-free license to the government. M.I.T. offered this invention to Research Corporation for management, and when Research Corporation did not wish to accept it, M.I.T. requested acceptance under the arrangement mentioned earlier, in which M.I.T. pays all expenses of the application. Before finally being granted, the Forrester patent was involved in an interference with an RCA patent. After losing before the board of patent interferences of the patent office, Research Corporation continued the interference in the United States District Court against RCA and then filed suit against IBM for infringement of the patent. At this point M.I.T. and Research Corporation severed contractual relations, since there were differences of opinion between the two organizations with regard to procedures in the Forrester and other cases. M.I.T. intervened in the two suits, and Research Corporation reassigned all rights in the Forrester patent to M.I.T. An agreement between M.I.T. and Research Corporation called for a lump sum payment to RCA for the Forrester invention and all other rights held by Research Corporation for M.I.T. In 1964 both suits were settled, and license agreements were executed with RCA and IBM. The agreements with those companies (as well as subsequent licensing agreements for the Forrester patent) have been nonexclusive, and each contains the grant of a royalty-free nonexclusive license to the U.S. Government. M.I.T.'s license income for the Forrester patent is now upward of $16 million, and most of the major computer manufacturers are licensed under this patent. As in all cases of M.I.T. inventions licensed for royalties, the inventor has shared in this income, and the Institute uses its share for general educational purposes. The Forrester patent has remained M.I.T.'s largest single source of patent income to date.

The Institute has done little or no foreign patenting in the past, but in cooperation with Arthur D. Little, Inc. in a recently initiated program, certain M.I.T. patents and inventions will be given review for possible licensing by companies outside the United States.

PRINCETON UNIVERSITY

Princeton University can serve as an example of a well-known, private university in the Eastern United States, which does extensive research supported by the university itself and also research sponsored by government and industry. The University Research Board was organized at Princeton in 1959, and its policies and decisions are implemented by the Office of Research and Project Administration, which assists departments and members of the faculty in the development and administration of research projects. The Office's work covers all departmental areas from aeronautical engineering to sociology, in other words, research in engineering, science, and humanities, including problems concerning inventions and patents and the mechanics of research grants and contracts.

The tradition of research at the University goes back to remarkable 19th-century personalities such as Joseph Henry, the discoverer of electrical induction (later Director of the Smithsonian Institute in Washington) and Charles A. Young, who made Princeton a center of American astronomical research.

The University-supported research is based on large endowments such as a scientific research fund, with an income of about $330,000 per year for the promotion of research in mathematics, physics, astronomy, chemistry, biology, and geology, endowing six professorships in these subjects. Another fund (Higgins Trust Fund) has a total income in 1967–1968 of $490,000. This is devoted to research in natural and physical science and engineering. Other funds make allotments to humanities and social sciences. Several special endowments are available for research in the engineering sciences.

Since World War II, research sponsored by outside sources, i.e., foundations, industry, and especially government agencies, has grown considerably. The large grants or contracts for research are organized in projects supervised each by a member of the faculty and involving other members of the faculty and other professional personnel, graduate students, and technicians. Besides these approximately 400 projects annually, there are two large undertakings of Princeton University which account for slightly less than one-half the total funds from outside sources. These each have a special organization: the Princeton-Pennsylvania Accelerator and the Plasma Physics Laboratory.

The Accelerator Laboratory since 1963 has been engaged in the study of production and properties of fundamental particles and nuclear structure with the help of a 3 BeV proton synchrotron. The equipment is used by scientists from the University of Pennsylvania, Princeton, Rutgers, Lehigh, Columbia, and other universities. University of Pennsylvania and Princeton University share the management of the Laboratory. The Laboratory has its own staff of physicists, engineers, technicians, and administrators, but research is carried on by members of the University and of other universities throughout the nation. The accelerator is located on the Forrestal campus, about three miles from the main campus. Members of the Princeton faculty and graduate students using the accelerator have offices in the Laboratory or in the Chemical Sciences building on the same campus as well as on the main campus. Experimenters from other universities are also housed at the Forrestal campus Laboratory when using the accelerator.

The Plasma Physics Laboratory has as an ultimate purpose to develop a controlled thermonuclear reactor which by extracting energy from fusion of deuterium nuclei would make available an almost unlimited source of energy. A small amount of confined ionized deuterium has to be heated to about one hundred million degrees, and the hot plasma must be isolated from the walls of the container by a magnetic field.

The staff of this Laboratory is about 400. The entire cost of the facility is borne by the Atomic Energy Commission: about $10 million for buildings, $25 million for equipment, and $6.8 million annually for operation.[43]

Besides these two major research programs, considerable research is carried out by the Department of Aerospace and Mechanical Sciences, and research facilities exist for the fields of subsonic aerodynamics, rotary-wing aircraft, aerospace propulsion, combustion, supersonic and hypersonic aerodynamics, aircraft structures, and instrumentation. In addition, several smaller research programs are carried on at Forrestal campus, closely connected with departments on the main campus of the university.

Private foundations supported 68 projects in 1966–1967 with new pledges for $612,000, mainly in the fields of chemistry, economics, and the humanities. Industrial corporations sponsored 29 projects with new pledges of $369,000, especially in fields of aerospace, electrical, chemical, and mechanical engineering. Total expenditures for research projects on the main campus were $11.760 million, and for those on the Forrestal campus, $17.541 million.[44]

Finally, the Computer Center was organized as a powerful help to research. The major installation operates an IBM 360 Model 67 with several converted Model 20's for remote access. This was to be replaced in 1969 by an IBM 360 Model 91. The Computer Center staff also provides training seminars and individual help for specific problems.[45]

Before discussing Princeton University patent policies, some comparative figures are presented to illustrate the financial scope of sponsored research during recent

[43] Princeton University, General Catalogue, 1968–1969, p. 441.
[44] *Annual Report of the University Research Board and Office of Research Administration* 1966–1967, Appendix B.
[45] Princeton University, General Catalogue 1968–1969, p. 443.

Table 6.2   Summary of Princeton Sponsored Research

	1962–1963	1963–1964	1966–1967
New Pledges (in millions)	$26.7	$27.1	$33.7
Number of projects	322	329	411
Cost of facilities and equipment (in millions)	$3.2	$4.7	$2.1
Expenses (in millions)	$9.2	$10.2	$10.2
Salaries (in millions)	$7.4	$8.7	$10.7

Source: *Annual Report of the (Princeton) University Research Board and the Office of Research Administration*, 1966–1967. Appendix B.

Table 6.3   Princeton Research Projects by Sponsor, 1966–1967

	New Pledges (millions)	Spent and Committed (millions)
Atomic Energy Commission 23 projects	$16.093	$15.367
Department of Navy 44 projects	$2.643	$1.604
Department of Air Force 25 projects	$2.255	$1.380
Department of Army 15 projects	$0.464	$0.524
National Science Foundation 107 projects	$4.099	$3.361
National Aeronautics and Space Administration 24 projects	$4.998	$4.460
Public Health Service 47 projects	$1.794	$1.116
Other Government Agencies 15 projects	$0.322	$0.128

Source: *Annual Report of the (Princeton) University Research Board and the Office of Research Administration*, 1966–1967. Appendix B.

years. Table 6.2 summarizes some major costs. Table 6.3 presents a breakdown by sponsor.

For private foundations such as the American Cancer Society, the American Philosophical Society, Brookings Institution, Ford Foundation, and Research Corporation, 68 projects were carried out in 1966–1967 with new pledges of $612,000. For industrial organizations, 29 projects were carried out with new pledges of $369,000. The vast majority of these latter projects were concerned with engineering research, especially in the field of aerospace, chemistry, and geology, involving also mechanical and electrical engineering. For the year 1966–1967 the university accounts totaled $11.8 million for expenditures for sponsored research on the main campus, with 355 projects involved; and $17.5 million for 56 projects at the Forrestal Research Center (including the Accelerator and Plasma Physics Laboratories). The total expenditures for the fiscal year 1966–1967 were more than $29.3 million.[46]

General University Patent Policy

Against this background of funds and projects the question is put: What is the patent policy of Princeton University? As approved by the Faculty and Trustees of the University, every faculty member, employee, and student is required to report to the University all patent applications filed on inventions made while the individual is a member of the University, regardless of the fact that the University may have an equity only in certain cases. The patent policy further states: (1) that the University has an equity in any invention that results from research supported by funds or utilizing facilities administered by the University, and (2) that any agreement to assign or license an invention in this category must be approved by the University.[47] (The statement on equity means that the University is entitled on principle to part of the income arising from all inventions created under patent agreements.) The University stated as the basic objectives of its patent policy, as approved by the Board of Trustees May 12, 1961, the following points:

1. To maintain the University's academic policy of encouraging research and scholarship as such without regard to potential gain from royalties or other such income.

2. To make inventions developed in the course of University research available in the public interest under conditions that will promote their effective development and utilization.

3. To assure that inventions developed in the course of University research will not be used to the detriment of the public interest by the unnecessary exclusion of any qualified user or by any other means.

4. To provide adequate recognition and incentive to inventors through a share in any proceeds from their inventions, since University salary scale is not based on its expectation of income from inventions, as is commonly the case in industries.

[46] *Annual Report of the University Research Board and the Office of Research Administration,* 1966–1967, Appendix B.
[47] *Official Register of Princeton University, Graduate School Announcement,* 1964–1965, pp. 27–28.

5. To encourage research within the University with the funds accruing from its equity in inventions. This applies to inventions developed in the course of research supported by funds or utilizing facilities administered by the University, or to other inventions which are handled through the University.

6. To recognize the equity of any outside sponsor of research within the University by making reasonable and equitable provision for the granting of limited patent rights to the sponsor, consistent with the University's basic objectives here outlined.

It is not the University's policy to take title to an invention or patent. The University has, however, entered into an agreement with Research Corporation, whereby if the University recommends the assignment of an invention to Research Corporation and the Corporation accepts this assignment, then the Corporation patents and commercializes the invention without expense to the inventor and agrees to pay a share of the gross income to the inventor. The net income from the invention after the payment of the inventor's share and special expenses in connection with the invention is shared between the University and Research Corporation. The inventor receives 15 percent of the gross income obtained by Research Corporation, and the University takes its share of the net income remaining. If the inventor patents on his own initiative, the University's equity is 40 percent after expenses. For inventions not developed in the course of research supported by the University but handled through the University and Research Corporation, the University receives 10 percent of the gross income made by Research Corporation, and the inventor and the Corporation share the rest—the inventor getting 47.5 percent and the Corporation 42.5 percent after expenses. The University in turn allocates its share of net income received from the Corporation for further research and scholarship, the Board and the President making the allotments. In doing this, preferential consideration is given to proposals by those working in the field of research from which the invention arose.

In the interests of the individual, because of the complexities and expenses involved in handling patents, and in the interests of the University, because of its equity in inventions, the University recommends that a faculty member, employee, or student who makes an invention refer it to the Office of Research and Project Administration for handling through Research Corporation, as just outlined. The University reserves the right to consider every invention on its merits in order to decide whether it should be presented to Research Corporation for consideration. Although the majority of the submitted inventions are referred to Research Corporation, a few also go to Batelle Development Corporation in Columbus,

Ohio, for conclusion of assignment and profit-sharing agreements. Disputes between an inventor and the University are referred to the Board of Arbitration composed of one representative nominated by the inventor, one by the University, and a third selected by the two chosen representatives.

Inventions of university employees which have their origin in connection with government research contracts are subject to current government patent rules. For the Atomic Energy Commission, the biggest source of Princeton research funds, this means acquisition of complete title to all inventions made at Princeton laboratories which are considered exclusively in the atomic energy field, except in a few cases where AEC waives its title rights. The other government sponsors apply a different patent policy. NASA changed its patent policy (starting in 1964) to offer a choice between acquiring full title, waiving title at the time of entering the contract, or deferring decision until a tangible invention exists which can be submitted. The Department of Defense (covering contracts entered into by Air Force, Army, and Navy Departments) since 1964 has given inventors producing inventions under their contracts a choice of three different ways to handle their inventions. The National Institutes of Health (Department of Health, Education, and Welfare) has agreements with a number of institutions which have approved patent policies to leave title to the institutions under certain prescribed conditions.

Apart from the patent policy practiced by Princeton University for research initiated and financed by itself, there is also a need for a formalized patent policy for all sponsored research arising from industrial grants or outside consulting agreements. The essential part of these policies is outlined here:

The policy for sponsored research is based upon the premise that the primary objectives of such research are the education of students, the advancement of knowledge, the preservation and dissemination of the knowledge acquired, and the advancement and protection of the public interest. In accepting a research contract the University, the department, and the members of the faculty or staff agree to furnish an appropriate share of their time and talent as well as an appropriate share of the University's administration, reports, and publications describing research performed and results achieved. Finally they agree to comply with any terms and conditions of the grant covering patent, copyrights, or fiscal requirements. The University further states that the terms of any contract shall permit flexible operation under regular University policies, shall permit free publication of results, shall reimburse the indirect as well as direct costs of research, and shall conform to the principles of the University patent policy. The Research Board obtains an invention agreement from each individual who participates in sponsored research, which recognizes the requirements of any sponsor or any changed requirements (as may be current for the Atomic Energy Commission, NASA, Department of Defense). The agreement covers any invention, improvement, or discovery in connection with work under one or more contracts, subcontracts, or agreements between Princeton University and a sponsor, made, conceived, or first actually reduced to practice by the signee in the course of any such contract. The signee agrees to furnish complete information on inventions, and agrees to answer questions regarding filing of patent applications, the disposition of title to applications, or claims for payment of award or compensation in accordance with the stated patent policy of the University and provisions of the contract.

With regard to grants for research from industrial organizations to Princeton University, the following policies are applicable: The inventor is to disclose and to publish information on the results of research, except for information classified from the standpoint of United States Government security. If requested, he must furnish information revealing the specific application of the results to operations of the sponsor. As to inventions and patents, Princeton grants to the sponsor irrevocable licenses under all patents resulting from the performance of research under the agreement. No payment of royalties is required from the sponsor for the use of such patents until the total amount of royalties that would have been paid equals twice the amount furnished by sponsor for support of the research. Disagreement as to reasonable royalty rate or royalty-free period is submitted for arbitration under rules of the American Arbitration Association. For certain kinds of work and inventions a provision may be added that Princeton will not grant licenses to others for a specific period. This period of immunity will be no less than three years and no longer than six years from the date of first marketing the patented product. Such an exclusive arrangement is warranted because of considerable investment in regard to the invention or because patent application has been made at expense and election of the sponsor. If, however, the sponsor should not diligently develop or utilize an invention or prosecute the patent application, Princeton may, after one notice, grant licenses to others.

In connection with outside consulting agreements entered into by members of the University, possible conflicts can arise with the established University patent policy. Such consulting agreements generally ask for licensing or assignment of inventions arising out of the consulting work, but such inventions can result from research supported by University funds or utilizing facilities administered by the

University in which the University has an equity. In this case consent by the University is required. The University has agreed that the word "facilities" means primarily laboratory facilities and does not include library facilities. Further consulting patent provisions in conflict with contractual obligations of the University to sponsors will not be granted.[48] Similar situations can also arise in connection with retainer agreements or part-time employment contracts of members or employees of the University. The University states in its patent policy statement that it has no intention of encouraging "patent consciousness" or the filing of patents for their own sake; neither does it require that inventions must be disclosed to the University (except in the event an inventor wants to apply for a patent). The situation is, of course, different in the case of many sponsors, especially government, which require disclosure of all inventions by contract.

Patent Activity

On the main campus in 1967–1968, 355 projects were carried out at an expenditure of $11,760,000 and 56 at the Forrestal campus for $17,541,000.[49]

As an example of patent activity at Princeton, the office of Princeton Research and Project Administration initiated on 13 "potential" (i.e., probably patentable) inventions during the year 1968–1969. At the same time Research Corporation and Batelle Development Corporation handled questions of patenting and licensing on a number of earlier inventions. The total income on patents from 1946 to 1964 was about $55,000 from six patents, the two most successful being a mass spectrometer invented by Walker Bleakney (application filed before the war) and a molecular model for teaching purposes invented by Hugh Taylor. As described earlier in this section, the University Research Board mediated contracts of employed inventors with Research Corporation in New York. In 50–75 cases since 1940 this led to an agreement with Research Corporation resulting in patents by them. Since Research Corporation does not do any development work on assigned inventions, other nonprofit organizations such as Batelle Development Corp. may be approached, or Arthur D. Little, Inc., a private firm. The Office of Research and Project Administration also assists inventors on the Princeton faculty or staff to receive a waiver of title to inventions made under government contracts, especially from AEC and NASA, on the basis of the respective special federal Acts.

[48] Sometimes specified fields of science or technology, in which inventions must be assigned, can overlap to cover both consulting work and research supported or sponsored by funds, as well as facilities administered by the University.

[49] *Annual Report of the University Research Board and The Office of Research Administration* 1966–1967, Appendix B. Other information in this section from a letter to the author from Office of Research Administration, December 1968.

For each project under government contract an invention report must be filed annually by the Princeton Research Board. This is done in about 300 cases annually. Further administrative checking and advising activities arise for the Research Board from the fact that in many Princeton government-sponsored projects the "hardware" is developed by industrial subcontractors of the University. The Astrophysics Department, for instance, subcontracts about $4.5 million to industrial firms, especially in electronics and optics. Inventions may be produced in the course of the work by employees of subconstracting firms. In most cases these belong to the employing firm on the basis of assignment agreements signed by all employees of these subcontractors, but they must be forwarded to the respective government agency by the University as a prime contractor.

Copyright Procedures

Finally, there are also legal problems in the field of copyright to printed publications produced by faculty members and staff of the University. The University does not claim any equity in income derived from copyrighted publications of employees. However, for publications originating from employees under government contract grants the University has to surrender a royalty-free license to the respective government agency to publish, use, reproduce, or translate in any desired way. There is a limit to these obligations toward government in contracts between the University and the Department of Defense. In these cases government will not sell such publications in competition with the University or with a commercial publishing house that may have acquired the remaining copyright from the author by contract. The University would desire similar arrangements with other government agencies, for instance with NASA. In the case of publications produced by University members, in which these employees have signed a contract with the National Science Foundation to write certain textbooks for teaching of secondary school science projects, copyright goes entirely to the Foundation, and neither the University nor the authors are allowed to keep any part of this right.

UNIVERSITY OF CALIFORNIA

The University of California is one of the largest universities of the Western world in terms of number of teachers, number of students, and acreage. In 1967 the full-time teaching staff was 5886; there were almost as many part-time teachers (5190), and a total staff of 54,405. The latter number includes research and professional personnel as well as clerical, administrative, manual, and technical employees (but not employees of the three laboratories managed under contract between the Atomic Energy Commission and the University, comprising a total of roughly 13,000 persons). Resident enrollment in regular session was at the same time 84,317 of which 26,822 were graduate students. There are 8 general campuses: in Berkeley, Davis, Los Angeles, Riverside, Santa Barbara, Irvine, Santa Cruz, and San Diego, and in addition the medical center in San Francisco.[50]

The Ernest O. Lawrence Radiation Laboratory is world-famous. It was established in 1936 as a part of University's department of physics and was a pioneer in the design and development of nuclear accelerators and associated research tools. The profusion of Berkeley discoveries include plutonium and 12 other new elements, hundreds of radioisotopes, the antiproton, and the antineutron. Here Ernest Lawrence and his staff in the 1930's worked out techniques of group research that brought together, probably for the first time in a serious way, the engineer and the basic research scientist.

There are two sites of the Lawrence Radiation Laboratory: at Berkeley, on the hills above the campus, where basic, unclassified research is done in the academic tradition; and at Livermore, 40 miles to the east, where the emphasis is on applied research, including a classified weapons program. It is almost completely supported by the Atomic Energy Commission. Prior to World War II it was built up and financed by private grants and University funds. The largest of these was in 1940 for the construction of the 184-inch cyclotron, and included $1,150,000 from the Rockefeller Foundation as well as $250,000 from other sources.[51]

The Los Alamos Scientific Laboratory at Los Alamos, New Mexico, was begun during early World War II under the leadership of Robert Oppenheimer and others from the Berkeley campus. It too is operated by the University under a contract with AEC, and in addition to research in nuclear weapons, conducts a broad program of fundamental research in the physical sciences, including space nuclear propulsion and controlled thermonuclear reactions. The Laboratory has a staff of about 4,000.

The third major laboratory operated under AEC contract is the much smaller Laboratory of Nuclear Medicine and Radiation Biology, located on a portion of the UCLA campus. It has a staff of nearly 200.

In 1966–1967 the University's organized research expenditures totaled $142 million. Expenditures by the three major AEC laboratories added $243 million. The organized research costs of $142 million came to about 28 percent of total University expenditures. Federal funds financed approximately two-thirds of these expenditures for research.[52]

[50] *University of California Statistical Summary,* 1966–1967.
[51] *Free Enterprise and University Research,* June 1954, p. 102.
[52] Communication to author from Director of Contracts and Grants, October 1968.

General University Patent Policy

The Regents of the University of California, consisting of 24 citizens, 8 of whom are *ex officio* members,[53] have adopted a formalized patent policy for the University, administered by the University of California Board of Patents. This Board deals with uniform procedures and other aspects of patents for discoveries and inventions made by faculty members and other employees of the University.[54] Carefully redrafted detailed regulations were approved by the Board of Regents in May and November 1963, and July 1967. The preamble of this regulation (University Regulation 23) states that the Regents are disposed to assist members of the faculties and employees of the University in all matters relating to patents based on discoveries and inventions developed in situations where the invention was conceived or developed by them. The Regents recognize that such inventions may involve equities beyond those of the inventor himself. A complex of interrelated equities or rights may exist, involving the inventor, the University, and some cooperating agency. The Regents further point to a resolution adopted by the fifteenth All-University Faculty Conference of 1960 urging further use of inventions as a source of funds for research within the University. A patent policy is adopted to appraise and determine relative rights and equities of all parties concerned. The Board of Patents also takes care of patent applications, licensing, equitable distribution of royalties, and obtaining funds for research. It provides a uniform procedure in patent matters originating within the University.

The statement of patent policy is collected in eight sections in Regulation 23. Sections 1 and 2 are concerned with the administrative body (the University of California Board of Patents): it must meet at least once a year and its members serve without extra compensation for a normal term of three years. The Board consists of eleven persons selected from the faculties, the administration and other groups determined by the Regents. The chairman and an administrator of patents shall be approved by the Regents upon the recommendation of the President.

The powers and duties of the Board are then listed. Some of the principal ones are as follows:

1. To appoint a committee of experts to examine the merits of each potentially

[53] *Ex officio* members are the Governor of California, the President of the Mechanics Institute, the President of the University, the Lieutenant Governor of California, the Speaker of the Assembly, the State Superintendent of Public Instruction, the President of the State Board of Agriculture, and the President of the Alumni Association of the University of California.
[54] *Handbook for Faculty Members of the University of California,* February 1963, p. 33.

patentable invention and to cause such committee to report its findings to the Board.

2. To determine the relative equities or rights held by the inventor and the Regents or by a cooperating agency and to reach an agreement among them of all parts concerned.

3. To authorize applications for patent and retain patent counsel.

4. To release patent rights to the inventor in unusual circumstances subject to a shop right to the Regents.

5. To negotiate licenses and other agreements for the manufacture, use, sale, or lease of patented articles or processes.

6. To arrange for collection and distribution of royalties and fees.

7. To assist in negotiation to obtain agreements from cooperating agencies concerning patents to inventions made as a result of research carried on under grants or contracts.

At the heart of Regulation 23 is the rule that an agreement to assign inventions and patents to the Regents of the University is mandatory for all employees, academic and nonacademic. Expected are inventions resulting from permissible consulting activities without use of University facilities. Releases of rights are executed by the Board of Patents "where the equities so indicate." University faculty and staff members who are employed under research contracts, grants-in-aid, service to industry agreements, or by special State appropriations covering specific activities shall make such assignment in each specific case, but all faculty and staff may be required to assign inventions.[55] In consideration of said assignment of patent rights, the Regents agree to pay annually to the inventor 50 percent of the royalties and fees received by the Regents, after a deduction of 15 percent for overhead costs plus a deduction for cost of patenting and protection of patent rights. In the event of litigation or other action to protect patent rights the Regents may withhold distribution of royalties until resolution of the matter. As to patenting of inventions, the Regents state that they are averse to seeking protective patents and will not seek such patents unless the inventor can demonstrate that the securing of the patent "is important to the University."[56]

Finally, it is stated in the regulation that, in the disposition of any net income accruing to the Regents from patents, first consideration will be given to promotion of research.

[55] The quoted policy overrides the right of the inventor to share in royalties in cases where the sponsor so insists.
[56] The regulations do not further define the term "important to the University." The

In a letter of May 17, 1963 from the Office of the President to the members of the Committee on Finance, Regulation 23 was further implemented. The mandatory assignment of inventions was incorporated into the employment form of the University, and all new employees are now asked to execute the form as part of the employment documents. All inventions made by staff and faculty must be reported by them. Release of patent rights to the inventor, providing a shop right to the University, is based upon the following criteria:

1. Where the invention has been conceived *and* reduced to practice without any University support, without the use of University facilities, not on University time, and where the invention is not within the scope of the inventor's assigned University activities (but is within the scope of permissible consulting activities under Regulation 4).

2. Where the invention has been conceived *or* reduced to practice with University support, or while using University facilities (exclusive of libraries), or on University time, or where the invention is within the scope of the inventor's assigned University activities, *if* the Board of Patents believes the invention does not justify the University's expenditure of patent prosecution costs from the standpoint of probable financial return or importance to the University to secure a protective patent.

The Board of Patents also prepares and revises necessary standard forms for all employees in the patent field, such as patent agreements and reports "of possibly patentable device, process, or product." The Patent Agreement is executed by the employees "in part consideration" of the employment and of wages and/or salary to be paid during employment by the University and/or utilization of University research facilities by the employee. The signer of the Patent Agreement agrees that every possible patentable device, process, or product conceived or developed while employed by the University, or during the course of utilization of any University research facilities shall be examined by the University to determine rights and equities therein. The employee further agrees to enable the University to perform its obligations to grantors of funds for research or contracting agencies (which means, in the case of government research contracts, obligation to report all inventions and discoveries and leave required right for them to the respective department or agency). The University may relinquish to the employee all or part

reasons may be purely economic, or they may involve protection of the research activities of the University against third parties. Sometimes the reasons may be of personal "honorary" character regarding the employed inventor.

Table 6.4   Patent Activity, University of California

	1962–63	1967–68
Inventions reported	50	207
Applications for patent filed	14	8
Patent licenses issued	5	12
Patent licenses in effect	33	53

Source: Communiction from Director of Contractors and Grants, University of California, 1968.

of its rights to any such invention, but according to the text of the agreement the employee does not waive any rights to a percentage of royalty payments received by the University according to Regulation 23. This agreement is binding for the signer during any periods of employment or any periods of utilization of University research facilities.

Patent Activity

How does the patent policy just described work out in practice? Table 6.4 compares 1967–1968 to 1962–1963.

For a working staff of more than 50,000 people these figures appear modest, but there may be a number of explanations. One is, of course, that neither clerical employees nor the huge faculties for Arts, Letters and Science, Education, Law, or Administration are active in fields which produce patentable inventions. Another explanation is that in mathematics, physics, and chemistry, discoveries and other scientific working results as a rule are purely scientific and fall outside the legal framework of patents. The same applies to nuclear weapon improvements. A further reason is that inventions under the major AEC contracts are not counted in these figures. Finally, many members of the research staff prefer publication over patenting as professional qualification. However, the two do not exclude each other. The official University policy in the publication field, which from a legal point of view may involve problems of copyright, is not known to the author.

Patent expenses for the University have increased over fiscal year 1962–1963 by approximately $12,500 (144 percent). This may be accounted for partly by the fact that the University has had to cope with increased administrative work as a result of the implementation of the Kennedy Memorandum of October 1963, which required more reporting to research-supporting government agencies. Note the sharp increase in expenses for fiscal year 1963–1964 as shown in Table 6.5.

Income from patents is organized in the following way. In 1952 the Regents

Table 6.5   Patent Expenses, University of California

1962–63	$28,206
1963–64	$39,433
1964–65	$46,169
1965–66	$37,125
1966–67	$41,173
1967–68	$40,727

Source: Director of Contracts and Grants, Univ. of California.

established the University Patent Fund for investment of accumulated earnings of University-owned inventions in the General Endowment Pool of the University. Object of the Fund is to finance patent expenses and research activities. Since that time income from such inventions has been sufficient to finance all patent expenses and to provide significant additions to this Fund. Investment income of the Fund has been used primarily for financing graduate student research. In 1968, $180,000 was distributed among all campuses to assist needy graduate students. Investment income from the Fund in 1967–1968 was $112,168 and income from royalties was $186,441.[57]

No collected material is available regarding the inventive efforts of the individuals, faculty members, and university staff for which the patent policy was drafted. Especially fruitful fields of inventions and discoveries are traditionally atomic energy research and agricultural engineering, the first field widely supported by federal appropriations (Atomic Energy Commission), the second geared to the direct needs of the state. Title to AEC inventions are vested in the AEC and not the University inventor. A long series of world-famous scientists, temporarily or permanently working at the Lawrence Radiation Laboratory in Berkeley and Livermore, and at the Los Alamos Scientific Laboratory have made basic discoveries in natural sciences, in many cases accompanied by new techniques usable in industrial production. For example, Glenn T. Seaborg found a separative method to produce plutonium, the inventions for which are owned by the Atomic Energy Commission by assignment and led in 1955 to an award of $400,000 for Seaborg and his three faculty coworkers of that time, Joseph Kennedy, Arthur Wahl and Emilio Segré.[58] Besides nuclear science, the Lawrence Radiation Laboratories have strong engineering departments with approximately 200 professional engineers at Berkeley and 760 at Livermore. The Livermore Laboratory has a staff of more than 5500 engaged not only in the weapons program but in other broad areas

[57] Director of Contracts and Grants, University of California, October, 1968.
[58] See case study of Atomic Energy Commission, Chapter 5.

of nuclear research for peacetime application, including the development of industrial applications of nuclear explosives, and energy production from controlled thermonuclear reaction.

University inventions by faculty members in agricultural engineering include a tomato harvester by Coby Lorenzen and Steven Szulka and a lettuce harvester by Roger Garrett. Both were made on the Davis campus. Calcium pantothenate, similar to sodium pentothenate and used to remedy deficiencies that lead to some dermatitises and neuritises, was invented by Sidney Babcock. On the Los Angeles campus a number of separate inventions resulted in a reverse osmosis desalination process. Here also Richard Kopa invented a fuel-atomizing carburetor.

In contrast to the plan of May 1963, referred to previously, to publish timely news items about individual accomplishments, the Board of Patents declared in June 1966 that "due to certain, not here relevant, factors these figures (on the University's Patent Fund and patent operations) are no longer published or available for dissemination. The same situation prevails as regards facts and figures regarding individual inventors, perhaps because there is still a fear that patent consciousness may override the true research effort of an educational institution."[59] At the same time the Board assures that the numbers of disclosures and licenses are increasing steadily and that the patent program is fulfilling its purpose of introducing technology into commerce. In an earlier communication (January 1966) the Board reported that gross royalty income from University patent licenses continued to climb.

Important comments illustrating the problems of University patent policy in relation to government agencies were made by Mark Owens, the Patent Administrator of the Regents of the University, in a lecture before the National Association of College and University Attorneys in July 1964, where he said:

Most of the inventions which occur at the University of California, or any other educational institution which does not maintain product engineering facilities, are usually developed on laboratory scale; they are not production engineered or refined for the commercial market. In this situation the institution cannot hope to find licensees unless it can assure them of a period of exclusivity to permit their recovery of engineering and development costs.[60]

When university inventions are the result of government sponsorship, they are

[59] Letter to the author from Board of Patents, 1966.
[60] Title of the lecture: "Effect of the Presidential Patent Policy, Statement of October 10, 1963, on Educational Institutions with an Interest in Patents, its Implementation by Federal Agencies," p. 142.

subject to the regulations prescribed by their respective departments or agencies. According to Owens, the interpretation of the purpose of the Policy Statement of the President, as expressed in the Armed Services Procurement Regulations, coincides with that of the University of California and most other educational institutions that maintain patent programs.

UNIVERSITY OF FLORIDA

General University Patent and Copyright Policy

At the University of Florida the disposition of funds for research and the industrial property rights emanating from such supported research are tightly bound by express provisions of Florida state law.[61] This type of policy is described later.

In 1968–1969 the University had an enrollment of just over 20,000 and a total full-time teaching staff of 1400. The University operates a number of experiment stations doing diversified research, especially in engineering and agriculture. At the Florida Engineering and Industrial Experiment Station of the University in Gainesville, research is carried out in aerospace, chemistry, civil engineering, coastal engineering, electrical engineering, engineering science and mechanics (vibrations, experimental stress analysis, shell buckling, thermal effects research), industrial and systems engineering, mechanical engineering (air conditioning, solar energy, internal combustion engines, survival shelter research), metallurgical and materials engineering, and nuclear engineering (including radiochemistry).[62]

Some of this engineering research is sponsored by federal funds, such as research in production of electricity directly from chemical energy, by the Department of Defense; or survival shelter research, by the Office of Civil Defense.[63] The dis-

[61] In *Patents and Nonprofit Research,* Study No. 6 of the Subcommittee on the Judiciary, U.S. Senate, 85th Cong., 1st sess., Washington, D.C., 1957, Archie Palmer refers to several state universities whose patent policies have been established by legislative action and are part of the laws of their states, as Connecticut, North Dakota, and Ohio, p. 7. Further, Palmer points to the similarities between the policies of the University of Florida and the University of Kansas (p. 5, footnote 14). A long series of universities and colleges (85 in 1957, according to Palmer) have adopted general research and patent policies as a definite course of action expressed in a systematic statement, "by the boards of control, State legislatures, or other governing bodies" (p. 45).

[62] *Research Facilities of the Engineering and Industrial Experiment Station* ("Engineering Progress at the University of Florida"), Vol. 18, No. 1, leaflet 168 (January 1964), Gainesville, Fla.

[63] Similiar state engineering experiment stations were operating in 44 states in 1957. Besides obvious uses for engineering education and training, the research conducted there is usually aimed to be of immediate value to farmers and industrial organizations within the state, but many inventions and discoveries have also contributed to national welfare and security. Palmer, "Patents and Nonprofit Research," pp. 17–18.

covery of an antibiotic against viruses by Ysolina Centifanto, an instructor at the
University's College of Medicine, was made at the state experiment station.[64]

As in most other states, the Agricultural Experiment Station of the University of
Florida promotes farm productivity and improves standards of farm work and
farm living with special regard to the needs and conditions of the state. The main
station is in Gainesville, but branch stations are situated throughout the state.
Activities are financed largely through state appropriations supplemented by
federal grants. The Experiment Station was originally organized through federal
funds authorized by the Hatch Act of 1887,[65] and agricultural research there is
still financed by funds available under this act. On the basis of this federal act,
allotments are made to the state university stations to encourage suitable agricultural research. However, conflicts have arisen regarding ownership of inventions
made by University employees during employment at such experiment stations.

Dollar investment in University research from federal funds, state funds, industry,
and other sources in 1966 was $17,216,650.[66]

A formalized patent policy was adopted by the University of Florida as early as
June 1924 and amended in August 1944.[67] The legal basis for this policy are
Chapters 240 and 272 of Florida Statutes, and some case law made by the Supreme
Court of Florida in the 1940's.

Chapter 240 of the Florida Statutes authorizes the Board of Regents (formerly
Board of Control) to make all rules and regulations necessary for the governing
and management of the University in the State University System. Chapter 272,
sections 272.01 and 272.02, gives the Board of Commissioners of State Institutions
certain definite rights with regard to any patent, trademark, or copyright (or
application for the same), owned or held by the state, or any of its boards, commissions, or agencies.[68]

Section 272.01 of the Statutes vests the legal title of all these industrial property
rights in the Board of Commissioners for the use and benefit of the state. Section
272.02 gives this Board the authority to perform everything necessary to secure
patents, trademarks, or copyrights and to enforce the rights of the state therein.
The Board may license, lease, assign, or otherwise give written consent for the

[64] *The New York Times,* June 26, 1966.
[65] 24 Stat. 440.
[66] *Industrial Research,* April 1967, p. 69.
[67] Palmer, *University Research* (1962), p. 84.
[68] This Board is made up of the cabinet members of the state government.

manufacture or use thereof, on a royalty basis, or for other proper consideration. It may also sell such rights. The University complies with these state law provisions by assigning all patents and similar rights to the Board of Commissioners of State Institutions through its Research Council.

The policy of the University of Florida concerning patents and copyrights resulting from research, as revised and approved in 1950, is described here. Regarding patents, four types of support of investigations are distinguished:

1. *Investigations financed wholly by the University* and carried out by public funds and persons paid by the University. All workers on such projects shall be under contract with the Board of Regents whereby, at the option of the Research Council, they may be required to patent their inventions and assign them to the Board of Commissioners. In this event the University pays the costs of obtaining patents.

2. *Investigations financed partly by the University* in material requirements or personnel service, the remainder being contributed by an organization of industrial or other character, or by an individual not connected with the University. Projects of this type are undertaken only on written agreement stipulating patent and publication rights.

3. *Investigations financed wholly by an industry* or other organization, or by an individual not employed by the University. Such research shall be prosecuted under a contract stating the rights and ownership of patents which may result from such research.

4. *Investigations financed by an employee of the University* and conducted on his own time. Two types of investigations are distinguished here:

Type A. When an invention is made outside the field in which the inventor is employed by the University, the results of such research are the private property of the investigator.

Type B. When an invention is made in the field in which the inventor is employed by the University, the investigator shall present to the Research Council an outline of the project and the conditions under which it was done. The Council shall then recommend a suitable policy for handling the material with respect to patent rights.

For the purposes of patent application, development, and management, the University reserves the right to enter into contracts with agencies for patent management and development such as Research Corporation. A decision as to whether the University and/or its patent-management contractor will prosecute the patent will be made within 120 days from the day the invention is announced to the Research Council. If the University will not undertake to pay the cost of obtaining a patent, all rights to the invention shall be the property of the inventor. If the patent-management firm develops the patents, the University gets a percentage of the profits.

Proceeds from the disposal of a patent between the contracting parties and the inventor in such contracts can be distributed in three ways.

1. In no case shall the proceeds allotted to the inventor be less than 15 percent of the gross proceeds, except as modified by specific recommendation for situations arising under (2), (3), and (4B).

2. If the patent is handled directly by the University, the share allotted to the inventor shall be not less than 25 percent of the net proceeds, with exceptions as noted in 1.

3. If the material involved in the patent comes from research done on doctoral dissertations (or in connection with dissertation problems), two-thirds of the amount allotted to the inventors shall go to the faculty member who directed the research and one-third to the graduate students who helped with the work.

All University profits derived from patents shall go to a "Research Fund" to be administered for the further promotion of research.[69]

Policies and regulations of the University regarding copyrights are divided into two parts, distinguishing two different types of university employees.

1. *Teaching faculty*. It has long been the privilege of these faculty members "to write articles, pamphlets and books, or to present papers before learned societies, to enter into contract for the publication of their works, to procure copyrights for their products, and to receive royalties resulting from their sales where the ideas came from the individual, where the products were the result of independent labor, and where the University was not responsible for the opinion expressed." The regulations say that it would be a violation of academic rights to propose a variation of this policy. Writings of part-time teachers and part-time researchers are included herein.

2. *Nonteaching faculty*, including research workers and employees on special status. When such persons are engaged in regular line of duty in projects assigned to them by the University, it shall be the policy of the University to present the claims of these employees for the use of copyright to the Research Council. The

[69] The Florida Statutes provide for a number of University funds (University research contracts trust funds, a permanent sponsored-research development fund and a working-capital trust fund).

Council shall then make a recommendation to the Board of Commissioners of State Institutions for the use of the state of Florida and the individual concerned.

This patent and copyright policy is implemented by standard forms such as a general patent waiver to be signed by all employees, and a Florida Engineering and Industrial Experiment Station contract with elaborate patent provisions. The patent waiver provides that the signee in consideration of his employment by the Board of Regents of Florida and the salary paid by the said Board agrees that "all writings, designs, productions, inventions, discoveries and developments" made by him during his employment, as well as "any copyright or patent rights arising therefrom" shall be held and owned, and the patent or copyright be assigned in accordance with existing University regulations, with the right of the signee to receive compensation allowed by said regulations.

In the Florida Experiment Station contract patent provisions play a considerable role. One part of the contract, called "Patent Options," contains three alternative patent procedures. The contracting employee must select one of these at the time the contract is signed, and this is not subject to change thereafter. The main features of these three options are:

1. If the University obtains a patent on the subject matter of the contract, payment of costs of this project entitles the individual signee to an irrevocable, nonexclusive, nontransferable, free license to make, have made, use and sell the articles, machines, or devices under all patents that may be granted to the Board of Commissioners of State Institutions of the State of Florida, or to the University upon any invention resulting from said research work. Neither the University nor the inventor shall be under any obligation to prosecute any patent application.

2. All inventions resulting from the work done in connection with the agreement shall be the joint property of the University and the signee. All patent expenses shall be borne by the individual signee, and he shall receive a free, nonexclusive license. Any moneys received from other licenses shall go first to compensate the signee for his actual expense of obtaining the patent, after which 50 percent of subsequent proceeds shall go to the signee and the remaining 50 percent to the University (these latter proceeds to be expended in accordance with the Patent Regulations of the University).

3. If the individual signee pays an additional "patents charge" in addition to the specified research charges (for technical assistance, equipment, travel, or service charges as specified in an earlier section of the contract), then in the event that patentable inventions are made in the performance of his research he has the

option to acquire ownership of patents (at any time within six months after the invention is reported to him in writing) under the following conditions: (a) he shall, at his expense, prepare and prosecute patent applications, having determined that patent applications shall be filed, (b) when the signee is not the inventor, he shall pay an inventor's fee of $100 to the University to the account of the inventor at the time each application is executed by the inventor. Payment of this fee for any application in any country entitles the signee to make applications, upon the claims covered, in all other countries, (c) the signee shall grant to the Board of Commissioners of the State Institutions of the State of Florida, and to the Board of Control, an irrevocable, nonexclusive, and nontransferable license to make, have made, and use for governmental purposes of the State of Florida articles, machines, or devices embodying inventions developed during the performance of the contract. License to sell such articles, machines, or devices is limited to sale of surplus or obsolete property according to Florida state law, but does not extend to sales "for the purpose of sale."

4. The six months option mentioned in point 3 is deemed to begin when the University has reported the invention to the individual signee and called upon him to elect to exercise his option.

5. If the individual signee fails to elect to prosecute said patent application within six months from the date of reporting, the Board, the University, or the inventor may prepare and prosecute the application. In this event the signee shall receive only the nonexclusive free license described in point 1.

In addition to the patent options, the contract contains an "Inventor's Agreement." This agreement, one short section of the contract, states that the Florida Engineering and Industrial Experiment Station, as one party to the contract, agrees to use only such employees in carrying out the research work as have signed a patent agreement obligating them to report all inventions, execute patent applications and assignments thereof, or grant licenses in accordance with this agreement.[70]

If the option to renew the research contract shoud expire through fault of the signee, the University reserves the right—if subsequent patentable information on the subject matter of the contract be obtained within two years from the time the contract expired—to grant the signee a free, nonexclusive license on all patents granted to the University or the Board of Commissioners. Should such subsequent information be obtained later than two years from the date of expiration the signee shall have no right in such patentable information.

[70] According to the contract, the signee agrees to report progress of the project and, in the event of a discovery or an invention believed to be patentable, to report the same and to disclose data and information relating to it.

Regarding publicity, the agreement provides that the University will prevent the disclosure of any facts or data furnished by the individual signee, but after mutual agreement publication of the results of the research project will be made "for the benefit of Science and Engineering." In preparing publications due regard will be given to the patent protection elected according to the patent options.

The implementation of the patent policy of the University toward employees of the Agricultural Experiment Station was influenced by three Florida State court decisions: *State Board of Education et al.* v. *Bourne,* of 1942[71]; *State et al.* v. *Neal et al.,* of 1943[72]; and *Suni-Citrus Products Co.* v. *Vincent,* of 1947.[73] The first case concerned a plant physiologist employed as a member of the research staff of the Everglades Experiment Station of the University of Florida. The State Board sued Bourne to assign to the Board certain federal plant patents granted to him. Judgment was given for the employee. Bourne's contract of employment was "general," i.e., he was assigned to a project which was limited to the breeding of syrup. He was not employed specifically to develop new kinds of sugarcane (as covered by his patent). The employer had no right to the patent "unless the contract of employment by express terms, or unequivocal inference shows the employee was hired for the express purpose of producing the thing patented."

The second case concerned Mr. Neat, an assistant in Animal Nutrition at the Agricultural Experiment Station of the University. The State of Florida sued for a decree that plaintiffs should own a federal patent granted to Neal. In 1933 Neal was assigned to a project under the Purnell Act to study the digestibility and feeding value of dried citrus waste. The project was later extended by verbal instruction to include methods by which dried citrus waste could be made available as a dairy feed by further dehydration. Neal developed such a method in 1935 while working on the project. Isolated factors in the case support the conclusion that his contract was a general one without obligation to assign his patent, but when looked at in a wider light a different view prevailed. The project was set up under the Purnell Act allotting funds to the state to pay the expense of conducting investigations or making experiments bearing directly on the production, manufacture, preparation, use, distribution, and marketing of agricultural products. Neal was placed in charge of the project and conceived the improved method for drying citrus waste. Neal employed the laboratories and other facilities of his

71 150 Florida 323; 7 Southern Reporter, 2nd Series, 838 (1942).
72 152 Florida 582; 12 Southern Reporter, 2nd Series, 590 (1943); cert. den. 320 U.S. Reports, 783; 64 Supreme Ct., 191; 88 Lawyer's Ed. 470; rehear. den. 320 U.S. Reports 814; 64 Supreme Ct. 259; 88 Lawyer's Ed. 492 (42).
73 D.C. 72 Fed. Supp. 740 (1947), reversed (on other grounds) 170 Fed. Reporter, 2d Series 850.

employer, and patent expenses, including a trip to Washington, were paid from the Purnell Fund by the employer. When given charge of the project, Neal was instructed to conduct research with the view of developing a better method. The modification of the project from time to time and the unanimity with which Neal and his employer construed it (as shown by correspondence and other evidence) support the view of the court that the invention in question was the product of Neal's contract of employment, and it was held that the invention inured to his employer. The decree appealed by the defendant (Neal) was reversed in favor of the appellants (the state).

In the third case it was held that the ownership and control by the state of Florida of a patentable process developed by a state employee in the Agricultural Experiment Station were not affected by the fact that Purnell Act funds were used in development of the process (and partially supported the experiment station) and in payment of employee's salary.

Compared with the biggest state universities and private universities of the United States, the patent activities of the University of Florida are not large, but the interest in the details of its regulations remains. Since 1963 one patent application was processed by the University, one jointly by the University and the sponsor of the research, and one submitted to Research Corporation for further development and patenting. Three employee inventions were released to the inventors. At the end of 1968, 16 patents were held by the University through Research Corporation. Very few inventions are conceived on the campus of the University of Florida which are not covered by specific government regulations.[74]

UNIVERSITY OF WISCONSIN

This university may serve as an example of a large Midwestern State university. It was established July 1848 under the provisions of the state constitution and embraced from the beginning departments of science, literature, law, and the arts. Mathematics, chemistry, "natural philosophy," and "natural history" were covered by early professorships, and specialized professional and vocational training, especially in cultivation of land and breeding and feeding of animals developed after the Civil War. The passage of the Hatch Act by Congress in 1887 gave strength to a College of Agriculture and its Experiment Station.[75] Close contact with actual problems of Wisconsin farmers and of industries especially related to

[74] Communication from the Director of Research of the Division of Sponsored Research of the University of Florida to the author, in July 1965.
[75] M. Curti and V. Cartensen, *The University of Wisconsin, A History 1848–1925* (Madison, Wis.: Univ. of Wisconsin Press, 1949), Vol. I.

agriculture has been a tradition of the University of Wisconsin. Organizations like the Wisconsin Pea Packers Association, the Quaker Oats Company, and the Wisconsin Association of Manufacturers have financially supported research to be carried out by the University. In the 1920's important scientific discoveries were made by faculty members of the College of Agriculture, especially by Stephen Babcock (milk-fat test) and Harry Steenbock. Steenbock, a professor of biochemistry, discovered first a way to recover vitamin A in its pure form and later found a method for creating vitamin D in foods by irradiation with ultraviolet light. His inventions from the beginning had commercial value, and he wished to protect his results by patent, but the University was not willing to play a more active role in supporting this part of the development. "The University tardily and even reluctantly appropriated a small sum for the payment of some of the expenses involved in securing a patent," say Curti and Carstensen, and they go on to characterize Steenbock's attitude to his discoveries as follows:

On the one hand, Steenbock knew that his application for a patent was open to the criticism that scientists might be tempted away from basic research in the hope of striking it rich. He knew, moreover, that a staff member in a state institution was looked on as a public servant. On the other hand, Steenbock resented the assumption that an investigator was in duty bound to hand over to the University the product of his researches. He also realized that the control of industrial firms subsidizing research was in no sense always easy, and that some universities had already forfeited control over scientific policy as a result. The patenting of his process would also protect the public against its unscrupulous use. The hesitation of the regents to take action on being informed that offers had been made for patenting the process, that unauthorized use of irradiation had already begun, and that if granted the patent would be assigned to the University, led Steenbock to propose the establishment of a trust to take over the patent.[76]

This was the starting point for the creation of an organization able and willing to protect by patents the inventive research results of University members, to develop them commercially, and to return income from development and investment to the University for research purposes. Thus the Wisconsin Alumni Research Foundation (WARF) was formally organized in November 1925, authorized by the Board of Regents of the University. According to the charter, WARF was to be a corporation to promote scientific investigation and research within the University of Wisconsin and was not for private profit. It was the first foundation in the country to manage patentable University research results on such a basis. Contributions of $900 from the nine original members of the Foundation and Steenbock's patent application were the sole initial assets. From this it can be

[76] *Ibid.,* pp. 421–423.

seen that the Foundation was from its start a separately incorporated undertaking but with close personal ties to the administration of the University. The University is still not represented on WARF's Board of Trustees, which consists of 13 members, of which 6 are Wisconsin businessmen, and 7 represent professional groups or industrial firms in other parts of the country. All are graduates of the University, however.

In addition to income returned to it by WARF, the University is helped to support research by extensive grants from federal agencies. The contracts regarding these grants confront the administration with sets of strict regulations governing inventions and discoveries originating from University employees in the course of such research programs.

The University of Wisconsin had in 1967 a full-time academic staff of 4358. In the same fall term there were 57,052 full-time students on all campuses.[77]

General University Patent Policy

The University patent policy in recent years is best characterized by a statement made in October 1963.

In dealing with inventions and discoveries emerging from its research program, the University of Wisconsin seeks to achieve two goals: to protect the public interest through rapid and wide utilization of research results, and to preserve the academic freedom of the research worker.
1. A considerable portion of the research effort at the University is supported by grants from federal agencies or from certain private foundations under agreements which specify how discoveries and inventions are to be handled and which make provision for the disposition of any patent rights that may arise. The terms of these various agreements determine the procedure to be followed. In virtually all of these agreements, the University accepts the primary responsibility for compliance with the terms; and the central administration will, therefore, in cooperation with the appropriate deans, develop and carry out such procedures as are necessary to fulfill these responsibilities.
2. Where research is supported by unrestricted funds or by grants which contain no specification as to the handling of discoveries or inventions, the widest possible publication of the results will normally achieve the goals set forth above and University policy is to encourage such publication.
3. Where there is evidence that the public interest is best served by the controls offered by means of patents or that the availability of discoveries to the public will be expedited by commercial development under patent protection, the University's goals are achieved by encouraging the investigator to assign his patent rights to the University or to an agency associated with the University. In such cases, the University undertakes to protect both the public interest and that of the investigator as well as to fulfill any contractual obligation it may have entered with the grantor of research funds.[78]

[77] Office of Business and Finance, University of Wisconsin, 1968.
[78] Official Statement of the University, October 1963.

Points 2 and 3, referring to "encouragement" of publication and of assignment of patent rights (to the University or to WARF) make it clear that the policy is not mandatory for University employees. In principle, university inventors may resort to any other organization or business firm when assigning their invention rights, and they have done so in some cases.

In the case of research funds and grants from federal agencies and from certain private foundations where handling and disposition of invention rights are specified, the University accepts responsibility to comply with their terms. As in most other universities, this obligation has increased gradually in recent years with increased allocation of government research funds to the University.

An office of Research Administration was organized by the University in July 1966 in the Office of the Vice President for Business Affairs. It was made responsible for financial cooperation with outside sources of support, but the University of Wisconsin has no centralized patent administration. One Assistant to the President (a professor) is authorized to handle as "patent officer" all employee-invention matters with government agencies and WARF.

At the same time certain schools and departments of the University administer questions in the field of faculty and staff inventions themselves, on the basis of the individual awards and grants they receive. The Deans of the Graduate Schools (in Madison and Milwaukee) are, for instance, active in this way as receiver of WARF funds.

Under the influence of growing problems in connection with research funds from outside sources, the University Regents adopted on March 5, 1965, a resolution authorizing the University to enter into a formal agreement with the Wisconsin Alumni Research Foundation. The resolution reads as follows:

Whereas, a substantial and growing portion of the University research effort is now supported by grants and contracts from agencies of the Federal Government; and

Whereas, these agencies impose diverse and presently changing conditions and obligations governing the assignment and disposition of rights to inventions or discoveries which may be conceived or reduced to practice by University personnel while engaged in research supported wholly or partly by these Federal agencies; and

Whereas, under the terms of present Federal regulations the University is held primarily responsible for the fulfillment of any and all terms governing grants and contracts, and

Whereas, in fulfillment of these responsibilities, the University is obliged to consider in the case of any and all inventions or discoveries made by its personnel whether and to what extent rights in these inventions and discoveries reside in any Federal agency; and

Whereas, for many years the Wisconsin Alumni Research Foundation has provided University personnel with an avenue for evaluating, patenting, and developing inventions:

Now, therefore, be it resolved that the University Administration be and it is hereby authorized in behalf of the Regents to enter into such agreement or agreements with the Wisconsin Alumni Research Foundation, or other patent evaluating and developing agencies, and, where feasible, with granting agencies, in order that the University may fully discharge all of its obligations to granting and contracting agencies, and also protect the interests of the public and of the University staff in discoveries made in connection with University research.

University Policy in Relation to WARF

As a next stage in connection with this resolution, the Regents of the University on June 22, 1965, executed a formal agreement with the Wisconsin Alumni Research Foundation which "provided the avenue for evaluating, patenting and licensing inventions originating with University personnel, for the benefit of the University and the public."[79] This was the first formal approach to the cooperation in the patent field between the University and WARF which in practice had existed for almost 40 years. This late move in formalizing the relations with WARF probably originated from the growing number and variety of federal contracts, as was stated in the resolution adopted by the Regents.

An important requirement of the agreement is that inventions conceived and reduced to practice by University personnel and which may ultimately be offered to WARF must first be reviewed by the University in order to determine whether and to what extent proprietary rights in such inventions reside in any particular federal agency. If such inventions are reported to WARF in the first instance, WARF will advise the inventor to report to the University. If after University review there is considered to be no obligation to federal agencies, WARF is free to pursue a course deemed to be to the best interests of all concerned and consistent with its public responsibilities. Where at least one federal agency has some proprietary right, WARF may proceed with patenting and development of such invention only with the approval of that agency, subject to its conditions and the terms established between the University, WARF, and the agency. Requests for release of any patent rights to WARF have to be prepared jointly by the University and WARF. The University asserts that it will protect the academic freedom, conserve the public interest, fulfill its obligations to supporting agencies, and preserve "the traditional autonomy of WARF and its staff." WARF asserts that it will adhere to a number of specified policies in patenting, development, and licensing of assigned inventions. One of the important provisions is that inventors are entitled to receive from WARF

[79] From the preamble of the agreement.

an aggregate amount (in the case of joint inventors) not to exceed 15 percent of net royalties or other remuneration received. The balance of the net royalties received by WARF is turned over to the University for scientific investigation and research. WARF will also do the following:

1. Grant licenses which in the public interest will result in the broadest distribution of the products or processes embraced within the patent (right) involved.

2. Generally grant nonexclusive licenses to that number of licensees which will reasonably be expected to produce the widest possible distribution of the invented product.

3. Require all licensees developing inventions to show diligence in pursuing such development and report progress.

4. Grant exclusive licenses, usually for a limited period, if this is the only practical manner by which the invention will be adequately and quickly developed for widest use for the benefit of the public. (The usual case is when substantial development must be completed, and such license is necessary to induce licensee to undertake it.)

5. Grant licenses upon the basis of reasonable royalties consistent with normal trade practices.

6. Make periodic reports to the University about its licensing activity, income and expenses.

Except for the regulation of royalty payment, it is obvious from the other provisions listed here that the agreement transmits to WARF the obligations required of the University by government agencies supporting University research.

WARF *Activities*

The articles of organization of WARF stipulate that it is the business of the Corporation to provide the means and machinery by which the scientific discoveries and inventions by faculty, staff, alumni, and students of the University, and those associated therewith, may be developed and patented. WARF may receive assignments of inventions from the individuals just mentioned and also from faculty, staff, alumni, and students of other universities, or from any person or corporation. In spite of this broad authorization, the Foundation has in the past confined its patent management almost exclusively to inventions made by faculty members and students of the University. Currently, it accepts only inventions arising from University of Wisconsin research or from its own laboratory, now a separate subsidiary. As a rule, a "Memorandum Agreement" is executed between the faculty or staff member and WARF, whereby the inventor assigns to WARF his invention and all improvements thereon in consideration of the prosecution of a U.S. patent application by WARF at its expense. The Foundation pays to the inventor 15 percent of the "net avails of monies" received from license fees, royalties, or the sale of the invention and patents thereon. "Net avails" is defined as that amount of money received by the Foundation less all expenditures connected with the securing, maintenance, and defending of the patent or patents so assigned, and expenses incurred in securing income arising therefrom.

On January 1, 1968, WARF owned 130 unexpired United States patents and 131 foreign patents, in addition 9 pending U.S. patent applications and 55 pending foreign patent applications, all on the basis of inventions assigned to WARF by faculty and students of the University of Wisconsin. A considerable number of U.S. and foreign patents owned by WARF have expired.

During recent years the number of invention disclosures received by WARF from University personnel has been severely reduced (71 disclosures in 1961, 22 in 1963, 14 in 1964, 11 in 1965, 10 in 1966, 8 in 1967, and 17 in 1968).[80] The situation under which WARF has flourished as sole owner of inventions from all University personnel desiring to assign their invention to it does not exist any more. Yet a broad basis of invention input is necessary for a successful business program, in view of the high mortality of projects. The fact is that most University research programs are now supported, at least in part, by research grants from federal agencies, which means that ownership of grantee inventions goes to government. Other reasons, too, may have some impact on this development, such as fewer patentable inventions being produced, or decisions to publish, to dedicate, or to keep secret inventions, or to assign them to someone else. Petitions to release and waive government ownership of rights are made by the University together with WARF in certain cases but have not resulted in any considerable increase of WARF-owned patents. The main income from assigned patents stems from licensing the "active" inventions to other companies. WARF does not feel anxiety about its licensing potential for the next ten years or so, considering the number of un-expired U.S. patents in its possession, but after this period development is uncertain.

Since 1927 WARF has granted considerably more than 600 licenses under the patents owned by it, of which nearly 500 were accounted for by the Steenbock vitamin D patents. In the 1960's, the most significant inventions in terms of income to WARF are the anticoagulant drugs discovered by Karl Link, Warfarin

[80] The number of University-employee inventions that did not go to WARF is not known.

and Dicumerol, and later Warfarin sodium.[81] In 1968 they yielded about 74 percent of WARF's net royalty income. The type of license granted has changed over the years. Originally, exclusive license agreements were executed, but later a policy of only nonexclusive licensing was adopted. In recent years exclusive licenses with a time limit of some years of use were granted to commercial companies. WARF's gross income from "income-producing inventions" until 1957 was $19,456,683, of which $13,966,919 arose from the commercial licenses for Steenbock's vitamin D patents and $3,232,766 from licenses for the Link patents. Thirty-one "active inventions" were under license by WARF through 21 years, from 1946 to 1960.[82] Total gross royalty income from 1944 to 1964 for assigned patents was $7,810,528 and net royalty income for the same period $3,850,413. Adding four more years (including 1968) gross royalty income for 1944–1968 increased to $10,670,629 and net royalty income for the same period to $5,453,825.

Other faculty inventors who assigned their inventions to WARF are the following:
Edwin B. Hart, a compound of iron and copper salts useful in treatment of secondary anemias, and a means of stabilizing iodine.
Ray Herb, of the physics department, a high-vacuum pump.
Carl Ernstrom, of the Dairy and Food Industries Department, a cottage cheese process.
Dale Wurster, of the School of Pharmacy, a process of applying protective coating to small particles.
James Asplin, a technician of Soils Department, a laboratory soil-grinding apparatus.
Farrington Daniels, of the Department of Chemistry, thermal luminescence of crystals.
Walter Price et al., formerly of the Dairy and Food Department, a new type of cheese.

The total gross royalty income for licenses to WARF under these inventions (with the exception of Hart's antianemia compound, Herb's pump, and Wurster's coating process) has been under $20,000 per invention. Other additional patents have brought in varying amounts, many patents less than the expenses incurred by the

[81] The unusual history of the discovery of the anticoagulant drug Dicumarol has been described by its discoverer K. P. Link in No. 16, *Proceedings of the Institute of Medicine of Chicago* 15, No. 16 (October 15, 1945); and in "A History of Anticoagulants, A Symposium," I.S. Wright, ed., *Circulation* 19, No. 1 (January 1959) pp. 97 ff.
[82] Thirteen income-producing inventions were being handled by WARF as of the end of 1968. Five others had been licensed to commercial firms by WARF but were not income-producing at that time.

Table 6.6   WARF Research Grants to the University of Wisconsin
1938–1969

1938–39	173,175	1949–50	514,604	1959–60	1,731,383
1939–40	159,000	1950–51	611,000	1960–61	1,694,826
1940–41	195,000	1951–52	668,110	1961–62	1,772,036
1941–42	193,232	1952–53	737,673	1962–63	1,684,326
1942–43	212,500	1953–54	755,125	1963–64	1,695,035
1943–44	225,232	1954–55	833,442	1964–65	1,864,562
1944–45	218,232	1955–56	909,500	1965–66	2,496,712
1945–46	289,091	1956–57	1,007,147	1966–67	2,053,936
1946–47	391,232	1957–58	1,304,600	1967–68	2,911,121
1947–48	425,232	1958–59	1,389,218	1968–69	2,889,000
1948–49	493,232				

Total Research Grants 1938–1969 = $33,330,846.

assignee. How these inventors were influenced or stimulated by their respective agreements with WARF is not known. Their actual income—15 percent maximum of net royalty income—is obviously low.

The University has totally received about $49 million in total research and building grants from Foundation income between 1928 and December 31, 1968. Table 6.6 shows a breakdown of research grants 1938–1968, and Table 6.7 shows some of the uses of the grants for buildings and equipment over the same years.

The large grants shown in Tables 6.6 and 6.7 are the result of the handling of WARF's income based on university (faculty and staff) inventions. Over the forty-three years since its organization, WARF has granted to the University of Wisconsin for research and research buildings and equipment more than its total net income from all sources (except capital gains).

In 1962 WARF was challenged by the Internal Revenue Service on the question whether it was a corporation operated exclusively for charitable, educational, or scientific purposes according to the Internal Revenue Code of 1954 (sec. 501(c)(3)) and was therefore exempt from income taxation.[83] The tax question was settled in 1968 when the Internal Revenue Service reaffirmed WARF's tax-exempt status. The development of WARF in the mid-1960's, with the slowdown of newly assigned inventions on the one hand and the solid income-bearing result of large successful

[83] The Treasury Department adopted in 1961 certain regulations in which it defined in detail under what conditions an organization retaining ownership and control of patents is regarded as organized and operated for the purpose of carrying on scientific research in the public interest (Final Regulations, Exempt Organizations, Internal Revenue Code, *CCH Current Law Handbook,* Edition 1965.

Table 6.7 WARF Grants for Buildings and Equipment 1938–1968

	Total Grant	Year of Grant
Chemistry addition (Charter Street)	$ 66,000	1938
Biochemistry—two additions	137,500	1938
	1,300,000	1954
Chemical engineering	500,000	1950
University Houses (faculty housing, 150 units)	2,710,839	1951
Astronomy observatory (Pine Bluff)	200,000	1955
Birge Hall (biology)	250,000	1955
Sterling Hall addition (mathematics center)	1,200,000	1955
Service Memorial Institutes (Medical School)	750,000	1956
Enzyme Institute	350,000	1948
	300,000	1957
Primate Laboratory and addition	160,462	1953
	300,000	1957
Chemistry research	1,454,000	1959
Computer equipment	500,000	1960
Genetics Laboratory	850,000	1960
Van Vleck Hall (mathematics)	150,000	1961
Zoology research	750,000	1961
Veterinary Science Research	475,000	1961
Molecular biology and biophysics	1,100,000	1963
Elvehjem Art Center	400,000	1965
Engineering research	185,000	1966
Agriculture Life Sciences Library	1,207,000	1967
Total Building Grants Through 1968–1969	$15,295,801	

SOURCE: *Wisconsin Alumnus*, February 1968.

investments on the other hand, has led to a situation in which "the tail wags the dog." There is no doubt that the regular grants to the University and the royalty payments to the inventors are at the core of this cooperation between WARF and the University. WARF's function to develop inventions, promote their scientific and commercial value to the public, and render aid in maintaining patents for them will be negated if submission of disclosures continues to fall off. The future trend probably is that the majority of all inventions and discoveries will be produced by University faculty and students under governmnet contracts and will have to be assigned to government agencies. In this case there may be no need for WARF to develop inventions on a private commercial basis or disseminate them by broad commercial use, and no extra income or other financial incentive will obtain for University inventors in this respect. Faculty members will probably not worry about this, but professional staff members or students who have not reached any high degree of economic stability or professional standard may feel differently about this loss of opportunity.

It is clear that in the case of WARF only a few assigned inventions "hit the jackpot" (substantially the ones emanating from professors Steenbock and Link). That such individual successes may represent a continuing and broad-based stimulus to all other inventing university employees is doubtful. Moreover, the successful exploitation of an invention always depends on a number of factors such as novelty, practical usefulness, and time of appearance on the market.

University Policy in Relation to Government Agencies

The fact that the University receives large amounts of money from the federal government explains the necessity for the University to supervise inventive research results produced by its employees.

For the fiscal year which ended June 30, 1967, the University received the following funds from government departments (the eight largest receipts ranked in round numbers by size)[84]:

1.	U.S. Public Health Service, National Institutes of Health	$ 22,531,000
2.	National Science Foundation	10,977,000
3.	Office of Education	7,074,000
4.	Department of State	3,134,000
5.	Atomic Energy Commission	3,073,000
6.	National Aeronautics & Space Administration	2,851,000
7.	Department of Defense	2,685,000
8.	Office of Economic Opportunity	2,633,000

Source: Financial Report of the University of Wisconsin for the year ending June 30, 1967.

Federal contract funds received for the fiscal year ending 1967 paid for research expenditures to the tune of $30.183 million, and federal land grant funds accounted for $1.239 million. These figures can be seen in the context of total research expenditures at the University, $50.693 million, and total for all expenditures, $180.968 million. The strong impact of research financed by the National Institutes of Health (and directed to wide fields of medicine, biology, animal science, biochemistry, biophysics, and psychology) is obvious.

A logical consequence of this input of federal funds is that a satisfactory cooperation with government and a strict pursuance of government regulations regarding inventions and discoveries made by University staff is a paramount task for the

[84] Communication to author from Vice President for Business and Finance, October 1968.

University administration. Government (represented in the case of NIH by the Surgeon General) is a strict principal when giving away research funds. If dissatisfied it can resort to sanctions by decreasing or cutting off federal research money unless Congress has expressly specified the conditions of use. As primary source of support, therefore, federal research grants demand careful attention in their administration. At the same time, the University wishes to give its faculty members a large amount of freedom to act on their own as discoverers and inventors. The fundamental policy of noninterference can be changed only gradually. Any future patent policy of the University is held to be one "to live with" and never one of complete control of employee inventions.

However, it is felt that there is a need to assert rights of the University and its members against too extensive government claims to invention rights. One practical problem concerns, for instance, the role of University facilities used in government-sponsored research projects. The stockrooms provided for and operated by the University for chemical and medical research contain large amounts of chemicals and replaceable equipment. Ten such stockrooms may supply working material for fifty projects at the same time. No detailed accounting for current use of these supplies for individual projects is carried out, since the University budget of supplies is pro rata. No consideration is given to this contribution of facilities by the University when invention rights of supported research are assigned to the Surgeon General as representative of the Public Health Service. On the other hand, research apparatus paid for to a generous extent by government agencies can be used in a number of different University projects.

In some cases of faculty inventions in the pharmaceutical field the University and WARF made petitions in common to the Surgeon General to make a rights determination under section 8.2(b) of the Patent Policy Regulations of the Department of Health, Education, and Welfare. The petitioners to the Surgeon General requested in one case assignment of the invention to WARF with the purpose of interesting a commercial firm in the necessary development program under a limited exclusive patent license. Total development costs for the invention, a new pesticide, were estimated at $1,000,000. A firm known to have extensive capabilities in research, production, and sales of agricultural chemicals was suggested as licensee; this seemed the best avenue by which to bring the benefits of the invention to the public. It was suggested that royalty from the licensee should not exceed 10 percent of its net sales of licensed products. At the same time government was offered a nonexclusive, irrevocable, royalty-free license for its own purposes. The

Surgeon General determined that "the greater public interest will be served by encouraging a qualified manufacturer to develop, manufacture and distribute the invention in the public interest." The terms of the petition were accepted, with the exception that the desired five-year period of market exclusivity to permit the commercial developer to recoup costs of development was limited to three years with the possibility of extending to five years upon written justification. Approval was granted to WARF for development and administration of the invention, and the inventors were ordered to assign the invention to WARF. The standard royalty of 15 percent of the net from royalties received was probably applied. The commercial firm, however, did not take over the development work.

There are no overall statistics on inventions disclosed by University employees, showing whether they were submitted to WARF or sponsoring government agencies, or prosecuted on the inventor's own initiative. According to the University administration about 50 invention disclosures were offered to WARF during the years 1963 to 1965. More detailed information from the University is needed, in order to evaluate the effect of its invention policy and that of WARF.

IOWA STATE UNIVERSITY OF SCIENCE AND TECHNOLOGY

The Iowa State University of Science and Technology in Ames lies in the heart of the agricultural part of the United States. It is one of the oldest in the country doing agricultural research on state-wide and nationwide problems. Most faculty engage in research pursuits as well as teaching. In 1968 Iowa State had 955 professors, associates, and assistants, and an instructional staff of 910, including instructors.[85]

Basically, there are six research institutes:
Agricultural Experiment Station
Engineering Research Institute
Sciences and Humanities Research Institute
Veterinary Medicine Research Institute
Home Economics Research Institute
Institute for Atomic Research

The Agricultural Experiment Station dates its formal beginning from 1887 when the Hatch Act initiated federal support to agricultural investigations concerned, for instance, with livestock, crops, and horticulture. Additional federal, state, and private support is now available in the field. More than two dozen research workers are active in U.S. Department of Agriculture research, working on entomology,

[85] Iowa State University Catalogue, 1967–1968.

new crops, plant pest control, soil conservation, farm products economics, marketing economics, and forest service projects.

Engineering research is supported by state appropriations and by industrial and government research grants and contracts. An Institute for Atomic Research was authorized by the Iowa State Board of Regents on November 1, 1945.[86] The work is carried out by the Ames Laboratory of the Atomic Energy Commission which hires buildings for research in metallurgy and metal development and runs a research reactor on campus.

Veterinary medical research is carried on as cooperative research with other departments of the University, particularly bacteriology, animal science, poultry science, zoology, and food and nutrition. Emphasis is placed on animal diseases, of importance to the livestock industry of the State. In 1967 Iowa State's total expenditure for R&D was $23 million, of which federal funds accounted for almost $16 million, state appropriations roughly $5 million, and private sources $2 million.[87]

General University Patent Policy

The University's general patent policy is bound by state law. Section 262.9, paragraph 10, of the Code of Iowa describes the powers and duties of the State Board of Regents in regard to patents and copyrights on inventions and writings produced by students, instructors, and officials of the University. Paragraph 10 states that the Board shall

. . . with consent of the inventor and in the discretion of the board, secure letters patent or copyright on inventions of students, instructors and officials, or take assignment of such letters patent or copyright and may make all necessary expenditures in regard thereto. That the letters patent or copyright on inventions when so secured shall be the property of the state, and the royalties and earnings thereon shall be credited to the funds of the institution in which such patent or copyright originated.

Under this provision the University has seen fit not to accept patents from employed or studying University inventors but instead encourages the assignment of rights to the agency established by the University to administer the patents, either by dedicating the patent to the public or by licensing its use, whichever is believed will best serve the public interest. The agency created in 1938 for this purpose by

[86] During World War II scientists at Iowa State University developed a new process for making high-purity uranium metal as a vital war material, and after the war the program was carried forward to develop peacetime uses of atomic energy.

[87] Communication to author from Iowa State Vice President for Business and Finance, October 1968.

the University is the Iowa State University Research Foundation (originally Iowa State College Research Foundation).

According to its Articles of Incorporation the purposes of this Foundation are exclusively scientific, educational, and literary, and are to be accomplished by aiding and promoting scientific research at the University in all departments by the members of faculty, staff, alumni, and students. The Foundation shall furnish means by which the discoveries and inventions developed in such research may be applied and patented and their uses determined and safeguarded for the public. The Foundation has the power to prosecute domestic and foreign patent applications, to acquire, sell and dispose of inventions as well as acquire and grant licenses to others for patents resulting from research by members of faculty, staff, and students. It may receive and collect royalties or other considerations for patent rights.

The net income of the Foundation "shall be used exclusively for scientific study, education and research in each of the departments of Iowa State College (now University), and for the education and training of persons in said College" (article II). The members of the Foundation are limited to eleven, of whom one shall be the President of the University and one a member of the Iowa State Board of Regents; six shall be members of the faculty or staff and the remaining three alumni of the University (article V). There are no outside (industrial or other) members.[88]

On November 1, 1950, the University issued a policy statement with reference to patents, copyrights, and trademarks, in which it set down the principle that it is desirable to insure the control, for the benefit of the public, of the inventions that grow out of the scheduled work of members of the staff. Publication alone does not always accomplish this control because university publications "are scrutinized closely by industrial research organizations," and published results "may become the basis of patents held by others." The only feasible method of control is said to be patents held by the University or by an agency established by it.

Inventions and discoveries that come to the attention of administrative officers of the various divisions, stations, and departments of the University, having been submitted to them by members of staff, are expected to be reported to the President or to a committee set up by him. Desirability of securing a patent is investigated by a faculty patent committee, set up by the President and consisting of five members, who take into account the relation of the invention to agriculture and to other

[88] This is in contrast to the Wisconsin Alumni Research Foundation (WARF), a majority of whose members come from industrial and banking circles of the country.

industries in the state and its possible relation to the life and health of the people of the state.

Inventions that are the outgrowth of research conducted at the University in cooperation with industrial corporations may be patented, but ownership of patent, licensing, and details of control must be fixed by agreement before the research is undertaken. In all cases the University shall reserve the right of publication of the results of research. All such agreements must conform to the principles of research contracts promulgated by the University (in a separate statement).

When a member of the University staff has assigned a patent to the University or to the agency established by it, this member will "receive a bonus in a sum equal to 15 percent of the net receipts from the licensing of the patent, such bonus to be paid annually as accrued." "Net receipts" are defined as receipts after the expenses of securing and licensing the patent. The current year's cost of administering the patent is deducted from the receipts from licensing, and in addition a reserve not to exceed 5 percent of the gross receipts is set aside in a litigation fund.

The policy statement of the University prescribes the use of the Research Foundation's funds. In this respect it says that the expenses of the Foundation are paid from the receipts from the licensing of patents and that net earnings from patents are to be employed exclusively for the promotion of research at Iowa State University. Allocation from such funds to specific research projects shall only be made upon the recommendation of the President. He may also recommend employing all or a portion of such net earnings to accumulate an endowment fund to promote research.

When a particular case requires that copyrights or trademarks be secured to protect publications or products that are the outgrowth of the work of the University, these are handled in the same general manner as inventions.

Patents for inventions developed upon a staff member's own initiative and time without direct relation to any research he has been engaged in for the University, or copyright on book manuscripts or other literary or artistic productions are not expected to be assigned to the University.

Practical Operation of Patent Policy

The Research Foundation, as the patent management arm of the University and under its direct control, uses a standard assignment agreement for the inventions submitted to it by University personnel, which is entirely in agreement with the conditions indicated in the University's statement of policy of 1950. The assignment agreement also specifies compensation paid to employees for the assignment of

Table 6.8   Four-Year Comparative Statement of Income, ISURF[1]

	1964	1965	1966	1967
Income from royalties	$404,404	170,908	196,348	197,843
Grants-in-aid expenses	149,500	445,550	197,557	343,695
Royalties to inventors	51,253	21,339	24,484	24,798
Net income or (loss)	224,927	(290,102)	(15,221)	(171,806)

[1] Project expenses, administrative expenses, interest, dividend, and returns from sale of securities are not shown in this condensed schedule.

Source: Iowa State University Research Foundation, Inc.

Table 6.9   ISURF Project Expenses 1965–1967

	1965	1966	1967
Invention disclosures	$1,737	$ 6,283	$10,565
Patent applications	6,628	4,455	6,666
Patents	583	375	600
Copyrights	–	30	–
Total	$8,949	$11,144	$17,831

patents yielding any income. An additional provision of the assignment agreement refers to the special case where "unsegregated gross income" results from the joint licensing or assignment of more than one patent.

The annual reports of the Iowa State University Research Foundation (ISURF) give a good idea of current size and trends of its patent activities. (See Table 6.8.)

Obviously royalty income from patent licenses is irregular. It depends on a number of nonrepeating factors. Project expenses also vary considerably. For the years 1965–1967 they were as shown in Table 6.9.

The portfolio of the Foundation was (on June 30, 1968) 85 patents, with 42 patent applications pending. In 1967, 39 inventions were reviewed.

Diethyl stilbestrol, a growth-stimulator for beef cattle, whose use was improved by an invention of Wise Burroughs, has been one of the largest income producers of the Foundation's patents. Its royalty income has been approximately $200,000 per year even though the market price for the licensed product has fallen, through the entry of a large manufacturer as exclusive licensee in the field. This licensee has guaranteed the Foundation a minimum royalty of $150,000 per year until 1969. (The patent will expire in 1973.)

Table 6.10   ISURF Research Grants to Iowa State University

1958–59	$ 42,000		1963–64	$ 149,500
1959–60	43,000		1964–65	280,350
1960–61	23,000		1965–66	366,988
1961–62	91,500		1966–67	177,319
1962–63	48,440		1967–68	166,000

The Foundation has also negotiated patent license agreements on foamed asphalt, a soybean growth regulator, an atomizer burner, and a mechanism for relief of respiratory syndromes in babies. The latter, invented by David Carlson, was licensed to Bourns Inc., and in 1968 there were about 60 of them in use. A magnetic memory device, a quick-curing process for superphosphate, a method for reductive decomposition of calcium sulfate, and an oxygen utilization analyzer are other examples. Inventors who have assigned their inventions in these fields are employees or students of different faculties of the University. Grants of Iowa State University Research Foundation to the University for the ten years 1958–1959 through 1967–1968 are shown in Table 6.10.

The Research Foundation since its start has brought Iowa State University more than 1.5 million. These funds have been used for University research in dairy industry and agricultural engineering, for establishment of laboratories and buildings, purchase of scientific equipment, and financing of graduate fellowships and visiting professorships.

Like other universities and university patent management organizations, ISURF has been confronted with problems raised by the federal government relative to the ownership and handling of patent rights that accrue by virtue of grants or contracts made by it with educational institutions. Assignment of title or dedication of patent rights to the public as prescribed in government contracts leaves practically no scope for other nongovernmental exploitation of university employee inventions.

On a state level, ISURF has contacts with the Iowa Development Commission concerning the development of patents arising out of research at Iowa State University.

As at the University of Wisconsin, a question of importance for successful invention utilization by the Research Foundation is its tax status under the Internal Revenue Code as a corporation operated exclusively for scientific purposes.

The Internal Revenue Service ruled that the Iowa State University Research Foundation is not tax exempt under sec. 501(c)(3) of the Internal Revenue Code. However, the Internal Revenue Service suspended the requirement that the Foundation file federal income tax returns so long as it confines its operation to providing services to Iowa State University relative to inventions arising from University research.

SUMMARY OF UNIVERSITY PATENT POLICY

Of seven universities selected for case studies, six have a formalized patent policy with uniform procedure. (The exception is Harvard.) In summarizing these university policies, we can ask the following questions:

1. Who adopts the policy?
2. Who administers the policy?
3. How is the policy implemented?
4. What are the declared purposes of the policy?
5. What are the actual features of the policy?

The term "patent policy" is used by many universities to cover all kinds of legally protectable employee working results including all kinds of publications which can be protected by copyright. However, copyright issues play a relatively subordinate part in the university relationship to its staff.

1. Who Adopts the Policy?

The answer depends on the structure and organization of the whole university. We find that at the state universities in California and Wisconsin the patent policy is adopted by the Regents of the university, at M.I.T. by the Executive Committee of the Corporation, at Princeton by the Faculty and the Trustees, at Florida by the Board of Commissioners of State Institutions, at Iowa by the State Board of Education. At Harvard the President and Fellows have abstained from issuing a formal patent policy for the use of the entire university.[89]

2. Who Administers the Policy?

With the increasing amount of research funds the university's responsibility to supervise disclosure and delivery of research results produced by faculty members and university staff (especially to federal agencies which now supply large funds) has increased. Offices have been created for the purpose of formulating employee-invention policy: an Office of Research Administration at Princeton, a Research Administration in the Office of the Vice-President for Business Affairs at Wisconsin,

[89] The particular body formally responsible for the policy is in many cases not identical with the persons or groups of persons actually pushing the policy.

a Research Council in Florida, and a Research Foundation in Iowa. Offices exclusively for patent management have been organized by the University of California (U.C. Board of Patents) and M.I.T. (Office of Patent Administration, under the Vice-President in charge of Research Administration). Harvard has an Office of Research Contracts which is not officially concerned with questions of a uniform patent policy but is likely to run into patent matters.

3. How Is the Policy Implemented?

The regulations concerning employee-invention policy are often described as part of the general rules and regulations of the university, accessible in printed catalogues, announcements, or bulletins. This is the case at Princeton, M.I.T., and California. Special pamphlets exist at the other universities. At all the universities described, with the exception of Harvard and Princeton, university employees, especially full-time research employees, have to sign patent agreements when starting employment.

4. What Are the Declared Purposes of the Policy?

Some universities list a number of purposes of the patent policy without separating primary and secondary principles. However, the declared purposes can be roughly classified in three groups: safeguarding the public interest in inventions, providing general service to the academic community, and offering incentive and recognition to the inventing academic employees. There may be combinations of these purposes, but making money for the university or stimulating utilization of inventions are not expressly cited.

Most specific of the institutions analyzed here is M.I.T. which states four principles to be insured by its patent policy: (1) to utilize inventions in a manner consistent with the public interest, (2) to direct attention to effective individual accomplishment in science and engineering, (3) to make Institute inventions available to industry and the public on a reasonable and effective basis, and (4) to provide adequate recognition to inventors. (There would seem to be considerable duplication between (1) and (3) and between (2) and (4).) These principles must be valid at all universities, even if they are not expressly stated. Widest possible publication of all working results (patentable or not) is naturally encouraged by many universities as in line with long-standing traditions in the academic world. Florida emphasizes its right to legal title of university patents for the use and benefit of the State including direct or indirect commercial exploitation. To serve the public interest by expediting commercial development and commercial use of university inventions is expressed by several universities.

To collect income from university-employee patents is never a declared primary purpose of any university administration. *If*, however, university-employee inventions turn out to have prospective market value, a number of universities consider it to be one of the purposes of their patent policy to work actively— through their own institutions, associated organization or outside corporations— for adequate patent protection, to negotiate with third parties, including government agencies, on behalf of the inventors about waiving property rights to the inventor and possibly administering income derived from licensed or sold inventions. A policy encouraging "investigators" to assign their invention rights "to an agency associated to the university" has been practiced by the University of Wisconsin for 40 years and is discussed in point 5.

5. Patent and Copyright Policy in Practice

There is often a gap between professions and actualities when comparing declared purposes of a university patent policy and a patent policy translated into efficient day-to-day work. The following points help the reader sort out the actual operation by institution.

Allocation of Ownership of Rights   At Iowa State University of Science and Technology the State Board of Education in its discretion takes assignment to inventions produced by students, instructors, and officials, with the consent of the inventor. In practice the University encourages the assignment of inventions to the agency established by it, the Iowa State University Research Foundation. The assignment of rights seems to be voluntary on the side of the inventor.

At the University of Florida the Florida statutes vest legal title to all industrial property rights of any state institution in the Board of Commissioners of State Institutions. The University, as such an institution, complies with state law by requiring, in all contracts for research financed wholly by the University, assignment of inventions to the Research Council of the University.

The University of California has ruled that an agreement to assign inventions and patents to the Regents of the University is mandatory for all employees, academic and nonacademic. Faculty and staff members employed under research contracts, grants-in-aid or service-to-industry agreements, or state-supported specific activities must make assignment in each specific case.

The University of Wisconsin encourages investigators to assign their patent rights to the University or to an agency associated with the University, when there is evidence that the public interest is best served by the controls offered by means of patents or when the availability to the public will be expedited by commercial development under patent protection. In 1965 the Regents of the University executed a formal agreement with the Wisconsin Alumni Research Foundation (WARF) as an organization providing "the avenue for evaluating, patenting, and licensing inventions originating with University personnel, for the benefit of the University and the public." Assignment of employee inventions to this organization is voluntary, but if made it is subject to University review to check for conflict with government proprietary rights. The agreement fixed a practice prevailing for more than one generation but increased University control of government contracts.

The Massachusetts Institute of Technology reserves the sole right to determine disposition of inventions made by staff and students and resulting from supported research programs.[90] The Institute, however, exercises this right only when the basic aims of the Institute would be furthered by acquisition of these rights. Otherwise it waives the rights to the inventor, to the government, or other sponsors. In cases of projects sponsored outside the Institute, assignment of inventions to the Institute may be required.

At Princeton University faculty members and employees may voluntarily refer inventions to the University and assign them to the Princeton Office of Research Administration, which is part of the University administration. The University may have an equity in inventions developed in the course of research supported by funds or utilizing facilities administered by the University. The equity is established in conference with the inventor. Assignment of employee inventions to the nonprofit organization Research Corporation is recommended by the University which, naturally, means acceptance of this organization's rules for licensing and division of income from assigned invention rights. Any agreement to assign or license employee inventions entered into by faculty members, employees, or students needs written consent of the University.

Harvard University, finally, does not take title to or ask for assignment of any employee inventions in any fields. Inventions made by members of the university "primarily concerned with therapeutics or public health," for which the inventor intends to file patents, must be reported to the Dean, and patenting is allowed only with the consent of the President and the Fellows.[91] No assignment of rights to the University is involved in this field either.

When talking about allocation of invention rights by universities one may never forget the fundamental change in this situation caused by the ever-increasing

90 The legal basis for this approach is not known.
91 The legal basis for this policy is not known.

percentage of government-supported university research. Government contracts with universities include, as a rule, provision that title to all inventions and discoveries made by university employees of any status engaged in this work be reserved to government.[92] Applications asking waiver of these government rights must be filed in each individual case. Some universities, such as Princeton, assist their employed inventors in asking for release of title to inventions made under government contracts. The percentage of government-bound research at the seven universities studied in this chapter was as follows in 1966[93]:

M.I.T.	89
Princeton	88
California	88
Wisconsin	59
Iowa	56
Florida	43
Harvard	not available.

Supposing that this supported research emanates from federal agencies requiring title to all patent rights from contractors, there is little margin left for a meaningful individual university patent policy.

Allocation of Income from Invention Rights and Copyrights   Where there is no transfer of rights from university inventors or writers to the university, there is no allocation of income. This is the case at Harvard, which stays away from any commercial cooperation with its employees. All other six universities analyzed have some arrangements with inventors for sharing income from licensing or selling employee invention rights.[94]

Iowa State University provides that when a staff member assigns a patent to the University or an agency established by the University and the patent is licensed, he shall receive an annual bonus equal to 15 percent of the net receipts from such licensing. The Iowa State University Research Foundation, as administrator of University inventions, agrees to pay this amount less 15 percent for general overhead administration and operation expenses and less the actual incurred

92 The government invention title policy is in a state of transition and tending to comprise more and more departments.
93 *Industrial Research*, April 1967, Tables pp. 69–71.
94 Exact comparison of the economic significance of the arrangements at different universities would demand careful study of the definitions of financial terms such as "net receipts," "proceeds," "net avails," "all monies received," "gross income," "net royalties," etc.

patenting, licensing, or assigning, and litigation expenses for the licensed or assigned patent applications and patents. (A reserve not to exceed 5 percent of the gross receipts is set aside in a litigation fund.) The net earnings of the Research Foundation from the income go exclusively to the promotion of research at Iowa State University. They can eventually be accumulated in a specific endowment fund.

The University of Florida distinguishes between three ways of distributing the proceeds from the disposal of assigned employee patents:

1. In no case shall the proceeds allotted to the employed inventor be less than 15 percent of the gross proceeds from investigations wholly financed by the University.

2. If the assigned patent is handled by the University and if the investigations are financed by the University, the share allotted to the inventor shall not be less than 25 percent of the net proceeds.

3. If the material involved in the assigned patent comes from research on dissertations, the amount allotted to the inventor shall be divided two-thirds to the faculty member who directed the research, and one-third to the graduate students who helped with the work.[95] All university profits from employee inventions go to a research fund for further promotion of research.

The University has special regulations regarding royalty income from sale of copyrighted material. Two groups of employees are distinguished here: teaching and nonteaching faculty (the latter including research workers and employees on special status). The group of academic employees may keep all royalties resulting from their sales where the ideas come from the individual, where the products were the result of independent work, and where the University was not responsible for the opinion expressed. The second group of employees shall present their claims to the Research Council of the University, and the Council shall make a recommendation as to these rights to the Board of Commissioners of State Institutions, for use by the State and the individual.[96]

The University of California holds that it is one of the duties of the University of California Board of Patents "to arrange for collection and distribution of royalties and fees" (for all patented inventions assigned to the University, and licensed or sold). According to their approved regulations the Regents of the University agree to pay annually to the inventor of assigned patents 50 percent of the royalties and fees received by the Regents, after a deduction of 15 percent thereof for overhead

95 The decision appears to be arbitrary and may give rise to conflict.
96 I do not know how this provision operates in practice or whether any controversies have arisen.

costs plus a deduction for cost of patenting and protection of patent rights (in case of litigation, to protect patent rights the Regents may withhold distribution of royalties until resolution of the matter). In disposing any net income accruing to the Regents from patents, first consideration will be given to promotion of research. If the Regents relinquish all or part of their patent rights to other grantors they do not waive any rights to a percentage of royalty payments received from such patents by the University. A special fund, the University Patent Fund, exists for investment of accumulated earnings of university-owned inventions in the General Endowment Pool of the university. Object of the Fund is to finance patent expense and research activities (especially graduate student research).

The University of Wisconsin does not itself allocate income from employee-invention rights or make any direct payments of patent income to inventors. This is left to Wisconsin Alumni Research Foundation (WARF), with which the Regents of the University executed a formal agreement in 1965 as an agency to evaluate and develop patents. WARF may exploit assignable employee inventions through licensing under a number of conditions confirmed in the agreement with the University. Income from exploited inventions is shared by WARF between University inventors, the University, and itself. Inventors of such inventions are by direct contract with WARF awarded (in an aggregate amount, if there are joint inventors) a bonus not to exceed 15 percent of net royalties (net avails) or other remuneration received by WARF. The balance of net royalties received by WARF is turned over to the University for scientific investigation and research within the University or its departments. The administration of patent income by WARF is organized in such a way that after payment of 15 percent royalty on net avails to inventors and reimbursement of patent costs to WARF, the remaining 85 percent of net returns are invested by WARF, mainly in stocks and in land. Income from such investment is then annually turned over to the University for the uses described in the contract. All expenditures connected with the securing, maintenance, and defending of assigned patents and expenses incurred in securing income therefrom may be deducted by WARF from money received by the Foundation as income.

Until 1959, the Massachusetts Institute of Technology referred assigned employee inventions for exploitation (and possible patent prosecution) to Research Corporation.[97] At present, in accord with the principle that the inventor should participate financially in any proceeds from his invention (even if it results from a program

[97] Why M.I.T. ceased to operate through Research Corporation is told in the M.I.T. case study.

administered by the Institute) normally 12 percent of received gross royalties are paid him by M.I.T. The Institute retains the net income after expenses (including payment to inventors) and uses it for its general educational purposes.

Princeton University has among its declared basic objectives of patent policy (as approved in 1961) "to provide adequate recognition and incentive to inventors through a share in any proceeds from their inventions," and on the part of the University itself: "to advance and encourage research within the University with the funds accruing to the University from its equity in those inventions which are developed in the course of research supported by funds or utilizing facilities administered by the University."

We can distinguish four main types of arrangements:

1. Employee inventors usually assign their inventions to some nonprofit organization for exploitation, preferably Research Corporation of New York. The University then pays the inventor 15 percent of the gross income received by Research Corporation. The University's own equity is considered "to be its share of net income remaining."[98]

2. For employee inventions referred to the University but handled "in some other manner than through Research Corporation" the relative equities of the inventor and the University will be comparable to the ones assigned to the Corporation.

3. In the case of inventions not referred to the University but patented by the inventor on his own initiative, the University considers its equity to be "40 percent of all monies received from the assignment, license, or use of the patent after expenses incurred by the inventor are deducted."

4. For any invention which is not developed in the course of research supported by funds or utilizing facilities administered by the University, but which the University inventor elects to handle through the University and Research Corporation, the University keeps 10 percent of the gross income realized by Research Corporation. The inventor receives 47.5 percent and Research Corporation 42.5 percent of the net income remaining after deduction of special expenses incurred by Research Corporation (with approval of the inventor). Total income for Princeton University from employee patents since 1946 has been modest (considerably under $100,000).

Utilization of University-Owned Invention Rights   It will probably not be a

98 Since the agreement between Princeton University and Research Corporation only provides for payment of 15 percent of the gross income by the Corporation to the inventor, any amount in excess of this is paid by the university to the inventor from the university's normal share.

wrong guess that the majority of persons responsible for the administration of a university consider the providing of commercial use of university-owned invention rights to be entirely outside their functions.[99] As a rule, there has not been in the past any machinery at any university to handle work of this type. There is also considerable "ideological resistance" toward commercial activities related to patent rights. University patents rights can be utilized in principle by dedication to the public, by different types of patent licenses, or by outright sale of patents.

The situation is different when presenting inventions and similar research results by publishing. A publication often satisfies both the public interest in fast unrestricted dissemination of new inventions and discoveries and the interest of individual recognition to the author and inventor. However, personal credit is not always given to all cooperators in publications about large research projects, whereas citation of names (of inventors) is guaranteed by law in patent letters.

Attempt to utilize university-owned employee inventions commercially, with the university as an active direct partner, was found at three universities of the case studies in this chapter: the University of California, the Massachusetts Institute of Technology, and the Iowa State University.

The Board of Patents of the University of California counts it among its duties to negotiate licenses and other agreements for the manufacture, use, sale, or lease of patented articles or processes owned by the University, and to assist in negotiation to obtain patent agreement from cooperating agencies. (In 1964, the University employed a special patent-licensing agent for a year to place commercial licenses for university-owned patents on the market.)

Massachusetts Institute of Technology, after using Research Corporation as agent for commercializing Institute patents, has now since 1959 administered and licensed these patents mainly in its own regime through its Patent Administration. Some inventions made under common sponsorship of M.I.T. and the firm Arthur D. Little are assigned to this firm for management and commercial utilization.

Iowa State University also undertakes to find commercial use for employee inventions through its own Research Foundation. This Foundation has placed a number of royalty-earning patent licenses on the market.

Most of the other universities analyzed give their employees more or less extensive advice, free of cost, on how to cooperate with professional outside nonprofit or profit organizations to achieve commercial use of their inventions. The University

[99] For a brilliant presentation of some main subjects of the economics of a university and the attitude of professors to such economic problems, see Allan M. Cartter, "Economics of the University," in *American Economic Review* 55, No. 2 (May 1965): 481 ff.

of Wisconsin offers the most explicit service of this kind to its inventive employees. With a detailed formal agreement with the Wisconsin Alumni Research Foundation (WARF) as an "avenue for evaluating, patenting, and licensing inventions originating with University personnel," University of Wisconsin inventors can take advantage of an experienced organization. There is, however, no compulsion for the University or its employees to make exclusive use of this special way of utilizing University invention rights.

Also Princeton University mediates commercial utilization of employee inventions, primarily with Research Corporation of New York, and offers negotiation and prosecution of business on behalf of University inventors through the University's own office of Research Administration.

The University of Florida reserves the right to enter into contracts "with recognized patent management and development agencies, such as the Research Corporation" for the purpose of patent application, development, and management for University research patents. The University reserves the same right for copyrights.

Harvard University gives no active patent work or advice to University members regarding commercial use of patents. Patents on discoveries or inventions bearing on health and therapeutics will not be taken out by the University itself "except for dedication to the public." An agreement with Research Corporation "for patent protection and development" does, however, exist even here and is open to all inventing employees.

EVALUATION OF UNIVERSITY EMPLOYER INVENTION POLICY

Suggestions for a University Patent Organization and Its Tasks

1. There should be some kind of formalized university-employee invention policy and program handled by a permanent university office or an office authorized by the university in all universities with research activities.

2. The program should be administered by a full-time legal staff, assisted and supervised by a committee of faculty, research staff, and graduate students.

3. The office should preferably have six main functions:

a. To publish (and from time to time update) general regulations in the invention field for the information of all faculty members, employees, students, consultants, and temporary guests; to prepare standard forms for important invention procedures, such as invention assignments, filing of patent applications and invention disclosures; and to provide guidelines in general patent law.[100]

100 This could be carried out with the assistance of law professors and students to inspire them to study this special field of law and to lecture about it, especially in universities with science and engineering departments.

b. To assist all types of university employees working under federal government and state research contracts and grants in fulfilling contract requirements concerning inventions and data, including the drafting and prosecuting of waiver applications to respective departments, agencies, or other supporting bodies or organizations.

c. On application, to assist employees in domestic and foreign patent prosecution and in getting into contact with one or more nonprofit or profit invention-exploiting institutions or firms.

d. If supported by the regents of a university or a majority of faculty members, to procure the utilization of university-employee inventions by licensing or selling nongovernment-owned patents through the university office or a delegated body and to administer the income from such activities for the benefit of the university and the inventors.

e. To create a loose, nationwide head organization of all university and college administrations in the invention field, which would have annual meetings for the purpose of exchanging experiences, would publish pamphlets in this field, and would cooperate with public service institutions such as the Civil Service Commission's Office of Career Development (Section of Federal Incentive Awards Program), the Federal Council for Science and Technology of the Department of Commerce, and the Patent Office.

f. On application, to assist employees in placing copyrightable material commercially, for instance with domestic and foreign publishers, schools, educational institutions, film and educational equipment producers, or manufacturers of various kinds.

4. State laws and regulations concerning the handling and allocation of industrial property rights produced by employees of state institutions should be made more uniform.

Suggestions Regarding Rights and Duties of University Inventors

1. University inventors should have to disclose to the university administration all inventions made during ordinary service or employment, including inventions made in the course of special research projects where the inventor has used university facilities.[101]

2. If a university inventor is unable to analyze the character of his own invention he should have to consult the invention office of his university.

[101] The administrative, legal, and economic relations between a university inventor and his employer depend on the character of the invention and the circumstances under which it was made.

3. Unless prohibited by government contract, a university inventor should always be entitled to a substantial share of income (profit) from inventions made by him and assigned and commercially exploited by the university, a licensed enterprise, or a licensed institution.

4. The percentage distribution of income from university inventions between the parties cannot be generally fixed in advance. It depends, among other things, on who is paying for the costs of patenting, negotiating, licensing, or sale, and eventual additional development costs for producing a marketable product or process.

5. Net income retained after expenses by a university from assigned employee inventions should be used for general university purposes, substantially to promote those research fields most useful in terms of broad educational objectives, including the school from which income from invention was received.

6. Income from employee inventions should not affect salary and other official income to which a university employee is entitled.

7. In all financial or other economic arrangements between a university administration and university inventors, due concern should be given to the public interest, since most universities are public institutions.

8. Disputes between university inventors and the university about correct analysis of the type of invention made, allocation of right, patenting and exploitation of inventions, and distribution of income from licensed or sold inventions should be referred to a special federal board or court deciding such questions for all nonprivate employees, i.e., government, state, or municipal employees. Employees of private universities enjoy the same right.[102]

102 Compare "Evaluation of Government Employer Patent Policy," point 6, p 390.

Anderson, Roland A. "If There Is an Invention under a Government Contract—Who Should Get It?" *Federal Bar Journal* 21 (1961): 64–66.

Ansell, Edward O., and Alfred L. Hamilton. "Security Considerations in Filing Patent Applications Abroad." *American Bar Association Journal* 50 (1964): 946.

Bambrick, James J., Jr., and Albert A. Blum. "Patent Agreements in Union Contracts." *Management Record,* June 1956.

Bambrick, James J., Jr., Albert A. Blum, and Hermine Zagat. *Unionization among American Engineers.* National Industrial Conference Board Studies in Personnel Policy, No. 155. New York.

Banta, P. M., and M. B. Hiller. "Patent Policies of the Department of Health, Education, and Welfare." *Federal Bar Journal* 21 (1961): 88–98.

Banzhaf, John. "Copyright Protection for Computer Programs." *ASCAP Copyright Law Symposium,* No. 14, 1966.

Barber, Richard J. *Politics of Research.* Washington, D.C.: Public Affairs Press, 1966.

Bate, Gordon. *Criminal Prosecution in Respect of Trade Secrets.* Practicing Law Institute, 25th Annual Summer Session, 1966.

Baumes, Carl. *Patent Counsel in Industry.* National Industrial Conference Board Policy Studies, No. 112. New York: 1964.

Beach, Robert E. "A Question of Property Rights: The Government and Industrial Know-How." *American Bar Association Journal* 41 (1955): 1024.

Bender, David. "Computer Programs: Should They Be Patentable?" *Colorado Law Review* 68 (1968): 241.

Bishop, Arthur N., Jr. "Employers, Employees, and Inventions." *Southern California Law Review* 31 (1957): 52–54.

Blake, Harlan M. "Employee Agreements Not to Compete." *Harvard Law Review* 73 (1960): 625–691.

Bowen, William. "Who Owns What's in Your Head?" *Fortune,* July 1964, p. 175.

Bowes, T. L. "Forum," *Journal of the Patent, Trademark and Copyright Foundation* 5 (1961): 269ff.

———— "Patents and the Corporation." *IDEA: The Patent, Trademark, and Copyright Journal of Research and Education* 10 (1966): 75ff.

Bown, Ralph. "Inventing and Patenting at Bell Laboratories." *Bell Laboratories Record,* January 1954, pp. 5–10.

Brooks, J. "Annals of Business—One Free Bite." *New Yorker,* January 11, 1964, p. 37.

Brooks, Overton. "Ownership and Use of Space Age Ideas—A Legislative Approach." *Federal Bar Journal* 21 (1961): 26ff.

Brown, Donald L. "Protection through Patents: The Polaroid Story." *Journal of the Patent Office Society* 42 (1960): 439 ff.

Calvert, Robert T. *Encyclopedia of Patent Practice and Invention Management.* New York: Reinhold, 1964.

Carter, Charles M. "Trade Secrets and the Technical Man." *IEEE Spectrum,* February 1969, p. 54.

Cartter, Allan M. "Economics of the University." *American Economic Review* 55 (1965): 481.

Caruso, Lawrence R. "Inventions in Orbit: The Patent Waiver Regulations—The National Aeronautics and Space Administration Revisited." *Howard Law Journal* 12 (1966): 35.

———. "A Study in Decision-Making: The Patent Policies of the National Aeronautics and Space Administration." *Howard Law Journal* 7 (1961): 93ff.

Chamberlain, Neil W., and J. W. Kuhn. *Collective Bargaining.* New York: McGraw-Hill, 1965.

Clesner, Herschel F. "Innovator's Payment Determination in the U.S.S.R." *IDEA: The Patent, Trademark, and Copyright Journal of Research and Education* 6 (1962): 225, 227–228.

———. *Patent Practices of the Department of Agriculture: Preliminary Report.* U.S. Senate Committee on the Judiciary Subcommittee on Patents, Trademarks, and Copyrights, 87th Cong., 1st sess., 1961.

Cohen, Ephraim K. "Rights of Employer and Employee in Patentable Inventions." *American Patent Law Association Bulletin,* April–May 1966, pp. 193–196.

Coleman, Lawrence A., and Charles B. Cole. "The Effect of Shifting Employment on Trade Secrets." *Business Lawyer* 14 (1959): 319.

Collins, W. T., III. "Injunctions to Protect Trade Secrets: The Goodrich and Du Pont Cases." *Virginia Law Review* 51 (1965): 932–933.

Commons, John R., ed. *Documentary History of American Industrial Society.* Cleveland: Arthur H. Clark, 1910.

Costa, Jasper Silva. *Law of Inventing in Employment.* Brooklyn, N.Y.: Central Book Co., 1953.

Cox, Archibald and Derek Curtis Bok, eds. *Cases and Materials on Labor Law.* Brooklyn, N.Y.: Foundation Press, 1965.

Daddario, Emilio Q. *Government and Science.* Hearings before the U.S. House Committee on Science and Astronautics Subcommittee on Science, Research, and Development, 88th Cong., 1st sess., 1964.

———. *Ownership of Inventions Developed in the Course of Federal Space Contracts: Report.* U.S. House Committee on Science and Astronautics Subcommittee on Patents and Scientific Inventions, 87th Cong., 2nd sess., 1962.

———. "A Patent Policy for a Free Economy." *American Bar Association Journal* 47 (1961): 671ff.

David, L. M. "Major Collective Bargaining Settlements." *Monthly Labor Review* 89 (1966): 372ff.

Davis, Ross D., and Eugene J. Davidson. "Government Patent Policy—Another Look at an Old Problem." *Federal Bar Journal* 21 (1961): 77.

Davis, Kenneth Culp. Administrative Law. St. Paul, Minn.: West Publishing Co., 1965.

Dinkins, C. M. *Patent Practices of the Department of Health, Education, and Welfare: Preliminary Report.* U.S. Senate Committee on the Judiciary Subcommittee on Patents, Trademarks, and Copyrights, 86th Cong., 1st sess., 1960.

Doskow, Ambrose. ed. "Notes," "Rights of Employers in Inventions of Employees." *Columbia Law Review* 30 (1930): 1172, 1176–1177.

Drucker, Peter. *The Concept of the Corporation.* New York: New American Library, 1964.

Dulles, Foster Rhea. *Labor in America.* New York: T. Y. Crowell, 2nd ed. 1960.

Dvorak, Eldon J. "Symposium: Will Engineers Unionize?" *Industrial Relations* 2, no. 3 (1963): 45.

Dykman, H. T. "Patent Licensing within the Manufacturers Aircraft Association (MAA)." *Journal of the Patent Office Society* 46 (1964): 656ff.

Eaton, William. "Patent Problem: Who Owns the Rights?" *Harvard Business Review* 45, no. 4 (1967): 10.

Ellis, Ridsdale. *Patent Assignments.* 3rd ed. Mt. Kisko, N.Y.: Baker, Voorhis, 1955.

———. *Trade Secrets.* Mt. Kisco, N.Y.: Baker, Voorhis, 1953.

Federico, P. *Distribution of Patents Issued to Corporations 1939–1955: Study No. 3.* U.S. Senate Committee on the Judiciary Subcommittee on Patents, Trademarks, and Copyrights, 84th Cong., 2nd sess., 1957.

Finnegan, Marcus B., and Richard W. Pogue. "Federal Employee Invention Rights—Time to Legislate." *Michigan Law Review* 55 (1957): 903, 917–924; or *Journal of the Patent Office Society* 40 (1958): 322.

Forman, Howard I. "Forgive My Enemies for They Know Not What They Do." *Journal of the Patent Office Society* 44 (1962): 274.

———. "Government Patent Policy—Yesterday, Today and Tomorrow." *Journal of the Patent Office Society* 50 (1968): 32, 35.

———. "The Government Patents Board—Determination of Patent Rights in Inventions Made by Government Employees." *Journal of the Patent Office Society* 35 (1953): 95, 101.

———. "The Impact of Government's Patent Policies on the Economy and the American Patent System." *Patent Procurement and Exploitation.* Institute on Patent Law. Washington, D.C.: B.N.A., Inc., 1963.

———. *Patents, Their Ownership and Administration by the United States Government.* Brooklyn, N.Y.: Central Book Co., 1957.

———. "President's Statement of Government Patent Policy: A Springboard for Legislative Action." *Federal Bar Journal* 25 (1965): 4–23.

————. "Wanted: A Definite Government Patent Policy." *IDEA: The Patent, Trademark, and Copyright Journal of Research and Education* 3 (1959): 399.

Gellhorn, Walter. *Security, Loyalty and Science.* Ithaca, N.Y.: Cornell University Press, 1950.

Goldberg, Arthur S. AFL–CIO, *Labor United.* New York: McGraw-Hill, 1964.

Goldstein, Bernard. "Some Aspects of the Nature of Unionism among Salaried Professionals in Industry." *American Sociological Review* 20 (1955): 199.

Gordon, B. "Government Patent Policy and the New Mercantilism." *Federal Bar Journal* 25 (1965): 24–31.

Graham, Max W. J., Jr. "Process Patents for Computer Programs." *California Law Review* 56 (1968): 466.

Greenberg, Daniel S. *The Politics of Pure Science.* New York: American Library, 1967.

Haddad, James A. "An Executive's View of the Employed Inventor." *Journal of the Patent Office Society* 47 (1965): 476, 478.

Hafstad, Lawrence R. "Lay Comments on the Proposed Patent Law." *IDEA: The Patent Trademark, and Copyright Journal of Research and Education* 11 (1967): 161–173.

Harbridge House, Inc. *Government Patent Policy Study, Final Report.* 4 vols. Washington, D.C.: Government Printing Office, 1968.

Harrison, Gladys A. *An Analytical History of the Patent Policy of the Department of Health, Education, and Welfare.* Study No. 27. Washington, D.C.: Government Printing Office, 1961.

Hayes, A. J. "The Independent Inventor's Interest." *Journal of the Patent Office Society* 47 (1965): 298ff.

Holman, Mary A. "Government Research and Development Inventions: A New Resource?" *Land Economics,* August 1965.

————. "The Utilization of Government-Owned Inventions." *IDEA: The Patent, Trademark, and Copyright Journal of Research and Education* 7 (1963): 109.

Holman, Mary A., and D. S. Watson. "Patents from Government-Financed Research and Development." *IDEA: The Patent, Trademark, and Copyright Journal of Research and Education* 8 (1964): 199.

Howard, Frank. "Patents and Technical Progress." *IDEA: The Patent, Trademark, and Copyright Journal of Research and Education* 4 (1960): 57, 60.

Howell, Herbert A. *Howell's Copyright Law.* Alan Latman, ed. Washington, D.C.: Bureau of National Affairs, 1962.

"Incentive Awards Act of 1954." *Congressional and Administrative News* 3 (1954): 3825.

Jewkes, John, David Sawers, and Richard Stillerman. *The Sources of Invention.* Cambridge, Mass.: Harvard University Press, 1966.

Jibrin, Barbara H., and Catherine S. Corry. "Government Assistance to Invention and Research: A Legislative History." Patent Study No. 22, 1960.

Johnson, John A. "Rights to Inventions under NASA Contracts." *Federal Bar Journal* 21 (1961): 37ff.

Kassalow, Everett M. "The Development of Western Labor Movements: Some Comparative Considerations." In *Labor: Readings on Major Issues*, Richard A. Lester, ed. New York: Random House, 1965.

———. "White Collar Unionism in Western Europe." *Monthly Labor Review* 36 (July 1963): 765, and 86 (August 1963): 889.

———. "Prospects for White Collar Union Growth." *Industrial Relations* 5, no. 1 (1965): 37.

Kidd, Charles V. *American Universities and Federal Research*. Cambridge, Mass.: Harvard University Press, 1960.

Koenig, Gloria K. "The Shop Right—Time for Limitation." *Journal of the Patent Office Society* 49 (1967): 658.

Kuhn, James W. "Success and Failure in Organizing Professional Engineers." *Proceedings of the 16th Annual Meeting, Industrial Relations Research Associates*. Madison, Wis.: 1964.

"Labor, Inventions, and Patents." *American Patent Law Association Bulletin,* June 1962, pp. 211ff.

Landis, James M. *Cases on Labor Law*. 2nd ed. Chicago: Foundation Press, 1942.

Lassagne, Louis. "The Legal Rights of Employed Inventors." *American Bar Association Journal* 51 (1965): 835, 838.

Leamer, Frank D. "Salary Administration of Scientific and Engineering Personnel at Bell Telephone Laboratories." *Research Management* 7, no. 2 (1964): 91–106.

Leonard, John W. "The Protected Rights of the Employee Inventor in His Invention." *Journal of the Patent Office Society* 49 (1967): 357, 360.

Lewis, R. David. "Contracts in Restraint of Trade: Employee Covenants Not to Compete." *American Law Reports* 21 (1967): 214.

Lockwood, E. T. "Bell System Patents: Why Do We Have Them? How Are They Used?" *Bell Telephone Magazine*, Winter 1959–1960, pp. 16–23.

Long, Russell. "Federal Contract Patent Policy and the Public Interest." *Federal Bar Journal* 21 (1961): 7–25.

———. "A Government Patent Policy to Serve the Public Interest." *American Bar Association Journal* 47 (1961): 675–681.

Lunch, Milton F. "The Engineers in a Changing Society." BNA White Collar Report No. 470, March 10, 1966, C-1.

McTiernan, Charles. "Employee-Inventor Compensation Plans." *Journal of the Patent Office Society* 46 (1964): 475, 483–489.

Maltby, Wilson. "A Government Patent Policy for Employees Inventions." *Federal Bar Journal* 21 (1961): 127ff.

———. "Need for a Federal Policy to Foster Invention Disclosures by Contractors and Employees." *Federal Bar Journal* 25 (1965): 32ff.

Marcson, Simon. *The Scientist in American Industry.* New York: Harper & Row, 1960.

Marcy, Willard. "The Endowment of Science by Invention." *Research Management* 9 (1966): 371, 377.

Markham, Jesse. "The Value of the American Patent System: An Inquiry into Possible Approaches to its Measurement." *IDEA: The Patent, Trademark, and Copyright Journal of Research and Education* 1 (1957): 20, 33.

Metz, H. *Management and the Professional Employee.* Addresses on Industrial Relations, 1954 Series, Bulletin No. 22. Ann Arbor, Mich.: Bureau of Industrial Relations, 1954.

Miessner, B. F. "Engineers and Patentry." Paper delivered before the Miami section of the Institute of Electrical and Electronic Engineers, July 23, 1963.

———. "Today's Inventor—A Study in Frustration." *American Engineer* 33, no. 4 (April 1963): 38–40, 55–59.

Milgrim, Roger. *Trade Secrets.* New York: Matthew Bender, 1968.

Morse, Gerry E. "Engineering Ethics from the Viewpoint of Industry." *Journal of Engineering Education,* November 1954, p. 214.

Morsell, Curt, Jr. "A Company's Right in the Invention of an Employee." *Wisconsin Bar Bulletin,* 1968, p. 11.

Morton, Jack A. "The Innovation Process." *Bell Telephone Magazine,* Autumn 1966, pp. 2ff.

———. "From Research to Technology." *International Science and Technology,* May 1964.

———. "A Systems Approach to the Innovation Process." *Business Horizons,* Summer 1967.

National Academy of Sciences, Committee on Utilization of Scientific and Engineering Talent. *Toward Better Utilization of Scientific and Engineering Talent: A Program for Action,* 1961.

Neumeyer, Fredrik. "The Employed Inventor—Part II, The American Situation." *Lex et Scientia* 2 (New York, 1965): 234.

———. "Employees' Rights in Their Inventions." *International Labour Review,* January 1961, p. 35.

———. "Employees' Rights in Their Inventions." *Journal of the Patent Office Society* 44 (1962): 674, 707.

———. *The Law of Employed Inventors in Europe.* Study No. 30. U.S. Senate Committee on the Judiciary Subcommittee on Patents, Trademarks, and Copyrights. Washington, D.C.: Government Printing Office, 1963.

Nimmer, Melville B. *Nimmer on Copyright.* New York: Matthew Bender, 1967.

O'Brien, Gerald D. "Federal Patent Policy." Speech before the North Carolina Inventors Congress, May 20, 1965, Raleigh, N.C.

O'Brien, Gerald D., and Gayle Parker. "Property Rights in Inventions under the National Aeronautics and Space Act of 1958." *Federal Bar Journal* 19 (1959): 255ff.

O'Connor, R. "Incentives for Inventors." *Management Record,* October 1953.

———. "Patent Policies for Employees." *Management Record,* August 1952.

O'Meara, J. Roger. "Company Patent Practices Challenged." *The Conference Board Record.* New York: National Industrial Conference Board, June 1964.

———. *Employee Patent and Secrecy Agreements.* New York: National Industrial Conference Board Studies in Business Policy, No. 199, 1965.

———. "Safeguarding Confidential Information." *Management Record,* December 1957.

Owens, Mark. "Effect of the Presidential Patent Policy Statement of October 10, 1963, on Educational Institutions with an Interest in Patents, Its Implementation by Federal Agencies." Lecture before the National Association of College and University Attorneys, July 1964.

Palmer, Archie M. *Patents and Nonprofit Research: Study No. 6.* U.S. Senate Committee on the Judiciary Subcommittee on Patents, Trademarks, and Copyrights, 85th Cong., 1st sess., 1957.

———. "Survey of University Patent Policies." Washington, D.C.: National Research Council, 1948.

———. *University Research and Patent Policies, Practices and Procedures.* Washington, D.C.: National Research Council Publication 999, 1962.

———. "University Patent Policies." *Journal of the Patent Office Society* 16 (February 1934): 96–131.

———. "University Patent Policies and Practices." Washington, D.C.: National Research Council, 1952; Supplement, 1955.

Patents and Technical Data. Government Contracts Monographs, No. 10. Washington, D.C.: George Washington University, 1967.

Prager, F. D. "Agawam v. Jordan, Annotated." *Journal of the Patent Office Society* 22 (1940): 737, 771–775.

Rabinow, Jacob. "Experiences in Electrical Invention." *Journal of the Patent Office Society* 47 (1965): 580.

———. "An Inventor's View." *Journal of the Patent Office Society* 47 (1965): 469, 474–475.

The Rate and Direction of Inventive Activity: Economic and Social Factors. Princeton, N.J.: Princeton University Press, 1962.

Research Institute of America. "How Safe Are Your Trade Secrets?" *Recommendations,* September 6, 1968.

Riegel, John W. *Collective Bargaining as Viewed by Unorganized Engineers and Scientists.* Ann Arbor, Mich.: Bureau of Industrial Relations, 1959.

————. *Intangible Awards for Engineers and Scientists.* Report No. 9. Ann Arbor, Mich.: Bureau of Industrial Relations, 1958.

"Rights of Employer and Employee in Patentable Inventions." *APLA Bulletin,* April–May 1966, p. 178.

Rossman, Joseph. *Industrial Creativity: The Psychology of the Inventor.* New Hyde Park, N.Y.: University Books, 3rd ed., 1964.

————. "Note on Trade Secrets." *IDEA: The Patent, Trademark, and Copyright Journal of Research and Education* 3 (1959): 211.

————. "Rewards and Incentives to Employee-Inventors." *IDEA: The Patent, Trademark, and Copyright Journal of Research and Education* 7 (1964): 436ff.

————. "Stimulating Employees to Invent." *Industrial and Engineering Chemistry* 12 (1935): 1512.

Ruf, Ernst H. "U.S. Patent Concepts v USSR Patent Concepts and Inventor's Certificates—A Comparison of Public Policies and Social Objectives." *Journal of the Patent Office Society* 49 (1967): 15, 30–31.

Rush, D. R. "A Stout Man to Bear On." In *Power to Produce, The Yearbook of Agriculture.* Washington, D.C.: U.S. Government Printing Office, 1960.

Schairer, Otto S. *Patent Policies of Radio Corporation of America.* New York: rca Institutes Technical Press, 1939.

Schauer, C. H. "Research Corporation—Experiment in Administration of Patent Rights for the Public Good." *Research Management* 5, no. 4 (1969): 229.

Scherer, Frederic, et al. *Patents and the Corporation.* Harvard Business School, 1959.

Schmookler, Jacob. *Invention and Economic Growth.* Cambridge, Mass.: Harvard University Press, 1966.

Seaborg, Glenn T. Talk before the Swedish Engineering Academy of Science, September 14, 1962, in Stockholm, Sweden.

"Sections 184 and 185 of the Invention Secrecy Act—An Ambiguous and Unnecessary Obstruction to Foreign Patenting." In "Notes." *Michigan Law Review* 64 (1966): 496.

Seidman, Joel and Glen G. Cain, "Unionized Engineers and Chemists: A Case Study of a Professional Union." *Journal of Business of the University of Chicago* 37, no. 3 (1964): 238.

Selby, R. T. and M. C. Cunningham. "Grievance Procedures in Major Contracts." *Monthly Labor Review,* October 1964, p. 1125.

Shockley, William. "On the Statistics of Individual Variations of Productivity in Research Laboratories." *Proceedings of the IRE,* March 1957, pp. 279ff.

Sloan, Alfred P., Jr. *My Years with General Motors.* New York: Macfadden-Bartell, 1965.

Smyth, Henry de W. "Role of the University in Basic Research." *Proceedings of a Conference on Academic and Industrial Basic Research,* Princeton University, November 1960, NSF 61–39.

Soans, Cyril A. "Who is the Inventor?" *Journal of the Patent Office Society* 28 (1946): 525.

Solo, Robert A. "Patent Policy for Government-Sponsored Research and Development." *IDEA: The Patent, Trademark, and Copyright Journal of Research and Education* 10 (1966): 143–206.

Stedman, John C. "The Employed Inventor, the Public Interest, and Horse and Buggy Law in the Space Age." *New York University Law Review* 45 (March 1970): 1.

———. "Rights and Responsibilities of the Employed Inventor." *Indiana Law Journal* 45 (Winter 1970): 254.

Strauss, George. "Professional or Employee-Oriented: Dilemma for Engineering Unions." *Industrial and Labor Relations Review* 17 (1964): 519.

Sturmthal, Adolf, ed. *White-Collar Trade Unions, Contemporary Developments in Industrial Societies.* Urbana, Ill.: University of Illinois Press, 1966.

Sutton, John P. "Trade Secrets Legislation." *IDEA: The Patent, Trademark, and Copyright Journal of Research and Education* 9 (1965): 587, 607.

Taft, Philip. *Organized Labor in American History.* New York: Harper & Row, 1964.

Thurman, Ronald V. "Adequate Legal Protection for Computer Programs." *Utah Law Review,* 1968, p. 369.

"Trade Secrets: The Technical Man in Legal Land." *Chemical & Engineering News,* January 18, 1965, p. 81.

Turner, Amédée. *The Law of Trade Secrets.* South Hackensack, N.J.: Fred B. Rothman, 1962.

U.S. Civil Service Commission. *Changes in the Incentive Awards Program.* Bulletin No. 451-1. March 4, 1969.

U.S. Congress, House, Committee on the Judiciary, Subcommittee No. 2. *Proposed Government Incentives, Awards and Rewards Program with Respect to Government Employees: Hearings on H.R. 7316.* 82nd Cong., 2nd sess., March 10, 1952.

U.S. Congress, House, Committee on Science and Astronautics, Subcommittee on Science, Research, and Development. *Report No. 1: A Statement of Purpose.* Washington, D.C.: U.S. Government Printing Office, 1963.

———. *Report No. 2: Fiscal Trends in Federal Research and Development.* Washington, D.C.: U.S. Government Printing Office, 1965.

U.S. Congress, House, Select Committee on Small Business. *Proprietary Rights and Data: Report No. 2230.* Washington, D.C.: U.S. Government Printing Office, 1960.

U.S. Congress, Joint Committee on Atomic Energy. *Hearings on Atomic Energy Patents.* 86th Cong., 1st sess., 1959.

————. *Hearings on Development, Growth, and State of the Atomic Energy Industry.* 84th Cong., 1st sess., 1955.

U.S. Congress, Senate, Committee on the Judiciary, Subcommittee on Patents, Trademarks, and Copyrights. *Government Patent Policy: Hearings.* 89th Cong., 1st sess., 1965, p. 329.

————. *National Patent Policy: Hearing.* 87th Cong., 1st sess., 1961.

————. *Patent Practices of Government Agencies—Preliminary Reports:*
Department of Agriculture, 87th Cong., 1st sess., 1961

Department of Commerce, 87th Cong., 1st sess., 1961

Department of Defense, 87th Cong., 1st sess., 1961

Department of HEW, 86th Cong., 1st sess., 1960

Department of Interior, 87th Cong., 2nd sess., 1962

Department of Treasury, 86th Cong., 2nd sess., 1960

Federal Aviation Agency, 86th Cong., 2nd sess., 1961

Federal Conservation Commission, 87th Cong., 2nd sess., 1962

General Services Administration, 86th Cong., 1st sess., 1959

Government Printing Office, 86th Cong., 2nd sess., 1960

National Science Foundation, 85th Cong., 2nd sess., 1959

Post Office Department, 86th Cong., 1st sess., 1959

Tennessee Valley Authority, 85th Cong., 2nd sess., 1959

Veterans' Administration, 86th Cong., 1st sess., 1959

————. *Patent Practices of the Government Patents Board: Report.* Washington, D.C.: Government Printing Office, 1959.

————. *Proposed Government Incentives, Awards and Rewards Program with Respect to Government Employees: Hearings on S. 2157 and H.R. 2383.* 84th Cong., 2nd sess., June 7, 1956.

U.S. Congress, Senate, Select Committee on Small Business, Subcommittee on Monopoly. *Economic and Legal Problems of Government Patent Policies.* Washington, D.C.: Government Printing Office, 1963.

————. *Economic Aspects of Government Patent Policies.* 88th Cong., 1st sess., 1963.

————. *Patent Policies of Government Departments and Agencies, 1960.* 86th Cong., 1st sess., Washington, D.C.: Government Printing Office, 1960.

U.S. Congress, Temporary National Economic Committee. *Investigation of Concentration of Economic Power: Hearings, Part I, Economic Prologue.* 75th Cong., 3rd sess. Washington, D.C.: Government Printing Office, 1939.

U.S. Department of Health, Education, and Welfare. *Program and Management Progress: A Report to the President.* Washington, D.C.: Government Printing Office, 1965.

U.S. Department of Justice. *Investigation of Government Patent Practices and Policies, Report and Recommendations of the Attorney General to the President.* 3 vols. Washington, D.C.: Government Printing Office, 1947.

U.S. Department of Labor, Bureau of Standards. *Growth of Labor Law in the United States.* Washington, D.C.: Government Printing Office, 1967.

U.S. Federal Council for Science and Technology. Annual Reports on Government Policy 1964–1968. Washington, D.C.: U.S. Government Printing Office.

U.S. National Aeronautics and Space Administration. "An Evaluation of the Patent Policies of the National Aeronautics and Space Administration." Prepared by the Department of Economics, George Washington University. *The George Washington Law Review* 27 (1958): 49–75.

———. *Program Review Document.* Prepared by the Office of the General Counsel. Washington, D.C.: Government Printing Office, 1966.

U.S. National Science Foundation. *Employment of Scientists and Engineers in the United States 1950–1966.* NSF 63–30, September 1968. Washington, D.C.: Government Printing Office, 1968.

———. *Federal Funds for Research, Development, and Other Scientific Activities.* NSF 67–19. Washington, D.C.: Government Printing Office, 1967.

———. *Federal Support to Universities and Colleges 1963–1966.* NSF 67–14. Washington, D.C.: Government Printing Office, 1967.

———. *Reviews of Data on Research and Development.* Nos. 31, NSF 61–52; 34, NSF 62–16; 38, NSF 63–12.

———. *Reviews of Data on Science Resources.* Nos. 9, August 1966; 12, January 1968.

———. *Scientific and Technical Personnel in Industry.* NSF 61–75, 1961. Washington, D.C.: Government Printing Office, 1960.

———. *Scientific and Technical Personnel in the Federal Government, 1966.* NSF 68–16. Washington, D.C.: Government Printing Office, 1968.

"Validity and Enforceability of Restrictive Covenants in Contracts of Employment." *American Law Reports* 9 (1920): 1467–1468.

Vaughan, Floyd. *Economics of the Patent System.* New York: Macmillan, 1925.

von Kalinowski, Julian O. "Key Employees and Trade Secrets." *Virginia Law Review* 47 (1961): 583, 595.

Wade, Worth. *Business and the Professional Unions.* Ardmore, Pa.: Advance House, 1961.

———. *Industrial Espionage and Mis-Use of Trade Secrets.* 2nd ed. Ardmore, Pa.: Advance House, 1961.

Walton, Richard E. *The Impact of the Professional Engineering Union.* Boston: Harvard Business School, 1961.

Watson, Robert C., and Mary A. Holman. "Soviet Law on Inventions and Patents." *Journal of the Patent Office Society* 43 (1961): 5, 35–39.

Watson, Thomas J. *Think Magazine,* December 1960, p. 18.

Webb, James E. Keynote address to the Second NASA-Industry Program Plans Conference, February 11–21, 1963, Washington, D.C.

Wirtz, W. Willard. "Constructive Bargaining." Talk given at the National Academy of Arbitrators, February 1, 1963, Chicago, Ill.

———. *Labor and the Public Interest.* New York: Harper & Row, 1964.

Wolk, I. Louis. "An Attorney's View of the Employee Inventor." *Journal of the Patent Office Society* 47 (1965): 483, 487.

Woodward, W. R. "Tax Aspects of Patents, Copyrights and Trademarks." *Current Problems in Federal Taxation.* New York: Practicing Law Institute, 1960.

DATE DUE